Missions

A Literary Directory

MW01518449

Cross /
Cultures

Readings in the Post/Colonial Literatures in English

58

Series Editors:

Gordon
Collier
(Giessen)

Hena
Maes-Jelinek
(Liège)

Geoffrey
Davis
(Aachen)

ASNEL Papers appear under the auspices of the
Gesellschaft für die Neuen Englischsprachigen Literaturen e.V. (GNEL)
Association for the Study of the New Literatures in English (ASNEL)
Heinz Antor, President
(English Seminar, University of Cologne, Albertus-Magnus-Platz,
D-50923 Cologne)

Amsterdam - New York, NY 2002

Missions of Interdependence

A Literary Directory

edited by

Gerhard Stilz

ASNEL Papers 6

The paper on which this book is printed meets the requirements of
"ISO 9706:1994, Information and documentation - Paper for documents -
Requirements for permanence".

ISBN: 90-420-1429-6 (bound)
©Editions Rodopi B.V., Amsterdam - New York, NY 2002
Printed in The Netherlands

Contents

Introduction

THIS VOLUME PRESENTS A SELECTION of papers read at the international conference "Colonies – Missions – Cultures," which was convened in Tübingen on 6–11 April 1999 and was arranged by the Association for the Study of the New English Literatures (ASNEL) and the European Association for Commonwealth Literature and Language Studies (EACLALS). Authors and critics from five continents attended this event. The aim was to come to terms with the cultural dialectic of Christian missions under colonialism and their modes of survival or secular transformation in a postcolonial world. While the theoretical implications and comparative issues of the conference topic have been published under the title *Colonies, Missions, Cultures in the English Speaking World: General and Comparative Studies* (Tübingen: Stauffenburg, 2001), the present collection assembles literary case studies devoted to particular regions, authors, or individual texts. All of them are concerned with reconsidering and re-evaluating the elements of a process initiated by colonialism and European missionary activities and which, by moving from dependence through independence to interdependence, has, on a global scale, led to international relations largely based on ideals of partnership, equality and respect. This process, however, has not been a universally smooth development, and it has not yet produced satisfactory results in all parts of the world. Political repression and social discrimination, economic exploitation and cultural alienation continue to be critical issues, even under allegedly 'postcolonial' conditions.

The driving forces of neocolonialism are now usually identified with global capital and international business. These forces no longer need to be supported by nations, empires or religious creeds, being based universally on pragmatism, expediency and profit. But even if their missionary impetus may no longer be reinforced by imperial rule and religious agency, Western imperialism and Christian missions have been made responsible for the perpetuation of the inequalities and depressions that disturb, accompany and undermine our efforts at global comfort and security. At the beginning of the twenty-first century it has become obvious that we will need to combine the urge for individual emancipation and the social practice of humanism in a productive dialectic, in order to help the world survive both the ancient pitfalls of particularist terrorism and the levelling tendencies of cultural indifference spread by the new hegemonial arrogance of global capital.

In this demanding sense, this book, with its goal of tendering a revised and multiple strategy of cultural conciliation, may be termed a literary directory. Thirty-five scholars address and negotiate, in a spirit of learning and understanding, an exemplary variety of intercultural splits and fissures found in the English-speaking world. Their methodological endeavour can be seen to constitute a seminal field of intellectual signposts. They point out the ways and means of conscientiously and responsibly assessing colonial predicaments and postcolonial developments in six regions shaped in the past by the British Empire and still associated today through their allegiance to the idea of a Commonwealth of Nations. They show how a new ethos of literary self-assertion, interpretative mediation and critical responsiveness can remove the old, deeply ingrained prejudices, silences and taboos established by forms of discrimination against race, class and gender.

The conference participants, while aware of the uncomfortable fact that they were using English as a lingua franca, were also united in their trust that even an old colonial language could function as an acceptable postcolonial medium. Unquestioningly, they agreed that this was a valid presumption, taking for granted that, in matters of language, there is a message beyond the medium. After all, they would also have needed to plead this exemption from Marshall McLuhan's famous formula for using any other language.

In view of the wide spaces and horizons addressed in the papers, a prime subdivision by regions has been deemed appropriate. Under the headings "North America," "Caribbean," "Africa," "India," "Australia" and "New Zealand and the Pacific," the articles have been arranged by considerations of time and scope. Papers addressing early texts or providing a survey have been given precedence over more recent issues or studies in detail. On a systematic account, it can be seen that all articles assess or revise the fictional or factual missions which characters, narrators or authors, in their discursive treatment of colonization and decolonization, may have proposed or followed. Their strategies of coming to terms with colonial and postcolonial missions can therefore be regarded as route markings on the map of our literary directory.

ULLA HASELSTEIN, in her essay on "Puritans and Praying Indians: Versions of Transculturation in Mary Rowlandson's *Captivity Narrative* (1682)," approaches the earliest text to be dealt with in this volume. She notes how immensely difficult it was for Puritans, during the early days of British colonialism in North America, to accept the fact that Christianity could be claimed by Indians as a mission for racial and cultural equality and interdependence. Even a hundred and fifty years later – as PILAR CUDER DOMÍNGUEZ shows in her exemplary study of James Russell's

Matilda; or, The Indian's Captive (1833) – a mission of interdependence is still far from springing up in colonial Canada. On the contrary: the ordeal of captivity, which temporarily exposes innocent Europeans to darkness and despair, is about to form one of the pillars of British North-American imperial consciousness. In fact, as MIRKO JURAK holds in his essay on national identity in Canadian literature, the idea of Canadian integrity, beyond accepting the uneasy link between the "two solitudes" of Franco- and Anglo-Canadians, only gradually developed during the decades following the Second World War. Canada needed creative writers and critics such as Northrop Frye and Margaret Atwood to formulate her independence and redefine her social and ethnic diversity as well as her international position. Frye's conclusion that "all human beings want the same things, freedom, dignity and decent living conditions" can serve as a yardstick of liberal egalitarianism on a level of both personal and international relations. Timothy Findley, according to MAYA PETRU-KHINA, endorses such a credo. He exposes war as the manifest consequence of the failure of human values and human relationships. Evidently, this ethos leading to intercultural compromise is not solely a product of white Canadian complacency. MARK SHACKLETON, in his contribution, convincingly argues that the message pervading the work of Tomson Highway, despite his denunciation of the colonizing aspects of Christianity, is the creative regeneration and imaginative fusion of cultures. Less confident, but in effect moving in the same direction, is the current revised understanding of the Canadian internment and ghetto experience suffered by the Japanese minority during and after the Second World War. MARI PEEPRE, in "Crossing the Fields of Death in Kerri Sakamoto's *The Electrical Field*," emphatically endorses this appeal to integrate the repressed and betrayed border zones of diasporic minority groups into the Canadian multicultural mosaic.

In the West Indies, integration of the cultural mosaic was a social, political and creative issue long before it came to be theorized elsewhere in the earlier British colonies. Authors from the Caribbean, perhaps more than others, therefore connect historical processes of hybridity and creolization with their existential predicament. BRUCE KING, whose biography of the Nobel Prize-winner Derek Walcott has recently appeared, traces Walcott's universalist 'making' to its roots in the colonial micro-history and liberal education offered by the motley ethnic and religious set-up of St Lucia. JOHN THIEME investigates the representation and transformation of Christianity in Walcott's poetry and examines this author's integral view that poetry is inseparable from religion "in the broadest sense." Hybridity is the dominant feature of West Indian cultural theory and practice. In this regard, ULRIKE ERICH-SEN concentrates on Erna Brodber's novel *Myal* (1988), finding that liberation from the alienating effects of the colonial encounter can be most easily envisaged by "borderline existences." These carry with them "more than one culture" and are thus able to embody a mission of interdependence. That such borderline existences do not necessarily produce positive solutions and integrative discourses is suggested by ANNE COLLETT in her study of the subversiveness of Jamaica Kincaid's gardening column the *New Yorker*; she here concurs with Diana Brydon's statement that a creative new globalism does not unfailingly give pat answers but, rather, "seeks a way to cooperate without cooption" by subscribing to myths that thrive on inter-action that 'contaminates' without homogenising." Such contaminations can also be seen in Pauline Melville's *The Ventriloquist's Tale* (1999). SARAH LAWSON WELSH investigates how, in this novel, Amerindian cultures and European narratives collide while still colluding in a critical assessment of both cultures, on a level of mutual acknowledgement of and respect for their correspondences. One of the missions of interdependence repeatedly approached by West Indian authors is love – a notion developed in most religions. BÉNÉDICTE LEDENT, in her study of Caryl Phillips's "diasporic philosophy," discovers this metaphorical secularization of religion. Like Derek Walcott's equation of poetry and religion "in its broadest sense," Phillips's "philosophy" contributes to a claim of triadic interdependence between love, reli-gion and poetry. Interestingly, this seems to revive Romantic notions of logical, moral and aesthetic unitarianism.

Turning to our African focus, we are particularly grateful for having been offered the bequest of JACQUELINE BARDOLPH's excellent essay on the two printed ver-sions of Ngugi's *A Grain of Wheat* (1967 and 1986). Shortly after the Tübingen conference, we received the sad news of her passing. As in her many other essays on African writing, she approached a gritty problem, one last time, with great scholarly discernment and moral candour. Ngugi wa Thiong'o's position in the militant revision of his novel (whose earlier version had subscribed to Christian imagery and frames of reference) cannot easily be reconciled with a mission of interdependence. Rather, it reflects the impatience and despair of an African intellectual who wit-nessed the fact that twenty years of independence had failed to bring about the desired freedom from colonialism. A different aspect of the ongoing colonial conflict is elucidated by THENGANI NGWENYA in a discussion of ideology and self-representation in Katie Makanya's autobiography, where the collaborative compact between ethnographic mediator and his or her (auto)biographical subject inevitably involves ideological collisions which become evident in conspicuous discursive tensions within the negotiated text. That such hybridity can be productively used in order to represent and activate a polyperspectival culture of understanding is the claim put forth by HEILNA DU PLOOY, who argues that A.H.M. Scholz's *Vatmaar* (1995), a novel initially written in English but published in Afrikaans, constitutes a multifacetted history of communal interdependence during and after the Anglo-Boer war, employing a polyphony of voices to assess the wrongs of the past. Giving voice to those who have traditionally been suppressed and marginalized has, of course, long been a literary instrument of social reform. This strategy has in recent years been given new validity in numerous novels and life stories from Southern Africa. It is particularly the female voices that contribute new aspects and values to the grand heroic tales about the struggle for independence, as EVA HUNTER points out in her study of the fiction of Yvonne Vera. Whether female authors and characters are better equipped than males for sustaining a hybrid position in an unresolved conflict may be debatable. In a Nigerian context, JOHN C. HAWLEY would seem to support this proposition. While Ngugi wa Thiong'o, under duress, radicalized his position in the second version of *A Grain of Wheat* (1986), Hawley shows how Tsitsi Dangarembga, in *Nervous Conditions* (1988), avoids the trap of militant disambiguation by opening up her protagonists to creative, hybrid missions of interdependence.

It may be that the colonial history of India, which, starting with the Aryan invasions, can be dated back well beyond the British Raj, has fostered a cultural disposition that makes people in South Asia not only sharply responsive to social rifts and differences, but at the same time particularly fit for coping with such fissures and asymmetries through strategies of ironical submission and artful subversion – in short, mimicry. Literature has its place in this vital process of hybrid dissimulation, which figures, according to Homi Bhabha, in its non-violent act of negotiation, as the cutting edge of culture. Several contributors have investigated such strategies and effects in Indian English and even Anglo-Indian literature. On the one hand, HYCINTH CYNTHIA WYATT points out the intricate web of ironic resistance built into R.K. Narayan's seemingly simple English texts. On the other, ISABEL ALONSO BRETO, in her reading of Ruth Prawer Jhabvala's *Heat and Dust*, describes how a migrant author, sensitized to Indian ambiguities, softens and relativizes manichaean opposites in the ironic light of mimicry. Reflecting on the mentality of the colonizers, RAJIVA WIJESINHA notes that – at least in Paul Scott's Raj Quartet – it is the women characters who, being acutely aware of both the colonial concept of mission and its failure, are ready and able to explore the spaces between their conflicting allegiances, facing love or despair. Authorial irony, however, is not the only instrument in Indian-English fiction to promote a postcolonial sense of interdependence. Polycentric narrative and multivocal competition have entered recent novels. CHITRA SANKARAN, in her essay on Nayantara Sahgal's *Rich Like Us* (1983), shows how the narratological play between (male) omniscient narrator, (female) first-person narrative and the retrieved voice of an historical diary constitute a polyperspectival postcolonial history. Inevitably, this undercuts a unified moral and logical position which would have required an unchallenged authorial self. A different mode of "widening the discursive space" for the purposes of demonstrating a postcolonial mission of interdependence is traced by ROCÍO G. DAVIS in

Amitav Ghosh's *In an Antique Land* (1993). By crossing the frontiers of traditional ethnographic travel writing and blending "autobiography and biography, investigative reporting and palæography, cultural studies and travel guide," Ghosh is shown to blur and thereby dissolve the generic and territorial boundaries attributed to colonialism and its divisive culture. "Dissolving boundaries" is also the guiding notion behind ROBERT ROSS's essay on the fiction of Chitra Banerjee Divakaruni. In his critical appreciation of a 'debutant' author who, like Bharati Mukherjee or Bapsi Sidhwa, is caught between her Indian childhood and her adolescent experiences and American exoticist demands, Ross envisages a space for "cosmopolitan interdependence" offered to diasporic authors in the USA. ALEXANDRA PODGÓRNIAK assesses a recent triumph of cross-cultural submergence, Arundhati Roy's Booker Prize-winning novel *The God of Small Things* (1997), which she sees as an Indian version of magical realism, mimicking and exploiting relativism in a postcolonial gesture of resistance developed earlier by, above all, Gabriel García Márquez and Salman Rushdie.

In Australia (as in Canada) the literary missions of interdependence seem to be directed at healing three kinds of colonial rift: The first can be seen as a process of emancipation operating mainly between European immigrants and their home countries; the second is the movement of multiculturalism trying to cope with the divisions between the different ethnic immigrant groups; the third is the process of reconciliation initiated between immigrants and natives on account of the poisoned relations arising from a past policy of conquest, subjection, contempt and cultural alienation. OLGA SUDLENKOVA, in her study of early nineteenth-century verse, brings to life the frustrations, fears and hopes that moved and accompanied Australian settlers on their passage from Britain to the Antipodes. MARC DELREZ, in his critical essay on David Malouf's *Fly Away Peter*, holds that white Australian postcolonial writing should move away from the culturally insincere attitude of regarding the "First World" as an object of resistance. Instead, Australian writers should be concerned with a discourse that no longer "identifies with the conquered land" as a new possession. By "renouncing ownership," they might come to terms with the Aboriginals and subscribe to the more appropriate postcolonial claim of being joint custodians of a territory that does not 'belong' to anyone. The "cultural schizophrenia inherent in a settler culture" (Delrez), with all its ambiguous potential, obviously shapes the Australian idea of utopia, as RALPH PORDZIK demonstrates. While Pordzik finds that "utopian novels in Australia lack a clear sense of faith in the creation of an improved society in which peace and stability are [...] obtained," Peter Carey in his novels is seen to "put an end to the apocalyptic state of siege that prevents humans from getting anywhere in the future." Carey's discursive strategy in his novel *Jack Maggs*, SIGRUN MEINIG observes, is a confident mode of playful, creative, exuberantly fabulating intertextuality. Carey refers to traditional stereotypes and delimits them by playing on their potential for polyvalency, complexity and ambiguity. That steps had already been taken toward redeeming Australia's Second-World schizophrenia from colonialist embroilments and collusions is emphasized by CYNTHIA VANDEN DRIESEN in her exploration of Australian paradigms in Katharine Susannah Prichard, David Malouf and Patrick White. She is able to show that Joseph Conrad's phobic image of black natives has, since the 1920s, been gradually transformed by Australian writers into fictional relations of interest, respect, admiration, and even physical and mental intimacy. Although these tentative modes of understanding might still be marred by eurocentric attitudes and ambivalent implications of superiority, they have certainly been instrumental in supporting the Australian mission of postcolonial interdependence. Such a mission, however, cannot be effective and successful without the readiness of Aboriginals to accept white admissions or apologies and share in the forging of a new social contract. In the literary realm, such a movement was prepared by Kath Walker (Oodgeroo Noonuccal). Her encouragement of many Aboriginal writers was seminal in voicing a black Australian consciousness and its readiness for reconciliation. One of the leading lights in this movement was Colin Johnson, whose presumed Aboriginality as "Mudrooroo Narogin" has unfortunately come under attack. Mudrooroo's creative work and personal predicament are addressed here in two essays. EVA RASK KNUDSEN deals with the literary politics of genre and form in Mudrooroo's novels and is appropriately "concerned with the missions of cultural survival and human integrity rather than with the mission of conquest"; GERRY TURCOTTE shows how the Gothic as a eurocentric notion of Aboriginality is turned back by Mudrooroo on the "otherworldly" European "ghosts," in order to prepare for a new encounter between the two conflicting cultures in a spirit of fairness and mutual respect.

New Zealand and, to a certain extent, the Pacific are seen to share with Australia at least two major postcolonial missions of interdependence: the settlers' mission of defining a new political and cultural identity, being critically aware of the fact that their islands, for two centuries or more, were transformed by European invaders; and the mission of native representatives to revive and revalidate their old native cultures in the face of an imposed colonial education, with the idea of syncretism as an integrative project. The first issue is raised by BÄRBEL CZENNIA, who traces features of 'identity formation' from the 1860s to the 1890s in poems by John Barr, Jessie Mackay and Thomas Bracken. PETER MARSDEN follows up with an investigation of the European myth of New Zealand as an antipodean place of "Nowhere." This notion was effectively introduced into literature by Samuel Butler's ambivalent utopian novel *Erewhon* (1872) and later acquired the role of a leitmotif expressing a recurrent sense of disorientation in Pakeha (white settler) poetry. The second issue, pressing towards a policy of recognizing and appreciating the native cultures of the Pacific on an equal basis, is authentically promoted by REINA WHAITIRI, who, with reference to literary texts by Patricia Grace and others, argues that a debt is owed to Maori women, and an apology. Finally, JEAN–PIERRE DURIX, in his examination of Albert Wendt's vision of a "new Pacific," presents a profoundly critical and at the same time powerfully constructive position which suggests that the political and social success of Christian missions in Samoa and the revival of old Pacific myths from Samoa's "hidden spiritual geography" should be creatively merged and integrated in a "syncretic modernity."

All the contributions to this volume converge on one critical argument: In our 'postcolonial' world, divided between hegemonial blindness and sectarian fundamentalism, voices in the humanities, liberal arts and education that have argued for an ethos of enlightenment have for too long remained unheeded. This book is intended to serve as an indicator of the diversity of mediating voices in fields of cultural conflict and their readiness to bridge the rifts of difference in a spirit of responsible intellectual compromise and constructive understanding.

❧

My gratitude for having been able to compile, edit and publish this book goes, above all, to its contributors. Their diligence has been complemented by their patience in responding to editorial requests. I am also obliged to the professional judgement offered by Geoff Davis, Sigrid Markmann and Norbert Platz, without whose good advice this selection of conference papers would have been much harder to make. The volume went to print with the support of ASNEL/GNEL. For its inclusion in Cross/Cultures, I extend my thanks to the series' Co-Editors and publisher. The massive editorial job would not have been manageable without the good services of Assia Harwazinski, Lars Eckstein and Julia Mussgnug. Tanya Davidson, Kate Tomes and Heidi Plucknett deserve much of the praise for suggesting stylistic and linguistic improvements. In addition, the Technical Editor of the Cross/Cultures series, Gordon Collier, put the finishing touches to the volume, in language, style and layout. Finally, a vote of thanks goes to the major sponsors of the Tübingen conference: the Deutsche Forschungsgemeinschaft, Bonn; the Australia Council, Sydney; the Canada Council, through the services of the Gesellschaft für Kanadastudien; the British Council, London; the New Zealand Embassy in Bonn; the University of Tübingen; the Ministerium für Wissenschaft, Forschung und Kunst, Baden–Württemberg; DaimlerChrysler AG, Stuttgart; Robert Bosch GmbH,

Stuttgart; Herr Eberhard Renz, Landesbischof der Evangelischen Kirche in Württemberg, Stuttgart; and Herr Reinhold Würth, Künzelsau. All have contributed substantially to the missions of interdependence outlined in this book.

GERHARD STILZ

TÜBINGEN, NOVEMBER 2001

North America

Puritans and Praying Indians
Versions of Transculturation in
Mary Rowlandson's *Captivity Narrative* (1682)

ULLA HASELSTEIN

T OGETHER WITH SPANISH ACCOUNTS by Juan Ortíz and Cabeza de Vaca about their Indian captivity and John Smith's story of his captivity and liberation by Pocahontas in his chronicle of Virginia, Mary Rowlandson's narrative of her Indian captivity during the so-called King Philip's War (1675–76) in New England is one of the first texts in which a European writes about his or her experiences with a New World culture in a proto-ethnographic manner: ie, from the position of a participant observer.[1] All these texts describe a rather dramatic encounter with cultural Otherness. While the survival of the captives typically depends on whether they are able to perform cultural mimesis, their texts explain and legitimize such behaviour by discussing its moral ground, its hermeneutic strategies and its limits. Negotiating cultural difference, the captives' tales articulate the various social forces operative in the early colonial encounters in rich historical detail.

The first edition of Rowlandson's book from 1682 has been lost, but two later editions dating from the same year have been preserved.[2] While the title printed by

---

[1] On the status of captives as proto-ethnographers see Mary Louise Pratt, "Fieldwork in Common Places," in *Writing Culture: The Poetics and Politics of Ethnography*, ed. James Clifford & George E. Marcus (Berkeley: U of California P, 1986): 27–50. Cf. also Stephen Greenblatt's remarks on "go-betweens" in *Marvelous Encounters: The Wonder of the New World* (Oxford: Clarendon, 1991): ch. 5. James Clifford's recent list of possible ethnographic sources is more comprehensive: "missionaries, converts, literate or educated informants, people of mixed blood, translators, government officials, police, merchants, explorers, prospectors, tourists, travelers, ethnographers, pilgrims, servants, entertainers, migrant laborers, recent immigrants"; Clifford, *Routes: Travel and Translation in the Late Twentieth Century* (Cambridge MA: Harvard UP, 1997): 25.

[2] Kathryn Zabelle Derounian, "The Publication, Promotion and Distribution of Mary Rowlandson's Indian Captivity Narrative in the Seventeenth Century," *Early American Literature* 23 (1988): 239–61.

Samuel Green in New England stressed the theological message ("The Sovereignty and Goodness of God, together with the Faithfulness of His Promises Displayed: being a narrative of the Captivity and Restauration of Mrs Mary Rowlandson, written by her hand"), the London edition gave a more detailed summary of its content:

> A True History of the Captivity and Restoration of Mrs Mary Rowlandson, A Minister's Wife in New England. Wherein is set forth, The Cruel and Inhumane Usage she underwent among the Heathens, for eleven weeks time: And her Deliverance from them. Written by her own hand, for her private use: and now made publick at the earnest Desire of some friends, for the benefit of the Afflicted. Whereunto is annexed, a sermon of the Possibility of God's Forsaking a People that have been near and dear to him, Preached by Mr Joseph Rowlandson, Husband to the said Mrs Rowlandson: It being his Last Sermon.[3]

A quotation from the Bible, Deuteronomy 32:39, aptly stressing the omnipotence of God, concludes the title page.

Since the title page functions as a precept of how to read the narrative, it has kept setting the frame for textual analysis and historical evaluation until today. As a piece of autobiographical writing, the text belongs to the discourse of Protestant spiritual self-scrutiny, as is indicated by the term "for private use." Since the narrative is proclaimed to carry exemplary meaning, its publication "for the benefit of the afflicted" was seen fit. Finally, the quotation from the Bible inscribes the author's individual experience in the discourse of typology and translates it into the temporal framework of Providence. In this way the text announces itself as a sign of Grace that provides not only the author herself, but Puritan society as a whole with proof of an ongoing rapport with God. Completed and elaborated by the husband's sermon and edited by one of the eminent Puritan dignitaries of the time, Rowlandson's text achieved quasi-official status with the religious authorities in New England. As a true report about frontier conditions with sensationalist qualities, it has remained in print ever since the seventeenth century.

Setting civilization against a background of Indian barbarity, Rowlandson's narrative anticipates some of the rhetoric of manifest destiny and, accordingly, has been seen as a premature example of colonial racism.[4] Evoking fear of Indian violence as the emotional trajectory of the narrative and mustering the authority of Scripture in response, Rowlandson presents a powerful model of militant Protestant self-fashioning to her readers. Using the Christian itinerary of humiliation and redemption, the

---

[3] Alden T. Vaughn & Edward W. Clark, ed. *Puritans Among the Indians: Accounts of Captivity and Redemption, 1676–1724* (Cambridge MA: Harvard UP / Belknap, 1981). Further page references are in the main text.

[4] Jane Tompkins, "'Indians': Textuality, Morality, and the Problem of History," in *"Race," Writing, and Difference,* ed. Henry Louis Gates, Jr. (Chicago: U of Chicago P, 1986): 59–77.

text calls for identification with the captive, her afflictions and her ultimate triumph, and helps construct cultural unity within Puritan society. Obviously, this textual ritual translates into a conceptual and institutional framework of domination, as the invocation of the word of God by Rowlandson conceives of the "Other" as alien to God and God's chosen people and provides the legitimation to expropriate, expel and, if necessary, exterminate them.[5]

No doubt this is a script which can be found at work in much colonial discourse all over the world. However, it remains to be seen how the local relations of production and domination, practical and symbolic, engraved themselves into the experience of the concrete 'others' upon which Western selfhood was built, and how their agency and imagination in turn exerted a formative influence upon such relations. While it will not be possible to unveil the natives' point of view in my reading of Rowlandson's text, I will attempt to show, however, that it registers the dissonant voices of the Other in an effort to contain and control; this effort fails for reasons easily discernible in the text. As a consequence of this failure, the text as a whole produces an increasingly self-reflexive and sometimes self-contradictory discourse on cultural difference.

For what provokes the captive's repeated acts of demarcating two distinct cultural entities in the first place is the recognition of hybridity in Indian society, engendered by commercial exchange and christianization. What she repeatedly tries to break apart and think away, however, returns within the space of her own narrative, as she reports her various means of securing survival which depend on the very fact of this hybridity. Ironically, in the course of her narrative Rowlandson herself becomes an agent and a figure of hybridity while arguing passionately against it.

Treacherous Praying Indians

The title page quoted above makes it clear that Rowlandson's captivity narrative was written as an allegory of Puritans in peril, and that the report of the captive's eventual rescue was to be read both as a token of her individual redemption and as an affirmation of the renewed covenant between God and his Chosen People. This accounts for the two-levelled structure of the text: On the one hand, Rowlandson provides the reader with a "realist" description of the incidents of her captivity, of

---

[5] Roy Harvey Pearce, *Savagism and Civilisation* (1953; Berkeley: U of California P, 1988); Richard Slotkin, *Regeneration Through Violence* (Middletown CT: Wesleyan UP, 1974). See also the essays on captivity narratives collected in Frank Shuffleton, ed. *A Mixed Race: Ethnicity in Early America* (New York: Oxford UP, 1993); Benedict Anderson, "Exodus," *Critical Inquiry* 20 (1994): 314–27. The religious force of Rowlandson's narrative is explored in David Downing, "'Streams of Scripture Comfort': Mary Rowlandson's Typological Use of the Bible," *Early American Literature* 15 (1980–81): 252–59; Gary Ebersole, *Captured by Texts: Puritan to Postmodern Images of Captivity* (Charlottesville: U of Virginia P, 1995): ch. 1.

the physical and emotional hardship she suffered during that time, and of her ingenious ways to remain alive and keep firm in her belief. On the other hand, she completely denies human agency in history and hence also in her captivity and her final release. Claiming the status of a passive victim makes her the object of the readers' sympathy[6] and turns her into a figure of divine will. While this latter argument typically gives utmost significance to such details to which some providential meaning can be ascribed, both ways of rendering the experience of captivity pay hardly any attention to the actual strategies of war employed by either of the two groups.[7]

Religious discourse is used throughout the text not only as a theological evaluation of the course of action, but as a dictionary that allows for the translation of an otherwise unintelligible traumatic experience. The Bible, however, not only provides the typological structure of narration and teleological closure, but is literally, almost fetishistically present in the narrative in the form of a Bible which Mary Rowlandson consults whenever she feels the need for consolation. Her reading of Scripture in the midst of the Indian camp thus sustains a writing that is constituted by the deciphering of her experience in the holy book.

The Bible, however, had been given to her by a Praying Indian who had turned traitor to the English (as the latter would have it) and had joined the ranks of the 'savage heathen' fighting against the colonists. He had brought the Bible into his possession by looting an English village. The subsequent itinerary of this Bible, and the fact that it comes to her as a gift, are used by Rowlandson in a complex allegory which predicts the final outcome of both her own and her community's affliction while simultaneously laying down and reinforcing the governing principles of the Puritan symbolic order. Firstly, it is not to the Indian, but to God that Mary Rowlandson must address all gratitude for this most welcome gift, since HE alone is responsible for all that is. But apart from gratitude as a recognition of the gift, and the obligation it brings about, there is nothing which can ever be given back to HIM. God's transcendent position makes it impossible to put him under obligation in any way. God cannot be moved (bribed, as the Puritans would have it) to give by either

---

[6] Leonard Tennenhouse and Nancy Armstrong suggest that captivity narratives are an important generic source for the novel; *The Imaginary Puritan: Literature, Intellectual Labor, and the Origins of Personal Life* (Berkeley: U of California P, 1992). Michelle Burnham elaborates this point in terms of an American cultural history of the novel in her *Captivity and Sentiment: Cultural Exchange in American Literature, 1682-1861* (Hanover NH: UP of New England, 1997).

[7] On the King Philip's War, see the antagonistic representations by Edward Leach, *Flintlock and Tomahawk: New England in King Philip's War* (1958; New York: W.W. Norton, 1966) and Francis Jennings, *The Invasion of America: Indians, Colonialism, and the Cant of Conquest* (New York: W.W. Norton, 1976); Russell Bourne, *The Red King's Rebellion: Racial Politics in New England, 1675–1678* (New York: Atheneum, 1990); Jill Lepore, *The Name of War: King Philip's War and the Origins of American Identity* (New York: Alfred A. Knopf, 1999).

sacrifice, good behaviour, prayer or ardent belief. Secondly, God uses the Indians as his unconscious instruments. Therefore not only their benevolent gifts, but also the afflictions brought about by them, the burning, looting, and killing, have to be regarded as God-sent, and consequently require humble acceptance. As a consequence, historic agency must be denied to the Indians. While it thus remains possible to hate Indian perpetrators as worshippers of Satan and bloodthirsty heathens who deserve punishment, Indian benefactors do not deserve gratitude. Thus, for Rowlandson, the Bible, as a most precious gift from the Indian, is not a gift at all, but the return of something the Indian had stolen from the Europeans and therefore something which by right belongs to her. Thirdly, Rowlandson's representation of this exchange not only illustrates this system of symbolic book-keeping, but also translates the theological argument into a political one. The fact that the object in question is a Bible finally suggests a reading in which the Indian collecting the Bible as loot and then giving it away to the captive signifies an arrogant refusal of the Puritan gift of true religion and the incorrigibility of Indian savagery.

For Rowlandson, the concept of christianization as a means of peaceful colonization has utterly failed, and she cites ample evidence for this proposition:

> There was another praying Indian who, when he had done all the mischief he could, betrayed his own father into the English hands therby to purchase his own life. Another praying Indian was at Sudbury fight, though, as he deserved, he was afterwards hanged for it. There was another praying Indian so wicked and cruel as to wear a string about his neck strung with Christian hands. Another praying Indian, when they went to Sudbury fight, went with them and his squaw also went with him with her papoose at her back. (62)

Again and again Rowlandson embarks on diatribes against the treacherous Praying Indians, and, by implication, against the misguided efforts of the Puritan missionaries John Eliot and Daniel Gookin who had translated the Bible into Algonquin, taught the Indians how to read and write, made them wear European clothes and founded Praying Indians' towns. Clearly, for her, the aim to bring the Gospel to the natives, as it was proclaimed by the official seal of the Bay colony – which showed an Indian and bore the caption: "come over and help us" – should be given up. On the eve of King Philip's war, superintendent Gookin had boasted "that there is none of the praying Indians, young or old, but can readily answer any question of the catechism."[8] Rowlandson's narrative gives this assertion of Gookin's a grim twist. For when she engages in theological exegesis with one of her captors, she finds the

---

[8] James Axtell, *The Invasion Within: The Contest of Cultures in Colonial North America* (New York: Oxford UP, 1985): 224. See also also Henry Bowden, *American Indians and Christian Missions* (Chicago: U of Chicago P, 1982): 124: "Under Puritan tutelage many [Indians] learned to treat religious prepositions with the gravity of systematic theologians."

Indian incapable of understanding the spirit of the letter. Instead he produces a reading of the Bible which seems to her as perverse as it is finely argued and systematic, hence irrefutable by Rowlandson:

> There was another praying Indian who told me that he had a brother that would not eat horse; his conscience was so tender and scrupulous (though as large as hell for the destruction of poor Christians). Then he said he had read that scripture to him, 2 Kings 6:25, "There was a famine in Samaria, and behold they besieged it, until an ass's head was sold for fourscore of silver, and the fourth part of a kab of doves' dung for five pieces of silver." He expounded this place to his brother and showed him that it was lawful to eat in a famine which is not at another time. And now, says he, he will eat horse with any Indian of them all. (62)

Rowlandson's ironic aside cannot completely suppress the suggestion of irony on the Indian's part. Indeed, she seems more than dimly aware that his theological finesse echoes her own reading strategies.

Cultural Mimicry

My second example of deconstructive dynamics in the narrative concerns another encounter with Indian hybridity: the weaving and wearing of clothes as a technique and a practice of civilization taught by the missionaries. Again, Rowlandson argues against such efforts of transcending cultural boundaries: Just as the praying Indians accepted the gift of religion only in the most superficial manner and turned it into a rhetorical weapon against the English, they accepted the gifts of civilization and knowledge only in order to appropriate them for their hellish designs. The Indians' responses to the benevolence and generosity of the missionaries are violence and scorn; instead of producing pious proselytes, the missions have created a mock-image of civilization. For now Indians ride horses, possess livestock, use English weapons, they live in English-style houses, write letters and imitate the English in every way.[9] The home production of civilized clothes or the purchase of such clothes by selling beaver makes it even possible for the Indians to look like Europeans, while indeed they are as savage and cruel as ever:

> In that time came a company of Indians to us, near thirty, all on horseback. My heart skipped within me, thinking they had been Englishmen at the first sight of them, for they were dressed in English apparel, with hats, white neckcloths and sashes about

---

[9] See James Axtell, *The European and the Indian: Essays in the Ethnohistory of Colonial North America* (New York: Oxford UP, 1981), and "Some Thought on the Ethnohistory of Missions," in *After Columbus: Essays in the Ethnohistory of Colonial North America*, ed. Axtell (New York: Oxford UP, 1981): 39–68; Neil Salisbury, "Red Puritans," *William and Mary Quarterly* 31 (1974): 27–54; Virginia Dejohn Anderson, "King Philip's Herds: Indians, Colonists and the Problem of Livestock in Early New England," *William and Mary Quarterly* 51 (1994): 601–24; Walter T. Meserve, "English Works of Seventeenth-Century Indians," *American Quarterly* 8 (1956): 264–76.

their waists, and ribbons upon their shoulders, but when they came near there was a vast difference between the lovely faces of Christians and the foul looks of those heathens which much damped my spirit again. (58–59)

Almost obsessively, Rowlandson returns again and again to the topic and recounts numerous instances when Indians kill the English for clothes or strip dead colonists and rob them of their clothes. Indeed, when her captors eventually begin negotiations with the English about Rowlandson's release, the ransom they demand consists of money, liquor and trading cloth.

The most obvious reason why clothes should increasingly become a central topic in the narrative is rhetorical: Clothes constitute an apt metaphor by which the missionaries' work is characterized as purely superficial. In basic accord with her arguments about the impossibility of christianizing the savages, Rowlandson tries to redefine the difference between the Indians and the English not as a cultural but rather an ontological one. In this way she attempts to come to terms with the effects of cultural contact, which, she admits, threatens the conceptual and religious framework of European domination instead of enforcing native submission.

Yet in spite of her eloquence and her ability to cite her harsh experiences as proof, Rowlandson ultimately fails in her effort to contain and control what she sees as treacherous Indian mimicry. When she makes the case of the correct reading of Scripture, Rowlandson's argument is inhibited by her own problematic status as a woman author, as women were denied the authority to preach in Puritan society after the Hutchinson crisis. Rowlandson's effort to discuss theological matters with the Praying Indian lacks institutional backing, and sometimes she must resort to rhetorical rather than doctrinal means of refutation. But then Rowlandson is far from being the fine example of a Puritan saint she casts herself to be. There is more than one instance when she gives in to the Indians' demands and violates the rules of her cultural upbringing: Just as the Praying Indian she quotes and ridicules, she also comes to accept horse liver and other food she had first refused as abominable. A graver offense is her eventual willingness to work for her master even on the Sabbath, although she regards an earlier instance of this sin as one of the reasons why God had sent her the affliction of captivity in the first place. Finally, such transgressions under duress give way to a conscious strategy of cooperation. Rowlandon's narrative reveals a side to her life with the Indians which the Puritan vocabulary for cultural Otherness cannot account for. In this context the topic of European clothes worn by Indians acquires a completely different meaning.

For when Rowlandson recognizes her dependency on the goodwill of her captors, she makes the effort to create alliances with certain powerful individuals. She observes Indian everyday life and in the process ignores her reductionist cognitive patterns. As she tries to establish social relations with her master and mistress (finding her master approachable and protective, whereas she felt that she could not expect anything from her proud and vain mistress Weetamoo), she becomes poignantly aware that she is still far from understanding them: "Sometimes I met with favors and sometimes with nothing but frowns" (50), sometimes she was given something to eat, and then sometimes she was not. In this frightening situation of failing hermeneutics (both official and self-devised), Rowlandson found a way to transform what seemed to her Indian inconsistency and irresponsibility into more stable and more transparent relationships on which she could act and influence her condition: She began to knit and sew for the Indians, opening up a European site of production and trade within in the Indian economic system. She would exchange her commodities for food or even money, thus securing her survival by trade;[10] and she would use an eventual surplus by giving it away as a gift to her master and mistress in an effort to enhance their obligation to her. In this way, she herself supported the Indian craze for European clothes and provided them with the means of transgressing cultural boundaries.

Gift-Exchange

Mary Rowlandson continued to belive herself to be subjected to divine will, and she continued to hope to be exchanged and reunited with her husband, if favorable terms could be obtained by the Indians. As entrepreneur, however, she had become a subject of exchange and when, finally, her husband made an offer for her, she even had a say in the final ransom paid for her. She resented the Praying Indians immensely, but was dependent on their goodwill as it was they who wrote the letters of negotiation that brought about her release.[11] And, despite her resentment, Rowlandson's knitting and sewing contributed to the threat of cultural ambiguity which she denounced so eloquently.

At the end of the narrative, when Rowlandson describes her journey towards the final ceremony of exchange and release, some very intricately argued passages suggest how the author and the Indians acknowledged the captive's position between the two cultures. Until this moment she had observed the chronology of events; at the crucial moment of departure from the Indians, at the moment of imminent return, she engages in a series of digressions and flashbacks.

---

[10] Mitchell Breitwieser comments: "Her entry into exchange lifts her out of the abjection of being on the dole, and thus creates a measure of equality between herself and the captors, with whom she can now barter, that is, set terms, rather than only accept"; *American Puritanism and the Defense of Mourning* (Madison: U of Wisconsin P, 1990): 146.

[11] In fact, one of them, James the Printer, after the war returned to Boston where he had worked in a printer's shop, and was involved in the printing of Rowlandson's narrative (Meserve, "English Works of Seventeenth-Century Indians," 267–77).

> In my travels an Indian came to me and told me if I were willing, he and his squaw
> would run away and go home along with me. I told him no. I was not willing to run
> away but desired to wait God's time that I might go home quietly and without fear.
> And now God hath granted me my desire. (70)

This earlier refusal to act is justified as the only appropriate behaviour of passively awaiting God's deliverance. Still, Mary Rowlandson does not place this incident in the chronological sequence of events, but mentions it only after the fact of her deliverance, when Providence has decided her fate. If reported earlier, this refusal of going home would have acquired a different meaning. Her argument is running a certain risk here, and she therefore makes an additional effort to prove her point. For by rendering the Indian's proposal as "run[ning] away and go[ing] home [...] with me," she effectively appropriates the Indian as a figure for her cause. This tropological strategy is repeated in what may be regarded as the manifestation of the textually repressed:

> O, the wonderful power of God that I have seen and the experience I have had! I have
> been in the midst of those roaring lions and savage bears that feared neither God nor
> man nor the devil, by night and day, alone and in company, sleeping all sorts together,
> and yet not one of them ever offered me the least abuse of unchastity to me in word or
> action. (70)

As before, this civil Indian behavior does not lead to a revision of the notion of the "savages," but is ascribed to God's miraculous power. But it is obvious that Rowlandson had to face the problem to convince her community that neither rape had taken place (a practice the Indians during this war were commonly accused of), nor had she consented to a sexual relationship with the "one-eyed sachem," as some rumours told by other Puritan sources would have it.[12]

> Though some are ready to say I speak it for my own credit, I speak it in the presence
> of God and to His glory. God's power is as great now and as sufficient to save as
> when He preserved Daniel in the lion's den or the three children in the fiery furnace.
> I may well say as his Psalm 107:12, "Oh, give thanks unto the Lord for He is good,
> for His mercy endureth forever. Let the redeemed of the Lord say so whom He hath
> redeemed from the hand of the enemy, especially that I should come away in the
> midst of so many hundreds of enemies quietly and peaceably and not a dog moving
> his tongue. (70)

If not an Indian dog moved his tongue, how dare the Puritans? When the sequence ends by finally taking leave, it resonates with ambivalence: "So I took my leave of them, and in coming along my heart melted into tears more than all the while I was with them, and I was almost swallowed up with the thoughts that ever I should go home again" (71).

---

[12] See esp. Nathaniel Saltonstall's reports on King Philip's War.

When the Indians finally release her for money and liquor (the trading cloth having been stolen before the transaction took place), and all the accounts are settled, they present her aptly with the parting gift of – clothes. The origins of this gift – a hood and a scarf – remain unknown; but be they Indian or European, they stress the ambiguity of Rowlandson's cultural identity. While hood and scarf certainly suggest European dress codes, they have become tokens of cultural alienability. In a similar way, this gift casts the earlier transactions into a different light. What had appeared as barter and trade of commodities now acquires the meaning of a gift exchange, which, with its symbolic meaning of mutual obligations, suggests Rowlandson's incorporation into Indian culture.[13]

Conclusion

There seems to be a structural similarity between Rowlandson's production of textiles and her textual production, since they serve the same function of survival and integration in both cultures respectively. In the text, however, she attempts to counterbalance the deceitful effects of her knittings by constantly expanding on the irreducible gap between Christians and heathen, between a civilized and a barbaric people. The text thus reveals and replaces the textiles which circulate across the cultural border in both directions, blurring differences and creating uncertainties with respect to property rights and cultural propriety.

While this substitution of the text for the textiles is meant as a way to re-establish codes of signification, it cannot but call attention to the textual structures which make such codes fragile in the first place. Once the theme of deceit and treachery masquerade is introduced with the Indians dressed up as Europeans and their false reading of Scripture according to their needs, one cannot but recognize in them the distorted mirror figure of Mary Rowlandson herself. This folding of the text onto itself disrupt the hermeneutical operations that were designed to keep the narrative within the boundaries of orthodox Puritanism. A suspicious reader might even read Rowlandson's orthodox religious hermeneutics themselves as a ruse.

It is no accident, however, that Mary Rowlandson has received all signs and attributes of her cultural identity (the Bible; her non-violation; hood and scarf) from the Indians. In one way or another, all the features of the text I have commented on are related to the impossible position of a subject caught between conflicting symbolic orders. In her writing, Rowlandson succeeds in transforming her experience as an object of exchange between the two cultures into a drama of Puritan exile and redemption in which she figures as the exemplary signifier. No doubt this trans-

---

[13] I have elaborated this point in "Die Gabe der Wilden: Mary Rowlandson's *Captivity Narrative*," in *Ethik der Gabe: Denken nach Jacques Derrida*, ed. Michael Wetzel & Jean-Michel Rabaté (Berlin: Akademie, 1993): 157–72.

formation affirms and perpetuates the dominant discourse, but to produce it convincingly Rowlandson must claim an authority otherwise not granted to women. For this reason, her husband's sermon and the anonymous introduction by a "friend" seek to supplement her challenged and fragile authority with theirs. The logic of this supplement, however, unfolds presently, for it draws attention to the way her narrative presents a passage from the needle to the pen that is apt to subvert the order she sets out to reconfirm.

WORKS CITED

Anderson, Benedict. "Exodus," *Critical Inquiry* 20 (1994): 314–27.

Anderson, Virginia Dejohn. "King Philip's Herds: Indians, Colonists and the Problem of Livestock in Early New England," *William and Mary Quarterly* 51 (1994): 601–24.

Armstrong, Nancy, & Leonard Tennenhouse. *The Imaginary Puritan: Literature, Intellectual Labor, and the Origins of Personal Life* (Berkeley: U of California P, 1992).

Axtell, James. *The European and the Indian: Essays in the Ethnohistory of Colonial North America* (New York: Oxford UP, 1981).

——. *The Invasion Within. The Contest of Cultures in Colonial North America* (New York: Oxford UP, 1985).

——. "Some Thought on the Ethnohistory of Missions," in *After Columbus: Essays in the Ethnohistory of Colonial North America*, ed. Axtell (New York: Oxford UP, 1981): 39–68.

Bourne, Russell. *The Red King's Rebellion: Racial Politics in New England, 1675–1678* (New York: Atheneum, 1990).

Bowden, Henry. *American Indians and Christian Missions* (Chicago: U of Chicago P, 1982).

Breitwieser, Mitchell. *American Puritanism and the Defense of Mourning* (Madison: U of Wisconsin P, 1990).

Burnham, Michelle. *Captivity and Sentiment: Cultural Exchange in American Literature, 1682–1861* (Hanover NH: UP of New England, 1997).

Clifford, James. *Routes: Travel and Translation in the Late Twentieth Century* (Cambridge MA: Harvard UP, 1997).

Derounian, Kathryn Zabelle, "The Publication, Promotion and Distribution of Mary Rowlandson's Indian Captivity Narrative," *Early American Literature* 23 (1988): 239–61.

Downing, David. "'Streams of Scripture Comfort': Mary Rowlandson's Typological Use of the Bible," *Early American Literature* 15 (1980–81): 252–59.

Ebersole, Gary. *Captured by Texts: Puritan to Postmodern Images of Captivity* (Charlottesville: U of Virginia P, 1995).

Greenblatt, Stephen. *Marvelous Encounters: The Wonder of the New World* (Oxford: Clarendon, 1991).

Haselstein, Ulla. "Die Gabe der Wilden: Mary Rowlandson's *Captivity Narrative*," in *Ethik der Gabe: Denken nach Jacques Derrida*, ed. Michael Wetzel & Jean–Michel Rabaté (Berlin: Akademie, 1993): 157–72.

Jennings, Francis. *The Invasion of America: Indians, Colonialism, and the Cant of Conquest* (New York: W.W. Norton, 1976).

Leach, Edward. *Flintlock and Tomahawk: New England in King Philip's War* (1958; New York: W.W. Norton, 1966).

Lepore, Jill. *The Name of War: King Philip's War and the Origins of American Identity* (New York: Alfred A. Knopf, 1999).

Meserve, Walter T. "English Works of Seventeenth Century Indians," *American Quarterly* 8 (1956): 264–76.

Pearce, Roy Harvey. *Savagism and Civilisation* (1953; Berkeley: U of California P, 1988).

Pratt, Mary Louise. "Fieldwork in Common Places," in *Writing Culture: The Poetics and Politics of Ethnography*, ed. James Clifford & George E. Marcus (Berkeley: U of California P, 1986): 27–50.

Salisbury, Neil. "Red Puritans," *William and Mary Quarterly* 31 (1974): 27–54.

Shuffleton, Frank, ed. *A Mixed Race: Ethnicity in Early America* (New York: Oxford UP, 1993).

Slotkin, Richard. *Regeneration Through Violence* (Middletown CT: Wesleyan UP, 1974).

Tompkins, Jane. "'Indians': Textuality, Morality, and the Problem of History," in *"Race," Writing, and Difference*, ed. Henry Louis Gates, Jr. (Chicago: U of Chicago P, 1986): 59–77.

Vaughn, Alden T., & Edward W. Clark, ed. *Puritans Among the Indians: Accounts of Captivity and Redemption, 1676–1724* (Cambridge MA: Harvard UP / Belknap, 1981).

❧

Colonial Canada's Forgotten Captivity Narratives
James Russell's *Matilda; or, the Indian's Captive* (1833)

PILAR CUDER DOMÍNGUEZ

I N *THE IGNOBLE SAVAGE* (1975), Louise K. Barnett defines a captivity narrative as one that typically "begins with an Indian raid in which some whites are massacred, usually in brief but revolting detail, and some, including the author, are carried away. The main body of the account is devoted to the hardships of the captivity period, which concludes with the author's return to civilized society."[1] According to classic studies of this genre, the pattern established in seventeenth and eighteenth century narratives degenerated into the frontier romance, in which the emphasis shifted from the captive (and his or her true account) to the rescuer. Central to this understanding of the evolution of captivity narratives is the assumption that they were "polluted" by foreign conventions, and particularly those of the English novel of sensibility and the historical romance. Recent criticism, however, has found fault with these ideas, and has highlighted instead the hybridity of the genre since its inception, both in its status as cultural document and as stylistic artifact: Christopher Castiglia's focus on the gendering of these narratives underlines the challenge they pose to the fixity of race and gender, so that "the captives ultimately subvert their intended function as symbols of the stable nation,"[2] whereas Michelle Burnham convincingly argues against the traditional separation of genres, and suggests that sentimentalism surfaces in colonial captivity narratives, sentimental novels and slave narratives of the period because the " ' moving' qualities" of these texts

> are inextricably linked to the movements in and by the texts themselves across various
> borders. In their narrative content as well as in their circulation as print commodities,

---

[1] Louise K. Barnett, *The Ignoble Savage: American Literary Racism, 1790–1890* (Westport CT: Greenwood, 1975): 7.

[2] Christopher Castiglia, *Bound and Determined: Captivity, Culture-Crossing, and White Womanhood from Mary Rowlandson to Patty Hearst* (Chicago: U of Chicago P, 1996): 9.

these texts traverse those very cultural, national, and racial boundaries that they seem
so indelibly to inscribe. Captivity literature, like its heroines, constantly negotiates
zones of contact such as the 'frontier,' the Atlantic Ocean, the master/slave division,
and the color line.[3]

Accepting, even provisionally, the implications of these arguments, should lead us to
problematize our reading of captivity stories – both true accounts and fictions –
although the prominent role they play in the nation-building project on the North
American continent is left fairly untouched. To add to these lines of enquiry, I would
like to bring into light a Canadian novel, James Russell's *Matilda; or, the Indian's
Captive*, published in Three Rivers (Quebec) in 1833.[4] Little is known about the
author: Mary Lu MacDonald lists him as an English immigrant in Canada, of unknown occupation, religion, or politics;[5] *Matilda* would be his only published work,
and it has the dubious honour of being the second novel ever published in Canada,
after Julia Hart's *St Ursula's Convent* (Kingston, Ontario, 1824).

Russell's novel must have been intended to capitalize on the already wide public
appeal of the captivity narrative, as the title clearly promised its potential readership
the titillation of a heady mixture of sex and violence. True to form, the "Preface"
addressed the readers in order to assure them that the story was founded on fact, "the
author having heard the outlines from the lady herself, who was really taken by the
Indians at the period mentioned in this work," to deny that the narrative might be
influenced by literary sources, and to finally promise a happy ending in which
Divine Providence would make itself felt (i–iii). This last assertion is true, but that
the former are simply conventional claims, even the most superficial reading cannot
fail to notice.

Matilda; or, the Indian's Captive spans approximately twenty years, from 1764
to 1783, an extremely eventful period which saw conflictive white and Native allegiances that finally crystallized in the emergence of the USA and British North
America, later Canada. Russell's choice of a period for his tale is therefore far from
accidental, and accordingly the story moves across several, but unclear, borders: first
Lower Canada, then New York State, later Upper Canada, once again New York, and
eventually, after a transatlantic passage, England.

At the beginning of the novel, Matilda Milford is a four-year-old girl born to an
Englishman and his Canadian wife, living in "a remote part of Lower Canada." As
she is happily playing on a river bank and her parents leave her unsupervised for a

---

[3] Michelle Burnham, *Captivity and Sentiment: Cultural Exchange in American Literature,
1682–1861* (Hanover NH: UP of New England, 1993): 3.

[4] Quotations are taken from the facsimile edition (New York: Garland, 1977).

[5] Mary Lu MacDonald, *Literature and Society in the Canadas 1817–1850* (Lewinston, Ont.:
Edwin Mellen, 1992): 280.

few minutes, an Indian family steal her and take her away. Unable to find out their daughter's whereabouts, the mother dies of grief in a week, and the father returns to England. A few months later, Matilda is spotted near the falls of Niagara by a kind American couple, the Wilsons, who manage to buy her from her captors, and, being childless, decide to adopt her. Matilda soon forgets her captivity, and is brought up as Matilda Wilson, until one day, when she is fourteen and has wandered too far from home, a young Indian attempts to kidnap her, allegedly she had been meant for his wife when she was stolen. The attempt fails due to the timely intervention of a young English gentleman, Captain Clifford, who is a prisoner of war to the Americans (the War of Independence being then in full swing). Afraid that the Indians may return once more to claim Matilda for their own, the Wilsons decide to move right away as far and as quietly as possible. They settle in Kingston, Ontario, where, two years later, Matilda will again be the victim of an attempt on her life and honour, this time by one Captain Fitzgibbon whose offer of marriage she rejected. Though he had stayed behind in New York, Captain Clifford manages to make another timely entrance, and deliver her from the unwanted suitor. The death of Mr Wilson's father in Albany brings the family back to the States in 1783, when Matilda is yet once more in danger, this time due to a carriage accident. She is duly rescued by Captain Clifford, who was on his way to Kingston to visit them, once he was free. His providential rescues are interpreted as a sign from Heaven, and thus they are promptly joined in holy matrimony, but not before the Wilsons have disclosed to both the secret of Matilda's unknown origins. A fortnight after the ceremony, Matilda's Indian captor happens to pass by. Recognized by Mr Wilson, he manages to gather some information that may lead to the discovery of Matilda's parentage, particularly because he retrieves from the Indian a picture book bearing her name and date of birth which she had been playing with at the time of her capture. The newly-wed couple is then called to England to claim Clifford's inheritance after his father's death, and there Matilda comes across her true father, a wealthy nobleman who never remarried and now acknowledges her as his long lost daughter and only heir. The novel thus brings Matilda from Indian captivity in the New World to the peak of rank and fortune in the Old, as the author remarks:

> Witness reader, the once poor and forlorn Indian's captive has now become the adored wife of a gentleman of the first standing in society, both for personal accomplishments and wealth, and is likewise the sole heiress to an immense property by her father, all which blessings, we hope she will be grateful for, and appreciate their value in a true light. (203–04)

The most remarkable feature of the novel is the complication of the plot, which is made up not just of one captivity, but of several similar episodes which endanger the protagonist. The captivity period itself – ie, the few months the child Matilda spends with her captors – receives little attention, and is painted with just enough strokes to emphasize the Indians' cruelty. It is known, for instance, that they beat the child very often (24). The main function this episode fulfils in the novel is no other than to separate Matilda from her parents and her rightful place in the world, an obstacle that the narrative will have to remove at the end, thus proving that a providential justice underlies even the most extraordinary events and the most awful misfortune. In order to assert this super-natural, all-encompassing order, the author is not afraid to challenge all laws of the natural order, and even the most basic rules of veri-similitude. Though in the history of European settlement on the North American continent it was not infrequent for Natives to capture children so that Matilda's story fits in the usual pattern, the details Russell works into the narrative contradict both the historical data and the true accounts of captives.[6] Thus, for instance, the closeness that tended to develop between captors and captive is abandoned for a less ambiguous dread of the Other. When Matilda is found by Mr and Mrs Wilson, she immediately takes to them, and eyes "the Indians with the greatest dread, and every motion of theirs seemed to excite the deepest anxiety in her young breast" (18).

Russell's lack of interest in the phenomenon of captivity itself, and his deployment of this motif only insofar as it imparts an exotic, mysterious quality on his main character, is also noticeable in his treatment of the Indians. They are at best agents of Destiny, in that they represent the unpredictable forces of life; at worst, they are demonized into cruel, threatening evildoers. Most frequently they are referred to as "savages." As Leslie Monkman[7] has pointed out, this treatment of Indians as savage antagonists to white settlers is characteristic of English-Canadian literature before 1840, Richardson's *Wacousta* being the best example (8–22).[8]

However, the absence of a real captivity period forces Russell to find other ways to maintain the readers' interest, and he tries to do so by means of an accumulation of episodes which place the sweet Matilda in danger: not just the one isolated kidnap, but two other attempts – one by the young Indian male and another by an unprincipled officer, Fitzgibbon – and finally, when one more attack would seem too

---

[6] James Axtell, *The European and the Indian: Essays in the Ethnohistory of Colonial North America* (New York: Oxford UP, 1981): 168–206.

[7] Leslie Monkman, *A Native Heritage: Images of the Indian in English-Canadian Literature* (Toronto: U of Toronto P, 1981).

[8] Daniel Francis' more recent study *The Imaginary Indian: The Image of the Indian in Cana-dian Culture* (Vancouver: Arsenal Pulp Press, 1992) is at odds with Monkman's. Francis contends (after the views of ethnohistorian Bruce Trigger) that "as long as Aboriginals were important in the life of the country – as traders and military allies – they received reasonably fair treatment at the hands of historians. Only after about 1840, when Native people had ceased to play much of a role in Canadian society, did historians begin to marginalize and demonize them" (166; cf also, on this point, his "Introduction"). Probably both positions make too general a statement to apply in all cases.

far-fetched even for the most gullible reader, a life-threatening accident. At the same time, he is at pains to contrive the means to effect Matilda's deliverance – since, needless to say, this sentimental heroine is utterly incapable of self-preservation, and faints at each and all high points of her story. As a succession of knights-errant would be too unlikely, Russell settles for just one, Captain Clifford, thereby reinforcing the sense of pre-destination and destiny that pervades the novel.

A further result of the plot is an extremely conservative position concerning gender issues. Captivity narratives, according to Castiglia, offered women

> a female picaresque, an adventure story set [...] outside the home. In the American "wilderness," white women could demonstrate skills and attitudes of which their home cultures thought them incapable. As it evolved from a religious document of the seventeenth to a feminist plot of the twentieth century, the captivity narrative allowed women authors to create a symbolic economy through which to express dissatisfaction with the roles traditionally offered white women in America, and to reimagine those roles and narratives that normalize them, giving rise ultimately to a new female subject and to the female audience on which she relies. (4)

But nothing of the sort takes place in *Matilda; or, the Indian's Captive*. On the contrary, Matilda is, in her passivity, the paragon of perfect femininity. She is idealized to the point of utter invisibility. The dangers that surround her do not humanize her; they serve only to encourage and justify the existence of mechanisms of male surveillance. She needs to be constantly watched over, supervised, protected, and eventually rescued. In her total dependence, she has to pass from the care of her adoptive parents to that of her husband. The perils lurking around a woman, threatening not just her life but, most importantly, her honour, prevent all female autonomy in the novel and strengthen male control, whereas women's mute submission is shown to be the safest road to the highest rewards.

Nevertheless, the romantic lineaments of the tale and their apparent arbitrariness cannot completely obscure the complex web of political allegiances at their heart. To start with, the episodes that make up Matilda's story overlap with crucial moments of the history of the continent. She was born in Lower Canada, i. e. New France, in 1764, months after the end of the Seven Years' War which made the *belle province* an English possession. Her father, described as an Englishman who came from the USA, must have been part of that first wave of settlers the British government encouraged in order to quickly outnumber the French-speaking, catholic population of the new colony.[9] Matilda was captured by the Indians in 1768, during a period of Native unrest,[10] and she suffered her first failed kidnap attempt in 1778, in the

---

[9] See J.M. Bumsted, *A History of the Canadian Peoples* (Toronto: Oxford UP, 1998): 75.

[10] Peter N. Carroll & David W. Noble, *The Free and the Unfree: A New History of the United States* (New York: Penguin, 2nd ed. 1988): 106–107.

middle of the American War of Independence. Her adoptive father's decision to go north and settle in Upper Canada – allegedly to lose Matilda's Indian captors – makes him a Loyalist, a fact which is hinted in the novel: "as [Mr Wilson] himself had never been called upon to swear allegiance to either the British or American Governments (being so far from the seat of war) there was nothing to prevent him from removing to the British territories, particularly as he was still partial to that constitution" (53). Captain Clifford himself, Matilda's full-time rescuer, has fought in the war on the British side: "Matilda's deliverer informed them that his name was Clifford, that he was a Captain in the British army, that he had been wounded and taken prisoner at the battle of Bunker Hill, on 17 June 1775, by the Americans; and that he was on parole not to serve again during the present war" (45–46). Finally, Matilda's Indian captor happens to have fought on the American side, as he reveals in his timely arrival, near the end of the novel (158). As a result, all the caring, benevolent, refined characters in the novel happen to be British or Canadian in origin and / or sympathies, while cruel or unrefined ones must inevitably be Americans or Natives with American leanings.

The polarization of the novel's characters indicates that the sentimental tale can and should be read as a political document as well. By providing clear-cut binary distinctions, male / female, good / evil, British / non-british, white / non-white, high-class / low-class on his characters, Russell is superimposing borders where there are in fact only few and blurred limits. He thus manages to turn a mixed contact zone into a British dominion, though only provisionally, for the only clean space where duties and alliances are clear, and where the self is unthreatened, lies beyond the sea, in Britain, the site of stable identity for the colony.

Consequently, Russell's *Matilda; or, the Indian's Captive* comes to read as an allegory of national identity, a blueprint for Canadianness.[11] It is not unheard-of for women to be the living symbols of a nation, just as other bigger-than-life abstractions (justice, freedom, etc) are often represented in female shape in the arts and letters (Delacroix's famous painting "Liberty leading the people" would be a well-known example of such gendered discourse). What's more, other Canadian works of the period, and especially sentimental novels, concur in this discursive genderization of a Canadian essence. Quite a few of them, like Rosanna Leprohon's *Antoinette de Mirecourt; or Secret Marriage and Secret Sorrowing* (1864), encode the political

---

[11] On the connections between nation and literature, especially as pertaining to the case of Canada and the USA, see Sarah M. Corse, *Nationalism and Literature: The Politics of Culture in Canada and the United States* (Cambridge: Cambridge UP, 1997).

alliance between the French and the English peoples inside the nation as the personal partnership of husband and wife in marriage.[12]

In the case of Russell's novel, the historical connections I have pointed out above serve the ultimate aim of endowing the fate of Matilda with political and national relevance, so that little by little, by sheer accumulation, the parallelisms between the position of young woman and new nation can be inferred. Just as the innocent Matilda is exposed to unspeakable dangers, the colony too is in need of protection. Just as this sweet woman depends on her powerful male guardians – father and/or husband – for material comforts and rewards, Canada too will reach her highest destiny if only she accepts to be dependent on Britain, the "wife of," the "sole heiress to." In exchange for submission, Matilda/Canada gains a stable sense of self, free from the conflict of having to choose a subject position. The unnamed and unknown Matilda of the beginning of the novel eventually becomes the worthy Mrs Clifford and takes her rightful place in the world, an appealing image of success for colonial subjects, a dream come true. James Russell wrote for an imagined community of British imperialists, who would share his vision of a triumphant Britishness in North America, a space decidedly non-American, non-Native, aristocratic in intent and moral views. *Matilda; or, the Indian's Captive* is thus the site of an authoritative colonial and colonialist discourse. Unlike other authors of captivity narratives, James Russell deploys the ready-made captivity mythology not in order to question standard values, but only in so far as it allows him to confer a name, define an origin, police a border, construct a culture.

WORKS CITED

Axtell, James. *The European and the Indian: Essays in the Ethnohistory of Colonial North America* (New York: Oxford UP, 1981).

Barnett, Louise K. *The Ignoble Savage: American Literary Racism, 1790–1890* (Westport CT: Greenwood, 1975).

Bumsted, J.M. *A History of the Canadian Peoples* (Toronto: Oxford UP, 1998).

Burnham, Michelle. *Captivity and Sentiment: Cultural Exchange in American Literature, 1682–1861* (Hanover NH: UP of New England, 1997).

Carroll, Peter N. & David W. Noble. *The Free and the Unfree: A New History of the United States* (New York: Penguin, 2nd ed. 1988).

---

[12] On this topic, see Carl Murphy's article "The Marriage Metaphor in Nineteenth-Century English-Canadian Fiction," *Studies in Canadian Literature* 13.1 (1988): 1–19, on what he has termed "the marriage metaphor" in other Canadian novels, and my article "Negotiations of Gender and Nationhood in Early Canadian Literature," *International Journal of Canadian Studies* 18 (1988): 97–113.

Castiglia, Christopher. *Bound and Determined: Captivity, Culture-Crossing, and White Woman-hood from Mary Rowlandson to Patty Hearst* (Chicago: U of Chicago P, 1996).

Corse, Sarah M. *Nationalism and Literature: The Politics of Culture in Canada and the United States* (Cambridge: Cambridge UP, 1997).

Cuder Domínguez, Pilar. "Negotiations of Gender and Nationhood in Early Canadian Literature." *International Journal of Canadian Studies* 18 (1998): 97–113.

Francis, Daniel. *The Imaginary Indian: The Image of the Indian in Canadian Culture* (Vancouver: Arsenal Pulp Press, 1995).

MacDonald, Mary Lu. *Literature and Society in the Canadas 1817–1850* (Lewinston, Ontario: Edwin Mellen, 1992).

Monkman, Leslie. *A Native Heritage: Images of the Indian in English-Canadian Literature* (Toronto: U of Toronto P, 1981).

Murphy, Carl. "The Marriage Metaphor in Nineteenth-century English-Canadian Fiction," *Studies in Canadian Literature* 13.1 (1988): 1–19.

Russell, James. *Matilda; or, the Indian's Captive* (Three Rivers: George Stubbs, 1833;New York: Garland, facsimile ed. 1977).

ༀ

Northrop Frye and Margaret Atwood
On National Identity in Canadian Literature

M IRKO J URAK

I
N 1972 M ARGARET A TWOOD PUBLISHED a collection of essays entitled *Survival*. In this "thematic guide to Canadian literature" she established a close link between the development of Canadian literature and questions concerning the development of Canadian national identity and integrity. Although such themes had been present for some time in different writings and particularly in public discussions in Canada, they had not been definitely settled. As a result, they were opened again and again by Canadian authors, who each interpreted them differently and offered various solutions. If a generalized conclusion of these views is made, two completely opposite views can be established: On the one side there are authors and critics who assert that Canadian literature is only a kind of extension of two other literatures, namely English and French literatures. They claim that in this way Canadian literature is really becoming international, because it is forced to accept aesthetic criteria of world literature as the only qualification of its value. There are, on the other side, authors who believe that individual features of Canadian literature – particularly in the twentieth century – can easily be observed and that Canadian literature cannot be measured only by the degree of its international orientation or its similarity with English (or American) literature. These authors maintain that a new stage of development in Canadian literature has been reached and that this achievement should also be reflected in school syllabi. They argue that the syllabi should be changed in favour of Canadian authors whose works should not only be studied only in elementary and secondary schools, but also at the university level. In spite of the fact that some changes in reading syllabi have taken place during the last few decades in Canadian schools, Margaret Atwood noticed even in 1995 that pupils in secondary shools still preferred reading J.D. Salinger's novel *The Catcher in the*

Rye to Canadian youth fiction, although Canada is particularly rich in the field of youth literature.[1]

Margaret Atwood was especially shocked when she discovered – but this happened only after her graduation – that Canadian literature was not just "British literature imported or American literature with something missing, but that it had a distinct tradition of its own."[2] She realized then that Canadian literature had its own characteristics, which had not been openly and clearly presented to the world but which were shyly hiding behind the image of English literature. The damage done by taking such a position, says Atwood, is not only the attitude authors (and critics) take towards their own work, but also that it diminishes or even negates the endeavours and achievements made by previous generations of Canadian authors which established the present cultural and intellectual image of Canada.

Discussions relating to these questions are frequently made even more complicated because Canada is a multi-ethnic society, which can be well illustrated by some historical, social and linguistic facts. In the 1991 Census, more than one hundred ethnic groups were identified in Canada.[3] Although British and French ancestors were still the most common in this census, almost one third of the population declared their origin to be other than British or French; and more than four million Canadians also reported that their mother tongue was neither English nor French. As early as October 1971, Canada announced its multicultural policy, according to which it would support "programs aimed at retaining, developing and sharing these cultures on a larger scale and programs which encourage mutual appreciation and understanding among Canadians."[4] In practice, this means that the Canadian government has accepted an obligation to provide assistance to different ethnic groups in maintaining and developing their cultural heritage, to support cultural-linguistic courses, to enable the training of instructors and so on. These measures should help emigrants to preserve their cultural heritage and indirectly, to integrate more easily into Canadian society. Canada's Constitution Act (1982) recognizes the Aboriginal ancestry of three groups: North American Indians (461,000), Inuit (36,000), and Métis (135,000), the latter being of mixed European and North American Indian descent. In the above-mentioned Act, Canada recognizes two official languages, English and French, which are equal. However, only about four million Canadians can converse in both French and English. This represents about 16 percent of the population, which, on 1 July 1995, reached nearly thirty million

---

[1] Margaret Atwood, *Strange Things: The Malevolent North in Canadian Literature* (Oxford: Oxford UP, 1995): 10.

[2] Atwood, *Survival* (Toronto: Anansi, 1972): 237.

[3] *Canada Handbook 1997* (Ottawa: Statistics Canada, 1996): 68.

[4] *Canada Handbook* (Ottawa: Canadian Government Publishing Centre, 1984): 61.

people.[5] The complexity of ethnic and linguistic questions in Canada has undoubtedly had a strong impact on Canadian culture. Still, the most relevant relations between what can be referred to as 'Canadian literature' and other literatures are still mainly limited to influences coming from English, French and American literature.

In regard to Canadian identity and its representation in Canadian literature, Atwood points out in *Survival* that "Canadian content" can not be considered as a decisive criterion for recognizing a work of art as "Canadian." Readers should find in this literature a universal meaning as well as specific types of images, and it is the totality of its spiritual, aesthetic, and formal features of the work, which places it in the framework of Canadian life and art. Margaret Atwood also rejects the claim that Canadian writers should primarily deal with themes stressing the Calvinistic and the Colonial belief that heroes in Canadian life and literature are "doomed and powerless." Instead, she asserts the opposite: the writer should name the real causes of victimization and not link them with Fate or Cosmos. Atwood sees as a more likely cause of the country's uncertainty Canada's long dependence on England and France, and, in modern times, on the USA. She explains that such a position regarding Canada only as an extension of other nations was favourably looked on by these countries because they wished to retain Canada in their political, cultural and economic domain. Canadians should be aware of the fact that "big nations" have no special sympathy for "small nations" when they wish to become independent. Canadians should therefore be more self-aware and more affirmative of their national and cultural identity, because this awareness is really one of the most important factors contributing to the self-image of a country. It is interesting to see that in this argument Atwood links Canada with "small nations caught between big ones when the former try to preserve their own identity."[6] A parallel can be found with Australia where the movement for complete sovereignty of the country is relatively strong, and well-known writers, like Thomas Kenneally, may be found in its ranks. Although Canada and Australia are, historically speaking, among 'new' nations, their images in the eyes of many European observers are far from being "small nations." It is very likely that the self-image of Canadians and Australians has changed favourably during the past few decades and that their self-respect has grown to the role their countries play not only in the economic and political fields of our global village but also in proportion with their artistic achievements.

The question of Canadian national and cultural independence appeared already in the nineteenth century, and several Canadian authors wrote about it or mentioned it in different studies, in introductions to their works (or works which they edited), in

---

[5] *Canada Handbook* 1997: 33, 59)

[6] Atwood, *Survival*, 239–41.

literary histories, and so on.[7] Among the early writers who reflected upon these issues are, for example, Susanna Moodie, Sir Daniel Wilson, Bliss Carman, Duncan Campbell Scott. In their view English literature had too strong an influence on Canadian literary creativity, so that many authors simply copied English writing instead of contributing original writing about problems Canadians had to face in the cold North or in the prairies. This new approach might bring at first a lowering of the standard of literary aesthetics, but it would be profitable in the long run. The Canadian existence, they said, should not only be a copy of British rural or urban life, but a reflection of their own environment and their own existential dilemmas. This question of democratic patriotism was also noticed at the outbreak of both the First and Second World Wars. The Canadians did not feel that these wars were their 'own wars,' and they therefore introduced conscription rather late, in 1917 and in 1944 respectively, when the wars were already in full swing.

It is a well-known fact that international policy as led by the USA became rather influential in Canada in the twentieth century. Many Canadians began to worry that Canada was beginning to be an American protectorate, not only as far as politics and the economy were concerned, but also in regard to cultural and intellectual life generally. This fear spread particularly after 1988, when Canada signed a free trade agreement with the USA. This is undoubtedly one of the reasons why the Canadians sometimes see the USA as a force which took the position previously held by Britain and France, even in literary matters.

Lionel Stevenson, with his *Appraisals of Canadian Literature* (1926), is "one of" the early twentieth-century Canadian authors who recommended that Canadian writers should stand for specific Canadian cultural and social values in their works, avoiding at the same time the use of a propagandistic tone. A view somewhat different – yet still fairly close to the national agenda – was expressed by Frederick Philip Grove in his study *It Needs to be Said* (1929). Grove suggests that, in their fiction, Canadian authors should deal with general human questions; however, they should also pay more attention to regional characteristics of Canadian life. Such views were also taken by a number of other Canadian writers in the period between the two Wars.

However, opposing voices were also heard on the Canadian literary scene from the 1920s onwards. For example, A.J.M. Smith advocated the position that the search for Canadian national identity was meaningless in the period of a growing internationalism, adding that the goal towards the development of a typically Canadian *literature* could not add anything essential to Canadian *culture*. Smith first clearly expressed this opinion in 1943 and he repeated it afterwards in various

---

[7] William Metcalfe, ed. *Understanding Canada* (New York & London: New York UP, 1982); W.H. New, *A History of Canadian Literature* (Houndmills: Macmillan, 1989).

writings. The literary theoretician and critic, Marshall McLuhan (1911–80), whose views on modern society were most clearly expressed in his works *The Mechanical Bride: Folklore of Industrial Man* (1951), *The Gutenberg Galaxy: The Making of Typographic Man* (1962) and *Understanding Media: The Extension of Man* (1964), states that new technologies promote the progress of civilization on an international level, and that nowadays information reaches many more people through various new media and that the world has thus become "a global village." Technological communication has brought about the postnational era, in which the freedom of information has broken down many boundaries. Even though McLuhan's message is essentially correct, this does not mean that adherence to national values should be abolished; on the contrary, many nations have become aware of the fact that globalization is not only positive, but that it may bring with it a loss of individuality, not only on a personal but also on a national level, particularly for nations who are not among the economically and politically most influential states. This awareness has caused a reaction even in countries who are by no means poor, such as France or the Scandinavian countries, where acts of parliament have been enacted to protect the use of the official language, to protect and subsidize their own television productions and television programs, and to limit the proportion of foreign programs on television – all of these being measures to protect national cultural interests in television, which is the most influential mass media today.

Although the greatest Canadian literary critic Northrop Frye (1912–99) did not explicitly take the side of those authors and intellectuals who overtly defended 'Canadian literature and culture' *per se*, his sympathies expressed in his best known work *The Bush Garden* (1971) are undoubtedly in their favour. Frye did not see these writers as 'Canadian nationalists,' a label which is often used by the opponents of national independence and which frequently bears a negative connotation. (It is also wrongly used for authors who defend the right to preserve their national identity vis-à-vis extreme internationalism and unification, which is endangering man's ethnic and cultural independence and integrity.) In his essay "Canada and Its Poetry,"[8] Frye defends the need to unite contemporary Canadian literature with other world literatures, and he particularly stresses the necessity to apply those aesthetic criteria to it which are also used elsewhere for assessing the best literary works. According to his views, Canadian literature had been under foreign influence for a long time, and Frye thinks that the moment has come when both tendencies, national and international, should be more adequately represented. The time has come for the Canadians to get rid of "the creative schizophrenia" (133–34) of Canada's colonial past, which has dominated the inhabitants of this vast and in many ways so varied land for several centuries.

---

[8] In *The Bush Garden* (Toronto: Anansi, 1971): 129–43.

When interpreting the level of spiritual and intellectual consciousness of Canadian people, Frye pays serious attention to the so-called 'geographic component.' In Frye's understanding of a Canadian pioneer conquering the Canadian wilderness through the centuries, this undertaking must have left in the conqueror "an experience of complete agony" (146), which resulted in feelings of "terrifying loneliness" (146). But eventually the Canadians began to get rid of this anxiety, especially when they began to accept Canada as their own country, not only physically but also mentally. It is important to stress that Canada was conquered by the white man in a more civilized manner than the USA, although crimes against native inhabitants were committed there too. "The last frontier," which is a concept so typical of the USA, did not merely represent a geographical destination for the white conquerors, but an intellectual one, too. This concept has provided US-Americans with positive connotations, inducing them to new challenges and new visions.

The white people settled Canada step by step, trying to organize all aspects of life in centres which they built along their route from the East to the West They built cities around the military camps, and Frye believes that people were also influenced by the psychological effects of the Anglo-French wars, the fear of Indian attacks, of hostile nature, as well as of a restriction of social activities, which tended to destroy the creative impulse and produced a so-called "garrison mentality."[9] This means that the minds of Canadians were formed by their living in such secluded and fortified areas, which were geographically, historically and socially limited units producing also their specific cultural atmosphere. Frye's second premiss is that every national consciousness is essentially related to its cultural background and that therefore the Canadian national consciousness is not the same as that of the USA or any other country. This is also the reason why heroes in Canadian literature are very different from heroes depicted in the works of twentieth-century American authors: for example, in the novels of Sinclair Lewis, Upton Sinclair, F. Scott Fitzgerald, Ernest Hemingway, John Steinbeck and others. Protagonists in the works of these authors are mainly famous rebels in their environment, sometimes also rather specific characters, individualists, who create new vistas of American society on the basis of their experiences. They may also fail in their endeavours, but their experiences are undoubtedly the main stimulus in their individualistic view of the world. On the other hand, Frye states, heroes in novels written by Canadian authors, such as Hugh MacLennan, Morley Callaghan, Margaret Laurence, Robertson Davies, Mordecai Richler, Alice Munro, Mavis Gallant and Margaret Atwood, are ordinary people who stick to their environment. They fight with it, try to change it, but at the same time wish to preserve their individuality and their integrity within the framework of the

---

[9] *The Bush Garden*, 226, 236.

relatively diversified regional characteristics which make different impacts on Canadian reality.

Taking into account Frye's assertions, one sees that his views have influenced views expressed by Margaret Atwood in her essays on Canadian literature and also on Canadian national consciousness. She was Frye's student at the University of Toronto, and therefore it is not surprising that Frye's position regarding Canadian national identity may be found in the basis of her work, too, although serving her also for the creation of new ideas and new approaches. Margaret Atwood was among the first Canadian intellectuals to point out in her work that the former British influence in politics, economy and culture has slowly been superseded by the American way of life after the Second World War. The cultural tradition in Canada was no longer in equilibrium because of new tendencies coming from different parts of the world, and particularly from America, with its strong impact of anarchic liberal individualism. Atwood sees in these movements a dangerous practice of neocolonialism, which threatens Canada not only in the field of economy and technology, but also in the cultural sphere. Her views expressed in *Survival* became quickly known in Canada and consequently the book was reprinted several times and reached a wide readership.

Some years later, similar observations were made by Robin Mathews in his work *Canadian Literature: Surrender or Revolution* (1978). He sees the Canadians mainly as people who endeavour to form close links within the community in which they live, even though they are not immune from individuals representing extreme individualism, as it may be seen in America and as it is artistically presented in, for example, Edward Albee's *The American Dream* (1961). The second important element of comparison between the Americans and the Canadians noted by Mathews is in the degree of national consciousness, which is self-explanatory for nations with a large population. They often see the spread of their ideas as the victory of internationalism, whereas even the assertion of national identity by nations with a small population often becomes questionable not only to foreigners but also to their own population. It is true that the line between "national" and "nationalistic" tendencies may occasionally be a very narrow one; but the dangers of transgressing this line may be much greater if nationalism becomes the policy of a large or domineering nation. Mathews makes another point about endangering Canadian national integrity: He believes that this is nowadays more endangered because during past decades countries like Britain, France and the USA, with which Canada has had firm links, have acquired a monopoly in publishing and, more generally, in the mass media. This may have a stronger negative impact on life in Canada than, for example, economic links between these countries and Canada.

Among Canadian critics who have written about Margaret Atwood's literary work is Frank Davey, who indicates in the title of his work *Margaret Atwood: A Feminist Poetics* (1984) that he sees Atwood's stance regarding Canadian society as a typically female position. This may imply that there is a difference between Atwood's views as expressed in her essays and the portrayal of life in her fiction. However, this is not the case as far as the central question of this essay is concerned. Her protagonists, for instance the narrator in *Surfacing* (1972), Offred in *The Handmaid's Tale* (1985) or the three heroines in *The Robber Bride* (1993) are just as critical towards Canadian society as they are towards any kind of political, social or racial oppression. Margaret Atwood has repeatedly confirmed such a position in her interviews and conversations,[10] stating that there is still not a sufficient degree of positive identification of Canadian people with Canada, and that she is displeased with the fact that Canadians seek the causes of their faint-heartedness towards their national consciousness elsewhere, as for example in the overall supremacy of the USA, and not in themselves. Atwood's main argument is that the history of Europe has shown how nations can preserve their identity if they are under foreign rule for hundreds or even thousands of years as long as they preserve their cultural and spiritual independence.

Questions referring to Canadian identity and to the essential features of Canadian literature are also discussed in Atwood's collection of essays *Second Words* (1982). The importance of culture in Canada has changed, Atwood admits. The Canadian writer does not need to go to one of the big cities abroad, like London, New York or Paris, to create his or her masterpiece. Nowadays Canadian authors find enough inspiration for their creativity at home, but it still helps them and their publishers if they are recognized abroad. Canada has become a "real country," in which poets can become famous, so that the old saying that poets are recognized by Canadians only if "they are English or dead" is no longer valid.[11] However, when Margaret Atwood compares the national feeling of the Americans and of the Canadians, she still sees the advantage which the Americans have over the Canadians. While Americans see their country as the centre of the world, not many years have passed since Canadian children learnt at school about Britain and France, whereas the history of Canada was hardly mentioned. Atwood suggests that the Canadians lack some typical features of a national character which can be easily perceived in their southern neighbours, such as enthusiasm for their own achievements, optimism, belief in their creative power and their national energy. When this is achieved,

---

[10] See Alan Twiggs, *For Openers: Conversations with 24 Canadian Writers* (Madeira Park, B.C.: Harbour Publishing, 1981): 219–30.

[11] Margaret Atwood, *Second Words: Selected Critical Prose* (Toronto: Anansi, 1982): 86.

Canadians will have a greater degree of self-consciousness and pride on both an individual and a national level.

Despite various shortcomings which Margaret Atwood still finds in the attitude of the Canadians towards their nationality and national identity, she believes that the awareness of people has grown a lot and that Canadian writers have played a significant role in this process. She finds that the narrow concept of nationalistically oriented and isolationist attitudes, on the one hand, and nationally unidentified, completely open, nationally unaware societies on the other are two extremes, which are outlived and therefore unacceptable in modern times. Her suggestion is that both the individual and the nation should first establish and then constantly re-create their own identity. It is obvious that this can never be a once and forever finished process but that some equilibrium between the two extremes of national isolationism and international individualism has to be sought and constantly re-established.

The difficulty of this process has been reflected in the division among Canadian artists when the Canada–United States Free Trade Agreement was signed. On 19 November 1988, two groups of intellectuals and artists published letters to the editor in the newspaper *Globe & Mail*.[12] The first group, which included Adrienne Clarkson and Robertson Davies and thirty-seven other signatories, appealed to the Canadian people to reject this agreement, because it was anti-Canadian. The second group, with Mordecai Richler and sixty-one artists and writers, stated in their letter that the Agreement did not represent any "threat to our national identity […] Nor is there a threat to any form of Canadian cultural expression" and that "the spirit of protectionism is the enemy of art and thought." It is interesting to note that many well-known authors signed neither the first nor the second letter, which may well suggest that they accepted this agreement as a pragmatic, economic measure by the Canadian government and at the same time as a result of their belief that the national consciousness in Canada was now strong enough and that it could not be undermined by such a treaty.

Frank Davey also interprets the letters as the artists' interventions in the nation's political debate. Touching on the relationship between politics and art, he finds that both approaches, the "nationalist" and the "internationalist" homogenize, and in this case obviously also appeal to either the idealization of Canada or to the idealization of creativity, art and knowledge. In his view, the real conflict is more often to be found within a society than between it and other societies. Such exclusive views are also a denial of the heterogeneity of the Canadian discursive field and are in different ways counterproductive to a vigorous and "distinct" Canadian society. Both extremes are also paradoxical because, by developing a national identity, each piece

---

[12] Quoted in Frank Davey, "Beyond Disputation: Anglophone-Canadian Artists and the Free Trade Debate," in Davey, *Post-National Arguments* (Toronto: U of Toronto P, 1993): 4, 10–24.

of literature also acquires a place in universal culture. We should nevertheless admit that the question remains whether in the world of multinational business – which also rules culture – the political interest to resolve such issues is strong enough to provide space for any "endangered" literature, which, together with its culture is not "important" enough in global dimensions. There is no doubt that Canadian literature has one basic advantage over literatures written by writers who do not belong to a nation of a superpower, namely that it is expressed in two languages, English or French, each of which is a lingua franca of the modern world.

In the spring of 1991, Margaret Atwood delivered four lectures at Oxford University which in 1995 were published in a book entitled *Strange Things*. She points out in the "Introduction" that despite the fact that a few Canadian writers, for instance Michael Ondaatje, Robertson Davies, Mordecai Richler and Alice Munro, are also known on the other side of the Atlantic, "Canadian literature as a whole tends to be, to the English literary mind, what Canadian geography itself used to be: an unexplored and uninteresting wasteland, punctuated by a few rocks, bogs, and stumps [...] lacking the exoticism of Africa, the strange fauna of Australia, or the romance of India – [Canada] still tends to occupy the bottom rung on the status ladder of ex-British colonies."[13] Looking at Canadian literature and its reception from "the outside," this seems to be an understatement because the impact of Canadian authors – the writers she mentions and also others, including, of course, Margaret Atwood herself – is such that it cannot be overlooked these days. Atwood points out in her first paper that her lectures are not "an attempt to prove to you that such a thing as Canadian literature actually exists. If I'd been delivering them twenty or thirty years ago, they might have been" (10). Another point worth mentioning in connection with the topic dealt with in this paper is that she has concentrated on some "leitmotifs" (11) in her lectures which are told and retold in Canadian literature and which hold "a curious fascination both for those who tell them and for those who hear them," so that the story is approached from different angles and that a new meaning is discovered each time the story is given "a fresh incarnation" (11). Such are, in her view, stories dealing with the Canadian North and with its imagery, which are deeply embedded in the feelings of the Canadians and their identity. She enumerates some of her own works, which are connected with these themes, eg, her woman-in-the-woods in *Surfacing*, her poem sequence entitled "The Journals of Susanna Moodie," her short stories "The Age of Lead" and "Wilderness Tips." The Northern imagery is a reality, which has attracted the white Canadians and the natives for a long time, despite the difficulties and disasters brought upon them by this landscape. Thus Atwood's own writing is the best proof of how some recurrent themes characterize

---

[13] Atwood, *Strange Things*, 2.

Canadian people. There is no doubt that many other features could be found in Canadian writing which could also be described as typically Canadian.

In the lecture on Canadian identity and Canadian literature which Northrop Frye delivered at the Slovene Academy of Sciences and Arts in Ljubljana on 21 September 1990, just a few months before his death, he particularly stressed some of the points which he also mentions in his essays written during his last years.[14] In the modern world of "life-style culture," Frye finds little that is typical of Canada as a whole (and the same can be said for the whole Western civilization). But in the so-called "middle level of cultural identity," in which he includes tradition and history with the distinctive political, economic, religious and other institutions that shape Canada's life, Canada undoubtedly has distinctive features, although the influence of England, France and the USA cannot be neglected. However, Frye most strongly emphasizes the "upper level of culture," which is the product of Canada's creative powers, particularly literature, because he is convinced that a nation's identity is its culture and that only "the arts and sciences are stable social realities: everything else simply dissolves and re-forms." His conclusion is that "all human beings want the same things, freedom, dignity and decent living conditions" (205) and that they can only get this by applying their knowledge and creative energy. In the late 1980s and early 1990s the Slovene nation was in the process of asserting its own national consciousness through the creation of its own state, and this was one of the reasons why Frye's audience could easily identify with the similar search for Canadian national identity and integrity as presented by Northrop Frye and why his views were received with strong applause. However, in order to avoid any misunderstanding, let me stress once again that I find in Margaret Atwood's and in Northrop Frye's views the national consciousness and the universality of human longings as complementary, and not as mutually exclusive positions enabling man to be an individual and a global being at the same time. And this is – in my view – a position still worth fighting for.

WORKS CITED

Atwood, Margaret. *Survival* (Toronto: Anansi, 1972).

——. *Second Words: Selected Critical Prose* (Toronto: Anansi, 1982).

——. *Strange Things: The Malevolent North in Canadian Literature* (Oxford: Oxford UP, 1995).

Canada Handbook 1997 (Ottawa: Statistics Canada, 1996).

Canada Handbook (Ottawa: Canadian Government Publishing Centre, 1984).

Davey, Frank. *Margaret Atwood: A Feminist Poetics* (Vancouver: Talonbooks, 1984).

---

[14] Northrop Frye, *Mythologising Canada: Essays on the Canadian Literary Imagination*, ed. Branko Gorjup (New York: Legas, 1997).

———. *Post-National Arguments* (Toronto: U of Toronto P, 1993).

Frye, Northrop. *The Bush Garden* (Toronto: Anansi, 1971).

———. *Mythologising Canada: Essays on the Canadian Literary Imagination*, ed. Branko Gorjup (New York, Ottawa, Toronto: Legas, 1997).

Mathews, Robin. *Canadian Literature: Surrender or Revolution* (Toronto: Steel Rail Educational Publishing, 1978).

Metcalfe, William, ed. *Understanding Canada* (New York & London: New York UP, 1982).

New, W.H. *A History of Canadian Literature* (Houndmills: Macmillan, 1989).

Twiggs, Alan. *For Openers: Conversations with 24 Canadian Writers* (Madeira Park, B.C.: Harbour Publishing, 1981).

❧

Timothy Findley's Look into History and War

Maya Petrukhina

WRITERS OF FICTION usually demonstrate two ways of interpreting history – creating fictional heroes to play roles in major historical events, or treating actual historical figures as fictional characters: they constantly blend fact and fiction in their work.

Most of Timothy Findley's writings also address historic facts, signalling in one way or another the importance of their use in fiction. Yet most of his novels, plays and short stories (*The Wars*, 1977; *Famous Last Words*, 1981; *Not Wanted on the Voyage*, 1984; *The Stillborn Lover*, 1993; *The Trials of Ezra Pound*, 1995; *Stones*, 1988) testify to the possibility of highly original, innovative interpretations of facts which often challenge the credibility of what appears to many historians absolutely unquestionable in terms of clear historical evidence. Unlike historians, Findley's interest in the past itself is minimal, which seems to conform with the idea expressed by Pieter Geyl, the Dutch historian, for whom history was an open-ended argument.[1]

For Findley history is a great source for mythology, for the symbolic representation of what William Faulkner called "eternal verities."[2] Findley is searching for clues in history about human nature in general, about human motives and incentives. Fiction, however, provides him with the opportunity to add important things which are not supplied by historical facts, thus filling certain gaps left incomplete by history. In his book of essays *A Nation of One*, the writer, discussing the notion of the interface between fiction and lies, asks: "Did Shakespeare ever lie? You bet he did! [...] But while he may have winked at history, he never lied about human nature. He always told the truth about being alive."[3]

Findley's fascination with mythology can be accounted for – the way he puts it – "by the largeness of the gestures which have defined the twentieth century, the

---

[1] Quoted in Arthur Schlesinger, Jr., "History as Therapy," *The New York Times* (3 May 1996): 7.

[2] Quoted in John Gardner, *On Moral Fiction* (New York: Basic Books, 1978): 24.

[3] Timothy Findley, *A Nation of One* (Toronto: Harbourfront Reading Series, 1997): 10.

vastness of the landscape of these times."[4] Indeed, for the settings of his books, the writer prefers to choose huge political or historical events or upheavals. Large events allow him to portray people with their motives and foibles, tragedies of false aspirations, and comedies of claims for superhuman status in a society – all that he knows to the best of his perception and knowledge. These occurrences range from the early days of man's creation – the story of Genesis in *Not Wanted on the Voyage* to the events of the First World War in *The Wars*, and to the Second World War and beyond – in the novel *Famous Last Words*, in the novella *You Went Away* (1996), in the plays *The Stillborn Lover* and *The Trials of Ezra Pound*.

Real historical figures appear in most of the books (the Duke of Windsor and Mrs Wallis Simpson, Ezra Pound, famous politicians, diplomats, characters from the Bible, etc). *Famous Last Words* alone covered an extensive span of twentieth-century European history numbering over fifty historical figures. Through them the writer elucidates the human factor, in which even small details can matter a lot (for example, the character of Mrs Simpson is revealed by describing the way she sits and wears white gloves). The writer's chief task in portraying historical figures is to demythologize them, to debunk the icons and legends. This can be seen in *Not Wanted on the Voyage* (1984), particularly in the figures of the tyrannical Noah and the aging and irritable Yaweh, in *Famous Last Words* (1981), in the implicit idea of the Duke of Windsor's and his wife's collaboration with the Nazi, and in *The Butterfly Plague* (1969), where the fascist myth of self-perfection is devalued through the depiction of Hollywood stars whose search for paradise through perfectionism and physical beauty, taken to an extreme, often turns out to be a destructive evil.

Demythologizing in Findley's books is achieved by making use of intertextuality, transposition metaphors and allusions, parody, quotation, language games, and cinematic style. Each technique is called upon to promote and expand the reader's search of new and unconventional certainties and directions.

In *Headhunter* (1993), Marlow and Kurtz confront one another in a place and a situation different from those in Conrad's "Heart of Darkness," from which they re-emerge in Findley's novel. Yet there are allusions to, as well as quotations from Conrad's book, which help to convey the atmosphere of darkness and horror (Kurtz's beloved triptych in the office depicts men's severed heads high up on their poles, which brings to mind the scene where beheaded Africans are exposed in "Heart of Darkness"; the psychiatrists and the white members of the Club of Men in Findley's book practice methods of treating children which remind the reader of those savage and cruel practices seen in the African jungle; in both books Kurtz's beloved women are called "the Intended").

---

[4] Findley, *A Nation of One*, 10.

But the Marlow in Findley's book is rather different from Conrad's Marlow. In "Heart of Darkness," Marlow is observing the local people, their poverty, misery and ugliness at a distance, without ever communicating with them. To himself Marlow acknowledges the equality of the Other's world, but is unable to get rid of his own conventions and prejudice towards it, though he seems to understand their arbitrariness. In Marlow's relations with Kurtz there is almost no dialogue or reciprocal exchange, which makes it hard for Marlow to understand Kurtz. Marlow's monologues predominate in the book.

In Findley's book, the figure of Marlow is important because of his conversations with different people, including Kurtz, as seen in one of the final scenes. He makes an attempt to understand Kurtz's evil motives, which he terms "megalomania," although, as he maintains, this alone could hardly explain the whole of Kurtz. And he is striving to learn more about Kurtz because not knowing would be unforgivable: Marlow wants to get at the roots of evil in every man. These roots lie in man's desire to exercise absolute power, which is done at the expense of turning people into zombies.

Both characters in many ways embody the idea of good and evil in man's nature, which is the focal theme in Findley's moral universe. Unlike the setting in Conrad's book, here they meet in a contemporary world where insanity and violence have replaced humanity and reason, as can be seen in numerous scenes at local psychiatric institutes. Kurtz, the Director and Chief Psychiatrist of the leading Institute of Psychiatric Research, appears to be the harbinger of darkness in his experiments, the horror-master, the real headhunter.

Findley constantly involves the reader in certain imaginative work so that he finds himself interpreting history on his own account. The reader often becomes a co-participant in the text, demonstrating his ability to distinguish truth from lies. One of the dangers here though, both for the reader and the writer, may lie in the fragility of the lines between fact and fiction, which are blurred to an extent that problematizes the very notion of historical knowledge. One of the examples is the meaning that can be attached to Mauberley's "writing on the wall" in *Famous Last Words*. Here, an apocalyptic prophetic epigraph from the book of Daniel invites certain doubt concerning its judgement – is this all a part of conmanship or an attempt to expose it? This also raises the question of the range of interplay between objectivity and subjectivity in historical fiction. For example, in *Not Wanted on the Voyage*, Noah's ark is transformed into a curious place. There emerges some doubt as to whether people on this troubled vessel have managed to get their souls and bodies cleansed.

One of the real historical figures that appears to haunt the writer's imagination is that of the poet Ezra Pound, who repeatedly emerges in Findley's work. The play

The Trials of Ezra Pound fully addresses the issue of Pound's political posturing. Obviously it was important to Findley to understand how it was possible for the idea of fascism, with its notion of physical and mental self-perfection, to conquer the minds and hearts of so many intellectuals in Europe. (The figure of the Norwegian Nobel prize winner Knut Hamsun is another case in point.)

In search of an answer, Findley came to understand one thing for certain – that the seeds of fascism lie dormant within all of us. The cases of Ezra Pound and his poem's hero, Mauberley (a borrowed fictional creation in Findley's novel), show us how writers' politics can affect their imagination and their artistic perception – the two most important things that keep artists alive and human. The conflict between the demands of politics and aestheticism underlies many of Findley's works.

A committed anti-fascist writer and thinker, Findley is politically engaged; he always takes sides. His whole work testifies to this. As a writer he feels responsible for his art and his words, and he constantly wrestles with one of the perennial questions of mankind which had also been a focal point in Leo Tolstoy's and Mahatma Gandhi's works: how to oppose violence in a non-violent way.

It is little wonder, then, that war becomes an intrinsic part of history in his books. His fiction is haunted by the spectre of war, which is revealed in the various spheres of sexual, intellectual and family life. Specific wars permeate the fabric of his novels *The Wars* (1977) and *Famous Last Words* (1981); their implicit reference is felt in *The Piano Man's Daughter* (1995), *You Went Away* (1996), *The Trials of Ezra Pound* (1995) and others.

War is mostly used by Findley as a means of illustrating his characters' human condition, since in the world they live there is always strife, combat, and war going on. Social, domestic and familial relations appear warlike in nature. His characters' field of action is portrayed against the backdrop of such relations. In *The Wars*, Robert Ross, a sensitive nineteen-year-old, is compelled to join the army following domestic strife and betrayals within his own family. Recurring images of domestic wars and conflicts, as well as scenes of cruelty and violence, underpin the fabric of such novels as *Headhunter* (1993), *The Last of the Crazy People* (1967), *Not Wanted on the Voyage*, and *The Telling of Lies* (1986).

Themes of violence have always been a focal point in Findley's work. According to him, all wars are rooted in the systems of violence which exist in any culture: "I see it everywhere. It's the violence we do to each other; the violence of refusing to solve our problems or confront them [...] I'm caught up in it [...]. Every single thing I have written hinges, turns upon violence."[5]

---

[5] Quoted in Carol Roberts, *Timothy Findley: Stories from a Life* (Toronto: ECW, 1995): 96.

In *The Telling of Lies* – his most overtly political book – he speaks about his apprehensions concerning the relations between the USA and Canada, with references to McCarthyism and independent artists' prosecution, the disclosure by the CIA of secret brainwashing experiments in a Montreal hospital in the 1950s. In *The Butterfly Plague* he draws an analogy between the atmosphere under the Nazi regime in Germany and in Hollywood during the 1930s, linking the movies' rage for physical perfection with fascist ideas and ideals of a master-race.

The voice of horror, which is present in Findley's most acclaimed book *The Wars*, brings to mind other kinds of novels about the First World War – Richard Aldington's *Death of a Hero* (1929) and Erich Maria Remarque's *All Quiet on the Western Front* (1929). Robert Ross, the hero in *The Wars*, as well as his German and English young military counterparts, find themselves in the quagmire world of trench warfare which is described in the scenes of mud and smoke, chlorine gas and rotting corpses. They all become war captives. These three books can be called a memorial to a lost generation who hoped much and suffered deeply.

Aldington's hero, the young painter George Winterbourne, joins the army because he is deeply disenchanted with his own art and family relations. He suffers profoundly from the first days of the War until his death at the very end of it. When George sees one section of his soldiers wiped out by a heavy shell and others lying in agony begging to be killed, he springs to his feet to meet his death by a bullet.

Paul, the hero of Remarque's novel, is a young man of eighteen years who, together with his seven classmates, faces the cruelty of war, dreaming all the time of going home and feeling secure. He is the last of them to die on one of the days when everything is quiet on the western front. Before dying he is thinking of his fellow soldiers as a lost generation, a generation of frustrated hopes and aspirations.

Robert Ross, like George, feels deeply alienated from the family and the people around him. He is a loner, whose best friends in the war are horses and dogs. Whereas Paul joins the army because his family sees it his duty to do so, Ross enrols in order to run away from home. His search for a sanctuary in a world of fire ends in a last desperate act to desert the front, driving away horses from one of the military station yards.

What brings all these books together is the writers' apprehension that all wars are rooted in the tragic fragility of human relationships and human values in life. Wars are possible because people everywhere are still groping in the dark – this is the underlying message of the works.

This helps to explain why Findley's most favourite character is his great-great-grandfather, Nicholas Fagan, the "one who sings."[6] The character appears in many

---

[6] *A Nation of One*, 17.

of his novels, including *Headhunter*, where his role is that of a teacher of classic literature who believes in books as a way of enlightening people in regard to their social life and identity: "A book is a way of singing: a way of singing our way out of darkness. The darkness that is night – and the darkness that is ignorance – and the darkness that is fear. The people drawn on the page by the makers of literature are distillations of our thwarted selves. We are their echoes and their shadows."[7]

Reading Timothy Findley's books, some perennial questions referring to war and history remain unanswered. It is little wonder: There are no simple answers to them in life. The value of Findley's work lies in the very fact that he poses these questions and that, in doing so, he promotes debates targeted at their solution.

His own message is quite clear: Writers can be held responsible for their art in terms of moral decisions made; aggression and violence should be always opposed; hope and compassion should become part of any author's commitment.

WORKS CITED

Aldington, Richard. *Death of a Hero* (Moscow: Foreign Languages Publishing House, 1958).

Findley, Timothy. *The Butterfly Plague* (New York: Viking, 1969).

——. *Famous Last Words* (Toronto: Clarke, Irwin,1981).

——. *Headhunter* (Toronto: HarperCollins, 1993).

——. *The Last of the Crazy People* (Toronto: General, 1997).

——. *A Nation of One* (Toronto: Harbourfront Reading Series, 1997).

——. *Not Wanted on the Voyage* (Toronto: Penguin, 1984).

——. *The Piano Man's Daughter* (Toronto: HarperCollins, 1995).

——. *The Stillborn Lover* (Winnipeg: Blizzard, 1993).

——. *Stones* (Toronto: Penguin, 1988).

——. *The Telling of Lies* (Toronto: Penguin, 1986).

——. *The Trials of Ezra Pound* (Winnipeg: Blizzard, 1995).

——. *The Wars* (Toronto: Clarke, Irwin, 1977).

——. *You Went Away* (Toronto: HarperCollins, 1996).

Gardner, John. *On Moral Fiction* (New York: Basic Books, 1978).

Schlesinger, Arthur. "History as Therapy," *New York Times* (3 May 1996): 7.

Remarque, Erich Maria. *Im Westen nichts Neues* (Moskau, Krakau & Minsk: Zentralverlag, 1930).

Roberts, Carol. *Timothy Findley: Stories from a Life* (Toronto: ECW, 1995).

✍

---

[7] *A Nation of One*, 18.

Tomson Highway
Colonizing Christianity versus Native Myth –
From Cultural Conflict to Reconciliation

MARK SHACKLETON

A LTHOUGH MYTH MUST BE SEEN within its cultural contexts there is enough similarity between the myths of different world cultures to justify links and comparisons between different cultures through the study of myth.[1] There is also a great deal of cross-cultural appropriation of myth.[2] This is clearly shown by the appropriation of Native myths by non-Native writers, particularly in the last thirty years[3] or so, though as this essay will show the appropriation

---

[1] See Jeanne Rosier Smith, *Writing Tricksters: Mythic Gambols in American Ethnic Literature* (Berkeley: U of California P, 1997). In her discussion of literary tricksters Smith argues that neither literature not literary criticism can be separated from its historical and cultural contexts (3). She aligns herself with Estella Lauter, *Women as Mythmakers* (Bloomington: Indiana UP, 1984), and John W. Roberts, *From Trickster to Badman: The Black Folk Hero in Slavery and Freedom* (Philadelphia: U of Pennsylvania P, 1989) who also argue for the cultural specificity of myths. Smith does acknowledge, however, that much of the theory surrounding archetypal figures such as tricksters emphasizes the universality or timelessness of myth, eg, Radin, *The Trickster: A Study in American Indian Mythology* (New York: Schocken, 1956), Northrop Frye, *Anatomy of Criticism: Four Essays* (Princeton NJ: Princeton UP, 1957). She also outlines characteristics that tricksters from different cultures share and quotes approvingly the universalistic statement of Victor Turner, "Myth and Symbol," *International Encyclopedia of the Social Sciences*, ed. David L. Sills (New York: Macmillan, 1968): 576, that all tricksters are "liminal phenomena": ie, the "betwixt and between" state of transition and change that is a source of myth in all cultures.

[2] See, for example, Gary Snyder, "The Incredible Survival of Coyote," *The Old Ways: Six Essays* (San Francisco: City Lights, 1977): 67–93, and Patricia Clark Smith, "Coyote Ortiz: Canis latrans latrans in the Poetry of Simon Ortiz," in *Studies in American Indian Literature*, ed. Paula Gunn Allen (New York: Modern Language Association of America, 1983): 192–210, on the appropriation of Coyote by Anglo poets. For a strong criticism of Snyder's appropriation of Native American materials, see Leslie Marmon Silko, "An Old-Time Indian Attack Conducted in Two Parts," in *The Remembered Earth*, ed. G. Hobson (Albuquerque: Red Earth, 1979): 211–16.

[3] Leslie A. Fiedler, *The Return of the Vanishing American* (London: Paladin, 1972): 84–86, argues that the first wave of idealization of Native Americans by white American writers is in the

is not all one way. Tomson Highway, who grew up on Brochet Indian Reserve in northwest Manitoba, is a Cree Indian. He is Canada's most important Native playwright. His success as a dramatist is related to his skilful fusion of Native mythology and Western (or mainstream) dramatic structures. His plays point in two directions. On the one hand, they are intended to raise the consciousness of Native peoples to their own forgotten culture, primarily through the figure of the Ojibway/Cree trickster Nanabush/Weesageechak, who appears in both his published plays. On the other hand, his plays educate non-Native audiences about the reality – both the pains and the pleasures – of reservation life, employing classical allusions and dramatic frameworks reminiscent of Shakespearean comedy that would be familiar to a sophisticated Native and non-Native audience.

Dry Lips Oughta Move to Kapuskasing, first performed in Toronto in 1989, is Highway's most significant play to date. The play starkly contrasts Christianity with Native spirituality. The key scene of the play is a rape of a Native woman (who also represents the spirit of Nanabush) with a crucifix. The imagery and symbolism is clear in this scene: Colonizing Christianity has attacked Native peoples' language, land and culture. But the play does not end there. The rape scene must be placed within the context of the play as a whole, which ends in affirmation and hope. Structurally, the play is like a Shakespearean comedy: Potentially tragic events are introduced, but the resolution reaffirms the values of individual joy and social harmony. The audience realizes at the end of the play that the events of the play (including the rape) have been dreamt by the protagonist, the resourceful and responsible community leader, Zachary Keechigeesik. The closing tableau of the play is a naked Zachary holding up his newly-born baby with his wife by his side. The dark events of the play are the history of cultural abuse Native peoples have suffered, the rape of their culture they have experienced through white assimilationist policies. The future, though, is seen as one of hope. James Joyce wrote that "history is a nightmare from which I am trying to awake,"[4] and similarly Highway in his plays seeks to awaken his people from the trauma of their past and lead them towards a positive future. But Highway is aware, though, that before that future is possible, those who caused suffering in the past (or their heirs) must acknowledge responsibility for their actions, and the victims must also fully face up to what has happened to them. It is for these reasons that Highway's programme note to the premiere of *Dry Lips* quotes a respected elder, Lyle Longclaws, "Before the healing can take place, the poison must be exposed."

1920s; the second wave, also associated with "disavowing one's whiteness and becoming all Indian," occurs in the 1960s.

[4] The words of Stephen Dedalus in Joyce's *Ulysses* (London: Picador, 1997): 35.

In this first section, I shall briefly outline the history of the christianizing influence in Native education in Canada; Highway's own experience of being brought up in a Catholic residential school; and finally the effects of Christianity on Native culture – symbolized as a rape – in *Dry Lips Oughta Move to Kapuskasing*. The second part of the essay will argue that although Highway never denies the reality of the nightmare of the post-contact Aboriginal past, the interdependence of mainstream and Native cultures in the structure of Highway's work indicates that he wishes to move beyond the exploration of cultural clashes between ethnic groups to focus increasingly on individual freedom beyond limiting notions of ethnic (and gender) identity.

J.R. Miller's *Shingwauk's Vision* is the most recent study of the effects of Christian education on Native peoples in Canada. Formal European education of Indian children began in the early 1600s in New France, in mission schools operated by French religious orders such as the Recollets, Jesuits and Ursulines. The major goals of these schools were the "civilization" and christianization of Indians. From the 1830s the churches, mainly the Roman Catholic and Anglican denominations, began to establish residential (ie, boarding) schools for Indians. These schools, staffed by missionary teachers, were seen as the ideal system for educating Native peoples because they removed children from the influences of traditional family life. The prevailing policy of both the government and educational authorities was to assimilate Native peoples into white society. As Miller pointedly says, "Clearly, Canada chose to eliminate Indians by assimilating them, unlike the Americans, who had long sought to exterminate them physically."[5] Those Indian parents who agreed to send their children to residential schools did so with mixed feelings. Some saw Christianity as a positive force, but most wished their children to have the benefits of European skills, in particular literacy. Generally Indians regarded the regime of these schools as harsh and cruel: Corporal punishment was frequent and staff forbade the use of native languages and made the children feel ashamed of their Native identity. By the end of the 1960s the era of residential schools was over, and by 1973 the policy of "Indian control of Indian Education" was adopted as federal policy. By 1990 widespread sexual abuse in orphanages and residential schools was revealed (328). In the late 1980s and in the 1990s various religious denominations issued apologies to the Aboriginal peoples of Canada (340), and compensation was paid in proven cases of sexual abuse.

---

[5] J.R. Miller, *Shingwauk's Vision: A History of Native Residential Schools* (Toronto: U of Toronto P, 1996): 184.

As the *Globe & Mail* reporter Geoffrey York has written in *The Dispossessed* (1992),[6] the education system was of crucial importance in Canada's assault on Indian culture from the 1860s to the 1960s: "The schools were the chief weapon of the missionaries and the federal bureaucrats in their systematic campaign to destroy Indian culture" (27). The destructive effects of this policy have recently come to light, through the work of historians like Miller, through investigative journalism such as York's, through narrative histories by Native scholars such as Gerald Vizenor[7] and through works of autobiographical fiction like Richard Wagamese's *Keeper 'n Me* (1994) and Tomson Highway's *Kiss of the Fur Queen* (1998).

In the "Foreword" to York's *The Dispossessed*, Highway describes the Brochet Reserve where he grew up as "remote," but nevertheless "one that has not been left unscarred by the forces of social and spiritual destruction"; he writes that, like many others, "I went through the entire Indian residential school system – nine years at the Guy Hill Indian Residential School near The Pas, Manitoba – and the entire white foster home cycle."[8] *Kiss of the Fur Queen*, a magical-realist work, tells about the Okimasis brothers (Highway and his younger brother René) growing up in the Cree hunting and fishing culture and at the age of six and five respectively, being sent three hundred miles south to Birch Lake Indian Residential School, run by the Catholic Church. At the school, Champion Okimasis has his name changed to Jeremiah (a prophet who in the novel tells the pitiful tale of his people), and the younger Ooneemeetoo (meaning dancer) is renamed Gabriel (the angel of Death) referring to René Highway, an outstanding ballet dancer, who died of AIDS in 1990. Their hair is cut and they are savagely beaten for speaking (or singing) in their native language. Both boys are sexually abused by the principal of the school, Father Lafleur. Highway has rendered in fiction what actually took place in fact.

In the closing pages of Chapter 5 of *Kiss of the Fur Queen*, Highway describes Champion Okimasis' first day at school: "With what looked like a hundred bald-headed Indian boys, Champion found himself climbing up several banks of stairs made of grey, black speckled stone."[9]

---

[6] Geoffrey York, *The Dispossessed: Life and Death in Native Canada* (Toronto: Little, Brown, 1992).

[7] The section "Boarding School Remembrance" in Vizenor's *The People Named the Chippewa* (Minneapolis: U of Minnesota P, 1984): 98–112, provides accounts of forced attendance at federal boarding schools and mission schools by Chippewa children from Minnesota and Wisconsin. The first account, by one John Rogers, is close to Highway's response to white education. Rogers criticizes the fact that he was taught that his own culture was inferior, but he values the benefits of white education, such as literacy.

[8] Tomson Highway, "Foreword" to York's *The Dispossessed*, viii.

[9] Tomson Highway, *Kiss of the Fur Queen* (Toronto: Doubleday, 1998): 55.

Many reports of life at residential schools mention hair-cutting. Like hair-cutting in the army and prison, the aim is to reduce individuality, but in the case of Indian youths it also removes one of the symbols of cultural identity – the customary long hair of Native peoples. Miller's *Shingwauk's Vision* shows near-bald-headed Indian children at missionary schools, and a telling "before and after" photo of one Thomas More, showing Thomas as an Indian boy with long braided hair and tribal dress in one picture, and a short-haired youth in a suit in the next. These before-and-after contrasts were beloved by missionaries because they were visible proof of the "civilizing" effect of Christian education.

Highway goes on to describe Champion's first day: "Uniformly garbed in sky-blue denim shirts and navy denim coveralls, the boys marched out into a long, white passageway that smelled of metal and Javex – everything here smelled of metal and Javex – where lines of Indian girl strangers were marching in the opposite direction."[10] The school uniform is again reminiscent of prison, while the pervasive smell of Javex is a sly reminder of the old saying "Cleanliness is next to godliness." The "Indian girl strangers" is a reminder that the standard residential school featured rigid segregation of the sexes, often separating brothers and sisters.[11]

Out of this crowd of strangers appears Champion's sister, Josephine, with a "soup-bowl" haircut, showing that she too has been shorn, but he is not allowed to speak to her, and her image is replaced by: "Ghost-pale, tight-faced women sheathed completely in black and white [who] stood guarding each door, holding long wooden stakes that, Champion later learned, were for measuring the length of objects" (55). This skilful presentation of a child's perspective, reminiscent of Pip's in *Great Expectations* or Stephen's in *A Portrait of the Artist as a Young Man*, defamiliarizes potentially positive images of nuns and presents them through Champion's eyes as spectral and threatening. But this alien and threatening environment is transformed by art – in Champion's case by music:

> The echo of four hundred feet on a stone-hard floor became music: *peeyuk, neesoo, peeyuk, neesoo (Cree: one, two, one, two).* Until Champion became aware that music of another kind entirely was seeping into his ears. From some radio in one of these rooms? From some *kitoochigan (literally music maker: e.g. record player, piano, guitar, or any other instrument that makes music hidden in the ceiling?).* All he knew was that this music was coming closer and closer.
>
> Pretty as the song of chickadees in spring, it tickled his eardrums. Like a ripe cloudberry in high July, his heart opened out. He forgot the odour of metal and bleach [...] (55–56)

---

[10] Highway, *Kiss of the Fur Queen*, 55.

[11] Miller, *Shingwauk's Vision*, 193.

Music allows Champion to transform and transcend the god-fearing cleanliness and starkness of his surroundings, and returns him to the comfort of the natural sights, sounds and tastes of home.

> He looked with hope to see which doorway might reveal the source of such arresting sweetness. His forced march, however, left him with no option but to put words, secretly, to a melody such as he had never heard, "*Kimoosoom, chimasoo, koogoom tapasao*, diddle-ee, diddle-ee, diddle-ee, diddle-ee ..." (56) [which, in the glossary of the novel, Highway tells us is "a non-sensical musical rhyme" with the words: Grandpa gets a hard-on, grandma runs away, diddle-ee, diddle-ee, diddle-ee.]

As Helen Gilbert and Joanne Tompkins point out, music and song can be an active force for resistance, a subversive activity, a source of parody:

> hybrid song / music often function to protest the domination of the coloniser's linguistic / musical tradition by liberally interspersing it with the words, forms, or musical structures of a less well-recognised and validated system of communication.[12]

Champion's secret Cree ditty is subversive in two ways: First, he is using a forbidden language; secondly, the bawdy content directly contravenes the values of the religious community he finds himself in.

But Highway does not posit a simplistic opposition: Native = good; non-Native = bad. Champion's musical variations are based on white man's music, and the following extract povides a sense of his world enlarging. Previously Champion had been the champion accordion player of his village, now for the first time he encounters a piano:

> On a bench sat a woman in black, the stiff white crown stretched across her forehead, her hawk's nose and owl's eyes aimed at a sheet of white paper propped in front of her. Her fingers caressed the keyboard of the biggest accordion Champion had ever seen.
>
> Except that it didn't sound like an accordion: the notes glided, intelligent and orderly, not giddy and frothy and of a nervous, clownish character.
>
> He wanted to listen until the world came to an end. His heart soared, his skin tingled, and his head filled with airy bubbles. (56)

His ecstatic response sends his lungs like "two small fishing boats" soaring into the sky, and his veins "untwined, stretched and swelled" in musical orgasm (57). His sensual daydream is interrupted, though:

> Something soft and fleshy brushing up against his left shoulder made him flutter back down to earth, unwillingly. He turned to look. What met his gaze, to his great surprise, was the upper body of Jesus, nailed to a silver cross, wedged into a wide black sash.
>
> "Jeremiah," said Jesus, "class will be starting soon." Champion blinked at the thrice-punctured man, to be assured that he had indeed spoken, and could he please say

---

[12] Helen Gilbert & Joanne Tompkins, *Post-Colonial Drama: Theory, Practice, Politics* (1996), (London: Routledge, 1996): 194.

more? But the victim's mouth remained unopened, leaving Champion to look elsewhere for the source of these words. (57)

There are a number of surprises here. First the Christ who speaks from the crucifix
and then remains silent, and next the curious anomaly between something that is
"soft and fleshy" and the pierced flesh of the "thrice punctured man." The anomaly
is resolved in the short final paragraph that concludes this chapter: "Champion
turned his face upward until the little bones of his neck began to smart. There, way
up, hovered the giant, beaming face of Father Lafleur" (57). Lafleur, insidiously
benevolent, the flower who deflowers is the priest who sexually abuses both
brothers.

Kiss of the Fur Queen is, on the one hand, a painful account of the effects of cultural and sexual abuse at the hands of an educational system that allows power
without responsibility. In Champion's case this upbringing divorces him from his
own people; in his brother's case Father Lafleur's sexual abuse leads to Gabriel's
masochistic fantasies in childhood, his promiscuous homosexuality in adulthood,
and an eventual death from AIDS. On the other hand, the novel is generous in
acknowledging that white culture can open doorways that might otherwise be closed
– in Highway's case the gift of classical music. Highway has written of the support
he has received from white people and "the benefit of a first-class university education."[13] He can help his people, he says, because he is equipped with both the culture
of the white world (among others he mentions Homer, Shakespeare, Bach and
Beethoven) and with the wisdom of native visionaries (Big Bear, Black Elk, and
others) and the "power and beauty" of the Cree language. This attempt to move
beyond ethnic conflict in order to find individual freedom and social harmony in a
space "between cultures" (adopting the best of both) is also the message of Highway's play *Dry Lips Oughta Move to Kapuskasing* (1989).

Dry Lips, like *Kiss of the Fur Queen*, is about cultural clash, and specifically
about the clash between Christianity and Native spirituality. In Highway's novel, the
brothers' night journey through the Christian hell of the residential school is watched
over by the Fur Queen, a wily shape-shifting trickster, who at one point identifies
herself as "Miss Maggie-Weesageechak-Nanabush-Coyote-Raven-Glooscap-oh-
you-should-hear-the things-they-call-me-honeypot-Sees" (*Kiss of the Fur Queen*,
233–34).[14] She starkly contrasts the difference between the Christian and Native
world-view. For one "some grumpy, embittered, sexually frustrated old fart with a
long white beard hiding behind some puffed-up cloud" runs "the goddam show,"

---

[13] York, *The Dispossessed*: viii.

[14] Maggeesees is Cree for fox; Weesageechak is the Cree Trickster, Nanabush the Ojibway,
Coyote the Trickster of the plains and plateau Indians in the US west, Raven the trickster of the
Northwestern and Alaskan tribes and Glooscap is the Algonquin Trickster.

and for the other the presiding deity is an anarchic "weaver of dreams, sparker of magic, showgirl from hell" (234). In *Dry Lips* the weaver of dreams who watches over the play is the Ojibway trickster Nanabush. In the "preface" to the play Highway contrasts her/him with Christ:

> The dream world of North American Indian mythology is inhabited by the most fantastic creatures, beings and events. Foremost among these beings is the "Trickster," as pivotal and important a figure in our world as Christ is in the realm of Christian mythology.[15]

Nanabush and Christ are equivalent in their cultural significance, but they represent very different world views. Nanabush, like all native Tricksters is comic and clownish, mischievous and fallible. The world of Nanabush is chaotic, gross and physical, and because of this it is also optimistic and life-affirming. Listening to Trickster tales encourages detachment and judgment from the audience, we are not meant to always approve of what the Trickster does. As Highway pointed out in an interview given in 1989,[16] the figure of Christ is by contrast serious, infallible and demands obedience. Trickster myths are cyclical and imply regeneration; the Christian legend is linear, a progress towards heaven. Father and son preside in Christianity. Trickster figures, although often male, can transform themselves into any shape, and can take on female form. In Highway's earlier play *The Rez Sisters* (1986), Nanabush is a male dancer whose movements are like those of a bird. In *Dry Lips* Nanabush takes the form of three different reservation women.

In the "Preface" to his two reservation plays, Highway stresses the educational and ecological role of Nanabush: "his role is to teach us about the nature and the meaning of existence on the planet Earth"; likewise, he emphasizes the Trickster's role in maintaining culture:

> Some say that Nanabush left this continent when the white man came. We believe she/he is still here among us – albeit a little the worse for wear and tear – having assumed other guises. Without the continued presence of this extraordinary figure, the core of Indian culture would be gone forever.[17]

In *Dry Lips* Highway uncompromisingly presents the colonizing Christian Mission as a cultural rape. Indeed, rape as a metaphor for cultural destruction occurs throughout Highway's work. In this play we witness the rape of Patsy, one of the incarnations of Nanabush, with a crucifix. The rapist, Dickie Bird, is himself a victim figure. Cut off from his Native roots, he is the disastrous product of a cultural dis-

---

[15] Highway, *Dry Lips Oughta Move to Kapuskasing* (Saskatoon: Fifth House, 1989): 12.

[16] See William Morgan, "The Trickster and Native Theater: An Interview with Tomson Highway," in *Aboriginal Voices: Amerindian, Inuit and Sami Theater*, ed. Per Brask & William Morgan (Baltimore MA: Johns Hopkins UP, 1992): 134–36.

[17] Highway, *Dry Lips Oughta Move to Kapuskasing*, 12–13.

inheritance aided by two of white men's gifts: religion and alcohol. Dickie is retarded as a result of fetal alcohol syndrome. His very name alludes to the name of the tavern in which he was born of a Native mother (ironically a staunch Catholic) who had been drinking for three weeks. His father, Big Joey, has for seventeen years refused to acknowledge him as his son. Dickie Bird is torn between the conflicting forces of Christianity and Native spirituality, between the doomsday Christianity of the aptly named Spooky Lacroix and the call of the Native drum and dance of Simon Starblanket. Shortly before Dicky's mental collapse and his descent into violence a stage direction shows him physically "caught between Simon's chanting and Spooky's praying" (73), blocking his ears with his hands.

But the strength of *Dry Lips* is that the play does not end in violence and destruction. The violent rape of Patsy is enacted on stage, but when Nanabush / Patsy appears shortly after she is playful and mocking. Nanabush is a force for regeneration, a survivor, a shape shifter who absorbs the worst and moves on.

The ultimate message of the play could be taken to be the rejection of mainstream (white) culture and a conservative return to lost Native values, as embodied by Nanabush and evoked by the dance and the drum. But this would be a simplification. Firstly, not all aspects of mainstream culture are rejected, only the most abusive. As in the first day of school in *Fur Queen*, the residential schooling system is associated with repression and abuse, but it is also leads to widening horizons: He hears the harmonium for the first time, and realizes the musical limitations of the accordion. Champion's musical education expands from that point on. In *Dry Lips*, similarly, we hear the Native drum, but also the blues harmonica and Country and Western (Kitty Wells) music. In his plays Highway weds Native mythology and classical and canonical allusions from the mainstream culture. One of the key characters is called Zachary Jeremiah Keechigeesik (meaning "heaven" or "great sky" in Cree), and his wife is called Hera. Zachary, therefore, is correlated with Zeus, and his marital squabbles and difficulties replicate those of the Greek myth. A stage direction refers to Nanabush's "winter night's magic" (42) – a clue that this play is in fact a "Midwinter Night's Dream," the dark events of the night having been dreamed up by Zachary. But Zachary (alias Zeus) is also Bottom, tormented by Nanabush / Puck. Zachary's "ass" is the first visual image of the play, and in the play he makes a total "ass" of himself. Native Tricksters are deities, but they also have such human foibles as lust and incompetence. *Dry Lips* is thus thoroughly composed in the spirit of Trickster tales in which the highest can be brought low, and what is serious is made to appear ridiculous. However, these reversals are also a feature of the carnivalesque aspect of Shakespearean and indeed all comedy.[18]

---

[18] See, for example, Mikhail Bakhtin's "From the Prehistory of Novelistic Discourse" in *The Dialogic Imagination: Four Essays*, ed. Michael Holquist (Austin: U of Texas P, 1981): 41–83.

Dry Lips, despite its serious subject matter, is, in fact, formally a comedy. It weds the magical realism of Native mythology with the structural constraints of traditional Western comedy. In doing so, Highway takes great risks, balancing comedy with tragedy and realism with mystery. Near the end of the play, for example, Simon Starblanket lies dead, after accidentally shooting himself. Simon, being the hope of the future, is the only male character in the play who has the belief and drive to bring a vision of Nanabush back to his people. Zachary delivers a speech over his dead body and rails at the gods, a modernized version of Lear with the dead Cordelia, or Cleopatra and a dying Antony:

> Lord! God! God of the Indian! God of the Whiteman! God-Al-fucking-mighty! Whatever the fuck your name is. Why are you doing this to us? Why are you doing this to us? Are you up there at all? Or are you some stupid, drunken shit, out-of-your-mind-passed out under some great beer table up there in your stupid fucking clouds? Come down! Astum oota! ("Come down here!") [...] (116)

He then collapses over Simon's body and weeps, though towards the end of this speech a light comes up on Nanabush. The stage instructions are as follows:

> *she (Nanabush) is sitting on a toilet having a good shit. He / she is dressed in an old man's white beard and wig, but also wearing sexy elegant women's high-heeled pumps. Surrounded by white, puffy clouds, she / he sits with her legs crossed, nonchalantly filing his / her fingernails. Fade-out.* (117)

This is a tremendous coup-de-théâtre that encapsulates Highway's sophisticated use of both Native and mainstream materials. The god of the Christians is debunked, being replaced by a shape-shifting Native Trickster. An all-wise male God is supplanted by the scurrilous, gender-free Nanabush; the ethereal is replaced by the physical. But note, too, the reference to Nanabush "nonchalantly filing his / her fingernails," which alludes to Stephen Dedalus's Modernist view of the artist as like an invisible and indifferent God hovering above his handiwork, "paring his fingernails."[19] Highway opposes the adverse effects of colonizing Christianity, but makes telling use of his white education. His drama presents the effects of cultural rape, but moves toward the possibility of cultural reconciliation.

Throughout Highway's work there is as much allusion to mainstream culture as there is to Native culture. *Kiss of the Fur Queen* is like a Native version of *A Portrait of the Artist as a Young Man*, *Dry Lips* is a Native version of *A Midsummer Night's Dream*. Highway's work indicates that he has moved beyond the exploration

---

Bakhtin argues that, from classical times onward, tragic treatments in the arts were always accompanied by comedy, travesty and parody.

[19] The full quotation is "The artist, like the God of creation, remains within or behind or beyond or above his handiwork, invisible, refined out of existence, indifferent, paring his fingernails"; James Joyce, *A Portrait of the Artist as a Young Man* (St Albans: Granada, 1983): 194–95.

of cultural clashes between mainstream and minority groups to focus increasingly on the notion of creative individual freedom, basing his artistic strength on the imaginative fusion of cultures.

WORKS CITED

Bakhtin, Mikhail M. *The Dialogic Imagination: Four Essays*, ed. Michael Holquist (Austin: U of Texas P, 1981).

Fiedler, Leslie A. *The Return of the Vanishing American* (London: Paladin, 1972).

Frye, Northrop. *Anatomy of Criticism: Four Essays* (Princeton NJ: Princeton UP, 1957).

Gilbert, Helen, & Joanne Tompkins. *Post-Colonial Drama: Theory, Practice, Politics* (London: Routledge, 1996).

Highway, Tomson. *Dry Lips Oughta Move to Kapuskasing* (Saskatoon: Fifth House, 1989).

——. *Kiss of the Fur Queen* (Toronto: Doubleday, 1998).

——. *The Rez Sisters* (Saskatoon: Fifth House, 1988).

Lauter, Estella. *Women as Mythmakers* (Bloomington: Indiana UP, 1984).

Miller, J.R. *Shingwauk's Vision: A History of Native Residential Schools* (Toronto: U of Toronto P, 1996).

Morgan, William (1992). "The Trickster and Native Theater: An Interview with Tomson Highway," in *Aboriginal Voices: Amerindian, Inuit, and Sami Theater*, ed. Per Brask & William Morgan (Baltimore MD: Johns Hopkins UP, 1992): 130–38.

Radin, Paul. *The Trickster: A Study in American Indian Mythology* (New York: Schocken, 1956).

Roberts, John W. *From Trickster to Badman: The Black Folk Hero in Slavery and Freedom* (Philadelphia: U of Pennsylvania P, 1989).

Silko, Leslie Marmon. "An Old-Time Indian Attack Conducted in Two Parts," in *The Remembered Earth*, ed. Geary Hobson (Albuquerque: Red Earth, 1979): 211–16.

Smith, Jeanne Rosier. *Writing Tricksters: Mythic Gambols in American Ethnic Literature* (Berkeley: U of California P, 1997).

Smith, Patricia Clark. "Coyote Ortiz: *Canis latrans latrans* in the Poetry of Simon Ortiz," in *Studies in American Indian Literature*, ed. Paula Gunn Allen (New York: Modern Language Association of America, 1983): 192–210.

Snyder, Gary. "The Incredible Survival of Coyote," *The Old Ways: Six Essays* (San Francisco: City Lights, 1977): 67–93.

Turner, Victor. "Myth and Symbol," *International Encyclopedia of the Social Sciences*, ed. David L. Sills (New York: Macmillan, 1968) : 576–82.

Vizenor, Gerald. *The People Named the Chippewa* (Minneapolis: U of Minnesota P, 1984).

Wagamese, Richard. *Keeper 'n Me* (Toronto: Doubleday, 1994).

York, Geoffrey. *The Dispossessed: Life and Death in Native Canada* (Toronto: Little, Brown, 1992).

◈

Crossing the Fields of Death
in Kerri Sakamoto's *The Electrical Field*

MARI PEEPRE

D OMINANT NOTIONS OF DIASPORIC EXISTENCE today suggest that race and nationality are fluid, that migrants can let go of "home" and become deterritorialized and absorbed elsewhere as hybridized denizens of a transcultural world. In Canada, especially, the rhetoric of multiculturalism has led to a valorization of the diaspora writer as the spokesperson for an ideal syncretic society. However, the migrant's passage from one location to another is by no means always a positive transition toward greater individual flexibility and enrichment. This essay argues that Kerri Sakamoto's novel *The Electrical Field* contradicts much of recent diaspora theory by portraying a migrant reality which stands in opposition to dominant notions of hybridity and assimilation. The novel describes the experiences of first and second generation Japanese immigrants to Canada around World War II. By depicting the Japanese diaspora as inhabiting first an externally imposed ghetto of internment camps and later an internally enclosed metaphorical space of loss, death, and alienation, Sakamoto interrogates and subverts the Canadian ideal of syncretic co-existence.

Migrants leave behind their direct contact to their homeland and heritage culture when they move out into the diaspora and settle into a new place. According to diaspora theory, they enter a *border zone* of double subjectivity where they are accountable to and influenced by more than one location simultaneously – and they remain there until they have become acculturated into the host society. They are pulled toward the traditions, history, language and identity of their heritage culture even as they absorb the new values and adjust to the new physical surroundings of their host culture.

The rich variety of narratives which emerge from the diaspora illuminate the acculturation processes during which immigrants are obliged to adjust their world views, their culture, and their sense of self to the new environment. They must strug-

gle to construct bridges which will span the geographical and social distances that
they have travelled and, as Dolores de Manuel has pointed out, through their writing
immigrants can "perform an act of reinscribing themselves within a new world, not
merely assimilating to their environment in [North America], but rather creating for
themselves a fresh mode of relation toward their present and their past, a way of
seeing themselves within a new order."[1] In other words, the act of writing can help
the immigrant to find a new sense of integrated identity within the diaspora.

In most cases today the series of alterations and transformations which take
place during the acculturation process enable the immigrant to become a hybridized
product of his/her multicultural society, eventually passing out of the border zones
into mainstream life as an enriched person with a strong sense of personal identity.
This migrant becomes the kind of new "hybridized," "transnational," or "cross-cultural" individual hypothesized by many diaspora theorists today. Inderpal Grewal,
for example, writes about these individuals as having "syncretic, 'immigrant,' cross-
cultural, and plural subjectivities, which can enable a politics through positions that
are coalitions, intransigent, in process, and contradictory. Such identities are enabling because they provide a mobility."[2] These diaspora dwellers are theorized as
inhabiting new spaces *beyond* the border zones where they can free themselves of
the restrictions of past cultural baggage and can take new roots and find new possibilities for growth even as they create new versions of themselves.

Homi Bhabha begins his *The Location of Culture* with the statement: "It is the
trope of our times to locate the question of culture in the realm of the *beyond*." He
goes on to define *beyond* "as the moment of transit where space and time cross to
produce complex figures of difference and identity, past and present, inside and
outside, inclusion and exclusion. For there is a sense of disorientation, a disturbance
of direction, in the 'beyond': an exploratory, restless movement."[3] This movement
eventually leads to hybridization.

What Bhabha writes is true for much of contemporary diasporic existence and
literature. But there are also individuals or whole minority groups which are frozen
in the border zones. They are imprisoned in empty space and static time and their
borders have closed around them and they are not able to move freely toward acculturation in those "in-between spaces" so formidably argued by Bhabha – the same
spaces which "provide the terrain for elaborating strategies of selfhood – singular or

---

[1] Dolores de Manuel, "Imagined Homecomings: Strategies for Reconnection in the Writing of
Asian Exiles," in: *Ideas of Home: Literature of Asian Migration*, ed. Geoffrey Kain (East Lansing:
Michigan State UP, 1997): 39.

[2] Inderpal Grewal, "Autobiographic Subjects and Diasporic Locations: *Meatless Days and
Borderlands*," in *Scattered Hegemonies*, ed. Inderpal Grewal & Cora Kaplan (Minnesota: U of
Minnesota P, 1994): 234.

[3] Homi Bhabha, *The Location of Culture* (London: Routledge, 1994): 1.

communal – that initiate new signs of identity, and innovative sites of collaboration, and contestation, in the act of defining the idea of society itself."[4]

For many immigrants the acculturation process can be a long, arduous and frustrating one – not only because of difficulties in learning and accepting new languages, customs and world-views – but also because of external circumstances ranging from economics to class, political oppression, and racial discrimination. Kerri Sakamoto's *The Electrical Field* depicts an extreme case of failed acculturation. It describes the situation of Japanese migrants whose external circumstances have been harsh enough to destroy their selfhood and erase their concept of "home." They are people whose negative experiences of the border zones have left them frozen in a restricted emotional wasteland, in this case enclosed within the metaphorical borders of an oppressive and dominating electrical field. What kind of subject position is portrayed here and how does this text fit into recent theoretical stances on diasporic subjectivity? How does it compare with other locationally and historically similar texts by Japanese diasporan writers? Where Bhabha the critic–scholar speaks of open stairwells, interrogatory spaces and connective tissues, all arguing for hybridity, the translation of cultures and the fluidity of borders, Sakamoto the creative artist depicts a starkly enclosed space from which there seems to be no escape. Why is this so? My focus in this essay is to summarize the Japanese diasporan experience in Canada and to offer Sakamoto's *The Electrical Field* as an alternative reading of the location of culture and the border spaces of *beyond*.

The internment of 23,000 Canadians of Japanese ancestry during World War II was a tragic betrayal of Canadian human rights and principles. In a country which had always prided itself upon its democratic ideals and its dedication to protecting the rights of its citizens and to its principles of equality, it came as a shock to many to learn of how quickly, ruthlessly and efficiently an established and vibrant Japanese community on the West Coast could be broken up and dispersed around the country. The Canadians went even further than their neighbours in the USA: They seized and sold off many of the houses, cars, and fishing boats of these often Canadian-born citizens who suddenly became despised "enemy aliens" after the bombing of Pearl Harbour. The act was ruthless: Fed by a xenophobia rooted in old racial hatreds, it flared up in an act of destruction and was then buried under a shocked silence and wilful forgetting after the war. The Japanese who were dispersed and interned in labour camps were effectively silenced for a generation, and the rest of Canada wanted to forget the entire disturbing episode. This silence was not broken until the publication of Joy Kogawa's highly acclaimed *Obasan* in 1981 and *Itsuka* in 1992, two novels which finally gave voice to the silenced suffer-

---

[4] Bhabha, *The Location of Culture*, 1.

ing of Japanese-Canadians. The novels had a deep impact on Canadians – they were and they still are widely read today – and they helped to bring about official redress and apologies. They were soon followed by other novels, including Sakamoto's recent work *The Electrical Field* (1998). Each work is built around interpretations of the silence which descended upon the Japanese diaspora following the internment years. The literature which came out of this 'border zone' between cultures shows how a whole generation of people existed in a deathlike state of separation from the rest of Canada. They were pushed outside mainstream society by a shameful political act as well as by their race, culture, religion and language. There was no longer any way they could take comfort in their own heritage (Japanese) culture either. They were pushed outside history to exist in a no-man's land between locations, in a space which modern diaspora theory tends to ignore or forget.

Obasan first introduced the themes of loss and alienation, of silence and the search for selfhood, while *Itsuka* described the Redress Movement which eventually forced the Canadian government to apologize and financially compensate the Japanese community for their suffering. *The Electrical Field* (shortlisted for the Governor General's Prize for 1998 and the Commonwealth Writers Award for 1999) builds on the groundbreaking work of Joy Kogawa and develops her themes of shattered childhood and wasteland life in even more concrete and chilling terms. Her novel creates an image of the border zone as a deathlike space – as an empty wasteland between cultures. The border zone is projected metaphorically as a field of electrical towers, a barren, threatening and desolate landscape around which a small group of Japanese-Canadians huddle. Frozen in time and space, they are unable to free themselves from their past history and are even less able to move forward into their future.

The Electrical Field is narrated by a middle-aged spinster named Asako Saito, who sleepwalks through an empty life of meaningless drudgery in the service of her aged, bedridden father and her younger brother. They live in an old farmhouse on the edge of a large electrical field, directly across from a row of small bungalows which house two other Japanese–Canadian families. The story is told simply, in the deadened, emotionless tones of a first person narrator who has lost touch with her sense of self and is obviously severely traumatized by past events. Instead of the dual subjectivity of the hybridized borderland dweller hypothesized by Homi Bhabha and others, Asako Saito has no identity and no sense of self. She lives at a conjunction of personal and political loss and her borderland is one of death: the death of her beloved family members in the past, the death of her Japanese cultural heritage and her pride in it, and the near-death of her very humanity in the process. The borderland here has become a death zone marked by the monstrous, tangled steel icons of modern civilization.

Asako Saito is a *nisei*, a second-generation Canadian-born Japanese who spent part of her childhood in an internment camp up in the mountains of British Columbia. Her family was deprived of their home and possessions and their freedom for several years, after which they were shipped to Ontario to survive as best they could. And the living death of those years still envelops her today. She has pushed her memories of that harrowing time deep into the back of her mind, from where they only begin to resurface in short flashes during the crisis which is the centre of the novel's active present. These flashes slowly reveal how the traumas of the forced incarceration and the deep "shame" of being an alien Japanese person in Canada have warped her entire adult life too.

A series of dramatic shocks toward the end of the novel force Asako Saito to relive the key moments in her past and to remember the central trauma of her life: the death of her beloved older brother Eiji. She blames herself for his death, and his loss has become intertwined with the loss of home, security, "face," and language which she underwent during the years of internment. She internalized the grief of the displaced Japanese people and her family as a child and that, together with the paralysing grief she felt over her lost brother, combined to strike her down with a psychological trauma from which she has never recovered. The rest of her life has been lived in a kind of deathlike trance, acting out the role of obedient filiality as a daughter and a caring sister, but feeling nothing and going nowhere beyond the circumscribed boundaries of home, the electrical field, and the occasional shopping trip.

The metaphoric centre of the novel lies in the huge electrical field that looms across the road from her house. Asako Saito spends her days gazing out at the "bleak," "desolate," "monstrous" field of towers which she later describes as "Chisako's cages, my giants."[5] She returns to this field again and again in her narration, describing her walks in "the biting winds that swept across the field" (233) and especially the day "the wind howled around me," the day she grabbed at the steel rails and shook them (235). She shook those towers with the helpless, dumb rage of an encaged human being who cannot escape from her wasteland prison and the living death that it symbolizes for her and for all post-internment Japanese-Canadians. For Saito, the field is "a minefield of echoes" (255), as "I saw myself there, foolish and clinging, insignificant beneath those monstrous beams" (286). This death imagery is metonymically extended to echo through all aspects of their lives, from the *issei* past to the *nisei* present and even into the future of their *sansei* children. It comes to represent both the internal psychological barriers which they have raised to

---

[5] Kerri Sakamoto, *The Electrical Field* (Toronto: Alfred A. Knopf, 1998): 286. Further page references are in the main text.

protect themselves from the onslaught of harsh external reality as well as the constraints which are forced upon them by Canadian society.

Saito avoids the two other Japanese families who live across the field – her consuming shame at her racial heritage and history makes her avoid even the comfort of ghetto life with her own kind. This fact is one of the distinguishing features of the life depicted in *The Electrical Field*: While most diasporan narratives portray the social interactions of ghetto life as a positive force and a significant underpinning to the acculturation processes of ghetto inhabitants, these lonely denizens of the Asian diaspora have been so traumatized by their self-perceived "shame" that they exist in a kind of limbo, unable to move either backward or forward in time or space.

One of the men across the field is Masa Yano, who is also a survivor of the internment experience. He recognizes Saito's lonely suffering as an echo of his own despair and helpless rage and, being more active and belligerent about their fate, Yano insists on intruding into her private space and her empty, lifeless existence. He forces her to recognize his presence and to become a hesitant, reluctant participant in their more communal life on the other side of the field. Yano marches around the electrical field beside Saito, loudly shouting out the unspeakable: the shame and the suppressed anger which she has not even begun to recognize within herself. On one of their walks Yano in his turn attacks the towers head-on – grabbing and shaking them in a frenzied, helpless rage at the society which so shamed and destroyed his life and future.

Yano is a Don Quixote figure, taking on this modern version of the windmill and jousting ineffectually with a distant government, trying to put right the wrongs done to his people. Like the vociferous Aunt Emily in Kogawa's *Obasan,* Yano is one of the early proponents of the Redress Movement which grew among Japanese–Canadians in the 1970s to demand compensation and, especially, apologies from the Canadian government for their unjust dispossession and incarceration of Canadian citizens. Yano realizes that the shame which has crippled their lives can only be lifted by direct action and he urges the Japanese community to stop hiding, to break their silence and come together to fight for recompense. Yano recognizes that his life has been broken by Canadian society but, rather than hiding away behind a cloak of deathlike invisibility like Saito, Yano chooses to go out into Canadian society to fight his metaphorical windmill – in the name of justice.

However, escape from the borderland of shame and death is not possible for Yano. The zone is enclosed on all sides and he cannot move forward because of the hegemonies and negative realities of a dominant Anglo-Canadian society which will not listen and is determined to keep him in his place. The Japanese diaspora depicted in this novel is one that could be included among those defined by Antonio Gramsci as "subaltern," insofar as it is pre-hegemonic, and not unified in its resistance to the dominant power. Its history is fragmented and episodic, and can only be identified in hindsight by histories such as *The Electrical Field* (52). Any challenges to hegemony within this minority group are independent and local, such as the (unsuccessful) redress meetings arranged by Yano.

Nor can Yano move back to the security of his heritage culture either. After the war he was sent back to the "homeland" in Japan – where a bitter disappointment awaited him. Instead of the golden paradise of virtues and traditions which the immigrant community had mythologized in its dreams, he found a war-torn country in turmoil, one where he could no longer make a place for himself. Yano returned to Canada, bringing with him a Japanese-born wife, Chisako, who for him symbolizes *utsukushi*, an emotionally laden word which reappears throughout the text to signify 'beautiful' and 'attractive.'

For Yano, Chisako embodies the myth of past beauty and value; she represents his pure Japanese heritage and thus belongs to a past which he can never recover. He needs her as an antidote to the shame and bitterness inflicted upon him by the racialization and Orientalism of Canadian society. Yano considers her to be untainted by the shame and darkness which have descended upon their commur ˙ and says to Asako Saito: "Chisako didn't know how it felt to be ashamed to be nihonjin. Not like you and me" (229).

Chisako, on the other hand, had wanted to escape the ugliness and poverty of postwar Japan and when she returned with Yano, she cherished the immigrant hope of finding a better future in Canada. Her myth of beauty (her *utsukushi*) lies in the clean and bright future "paradise" (93) that Canada seems to offer, and she remembers her past as unattractive and undesirable; she wants to cross cultures in order to enter the mainstream and embrace Western ways as quickly as possible. Chisako does also have a strong sense of self, however. She is proud to be Japanese and takes a white lover with the expectation that he will carry her forward into a Canadian future. In an ironic comment on Orientalist stereotyping by the majority culture, the story sees Chisako transforming herself into a pretty "Asian doll" in order to attract her Anglo lover Spears. The two act out a stereotypical "exotic, submissive East meets powerful, dominant West" scenario – up to the point where her Canadian lover betrays Chisako and admits that he will never leave his white wife for his Asian mistress. The expected Madame Butterfly ending is thwarted by Yano, however, when he takes action and follows his Japanese heritage traditions of honour and justice by killing both.

The tragic events in this borderland drama take place because Chisako wants to look forward to a future in the host culture, while her husband Yano and especially her friend Asako want to gaze backward in contemplation of the broken blooms of their Japanese cultural heritage, as exemplified by the blossoming apple trees of springtime in the mountains. When she sleeps with another man who is of the *hakujin* – White – race, Chisako acts out a double betrayal of both her husband and her Japanese community. The shame of this betrayal is too much for Yano and in a desperate attempt to redeem his honour from the cumulative blows of a lifetime he kills Chisako and her white lover, his two children, and finally himself. His only connection to beauty, to heritage pride and to self-esteem is gone after her betrayal, and only this ultimate act of violence can wipe out the shame to the entire family.

Yano's dramatic act ignites a storm in the life of Asako Saito, shaking her out of her deep internal trance and bringing down the delicate structure of evasion and repression upon which she has built her life. As the protective barriers collapse, unwanted memories begin to resurface, and when she is forced out of her state of paralysis to go and save the life of the last young victim (Sachi – a young teenager who loves the son of Yano and Chisako) she begins to feel the early stirrings of life and hope for herself. The traumatic process of coming back to life also forces her to admit that the guilt she has always felt for everything bad in their lives, from her brother's death to the internment camps and their bleak life thereafter, is largely self-inflicted. As her dark borderland comes into focus, Asako is slowly forced to admit the truth of what Yano had said to her earlier about the shame of the Japanese-Canadians: "We're so full of shame, aren't we Asako? We hide away, afraid that they'll lock us up again [...] I can see it in you too. You hide in your house taking care of Papa and little brother. You should get on with your life" (231–32). Asako has been frozen in time, suppressing all emotion and repressing her natural instincts to a point where she could only function as a sleep-walking automaton under the spell of the towering beams. After the shattering events of Yano's murder–suicide, Asako breaks down emotionally and physically and then slowly and painfully begins to breathe again. At the end she is still a long way from healing but, with the help of her brother and his Filipino girlfriend Angela, she takes the first shaky steps beyond the deathlike field of her borderland when she goes out to visit the chicken factory where they work. The Japanese sakurai blossoms she admires out there are a metonymic extension of her awakening to life and beauty and the values of her own heritage. Asako is ready to cross over, to move out of her borderlands into a new life within Babha's "in-between spaces." But she finds the effort is exhausting: "This persistent fatigue that was, it occurred to me, like jetlag, though I'd never travelled far enough, never flown in a jet to know. Still I was sure it would feel like this: part of me here; part of me there, *never catching up*" (292; my emphasis).

This novel depicts an extreme example of the acculturation process. Asako's pain was externally caused but is now mostly internally perpetuated as penance for her perceived guilt about her brother's death. She was never able to deal with her grief and her shame and has thus never been able to catch up with herself or grow as a mature human being or progress through the border zone of the diaspora. The image of the electrical field is also an extreme, albeit chillingly accurate, one. Living under an electrical tower is known to blight human life and cause cancer and death. By placing her Japanese protagonists under the shadow of these towers Sakamoto intensifies her message about the emotional blight left on the lives of all Japanese Canadians who were subjected to the injustice and inhumanity of the Wartime Measures Act. The image of these monstrous towers gives metaphorical significance to the events of the novel and the very real human tragedies that are enacted in the blighted field beneath them.

The Japanese immigrants who in narrative live out their lives in an extreme state of "deterritorialisation."[6] They have been radically dislocated and distanced from their homeland and culture and live in an alienated space outside the borders of mainstream society. They have experienced exile and the deep psychic pain of the "unhealable rift"[7] of diasporan life, losing their identity as well as their direct contact to their own language. The space that they now inhabit has become a prison rather than a border zone they would normally pass through on their way to hybridity or assimilation or any of the more favourable states of *beyond* posited by contemporary diaspora theorists.

WORKS CITED

Bhabha, Homi. *The Location of Culture* (London: Routledge, 1994).

Chow, Rey. *Writing Diaspora: Tactics of Intervention in Contemporary Cultural Studies* (Bloomington: Indiana UP, 1993).

Deleuze, Gilles, & Felix Guattari. *Kafka: Towards a Minor Literature* (Minneapolis: U of Minnesota P, 1986).

de Manuel, Dolores. "Imagined Homecomings: Strategies for Reconnection in the Writing of Asian Exiles," in: *Ideas of Home: Literature of Asian Migration*, ed. Geoffrey Kain (East Lansing: Michigan State UP, 1997): 39–48.

George, Rosemary Marangoly. *The Politics of Home: Postcolonial Relocations and Twentieth-Century Fiction* (Cambridge: Cambridge UP, 1996).

Gramsci, Antonio. *Selections From the Prison Notebooks*, ed. and tr. by Quinton Hoare & Geoffrey Nowell Smith (New York: International Publishers, 1971).

Grewal, Inderpal. "Autobiographic Subjects and Diasporic Locations: *Meatless Days* and *Borderlands*," in *Scattered Hegemonies*, ed. Inderpal Grewal & Cora Kaplan (Minnesota: U of Minnesota P, 1994): 231–54.

---

[6] Gilles Deleuze & Felix Guattari, *Kafka: Towards a Minor Literature* (Minneapolis: U of Minnesota P, 1986): 17.

[7] Said, Edward. "Reflections on Exile," in *Out There: Marginalisations and Contemporary Cultures* (Cambridge MA: MIT Press, 1990): 357.

Kogawa, Joy. *Itsuka* (Toronto: Penguin Books, 1992).

——. *Obasan* (Toronto: Penguin Books, 1981).

Sakamoto, Kerri. *The Electrical Field* (Toronto: Alfred A. Knopf, 1998).

Said, Edward. "Reflections on Exile," in *Out There: Marginalisations and Contemporary Cultures* (Cambridge MA: MIT Press, 1990): 357–66.

✤

~ The Caribbean

Religion and Education
in Derek Walcott's St Lucia

BRUCE KING

I AM TIRED OF THE GENERALIZATIONS AND POLARITIES of contemporary postcolonial Theory with its simplified version of dialectics and
its polarized contrasts between white and black, dominant and dominated,
alien and native. Such ways of thinking lack nuance and misrepresent the actual
social and political complexities of the world. All cultures and people change, are
changing, are hybrid, the result of cross-breeding, foreign influences, trade, communications, the movements of people. This is especially true in such areas as the
Caribbean where almost all the population is 'new,' whether immigrant or originally
brought as slave, and where many cultures and ethnicities exist side by side and
bleed into each other producing new formations.

Rather than positing a guilty and rage filled world of masters and slaves, whites
and blacks, Western and the Other, we need micro-histories examining in detail how
local cultures have been produced, what they have made, their chronologies, their
real stories. Even those who recognize hybridity and change and understand the role
of appropriation usually speak of opposition to the colonizer or the West as if older
local cultures could not themselves be feudal, tyrannical, backward. We have tied
the flag of postcolonialism to anti-modernization, to a nativized authenticity, or to a
continuous historical role as a response of an imagined centre. As history it will not
do. It is too abstract to get at the truth, to tell us what happened and why, and it is
structurally reactionary and emotionally naïve and fundamentalist.

We need the opposite of such theories, we need micro-histories. We need to do
a similar job to those Victorian historians who could tell you what happened each
day concerning the subjects of their study. I do not want the Empire Writing Back,
I want recognition that each place has its own complex individuality, so that, say,
Jamaica is not thought of as the same as St Lucia, and both are seen as distinct
from Nigeria or Canada.

Being aware of local history is especially important in matters of the relationship of religion and education to the new national literatures. If we were to believe the kind of simplicities that are regularly made on the E-mail PostColonial List, simplicities based on Edward Saidian assumptions, then all forms of Western Education, culture, and Christianity would be seen as Western imperialism, and having said that there would be little more to say than deplore Christians and those schooled in colonies as imperialists or complicit with imperialism in contrast to some presumed native purity. A much more interesting and useful social and cultural history emerges when we examine in detail a movement such as Methodism in St Lucia or examine the role of Methodists and education in the West Indies during the colonial period. The following remarks are based on research for my biography of Walcott,[1] although here I discuss several matters only alluded to in the biography. I hope this will contribute towards an understanding of the culture of St Lucia that produced Derek and Roderick Walcott, and even towards an understanding of the brown elite that has ruled St Lucia and played an important role in West Indian culture and politics. Rather than assuming some dramatic uprising of the oppressed we should instead be concerned with how a new society and culture is formed in actual historical situations and the roles played by Western religions and the educational system which could vary from radical and progressive to conservative and reactionary. The dynamics of the relations between brown–black, anglophone–francophone, Creole–French, Protestant–Roman Catholic, and within the various church schools is too interesting and complicated to be treated in the terms Theory offers us.

St Lucia was ruled for many centuries by the French. When settlement began in the eighteenth century, there was a mixture of French and African cultures – the Africans coming from other French-speaking islands – and this produced a French Creole language and culture. French Creole culture developed its own traditions, with those of African descent divided into two African clans; there were two competing flower societies, and so on. It is an interesting culture that seems to have taken in a range of entertainments from African drumming to eighteenth-century French court dances. On top of this French Creole culture there was an official French culture of a few schools and the Roman Catholic Church. The start of British rule in the early nineteenth century changed little, as there were hardly any British settlers and the British were mostly interested in St Lucia for its harbour.

The St Lucia of Walcott's youth was basically a Catholic country with a Protestant minority centred in the capital Castries. The St Lucia of the first half of the century might be thought feudal, a bit like Ireland, but with a more interesting social composition. At the top was an extremely tiny white elite of French and

---

[1] Bruce King, *Derek Walcott: A Caribbean Life* (Oxford: Oxford UP, 2000).

English families that owned large estates and perhaps two-thirds of the land. There was a thin layer of British government officials and a small urban anglophone Protestant mulatto middle class to which the Walcotts belonged. Underneath there was a large Roman Catholic French Creole speaking black peasantry. Except for matters of foreign policy, St Lucia was largely ruled by a white French clergy led by the Archbishop of Trinidad. Catholic Church holidays were celebrated with feasts, processions with banners, and all the ceremony and display found in a Catholic country at the time such as Spain. There was an Administrator (rather than a Governor) on St Lucia, and no visible independence movement of the kind found on Jamaica or Trinidad.

Catholic domination began to be challenged during the Second World War when the British increasingly turned colonial administration over to local people and started the process towards decolonization. While the Administrator and his appointments continued to listen to the Archbishop, committees were Anglophone Protestants and especially Methodists. The dominance of the Church was being challenged by a secular culture in which education, morals, and the arts were areas of conflict. The Catholic Church fought against a common state approved syllabus, against hiring non-Catholic teachers, against teaching heretical poets.

One area of conflict was French Creole culture and language. This might have been expected to be a Catholic preserve as the priests were from France, but the Church had been trying to suppress what it saw as an immoral African-influenced pagan way of life in which children were usually born outside of wedlock. Marriage was always an important issue in St Lucia. At St Joseph's Convent girls born out of wedlock had to wear different school uniforms from those born from legal unions. The Methodists, while refusing the use of Creole in their schools, were sympathetic to the traditions of Creole culture, its festivals and its customs. Derek's mother was one of the founders of modern Carnival in St Lucia. Harry Simmons, from a leading Methodist family, was a student of local cultural traditions such as the Rose Festival and the history of the Creole language. Derek Walcott wrote some poems in Creole, while Derek and Roderick Walcott would use Creole words and stories in their plays. The renewal of Creole in St Lucia might be said to have its origins in the Methodists, who brought an outsider's interest to what had been a dying folk culture. Creole culture and language were taken on as part of a usable past, a national history which the Methodist minority, otherwise outsiders, usually recent brown immigrants from Anglophone islands, could otherwise be said to lack.

Although French Creole was spoken by almost everyone, its culture was increasingly that of rural black St Lucia as, during the twentieth century, English became the language of Castries (the only large town on the island), the civil service, the courts, and government. Those wanting to leave the farms and plantations and hoping that their children would go to school and eventually have a government job with a pension would need to learn English and become part of a minority English-speaking secular world. It was widely agreed in St Lucia that the best way to do this for both boys and girls was by attending first the Methodist Infant School and then the Methodist Primary School. Afterwards a lucky few would attend St Joseph's Convent school for girls, or St Mary's College, the only secondary schools on the island.

The role of the Methodists in the region was important from the days of slavery; whereas the Anglican church of Barbados denied Christianity to the black slaves as a way of enforcing authority and denying consideration, other denominations, such as the Quakers and Moravians, encouraged slaves to join. The Methodists were especially active and were viewed as anti-slavery agitators. Attempts were made to outlaw Methodism and in 1823 the Methodist Chapel in Bridgetown was destroyed by a mob. The Methodists were often preacher educators bringing schooling to the ex-slaves. When you talk to older people in the arts in the West Indians, it is amazing how often their parents were Methodist preachers. Unless you could somehow get higher qualifications, your choice of a non-labouring career was largely limited to teaching and preaching. As late as the 1950s most of the West Indian poets were teachers.

While there was some schooling in French in the eighteenth century, education in St Lucia is usually said to begin with the Mico Schools, based on an endowment from Lady Mico, established to redeem Christian slaves from "Barbary." There were soon Mico Teachers' Colleges in Antigua and Jamaica. A small brown Protestant elite with an enormous role in modern St Lucian history derives from the first Mico Trust school to be established there, in 1838. Such schools existed until 1891, when they became Government Schools. They soon were passed on to the churches or sold. At the end of the century St Lucian schools were denominationally Catholic (19), East Indian Mission (16), Methodist (2), and Anglican (2). The East Indian Mission schools eventually closed, except for a few which became Methodist. Education was still rare; perhaps only 13 percent of the population were enrolled in primary school, and average attendance was under 7 percent. As education became important in Castries society the Methodists, although a minority within the Protestant English-speaking minority, had a major role in the cultural politics of the island.

The history of the Methodists in St Lucia also begins with the Mico schools. During the 1880s, T.D. Gordon, a Congregationalist from Jamaica, took charge of the Mico school in St Lucia and brought together Free Church people including some Methodists from St Maarten. One result was the appointment of the first Methodist Missionary in 1888. When the Methodist Church took over one of the schools relinquished by the Mico Charity in 1891, T.D. Gordon became headmaster of a mixed-age school of 170 pupils ranging from 4 to 16 years. At first Methodist services were limited to Mico School, but after appointment of a minister they purchased a site on Chisel Street where in 1903 a school-chapel was erected – the building is still used for the Methodist Infant School. In 1910 the building stopped being used as a church and a partition began to separate Primary from the Infant School around the time Alix Walcott, Derek's mother, joined the school. She became its first Head Teacher and Principal.

The Walcotts were brown anglophone Protestant immigrants on a black francophone island where the Roman Catholics formed well over 90 percent of the population. Derek's grandfathers were white, his grandmothers were shades of brown. Derek's paternal grandfather Charles was a white from Barbados. Derek's father Warwick Walcott was born in St Lucia but raised as a Bajan, an imitation Englishman, and was an Anglican. Derek's maternal grandfather was of Dutch origin, from St Maarten, where Derek's light-brown mother, Alix, was born. The St Maarten van Romondts were Methodists who argued for the Bible to be taught to slaves; after the first St Maarten van Romondt became Governor in 1820 the local white elite began joining the Methodist church, which until then had been regarded as a church for slaves. Alix Walcott was brought as a child to St Lucia to finish her education at the new Methodist school, taken there by a Dutch Methodist trader who was part of a small St Maarten community in St Lucia. Her mother also moved to St Lucia, where she married a St Lucian. As soon as Alix finished primary school she began teaching Infant School in the same building.

There are obvious ways in which the St Lucian Methodists were like Jews or Chinese minorities, an energetic, talented, immigrant community with a belief in education and work. However, they were likely to be illegitimate, the result in the recent past of the union of white males and female black servants or brown women who occupied an in-between position in society. Education and mastery of white culture was a way to move up the social ladder. The Methodist community was small, in Walcott's youth probably no more than 200 in Castries, and the families all knew each other. Even the Anglicans numbered only about 500.

The importance of studying at the Methodist school can be seen from the scholarship examinations for secondary schools in 1944. Students from Castries Methodist School won five of six scholarships awarded including the two better paying Government scholarships. Others attending secondary school had to pay fees. By 1947 there were over 450 boys and girls in Methodist Infant School and Primary Schools in comparison to 1100 pupils in the Roman Catholic Boys and Girls Infant and Primary Schools. The Methodist two percent of the population was educating and influencing nearly half the number of students the Catholic schools were.

Although St Lucia did not have firm colour lines, it should be mentioned that the local Methodists were racially mixed. Although mostly brown or mulattoes they included whites and blacks and Asian Indians. Whereas in Trinidad the Indian community either converted to Presbyterianism in mission schools or remained in Hindu or Muslim communities, in St Lucia the Presbyterian schools and congregations were taken over by the Methodists. The Methodists were evangelical. Their school was at first used for a chapel and, as Catholics could be excommunicated for attending the Methodist church, the chapel was open on one side so that Catholics could listen to sermons without actually attending. Wealthy Catholic parents tried to avoid trouble with priests by sending their children to Catholic schools while paying for private English lessons with the Methodist teachers.

Before the late 1950s, the only secondary schools were St Joseph's Convent school for girls and St Mary's College. In 1890 St Mary's College for boys had been opened by Father Tapon. Whereas the Catholic clergy in St Lucia would long remain French, Tapon decided to follow the model of a British public school. He went to England for a year to improve his English and learn how English schools were run. In 1903 St Mary's College's grant from the government was doubled, provided that 10 scholarships be awarded each year on the basis of a competitive examination. The first scholarships to primary school were in 1906. Warwick Walcott, Derek's father, earned one. In 1918 Island Scholarships were introduced. At the age of eleven, Derek Walcott won one of the two St Lucia government scholarships to St Mary's College, 1941–47. Most students attended St Mary's for six years, from the age of 11 until 16, then a few, such as Derek, stayed on an extra two years to prepare for the advanced examinations which might gain them entry to British universities. There was a hierarchy including head master, assistant head master, prefect and monitor. The courses were French, Latin, English Literature, English Language, History, Geography, Religion, Arithmetic, Geometry and Algebra. The students sat Cambridge Examinations, London Matriculation, and other British-devised, administered and graded competitive tests used throughout the Empire.

Patrick Leigh Fermor, in *The Traveller's Tree*, reports a visit on Speech Day at St Mary's "a school justly famous throughout the Antilles." He saw

> a completely English atmosphere [...] The Inter-House trophies came next: Rodney had won the cricket and football, Abercromby the aquatics [...] the island fashions had remained faithful to Oxford bags. Those obsolete trousers were especially noticeable [...] When the last of the colours and prizes had been carried away, the curtain came down and after a minute or two, rose again on the Forum scene in *Julius Caesar* [...] A loudspeaker announced His Honour the Administrator, and Mr Stow, an elegantly dinner-jacketed figure in the blinding spotlight, rose, and made an excellent speech, which was answered by the Head Prefect in words [...] far better than any head prefect's speech I had ever heard at school.

Walcott was a Prefect and would a few years later be a Junior Master and direct scenes from *Macbeth*.

St Mary's took in about sixteen new students a year and was divided into four houses. Derek was in Abercromby House. St Mary's produced the national elite. George Odlum (later a representative to the UN) and Vincent Flossic (Chief Justice of OECS) were both in Abercromby. From an early age Derek had participated in some Methodist shows, including a pantomime when he was eleven, and he continued acting and then writing scripts at St Mary's for the weekly college speech night from which his early plays evolved. Derek edited the first Wall magazine, on which poems and other writings where exhibited and which was collected into an annual printed magazine. In 1946 St Mary's College was handed over to the (Irish) Presentation Brothers who told Walcott about the Abbey Theatre, James Joyce, and the leading role of culture in nationalism. Walcott began to see himself as a young Joyce or Stephen Dedalus, a rebel against the Church, someone who would in exile create the consciousness of his race.

There is a widely propagated romantic myth about schools alienating the young native from his or her society. The myth is at the heart of postcolonial theory. There might have been times and places where that is true, some original fall into cultural contact, but it is essentially a romantic complaint about education, about being in the school room rather than outside in nature. Walcott loved St Mary's, found it interesting, was encouraged by his teachers, and has spent his life teaching others whether as a Junior Master at St Mary's or now as a professor of Poetry and Drama at Boston University. Elites are formed in secondary schools not universities. St Mary's made Walcott part of an elite, an elite that until recently has governed St Lucia. Walcott still often attends events at St Mary's. When Walcott went on to the University College of the West Indies in Jamaica he hated it. Jamaica was an alien island and culture; he already had his education at St Mary's.

I do not want to offer an idealized view of St Mary's. Walcott was always aware that it was a Roman Catholic school. At times his classmates treated him as a heretic, shunned or made comments about him and his religion and told him that as a non-Catholic he was doomed to Limbo or Hell, and he could not understand religious matters. He always felt that he had no future as a teacher at St Mary's and would need to leave St Lucia for advancement. There were a number of incidents that reminded him that he was part of a religious and cultural minority. An early episode of this kind occurred when Derek, at the age of fourteen, published his first poem in the local newspaper. It was publicly criticized by a local priest, who saw it as pantheistic and against revealed religion and church authority.

By contrast, the literary world into which Walcott moved might be thought in part a secularized Protestant, often Methodist culture. The main local newspaper, the

Voice of St Lucia, which published Walcott's first poems during his teens and which would give publicity to his achievements, was started and owned by the same Gordon family that had started the Methodist school. Harry Simmons was for a time the editor. Simmons, who taught Walcott painting and did so much to promote the Creole language and culture, was part of an important Methodist family which included Ira Simmons, the first black governor. Harry Simmons might be said to have taught Derek the beauty of the local landscape and of black people in contrast to the subject matter of white European art. Simmons started an arts and crafts guild to encourage people to use local materials and subjects. Women should sew quilts decorated with local flowers and birds. Six years later Derek co-founded the St Lucia Arts Guild which was at first regarded as a continuation of the Junior Wesley Guild, members of which would meet on the veranda of Walcott's house to read the scripts of his plays. It was strengthened by other young people Walcott met at St Mary's, but its leadership was Methodist. It was co-founded by Maurice Mason, another Methodist. Maurice Mason's brother Lucius became Head of the Methodist school and David Mason became a Methodist minister. When Derek left for Jamaica his leadership of the St Lucia Arts Guild was taken on by his twin brother Roderick.

The leading personality in setting up the new University College of the West Indies was the poet Philip Sherlock, whose father was a famous Methodist preacher in Jamaica. When Walcott would move on to Trinidad his way would be eased by two generations of Woodings, the elder of whom was a Queen's Counsel, and part of the regional Methodist Synod. Walcott would have sung to him in 1946 as part of the Methodist choir. The younger Wooding, also a QC, became one of Derek's close friends in Trinidad.

From about 1940 and for two decades thereafter the Methodists occupied an unusually significant place in the process of West Indian modernization and regional decolonization. They were in the vanguard of brown culture until it was overtaken by black nationalism. Ask an older West Indian about the Methodists and you will probably draw a blank and be told such things do not matter; ask about the family religion of the Prime Minister and you might well be told, well yes, now that you mention it, he is Methodist but you would not know it. The Methodists had stopped being evangelical and had become part of the West Indian brown professional elite. (A Methodist is the current head of government in St Lucia.) In St Lucia, however, for decades a battle was waged between the Roman Catholic church and the Methodists for control of the schools, the syllabus, appointment of teachers, and the culture and morals of the people.

For the 1958 West Indian Arts Festival, the St Lucian Arts Guild planned to perform two one-act plays, Derek Walcott's *The Sea at Dauphin* and Roderick Walcott's *The Banjo Man*. To us, *The Sea at Dauphin* is an early nationalist–modernist play which uses some creole words; its portrayal of the peasantry is modelled on Synge's peasant plays. Derek's play was, however, denounced by the local priests as blasphemous, fatalistic and casting a bad light on the clergy. Roderick's *Banjo Man* concerns the celebration of local Creole culture as pagan, amoral and creative in contrast to the narrow rigid confines of marriage, especially for women. The hero, the Banjo Man, is a wandering folk artist, a Don Juan, sowing his seed among the otherwise mistreated women. In a country where legitimate birth was still not the rule, *The Banjo Man* could be seen as challenging the Church's moral authority and was so understood by the clergy, who told Catholics not to act in the play and avoid the Guild. As a consequence, the Guild had to withdraw its representation from the Festival and an argument raged for several months in the *Voice of St Lucia* in which Roderick Walcott and other members of the Arts Guild argued for the independence of art from religion and conventional morality. Part of the debate was over the value of French Creole culture, which the largely Methodist St Lucia Arts Guild promoted as a form of nationalism; it was partly about what we might call the modernization of society, the right of education, the arts, and culture to be outside religion.

To show the role of Methodism in the modernization of St Lucia and the creation of a cultural nationalism and to indicate Derek Walcott's formation, I have, as do so many arguments and intellectual histories, created my own dialectic of brown–black, anglophone–francopone, Methodist–Roman Catholic. Reality is more nuanced. Not all Roman Catholics were reactionary Francophones. While St Joseph's Convent and St Mary's College were both Roman Catholic schools, they were part of anglophone education (indeed, the only such secondary education) in St Lucia, and were often sympathetic to Derek Walcott, the St Lucia Arts Guild, and such attempts as the creation of a local theatre and local art. The most reactionary of the Catholic priests, and a leader of the Church against secular art and education, was a converted English Anglican intellectual, a Father Jesse, who himself had an interest in discovering the St Lucian past, made archaeological discoveries and wrote a standard history – still used – of St Lucia. The Methodist pastor at least once banned an Arts Guild play which was instead performed in a Roman Catholic school, and, as I indicated, Walcott learned from the new Irish priests in 1946 about the Irish nationalist movement and arts at the turn of the century. Social and cultural reality is a complex affair, wherever we go. We need detailed micro-histories of the Caribbean and other formerly colonized areas if we are to have a true foundation to discuss postcolonialism.

WORKS CITED

Anon. "Arts and Crafts Society Inaugurated," *The Voice of St Lucia* (Friday, 27 April 1945): 1–4. [Probably Harold Simmons]

——. "Arts Guild Formed," *The Voice of St Lucia* (Saturday, 11 March 1950): 8.

——. "Arts' Guild Withdraws Plays," *The Voice of St Lucia* (Saturday, 15 March 1958): 1.

——. "Methodist School Honours Ex-Principal," *The Voice of St Lucia* (11 February 1989): 2.

——. "New Methodist School Opened," *The Voice of St Lucia* (19 April 1952): 1–2.

——. "Patois phrases in Walcott's *Sea at Dauphin*," *The Voice of St Lucia* (Wednesday, 15 December 1954): 1.

——. "Statement by His Lordship the Bishop of Castries on the Incident of the 'Banjo Man' etc.," *The Voice of St Lucia* (Saturday, 22 March 1958): 8.

Easter, H. "Banjo Man," *The Voice of St Lucia* (22 March 1958): 4, 7.

Fermor, Patrick Leigh. *The Traveller's Tree: A Journey through the Caribbean Islands* (London: John Murray, 1950): 202–03.

Gray, Irvin. "Il Faut Paller," *The Voice of St Lucia* (8 March 1958): 7 (creole poem praising Walcott).

Jesse, Charles, Father, F.M.I. "The Agreed Syllabus," *The Voice of St Lucia* (Saturday, 2 September 1944).

——. "Catholicus Says – 'Plays Profane'," *The Voice of St Lucia* (Saturday 22 March 1958): 4.B.

——. Catholicus [C. Jesse]. "The Message of 'The Sea at Dauphin': a message of Morbid fatalism," *The Voice of St Lucia* (22 December 1954): 4.

——. *Outlines of St Lucia's History*, The St Lucia Archaeological and Historical Society (1956; fifth edition 1994).

——. "Reflections on Reading the Poem '1944'," *The Voice of St Lucia* (5 August 1944).

Lewis, Gordon. "The West Indies Middle Class & the Future," *The Voice of St Lucia* (6 September 1958): 4–5.

Monplaisir, Kenneth. "The Arts Guild and Its Struggle," *The Voice of St Lucia* (Saturday, 22 March 1958): 4, 7.

Seeker, A. "The Offending Poem," in *The Voice of St Lucia* (9 August 1944): 3.

Simmons, Harold. "The Flower Festivals of St Lucia," *The Voice of St Lucia* (Thursday, 27 August 1953): 2.

——. "The Need for an Arts and Crafts Society," *The Voice of St Lucia* (Saturday, 21 April 1945): 3–4.

——. "'Spotlight' On the Dungeon of Culture: *The Banjo Man*," *The Voice of St Lucia* (Saturday, 15 March 1958): 4.

——. "Suggestions For an English-Based Orthography for Creole," *The Voice of St Lucia* (19 April 1958): 6.

Walcott, Derek. "Ballades Creole pour Harry Simmons par Derek Walcott," *The Voice of St Lucia* (Saturday, 8 February 1958): 2.

——. "Inside the Cathedral" (29 pages, 1987, unpublished typescript, Walcott Collection, University of the West Indies, St Augustine, Trinidad).

——. "1944," *The Voice of St Lucia* (2 August 1944): 3.

——. *The Sea at Dauphin* (Port-of-Spain: Extra-Mural Department, 1954).

Walcott, Roderick, "The Candle In the Bushel/ Of Art and Immorality," *The Voice of St Lucia* (Saturday 29 March 1958): 4–5.

❧

Derek Walcott and the Light of the World

JOHN THIEME

SKED IN A 1985 INTERVIEW[1] whether he regarded himself as "a religious person," Derek Walcott answered in the affirmative, adding:

> I don't think one can be a poet and not be in some way religious in the broadest sense
> [...] because whatever the name of the force or the thing that inhabits one in the wish to
> make a poem, it's certainly beyond oneself; it can't be explained in terms of its
> chemical composition or the moment. [It's a] total surrender to a discipline that doesn't
> seem necessary.

At the same time, he rejected the notion of poetry as an act of religious inspiration as
"pretentious," said he regretted the "absurdity" of killing "in the name of God" and
expressed scepticism about the possibility of the after-life, while promising to "come
back and tell" the interviewer what he found.

In this essay I would like to try to locate Walcott's representation of Christianity
in his poetry in the specifics of his St Lucian upbringing and, more importantly,
examine his view that poetry is inseparable from religion "in the broadest sense," an
act of spiritual benediction which has little to do with institutionalized versions of
Christianity. My main emphasis is on Walcott's artistic mission, rather than forms
associated with colonial or anti-colonial missions in the Caribbean or elsewhere,
though I will discuss his response to Catholicism and Protestantism, particularly
Methodism; and I am mainly, but not exclusively, concerned with his later poetry,
especially his 1984 sequence *Midsummer* and poems in his 1987 collection, *The
Arkansas Testament*, particularly "The Light of the World," where the setting is St
Lucia, and the title-poem, where the site is the American South.

In *Midsummer*, the title-motif proves to be far more than a seasonal moment.
Midsummer heat is to be found in both the tropics and North America and seems to

---

[1] *Tongues of Fire*, interviewer Karen Armstrong; Griffin Production for Channel 4 Television;
directed by Ian Hamilton (1985).

be primarily, though not exclusively, associated with a mood of bored languor. The poet finds summer as "one-dimensional / as lust" (*Midsummer* X)[2] and on more than one occasion longs for the moment when the mood of torpor will be shattered by a flash of summer lightning (VI and IX). More frequently, though, midsummer is associated with a spiritual radiance that provides the raw material of art: Several poems make direct reference to European painters[3] and the pictorial impulse is always to the fore.[4] The eighth and ninth poems in the sequence crystallize the themes that lie at its centre.

Poem VIII opens with a vivid picture of searing midsummer heat ("A radiant summer, so fierce it turns yellow") and goes on to liken this to the moment before a holocaust, a motif which will reappear in *Midsummer* in a variety of guises (the fall-out of a nuclear war, the genocide of the Nazi concentration camps and the post-Columbian predicament of the Americas) and a recurrent concern of Walcott's writing since his early radio-play, *Harry Dernier*. As so often in Walcott, image is compounded with image, as the poet likens his act of composition to the activity of a general arranging lines (of troops?) and also to the "peace [...] of a gold-framed meadow in Brueghel or Pissarro." The use of artistic analogies, whether with the work of writers or painters, is by this point in his career a staple of Walcott's self-reflexive verse, but *Midsummer* sees him moving away from such parallelism, even as it uses it. Poem VIII continues with the persona rejecting the frame of the Brueghel or Pissarro painting which he has initially invoked, saying "let the imagination range wherever / its correspondences take it," proposing other artistic analogies and urging:

> let it [the imagination] come back to say that summer is the same
> everywhere. [...]
> The heart is housebound in books – open your leaves,
> let light freckle the earth-coloured earth, since
> light is plenty to make do with. (VIII)

So there appears to be an exhortation to turn away from art in favour of the radiant light of midsummer, which transcends cultural specifics ("summer is the same / everywhere") and which can illuminate "earth-coloured earth" – far from being a tired use of language, the repetition of the word "earth" in this phrase suggests the unchanging *quidditas* of matter until it is transformed by the light of a less "house-

---

[2] References to *Midsummer* (London: Faber and Faber, 1984) cite the poem number (with subsection if appropriate), since the collection is unpaginated.

[3] See particularly a group of poems which appears towards the end of the first of *Midsummer*'s two parts, XVII–XX.

[4] See esp. Robert Bensen, "The Painter as Poet: Derek Walcott's *Midsummer*" (1986), in Robert Hamner, ed. *Critical Perspectives on Derek Walcott* (Washington DC: Three Continents, 1993): 336–47.

bound" artistic vision. Although the imagination will persist in exploring "correspondences," it is licensed to roam at will, as a kind of Odyssean traveller,[5] in the
conviction that it will discover the underlying uniformity of the natural world represented by "midsummer." The poem concludes by seeing midsummer as the source of
poetry and suggesting that it confers a quasi-spiritual benediction on the writer:

> [...] Midsummer bursts
> out of its body, and its poems come unwarranted,
> as when, hearing what sounds like rain, we startle a place
> where a waterfall crashes down rocks. Abounding grace! (VIII)

In Poem IX Walcott's poetic persona returns to the subject of the difficulty of encompassing particular experiences in language, bemoaning the fact that "everything
I read / or write goes on too long" and longing for a transcendental signifier, such as
"God," which will synthesize everything "in one heraldic stroke." If at first this
poem seems to be simply a finely wrought exploration of the signifier–signified gap,
it becomes something more through the use of the image of lightning, which is seen
as a conduit for the task of bridging this gap: "Language never fits geography / except when the earth and summer lightning rhyme." Lightning, it seems, is a vehicle
for bridging the post-Babel gap between "language" and "geography." Like midsummer in the previous poems, it seems, at least sometimes, to offer the poet the
power to heal the wounds inflicted by Babel.

This theme comes to a head in Poem XLI, in which Walcott asks whether he
would have broken his pen when he began composing poetry forty years before, if
he had realized that "this century's pastorals were being written / by the chimneys of
Dachau, of Auschwitz, of Sachsenhausen." In this poem he returns to a central
theme of his poetic autobiography, *Another Life* (1973), the sense of election and
artistic vocation he felt as a young man:

> Forty years ago, in my island childhood, I felt that
> the gift of poetry had made me one of the chosen,
> that all experience was kindling to the fire of the Muse. (LI)

Asked about these lines, he reaffirmed his belief that he felt it was his "job" to give
voice to the unwritten beauty of the St Lucian landscape and people:

> I never thought of my gift – I have to say "my gift" because I believe it is a gift – as
> anything I did completely on my own. I have felt from my boyhood that I had one
> function and that was somehow to articulate, not my own experience, but what I saw
> around me. From the time I was a child I knew it was beautiful. If you go to a peak
> anywhere in St Lucia you feel a simultaneous newness and sense of timelessness at the

---

[5] Homeric and other Greek parallels, which are prominent throughout Walcott's poetry, are less
frequent in *Midsummer* than elsewhere in his work, but they do occur in certain poems, eg, XXV
and XXXIII.

same time – the presence of where you are. It's a primal thing and it's always been that way.[6]

The midsummer moment is the central expression of such "primal" beauty and time-lessness, just as the healing Homeric sea and St Lucian landscape have been in so many of Walcott's earlier poems and plays; and while "midsummer" is presented as a phenomenon which traverses national boundaries, it is finally associated with the Caribbean and the quintessential Walcott setting of a St Lucian beach. So a sense of *artistic* election replaces any Christian belief in election and this is particularly connected with St Lucia.

Walcott's own St Lucian upbringing had been of a particular kind. While St Lucia is a primarily francophone Catholic island, he was born into an English-speak-ing Methodist family and thus belonged to a "minority" community for reasons other than his racial origins. In a 1965 article, he conveys a sense of what it felt like to be a Methodist growing up in colonial St Lucia:

> I learnt early to accept that Methodists went to purgatory or hell, a Catholic hell, only after some strenuous dispensation. I was thus, in boyhood, estranged not only from another God, but from the common life of the island.[7]

Walcott has also associated Methodism with the Robinson Crusoe figure. In his early poem, "Crusoe's Journal," he begins by stressing the pragmatism of Defoe's text, arguing that "even the bare necessities of style are turned to use" and seeing Defoe as "hewing a prose / as odorous as raw wood to the adze." The poem goes on to use the trope of the artist as castaway to suggest the Caribbean artist's struggle to create from a vacuum: "We learn to shape from them, where nothing was / The language of a race."[8] So in this respect Defoe and Crusoe are seen as performing "Adam's task of giving things their name,"[9] a role which Walcott had pledged himself to as a young man. However, he also identifies with the plain carpentry of Defoe's prose style for another reason. Talking about the influence of his Methodist upbringing, he said:

> Decency and understanding are what I've learned from being a Methodist. Always, one was responsible to God for one's inner conduct and not to any immense hierarchy of angels and saints. In a way I think I tried to say that in some earlier poems. There's also a very strong sense of carpentry in Protestantism, in making things simply and in a utilitarian way.[10]

Elsewhere in the same interview, he talks of "the metaphor of the shipwreck" as "one of the more positive aspects of the Crusoe idea," saying that because all the

---

[6] Edward Hirsch, "The Art of Poetry" (1986), in Hamner, ed. *Critical Perspectives*, quoted 72.

[7] "Leaving School" (1965), in Hamner, ed. *Critical Perspectives*, 26–27.

[8] Walcott, *The Castaway* (London: Jonathan Cape, 1965): 51–52.

[9] Walcott, *Another Life* (London: Jonathan Cape, 1973): 53.

[10] Hirsch, "The Art of Poetry," 70.

races that have come to the region have "been brought here under situations of servitude or rejection [...] you look around you and you have to make your own tools" (74), a view which again suggests the relevance of Defoe's Protestant ethic in Caribbean contexts.

In contrast to his view that Protestantism fosters creativity, Walcott regards Catholicism as stifling. In the title-poem of *The Fortunate Traveller*, the ironically named eponymous narrator displays the nervous disquiet typical of the travelling Odysseus figure who is the dominant protagonist of Walcott's later verse: "There is no sea as restless as my mind,"[11] His journeying takes him from Europe to a place "where the phantoms live" (93). This is a church in the St Lucian town of Canaries, where he finds a "heart of darkness," not in the setting itself, but in the practices of the local Catholic church, which keeps the local population poor and uninformed. The first part of *The Arkansas Testament* also includes a group of poems which focus on Christianity and local folk beliefs and in so doing collectively contest the idea of definition through European analogy in a more adversarial manner than is usually the case in Walcott's verse. In "St Lucia's First Communion" the poet attacks the loss of innocence that Christianity has inflicted on the island; in "Gros-Ilet" he asserts that "There are different candles and customs here."[12] In "The Whelk Gatherers," the moonlight fishermen of the title insist they have seen the devilish folk figure of "Abaddon the usurper," not a devilfish, and reject "the prelate's modern sermon / [which] proves there is no evil" (36). This group of poems concludes with the powerful "White Magic," which provides a summation of the concerns of this section. It invokes a number of St Lucian folklore figures associated with magico-religious beliefs, among them the *loupgarou* (or werewolf), the *gens-gagée* (or sorceress who flies by night, leaving her human skin behind) and the forest-god Papa Bois, who had previously figured prominently in Walcott's play *Ti-Jean and His Brothers* (1958). Christianity has failed to "anachronise" (38) the hold these African-derived mythical figures exercise on the local imagination.

In another poem in *The Arkansas Testament*, "The Light of the World," light is quite explicitly associated with the spiritual benediction that art can provide. Travelling through the St Lucian countryside in a sixteen-seater transport, the poet contemplates his sense of having abandoned the local people. As the passengers board the transport at the depot, an old woman beseeches the driver, "*Pas quittez moi à terre,*" which he translates as both "Don't leave me on earth," and, by a shift of stress, "Don't leave me the earth" [for an inheritance] (50). He interprets the

---

[11] Walcott, *The Fortunate Traveller* (London: Jonathan Cape, 1982): 95. Further page references are in the main text.

[12] Walcott, *The Arkansas Testament* (London: Faber & Faber, 1988): 35. Further page references are in the main text.

phrase as a plea for "Heavenly Transport," born out of a sense of being habitually abandoned, and this leads to reflections on his own sense of having "abandoned" the local people (50). On the transport he is captivated by the beauty of an Afro-Caribbean woman, whom he thinks of as "the light of the world" (48). His various reflections converge into a meditation on his inability to communicate his "inexpressible love" and he leaves the van thinking:

> There was nothing they wanted, nothing I could give them
> – but this thing I have called "The Light of the World." (51)

So, like much of Walcott's later verse, the poem ends on a self-reflexive note, presenting itself as a substitute for religion. Given the position it occupies in *The Arkansas Testament* – amid a group of poems which suggest the stifling effects of the dominant forms of St Lucian Christianity – it seems reasonable to suggest that poetry is being viewed as a metareligious activity, an enlightening medium which can dispel the "darkness" of such forms of Christianity.

The Arkansas Testament concludes with a longer poem which gives the collection its title and provides one of Walcott's most searching explorations of the American condition, in this case specifically the situation of the contemporary American South seen in relation to the historical legacy of the Civil War. This poem is also a particularly fine example of Walcott's ability to infuse the most minute details with a welter of symbolic resonances which, for all his distrust of official historical and political discourses, suggest that history saturates everyday experience. Initially the poem appears to be little more than a careful poetic construction of a particular place, Fayetteville, Arkansas, on a particular winter morning, but during the course of twenty-four gently paced meditative stanzas, it evolves into a full-scale indictment of the racially divisive legacy of the Old South. Towards the end, the "I" persona of the poem says "only old age earns the / right to an abstract noun" and this provides the sanction for *his* Arkansas Testament, a metareligious statement on his "people's predicament" (116).

"The Arkansas Testament" opens with the persona checking into a cheap motel room in Fayetteville and contemplating the dead Confederate soldiers buried in a cemetery above the town. He reflects that the soldiers "have no names" (104) and as he signs the motel register momentarily considers changing his own name, before deciding to keep up "the game / of pretending whoever I was, or am, or will be [are the same]" (105–106). Identity is, then, seen as a fluid construct, stabilized only by one's complicity in the social fiction of the unitary self. What follows is recorded in a low-key circumstantial manner which seems a marked departure from the customary metaphoric density of Walcott's style:

> I dozed off in the early dark
> to a smell of detergent pine

and they faded with me: the rug
with its shag, pine-needled floor
the without-a-calendar wall
now hung with the neon's sign,
no thin-lipped Gideon Bible [...].

I crucified my coat on one wire
hanger, undressed for bathing,
then saw that other, full-length,
alarmed in the glass coffin
of the bathroom door. Right there,
I decided to stay unshaven,
unsaved [...].
On a ridge over Fayetteville,
higher than any steeple,
is a white-hot electric cross.

It burns the back of my mind.
It scorches the skin of night [...] (106–107)

The apparently naturalistic mode of this passage is, however, deceptive. The "pine" in the motel room replicates the pine of the hillside cemetery, suggesting the extent to which defining moments from the national past permeate the mundane present. The persona's crucifixion of his coat on the wire hanger links with the "white-hot electric cross" on the hillside and, while this is most obviously a memorial to the fallen soldiers, its scorching qualities which, he says, burn "the back of [his] mind," suggest another kind of southern cross, that of the Ku Klux Klan. The persona's decision to stay unshaven seems another commonplace detail, but its association with the word "unsaved" suggests it may be an image of the unredeemed post-lapsarian condition which figures prominently in Walcott's verse from the outset, a suggestion which is substantiated as the poem continues. Cumulatively the most ordinary details assume deeper significance, as Walcott develops a complex network of images which relate to race, religion and history. The emptiness of the motel room becomes a metonym for the spiritual vacuity of the contemporary South; there is not even a Gideon Bible, but the glare of the white cross still "scribble[s] its signature" (105) on the bare wall.

Awake at dawn, the poet goes in search of coffee, walking streets where he feels the repressiveness of what he sees as the enduring manichaean racial binaries of the South. Despite an appearance of Sabbath calm, the highway seems charged with a racist sub-text: He remembers "the Trail of Tears" taken by dispossessed Cherokee warriors (108)[13] and feels a similar sense of personal dislocation, as he imagines silent hostility directed towards him because of his skin colour:

> in an all-night garage I saw
> the gums of a toothless sybil
> in garage tires, and she said:
> STAY BLACK AND INVISIBLE
> TO THE SIRENS OF ARKANSAS [...]
> Your shadow still hurts the South,
> like Lee's slowly reversing sword. (109)

Even breakfast is colour-coded, as he watches "the shell / of a white sun tapping its yolk / on the dark crust of Fayetteville" and identifies with "the bubbling black zeros" of a decanter of coffee (110). The "grey calm" of the town offers no relief – grey is the colour of the uniforms of Confederate soldiers – and he feels that the semblance "of an average mid-American town" inhabited by "simple, God-fearing folks" (112) and the platitudinous pretence that old divisions have been healed thinly veil a situation analogous to Apartheid: Curfew laws have only recently been repealed and the sunrise is linked with "the doctrine of Aryan light" (111). However, again, the poem also uses light imagery to suggest the possibility of an alternative transformative vision, which is associated with a form of *spiritual* illumination.

At the beginning, as the persona collapses on the motel-room bed, he likens himself to Saul on the road to Damascus and the notion of a Pauline call to spiritual action recurs when he subsequently refers to the First Epistle to the Corinthians (108). So the "testament" of the poem is an apostolic benediction, which recognizes that it can do nothing to remedy the historic "stripes and [...] scars" (117) perpetuated in the American flag, but nevertheless strives through art to offer its own kind of enlightenment. This enlightenment it offers is associated with the colour amber –

> The light, being amber, ignored
> the red and the green traffic stops, [...]
> like the lasers of angels, went
> through the pines guarding each slab
> of the Confederate Cemetery,
> piercing the dead with the quick. (113)

– and the poem ends with television images of a journey across America in which the amber light spreads westwards re-enacting the nineteenth-century American belief in Manifest Destiny. Typically, Walcott's poems about historic divisions move towards resolutions which "obliterat[e] hurt" (*In a Green Night* [1962]: 19), but here the conclusion is more ambivalent since, while on the one hand the journey rejects

---

[13] The forced march westwards of a group of Cherokees in 1838.

"the neon rose / of Vegas" and concludes with the shafts of light reaching the Pacific and "huge organ pipes of sequoias" (117), the images that depict this are only media stills and it is a moot point whether they refer to the future or the past. The suspicion that America has forgotten its roots, "its log-cabin dream" (114) of democracy, remains to the last. Yet the poem itself is an act of atonement, an artistic offering which offers the benediction of an interracial vision. Walcott likens the light to a mongrel which charges towards the persona, displaying a warmth that is in marked contrast to the behaviour of the people he encounters:

> Abounding light
> raced towards me like a mongrel
> hoping that it would be caressed
> by my cold, roughening hand,
> and I prayed that all could be blest [...]. (110)

This dog is perhaps as much the Odyssean protagonist of "The Arkansas Testament" as the poet. Both cross boundaries and, like the amber light, resist the essentialism of static racial categories. This is the cautious religious benediction that the poem offers, but it remains far from sanguine about changing society.

The mongrel, the Odyssean traveller, the poet: These are all figures that offer the possibility of transgressing Manichean binaries through a vision of "Abounding light." But how should we read this vision of apparent spiritual illumination? I have argued throughout that it relates to Walcott's aesthetic practice, his artistic mission, but what does such a practice finally amount to? Should we see it as a project which privileges art over lived experience or as an attempt at humanist transcendence? Each reader will make up his or her own mind, but whatever each of us concludes, I would like to suggest that it is important to see it as rooted in the Defoe-like, Methodist carpentry of Walcott's finely wrought imagistic style. Whether or not there is finally a transcendental dimension in Walcott's artistic mission, it is an intervention which employs a materially grounded artistic practice to contest particular sociocultural phenomena, such as the Catholic mission in the Caribbean and the white supremacist ideology that lingers on in the American South.

WORKS CITED

Bensen, Robert, "The Painter as Poet: Derek Walcott's *Midsummer*," *Literary Review* 29.3 (1986): 257–68. Repr. in Hamner, *Critical Perspectives,* 336–47.

Hamner, Robert, ed. *Critical Perspectives on Derek Walcott* (Washington DC: Three Continents, 1993).

Hirsch, Edward, "The Art of Poetry," *Paris Review* 28 (1986): 197–230. Repr. in Hamner, *Critical Perspectives*, 65–83.

Walcott, Derek. *Another Life* (London: Jonathan Cape, 1973).

——. *The Arkansas Testament* (London: Faber, 1988).

——. *The Castaway* (London: Jonathan Cape, 1965).

——. *The Fortunate Traveller* (London: Jonathan Cape, 1982).

——. *Harry Dernier* (Bridgetown: Advocate Co., n.d. [1952?]).

——. *In a Green Night* (London: Jonathan Cape, 1962).

——. "Leaving School," *The London Magazine* 5.6 (1965): 4–14. Repr. in Hamner, *Critical Perspectives*, 24–32.

——. *Midsummer* (London: Faber & Faber, 1984).

——. *Tongues of Fire*. Interviewer Karen Armstrong. Griffin Production for Channel 4 Television. Directed by Ian Hamilton (1985).

——. "Ti-Jean and His Brothers," in *Dream on Monkey Mountain and Other Plays* (London: Jonathan Cape, 1972).

❧

"Planning a strategy
To beat back those spirit thieves"
Erna Brodber's Novel *Myal*

Ulrike Erichsen

I

T HE FACT THAT EUROPE CONSTRUCTED ITS COLONIES in the 'New World' as 'Other' has become almost commonplace in postcolonial criticism.[1] The notion of 'othering' typically implies an asymmetric power relation in which one side ascribes to the other certain, usually negatively connoted characteristics; it also implies that the hegemonic side can pose as the norm against which the other appears deviant. What seems to be neglected in this debate is the fact that processes of acculturation work both ways, even in asymmetric relationships. I will begin my argument in this paper by commenting on two widely used models for describing processes of acculturation which I will refer to as 1) the centre–periphery model and 2) the conflict model. Both these models, I shall argue, are reductive in predominantly describing the colonial situation in terms of economic and power relations. In neglecting the complexities of the colonial situation and colonial interaction, however, such models are ultimately reifying the power structures on which they are based.

I want to argue that processes of acculturation are not one-way-streets but work both ways because, despite all attempts to do so, the 'Other,' ultimately, cannot be contained, controlled or kept in its assigned place. The process of 'othering' relies on the use of stereotypes, according to Homi Bhabha, "a form of knowledge and identification that vacillates between what is always 'in place,' already known and

---

[1] Cf, for example, Francis Barker, Peter Hulme, Margret Iversen & Diane Loxley, ed. *Europe and Its Others* (2 vols.; Proceedings of the Essex Sociology of Literature Conference; Colchester: Essex UP, 1985), and Trinh T. Minh–ha, *Woman, Native, Other: Writing Postcoloniality and Feminism* (Bloomington: Indiana UP, 1989).

something that must be anxiously repeated [...]."[2] It is this ambivalence, I argue, that also characterizes the process of 'othering' and prevents ultimate control. Erna Brodber's second novel, *Myal*, which I will use as an illustration of my argument, very subtly emphasizes this point. *Myal*, published in 1988, explores the complex communications and cultural negotiations between colonizer and colonized. Brodber's novel provides the reader with various examples of cultural and racial alienation. In fact, the novel can be read as an allegory of the colonial enterprise. Yet it also emphasizes successful resistance against such alienation on the basis of mutual acceptance and spiritual solidarity between Europe and the Afro-Caribbean. Brodber manages to overcome the crucial but often counter-productive dichotomy[3] that lies at the heart of much postcolonial argument and which appears in various guises including, for instance, colonizer versus colonized, victor versus victim, centre versus periphery, or civilization versus barbarism. Like Homi Bhabha, who theorizes the colonial relationship as interdependent,[4] Brodber recognizes that influence in the colonial encounter is not one-directional.

II

The basis of all cross-cultural negotiations[5] is the perception of difference. This perception is always dependent on what counts as the norm and therefore as normal in a given culture. Thus, difference is never absolute but always relative to the position of the 'observer' and sometimes an expression of fear or anxiety.[6] Characteristics or

---

[2] Homi K. Bhabha, "The other question: stereotype, discrimination, and the discourse of colonialism," in *The Location of Culture* (London & New York: Routledge, 1994): 66.

[3] I do not wish to deny the importance of material power relations, but I believe that an exclusive focus on the dichotomy of colonizer versus colonized or any of its derivatives is disabling rather than productive because there are more aspects that need to be taken into account.

[4] Homi K. Bhabha, "The other question," and "Of mimicry and man: The ambivalence of colonial discourse," in *The Location of Culture*, 66–84 and 85–92. Although Bhabha regards the behaviour of the colonized as subversive the colonizer remains the norm against which the colonized and his or her mimicry (that is imitation with a difference) is measured. Moreover, Bart Moore–Gilbert raises the important point that "if the resistance inscribed in mimicry is unconscious for the colonized [...] it cannot function for the colonized as the grounds on which to construct a considered counter-discourse let alone as a means of mobilizing a strategic programme of material and 'public' forms of political action from within the oppressed culture"; Moore–Gilbert, *Postcolonial Theory: Contexts, Practices, Politics* (London & New York: Verso, 1997): 133.

[5] I borrow the term 'cross-cultural negotiations' from *Cultural Negotiations: Sichtweisen des Anderen*, ed. Cedric Brown & Therese Fischer–Seidel (Tübingen & Basel: Francke, 1998): 8. 'Cultural Negotiations' was the title of a symposium which took place at Düsseldorf University in 1996. According to the editors, the term 'negotiation,' rather than perception or reception, was selected because it emphasizes the mutual influence and the strategies of influencing which inform cross-cultural encounters.

[6] Cf Cedric Brown & Therese Fischer–Seidel, "Introduction" to *Cultural Negotiations*, 10.

positions ascribed to the 'other' are often only tenuous because the map that allo-
cates the positions of 'us' and 'them' can undergo decisive changes over a period of
sustained contact. Boundaries between 'us' and 'them' can be redrawn, and the
evaluation of certain features or characteristics can also change quite dramatically.

A widely used model for investigating and describing the interaction between
colonizer and colonized is the centre–periphery model. Its spatial imagery and the
connotations it evokes very clearly assign a secondary place to the colonized territory and its population. The periphery is seen to depend on the centre for its existence, although – strictly speaking – there cannot be a centre without periphery. The
centre–periphery model regards the process of acculturation as a one-way-process
resulting in cultural hegemony of the colonizing nation. The victor forces the victim
to adapt to his (or her) norms and standards; cultural domination is explained in
terms of economic and political power structures. Thus, the centre–periphery model
does not really address processes of cultural interaction and negotiation but regards
cultural domination as an extension of economic and political power. For the colonized population, the only possibility for success lies in becoming "little England,"
in internalizing the colonizer's standards, thereby reinforcing the interpretative categories of centre and margin.[7]

One obvious drawback of the centre-periphery model is the fact that is does not
seem to allow for successful resistance to the colonizing powers because cultural
hegemony is seen as a direct result of material conditions, that is economic power
and political influence. In order to allow for resistance or even subversion, the
centre–periphery model, with its emphasis on material conditions, needs to be modi-
fied. Discourse-based theories and models, mainly influenced by either Foucault's or
a New-Historicist understanding of the term, offer an alternative allowing for cultural activity and production without seeing this as a direct outcome of material
circumstances. Theories of discourse stress the productive aspect of all linguistic and
literary activity. Paul A. Bové defines 'discourse' as "the organised and regulated, as
well as the regulating and constituting function of language [...]: its aim is to describe the surface linkages between power, knowledge, institutions, intellectuals, the

---

[7] Bill Ashcroft, Gareth Griffiths & Helen Tiffin, with their emphasis on the abrogation of colonial power and appropriation of language, rely on such a centre–margin model based on material
conditions: "Both the available discourse and the material conditions of production for literature in
these early post-colonial societies restrain this possibility. The institution of 'Literature' in the
colony is under direct control of the imperial ruling class [...]." Even after the end of direct colonial
rule, the Empire continues to exert its cultural hegemony through the literary canon and through
Received Standard English. See Ashcroft et al., *The Empire Writes Back: Theory and Practice in
Post-Colonial Literatures* (London & New York: Routledge, 1989): 6, 7. The 'writing back' paradigm which, implicitly or explicitly, is widely used in postcolonial criticism leads to a similar problem in ascribing secondary or derivative status to the new literatures originating in the former
colonies.

control of populations, and the modern state as these intersect in the functions of systems of thought."[8]

Discourse-based theories regard the colonial encounter as a conflict between cultures. Their advantage – in comparison with the centre–periphery model – lies in the fact that the colonized population is seen as having a culture prior to the colonial invasion, a view often denied by the imperial mission which saw itself as bringing not only law and order but also culture and civilization to the 'primitive' lands. A conflict-of-cultures model allows for resistance and subversion, however it often fails to discriminate in a convincing way between different responses to the colonial invasion, between, for instance, submission, collaboration (active or passive) and resistance. Besides, this model lends itself to a reductive, or, rather, an over-generalizing, interpretation[9] which regards every utterance or verbal activity of the colonized as counter-discourse and thus, by definition, as subversive – the very construction of the model guarantees the desired outcome. In a sense, then, calling this model a conflict-model is inappropriate. Conflict there is, but the model cannot describe its negotiation and resolution. Strictly speaking, it is impossible to resolve such conflict as the colonizer's culture and the colonized's culture are set out as two distinct phenomena which do not or, rather, cannot mix; discourse and counter-discourse cannot be mediated but are locked in static combat. The model assumes, must assume, that cultures are pure entities, an assumption which cannot accommodate the hybrid or syncretic nature of cultures.[10] The notion of the general hybridity of all cultures does not seem to go along well with a counter-discursive impulse of post-

---

[8] Paul A. Bové, "Discourse," in Frank Lentricchia & Thomas Mc Laughlin, ed. *Critical Terms for Literary Study* (Chicago & London: of Chicago P, 1995, 2nd edition): 54–55.

[9] This is, at least to a certain extent, a problem in Helen Tiffin's, "Post-Colonial Literatures and Counter-Discourse," in *Kunapipi* 9.3 (1987), 17–34. Tiffin argues: "Thus the rereading and rewriting of the European historical and fictional record are vital and inescapable tasks. These subversive manœuvres, rather than the construction of the *essentially* national or regional, are what are characteristic of post-colonial texts, as the subversive is characteristic of post-colonial discourse in general. Post-colonial literatures / cultures are thus constituted in counter-discursive rather than homologous practices, and they offer 'fields' of counter-discursive strategies to the dominant discourse" (18).

[10] Tiffin claims: "Post-colonial cultures are inevitably hybridized, involving a dialectical relationship between European ontology and epistemology and the impulse to create or recreate independent local identity"; "Post-Colonial Literatures and Counter-Discourse," 17. Yet this seems to imply that there can be cultures, European cultures in this case, that are not hybrids which seems to be a problematic assertion. For a critique of essentialist notions of culture see, for example, Robert C. Young, *Colonial Desire: Hybridity in Theory, Culture and Race* (London & New York: Routledge, 1995), and Monika Fludernik, ed. *Hybridity and Postcolonialism: Twentieth Century Indian Literature* (Tübingen: Stauffenburg, 1998).

colonial agency. However, if all cultures are hybrids, then hybridity cannot be the location for, or mode of, a specifically postcolonial way of cultural intervention.[11]

What is needed in order to describe and analyse processes of acculturation is a model that takes the hybrid natures of cultures into account, without neglecting the impact of material conditions and power structures, a model that can describe complex processes of interaction and cross-cultural negotiation between hybrid cultures. In short, what is needed is a model that also takes into account the ambivalent and productive aspect of the 'other' culture. Brodber's novel *Myal* gives ample illustration of the microdynamics of cross-cultural negotiations. Being a work of fiction, it does not, of course, set out to provide a model for theoretical analysis. However, as an illustration of the complexity of cultural negotiations, the novel points to the shortcomings of some widely used theoretical models.

III

The setting for Brodber's novel is a small Jamaican community at the beginning of the twentieth century. British officials are conspicuously absent, the Empire exerts its influence through assimilated representatives and institutions: church, school, literature.[12] Despite the (relative) absence of white British characters,[13] the colonial influence is clearly felt. The area has an Anglican, a Methodist and a Baptist community pursuing their faith in peaceful coexistence, or so it seems. A second glance reveals that the Anglican Church has very little influence compared with its two dissenting competitors.[14] Parson and Teacher are not just professions but titles, and their bearers fulfil important functions within the community. Teacher Holness, for example, sees his mission not just in teaching "History, Geography and Civics," all by means of Kipling's poem "Big Steamers," but also "love for the Empire, so badly needed with England facing war."[15] Brodber does not set up a black-and-white divide but explores the effects of the colonial encounter within the black community,

---

[11] Cf. Moore–Gilbert's critique of Bhabha's generalizing notion of hybridity in *Postcolonial Theory*, 130.

[12] Kipling's poetry, which is recited at school functions, may serve as an example here. See Brodber, *Myal*, ch. 2.

[13] The only white and British-born character of the novel is Maydene Brassington, wife of the Methodist pastor, who is very critical of the colonial mission (secular and religious) and who becomes a member of the Myal-alliance.

[14] As the Anglican church has very little influence in the community, the name of its parson (Parson Getfield) is clearly an ironic misnomer.

[15] Erna Brodber, *Myal* (London & Port of Spain: New Beacon, 1988): 27. Further page references are in the main text. The novel deals with a period that coincides, more or less, with World War I. The very first chapter of the novel stresses the parallel temporalities. The healing of Ella O'Grady coincides with the end of World War I, yet the process of healing is also accompanied by great destruction; see Brodber, *Myal*, 4.

thereby avoiding a direct confrontation of colonizer and colonized as well as the trap of racial stereotyping. It seems to me as if Brodber very deliberately avoids setting up any of the well-known binaries like black/white, master/slave, colonizer/colonized. If the novel plays on any difference at all it is the difference between religious denominations, yet this is certainly not presented as a difference in dogma but rather in style or attitude. I would like to suggest, then, that the cultural difference between colonizer and colonized is projected onto the religious difference between the British-influenced Methodist Church and the Black Baptist Church. The process of acculturation, or of cross-cultural negotiation, is depicted in terms of a coming together of the representatives of the different religions. The religious difference, thus, metonymically foregrounds both the cultural difference and the common good or, rather, God. Whereas skin colour might have functioned as an indicator of race as a biological fact, the stress on religious allegiance emphasizes the ideological character of culture as a man-made construct. This is the context for Brodber's fictional investigation of 'spirit thievery,' her term for the racial and cultural alienation that results from 'othering' and in its most extreme case can lead to what the novel calls 'zombification.'

The novel's title suggests that Brodber's text is concerned with spiritual experiences that go beyond what is commonly understood as perception of reality. Myal or myalism is a residual and fragmented form of African religion commonly associated with Jamaica which expresses itself through dreams, visions, prophesying, and possession dances.[16] In contrast to obeah, another form of Afro-Caribbean belief, Orlando Patterson stresses the fact that myalism was "not an individual practice between practitioner and client, but was organized more as a kind of cult."[17] It is this

---

[16] Edward Kamau Brathwaite, "The African Presence in Caribbean Literature," *BIM* 17.65 (June 1979): 33–44. Brathwaite claims that the term 'myal' refers to the divination aspect of Afro-Caribbean religion (41), while according to Orlando Patterson the etymology of the term is unknown. See Patterson, *The Sociology of Slavery: An Analysis of the Origins, Development and Structure of Negro Slave Society in Jamaica* (London: MacGibbon & Kee, 1967): 185.

[17] Patterson, *The Sociology of Slavery*, 188. The ritualistic possession dances associated with the myal cult apparently show some similarity to Christian notions of death and resurrection. This might be one reason why, according to Patterson, myalism converged with Protestant revivalism to form the basis of modern Jamaican folk religion. Patterson, *The Sociology of Slavery*, 287. In the nineteenth century, Jamaica saw what Kamau Brathwaite describes as a " ' startling' phenomenon – the public reappearance of myalism." Brathwaite links this re-appearance of myalism to the importance of the Black Baptist churches, which, as he claims, functioned as semi-political organizations in the late nineteenth century. He argues: "Social and political unrest centered in the Baptist churches which the slaves had always preferred, mainly because of the 'African' nature of their adult baptism and the comparative freedom of their communal worship. [...] As a result, certain churches shifted away from a Euro-American kind of organisation into congregations that were not only run by blacks, but included African religious elements into their services"; Brathwaite, "The African Presence in Caribbean Literature," 37.

trans-individual and social aspect of myalism, its syncretic potential, and the fact
that the cult is associated with healing that make the concept and movement useful
to Brodber's critique of the results of the colonial encounter. More specifically, the
title refers to a group of characters within the novel, a secret Myal-alliance, and to
their activities. The alliance comprises various people of different creed, race, class,
gender, and occupation – the common denominator between the different members
of the group seems to be the absence of any such divisive principle. The group is
committed to healing the effects of the colonial mission presented in the novel in
terms of spirit thievery or zombification: "People are separated from the parts of
themselves that make them think and they are left as flesh only. Flesh that takes
direction from someone" (108). They are left as "empty shells – duppies, zombies,
living deads capable only of receiving orders from someone else and carrying them
out" (107). Spirit thievery separates body and mind and makes passive; it results in a
lack of agency, which the Myal-alliance tries to counteract.

IV

The most prominent and obvious case of spirit thievery, as a result of racial and
cultural alienation, is that of Ella O'Grady, a light-skinned girl of mixed racial
parentage, who for that reason attracts envy and resentment and remains an outsider
to the black community.[18] Ella's difference in skin-colouring, the fact that she is
neither black nor white, is the most obvious reason for the exclusion from her
culture of origin. And she is part of a family who has been considered different and
therefore 'strange'[19] for several generations: "three long face, thin lip, pointed nose
souls in a round face, thick lip, big eye country!" (8). Yet, in Brodber's novel, difference is an ambivalent concept: It also functions as a source of attraction,[20] in Ella's
case to the white US-American Selwyn Langley, her future husband, who regards
her 'otherness' as exotic, a positive asset to be exploited. Langley, the first person to
show any interest in Ella and her past, immediately recognizes the appeal of her

---

[18] This is not only the case with respect to her peer group: "The teachers didn't warm to her
either [...] and they said 'That child is odd. No fight at all. Suppose the colour will carry her
through.' And they were more than a little vexed at that and built up resentment against her. For it
was true [...] no one was going to give them with their black selves any job as a clerk in Kingston
or Morant Bay or any other town anywhere in the world. [...] So they stopped seeing her and she
too stopped seeing them"; Brodber, *Myal*, 10–11.

[19] The novel very subtly changes the connotations of the word 'strange' from expressing a negative reaction to expressing a specific sensitivity and a potential for spiritual growth. See Brodber,
Myal, 12, 13, 88.

[20] The same ambivalence can be seen with regard to the second character of mixed race, the
Reverend Brassington. While his colouring makes him deeply attractive to his later wife, his colour
and the assumption that, educated in Britain, he identifies with the British arouse suspicion in the
black community.

narration and decides to turn her story into "the biggest coon show ever" (80). The fact that Ella can neither belong to the black culture she is born into nor to the white American culture of her husband accounts for her extraordinary sensitivity (6), but also makes her behave like an actress in both contexts. Langley sees this pliability as Ella's specific potential – to him she is "a marvellously sculpted work waiting for the animator" (46).

Ella is the victim of several processes of 'othering': alienated from the community into which she was born because of her skin colour; alienated from her past through her husband's theatrical representation of her story as "the biggest coon show ever"; alienated from what she herself sees as her female destiny, namely pregnancy, Ella shows signs of mental dissociation[21] and, moreover, develops a pseudo-pregnancy to compensate for what she experiences as a constant draining of her resources.[22] Western or, more precisely, US-American medicine is unable to cope and regards her symptoms as a specifically Caribbean problem, so Ella is sent back to Jamaica. Again, her environment protects its own stability by means of exclusion. Through the collaborate healing effort of the myal-alliance and her adoptive family[23] Ella is restored to physical and mental health[24] and for the first time integrated into the community. For Brodber, myalism as an expression of ancestral knowledge and traditional community wisdom clearly is a positive force, a means of healing and achieving reconciliation not only on an individual but also on a community level. Ella is not only restored to health but also reconciled with her community. Her new position as assistant teacher brings out Ella's specific abilities to recognize discrimination even if it is very subtle. She complains about the colonial teaching materials that she is supposed to be using.[25] Her otherness, initially the reason for her exclu-

---

[21] In this respect, Ella is similar to Nellie, the protagonist of Brodber's first novel *Jane and Louisa Will Soon Come Home* (London & Port of Spain: New Beacon, 1980) who withdraws into what the novel calls the *kumbla* (= a 'cocoon'), displaying symptoms of psychic fragmentation which lead to mental breakdown.

[22] Brodber, *Myal*, 82–84. "If he could not show her how to fill the spaces he had created and give her too a chance to create, then what was the point of all this draining and changing and losing her friends?" (82).

[23] It is important to emphasize that Ella's adoptive family, the Reverend Brassington, his wife Maydene and their two sons, is also 'mixed' with regard to skin colour.

[24] Una Marson's play *Pocomania* (first performed in Jamaica in 1938) explores the practices and effects of another syncretistic religious ritual, pocomania (= a little madness), in a rural Jamaican community, yet the ending of her play, a repudiation of pocomania, suggests a less positive evaluation of the potential of Afro-Caribbean religion than Brodber's. See Elaine Campbell, "The Unpublished Plays of Una Marson," *Anglophone Karibik – USA: Peripherie und Zentrum in der 'neuen Welt'*, ed. Michael Hoenisch & Remco van Capelleveen (Hamburg & Berlin: Argument, 1991): 110–16. The volume also contains Marson's play (117–47).

[25] Her complaint is directed at a story about several animals living on Mr Joe's farm which is part of the Caribbean Primer used in teaching to read. Ella realizes that this story provides a

sion from the community, now becomes the source of her understanding the mechanisms of colonial exploitation as well as the ultimate condition for articulating her own subjectivity.

Brodber's novel presents the reader with a biography of spiritual growth and of increasing self-understanding. In fact, in *Myal*, it seems as if 'othering' and acculturation are complementary processes, two sides of the same coin. The difference that initially was the reason for exclusion from the community ultimately becomes the source of identifying with it. The novel develops this idea through subtly changing the connotations of the word 'strange,' from 'peculiar' or 'odd one out' in the beginning of the novel to 'extra-sensitive' with a 'specific potential for spiritual growth' (12, 13, 87–88). Similarly, the connotations of the so-called "new people" or "in-between colours people" (1, 3, 7–9, 23, 43, 109–10) change from troublemakers who belong neither here nor there to a positive evaluation: "Two special people. New people" (109). In a sense, the ending of the novel justifies a judgement that initially had been regarded as the statement of a cranky eccentric: "It was the mixture of black and white that would be most attuned to the new setting" (16).[26]

To conclude: In my reading, Brodber's novel is both an historical investigation of the effects of the colonial encounter and the articulation of a utopian hope. In *Myal*, it is the new people, the in-between-colours people, who are the bearers of hope for a better future. Their borderline existence is not a weakness but a strength. They combine the knowledge of more than one culture with an extraordinary sensitivity to the subtlest matters of discrimination. As the 'other' is 'always already' at the centre of any self-definition, Brodber's novel seems to suggest, it would be better to acknowledge and integrate rather than repress it. If all cultures are hybrids, no culture can afford to lose the creative potential of its 'other.'

WORKS CITED

Ashcroft, Bill, Gareth Griffiths & Helen Tiffin. *The Empire Writes Back: Theory and Practice in Post-Colonial Literatures* (London & New York: Routledge, 1989).

Barker, Francis, Peter Hulme, Margret Iversen & Diane Loxley, ed. *Europe and Its Others* (Proceedings of the Essex Sociology of Literature Conference, 2 vols.; Colchester: Essex UP, 1985).

Bhabha, Homi K. *The Location of Culture* (London & New York: Routledge, 1994).

---

parallel to the colonial situation: "They treat them as sub-normals who have no hope of growth." Moreover, she complains that the "children are invited into complicity" by the story (97); see also 105–107.

[26] Similar to Bhabha's understanding of the postcolonial intellectual and Salman Rushdie's notion of the migrant between cultures, Brodber's novel emphasizes the positive aspects and particular strengths of such a borderline mode of existence.

Bové, Paul A. "Discourse," in *Critical Terms for Literary Study*, ed. Frank Lentricchia & Thomas McLaughlin (Chicago & London: U of Chicago P, 2nd ed. 1995): 50–65.

Brathwaite, Edward Kamau. "The African Presence in Caribbean Literature," *Bim* 17.65 (1979): 33–44. Originally published in *Daedalus* 103 (Spring 1974): 73–109.

Brodber, Erna. *Jane and Louisa Will Soon Come Home* (London & Port of Spain: New Beacon, 1980).

——. *Myal* (London & Port of Spain: New Beacon, 1988).

Brown, Cedric, & Therese Fischer–Seidel, ed. *Cultural Negotiations: Sichtweisen des Anderen* (Kultur und Erkenntnis 19; Tübingen & Basel: Francke, 1998).

Campbell, Elaine. "The Unpublished Plays of Una Marson," in *Anglophone Karibik – USA: Peripherie und Zentrum in der 'neuen Welt'*, ed. Michael Hoenisch & Remco van Capelleveen (*Gulliver* 30; Hamburg & Berlin: Argument, 1991): 110–16.

Fludernik, Monika. *Hybridity and Postcolonialism: Twentieth Century Indian Literature* (Tübingen: Stauffenburg, 1998).

Minh–ha, Trinh T. *Woman, Native, Other: Writing Postcoloniality and Feminism* (Bloomington: Indiana UP, 1989).

Moore–Gilbert, Bart. *Postcolonial Theory: Contexts, Practices, Politics* (London & New York: Verso, 1997).

Patterson, Orlando. *The Sociology of Slavery: An Analysis of the Origins, Development and Structure of Negro Slave Society in Jamaica* (London: MacGibbon & Kee, 1967).

Tiffin, Helen. "Post-Colonial Literatures and Counter-Discourse," *Kunapipi* 9.3 (1987): 17–34.

Young, Robert C. *Colonial Desire: Hybridity in Theory, Culture and Race* (London & New York: Routledge, 1995).

~

A Snake in the Garden of the *New Yorker*?
An Analysis of the Disruptive Function of Jamaica Kincaid's Gardening Column

ANNE COLLETT

T HIS ESSAY OFFERS AN ASSESSMENT of the confrontation/contamination nexus of Jamaica Kincaid's work in the *New Yorker*. In a discussion of the notion of contamination as it might be applied positively to texts identified as creole, Diana Brydon has suggested that these texts are "searching for a new globalism that is neither the old universalism nor the Disney simulacrum," and that

> This globalism simultaneously asserts local independence and global interdependencies. It seeks a way to cooperate without cooption, a way to define differences that do not depend on myths of cultural purity or authenticity but that thrive on an interaction that "contaminates" without homogenising.[1]

In her reading of the work of Kristjana Gunnars and Mordecai Richler, Brydon makes what might be seen to be a somewhat idealistic or even naïve claim that "Although they recognise inevitable complicities, they choose contestation; they discover free spaces for resistance."[2] It is both the notion of 'free space' and the possibility of choice that I would interrogate in an analysis of Jamaica Kincaid's position and positioning in the *New Yorker*.

"Flowers of Evil," the first in a series of articles written by Kincaid under the title "In the Garden" in the *New Yorker* between October 1992 and June 1995, begins with the musing statement: "The way you think and feel about gardens and the things growing in them – flowers, vegetables – I can see must depend on where you

---

[1] Diana Brydon, "The White Inuit Speaks: Contamination as Literary Strategy," in *Past the Last Post: Theorising Post-Colonialism and Post-Modernism*, ed. Ian Adam & Helen Tiffin (Calgary: Calgary UP, 1990): 196.

[2] Brydon, "The White Inuit Speaks," 198.

come from [...]."[3] Jamaica Kincaid makes clear that this difference of perception is
not a difference of nationality as such but a difference of power – a difference that is
historical rather than geographical (although geography and history could probably
be said to be inevitably and irrevocably entangled). Towards the end of a piece of
writing that explores the dynamics of power, the complex and entangled relationship
of powerful and powerless, of conqueror and conquered, Kincaid describes, indeed,
addresses or even redresses, her own writing position, in terms of that same traffic in
power:

> As I started to write this (at the very beginning) I was sitting at a window that looked
> out over my own garden [...] and I took pleasure in that because in putting things
> together (plants) you never really know how it will all work until they do something
> like bloom [...]. Just now the leaves in the shade bed are all complementary (but not in
> a predictable way – in a way I had not expected, a thrilling way). And I thought how I
> had crossed a line; but at whose expense? I cannot begin to look, because what if it is
> someone I know? I have joined the conquering class: who else could afford this garden
> – a garden in which I grow things that it would be much cheaper to buy at the store?
> My feet (so to speak) are in two worlds [...] (159)

What, one might ask, is the possibility of getting those feet to operate co-operatively
if they are positioned "in two worlds"? Either they operate without relation to each
other, in which case you are likely, at best, to end up with mud on your face (propelled by an awkward gait that causes you to trip), at worst, to suffer a painful death
– split asunder by divisive desires, loyalties, loves, hates; or you find some way of
bringing those worlds into workable proximity which necessarily demands compromise, complicity and the threat of possible contamination. There is another possibility, that the division between the worlds is an artificial boundary constituting an
imaginary construct of limited use, traffic across which is so frequent (either covert-
ly or overtly) as to nullify the distinction between worlds almost completely. This is,
however, a dangerous idea in real terms (or in political terms) because it suggests the
possibility of conceiving of poverty, torture, starvation and death as equally imaginary – or that responsibility and liability are not only non-ascribable to any one or
any event in particular, but irrelevant or even absurd concepts; and I for one could
not go that far. The guiding interest of this discussion is not only a personal desire to
understand or at least confront and consider the complexity of Kincaid's political
and poetic position, but also to investigate her own understanding of that position as
revealed through a variety of textual discourse that is, as Helen Tiffin has recently

---

[3] In this essay, all words and phrases appearing in double quotation marks but unaccompanied
by page numbers are drawn from Kincaid's article "Flowers of Evil," *The New Yorker* (5 October
1991): 154–59.

used the term, inevitably "entangled."[4] Has Kincaid "stepped over the line" to join "the conquering class"? Or to put the question another way and suggest linkage with Gayatri Spivak's concerns, when is a subaltern not a subaltern?

Born on the Caribbean island of Antigua (that "small place" of which she writes in 1988),[5] Jamaica Kincaid began life as Elaine Potter Richardson, a name inherited in the usual fashion, signifying both the whims and desires of parentage. She left the incestuous suffocation of colonial island politics in 1965 and has spent the remainder of her life in the USA making the trip back home only rarely, one recent instance being the return to alleviate, but also to witness and perhaps bear witness, to the living death of a brother with AIDS, recorded in the most recent text, *My Brother* (1997). Perhaps, like James Joyce, Kincaid attempts to disentangle herself from an inherited history (to "fly by those nets" of "nationality, language and religion"[6] as expressed by Kincaid through the persona of Xuela as a refusal to belong to either race or nation.[7] Yet the processes of that disentanglement is only a further entanglement, because it is the life-writing of that relationship. In the words of Joyce, via Stephen Dedalus: "This race and this country and this life produced me [...] I shall express myself as I am [...]" This is an "I am" that both Joyce and Kincaid discover cannot be extricated from that country and that life. All Kincaid's work is autobiographical in the sense that it writes the story of her self as colonized Caribbean – the life of the defeated and the vanquished, yet neither defeated nor vanquished (as Joyce wrote the story of his self as colonized Irish). Elaine Potter Richardson created herself 'Jamaica Kincaid' as a writer for the *New Yorker*: she was like Xuela, orphan-born – born of herself. Kincaid remarks in an interview with Kay Bonetti: "By the time I made the effort to write I had changed my name, so I was never anything but Jamaica Kincaid as a writer." Her text is the struggle to disentangle herself

---

[4] Tiffin observes in a recent article on the work of Jamaica Kincaid, Olive Senior and Lorna Goodison, "as most disciplines move away from binarist models of colonizer versus colonized, imperium versus periphery – a political phase of disciplinary construction that was and is still a crucial one – it is the inextricably 'entangled' nature of the cultural products of that history which increasingly commands our attention"; "' Flowers of Evil,' flowers of Empire: Roses and Daffodils in the Work of Jamaica Kincaid, Olive Senior and Lorna Goodison," *SPAN: Journal of the South Pacific Association for Commonwealth Literature and Language Studies* 46 (April 1998): 58. The term "entangled" is cited as an echo of that used by Nicholas Thomas in his work on *Entangled Objects: Exchange, Material Culture, and Colonialism in the Pacific* (Cambridge MA: Harvard UP, 1991).

[5] *A Small Place* (New York: Farrar, Straus & Giroux, 1988).

[6] James Joyce, "A Portrait of the Artist as a Young Man," in *The Essential James Joyce*, ed. Harry Levin (Harmondsworth: Penguin, 1963): 211.

[7] Jamaica Kincaid, *The Autobiography of My Mother* (London: Vintage, 1996): 216.

from the mire of inheritance (Darwin's "tangled bank"[8]) – perhaps to 'discover' to
create 'free space'? But how might she best achieve this, if, as Virginia Woolf has so
eloquently claimed in *A Room of One's Own* (1929), the potential to write the self is
determined by material things. Is it possible to gain "a room of one's own" and the
freedom to write the self if one is poor, black and a woman, that is, 'subaltern'?
Could the *New Yorker* offer that 'free space,' that 'independent room'? The *New
Yorker* certainly offered Kincaid the material necessities, the possibility of survival
in terms of body and mind – the assumption of a powerful position from which to
speak – but speak to whom? – and subsequent to the question of audience is that
which asks if the subaltern can 'speak' from this central position any more effectively than from the margins.

Kincaid describes her initial relationship with the *New Yorker* as a matter of subsistence or even survival. When asked how she came to write for the *New Yorker*'s
"Talk of the Town," she describes the early days of that relationship in terms of
necessary exchange – necessary, that is, to the survival of body as much as spirit –
an exchange of sassy black words for "little cocktail things":

> How did I come to write for *The New Yorker*? George Trow befriended me – I think
> that is how I would put it – and was very generous and kind and loving. He thought I
> was funny, and he would take me around to parties. I was so grateful, because I was
> very poor. Sometimes the only meal I ate was those little cocktail things. He would
> write about me in "Talk of the Town." He took me to meet Mr. Shawn, and I started to
> write for *The New Yorker*. I gave George my impressions of an event, and they ap-
> peared in the magazine just as I wrote them. That was how I discovered what my own
> writing was.[9]

It is significant that the event of which she wrote that gave her the necessary start to
her writing career (and that, perhaps again significantly, is not mentioned by name in
this interview) was 'West Indian' carnival (in Brooklyn). From the outset, then,
Kincaid's relationship with the *New Yorker* is a trade in the erotic exotic, of which
the exchange of "sassy black" for "cocktail things" is signatory. The *New Yorker*
offers the luxury of a room (or in this case, a garden) of one's own (Kincaid makes
deliberate reference to "my own garden" in "Flowers of Evil") in exchange for black
rap, street cred, the violet-scented air of liberal humanism that cannot help but im-

---

[8] Charles Darwin's *Origin of Species* contemplates in conclusion "a tangled bank" and reflects
upon the complexity of relationship between the life forms, "so different from each other and
dependent upon each other." This entanglement is imagined as "the war of nature, a war that produces famine and death but out of which "the most exalted object which we are capable of conceiving, namely, the production of the higher animals, directly follows." Interestingly Kincaid's
article concludes with the somewhat opaque statement "I am not in nature."

[9] Kay Bonetti, "An Interview with Jamaica Kincaid" (1992), http://www.missouri.edu/ moreview/
interviews/kincaid.html (22 May 1998).

part the vaguely unpleasant whiff of *Pygmalion* (or *My Fair Lady*) – Kincaid playing a black Liza Doolittle to Shawn's Professor Higgins. What are the dynamics of power in what might be seen as a compromised or co-opted move from a subsistence existence as a flower seller (honourable sassy) to 'a Lady' (still sassy but somewhat tainted) who now has the knowledge and power to recognize and name the flowers in her own garden – but a garden bought at what price? Kincaid observes:

> This ignorance of the botany of the place I am from (and am of) really only reflects the fact that when I lived there, I was of the conquered class and living in a conquered place; the principle of this condition is that nothing about you is of any interest unless the conqueror deems it so. ("Flowers of Evil," 157)

Moving to a discussion of her present position (both in her new garden 'at home' in Vermont, and in her 'gardening column' in the *New Yorker*) Kincaid remarks "with a certain amount of bitterness" that now "I was in my garden": "a flower garden, a garden planted only because I wished to have such a thing, and that I know how I wanted it to look and knew the name, proper and common, of each thing growing in it." But what amount of control or power does Kincaid have in her literary garden? Is she the owner or the owned? Has the principle changed? Is Kincaid still only of interest because the conqueror deems it so? What are the politics and the poetics of a "cosmopolitan interdependence," and how might Jamaica Kincaid's garden patch as situated (or possibly insinuated) within the bounds of the larger, cosmopolitan, garden of the *New Yorker* be read, that is, to what degree does this Antiguan incursion disrupt or become party to the globalizing, colonizing 'ethics' of a northern American cosmopolitanism signified in the glossy consumerism of the *New Yorker*? What is the ironic disruptive potential of the article "Flowers of Evil" and to what degree does it refuse or embrace what might be seen as the commodification of liberal humanism?

This is a liberal humanism which might best be signified by the icon of the "gift wrapped buffalo" that attaches itself (as parasite to host) to an article published toward the end of the series (12 December 1994) entitled "Earthly Delights" and enjoins readers to "buy a bison through us, The American Friends Service Committee."[10] Readers are assured that their gift has a quantifiable value not only in terms of $$$ but weight: "Your gift, weighing 1,000 lbs, or more, will cost $500." And you are assured of delivery to Lakota/Sioux young people on the Pine Ridge "Reservation in South Dakota." Sounds like a worthy cause at a reasonable price? – an admirable charity through which, for a few hundred American dollars you might atone for the sins of the nation, and absolve yourself of inherited guilt and respon-

---

[10] AFSC is a Quaker organization founded by American and Canadian 'Friends' during the period of the first world war, primarily in order to find acceptable alternatives to military service for pacifists or 'conscientious objectors.'

sibility? It's a bargain, a particularly good bargain when this purchase might be seen not only to help the Lakota to "develop self-sufficiency and preserve their culture and religion" but, by colonial extension, to placate the wrath, dull the sting, divert the attack of the Caribbean gardener cum writer (a cultivator of word) who insists that "the world cannot be left out of the garden" and that "flowers are evil" not in themselves but in their uses, their meaning, their signification and representation.

Kincaid's article to which the AFSC buffalo attaches itself describes the "botanical garden" of a museum at Harvard, in which fruit and flowers of blown glass are displayed "to perfection" – the flowers are shown "without any blemish at all" and even those fruits representative of states of decay and degradation appear as "art," or as artifice – a beautiful yet curious falsity of simulacrum. Of this display, to which she admits she is strangely drawn ("captivated"), Kincaid observes:

> The creation of these simulacra is also an almost defiant assertion of will: it is man vying with nature herself. To see these things is to be reminded of how barefaced the notions of captivity and control used to be [...] How permanent everything must feel when the world is going your way! ("Earthly Delights," 64)

"How barefaced the notions of captivity and control *used to be*"? Are those notions of captivity and control even more dangerous now when they are less barefaced? Are they less barefaced? To take the *New Yorker* as an example...

The flowers, like the buffalo, the American Indian and the African slave who worked the plantations of South Carolina[11] and Antigua, might be seen to be conveniently gift-wrapped and controlled – conveniently rendered almost invisible, certainly lifeless, on reservations and in museums. Kincaid's pieces in the *New Yorker* have the effect of a slap in the face – they are "in ya face" – revealing the blemish in the beauty, the rot at the heart of an American imperial dream built upon, or to maintain a gardening motif, fertilized by the blood and bone of native and transplanted peoples; but given the context of contagious disease with which these digs are associated – the disease of rampant American consumerism – are her words inevitably sucked of life, consumed, controlled and rendered inaudible (unreadable, unspeakable) by a parasite that ultimately destroys its host? Which the host and which the parasite? The magazine admits (suffers?) advertisement in order that it might maintain (satisfy?) both its writers and its readership – or does it? Is Kincaid's work contaminated by the compromise of her own implicated position (of which she admits – "I have crossed the line") or does it function as a site and disseminator of disease?

---

[11] South Carolina is a reference to an advertisement for a weight loss clinic in "Valencia Road, Shipyard Plantation, South Carolina" ("Flowers of Evil," 159).

How do we read biting observations about the acquisitive greed of the colonizer and the destructive and demeaning ramifications for the colonized that lie within the parameters of such "barefaced" consumerism that speaks to and for the acquisitive greed of global capital founded upon 'cosmopolitan interdependence'? "Flowers of Evil" I set within the heart of a magazine Tom Wolfe debunked in the 1960s as "the national shopping news," claiming that under William Shawn's editorship the *New Yorker* had become an embalmed corpse, drained of its literary juices (ghost of its former self as expressed under Harold Ross's editorship). Wolfe makes the claim that the *New Yorker* is "nothing more than 'thin connective tissue' holding together the fancy ads for cognac, furs and ritzy places."[12] The magazine might in fact be seen to be a simulacrum – the cosmetic replication of a facile and increasingly self-interested, self-perpetuating, self-created monster of middle-class America – signified by the bumper-sticker "I shop therefore I am." Kincaid's 'flower garden' is nurtured by avaricious advertisements for "thick, juicy, world-famous Omaha Steaks" and organic "old-fashioned, flavorful" potatoes that jostle for attention with "Natural or Roasted Salted California Almonds fresh from our farm" and Vidalia Sweet Onions: this is a "little feast" – testimony to the luxury, comfort and power of the educated American middle class – to which Kincaid draws attention, indeed, makes acerbic comment upon, in her opening discussion of a writer's "angle of vision."[13] In this exploration of the relationship between gardening and conquest, Henry James's description of life as a "little feast" is contrasted with that of Tsitsi Dangarembga in which "the ingredients for a garden [...] do not lead to little feasts; they lead to nothing or they lead to work, and do not work as an act of self-definition, self-acclaim, but work as torture, work as hell" ("Flowers of Evil," 154). Does Kincaid's article work to unsettle the comfort of that sense of luxury, of "permanence" as exemplified not only by Henry James' text but by the *New Yorker*; or is it swallowed along with the potatoes and onions or the more exotic consumables of beach clubs in Hawaii, Inuit art, and most fittingly (ironically?) cruises in the Caribbean, holidays in the British Virgin Islands and a romantic getaway on a private island off St Vincent? But perhaps consumption is not so easy – perhaps the discomfort of this curious disjunction gives the reader indigestion, somewhat like the effect of *A Small Place*.

---

[12] George H. Douglas, *The Smart Magazine* (Hamden CT: Archon, 1991): 172–73.

[13] Virginia Woolf refers to this "angle of vision" in a paper read to the Brighton Workers' Educational Association in 1940, in which she observes of the male writer: "He sits upon a tower raised above the rest of us; a tower on his parents' station, then on his parents' fold. It is a tower of the utmost importance; it decides his angle of vision; it affects his power of communication"; quoted by Michele Barrett in her introduction to the Penguin edition of *A Room of One's Own* and *Three Guineas* (Harmondsworth: Penguin, 1993): xiv.

Perhaps Kincaid has not "crossed the line" but, rather, undermines the line. In the final paragraph of "Flowers of Evil," Kincaid reasserts the validity or the authority of the position from which she speaks, reaffirming her alliance with the colonized – "I do not find the world furnished like a room, with cushioned seats and rich-colored rugs. To me, the world is cracked, unwhole, not pure, accidental; and the idea of moments of joy for no reason is very strange" (159) – for no reason? The reader is brought full-circle to the opening contrasted images of conqueror and conquered in which an exemplification of Woolf's "angle of vision" takes the form of those complimentary contrasting images drawn from James and Dangarembga – images analogous to Woolf's symbols in *A Room of One's Own* of the benefits of power and wealth, where in Chapter One she contrasts "the little feast" of sole, partridge and sugar confection that gives rise to "the subtle and subterranean glow which is the rich yellow flame of rational intercourse" (10) to be enjoyed at the men's college in Cambridge, with the fare of plain gravy soup, custard and prunes of the women's college (15–16) that gives rise to not so subtle discontent and only rare moments of liberating enlightenment. Are these rare moments sufficient? The question of Kincaid's positioning by herself and others (a question in Woolf's terminology of the relative agency of an "angle of vision") leads inevitably to Gayatri Spivak's question, "Can the subaltern speak?" anywhere – can she speak any more effectively from the centre than from the margins? The problem of contamination and compromise that might be seen to 'come with the job' when one secures a position at centre, brings us again to Woolf and the question arising out of contrasted angles of vision that she posits but does not or cannot resolve in the concluding lines of the first chapter of *A Room of One's Own*:

> and I thought how unpleasant it is to be locked out; and I thought how it is worse perhaps to be locked in; and thinking of the safety and prosperity of the one sex and of the poverty and insecurity of the other and of the effect of tradition and of the lack of tradition upon the mind of the writer, I thought at last that it was time to roll up the crumpled skin of the day, with its arguments and its impressions and its anger and its laughter, and cast it into the hedge. (21–22)

The casting of the skin, albeit of the day, so carelessly and casually into the hedge serves to reinforce the constraints of Kincaid's position as one who cannot cast her skin as a snake might do (given time). She is inscribed and described by it – but might she not make use of an inheritance, an "angle of vision," that determines but does not necessarily undermine or render powerless her writing position? Kincaid's place in the *New Yorker* is a "small place" but it is not necessarily an ineffectual place. Perhaps, as indicated in Diana Brydon's reading of Richler's *Solomon Gursky Was Here*, although "the movements of peoples and interactions of cultures that have characterized the twentieth century have taken place as part of the military expansion of capital [...] there is always a space for resistance, for eluding control and surprising the enemy."[14]

How might we read Kincaid's article as resistance? Is my understanding of Kincaid's place in the *New Yorker* unnecessarily, or unfairly, passive? Do I deny her the possibility of effect or of intent to disrupt because I perceive her as conquered and colonized? Might I learn something from Kincaid's exposition of her own perception of place and position through the words of her M / Other self, Xuela:

> I am of the vanquished, I am of the defeated. The past is a fixed point, the future is open-ended; for me the future must remain capable of casting light on the past such that in my defeat lies the seed of my great victory, in my defeat lies the beginning of my great revenge.[15]

Kincaid, in face like Xuela, affirms and decries a history that has determined her as "of the defeated" and "of the vanquished" but she is neither conquered nor vanquished. That was the past, this is the future – but time is a flow, its borders imaginary and permeable – like the text of the *New Yorker* in which images and ideas circulate 'in tension': they exist in dynamic relation to one another – a relationship out of which Kincaid might speak – not in spite of surrounding text, but in ironic relation to 'other' text, such that a discussion of the destructive ramifications of conquest of the Americas stands in ironic relation to that which feeds off and perpetuates the inequalities and insurgency of such conquest as figured in advertisements of Hawaii, the Caribbean and Inuit and Northwest Coast Indian art.

Must contamination then necessarily imply complicity or co-option? Although I have moved my understanding of Kincaid's work in the *New Yorker* from that of the idea of contamination that carries negative connotations of pollution or infection, and that which assumes an originary notion of authenticity or purity, this discussion of Kincaid's work has not been an exploration of the "creative possibility of cross-cultural contact,"[16] nor is the effect of this textual conjunction something as lacking in energy as that expressed by Lola Lemire Tostevin – that "Contamination means differences have been brought together so they make contact."[17] I would suggest that we need to understand literature or textual interrelationship as energy. The dynamic or energy of text lies in the quality of this 'making contact' – the rub, the irritation – the kind of energy that is associated with friction; or perhaps better, a metaphor of osmotic process that refuses the notion or possibility of discrete texts of body or consciousness might be helpful, giving expression to the idea central to Kincaid's work that the perceived limits of the text – the borders –

[14] Brydon, "The White Inuit Speaks," 199.

[15] *The Autobiography of My Mother* (London: Vintage, 1966): 216.

[16] Brydon, "The White Inuit Speaks," 191.

[17] Quoted by Brydon, "The White Inuit Speaks," 191.

are permeable – vulnerable yet not indiscriminatory. No space is 'free' but perhaps
it is possible to create, as opposed to discover speaking space – to manipulate and
manoeuvre room to move – even in a garden that is hedged in on all sides. Contamination is a term that does not adequately address the ironic function nor the
sometimes concealed tensile energy of 'contact.'

Kincaid's own discussion of her writing relationship with the *New Yorker* is an
acknowledgement, even a celebration, of the creative dynamic of entanglement.
Kincaid's response to the question, "How do you think the writing that you did for
'Talk of the Town' prepared you for the fiction?" is typically paradoxical (and fully
aware of its paradox):

> It did two things. It showed me how to write, and it allowed me to write in my own
> voice. *The New Yorker* no longer has that power, but at one time it could take any indi-
> vidual piece of writing, no matter how eccentric the writing was, and without changing
> so much as a punctuation mark, the piece became the standard of *The New Yorker*. It
> had such power of personality.[18]

Who holds the power, who wields the power – the *New Yorker* or "the piece"? The
last "it" here is deliberately ambiguous: Is "it" a reference to the power of personality of the *New Yorker* or of Kincaid's individual piece of writing? The notion of
"standard" is entangled: Does the piece become "the standard" of the magazine
because it reflects, imbibes or is contaminated by the larger text within which it lies
and through which it is given life, or does the piece of itself create "the standard" –
energizing and breathing life into what would otherwise be merely a vessel – body
without soul? Or is the relationship an entangled one, such that the effect of one
upon the other cannot be teased out. In biological terms, is the relationship parasitic
or symbiotic? At what point does the outsider become insider? At what point is the
relationship between author and editor nepotistic or even incestuous?

"So there I was," remarks Kincaid, "writing anonymously in this strange voice,
and it looked like the *New Yorker*. It was a wonderful thing for me because I was
edited by this brilliant editor, this brilliant man, Mr. William Shawn, who became
my father-in-law." Bonetti hurries in to disclaim the possible reading of nepotism:
"Later. We have to say later." And Kincaid continues, "Yes, he was very keen on not
appearing to practice nepotism. Anyway, I had this wonderful editor and what I had
to do to keep him interested was write clearly and keep my personality. And I did it.
I could make him understand what I had to say. I doubt very much that I would have
turned out to be the writer I am without him." So did Elaine Potter Richardson give
birth to Jamaica Kincaid, or was she born between the pages of a magazine – child
of an entangled and incestuous textual relationship?

---

[18] Kay Bonetti, "An Interview with Jamaica Kincaid."

Kincaid's gardening column in the *New Yorker* might be understood as a simulacrum of the garden she describes in "Flowers of Evil" – one in which "the leaves in the shade bed are all complimentary" – complimentary in the sense that the ostensibly separate texts (of advertisement and gardening column) speak to each other – "not in a predictable way" but "in a way I had not expected, a thrilling way": bodies of text collide, rub, caress, irritate, such that borders are merely "stenographic."[19] A line is crossed. And if we begin to look, as Kincaid would have us do, "at whose expense," I find myself on unstable ground, perhaps one of the dis-affected, but nevertheless one who has become entangled in the pleasure of the text, a pleasure is to be found, as Jamaica Kincaid asserts, in "putting things [words] together" because "you never really know how it will work until they do something, like bloom."

WORKS CITED AND CONSULTED

Bonetti, Kay. "An Interview with Jamaica Kincaid." (1992): http://www.missouri.edu/ review/ interviews/kincaid.html (22 May 1998).

Brydon, Diana. "The White Inuit Speaks: Contamination as Literary Strategy." in *Past the Last Post: Theorising Post-Colonialism and Post-Modernism*, ed. Ian Adam & Helen Tiffin (Calgary: Calgary UP, 1990): 191–203.

Deleuze, Gilles, & Felix Guattari. *Kafka: Toward a Minor Literature* (Minneapolis & London: Minnesota UP, 1994).

Douglas, George H. *The Smart Magazine: 50 Years of Literary Revelry & High Jinks at Vanity Fair, The New Yorker, Life, Esquire & The Smart Set* (Hamden CT: Archon, 1991).

Joyce, James. "Portrait of the Artist as a Young Man," in *The Essential James Joyce*, ed. Harry Levin (Harmondsworth: Penguin, 1963).

Kincaid, Jamaica. *The Autobiography of My Mother* (London: Random House / Vintage, 1996).

——. "Earthly Delights" ['In the Garden'], *New Yorker* (12 December 1994): 63–71.

——. "Flowers of Evil" ['In the Garden'], *New Yorker* (5 October 1992): 154–59.

——. *My Brother* (1997; London: Random House / Vintage, 1998).

——. *A Small Place* (New York: Farrar, Straus & Giroux, 1988).

——. "This Other Eden" ['In the Garden'], *New Yorker* (23–30 August 1993): 69–73.

Spivak, Gayatri Chakravorty. "Can the Subaltern Speak?" in *Colonial Discourse and Post-Colonial Theory: A Reader*, ed. Patrick Williams & Laura Chrisman (Hemel Hempstead: Harvester Wheatsheaf, 1994): 66–111.

——. "Subaltern Talk: Interview with the Editors," in *The Spivak Reader: Selected Works of Gayatri Chakravorty Spivak*, ed. Donna Landry & Gerald MacLean (New York & London: Routledge, 1996): 287–308.

Thomas, Nicholas. *Entangled Objects: Exchange, Material Culture, and Colonialism in the Pacific* (Cambridge MA: Harvard UP, 1991).

---

[19] "Stenographic" is an echo of Harold Ross's original conception of *The New Yorker* as "interpretive rather than stenographic"; quoted by George H. Douglas, *The Smart Magazine: 50 Years of Literary Revelry & High Jinks at Vanity Fair, The New Yorker, Life, Esquire & The Smart Set* (Hamden CT: Archon, 1991): 143.

Tiffin, Helen. "' Flowers of Evil,' Flowers of Empire: Roses and Daffodils in the Work of Jamaica Kincaid, Olive Senior and Lorna Goodison," *SPAN: Journal of the South Pacific Association for Commonwealth Literature and Language Studies* 46 (April 1998): 58–71.

Wolfe, Tom. "Lost in a Whichy Thicket," *New York Herald Tribune Magazine* (18 April 1965): 16.

Woolf, Virginia. *A Room of One's Own and Three Guineas* (Harmondsworth: Penguin, 1993).

❧

Imposing Narratives

European Incursions and Intertexts
in Pauline Melville's *The Ventriloquist's Tale* (1997)

SARAH LAWSON WELSH

T AKING AS MY STARTING-POINT David Dabydeen's provocative comments about the prevalent ignorance and scholarly neglect of "what is
oldest in the [Caribbean] region, namely our Amerindian cultures" in his
recent essay "Teaching West Indian Literature in Britain,"[1] my essay concentrates on
the latest novel by the Guyanese writer Pauline Melville, *The Ventriloquist's Tale*.

This highly significant silence or omission regarding Amerindian peoples from
the Caribbean or South America reflects a larger silence or omission within the academy, and within Caribbean studies as a subject area. It would therefore seem appo-
site that I undertake a little of my own evangelizing in highlighting Pauline Melville's novel. However, I also want to suggest that the *process* of reading *The Ventriloquist's Tale* is an uncomfortable one in many ways. As I was writing this essay I
had the uneasy sense that my every move, every articulation I could possibly make
had already been anticipated, and indeed, satirized or critiqued, by Melville in her
novel. As a white, female Caribbeanist based in the Western academy, I became
increasingly aware of just how far the fictional academic, Rosa Mendelson, in the
novel anticipated my own scholarly interventions. Indeed, I think Melville's novel
can and *should* be read as a salutary reminder of the exclusions, blind spots, and
omissions of our scholarly activity and of the need to recognize, in Jean Rhys's
words, that "there is always the other side,"[2] or at least *another* side.

Dabydeen's essay is an important one for pointing out the continued neglect of
Amerindian cultures:

> In Guyana we have many such living cultures – Wai Wai, Macusi, Arawak, Carib – but
> Western Caribbeanists know next to nothing of Amerindian languages, oral and written

---

[2] Jean Rhys, *Wide Sargasso Sea* (1966; Harmondsworth: Penguin, 1969): 106.

expressions, myths, religions, art, music, diet, political economy, gender relations, and so on. Evidence of the wilful neglect of Amerindian cultures is stark. [Amerindian] poem[s], chant[s], song[s], prayer[s] or proverb[s are not generally anthologised.] There is correspondingly a total ignoring of Amerindian ideas in books which purport to deal with the intellectual traditions in the region [...] The simple fact is that scholars who produce such texts – which form the basis of teaching Caribbean Studies in the Western academies – have rarely travelled into the interior to meet Amerindians, never mind studied the languages and cultures [...] The dismal truth is that Caribbeanists are still very much timid external observers of the cultures of the region. Herskovits's injunction that they should 'get down from their verandas' and live among the peoples they study falls on deaf ears. If the region has always been prey to piracy and quick plunder, today it endures new pirates from the metropolis – people who make quick visits, observe hastily and in fright of the native presence, then return to pronounce with authority in the centres in Britain.[3]

Dabydeen's essay was published in 1997, the same year in which Melville's first novel, *The Ventriloquist's Tale*, appeared to considerable acclaim. Dabydeen cites Melville as a writer whose works have "emerged from the plundering and silencing of her Amerindian ancestors."[4] Indeed, Melville's novel is centrally engaged with the way in which "the silenced subjects of oppression are spoken by the different discourses through which their story is inscribed."[5] I want to argue that Melville's novel deliberately stages, interrogates and probes the sore points of postcolonial debates surrounding the status, study and representation of indigenous peoples, with a specific focus on Amerindian peoples and cultures in a Guyanese context. The notion that fictional works can and do constitute significant interventions in relevant critical and theoretical debates is not a new one, at least not in postcolonial studies, and *The Ventriloquist's Tale* can be seen to contribute to debates on indigeneity in some valuable ways.

In this context, Melville's handling of both European and Amerindian literary and cultural intertexts deserves examination, as does the role of the intruding Europeans and their discourse(s) in the novel. The latter include Father Napier, a Jesuit missionary, Professor Wormoal, a structuralist anthropologist researching Amerindian myth, and Rosa Mendelson, a young literary scholar who is researching "the attitude to the colonies"[6] of an earlier interloper, the novelist Evelyn Waugh. All

---

[3] David Dabydeen, "Teaching West Indian Literature in Britain," in *Studying British Cultures*, ed. Susan Bassnett (London & New York: Routledge, 1997): 145.

[4] Dabydeen, "Teaching West Indian Literature in Britain," 138,

[5] Griffiths uses this phrase with reference to Michael Taussig's study of the Putumayo Indians in the early years of the twentieth century in his essay "The Myth of Authenticity," in *The Post-Colonial Studies Reader*, ed. Bill Ashcroft, Gareth Griffiths & Helen Tiffin (London & New York: Routledge, 1995): 238.

[6] Pauline Melville, *The Ventriloquist's Tale* (London, Bloomsbury, 1997): 44.

are on missions, in the widest sense of an "expedition for a particular purpose,"[7] and, significantly, all seek to represent the Amerindian peoples they encounter and to produce textual accounts of different kinds (letters, diaries, fiction, scholarly articles, lectures) as the outcome of their travel. They are all, therefore, implicated in the processes of colonization by textual means. Indeed, all of these figures in the novel construct 'imposing narratives' – potentially powerful and coercive accounts of Amerindian peoples, their cultures and cosmologies which act ultimately to foreground European anxieties and to render Amerindian peoples even more marginal and 'invisible.' However, Melville also deconstructs and decentres such 'imposing narratives,' in so doing she recovers a degree of agency and resistance for her Amerindian characters while remaining mindful of the dangers attendant on over-easy or over-simplified postcolonial literary recuperations of agency for indigenous peoples. In other words, her aim is not simply to invert the power relations operating within the manichaean opposition: 'putatively superior European' vs. 'inferior indigene'[8] nor to simply pit 'dynamic,' 'provisional,' 'authentic' Amerindian cultural intertexts against 'static,' 'totalizing,' 'inauthentic' European ones, but instead to examine the conflicted field of textual relations which crosses (and is crossed by) *The Ventriloquist' Tale*, as one which is deeply illuminating in relation to larger questions regarding the discursive formations of colonialism and postcolonial representations.

In her writing of fiction which actively contributes to key critical debates, Melville can be seen to be following in the footsteps of a number of Caribbean writers who are practising critics as well as creative writers, most strikingly her fellow Guyanese Wilson Harris. Harris, like Melville, claims part Amerindian ancestry and his literary and philosophical influence on Melville's work appears to be not insignificant.[9] Both Harris and Melville are concerned, in their fiction, with questions of

---

[7] *The Oxford English Dictionary* (Oxford: Oxford UP, 1992): s.v. "mission."

[8] These terms are Terry Goldie's from "The Representation of the Indigene" in *The Post-Colonial Studies Reader*, ed. Bill Ashcroft, Gareth Griffiths & Helen Tiffin (London & New York: Routledge, 1995): 233.

[9] I am indebted to Helen Tiffin for her helpful suggestions on extending the discussion of this aspect of Melville's work and for her incisive point on the possible significance of Professor Wormoal's name. In his essay "Carnival of Psyche" (1980) Harris argues that the "unstructured mediation or untameable force [of myth]" opens up our awareness of "the 'inarticulate' layers of community"; not only may this "unstructured mediation or untameable force [...] be equated with variables of the unconscious" but it may also be "consistent with recent discoveries in science – enigmatic black hole, ungraspable neutrino, quark etc.etc. – in which the term 'force' seems closer to reality, to ungraspable quantum leap, than 'studied sovereign mode'" (149). Such terms might equally be applied to the mode and subject matter of many of Melville's short stories. Stories such as "The Truth is in the Clothes" and "You Left the Door Open" in *Shape-Shifter* (1990), "Erzulie" and "The Duende" in *The Migration of Ghosts* (1998), explore exactly such "ungraspable" and perhaps also "untameable" aspects of human experience, extraordinary events or elements which

history, ancestry and complex overlapping identities in a Guyanese context. Both favour fictional techniques which could be termed magical realist, postmodernist, or, in Harris' case, the lineaments of a kind of visionary prose. Without overplaying these similarities I do want to suggest that, like Harris' fiction, Melville's writing occupies a particularly fruitful, but also at times fraught, border country between postcolonialism and postmodernism and seems to defy or elude simple categorizations within either camp.

Thus Melville's handling of both European and Amerindian literary and cultural intertexts in her novel can be read as part of its postmodern fictional strategies.[10] However, a postmodern framing of Melville's novel is not my intention in this paper. Instead, I want to suggest that Melville's use of literary and cultural intertexts in the novel reflects more than "that contestational wave of cultures which recent critical theory argues is the inescapable condition of all postmodernist experience."[11] Melville's handling of intertexts in her novel and her treatment of the intruding Europeans and their discourse(s) needs to be seen as part of a larger colonial imperative to represent, to textualize within the wider field of colonial (and postcolonial) discourse. For the purposes of this paper, consider the term 'mission' as one which is polyvalent, embracing individual projects as well as larger discursive and institutional structures. However, throughout I stress mission as a 'field of [textual] activity' (OED), one which involves the process of imposing narratives or the use of 'imposing narratives.'

I want to argue, then, that Melville's novel not only stages some highly topical, contemporary debates surrounding the status, study and representation of Amer-

---

refute, or at the very least force a radical reassessment of, our orthodox structures of understanding. Most explicitly stories such as "The Girl With the Celestial Limb" and "You Left The Door Open" from *Shape-Shifter* actually treat Harris' "enigmatic black hole, ungraspable neutrino, quark" as the *subject* of their narrative, and Melville's eye for scientific detail, especially in physics, is much in evidence elsewhere in her writing. In turn, Harris writes of the influence of Quantum theory on his own writing and offers an illustrative reading of Melville's "You Left the Door Open" in his essay "The Open Door." It may not be entirely coincidental then, that Melville chose to name her anthropologist Professor Wormoal, a name which ironically invokes the word 'wormhole' with its echoes of 'black hole' and suggestion of a Harrisonian capacity for cross-cultural movement between different times, spaces and dimensions. Wormoal clearly does not possess this Harrisonian insight or capacity for 'cross-cultural imagination.'

[10] Its other postmodern fictional techniques would include: its emphasis on multiple accounts and interpretations of events and the blurring of fact and fiction, its use of parody and pastiche (the fairly transparent portrait of Anita Roddick, Body Shop tycoon, as the 'Cosmetics Queen' encountering indigenous people in her search for new ingredients for her Body Shop products, is a good example), and the decentring of narrative authority through Melville's highly self-conscious and eccentric frame narrator, Sonny, the first and most prominent ventriloquist of the novel, with a playful talent for lies, imitations and camouflage.

[11] Gareth Griffiths, "The Myth of Authenticity," 240.

indian peoples but that it also historicizes that field, in terms of a complex network of discursive formations and (inter)textual relations. *The Ventriloquist's Tale* is one of a number of recent texts which might be inserted into Helen Tiffin's essay 'Post-Colonial Literatures and Counter Discourse' as an alternative example:

> [Texts such as] *Wide Sargasso Sea* [and, one might add, *The Ventriloquist's Tale*] directly contest [European] sovereignty – over persons, place, culture, language. [They] reinvest [their] own hybridized world with a [...] perspective [...] which is deliberately constructed as provisional since the novel is at pains to demonstrate the subjective nature of point of view and hence the cultural construction of meaning.

When "Jean Rhys writes back to Charlotte Brontë's *Jane Eyre* in *Wide Sargasso Sea*" or when Melville writes back to Evelyn Waugh's *A Handful of Dust*,

> Neither writer is simply 'writing back' to an English canonical text, but to the whole discursive field within which such a text operated and continues to operate in post-colonial worlds.[12]

Each of the central interlopers in *The Ventriloquist's Tale*, Father Napier, Evelyn Waugh, Rosa Mendelson and Professor Wormoal will therefore be considered in terms of the aims and wider implications of their different 'missions' the issues raised by their textualizing activity, and their intertextual positioning in the novel.

Father Napier

Father Napier's mission is perhaps the most straightforward, given that he is a Jesuit missionary, set on propagating the Catholic faith in South America. As a literary representation of missionary activity in a colonial context, he has much in common with Robinson in Mudrooroo's *Dr Wooreddy's Prescription* and is also a distant fictional cousin of the missionary figures in Achebe's *Things Fall Apart*. Indeed, his authority is similarly deflated in *The Ventriloquist's Tale* by his inadequate grasp of Amerindian languages (116) and a Wapisiana Indian's dubbing of him "the grass-hopper" after his eccentric and exaggerated posture playing the violin to the villagers. Napier's deluded and grandiose vision of his mission to convert the Amerindian peoples of the savannahs and his overweening pride in his first mission, St Ignatius, is fiercely dismantled in Melville's novel as Napier is poisoned by a Wai-Wai woman and embarks on an orgy of cruelty and destruction, burning down the very churches which he had built, and succumbing to total derangement in the latter stages of Melville's novel.

---

[12] Helen Tiffin, "Post-Colonial Literatures and Counter Discourse," in *The Post-Colonial Studies Reader*, ed. Bill Ashcroft, Gareth Griffiths & Helen Tiffin (London & New York: Routledge, 1995): 98.

Although, as Nicholas Thomas notes, in a number of historical contexts "the Christian missions [did] some of the groundwork for the colonial state" by converting large numbers to Christianity and thereby providing "conditions [which] enabled the colonizing project to take the form of 'improvement,' of constructive government rather than a destructive invasion"[13] there is little sense of this kind of intersection between missionary and colonial projects in Melville's novel. Father Napier badgers his bishop in Georgetown to be allowed to evangelize in the savannahs, and his mission, although ideologically underpinned by Jesuit teachings, seems a curiously isolated one. It is to his briefly mentioned successor and to Waugh, particularly in his non-fictional work, that we have to turn in order to see the "often close ties between the Church and the colonial state."[14]

Importantly, Father Napier can be located within a tissue of intertextual relations which are not purely literary. Like a number of the characters in *The Ventriloquist's Tale*, Father Napier has a pretextual life which can be traced as part of a wider discursive field, one which includes autobiographical texts, diaries and testimonies as well as fictional works. In the process of researching this paper, I unwittingly became Rosa Mendelson's non-fictional counterpart, by becoming increasingly intrigued by the complex nexus of intertextual relations which exist between all of Melville's non-Amerindian characters, the Melville family and the writings of Evelyn Waugh.

Waugh and the Melville Family

Waugh arrived in British Guiana in December 1932, stayed in Georgetown and travelled to a number of Amerindian settlements and missions in Guiana and Brazil, before his departure for England in April 1933. In 1929 he had converted to Catholicism and, increasingly, he was to show a keen intellectual interest in his new faith, which was to climax in the writing of a biography of the Jesuit martyr, Edmund Campion, in 1934 and his exploration of Catholicism and the English nobility in his 1945 novel, *Brideshead Revisited*.

Waugh's diary entries for the period of his stay in British Guiana also reveal this interest. In Georgetown, Waugh visited the Bishop of Georgetown, lunched with Jesuits and attended masses and other services. During his travels into the Guyanese and Brazilian hinterland, he visited a number of stations, ranches and missions where he had ample opportunity to meet missionaries and priests, or "Lascivious

---

[13] Nicholas Thomas, *Colonialism's Culture* (Cambridge: Polity, 1994): 124–25.

[14] Jan Nederve Pieterse, *White on Black: Images of Africa and Blacks in Western Popular Culture* (New Haven CT & London: Yale UP, 1992): 68. Cf "The new [Catholic] priest, just appointed, who had attended Stonyhurst College [a thinly veiled Stonehurst College] in England and knew several of Waugh's acquaintances"; *The Ventriloquist's Tale*, 288.

beasts" as he playfully dubbed them in his letters. Amongst those he met was Father Keary who bears some resemblances to Melville's Father Napier and one Father Mather, Catholic missionary at St Ignatius mission, close to Hart's ranch. In Melville's novel, Father Napier renames Zariwa St Ignatius, and chooses to build his church near McKinnon's ranch.

More strikingly, Waugh notes in his diary that he encountered members of the Melville family during his travels. On 19 January, at Annai, en route to Hart's ranch, he mentions the arrival of a "[Dealer] with wife, daughter of Melville." On arriving at the ranch on 22 January 1933, he wrote:

> several large buildings; the living house with ceilings and floors. Library of ill-assorted ant-eaten books – *Young Visiters*, *Sinister Street*, *Mill on Liberty*, *What a young man ought to know*, *Practical Joinery* etc [...] Hart away. [Similarly ant-eaten books are described in Mr. Todd's house in *A Handful of Dust*, 209.] Mrs Hart (Amy Melville), a brother, six boys and a dotty bastard nephew, son of John Melville by his three-quarter sister (went off with a Mr King).[15]

This would appear to be one of the possible starting-points for Melville's story, especially as Melville mentions details from Waugh's diary in her novel (eg, Koko Lupi, the native woman who claims she can fly, 288). Hart is replaced by Alexander McKinnon (who also goes away and leaves his family for periods of time); the incestuous liaison is between Beatrice and Danny McKinnon; their "dotty bastard son," Sonny, is also the frame narrator of Melville's novel; and Waugh, the historical entity, is replaced by a fictional counterpart of the same name.

The relationship between Melville's novel and Waugh's writings is, then, a highly intertwined and complex one. When Evelyn Waugh set off for South America in 1932, he had already published three novels and two travel books and was no stranger to foreign travel, having travelled to Abyssinia in 1930 as the *Times* correspondent covering the coronation of Emperor Haile Selassie. However, Waugh's mission in travelling to British Guiana appears to have been motivated by domestic factors: He left behind him in England – like Tony Last in his 1934 novel, *A Handful of Dust* – a failed marriage as well as a complicated, multiple love life. In Melville's novel the fictional Waugh is also escaping a failed marriage (287) and also travels to Guiana in search of new material for his writing. This is certainly corroborated by a letter written by Waugh to his parents dated 2 January 1933 and addressed to "Georgetown club." In it Waugh outlines his "trip up country" and mentions that he will be

> travelling up with the Commissioner for the Rupununi district – A Mr Haynes – we ride from the Berbice river to the Essequibo. It ought to be very interesting [...] I hope

---

[15] *The Diaries of Evelyn Waugh*, ed. Michael Davie (Harmondsworth: Penguin, 1979): 367.

to get to Takutu to a mission there. Anyway even if I don't get as far as that it should
be an interesting trip and give me material for writing.[16]

From his travels in British Guiana and Brazil, Waugh produced a number of articles,
a travel book, and notably a short story, "The Man Who Loved Dickens" which was
later worked into the novel *A Handful of Dust*. The latter famously features an
English gentleman, Tony Last, fleeing his disintegrating marriage and what Waugh
called the 'savages' of his own class in England to travel up the Amazon with a Dr
Messenger. When Messenger dies due to a fall down a pitiful ten foot drop, Tony
wanders on and is rescued by an eccentric and reclusive part-European, Mr Todd,
whose Barbadian father "came to Guiana as a missionary."[17] Missionaries, it would
seem, are replicated in a kind of *mise en abyme* effect in this tissue of intertexual
relations.

While Waugh's novel ends with Tony being forced to become Todd's companion
and to read the works of Dickens aloud to him, Melville's novel features Waugh
himself reading Dickens to a tolerant but rather uninterested Danny McKinnon.
While the encounter is apparently productive from Waugh's point of view (in giving
him new material for a short story, to be called "The Man Who Liked Dickens"),
from the perspective of the McKinnon family the meeting is rather less momentous;
Waugh is rather banally depicted requesting a haircut, and Nancy Freeman, the
schoolteacher, cuts his hair. Much later, when questioned by Rosa Mendelson, who
is researching into Waugh's "attitude to the colonies" (44), neither Nancy Freeman
nor Wilfreda McKinnon can remember anything interesting or distinctive about the
'great writer.' Instead, Nancy suggests to Rosa that "nobody really knew what the
hell he was doing there" and that "for all that [Waugh] was looking for material, he
missed one story that was under his nose [the story of Danny and Beatrice's relation-
ship]" (49). When Rosa responds, "Perhaps it was not Evelyn Waugh's sort of
story," Nancy replies: "Perhaps not. But it interested me" (49). The logical correlative is that Rosa's mission to uncover "Waugh's attitude to the colonies" (44) is also
misguided; what Rosa fails to see "under her nose" is that her focus only on Waugh
drowns out other potentially interesting narratives, or perhaps, more subtly, that
Waugh's response to and representation of Amerindian peoples is crucial to an
understanding of his attitude to the colonies.

This is just one of the ways in which Melville's novel acts counter-discursively
to decentre Waugh's presence in the novel and to undermine the putative authority of
Waugh's account of Guyana in his textual accounts. Throughout his diaries, letters
and to some extent his fiction too, Waugh subjects even the colonial figures he en-

---

[16] Evelyn Waugh, *The Letters of Evelyn Waugh*, ed. Mark Amory (London: Weidenfeld &
Nicolson, 1980): 69.

[17] Evelyn Waugh, *A Handful of Dust* (1934; Harmondsworth: Penguin, 1968): 207–208.

counters to fiercely satirical treatment. However, the emphasis on Waugh's most famous eccentrics and their Guyanese sources (such as Mr Christie, the prototype for Mr Todd in *A Handful of Dust*) has tended to occlude Waugh's representation of Amerindian peoples in his writing. The latter representations in his textual accounts (such as Rosa, the "pretty Indian girl" who Haynes, the District Commissioner, claims he can make sexually available to Waugh, or Koko Lupi, the "woman who pretends to fly" in the diaries) recognizably operate within what Terry Goldie has termed "the semiotic field of the indigene [...] a circular economy [in which the European interloper or non-indigene trades in] commodities – sex, violence, orality, mysticism, the prehistoric."[18] These representations act to silence and objectify the Amerindian, rendering him or her more invisible.

Rosa Mendelson

Surprisingly, there were no significant postcolonial readings of Waugh that I could discover, which makes Rosa Mendelson's aim, in Melville's novel, to construct such a reading even more intriguing. By making Rosa's mission one of discovering Waugh's 'attitude to the colonies,' Melville is able to stage, metafictionally, the very debates surrounding representation and intertextuality that I myself have been attempting to discuss. Rosa's problem is exactly my own: how to untangle Waugh's attitude to the colony of British Guiana and to the colonial project more generally.

Selina Hastings, a recent biographer of Waugh, argues that Waugh's attitude to the colonies – in particular his attitude to British Guiana – could hardly have been less engaged:

'What a snare this travelling business is to the young writer,' wrote P. G. Wodehouse referring to the South American sequences in *A Handful of Dust* 'He goes to some blasted jungle or other and imagines that everybody will be interested in it.' That Evelyn was aware of this widely held attitude, and himself not remotely interested in the 'blasted jungle,' is apparent from the defensive tone of most of his travel articles about it. Although admitting to a genuine fascination for 'distant and barbarous places, and particularly in the borderlands of conflicting cultures and states of development,' and whilst relishing some of the grotesque characters encountered in these borderlands [...] there can have been few travel writers [...] who show less curiosity about their surroundings. Although prepared to note the architecture, go to Mass, and drink with members of the expatriate population, Evelyn rarely displays more than a superficial inquisitiveness about the country or its indigenous inhabitants. In Guiana and Brazil, the spectacular jungle and lush riverside scenery are considered 'unendurably monotonous,' while the [American] Indians are cursorily dismissed as 'unattractive, squat and dingy, with none of the grace one expects in savages.' In [...] *Ninety-Two Days*,

---

[18] Terry Goldie, "The Representation of the Indigene," in *The Post-Colonial Studies Reader*, ed. Bill Ashcroft, Gareth Griffiths & Helen Tiffin (London & New York: Routledge, 1995): 236.

there is barely a glimmer of excitement or enjoyment [...] instead it was as though the whole expedition had been taken as a form of penance, with even the book's title sounding as if the sufferer had been counting off the hours and minutes as well as the days.[19]

This curiously distanced and uninterested position is just one of the factors that makes it relatively easy to mount a reading which aligns Waugh unproblematically with the ruling colonial class. For example, in a telling anecdote included in *Ninety-Two Days*, he recalls how he and his brother Alec, both writers, agreed to carve up the globe for their travel writing: "We made a compact each to keep off the other's territory; with a papal gesture he made me a present of the whole of Africa and a good slice of Asia in exchange for the Polynesian Islands, North America and the West Indies."[20] Similarly, the following letter to Waugh's friend, Lady Dorothy Lydon, written on his arrival in Georgetown and dated 1 January 1933, is illuminating. In it, Waugh constructs a fantastic portrait of his situation:

This club, if club it can be called so different it is from the gracious calm of Bucks & Bunchs, is a log shack on the edge of the jungle [...] The table has long ago been devoured by ants and I write on my knees crouching on an empty cask. Around me corrupt officials gamble away the bribes they have taken during the day and a few traders and missionaries seek release from their sufferings in the anodyne of rum. Outside in the night air I can hear the tom-toms of hostile Indians encamped around us and the rhythmic rise and fall of the lash with which a drink crazed planter is flogging his half caste mistress [...] The missionaries have long forsaken their vows and live openly with native women infecting them with hideous diseases.[21]

However parodic the tone of this portrait, and even taking into account its context as private correspondence, it reveals how far Waugh's class position and his affiliations with the governing elite of British Guiana facilitated the kind of unerring confidence and overweening cultural arrogance that place him within a longer tradition of gentleman interlopers' accounts of the colonies. Indeed, one is tempted to see Waugh's orientalizing gaze as one which can be traced back to Trollope, Kingsley and Froude, all gentleman travellers and observers who, to a greater or lesser extent, knew what they would find before they had barely set sail from Europe, let alone disembarked in the West Indies – and whom, like Dabydeen's fearful academics, rarely strayed off the beaten track.

Although Rosa's attitude to her subject is more enlightened than Professor Wormoal's, the fellow academic with whom she is anxious not to be bracketed, she does appear to share certain characteristics with Dabydeen's notion of the Western aca-

[19] Selina Hastings, *Evelyn Waugh, a Biography* (London: Sinclair–Stevenson, 1994): 269–70.

[20] Evelyn Waugh, *Ninety-Two Days* (Harmondsworth: Penguin, 1985): 15.

[21] Evelyn Waugh, *Letters*, ed. Amory, 68–69.

demic, one of those who "make quick visits, observe hastily and in fright of the native presence, then return to pronounce with authority in the centres in Britain."[22] She too will quickly visit and retreat having gathered her evidence. Although Melville stages Rosa's academic mission in some quite predictable ways – her 'native informant,' Chofy, also becomes her lover and some of the cross-cultural tensions of the novel are played out through this central relationship – Rosa's presence in the novel does raise some pertinent issues vis-à-vis postcolonial theory's articulation of the category of the 'indigene' and the epistemological and experiential dimensions of subalternity more generally.[23]

Professor Wormoal

Professor Wormoal is another visiting academic who, like a latter-day Casaubon, is attempting to construct a "scientific approach to [Amerindian] mythology." His reason for being in Guyana is to give a paper at the University in Georgetown. His most obvious key antecedent is the structuralist anthropologist Claude Lévi–Strauss, who also researched Amerindian myth and whose comments on eclipse myths (a subject also covered by Wormoal) form one of the epigraphs to *The Ventriloquist's Tale*; he may also be partly based on Walter Roth, government archivist and curator of the Georgetown Museum in the 1930s, who is best known for his anthropological research into the 'Guiana Indians' and whom Waugh met on New Year's Day, 1933.[24] Although Wormoal shows awareness of the problematical presence of the European anthropologist in the region and the eurocentric skewing of his studies of Amerindian cultures, his structuralist methodology is still seen to reduce and fix the

---

[22] "Teaching West Indian Literature in Britain," 145.

[23] Rosa's name also has intertextual resonances as there is a Rosa mentioned in Waugh's diaries and also an Amerindian guide called Rosa in *A Handful of Dust*.

[24] In the process of revising this essay for publication, I discovered this connection between Waugh and Walter Roth after reading Russell McDougall's article "Walter Roth, Wilson Harris and a Caribbean/Postcolonial Theory of Modernism," *University of Toronto Quarterly* 67.2 (Spring 1998): 567–91. McDougall mentions the meeting between Waugh and Roth only briefly, in order to discuss the latter's reputation. The main body of his article traces the "pivotal role of Roth's ethnology to the evolving postcolonial vision of [Wilson] Harris," examining the elements of Caribbean myth and ritual which Harris drew from Roth and which were to become so central to his writing. Appropriately enough, McDougall charts how Harris became interested in Roth after he discovered a passage from Roth's 1922–23 translation and annotated edition of Richard Schomburgk's *Travels in British Guiana 1840–1844* in the appendix to another book, Michael Swan's historical study *The Marches of El Dorado*, published by Jonathan Cape in 1961. This somewhat torturous resumé shows how thoroughly dense and complex the intertextual links between Waugh, Roth, Harris, Melville and a number of other writers are – all of whom were born, or spent time in Guyana/British Guiana.

Amerindian myths of eclipse which appear more fluidly and organically elsewhere in the novel.

The subjectifying eurocentricity of his gaze positions him securely within a longer history of colonial discourse, produced by the eurocentric gaze, and constitutes one of the permutations of blindness that Melville explores in her novel: "I think I probably know more about the Amerindian peoples than they know about themselves," he says to Rosa. Interestingly, he too has a close intertextual analogue, Dr Messenger in Waugh's *A Handful of Dust*, who confidently tells Tony, over his stash of mechanical tin mice designed to entice and curry favour with the Macusi people, "I *know* the Indian mind" (188). However, Melville's novel characteristically goes one step further by investing Professor Wormoal with a consciousness or self-awareness of his complicity in a problematic politics which Waugh's Dr Messenger emphatically lacks. Wormoal admits to Rosa:

> 'We try just to observe but our very presence alters things. Mine are the wasted talents of a secret agent. I have the entire map of this country in my head. I know about the history and movements of the indigenous peoples here, their kinship structures, occupations, philosophies, cosmologies, labour pattern, languages. We Europeans have access to all the books and documentation that they lack. And what do I do with it? I become a professor and enrich European and American culture with it.'
> Rosa looked at him curiously.
> 'You make knowledge sound like a new form of colonial power'
> [...]
> 'But of course. Information is the new gold. You, as a scholar, must know that. My knowledge of the Indians is a way of owning them – I admit it. We fight over the intellectual territory. But it's better than stealing their land, isn't it?'
> Confused, Rosa shrank from being bracketed with him. (79–80)

What Melville foregrounds in her novel is the role played by the imposing narratives of missionary, colonial, postcolonial and neo-colonial forces in marginalizing Amerindian peoples. The notion that the interloping European 'visitor,' whether missionary, scientist, anthropologist, historian, novelist or literary scholar, can either 'know the subject' of his or her study and evangelizing zeal in any meaningful way, or carry any kind of authoritative knowledge back to Europe, are both thoroughly deconstructed in *The Ventriloquist's Tale*. Indeed, all the interlopers are shown to be flawed in some way, their missions self-deluding or ineffectual.

I have shown how the incestuous union between Danny and Beatrice which lies at the centre of *The Ventriloquist's Tale* can be traced back to events in Melville's family history via a complex tissue of intertextual relations. However, the intertexts of *The Ventriloquist's Tale* are, crucially, neither exclusively written ones nor European, but also embrace a number of ancient Mayan and Amerindian myths concerning eclipse, incest and (pro)creation. In Melville's novel, a series of orally transmitted variants of indigenous myths create an alternative sense of narrative as locally inflected and provisional in status; narrative which is overlapping and resonant rather than discrete and linearly based and whose meaning is mobile and culturally constructed rather than static or universal. Such Amerindian and Mayan mythic narratives, in Wilson Harris' terms, "erupt through the narrative,"[25] decentering the textualizing accounts of European interlopers and other external commentators. They destabilize the imposed narratives which attempt to name, fix, categorize and interpret Amerindian peoples and cultures, or to repackage them for overseas consumption.

Melville's novel shows, according to Harris, that "Amerindian culture is not a dead culture; it is present in other, resonant ways."[26] Thus the moon / evening star / sun / moon eclipse and incest motifs at the heart of the novel are also interpreted and re-interpreted by the different Amerindian peoples themselves and are shown to be themselves re-tellings of more ancient narratives such as the Mayan story of the god Quetzalcoatl having to leave Mexico during an eclipse "because he made love to his sister." In this way, the European narratives are divested of some of their power. Not only are the European narratives surrounding incest and the significance of the eclipse shown to be ethnocentric, partial, biased and frequently based on false premisses (eg, that the Amerindian explanations are just myths, useless superstitions, the Amerindian peoples know no spirituality) but the written frame of the novel is also undermined by the hybrid oral traditions that run counter to it. Melville's novel shows how European anthropological and astronomical explanations have failed to take account of Amerindian explanations of the eclipse, dismissing them as mythical narratives of a lower order and lesser significance. In Melville's novel such potentially powerfully coercive European accounts are exposed as only one of a number of possible interpretations and the resort to the use of resistantly European discourses in the construction of 'imposing narratives' are shown to reveal, as the Amerindian scholar Desrey Fox has argued in a wider context,[27] as much about the Europeans' own anxieties as about the objects of their evangelism or study.

∼

---

[25] In the use of this observation I am indebted to Wilson Harris and a talk on "The Amerindian Legacy (Memory and Imagination)" given by him at a symposium on Amerindian Cultures held at the Institute of Education, University of London, 14–15 May 1997.

[26] "The Amerindian Legacy (Memory and Imagination)."

[27] Desrey Fox, "The Kanaimo as a Social Type within the Akawaian Society of Guyana," symposium on Amerindian Cultures held at the Institute of Education, University of London, 14–15 May 1997.

WORKS CITED

Ashcroft, Bill, Gareth Griffiths & Helen Tiffin, ed. *The Post-Colonial Studies Reader* (London & New York: Routledge, 1995).

Dabydeen, David. "Teaching West Indian Literature in Britain," in *Studying British Cultures*, ed. Susan Bassnett (London & New York: Routledge, 1997): 135–51.

Fox, Desrey. "The Kanaimo as a Social Type within the Akawaian Society of Guyana," symposium on Amerindian Cultures held at the Institute of Education, University of London, 14–15 May 1997.

Goldie, Terry. "The Representation of the Indigene," in *The Post-Colonial Studies Reader*, ed. Bill Ashcroft, Gareth Griffiths & Helen Tiffin (London & New York: Routledge, 1995): 232–36.

Griffiths, Gareth. "The Myth of Authenticity," in *The Post-Colonial Studies Reader*, ed. Bill Ashcroft, Gareth Griffiths & Helen Tiffin (London & New York: Routledge, 1995): 237–41.

Harris, Wilson. "The Amerindian Legacy (Memory and Imagination)," symposium on Amerindian Cultures held at the Institute of Education, University of London, 14–15 May 1997.

——. "Carnival of Psyche: Jean Rhys's Wide Sargasso Sea," *Kunapipi* 2.2 (1980): 142–51.

——. "The Open Door," *Journal of Modern Literature* 20.1 (Summer 1996): 7–12.

Hastings, Selina. *Evelyn Waugh, a Biography* (London: Sinclair–Stevenson, 1994).

McDougall, Russell. "Walter Roth, Wilson Harris and a Caribbean / Postcolonial Theory of Modernism," *University of Toronto Quarterly* 67.2 (Spring 1998): 567–91.

Melville, Pauline. *The Migration of Ghosts* (London: Bloomsbury, 1998).

——. *Shape-Shifter* (London: The Women's Press, 1990).

——. *The Ventriloquist's Tale* (London: Bloomsbury, 1997).

The Oxford English Dictionary (Oxford: Oxford UP, 1992).

Pieterse, Jan Nederveen. *White On Black: Images of Africa and Blacks in Western Popular Culture* (New Haven CT & London: Yale UP, 1992).

Rhys, Jean. *Wide Sargasso Sea* (1966; Harmondsworth: Penguin, 1987).

Thomas, Nicholas. *Colonialism's Culture* (Cambridge: Polity, 1994).

Tiffin, Helen. "Post-Colonial Literatures and Counter Discourse," in *The Post-Colonial Studies Reader*, ed. Bill Ashcroft, Gareth Griffiths & Helen Tiffin (London & New York: Routledge, 1995): 95–98.

Waugh, Evelyn. *Brideshead Revisited* (1945; Harmondsworth: Penguin, 1973).

——. *The Diaries of Evelyn Waugh*, ed. Michael Davie (1976; Harmondsworth: Penguin, 1979).

——. *A Handful of Dust* (1934; Harmondsworth: Penguin, 1968).

——. *The Letters of Evelyn Waugh*, ed. Mark Amory (London: Weidenfeld & Nicolson, 1980).

——. *Ninety-Two Days* (Harmondsworth: Penguin, 1985).

"One is exiled when one refuses to obey the commandments of Conquest Mission"
Religion as Metaphor in Caryl Phillips's Diasporic Philosophy

BÉNÉDICTE LEDENT

C ARYL PHILLIPS'S LATER NOVELS, from *Higher Ground* (1989) to *Crossing the River* (1993), have often been read in the context of what Paul Gilroy has called the Black Atlantic, as re-creations of slave-trading in Africa, plantation life in the Americas, and exile in European metropolises. Described by one commentator as "a vivid historian of slave experience,"[1] Phillips could even be called one of the major current chroniclers of this often silenced past, since "behind all of [his fiction] looms the dark history of slavery and its consequences."[2] For all its interest and relevance, however, this historicist approach has its own limitations. In the long run, it could indeed make us forget that Phillips's fiction, far from being exclusively concerned with elaborating a response to the wrongs of colonialism, among them slavery, aspires, like any self-respecting work of art, to express its own way of seeing the world: ie, its philosophy.

Unsurprisingly, therefore, a few reviewers were mystified when in his latest novel, *The Nature of Blood* (1997), Phillips seemed to distance himself from what they regarded as his fictional territory, and dealt with the European roots of exclusion and tribalism, particularly the Jewish Holocaust (which, incidentally, he had already addressed in a collection of travel essays, *The European Tribe* [1987], and in the last section of *Higher Ground*). As if, by leaving the literary ghetto to which the sacred rules of authenticity would have confined him, Phillips had claimed a more direct say on the human condition at large, and had thereby committed literary tres-

---

[1] Randall Stevenson, *A Reader's Guide to the Twentieth-Century Novel in Britain* (New York: Harvester, 1993): 131.

[2] J.M. Coetzee, "What We Like to Forget," *New York Review of Books* (6 November 1997): 38.

pass, an offence taken seriously by some mainstream critics. Such, at least, is the impression given in a review by Hilary Mantel, entitled "Black is not Jewish," where she objects to what she views as Phillips's inadequate tackling of the Jewish Holocaust:

> There is only one rule in postwar fiction: don't write about the Holocaust unless you are sure you can do it well. [...] If you can't match [the brilliant desolation of Cynthia Ozick's *The Shawl*], look elsewhere for a story. [...] Caryl Phillips – born in St Kitts and brought up in Leeds – has dwelled a good deal in his previous novels on the slave trade, which was a kind of prolonged Holocaust in itself. He therefore identifies himself with those wrenched from their homeland, with the dispossessed and the abused; his feelings, surely, do him credit. He has been quoted in an interview in *The Bookseller* as saying he agrees with James Baldwin: 'that when anyone talks about a Jew, that person is talking about me.' This is the devil's sentimentality: it is demented cosiness, that denies the differences between people, denies how easily the interests of human beings become divided. It is indecent to lay claim to other people's suffering: it's a colonial impulse, dressed up as altruism.[3]

This piece of criticism may demonstrate "the white man's profound desire not to be judged by those who are not white."[4] Moreover, I find it ironical that, while being painfully ignorant of artistic freedom, such a commentary, by ghettoizing Phillips as it does, should enact one of the main themes of the novel: ie, the fact that throughout history humans have felt the need to define themselves by defining the others.

A similar fate doubtless threatens other writers from the former British Empire who, like Phillips, refuse the role of mere exotic appendages to Western literature, insisting on being viewed as going beyond the purely representational, as exploring the deeper layers of the human psyche. Their writing tends to be read from the narrow angle of a "supposedly homogeneous and unbroken" national tradition,[5] which is not only oblivious of the plural affiliations of these often displaced artists, but, more importantly, of their contribution to the world of ideas in general. Caryl Phillips, for one, has always opposed what he calls "the missionary approach": ie, "the idea that the black writer should explain black people to white people."[6] To him, the purpose of literature is rather "to dare to imagine into regions that help to expand not only [the writer's] understanding of the human condition, but help the

---

[3] Hilary Mantel, "Black is not Jewish," review of *The Nature of Blood*, by Caryl Phillips, *Literary Review* (1 February 1997): 39.

[4] James Baldwin, *The Fire Next Time* (1963; Harmondsworth: Penguin, 1979): 81.

[5] Salman Rushdie, "'Commonwealth Literature' does not exist," *Imaginary Homelands: Essays and Criticism 1981–1991* (London: Granta, 1991): 67.

[6] "Living and Writing in the Caribbean: an Experiment," *Kunapipi* 11.2 (1989): 47.

reader to understand and expand their own notion of what constitutes the human condition,"[7] one aspect of which is faith or the capacity to believe.

My purpose in this essay is to discuss the place of religion in Caryl Phillips's fiction, a theme that metaphorizes not only his own position towards what Wilson Harris has called the "commandments of Conquest Mission"[8] – the artistic standards imposed on the postcolonial writer, but also the ambivalent interplay between dependence and independence, submission and resistance in postcolonial societies. To do full justice to this multifaceted topic, my reading will have to take into account the social and historical realities underlying Phillips's vision, while being also attuned to his characters' inner states; a reading, in short, that combines both 'secular' and, appropriately here, 'religious' criticism. In *The World, the Text, and the Critic*, Edward Said pits these two forms of criticism against each other. Secular criticism, he argues, relies on the fact that texts "are worldly [...], and, even when they appear to deny it, they are nevertheless a part of the social world, human life, and of course the historical moments in which they are located and interpreted."[9] Religious criticism, by contrast, does not find favour with him, for, as a religious discourse, it can serve "as an agent of closure, shutting off human investigation, criticism, and effort in deference to the authority of the more-than-human, the supernatural, the other-worldly" (290). While I agree with Said on the need for contextualization on the one hand and, on the other, on the necessary resistance to indoctrination, it seems to me that the dichotomy he sets up is not easy to play out, all the more so because, as T.S. Eliot reminds us, literature affects us as "entire human beings," endowed both with reason and with imagination and emotions.[10]

In the case of Phillips's fiction, as we shall see, a separation between the secular and the spiritual, the historical and the existential, the collective and the individual, would be pointless, if not downright misleading. Moreover, as the examples given above can show, secular criticism can occasionally take on a religious garb and lead to closure when it derives, as religious criticism does for Said, from "organized collective passions,"[11] be it a blind commitment to orthodox postcolonialism which would see in every novel by Phillips a counter-discursive response to slavery or a form of literary racism that would exclude writers like him from the preoccupations of the so-called centre. Inversely, religious criticism, as a means of investigating what is beyond the strictly historical, social and secular, should not always be asso-

---

[7] "The Other Voice: A Dialogue between Anita Desai, Caryl Phillips, and Ilan Stavans," *Transition* 64 (1994): 88.

[8] Wilson Harris, *Jonestown* (London: Faber, 1996): 14.

[9] Edward Said, *The World, the Text, and the Critic* (1984; London: Vintage, 1991): 4.

[10] T.S. Eliot, "Religion and Literature," *Selected Prose*, ed. John Hayward (1953; Harmondsworth: Penguin, 1963): 38.

[11] Said, *The World, the Text, and the Critic*, 290.

ciated, as Said suggests, with "systems of authority" or "canons of order."[12] As I will attempt to demonstrate in this paper, it can help to plumb the inner feelings of individual characters and their discovery of the sacred which, in Phillips's fiction, never conveys an unconditional deference to a supernatural order, but rather a deep respect for the human as expressed through insecure individual minds who probe self-awareness outside a coercive system of thought.

Phillips's novels have repeatedly dramatized the crucial role of Christianity in the various stages of the colonizing process: "Heartland," the first section of *Higher Ground*, shows how the Bible, combined with the apparently more aggressive sword, was part of the so-called civilizing mission of the early European settlements in Africa, meant to help the native "raise [himself] up above the animal"[13] and eradicate his pagan customs; the journal of the English slave-trader, Captain Hamilton, in *Crossing the River*, alludes to the ambiguous part played by Christian religion in the enslavement of those who were mere cargo in the eyes of the European believers, a shameful complicity that the Western churches are still refusing to recognize officially today in spite of appeals from African theologians;[14] both *Cambridge* (1991) and *Crossing the River* depict the ambivalence of the converted slaves Cambridge and Nash Williams, who, once "blessed with rational Christian minds,"[15] turn into missionaries for their own "heathen" people. Finally, *The Nature of Blood* denounces the hypocrisy of a religion which contributed to a destructive sense of European superiority and hence to the exclusion from what James Baldwin has called "God's citadel" of those "neither civilized nor Christian,"[16] be they the "infidel Turks"[17] or the Jews.

Imposed from the outside and smacking of paternalism, Christianity is presented in these novels as a major factor of alienation since it makes colonial converts believe that, if they leave paganism behind, they can get access to the "centre," reach a higher level of humanity, or even "renounce [their] devilish likeness":[18] ie, get symbolically whitened. In practice, however, this religion seems to be a powerful means to keep them in their "rightful place" (*C* 73) and instil in them a sense of dutiful resignation to divine order, in a world regulated by Christian Providence.

---

[12] Said, *The World, the Text, and the Critic*, 290.

[13] Phillips, *Higher Ground* (London: Viking, 1989): 53. Henceforth in the main text as *HG*.

[14] C. Panu–Mbendele, "Le Silence des Eglises sur la Traite des Noirs," *Le Soir* (16 February 1999).

[15] Phillips, *Crossing the River* (London: Bloomsbury, 1993): 9. Henceforth in the main text as *CR*.

[16] Baldwin, *The Fire Next Time* (1963; Harmondsworth: Penguin, 1979): 50.

[17] Phillips, *The Nature of Blood* (London: Faber & Faber, 1997): 49. Henceforth in the main text as *NB*.

[18] Phillips, Cambridge (London: Bloomsbury, 1991): 151. Henceforth in the main text as *C*.

where man "[is] nothing and can do nothing" (*CR* 21) without God. This is why Cambridge, after being captured by slave traders for the second time on his way to Africa, is able to believe that "through hard work and faith in the Lord God Almighty, [his] bondage would soon cease" (*C* 157).

Far from being enlightening, then, Christianity proves the efficient handmaiden of oppression, whether slavery, the Holocaust or the daily exploitation of man by man. Cambridge, to take his example again, remains unaware of being lured, and keeps seeing Christianity as a "magical opportunity of improvement" (*C* 143), a means of escaping his natural African "barbarity" (*C* 143) and gaining access to "the laws of civilization" (*C* 149), while being repeatedly victim of the moral bankruptcy of the West, be it greed, lust or sheer dishonesty.

If, at the start, Nash is, like Cambridge, brainwashed by Christian dogma, as he enters deeper into the heart of Liberia, he gradually loses faith in the redemptive powers of his master's creed, even though he believes till the end in an afterlife. While his relationship with his master Edward illustrates how religion intersects with love, his narrative and the failure of his experience as a missionary also highlight an important feature of religion as seen by Phillips: ie, its highly cultural content. Phillips shares this theme with Shûsaku Endô, one of his favourite writers,[19] whose novel *Silence*, set in seventeenth-century Japan, explores the nature of transplanted Christianity and wonders whether as "a religion that developed largely out of European ways of thinking, [it] can ever take root in Japan."[20] A similar interrogation crops up in *Crossing the River* when Nash concludes, in the last letter he addresses to his master in America, that

> this missionary work, this process of persuasion, is futile amongst these people, for they never truly pray to the Christian God, they merely pray to their own gods in Christian guise, for the American God does not even resemble them in that most fundamental of features. The truth is, our religion, in its purest and least diluted form, can never take root in this country. Its young shoots will wither and die, leaving the sensible man with the conclusive evidence that he must reap what grows naturally. (*CR* 62)

If such a statement questions the efficiency of missionary work and the notion of a "pure" religious tradition to be handed down, it acknowledges at the same time an (essential) "natural" religious feeling that cannot be imposed from the outside, but exists on its own, regardless of a specific creed. That a cultural barrier remains in spite of a universal need for spirituality is again evoked at the end of Edward's "pilgrimage" (*CR* 66) to the squalid place where Nash died, when he decides to "sing an hymn, in order that he might calm his beleaguered mind" but "as [his] lips

---

[19] Interview by Louise Yelin, *Culturefront* 7.2 (1998): 80.

[20] Shûsaku Endô, *Foreign Studies* (1965; London: Sceptre, 1990): 9.

formed the words, [...] no sound was heard. Still Edward continued to *sing* his hymn"; but while Edward needs the spiritual sustenance of the hymn, even without lyrics, irrelevant in this African context, the natives fail to understand him and wonder "what evil spirits had populated this poor man's soul" (*CR* 69).

This being said, it is difficult, if not vain, for individuals to negate the influence of Christianity on their minds, if only because of the extent to which this religion has affected their culture, as Phillips's fiction itself testifies. It contains numerous Biblical references. For instance, the titles *Higher Ground* and *Crossing the River* have clear Judaeo-Christian overtones. Also, the compassion at work in Phillips's writing can be said to be of Christian origin, although the suffering of his characters never has a redemptive quality. It is no use denying this legacy, Phillips seems to suggest, because it is part of who we are, and even as "there is no return" (*CR* 237) for the children of the African diaspora, it is not possible to go back to pre-Christendom times, as substantiated by the case of Rudi, a black American prisoner in "The Cargo Rap," the second section of *Higher Ground*. While he claims to "have no religion" (*HG* 95) and radically dismisses Christmas cards as "images of the enemy" (*HG* 65), he is unaware how deeply his discourse is influenced by Christian rhetoric. Ironically, though he wants to escape white Christianity at all costs, he ends up embracing racial bigotry, which like some other theologies, that of the Nation of Islam, for example, aims at "the sanctification of power."[21]

While focusing on the cultural and existential alienation induced by Christianity, Phillips also challenges other concepts associated with religious doctrines at large, namely those of belonging and novelty, which are to be found in the major myths of humanity, but are also part of the mythology of literary criticism, as we have seen.

Religion, which etymologically relates to that which binds or brings together, relies traditionally on a rhetoric of love and community since, as Cambridge points out at the end of his testimony, " '[the Lord] hath made of one blood all nations of men for to dwell on all the face of the earth' " (*C* 167). Yet Phillips's novels repeatedly show that, in its institutionalized form at least, it is a system that separates rather than gathers, that excludes rather than includes human beings. First, it seems to promote gender discrimination, since as Cambridge says "a Christian man possesses a wife, and the dutiful wife must obey her Christian husband" (*C* 163). Then, it also favours divisiveness over reconciliation insofar as God Himself is "a God of all nations, provided they obey and dutifully serve Him" (*CR* 26) and his love is "for all, as long as they be Christian and part of His World" (*C* 145). Therefore, when Cambridge's first wife and his baby die, the minister initially refuses to bury them together because the child has not been baptized. In *The Nature of Blood*, the Jews'

---

[21] James Baldwin, *The Fire Next Time*, 48.

fear of exogamy (which is, according to Eva's mother, "the greatest crime that a person could commit," *NB* 70) partakes of a similar suspicion of the stranger induced by religion. In this regard, it is interesting to note, with Julius Lester, that "racism is a group's idealisation of itself in society, the world and the universe. It confers religious identity in secular garb."[22]

Religion, not only Christianity but Judaism as well, is also replete with the notion of newness: Born-again Christians are given a new name; the Promised Land of the Jewish tradition is a new world. The same could be said of the secular avatars of these two creeds, one example of which is the transportation of the Ethiopian Falashas to Israel, which for all its benevolence fails to take the Ethiopian past into account. Yet, as *The Nature of Blood* powerfully demonstrates, this idea of starting all over again, of "[putting] things behind [oneself]" (*NB* 178), is a myth because men carry their past within themselves however hard they try to shed it. So, if the Bible does open up new horizons for the colonial converts, these should not forget, as Othello seems to do when he reaches the "heart" (*NB* 145) of Venetian society, that the Holy Book also contains the story of Ham and his curse, which, James Baldwin reminds us, has sealed the fate of the black man since the beginning of time.[23]

If Phillips denounces the hold of institutionalized religion and its secular missions on the individual, he also points out that "there is a terrible paradox with religion. It both enslaves and it liberates."[24] As the history of slavery has shown, Christianity proved "a medium of independent black expression and identity."[25] In the case of Cambridge and Othello, for example, it means literacy and thus the possibility of making oneself heard in the language of the master, even if the psychological price to be paid for this avenue of expression is very high indeed. The ironically named Christiania, an obeah-wielding slave, embodies what Cambridge, her educated partner, both wins and loses by his Christian education, for if her voice is never heard throughout the novel, she nonetheless remains "spiritually powerful" (*C* 158) and, unlike Cambridge, survives the violence of the plantation. Though her obeah is dismissed by an English clergyman as "a primitive belief in witchcraft which operates upon the negroes to produce death" (*C* 98), it empowers her because it puts her beyond the colonizer's rational grasp and symbolizes her refusal to take

---

[22] Julius Lester, "The Outsiders: Blacks and Jews and the Soul of America," *Transition* 68 (1995): 79.

[23] Baldwin, *The Fire Next Time*, 38.

[24] "See you on the Plantation," interview [with Phillips] by Aaron Ashby and Artress Bethany White, *ARK/angel Review* 9 (1994): 100.

[25] James Walvin, *Questioning Slavery* (London & New York: Routledge, 1996): 154.

part in the master's grand schemes, be they the Christian religion or the breeding system supposed to compensate for the end of the slave trade (*C* 67).[26]

But when Phillips says that religion can liberate too, he may have in mind a religious feeling of an even more marginal and unobtrusive type than obeah: ie, what he calls "faith," which does not necessarily have "a religious gloss," but is "the ability to actually acknowledge the existence of something that you believe in, something that helps you to make sense of your life."[27] Such a feeling, which is essentially interior and comes with none of the trappings of official religions, affects all of Phillips's characters, even the most obnoxious ones, like Captain Hamilton or Edward Nash. It also connects them with each other, involving them in a spiritual community, as in *Crossing the River* where the characters relate to an ambivalent father figure, in turn God, master and ancestor. However, this inner belief seems to be more developed in Phillips's female protagonists, who are, on the whole, more critical of the religious establishment (perhaps because they are its first victims) and have more introspective capacities than his male characters. There is Irena in *Higher Ground* who imagines God as a cannibal "shaking a celestial salt-cellar before he ate up his children" (*HG* 176); Martha, in *Crossing the River*, who "could find no solace in religion, and was unable to sympathize with the sufferings of the son of God when set against her own private misery" (*CR* 79); or Joyce, in the same novel, whose wide-ranging iconoclasm is a direct response to her mother's selfish bigotry. Though the distance of these women from religion can be, at first, a source of sadness and isolation, there is nevertheless in all of them a love, whether filial or sexual, that drives them on and helps them to find a purpose in life, if only temporarily. This passion, in Phillips's words, this "annealing force [coming] out of fracture,"[28] has much in common with the profane spirituality that characterizes soul music which a critic sees as "a saviour of self-esteem [...] by creating a private world as an escape from the one that is giving you grief."[29] It would require another paper to demonstrate how deeply this musical style has shaped Caryl Phillips's writing, but suffice it to say here that it is the "ability to combine passion with social acumen"[30] of an artist like Curtis Mayfield that fascinates Phillips. The same could be said of Marvin Gaye, Stevie Wonder and many others.

It is probably through Emily, a nineteenth-century Englishwoman in *Cambridge*, who goes to the Caribbean to supervise her father's plantation, that Phillips's sensi-

---

[26] The girl in "Heartland" (the first section of *Higher Ground*) also possesses a "boldness of spirit" (35), an "inner stillness" (29) which her converted, male counterpart has lost.

[27] Interview [with Caryl Phillips] by Graham Swift, *Kunapipi* 13.3 (1991): 103.

[28] "Crossing the River: Caryl Phillips Talks to Maya Jaggi," *Wasafiri* 20 (1994): 28.

[29] Lloyd Bradley, "Introduction: What is Soul?" in *Soul on CD: The Essential Guide* (London: Kyle Cathie, 1994): 2.

[30] Donna Bailey Nurse, "Caryl Phillips' Riffs on Freedom," *Globe & Mail* (21 May 1997).

tive exploration of the female psyche shows best how an inner sense of the sacred helps people to preserve their dignity and assert their individual self, albeit sometimes modestly. At the beginning of the novel, Emily's faith in a loving, protective but powerful God (*C* 13, 45) does not really impinge on her view of the island, which she observes from an apparently desacralized, rational perspective, trying to give objective causes to the phenomena she observes, both natural and human. However, as the novel unfolds and her certainties are shaken, she relinquishes her pseudo-scientific discourse, and her voyage into self-awareness goes hand in hand with the realization of the numinous dimensions of the world around her as "her vision had begun to pulsate with a new and magical life, her mind had become a frieze of sharp stabbling colours. Love, love, love" (*C* 182). This love, or faith, should be understood "as a state of being, or a state of grace" in the "tough and universal sense of quest and daring and growth."[31]

The two religious forms, one institutionalized and the other private, which I have attempted to outline may well suggest what has been called the Caribbean "inability to integrate inner and outer space," the fragmentation of Caribbean philosophy between its European and indigenous roots.[32] To me, however, the tension and interaction between the two partake of a diasporic philosophy in which displaced individuals are shown as potentially able to tap their own imaginary resources and build their own spiritual frames away from the religious or secular missions which would like to put an end to their wandering by imposing a spiritual order on their marooning imagination. As *The Nature of Blood* obliquely suggests, it is when the Jewish people give up exile for the elusive sense of belonging afforded by the foundation of the nation state of Israel that their religious faith tends to harden into dogma. Exile, and the marginality it entails, carries an awareness and a yearning which, as Phillips's female characters testify, can be a source of anxiety but also constitute the basic "building blocks of open-mindedness and an ability to question given truths."[33]

WORKS CITED

Baldwin, James. *The Fire Next Time* (1963; Harmondsworth: Penguin, 1979).

Bradley, Lloyd. "Introduction: What is Soul?" *Soul on CD: The Essential Guide* (London: Kyle Cathie, 1994).

Coetzee, J.M. "What We Like to Forget," *New York Review* (6 November 1997): 38–41.

---

[31] Baldwin, *The Fire Next Time*, 82.

[32] Paget Henry, "Rex Nettleford African and Afro-Caribbean Philosophy," *CLR James Journal* 5.1 (1997): 58.

[33] Susan Greenberg, "Jews against Israel," *Prospect* 31 (1998): 12.

Eliot, T.S. "Religion and Literature," *Selected Prose*, ed. John Hayward (1953; Harmondsworth: Penguin, 1963): 31–42.

Endô, Shûsaku. *Foreign Studies* (1965; London: Sceptre, 1990).

——. *Silence* (1966; Paris: Denoël, 1992).

Gilroy, Paul. *The Black Atlantic: Modernity and Double Consciousness* (London & New York Verso, 1993).

Greenberg, Susan. "Jews against Israel," *Prospect* 31 (1998): 12–13.

Harris, Wilson. *Jonestown* (London: Faber & Faber, 1996).

Henry, Paget. "Rex Nettleford African and Afro-Caribbean Philosophy," *CLR James Journal* 5.1 (1997): 44–97.

Lester, Julius. "The Outsiders: Blacks and Jews and the Soul of America," *Transition* 68 (1995): 66–88.

Mantel, Hilary. "Black is not Jewish," review of *The Nature of Blood*, by Caryl Phillips, *Literary Review* (1 February 1997): 39.

Nurse, Donna Bailey. "Caryl Phillips Riffs on Freedom," *Globe & Mail* (21 May 1997).

Panu–Mbendele, C. "Le Silence des Eglises sur la Traite des Noirs," *Le Soir* (16 February 1999).

Phillips, Caryl. *Cambridge* (London: Bloomsbury, 1991).

——. *Crossing the River* (London: Bloomsbury, 1993).

——. "Crossing the River: Caryl Phillips Talks to Maya Jaggi," *Wasafiri* 20 (1994): 25–29.

——. *The European Tribe* (London: Faber & Faber, 1987).

——. *Higher Ground* (London: Viking, 1989).

——. Interview by Graham Swift, *Kunapipi* 13.3 (1991): 96–103.

——. Interview by Louise Yelin, *Culturefront* 7.2 (1998): 52, 53, 80.

——. "Living and Writing in the Caribbean: An Experiment," *Kunapipi* 11.2 (1989): 44–50.

——. *The Nature of Blood* (London: Faber & Faber, 1997).

——. "The Other Voice: A Dialogue between Anita Desai, Caryl Phillips, and Ilan Stavans," *Transition* 64 (1994): 77–89.

——. "See You on the Plantation," interview by Aaron Ashby and Artress Bethany White. *ARK/angel Review* 9 (1994): 92–106.

Rushdie, Salman. "'Commonwealth Literature' does not exist," *Imaginary Homelands: Essays and Criticism 1981–1991* (London: Granta, 1991): 61–70.

Said, Edward W. *The World, the Text, and the Critic* (1984; London: Random House / Vintage, 1991).

Stevenson, Randall. *A Reader's Guide to the Twentieth-Century Novel in Britain* (New York: Harvester, 1993).

Walvin, James. *Questioning Slavery* (London & New York: Routledge, 1996).

❧

Africa

Moving Away From the Mission
Ngugi wa Thiong'o's Versions of *A Grain of Wheat*

JACQUELINE BARDOLPH

WHEN NGUGI FINISHED WRITING *A GRAIN OF WHEAT* in November 1966, he was in Leeds doing postgraduate studies. The date corresponds to a moment of qualified optimism in African history: Nkrumah was still in power. Obote had not yet taken over in Uganda. That same year, Oginga Odinga published *Not Yet Uhuru*, a socialist analysis of the way in which he considered the rural masses were being cheated of the benefits of independence. Ngugi was educated in a religious context before going to university at Makerere. One must also underline that during the years of Emergency, the churches as a whole were on the side of the British government, in particular helping with the propaganda that described Mau Mau as terrorists, violent outsiders refusing Christian and human values for the sake of atavistic regression. The villagers, suspected of helping the forest guerrillas, and the inmates in detention camps, were subjected to intensive re-education, told to confess, to seek rehabilitation. Moral Rearmament was explicitly involved in the campaign to cultivate guilt feelings among the people, and pacifist Revivalist currents encouraged them to 'see the light' at public meetings. The detainees who agreed to begin new lives were gradually restored to freedom, "going through the pipe-line," their card symbolically changing from black to grey and to white.

With this in mind, one can read *A Grain of Wheat* (published in 1967)[1] as a novel written by the man still called James Ngugi. The revised edition produced twenty years later by Ngugi wa Thiong'o (1986) paradoxically helps one realize how strong some Christian elements were for the more politically aware mature writer who, by that time, had grown to consider them as unacceptable. Under the

---

[1] Ngugi wa Thiong'o, *A Grain of Wheat* (London: Heinemann, 1967). All page references to this edition unless otherwise indicated.

phrase "Christian elements," we include here several levels: the beliefs and practices of ordinary people of the time, the picture of the struggle as indicated by the combination of government and official churches, and the overall Christian vision that shapes the book, whether as expression of belief or as convenient parable.

The novel published by Heinemann seems at first to fit into the pattern set by Achebe's village novels. When one examines what has been cut out from the original manuscript (kept at the School of Oriental and African Studies in London), whether as a change of mind or under guidance from the publisher, several features become apparent. The early text has an even more nightmarish quality than the final version. Eliminated passages show characters suffering from one another's sneers or mocking gaze. Disgust is stressed in sentences that speak of bad smells, excrement and slime. The drop that moves towards Mugo's eyes in his opening dream is also a slug.[2] Physical repulsion is connected with humiliation, and the humiliation is always of a sexual nature. The main elements which did not find their way into the published book have to do with rape fantasies of a twisted nature. The novel is framed by two instances when Mugo feels anger and disgust towards an old lady: first the aunt that brought him up, then at the end the old woman, the mother of the deaf and mute that was shot. These figures with their potential evil eyes are close to castrating witches. The early text adds a weird element to Mugo's irrational emotions. When he feels like throttling the aunt, the imaginary assault is told in terms of climax and release. He sees her with her legs in the air.[3] At the end of the book he kills an old lady, in the same paroxystic mood, and sets her on a stool "burying her feet wide apart in the ashes."[4] Another very long passage, in fact a whole chapter, dealing mostly with Thompson, has been eliminated. The man feels horribly guilty because he once saw a little girl sleeping on a bed in London and felt a strong desire to take her then and there. Years later in Kenya, ashamed of this fantasy, he starts scribbling at night in a notebook, wanting to confess and feel free again. His confession also includes the tortures inflicted as he was responsible for the detention camp

---

[2] "A slug started moving towards him" (MS 3).

[3] "He watched her struggles like a fly in a spider's hands, saw her kick her legs in the air" (MS 14).

[4] "The new rage now fully possessed him, his body shook violently. But as in the meeting, he was clear about his next action. He knew he would put his hand around his neck. Would she groan? Anyway he would press, harder, and she would feel the power of his hands. He felt almost triumphant as he beheld the future, this little future he had just planned.

And that is what he did.

The old woman did not scream.

She fell from his hands onto the ground as if she had died at his touch... He bent down and raised the inert body from the ground. He placed it on the stool near the fire-place, making her head and hands rest on the stone. He then buried her feet, wide apart into the ashes. He stood back to survey the work of his hands" (MS 351).

of Rira. His exalted mood when he wants to liberate himself by this written account is described in the same terms as that of Mugo.[5] The parallel is so strong that some terms could apply to either character. The intricate black and white pair, both feeling guilty and afraid of the other's sneer is not very far from the Munira / Inspector Godfrey pair at the beginning of *Petals of Blood*. Both are involved in the writing down of guilt, as a mode of atonement. Mugo has several nocturnal doubles, Kihika, Karanja, or Thompson, in fantasmatic couples which are clear echoes of Conrad. On the whole, the world in the early manuscript is more irrational, more anguished. All the characters, colonized or colonizers, are locked in nightmares and guilt, distrustful of one another – the parallel between the two adulterous couples, Gikonyo and Mumbi, Thompson and his wife, is underlined – and ultimately alone with their shameful past and oppressive fantasies.[6]

The published novel focuses on a group of people of the same generation. There are three men, Karanja, Mugo, and Gikonyo, and one woman, Mumbi, a pattern that will be repeated in *Petals of Blood*, as will be the confession theme. The others are peripheral to this central plot devoted to ordinary rural young people. There is the group of rebels, Koinandu, General R, Kihika, the politicians of the Party, and the whites. The older generation are here witnesses more than actors. Several fathers are missing or contested. The general atmosphere is one of fear, guilt and exhaustion on the eve of the independence. The village is coming to terms with the meaning of loyalty, courage and betrayal after a period where sides had to be taken but distinctions were often blurred. The process is helped by a chain of confessions, first private then public that help words to regain their meaning as they liberate the actors of this troubled period one after the other.

In 1986, Ngugi, who had not returned to Kenya since 1982, was well-known for his fiction and for the cultural and political positions contained in his collections of essays. Writing directly on an early copy of *A Grain of Wheat*, he brought several types of changes to bear on the novel. The situation of the 1950s and the 1960s is analysed differently. The simple terms, which were close to the world view of the villagers then, are replaced by more general terms: The Party, which is too close to Kenyatta's politics, is replaced by the Movement, which is of a more general nature. The pair of "traitors and collaborators" recurs repeatedly: There is no half-judgment

---

[5] "He wrote in fury. Images flowed, merged, clashed. It was as if he had only a few minutes to live and wanted to purge his soul of filth, a confession to a priest before the gallows fell" (MS 267).

[6] Robson (who becomes Thompson): "I want to know what went wrong that even my wife laughs secretly at me" (MS 264). On Mugo: "At night, in the morning, I saw the grin, the sneer, the secret laughter, the face was everywhere" (MS 267). Mugo: "Mugo felt the woman look at him with a glint, the glint as of a puzzled recognition transformed her into Mugo's idea of a witch. The luridness seemed to ooze from her eyes and creep towards his flesh" (MS 10).

(25, 60). Some elements of economic analysis are added, in particular concerning the relationship with Asians and Europeans. The possibility of ambivalent assessments is reduced through complete changes in some characters. In the first version, Gatu, a strange man in the detention camp, is full of wisdom, courage, but also despair, a kind of sad clown who commits suicide. His bleak assessment of human capacities is now replaced by certainties. The character who so disturbed Gikonyo is killed by the camp authorities who try to pass this as suicide. General R is, like all rebels in the early novel, a frightening figure (think of Boro in *Weep not Child*). The novelist has been at pains to find motivations for the violence of the forest fighters. In the 1967 version, General R who used to be a tailor, is an outcast because he has committed a major transgression by hitting his father. He is no longer part of his community. His motive for fighting is connected to personal pride and an inflated sense of honour. In the 1986 version, this disappears from the presentation of the character who becomes an articulate anti-colonial fighter. Koinandu is so altered that, in the 1986 version, he gets a new name, Koina. In 1966, Ngugi was trying to understand the violence committed against white people. He presented the rape of an unattractive spinster by her houseboy as such an extreme case, caused by envy, greed and a distorted sense of manhood.[7] The odd thing is that, although such rapes featured widely in the anti-Mau Mau propaganda of the time, I have not been able to find historical accounts that would match the story. It is as if the young Ngugi still saw the guerrillas as they were presented by propaganda, as creatures totally beyond moral redemption, and tried to find motives and attenuating circumstances. Yet Koinandu remains a thug to the end, motivated by envy and fear. The new Koina does not rape Mrs. Lynd. He just hacks her dog to pieces and finds equalitarian justifications for his resentment.

There is however a very significant change. In the 1967 version, the Reverend Jackson is a minister, a true believer. He is respected by all, in particular the elders and preaches against Mau Mau. He becomes involved in the Revivalist movement. His position is described in a rather non-committal way, close to the point of view of the villagers. He dies at the hands of General R in a manner which can be read as martyrdom, and haunts the conscience of the ex-guerrilla. He is one of the Christ figures of the book, an element in the collective suffering. Any ambiguity there might have been in the interpretation of this important character is lifted by the way Ngugi modifies his presentation radically twenty years after. In 1986, the church minister who has been an informer is justly executed. The recent version is firmly didactic and shows as far as possible the people as more conscious, more united. The

---

[7] "He found his tongue and revealed his thoughts to other people: she was alone, it was not right for a woman to live alone, Man, I'll break her in. I'll swim in that hole. The others laughed at Koinandu's delightful tongue" (185).

charismatic forest leader, Kihika, is no longer a marginal or ambivalent figure, a man his sister refused to see avenged.[8] He is closer to the full national hero, Dedan Kimathi, as presented in the 1977 play.

The modifications point at some of the elements in the 1967 novel, which perhaps readers at the time had not analysed in the same way. Let us read again the system of values which is represented there and the part played by Christian churches and their teaching. It is obvious now, especially if one compares this with the unpublished extracts, that the main value system rests on manhood.[9] When the moment of decision comes, a man tests whether he is true to his circumcision. The characters feel threatened by the laughter of young women and the all-seeing eyes of old ones, the sneers and sexual taunting on the part of white people. Kihika is admired for his courage in tackling a whiteman single-handed. Both Karanja and Mugo are grateful at some point to a white man who has saved them from humiliation, while at others they feel debased, un-manned by their oppression. Humiliation in the hands of representatives of the colonial power is always shown here as sexual in nature; all examples of torture are to do with castration and penetration. Virility, the capacity to engender males and look after one's honour is the core value. The young people do not seem to have other ethical codes to guide their behaviour. They often live in a spiritual vacuum, especially at the end of the years of Emergency. The novel is about spiritual drought, the kind of moral lassitude one sees after conflicts which in some aspects were a form of civil strife, as in the postwar fiction of Zimbabwe. Mumbi has "no words. No feelings. Nothing" (181). She wants Mugo to forget about the dead, but to "Speak to the living. Tell them about those whom the war maimed, left naked and scarred: the orphans, the widows" (161). There is no definite political consciousness in any of the ordinary people, whether they are loyalists, rebels or ordinary people caught in between. The central couple, Gikonyo and Mumbi, named after the mythical founding couple of the Kikuyu, have gone through the terrible period by trying to survive, both attempting to save some personal happiness in the chaos.

What, then, is the part played by organized religion and by the Christian vision in the overall narrative? The experience told is that of a community, and it is described in the terms used by the majority in their discussions, comments and songs. The Bible, the Old Testament in particular, plays an important part in the way people perceive themselves and give shape to their predicament. Mumbi sees herself as Ruth, an earth figure waiting for a child (69). The songs quoted are those sung at the time. From the beginning, anti-colonial attitudes were expressed in Biblical terms: The oppressed were the people of Israel, and Kenyatta was to be the Moses who

---

[8] "But she did not want anybody to die or come to harm because of her brother" (181).

[9] Cf. pages 25, 31, 32, 106, 130, 157.

would deliver them. The whole economy of sacrifice is close to what is left of the Kikuyu traditional religion and to a sombre view of the Christian message which stresses suffering and sin more than beatitude. The Revivalist movement is described in a non-committal way, as a new development that helps some individuals. The violent figure of Kihika is redeemed by the fact that he always quotes from his Bible, which is true of his historical model. In such characters, the values of manhood can be reconciled with the Biblical vision.

The syncretic conception that equates Ngai with the Christian god and Gikuyu and Mumbi with Adam and Eve is part of the efforts of the missions to reconcile two visions and also part of the creed of the nationalist independent churches. In later works, Ngugi will use a more revolutionary mythical ancestor in Ndemi, an active Promethean figure. But here, the vision of the land to be fertilized again or of the allegorical woman to be impregnated is part of the agricultural rhetoric of the title. It is, however, to be noted that none of the main characters suffers from the loss of their land although repossessing land was the central claim for the people who rose against the power of the settlers.

At a deeper level, the narrative seems to be still permeated by the guilt feelings induced by the propaganda. We have seen how close the picture of the terrorists is to the way the rebellion was presented in Kenya and England, even if the young novelist tries to explain the humiliations and unjust treatments that drove some fighters to the forest. In a puritanical vision, sin is equated most of the time with the sin of the flesh. Suffering seems to be the only way forward, a system of atonement that can provide a fresh start when the world as it was known has collapsed. The image of crucifixion is used several times (152, 157). This is a major trope for Ngugi even when it appears in an inverted form in *Devil on the Cross*. The major characters go through a phase of soul-searching, then of confession that is close to the Revivalist method (86, 98). Ngugi's fascination with such emotional type of belief appears again, in a clearly distanced manner in the character of the barmaid in *Petals of Blood*.

Later in his career, when he publicly declared he was not a Christian and changed his name, Ngugi said he used the Bible as a source of metaphors and parables close to the culture of his people. It is true that, in the 1960s, a period when written literary Kikuyu was used essentially for the translation of the Good Book, references to the Bible served to establish a strong link between English, which he enjoyed in a guilty manner, and the popular rhetoric in his own language. The lyrical passages, the agricultural metaphors that give dignity to the simple English used here owe much to the psalms and parables, as well as to the songs composed at the time of the Emergency (75, 85, 126).

The enigmatic character of Mugo can thus be explained by the ambivalent attitude to the power and poetry of the Biblical text. When he speaks like a Messiah, a Moses, he is clearly deluded by a sense of his lonely elite position, like other similar protagonists in Ngugi's fiction. The pastiche of prophetic pronouncements is blasphemous in a man who knows his guilt, whereas others think of him as a saint, who is able to talk with God (108, 110, 112, 139, 164, 173, 188). His betrayal echoes all the other betrayals, however: Mumbi had no real excuse to give herself to Karanja; Gikonyo betrayed the oath because he had a wife to love, a selfish human motive for an act that weighs on them later. Mugo is more ambivalent, excessive in his courage and in his cowardice. Paradoxically, he betrays Kihika in order to save himself for his destiny as a saviour. There is no doubt yet that he is a fraud, and he knows it. He accepts in advance the trial and judgment by the couple of ex-fighters, even if they are not very positive figures. But somehow the book seems to imply that, for all his delusions and weaknesses, he ultimately embodies the major values of the community. His confession is the sacrificial act that allows regeneration: Mumbi and Gikonyo can come together again. And, in his choice to offer himself as a sacrificial victim, "he is a man of courage" who comes close to the manly virtue of a circumcised man. In some ways, Mugo's confession and his feeling of indignity are duplicated by the writing of the book itself. The long conflict has profoundly shaken everyone, divided families, encouraged individual acts of survival at the expense of solidarity. If one refers to similar situations around the world one sees how silence – Kenyatta's "Forget and Forgive!" – can be in itself destructive. The worse moments have to be faced, spoken about, and when one thinks how close to the actual events the 1967 novel is, one can only admire the courage of the young man who chose to give such an image of his people. Later on, political tools were acquired that helped him to analyse the factors differently and present a more militant text based on a clear idealization of fighters as opposed to "traitors and collaborators." It is much easier to see the choices that could have been made, the reasons that could have been given.

The first title of *A Grain of Wheat* was to have been *Wrestling with God*, a phrase taken from the struggle between Tobias and the angel as quoted in a letter by Conrad, referring to the act of fictional creation.[10] The book does not just refer to the world view of Christian villagers seen from a detached position. It is written in the margins and between the lines of the Bible. It reflects some aspects of the colonizer's ideology as taught in a school system that conveyed good and bad together, the vision of the missions, the visions of independent churches and the syncretic popular narratives. But it mostly creates a highly personal world, the

---

[10] Jacqueline Bardolph, "Ngugi wa Thiong'o's *A Grain of Wheat* and *Petals of Blood* as Readings of Conrad's *Under Western Eyes* and *Victory*," *The Conradian* 12.1 (1987): 32–49.

tortured self-searching and ironical distance of one who worked on Conrad and found there a pessimism to which he could relate. The end is very bleak, with isolated figures in the drizzle. In detention, Gikonyo has come to the conclusion that "to live and die alone was the ultimate truth" (102). On his return he finds it difficult to regain any kind of faith. All the heroes, even the near mythical couple, are at a loss. The only fruit of the period is an illegitimate child, but he is there, he is ill and needs attending to. The sick child, like in *Petals of Blood*, is an image of the pain of the world. In spite of the rewriting of *A Grain of Wheat* in 1986 to give positive examples to people in their present resistance, the novel remains complex, alive and fraught with deep contradictions. The Christian mode of narrative, whether a grand metaphor or the expression of a deep belief, is the only element that makes sense in this picture of a world that suffers spiritually from its division more than from external oppression.

RELEVANT DATES

1938	Ngugi's birth. One of twenty-seven siblings, fifth child of Thiong'o's third wife.
1947–48	Attends Church of Scotland Mission School.
1948–55	Attends Independent School, which becomes government school
1952	State of Emergency declared.
1953	Ngugi is circumcised.
1954	His deaf and dumb brother is shot dead. Wallace joins Mau Mau with whom he stays until 1956.
1955–56	Attends Alliance School, a secondary school run by Allied Protestant Missions for East Africa (Siriana).
1955	Ngugi finds house and village razed to the ground on returning home from school.
1956	Public execution of Dedan Kimathi.
1959	Ngugi enters Makerere.
1960	End of Emergency.
1961	Ngugi writes *The River Between*.
1962	Ngugi writes *Weep not Child*.
1963	Independence of Kenya.
1964	Ngugi graduates. Works on Conrad. Goes to Leeds University. Writes *Wrestling with God. Weep not Child* published.
1965	*The River Between* published.
1966	*Not Yet Uhuru* by Oginga Odinga published. Ngugi finishes *A Grain of Wheat*.
1967	*A Grain of Wheat* published.

WORKS CITED

Bardolph, Jacqueline. "Ngugi wa Thiong'o's *A Grain of Wheat* and *Petals of Blood* as Readings of Conrad's *Under Western Eyes* and *Victory,*" *The Conradian* 12.1 (1987): 32–49.

Ngugi wa Thiong'o. *Devil on the Cross*, tr. from Gikuyu by the author (London: Heinemann, 1982).

——. "A Grain of Wheat" (original MS, kept at the School of Oriental and African Studies in London).

——. *A Grain of Wheat* (London: Heinemann, 1967).

——. *A Grain of Wheat* (London: Heinemann, rev. ed. 1986).

——. *Petals of Blood* (London: Heinemann, 1977).

——. *Weep Not Child* (London: Heinemann, 1964).

Odinga, Oginga. *Not Yet Uhuru* (London: Heinemann, 1966).

❧

Ideology and Self-Representation in Autobiography
The Case of Katie Makanya

THENGANI H. NGWENYA

S
OCIAL HISTORIANS AND ANTHROPOLOGISTS who have studied the social and cultural consequences of the encounter between Africa and the colonizing Western countries have commented on the characteristic world-view of the Africans who embraced the colonizer's religion and its underlying cultural and political outlook.[1] (As also shown in their own writings and utterances, Africans who converted to Christianity during the nineteenth and early twentieth centuries seem to have understood the implications of accepting the religion of the Christian missionaries and the lifestyle associated with it: They were expected to renounce or radically re-define their own traditional belief systems, values and cultural practices and to adopt an alien world-view which was presented as having universal applicability and validity. This process of cultural and moral transformation which has been variously described as assimilation, deculturation, acculturation and, most recently, as transculturation, was characterized by numerous inherent ambiguities and contradictions.

As demonstrated by Katie Makanya's self-portrayal in her autobiography,[2] the underpinning ideology of a civilization the code words of which were 'rationality,' 'enlightenment,' 'progress,' 'morality' and 'justice' slowly gained acceptance among the converted Africans and provided the language or, more appropriately, a discourse

---

[1] See Norman Etherington, *Preachers, Peasants and Politics in South East Africa, 1835–1880* (London: Royal History Society: 1978); Gail M. Gerhart, *Black Power in South Africa: The Evolution of an Ideology* (Berkeley: U of California P, 1978); Shula Marks, *The Ambiguities of Dependence in South Africa: Class, Nationalism, and the State in Twentieth-Century Natal* (Johannesburg: Ravan, 1986); Absalom Vilakazi, *Zulu Transformations: A Study of the Dynamics of Social Change* (Pietermaritzburg: U of Natal P, 1965); Bernard Magubane, *The Political Economy, Race and Class in South Africa* (New York & London: Monthly Review Press, 1979).

[2] I distinguish between Katie Makanya's two roles as author and character by using her surname to refer to the former role and her first name to denote the latter.

of self-definition for the converted African Christian community. As a way of reinforcing their newly acquired identities, the converts often presented themselves as having a fundamentally different moral and cultural outlook from the traditionalists. As Paul la Hausse rightly points out, there was an unbridgeable chasm between traditionalists and the christianized African (Zulu) community of the late nineteenth and early twentieth centuries:

> As 'civilised', 'progressive' and, most importantly, 'respectable' members of colonial society who had left the 'backward' cultural and social organisation of pre-capitalist Zulu society behind them, the *kholwa* faithfully believed in the 'promise of Queen Victoria.'[3]

This essay examines the effect of colonial ideology in shaping self-conception and self-portrayal within the mode of collaborative autobiography.[4] *The Calling of Katie Makanya* (1995)[5] is a text which straddles the divide between biography and autobiography and displays many structural and thematic affinities with the kind of life-writing that Mary Louise Pratt has described as 'autoethnography'[6] which she defines as follows:

> If ethnographic texts are a means by which Europeans represent to themselves their (usually subjugated) others, autoethnographic texts are those the others construct in response to or in dialogue with those metropolitan representations. (7)

---

[3] Paul la Hausse, "So Who Was Elias Kuzwayo? Nationalism, Collaboration and the Picaresque in Natal," in *Apartheid's Genesis 1935–1962*, ed. Philip Bonner, Peter Delius & Deborah Posel (Johannesburg: Ravan / Witwatersrand UP, 1993): 195–228.

[4] For an informative discussion of the political implications of collaborative life-writing of black women in South Africa, see Carole Boyce Davis, "Collaboration and the Ordering Imperative in Life-Story Production," in *De / Colonising the Subject: The Politics of Gender in Women's Autobiography*, ed. Sidonie Smith & Julia Watson (Minneapolis: U of Minnesota P, 1992): 3–19, and Anne McClintock, " ' The Very House of Difference': Race, Gender, and the Politics of South African Women's Narrative in Poppie Nongena," in *The Bounds of Race: Perspectives on Hegemony and Resistance*, ed. Dominick LaCapra (Ithaca NY & London: Cornell UP, 1991): 196–230. On collaborative autobiography in general see Philippe Lejeune, "The Autobiography of Those Who Do Not Write," in *On Autobiography*, ed. Paul John Eakin, tr. Katherine Leary (Madison: U of Wisconsin P, 1989): 185–215, and John Beverly, "The Margin and the Centre: On Testimonio (Testimonial Narrative)," in *De / Colonising the Subject*, ed. Smith & Watson, 91–114.

[5] Margaret McCord, *The Calling of Katie Makanya* (Cape Town: David Philip & New York: Dan Wiley, 1995). Page references are in the main text.

[6] Mary Louise Pratt, *Imperial Eyes: Travel Writing and Transculturation* (London & New York: Routledge, 1992). See also Joseph Hogan & Rebecca Hogan, "Autobiography in the Contact Zone," in *True Relations: Essays on Autobiography and the Postmodern*, ed. Thomas Couser & Joseph Fichtelberg (Westport CT & London: Greenwood, 1998): 83–95, for an illuminating discussion of the concept of 'autoethnography' and Françoise Lionnet, *Autobiographical Voices: Race, Gender, Self-Portraiture* (Ithaca NY & London: Cornell UP, 1989), esp. ch. 2 ("Autoethnography: The An-Archic Style of Dust Tracks on a Road," 97–129).

Pratt goes on to point out that "autoethnographic texts are not [...] what are usually thought of as 'authentic' or autochthonous forms of self-representation [...]. Rather, autoethnography involves partial collaboration with and appropriation of the idioms of the conqueror" (7). In the case of Makanya's life story, metropolitan representations of the colonized other are reinforced and validated by what seems to be her deliberate reliance on both the 'language' and the moralistic philosophy of the missionaries in describing her own experience. Thus, instead of offering a counter-hegemonic interpretation of her subjectivity as most autoethnographers would do, Makanya presents, through her editor, a self-portrait which largely reflects the ideology of moral and social transformation underlying the civilizing project of the missionaries.

As *The Calling* deals mainly with the life of an American missionary doctor and her African assistant, Margaret McCord, the writer, seems to have targeted both American and South African readers. The book was published by David Philip publishers in South Africa and by John Wiley publishers in America. When it appeared in South Africa in 1995, one reviewer described its publication as "a moving act of feminist retrieval."[7] A comprehensive review article which focused on the editor–subject relationship appeared in the *Southern African Review of Books*.[8]

Makanya's life story is the product of collaboration between Margaret McCord, the daughter of the American Board missionary doctor, James McCord who founded the McCord Zulu Hospital in 1909. Recognizing the historical significance of her 'calling' as Dr McCord's first assistant and the inherent value of her various social roles, Katie Makanya appealed to McCord's daughter to preserve her story in writing for future generations (*The Calling*, 3–4). The story was told orally and recorded on tape in 1954 and forty years later transcribed, edited and presented as a readable story in book form.[9] In keeping with the status of Makanya's book as a carefully researched quasi-ethnographic collaborative autobiography,[10] my discussion will focus on what I regard as her various subject positions provided by the analytical framework employed by McCord to interpret and 'write up' her friend's oral story.

---

[7] Shirley Kossick, "A Moving Act of Feminist Retrieval" (review of *The Calling of Katie Makanya*), *Mail & Guardian* (6–12 October 1995): 34.

[8] Thengani H. Ngwenya, review of *The Calling of Katie Makanya*, in *Southern African Review of Books* 39–40 (September–October / November–December 1995): 6–7.

[9] As a genre of life-writing, collaborative autobiography is becoming pupolar in South Africa. Editors or 'facilitators' include Shula Marks, *The Ambiguities of Dependence in South Africa: Class, Nationalism, and the State in Twentieth-Century Natal* (Johannesburg: Ravan, 1986); S. Bourquin, ed. *Paulina Dlamini: Servant of Two Kings* (Durban: Killie Campbell Africana Library, 1986); and K. Limakatso Kendall with Mpho 'M'atsepo Nthunya, *Singing Away the Hunger: Stories of a Life in Lesotho* (Pietermaritzburg: U of Natal P, 1996).

[10] In her note of acknowledgement, McCord mentions people who assisted her in various ways with the research which formed part of the writing process.

Although most African Christians of Makanya's time often displayed largely
ambivalent attitudes towards some aspects of Western culture, she seems to have had
no major reservations about what she saw as the inherent superiority of the imperial
culture. This is confirmed by her consistent self-portrayal as a Christian who has
completely renounced traditional beliefs and practices (*The Calling*: 178). However,
in the process of writing her story, McCord attempts to problematize issues of
identity and consciousness which Makanya would have taken for granted. Mainly
because she adopts the role of observer, writer and analyst, McCord offers a far
more nuanced and sophisticated analysis of Makanya's life than she herself would
have done. Thus, for McCord, editing the oral version of Makanya's story involves
more than merely giving the reader an 'accurate' account of Makanya's understanding of key events in her life. Among other things, the editing process entails the conscious deployment of interpretive and analytical skills, an attempt empathetically to
understand her subject's experiences, as well as reliance on the conventional techniques of storytelling such as plausibility, narrative sequence and credible characterization. Like an ethnographer, McCord assumes the apparently incongruous role
of participant-observer. As James Clifford rightly points out, the ethnographer combines the perspectives of "experience" and "interpretation":

> 'Participant observation' serves as shorthand for a continuous tacking between the
> 'inside' and 'outside' of events: on the one hand grasping the sense of specific occur-
> rences and gestures empathetically, on the other stepping back to situate these mean-
> ings in wider contexts.[11]

As shown in the editorial comments which form part of the text, McCord's recording
of her subject's oral self-narrative life involved constant interpretation and recon-
figuration of the latter's story as she was recording it and later when she was
preparing it for publication. It would not be inaccurate therefore to categorize
Makanya's life story as a mode of autobiographical writing which Paul John Eakin
has aptly called "the story of the story" in which "the story of the other, of the
informant [...], is accompanied by the story of the individual gathering the oral
history."[12] For McCord, interviewing Makanya also entailed re-living significant
events and occurrences in the history of her own family.[13] As I hope to show

[11] James Clifford, *The Predicament of Culture: Twentieth-Century Ethnography, Literature, and Art* (Cambridge MA: Harvard UP, 1988).

[12] Paul John Eakin, "Relational Selves, Relational Lives: The Story of the Story," in *True Relations: Essays on Autobiography and the Postmodern*, ed. G. Thomas Couser & Joseph Fichtelberg
(Westport CT & London: Greenwood, 1998): 63–81.

[13] See Thengani H. Ngwenya's review of *The Calling of Katie Makanya* for a discussion of
McCord's close relationship with Makanya and the interweaving of the process of reconstructing
Makanya's life into the published text. Significantly, it is Katie who gave Margaret her Zulu name,
Ntombikanina when the latter was still an infant.

McCord's interpretation of the life of her father's assistant and her (McCord's) attempts to render it into readable and interesting narrative involve an imposition of a recognizably postcolonial analytical paradigm underpinned by notions of transculturation and hybridity. Apparently, the anticipated readership of the book included sophisticated social historians, feminists, and literary critics.

Formative Experiences

Although *The Calling* is presented to the reader as a "true story" like most autobiographies, it could also be easily categorized as "fiction."[14] Makanya's moral outlook is so typical of the westernized African elite of the late nineteenth and early twentieth centuries that McCord could easily have created a fictional yet credible character of Katie Makanya on the basis of historical accounts of the behaviour patterns and attitudes of her social group. Clearly, Makanya's autobiography is not simply a story of a woman who was "called" into the Christian faith to serve as a missionary doctor's general assistant as suggested by the book's title, but it is also a story which provides valuable insights into the discourses which in part 'created' and sustained the class of the converted Africans or the *amakholwa*, as they were in Natal.

Perhaps the most noticeable feature of converted Africans was their willingness to give up their African names and their eagerness to adopt 'Christian' names. The name change was emblematic of significant changes in moral consciousness and self-conception. As the children of 'progressive' parents, the Manye (Katie's maiden name) children all had 'Christian' names inscribed in the family Bible by their almost fanatically religious mother:

> Ma was not like other mothers who told their children they were born in the time of this war or that war. Ma was an educated woman. She wrote everything down in the family Bible. First the record of Charlotte's birth, and then "a second daughter, Katie, born on July 28, 1873 at Fort Beaufort in the Cape of Good Hope. [...] Pa was a Christian too, but not in his early years, and he did not altogether put aside the customs of his people. He called her by her home name, Malubisi – which means "Mother of Milk" – because she was born at milking time. (9–10)

As shown in the depiction of Katie's father in this passage, the editor's intention seems to be to give the two competing world views (African traditionalism and Western modernity) equal and balanced representation in the book even when this is

---

[14] James Clifford reminds us that the word 'fiction' "as commonly used in recent textual theory has lost its connotation of falsehood, of something merely opposed to truth. It suggests the partiality of cultural and historical truths, the ways they are systematic and exclusive." "Introduction: Partial Truths," in *Writing Culture: The Poetics and Politics of Ethnography*, ed. James Clifford & George Marcus (Berkeley: U of California P, 1986): 6.

not entirely warranted by the people and events she is describing. For example, Katie's African name was rarely, if ever, used outside the extended family and there is no mention in the book of any significant African custom of which the missionaries disapproved but which Katie's father did not give up. So it is not entirely accurate to say that "he did not altogether put aside the customs of his people" (16). However, portraying him in this manner is in line with the writer's analytical framework underpinned by the notion of transculturation which Pratt defines as follows:

> Ethnographers have used this term to describe how subordinated or marginal groups select and invent from materials transmitted to them by a dominant metropolitan culture. While subjugated people cannot readily control what emanates from the dominant culture, they do determine to varying extents what they absorb into their own, and what they use it for. (6)

Thus, apart from their function of giving added authenticity to the events described in the book, the photos which take up the first eleven pages of the book serve to reinforce Katie's 'transcultural' status. In their arrangement there seems to be a deliberate attempt on the editor's part to juxtapose images and symbols of traditionalism with those of modernity. Although there is ample evidence in the autobiography itself to suggest that Katie had, as far as this is possible, renounced African and, more specifically, Sotho customs and traditions (178), McCord consciously presents her moral sensibility as characterized by cultural hybridity which is often portrayed as a consequence of Katie's own choice. For instance, when Katie is with the traditional Batlokwa community of Soekmekaar whom she repeatedly refers to as "heathen," the editor, assuming the role of omniscient narrator, describes her as follows:

> As the days passed, Katie felt that even though she was a Christian girl, she belonged among the heathen Batlokwa. It seemed to her that all the years of her life had been one long journey home to Soekmekaar. (80)

Characterizing the young Katie in obviously self-contradictory terms as a "Christian girl" who also belongs to the heathen Batlokwa tribe is part of the editor's deliberate strategy to give the two competing world views a semblance of equality. Perhaps unwittingly casting doubt on her own assessment of Katie's moral awareness, the editor goes on to tell us how she could not adapt to the life-style of her age-mates in Soekmekaar and ultimately had to leave for Johannesburg to look for an educated Christian husband (90). The rural village of Soekmekaar could only be a symbolic cultural 'home' for Katie, her real home would be in the shanty towns and mission stations of Johannesburg and Durban where people of her class and aspirations had congregated in search of a way of life which suited their interests and aspirations.

When the Manye family went to settle among the Batlokwa tribe of Soekmekaar both Katie and her elder sister Charlotte had been to London as members of the

African Native Choir which toured England from 1891 to 1893. There is no doubt that Katie saw this episode in her life as an important landmark in the evolution of her social and moral consciousness. The membership of this choir included teachers, clerks, nurses, social workers and other educated Africans. The selection of Katie and her elder sister Charlotte who was already a trained teacher confirmed their class status as members of the very class-conscious emergent black petty bourgeoisie of the time. Mainly because of her Christian upbringing as well her exposure to British manners, Katie found it difficult to adjust to traditional life in Soekmekaar. When her playmates told her stories that were part of their community's folklore she would reciprocate by telling them about her experiences in London:

> They told Katie stories about Huveana, a little man who lived in the reeds and tossed a magic spell on anyone who came too near. In return Katie told them of all the wonders she had seen in London. The girls laughed at her stories, knowing such things to be impossible, just as Katie laughed at theirs. (81)

Katie is shown to be both an insider and an outsider in most of the groups or situations described in the book: She is a Christian who has discarded the customs of the 'heathen' relatives, yet she seems to appreciate the practical value of some traditional beliefs and customs. For instance, she finds the way the heathens treat unmarried mothers more humane than that of the Christians (81). She also seems to take her grandfather seriously when he says he would come back from the dead in the form of a snake to protect his family (85, 89).

Katie as a Domestic and Social Worker

After moving to Johannesburg in search of employment and a life that would accord with her tastes and interests, Katie joined the largely unskilled urban community in the informal settlement of Doornfontein. But the fact that she had been to England and could speak fluent English set her apart from the illiterate country girls who came to Johannesburg to sell their labour as domestic servants. Nevertheless, because of her lack of training the only job she was likely to get was that of a domestic worker. In her first job, when she accidentally mentioned things she was not supposed to know as a domestic worker, her employer suspected her of being a "witch" with magical powers. McCord describes her ambiguous status as follows:

> Everywhere she went it seemed that she was set apart – in England because her skin was black, in Kimberley because she had lived too long among the English, in Ramkgopa's village because she was a Christian, and now here in her work because Mrs Height thought she had magic powers. (103)

Mrs Height could not have guessed that Katie would never think of herself as even remotely connected with traditional African beliefs and cultural practices. The most articulate spokespersons of the *kholwa* community who saw themselves as mediators between the two cultures openly declared their opposition to traditional beliefs and customs. A typical comment in this regard was made by John L. Dube in his "Address to the Chiefs and People of the South African Native Congress," presented in absentia on his appointment as president in 1912:

> Upward! Into the higher places of civilisation and Christianity – not backward into the slump of darkness nor downward into the abyss of the antiquated tribal system. Our salvation is not there, but in preparing ourselves for an honoured place amongst the nations.[15]

There are numerous examples of McCord's conscious attempts to create "contact zones"[16] marked by mutual exchange or reciprocity between African traditionalism and European modernity. For example, Katie's grandfather (referred to as Old Man in the book) and the chief of the Batlokwa tribe (Ramkgopa) are presented as articulate spokespersons of the indigenous Sotho culture. By re-creating convincing dialogue between Katie's mother and the Old Man on such controversial topics as arranged marriages, ancestor worship and traditional medicine McCord ensures that the defining features of both cultures have an equal representation in Makanya's life story.

Katie's first job as a domestic worker was hardly consistent with her own chosen status as a member of the educated African elite. However, in an urban environment in which jobs were scarce she had to play the role of an unsophisticated country girl to keep her job. Things began to change when she joined her husband's church, the American Board Mission. She soon became an outspoken member of the Women's Association and was subsequently asked to act as an interpreter to Mr Dickson who had been hired by the Chamber of Mines to teach black workers about the dangers of intoxicating drink. Like her later role as Dr McCord's assistant, this was a job befitting her status and self-conception. In an attempt to reach mine workers most of whom were illiterate, Katie spoke to them in their various home languages using appropriate African imagery and exploiting their prejudices and fears:

> "Are you afraid of my words?" she shouted back in Xhosa. "Then you are right to be afraid. Because my words are not the words of a woman. I am the mouth of white *inyanga* who comes to warn you of the evil spirits waiting for you in all the drinks you buy from the old witches in this town. Pretty soon the spirits will burn you up inside until you die." (124)

---

[15] Quoted in Shula Marks, *The Ambiguities of Dependence*, 53.

[16] As Pratt rightly points out, "transculturation is a phenomenon of the contact zone"; *Imperial Eyes*, 6. Pratt describes contact zones as "social spaces where disparate cultures meet, clash, and grapple with each other, often in highly asymmetrical relations of domination and subordination – like colonialism, slavery, or their aftermaths as they are lived out across the globe today" (4).

Adopting the perspective of the enlightened social worker Katie spoke to her own people in what is supposed to be their 'language' – the language of superstition and apparently irrational fears and beliefs. Following the example of her sister Charlotte who was then an active member of the Temperance Movement in America, Katie began visiting women in other churches, schools and even shebeens (taverns) urging them to join her new Temperance Union. As a person who judged everything from a religious perspective, Katie regarded her job as having an inherent moral and social significance. She was always busy and apparently contented with her efforts:

> There were meetings to plan, parades to lead, and songs to teach to the children after school. At last her life was complete. Even without a high school education, she was doing important work. If Pa could see her now, he would be proud. Charlotte, too, would think she was doing an important work. (125)

In many ways Katie's involvement in social and humanitarian projects was in emulation of her sister Charlotte Maxeke who has been described as the "Mother of African Freedom."[17] Maxeke's achievements are nothing short of phenomenal: She was the first president of the Bantu Women's League, the first president of the National Council of African Women, the first African woman BA graduate in South Africa as well as the first African Social Worker in South Africa.[18]

Katie's Calling

When the Anglo-Boer War broke out in 1899, Katie and her family had to move to Amanzimtoti Mission reserve in Natal. Katie must have believed that her marrying a Zulu brought up and educated on an American Board Mission station was God's plan for her to meet Dr James McCord, for whom she worked for thirty-five years. From the perspective of hindsight, Katie could see everything she did prior to her meeting the missionary doctor, including her education and her visit to Britain, as forming part of the long preparation for her job as Dr McCord's assistant. Being a Christian who could read, write and speak English and other indigenous languages and who also had a keen interest in the improvement of her people's standard of living were her most outstanding credentials. In his own autobiographical account of his life in South Africa, Dr James McCord explains Katie's role as follows: "Katie Makanya faithfully carried out any work assigned to her, but her knowledge of six native dialects made her so invaluable as interpreter that I kept her much of the time in the consulting room."[19]

---

[17] Cherryl Walker, *Women and Resistance in South Africa* (Cape Town & Johannesburg: David Philip, 1991): 36.

[18] Walker, *Women and Resistance in South Africa*, 36–40.

[19] James B. McCord, *My Patients Were Zulus* (New York & Toronto: Rinehart, 1946): 119.

Although her relationship with Dr McCord was characterized by mutual under-standing, respect and loyalty, what really kept them together was their shared religious beliefs. According to Katie, Dr McCord was doing God's work and needed the support and assistance of educated Africans.[20] Ironically, the uneducated Zulus believed that Dr McCord must have trained secretly under a famous *inyanga* (Zulu traditional Zulu healer) because he understood and could treat what they regarded as uniquely African diseases, especially those caused by the dreaded 'evil spirits.' When Dr McCord jokingly asked Katie whether she also believed these stories about his secret initiation into traditional medicine she was deeply offended by what she saw as a sign of the doctor's failure to understand her moral outlook as an "enlightened" African. Katie's response to the doctor's question as paraphrased by McCord is worth quoting at length as it reveals the definitive features of both her moral consciousness and self-conception:

> He had no right to ask her such a question, not when he knew she was a good Christian like her mother and her grandfather and her great-grandmother [...] Not when he knew she had lived among white people in England. Not when he knew her own sister had graduated from a university in America and even now was building a school among the heathen in Soekmekaar. Not when she had also left her husband and her eldest son alone in the country to follow him in God's work. (178)

As a Christian, Katie was sceptical of the value of traditional healing methods and would not have anything to do with traditional healers. However, when her own son was suffering from what the doctors diagnosed as a nervous breakdown, she desperately tried all possible remedies. But when his condition did not improve she began considering something that would have been unthinkable to a person of her beliefs and convictions – seeking help from traditional healers. When she ultimately decided to consult an *inyanga*, she was prevented from entering his home by his messenger who told her to go back home as she was not welcome. This incident raises a number of questions not only about the veracity of McCord's presentation of this incident but also about the interpretive and selective nature of the editing process: Was Katie refused assistance because she was a known Christian, or because she worked for a white missionary doctor, or is this one of the instances of deliberate distortion of events by the editor for the sake of portraying Katie as consistent in her beliefs, or did Katie, for obvious reasons, prefer this version of this incident? Sadly, Katie's son was eventually sent to an institution for the incurably insane.

---

[20] McCord, *The Calling of Katie Makanya*, 178.

Katie's Political Outlook

Obviously, the influence of religion on African converts was not confined to spiritual matters. Katie's involvement in politics is thus in line with the dominant world view of moderate black leaders such as John L. Dube, the first president of the African National Congress. Like Dube, Katie regarded herself as a *hamba-kahle* (moderate) person as opposed to radical members of the Industrial and Commercial Workers Union such as Bertha Mkhise and Violet Makanya. Katie is therefore describing her own moderate political orientation when she says of Dube: "John Dube doesn't rush about like a wild bull, frightening everyone. He looks for the right path, one that may be a long way round but will in time take him safely home" (214). There seems to have been a direct correlation between the political outlook of leaders such as Dube and their religious beliefs. To most of them political problems which required militant political mobilization appeared as moral issues.

Besides moral reservations which provided an ideological deterrence to political agitation by the oppressed, there was also the obvious military superiority of the white man's army. Thus when the Zulu chief Bambatha led a violent rebellion against the British rulers of the Natal province in 1906, African Christians and other 'loyal natives' considered his actions not only foolhardy but also as unacceptable on moral grounds. As McCord remarks, Katie's views on this matter reflected those of the African elite in Natal:

> Katie, like most of the educated Christian Zulus, was dismayed. How can a little chief like Bhambatha do this when our great King Cetshwayo, failed? The people around Durban asked [...] to stop Bhambatha, some of the Zulus formed their own cavalry regiment, the Natal Native Horse, to fight on the side of the British. (180)

Dr McCord, urged by the white officers most of whom were sons of the missionaries, enlisted as a medical officer to care for the wounded in the Native army. This episode provides a graphic example of ideological divisions between the politically-aware and radical traditionalists on the one hand and christianized Africans on the other hand. The willingness of converted Zulus to take up arms against their own brothers is evidence of the unbridgeable chasm between these two groups. James McCord explains the attitude of Zulu volunteers in rather facile terms when he says, "none of our natives saw anything incongruous in fighting their own people, for the Zulus have always practiced intertribal warfare."[21] To attribute this division to Zulu military history, as James McCord does, is to ignore the potent role of ideology in shaping self-conception and social roles. Besides, McCord seems to have overlooked the obvious fact that this was intra-tribal warfare as distinct from what he terms "intertribal warfare."

---

[21] McCord, *My Patients Were Zulus*, 53.

To the numerous questions raised by a text which transgresses generic boundaries like *The Calling* literary critics can only provide provisional answers. Perhaps the most fruitful way to approach an edited life story that is narrated orally and then transferred into print is by way of cultural hermeneutics, which Clifford Geertz has aptly described as "the understanding of understanding."[22] In its constant self-reflexive commentary on its process of construction, *The Calling* draws our attention to the dual status of ethnography as a process and a product of qualitative research. Essentially, the book presents Margaret McCord's *understanding* of Katie Makanya's fascinating life.

WORKS CITED

Beverley, John. "The Margin at the Centre: On Testimonio (Testimonial Narrative)," in Smith & Watson, *De/Colonising the Subject,* 91–114.

Bourquin, S., ed. *Paulina Dlamini: Servant of Two Kings* (Durban: Killie Campell Africana Library, 1986).

Boyce Davies, Carol. "Collaboration and the Ordering Imperative in Life-Story Production," in Smith & Watson, *De / Colonising the Subject*, 3–19.

Clifford, James. "Introduction: Partial Truths," in *Writing Culture: The Poetics and Politics of Ethnography*, ed. James Clifford & George Marcus (Berkeley: U of California P, 1986): 1–26.

——. *The Predicament of Culture: Twentieth-Century Ethnography, Literature, and Art* (Cambridge MA: Harvard UP, 1988).

Couser, G. Thomas, & Joseph Fichtelberg, ed. *True Relations: Essays on Autobiography and the Postmodern* (Westport CT & London: Greenwood, 1998).

Eakin, Paul John. "Relational Selves, Relational Lives: The Story of the Story," in Couser & Fichtelberg, *True Relations,* 63–81.

Etherington, Norman. *Preachers Peasants and Politics in South East Africa, 1835–1880* (London: Royal Historical Society, 1978).

Geertz, Clifford. *Local Knowledge: Further Essays in Interpretive Anthropology* (New York: Basic Books, 1983).

Gerhart, Gail M. *Black Power in South Africa: The Evolution of an Ideology* (Berkeley: U of California P, 1978).

Hogan, Joseph, & Rebecca Hogan. "Autobiography in the Contact Zone: Cross-Cultural Identity in Jane Tapsubei Creider's *Two Lives*," in Couser & Fichtelberg, *True Relations,* 83–95.

Kossick, Shirley. "A Moving Act of Feminist Retrieval" (Review of *The Calling of Katie Makanya*), *Mail & Guardian* (6–12 October 1995): 34.

la Hausse, Paul. "So Who Was Elias Kuzwayo? Nationalism, Collaboration and the Picaresque in Natal," in *Apartheid's Genesis 1935–1962*, ed. Philip Bonner, Peter Delius & Deborah Posel (Johannesburg: Ravan & Wits UP, 1993): 195–228.

---

[22] Clifford Geertz, *Local Knowledge: Further Essays in Interpretive Anthropology* (New York: Basic Books, 1983): 5.

Lejeune, Philippe. "The Autobiography of Those Who Do Not Write," in *On Autobiography*, ed. Paul John Eakin, tr. Katherine Leary (Madison: U of Winsconsin P, 1989): 185–215.

Lionnet, Françoise. *Autobiographical Voices: Race, Gender, Self-Portraiture* (Ithaca NY & London: Cornell UP, 1989).

Magubane, Bernard. *The Political Economy, Race and Class in South Africa* (New York & London: Monthly Review Press, 1979).

Marks, Shula. *The Ambiguities of Dependence in South Africa: Class, Nationalism, and the State in Twentieth-Century Natal* (Johannesburg: Ravan, 1986).

——, ed. *Not Either an Experimental Doll: The Separate World of Three South African Women* (Pietermaritzburg: U of Natal P, 1987).

McClintock, Anne. " ' The Very House of Difference': Race, Gender, and the Politics of South African Women's Narrative in Poppie Nongena," in *The Bounds of Race: Perspectives on Hegemony and Resistance*, ed. Dominick LaCapra (Ithaca NY & London: Cornell UP, 1991): 196–230.

McCord, James B. *My Patients Were Zulus* (New York & Toronto: Rinehart, 1946).

McCord, Margaret. *The Calling of Katie Makanya* (Cape Town & Johannesburg: David Philip; New York: Dan Wiley, 1995).

Ngwenya, Thengani H. Review of *The Calling of Katie Makanya*, *Southern African Review of Books* 39–40 (September–December 1995): 6–7.

Nthunya, Mpho 'M'atsepo. *Singing Away the Hunger: Stories of a Life in Lesotho*, ed. K. Limakatso Kendall (Pietermaritzburg: U of Natal P, 1996).

Pratt, Mary Louise. *Imperial Eyes: Travel Writing and Transculturation* (London & New York: Routledge, 1992).

Smith, Sidonie, & Julia Watson, ed. *De / Colonising the Subject: The Politics of Gender in Women's Autobiography* (Minneapolis: U of Minnesota P, 1992).

Vilakazi, Absalom. *Zulu Transformations: A Study of the Dynamics of Social Change* (Pietermaritzburg: U of Natal P, 1965).

Walker, Cherryl. *Women and Resistance in South Africa* (Cape Town & Johannesburg: David Philip, 1991).

❧

New Voices Rewriting the Community

Dialogic History in South Africa; A.H.M. Scholtz's Novel *Vatmaar*

HEILNA DU PLOOY

Introduction

T
HE NOVEL *VATMAAR* BY A.H.M. SCHOLTZ was published in 1995. The title can be translated as 'For the taking,' or something like 'To be had' in the sense of 'You can take it' or 'You can have it.' The novel offers a perspective from a previously marginalized community and from a marginalized personal position, on a crucial period in South African history: namely, the period after the Anglo-Boer War which ended in 1902. The origins of the contemporary South African community and its cultural variety are described through the eyes of a 'brown' man focusing on the position of the so-called 'coloured' people as an interface between the white and black communities, highlighting problems which have come a long way and are still prevalent today. Apart from the extra-textual aspects of political, ideological and historical nature which have to be taken into account in a discussion of this novel, an analysis of the linguistic and literary characteristics of *Vatmaar* are essential for an adequate interpretation of the text.

Historical Background

It has become postmodernist commonplace that the world and all things in it – ontologically as well as representationally – should be regarded as relative and contingent. In this line of thinking three issues have to be kept in mind throughout the discussion of *Vatmaar*, because they determine the publication history as well as the thematic content of this novel:

1. History is almost always written by those in power, and the official history of a country like South Africa not only speaks about historical events but also reflects the attitudes of the different people ruling the country at different times. It is a

generally accepted fact that a change of government brings about a new way of
looking at the events of the past and the present so that each government and its
'official' and loyal historians tell the story of the country according to their own
master narrative or their own set of values.

2. Historiography presents the official and 'canonized' versions of great and
decisive events in a country and does not primarily concern itself with personal or
individual experience. In literature, however, individual versions of history and the
influence of events on the lives of ordinary people can be reflected in numerous
explicit or implicit ways and in varying degrees. Literature often contains, amongst
many other things, the small or little narratives of individuals irrespective of their
social standing and therefore also acts as a specific type of representation of history
and of the attitudes and dispositions of the people of a country.

3. In the third instance, language itself can be seen as a receptacle of historical
events and movements as language absorbs or forms words and concepts and ideas
referring to or representing events and attitudes. The languages of a country can be
seen to act as a radar dish simultaneously receiving and sending out signals in the
way the languages mirror as well as shape the community and its history.

In the case of South Africa it is important to keep these factors in mind, because over
the past three hundred and fifty years the country has been ruled and influenced by a
number of different powers. Political history not only had a profound influence on
the linguistic composition of the country, but the development and content of the
languages also reflect history in various ways.[1]

While the power to govern the territory passed repeatedly from the Dutch to the
English,[2] the interaction among those colonizers who became settlers, the slave
community and the indigenous people gave rise to the development of a new
language. This initially simplified form of Dutch developed into the language called
Afrikaans which is today a fully functional modern language with an extensive
literature, which reflects in its structure and vocabulary remnants of all the peoples

---

[1] P.H. Zietsman, *Die taal is gans die volk* (Pretoria: Unisa, 1992); Christo Van Rensburg et al.,
Afrikaans in Afrika (Pretoria: van Schaik, 1997).

[2] The elections of 1994 were the official and formal beginning of a new political era in South
Africa. But the history of the southern tip of the African continent is a drama in which power was
taken and given, distributed and redistributed by a series of players: ie, the Portuguese, the Dutch
(1652), the English (1795, 1806, 1902), and the Afrikaner nationalists (1948). It can be illustrated
how a series of colonizations and decolonizations have formed the central thread of the history of
the country for the past 350 years. In the twentieth century two distinct decolonizing movements
can be distinguished. Between 1910 and 1948 the Afrikaner people decolonized themselves from
English rule, and the black nations of the country decolonized themselves from Afrikaner rule from
1948 to 1994; see André P. Brink, "Op pad na 2000: Afrikaans in 'n (post-)koloniale situasie,"
Tydskrif vir Letterkonde 19.4 (1991): 1–12.

and all the historical events of the past three hundred and fifty years in South Africa. Words and phrases from Portuguese, Malay, German, French, Koi, San, Zulu, Xhosa, Sotho, Tswana and English were absorbed into the mainly Dutch structure and today form part of everyday Afrikaans.

The history of Afrikaans as a language is therefore intricately interwoven with the colonial history of the country, not only in the formation and development of the language but also because the language was repeatedly and officially undermined by imperialistic linguistic and cultural policies and processes of anglicizing.[3] Ironically, the resistance to imperialistic ideals added force and passion to the forming of a national identity by the speakers of the language. However, the greater irony is that the descendants of the people in interaction with whom the language initially developed were excluded from the nation-forming movement.

The remarkable and rather unique fact remains that a new language evolved in colonial circumstances. It was actually on account of colonial circumstances in South Africa that a language evolved which was and is of European origin, but which was and is influenced to such an extent by the environment and local conditions that the language itself tells the story of the country.[4] Moreover, the language has repeatedly been used as a focal point in political and ideological struggles, of which the revolt against Afrikaans as a medium of education in 1976 by black schoolchildren is well-known.

To understand the uniqueness of the novel *Vatmaar*, one has to take cognisance of the linguistic background. The Afrikaans language is spoken by 5.5 million people as their home language in South Africa and more or less half of the speakers of the language are either brown or black.[5] In large parts of the country, Afrikaans is the lingua franca, as well as the only language used extensively. The town of

---

[3] Important decisions concerning language policies under British rule were made public in 1806 when the Cape colony was annexed by England; in 1814 when Lord Charles Somerset became Governor, and especially in 1822 when by proclamation measures were put into action to make English the only language of the country, a process that would continue right until the end of the nineteenth century (see E.C. Pienaar, *Die triomf van Afrikaans* [Cape Town: Nasionale Pers, 1943]: 21–107) in 1897 and again in 1902 when Lord Milner introduced intensive policies to anglicize all institutions and schools and all the people of the country (Zietsman, *Die taal*: 27–58).

[4] Though the cultural contact in colonial situations has had a strong influence on language development in many countries, giving rise to a number of creole languages, creolites and dialects, Afrikaans is the only language that has developed from Dutch origins. Afrikaans has become a fully functional cultural language used in courts of law, in commerce, in religious practice and as an academic language. It also has an extensive corpus of oral and written literature; see E.H. Raidt, *Afrikaans en sy Europese verlede* (Cape Town: Nasau, 1991): 89–268.

[5] Afrikaans is the third-largest language of the eleven official languages in the country. Though the language is politically associated with Afrikaner people and with the policies of Apartheid, 15.9 million people (according to Van Rensburg) can speak the language in South Africa either as a first or second tongue.

Vatmaar is situated exactly in such a part of the country where Afrikaans is the dominant language.

The most important fact to be kept in mind here is that the Afrikaans-speaking component of the South African community is not a homogeneous group but consist (in racial terms) of white, black and brown people and (in cultural terms) of such divergent groups as the Griquas of the Northern Cape Province, the traditional Afrikaners, people of mixed blood and the Malay people of the Cape (who are the descendants of the slave community and are mostly Muslim). The language also has distinct varieties which are, however, mutually understandable.

The novel *Vatmaar* is intensely concerned with exactly this multifaceted history in a number of ways. The community from which the author comes and about which the story is told, as well as the language in which the book is written, form interfaces between the European heritage and the African context. In this article the personal circumstances of the author and the publication history of the book will be discussed briefly, but the main focus will be on the way in which the story is told and the implications of content and narrative strategy for the thematic value of the text.

The Author of Vatmaar

Scholtz's name reflects the hybrid nature of the South African community. Andrew Henry Martin – these are English names; but the surname Scholtz is quite common among Afrikaners and is of German origin. The first people by the name of Scholtz arrived in South Africa in 1719 from Bielefeld and were initially known as Schultze, though the name soon appeared in the Dutch form as Scholtz. Thus A.H.M. Scholtz carries the name of one of the oldest European families in the country.[6] Scholtz is a brown man, belonging to the group sometimes also called 'coloured,' the group of people that came into being through the contact between Europeans, the various indigenous peoples of Southern Africa and slaves from the east.

The brown communities in South Africa have been marginalized repeatedly in South African history and often say that they still experience themselves as being in-between, not really part of either the black or the white communities. Though most of them are Christians (apart from the very important Malay community in Cape Town) and though they speak Afrikaans, they have never in the past formed part of the Afrikaner community and feel that they have been regarded as socially inferior. These brown communities have a rich heritage of oral songs, rhymes and folktales, and though some prominent Afrikaans poets have incorporated elements from this

---

[6] E.C. De Villiers & C. Pama, *Geslagsregisters van die on Kaapse families* (Amsterdam: Balkema, 1966).

oral tradition in their work, not much of it has been written down, even less by brown writers themselves.

Though there are important brown poets who write in Afrikaans (such as Adam Small, S.V. Petersen and Patrick Petersen), *Vatmaar* was the first novel in Afrikaans by a brown author. Scholtz was 72 years old when the novel was published. He has had little education, and it can be assumed that the novel was written without extensive knowledge of canonical literature in Afrikaans.

What is even more remarkable is that the novel was initially written in English. The little schooling that the author had was in English and therefore, according to him, he did not have the confidence to write in Afrikaans, as he had never had any formal education in the latter language. He decided to use the language he had been taught in an English school, not trusting his ability to use his own mother tongue in writing. The editor to whom the novel was submitted, Dr Anneri van der Merwe of Kwela Books in Cape Town, realized that the novel was essentially Afrikaans, in linguistic structure as well as vocabulary. It seemed as if every word had simply been written down in English while the thought processes behind it were essentially Afrikaans. The language also contained many untranslatable words in Afrikaans. She also realized that the novel possessed a unique appeal.[7]

Eventually the book was reworked in Afrikaans by an experienced writer, Wium van Zyl, in close collaboration with Scholtz and was published in Afrikaans. Three years after publication a third edition appeared, which is an excellent record for any Afrikaans literary work.

This encouraged and inspired Scholtz to such an extent that he has since (within three years) published two more books, one with short stories and another novel. This shows how the author had to free himself from the ideological restrictions of the past which first denied him an education in his mother tongue and then disempowered him culturally, socially and politically.

Theme and Narrative Technique

The immediate appeal of the novel *Vatmaar* comes from the thematic content, where theme can be seen as that aspect of a narrative text which evokes a specific interpretation of the text that is meaningful and relevant to what the reader regards as important in his life.[8] The novel tells the story of the origin of a fictitious town in the north-western parts of South Africa, extending from the beginning of the century to the early 1930s. This town can be seen as a microcosm of the South African community at large because people from different origins have ended up living there: a

---

[7] Anneri van der Merwe, "Die ongewone geboorte van *Vatmaar*," *Insig* (January 1996): 26–27.

[8] M. Brinker, "Theme and Interpretation," in *The Return of Thematic Criticism*, ed. Werner Sollors (Cambridge MA: Harvard UP, 1993): 30.

British soldier who stays behind after the Boer War and marries a Tswana wife, a German woman from German South West Africa (now Namibia), Griqua people, a man from Lesotho, Indian people and others.

The story tells how these people build a community from nothing – they take what is left over by others, they use land which nobody really needs or wants, and out of these scraps (which are there to be taken, "*wat maar gevat kan word*" = *vatmaar*) they start constructing a new life. They develop a system of helping one another to buy a small plot of land, they build a church and later a medical clinic. With the little they have, they help those in need, taking in those who have nowhere to go, who have been rejected either by their families or the establishment. In fact, the evolution of the material, spiritual and psychological components of a community of true fellowship is described.

The fact that an author from a marginalized community should write a novel of substance about the origins of the South African people, as well as the linguistic history of the book, creates a set of circumstances of ideological and political nature which can partially account for the acclaim with which the book was received.[9] The same circumstances are seen by others as a paternalistic and belated attempt at compensation for the wrongs of the past.

To my mind, neither position takes cognizance of the stylistic and rhetorical nature of the text itself, "the distinction between what a discourse is *rhetorically about* and that which it may be taken to be *referentially about* when read metaphorically."[10] Talking about this novel only in ideological and political terms either positively or negatively would be simplistic and devoid of literary insight.

J. Hillis Miller states that while he admires and understands the reasons why literature is read in terms of social, psychological, historical and ethical relevance, literary study should be more than that. Reading should be seen as a negotiation, as a confrontation in which the extrinsic thematic relevance is facilitated exactly by and through the rhetorical structure of the text:

> In any case, *without the rhetorical study of literature*, focused on language, its laws, what it is, and what it can do, particularly on the role of figurative language in interfering with the straightforward working of grammar and logic, as the parasitical virus interferes with the working of the host cell, *we can have no hope of understanding what the role of literature might be* in society, in history, and in individual life.[11]

---

[9] In 1996 Vatmaar received the prestigious M-Net Award as well as the Eugene Marais Prize, which is awarded for a debut by the South African Academy of Arts and Science.

[10] M. Brinker, "Theme and Interpretation," 27.

[11] J. Hillis Miller, "The Function of Literary Theory at the Present Time" (1989), in Miller, *Theory Now and Then* (Durham NC: Duke UP, 1991) (my emphases).

The point is that an analysis of the structure and narrative technique[12] of *Vatmaar* reveals an ethical dimension which substantiates and reinforces the thematic content. The value system inherent in the novel is subtly underpinned by aspects of the narration, and this can be seen as a dominant characteristic of the novel.

Narrators and Focalization

In *Vatmaar* many stories are told. A panorama of village life is created by telling the stories of a great number of the people in the village. The narrator in the novel is a man remembering his youth in the village when he was about 12 years old, so that the basic point of view is that of a child of that age. But the narrator is actually only a master of ceremonies; he introduces a character and then the character tells his own story from his own point of view. There is frequent use of direct and indirect speech as well as free indirect speech, creating an impression of authenticity.

Characters are not described and portrayed only 'from outside,' either by the narrator or through the eyes of other characters. What is said about specific characters is substantiated or contrasted by what they say and tell about themselves because all characters are allowed to tell their own stories. Descriptions of the appearance of characters occur very sparingly. Characters come to life, so to speak, mainly through their own words or through a rendering of their words in indirect or free indirect speech.

I have translated a few phrases to illustrate how characters are used to mediate the action of the novel by telling their own stories. Words and phrases like "said," "told," "he told," "she said to me," which imply that one character is quoting another or retelling stories he / she has heard previously, abound throughout the novel.

> Later she told how she took a kalabas, filled it with water and started walking down the voetpad (pathway). (22)
>
> Oom Flip said that his people lived in Basotholand, a country he left as a piccanin [Then oom (uncle) Flip's story is continued in the first person.] I enjoyed my first trip on a wagon. (41)
>
> You'll be surprised how scared those people were of bayonets, Wonnie, said uncle Norman. (204)[13]

By having the same event described through different characters (38–140; 184–85; 222–24), the author indicates how different people see and experience events and

---

[12] My argument primarily concerns narrative technique and style as it could be argued that the linguistic nature or metaphor could be influenced by the linguistic transcription of the original MS. The novel also does not reflect linguistic varieties such as Griqua-Afrikaans or Cape Afrikaans.

[13] When this essay was first written, the book had not been translated into English (albeit into Dutch and German). An English translation is being published shortly, but for my present purposes I have had to do my own translation of the relevant phrases in the quotations.

situations in different ways. This shows how intensely conscious the narrator (and obviously the author) is of whose point of view is being represented, whose words are used to tell the story and, consequently, whose evaluation of a situation is given. The use of different narrators and different levels of narration as well as the authenticating use of a variety of focalizers becomes the most prominent feature of the novel.

Added to this is the fact that in every narrative situation there is also a listener present. Nobody simply talks to the reader or to himself or to nobody in particular, but every utterance functions in a triangular archetypal narrative situation. Ta Vuurmaak tells his stories to the children (5–10; 20–25), oom Flip talks to the narrator, tant Wonnie speaks to Susan and Bet to Wonnie (107; 41; 222).

A simple but quite touching sequence in the novel tells how oom Flip and his future wife, Bet, come to know each other. They usually meet by a specific tree. When she wants to think, Bet goes to this place and sits on a huge stone under the tree. But when she senses that Flip likes her and would like to talk to her about himself, she wants to listen.

> Bet got up from the stone and said: Sit down Flippus. She sat down across from him and folded her arms over her knees.
> Bana! said oom Flip. You know what? This girl wanted to know everything about me. (49)

At a subsequent meeting Flip realizes that something is bothering Bet, and the roles are reversed.

> This time Sis Bet found oom Flip waiting under the tree. Good day, Bet, he said. He stood up and pointed to the stone. (51)

The plurality of voices and points of view in the novel is remincent of Bakhtin's description of the polyphonic text, in which the narrator gives up his right to have the last word and grants his characters full autonomy and equal status to be and have a voice in "a plurality of independent and unmerged voices and consciousnesses, a genuine polyphony of fully valid voices." Bakhtin's position on this does not simply imply the relative value of all voices and is not only concerned with the mere existence and the non-hierarchical status of the voices. He indicates the importance of the active engagement of all voices and of true interaction: "the dialogue of the polyphonic novel is authentic only insofar as it represents an engagement in which, in various ways, the discourses of self and other interpenetrate each other."[14]

When oom Flip and Bet invite each other to talk with the implicit promise of truly listening, they acknowledge each other's "Otherness" in an essential way, not only affirming the other's "I" as an object but affirming the other person as another subject.

---

[14] Simon Dentith, *Bakhtinian Thought* (London & New York: Routledge, 1995): 42.

Characters are not explained in social-historical terms, but are provoked to "ultimate revelations of themselves in extreme situations" in an ongoing process (43).

In a community in which they are not important, in which they are not even properly noticed, in which their humanity and dignity are not acknowledged, oom Flip and Bet validate each other's existence and worthiness. According to Bakhtin, "single consciousness is a contradictio in adjecto. Consciousness is in essence multiple." The dialogic nature of all human communication is the essential point of departure when Bakhtin says "Two voices are the minimum for life, the minimum for existence" and "All utterances ought to anticipate the word of the other."[15]

There are passages in the novel where the white Afrikaner community is described, but this is done from 'outside': that is, from the position of the people of Vatmaar for whom the Afrikaners are the 'Other.' As a result, a rather negative view of these people is presented. This is understandable in view of the political situation in the country and is a realistic representation of the lack of contact and understanding between the groups in a politically divided society. However, at the same time it highlights the value of the polyphonic approach in the rest of the novel.

Though the people of Vatmaar are depicted with empathy and compassion, the narrator does not shy away from their bad characteristics. These people are neither absolutely good nor completely bad. There is an essential honesty in the novel that keeps it from being over-idealistic and sentimental. In the portrayal of people in their full humanity the falseness of the colonial hierarchies, even in a community such as this, is exposed. The grandchildren of Lance-Corporal Lewis, who becomes oom Lewies in Vatmaar, consider themselves superior to the Tswana and Griqua people even though they have a Tswana grandmother. A fairer complexion is coveted by all and is a common topic among them. In this manner, the novel breathes an air of integrity, of simplicity and unaffectedness. But artlessness should be seen in the right perspective here. Behind the simple surface of the text lies an archetypal sensitivity for human dignity and an appreciation and respect for the variety of lifestyles and perspectives which are present in every human community.

Archetypal Narrative

Specific aspects of the novel such as the emphasis on the narrative itself and the act of narration, as well as the absence of conscious literary devices, alert the reader to the basic archetypal nature of the novel. Thematically, *Vatmaar* is indeed concerned with archetypal human functions.

In his book *The Rituals of Life*, Langdon Elsbree argues that narration is an archetypal activity because human beings make sense of their world and their

---

[15]   Dentith, *Bakhtinian Thought*, 44, 46.

circumstances by making and experiencing narratives: "the making of stories –
acting, telling, writing – and the experience of stories – watching, listening, reading
– are both 'art' and 'life,' are neither more nor less natural than other significant,
distinctively human rituals." Elsbree identifies five archetypal actions which he considers to be the core of the plots of most great works of world literature: 1)
establishing and consecrating a home; 2) engaging in a contest or fighting a battle;
3) taking a journey; 4) enduring suffering; and 5) pursuing consummation.[16]

The novel *Vatmaar* is concerned with precisely such actions and issues. The
events which are extensively related in the novel are indeed those which can be
regarded as archetypal according to Elsbree's description:

1.   The allocation and distribution of the land, the building of houses and especially the consecration of the church – an event which is regarded as the pivotal
point in their history, providing the people of the small new community with a sense
of belonging to the place and the place as belonging to them – fill many pages in the
first part of the book.

2.   There are a number of stories about war-torn people coming to find rest in
Vatmaar, having struggled and fought to escape oppressive circumstances and
becoming engaged in new struggles to fight for their own dignity. But there is also
conflict within the community as such; for instance, Wonnie and her daughters have
a hard time fighting injustice and false accusations.

3.   Journeys undertaken by many inhabitants of the town are described and
related at length. Most of the inhabitants come from other places and many from far
away; some have come of their own accord, others through circumstances or force –
one could almost say that the town comes into being by acting as a container catching up all these drifting, travel-stained people, and accepting them without prejudice.

4.   All the inhabitants have known suffering, either in their past or in their
present.

5.   Love thrives in this community in a number of ways but the lovers have to
overcome many obstacles. A number of people also transcend the handicaps of their
circumstances by realizing their dreams.

Conclusion

Vatmaar is not a sophisticated novel, it is, rather, an archetypal act of narration, in
content and style. It tells the story of the village of Vatmaar, but it also represents a
phase in the history of South Africa. It is in fact concerned with cultural and social
problems and issues which are still unresolved in present-day South Africa. The

---

[16] Langdon Elsbree, *The Rituals of Life: Patterns in Narratives* (Port Washington NY: Kennicat
P, 1982): 3, 15.

inescapable heterogeneity of the country, the fact that the division between good and bad does not run between nations or races or social and cultural groups, but through the heart of every man, the need to acknowledge the dignity and every human being's right to a voice, the struggle to free people from fixed perceptions and stigmas, the emphasis on honesty, respect and love for one another without ignoring human failings and wilful transgressions – these basic human issues form the core of the novel.

The discursive style of the novel, the way in which the 'Otherness' of people is respected, the way in which all people are given a voice, the compassionate way in which people are allowed to show themselves, the honest look at people in their failings as well as their goodness and successes despite social standing – these things make the reading of this apparently simple text a rich and rewarding experience.

Essentially, the novel gives voice to a previously silenced community, and, apart from the polyphonic discourse within it, the novel as such inserts itself dialogically into the silence which has been imposed on the brown people of South Africa for such a long time. An historical perspective formerly unknown and unacknowledged is represented, elements of the historical panorama previously ignored or rejected are put forward to help fill the obvious voids in the national narrative. In this way the novel contributes to the rewriting of the story, the stories and the history of the country. By asserting the right to speak for itself, by stating the dignity of this component of the greater community of South Africa, the negations and silences of the past are challenged. In a dialogic narrative act the novel becomes one of the speaking voices of the country functioning as an opposing and complementary voice to the main discourses of the past, the present and the future.

All in all, the novel *Vatmaar* is a book of insight and wisdom opening up past and present with sincerity and a clear voice.

WORKS CITED

Bakhtin, Mikhail M. "The Hero's Monologic Discourse and Narrational Discourse in Dostoevsky's Short Novels," in Dentith, *Bakhtinian Thought*, 157–94.

——. "Heteroglossia in the Novel," in Dentith, *Bakhtinian Thought*, 195–224.

Brink, André P. "Op pad na 2000: Afrikaans in 'n (post)-koloniale situasie," *Tydskrif vir letterkunde* 29.4 (1991): 1–12.

Brinker, Menachem. "Theme and Interpretation," in *The Return of Thematic Criticism*, ed. Werner Sollors (Cambridge MA: Harvard UP, 1993): 21–37.

Dentith, Simon. *Bakhtinian Thought* (London & New York: Routledge, 1995).

Du Plooy, Heilna. "Die literatuur self is weer voor: *Vatmaar* van A.H.M. Scholtz," *Stilet* 9.2 (1997): 69–80.

De Villiers, C.C., & C. Pama. *Geslagsregisters van die ou Kaapse families* (Amsterdam: Balkema, 1966).

Elsbree, Langdon. *The Rituals of Life: Patterns in Narratives* (Port Washington NY: Kennikat, 1982).

Miller, J. Hillis. "The Function of Literary Theory at the Present Time" (1989), in *Theory Now and Then*, ed. Miller (Durham NC: Duke UP, 1991).

Pienaar, Eduard C. *Die triomf van Afrikaans* (Kaapstad: Nasionale Pers, 1943).

Raidt, Edith H. *Afrikaans en sy Europese verlede* (Kaapstad: Nasou, 1991).

Scholtz. A.H.M. *Vatmaar* (Cape Town: Kwela Boeke, 1995).

Sollors, Werner, ed. *The Return of Thematic Criticism* (Cambridge MA: Harvard UP, 1993).

Van der Merwe, Anneri. "Die ongewone geboorte van *Vatmaar*," *Insig* (January 1996): 26–27.

Van Rensburg, Christo et al. *Afrikaans in Afrika* (Pretoria: J.L. van Schaik, 1997).

Zietsman, Paul H. *Die taal is gans die volk* (Pretoria: Unisa, 1992).

❧

New War Stories
Women, Heroes and Violence in Yvonne Vera's Novels

EVA HUNTER

T HE ZIMBABWEAN WRITER YVONNE VERA, born in 1964, is among those African writers whose work is aimed at new, post-independence communities. She is also outstanding among such writers: Her first published title, *Why Don't You Carve Other Animals* (1993), a collection of short stories, was short-listed for the Commonwealth Writer's Prize (Africa Region) as was her first novel, *Nehanda* (1993); *Without a Name* (1994) was a runner-up in 1995 in the Best Book Category for this prize, which Vera won the following year for *Under the Tongue* (1996). This essay will examine Vera's challenges in her three novels, *Nehanda*, *Without a Name*, and *Under the Tongue*, to the inscription in Zimbabwean nationalist and populist discourses of sexual difference, as it affects conceptions of the hero and as it sanctions or proscribes acts of violence.

During liberation struggles in Africa and into post-independence times, the language and symbolism of nationalist rhetoric have seen the hero as necessarily male and have approved his use of forms of violence as expressions of political activism; femaleness, on the other hand, has been linked in a symbolic way with an abstract principle of liberation, whose expression in active form is accommodated only so long as it falls within conventional bounds of feminine behaviour. Women are linked with the fertile properties of the land and the continent itself, as in the concept "Mother Africa," and they function properly within liberation struggles when they do so as mothers, as nurturers of the true (male) warriors. A phenomenon complementary to women's elevation in relation to their fertility is the outlawing of the use of violence by women, even in the name of freedom. And, when women are on the receiving end of violent acts committed by their own menfolk, they are bound to silence, even (or, perhaps, especially) when those men are extolled as fighting for the liberation of all.

The ideology holds even if the reality of an armed struggle is very different. In Zimbabwe, for instance, during its War of Liberation from 1964 to 1980, many young women participated in the field, most as carriers, cooks and medical staff but some as guerrilla fighters, using weaponry alc ˙side the men.[1] Yet women were excluded from leadership roles in Zimbabwe's liberation movements, and, even when they managed to blur gender boundaries and assume leadership, as one or two Zimbabwean women did, their achievements were subsequently downplayed or ignored when, having triumphed, the movements recorded their histories and built their monuments. The only woman buried in Heroes' Acre in Harare is Robert Mugabe's dead wife. To date, neither these female war-heroes nor the mass of Zimbabwean women have been emancipated from traditional practices that subjugated women.

This is the context for Vera's new stories of Zimbabwe's struggles to free itself from colonial and settler occupation. In her first novel Vera re-writes the legend of a nineteenth-century resistance hero, Nehanda, to insist upon the part she played as a *leader* of the maShona peoples. Her subsequent novels, *Without a Name* and *Under the Tongue*, are set during the twentieth-century War of Liberation, and tell the stories of women who were non-combatants. Inserting into what she calls the "grand narrative of heroism" the previously silenced stories of 'ordinary' women, Vera destabilizes the authorized, public narrative by incorporating an unsanitized underbelly of the war, in which some of the male combatants, brutalized, assault their own women and children, in most cowardly fashion – and some of the women kill their own men and children, in revenge. By refuting both the universal nobility of men-heroes and the universal sainthood of mothers, Vera opposes the dominant male-constructed accounts of the war – for those who have told the stories of Zimbabwe's war of liberation have nearly all been men – to expose instead the ways in which gender has been structured into accounts of war.

Retelling the Past: Nehanda *(1993)*

In *Nehanda*, Vera turned to Zimbabwe's legends of the past to write the life-story of a female hero of the first phase of Zimbabwe's liberation struggle, which took place during 1896–97. Nehanda was one of several resistance leaders during this first rebellion against the British, which was called the First Chimurenga. "Chimurenga" means, figuratively, "flame," literally, it signifies an uprising or rebellion. Nehanda was a spiritual liberator. During visions, the ancestors revealed their wishes to her, and she interpreted their revelations for the maShona, inciting the people to rebel-

---

[1] Tanya Lyons, "Written in the Revolution(s): Zimbabwean Women in the National War of Liberation," Paper presented at conference on "Gender and Colonialism in Southern Africa," University of the Western Cape (13–15 January 1997).

lion. Given the persistent, iconic association of women with the spiritual rather than active aspect of freedom, it is vital to note that Nehanda did act as a *leader*: The British saw her as dangerous enough to hang her. Vera said in an interview that what she wished to emphasize was, precisely, the "actuality" of Nehanda's life, which had "vanished."[2]

> Nehanda was used to justify the struggle of the second phase but what emerged was another narrative that became patriarchal, although it was feminised by the Nehanda figure who epitomised the spiritual struggle. But the struggle had become a grand narrative of heroism.[3]

Vera suggests the 'actuality' of Nehanda's life through scenes such as the child Nehanda dipping water from a river with a gourd and her meetings, as an adult, with the warriors of the First Chimurenga, but much of the force of the narrative is invested in a densely metaphoric style that conveys an exhilarating sense of a life-force that flows through Nehanda, and specifically her voice, to transcend space and time, so ensuring continuity between past, present, and future, for both nineteenth-century auditors and for those who drew on her vision in the second phase of the struggle:

> Nehanda's trembling voice reaches them as though coming from some distant past, some sacred territory in their imaginings [...] but it is also the comforting voice of a woman, of their mothers whom they trust. Her voice throws them into the future, and she speaks as though they have already triumphed [...]. But again she abandons that voice and brings them back into their present sorrow.[4]

Nehanda's voice has continued to influence twentieth-century listeners – "Her death [...] is also birth" – through the vitality of legend:

> Her death, which is also birth, will weigh on those lives remaining to be lived. In the valley, where they have prayed all night for rain, is heard the beginning of a new language and a new speech. (112)

In a recent interview, Vera said that "people [left] to go and fight [in the Second Chimurenga of the late 1970s] with the belief that even if bullets were shot at them they would not die" because of protection afforded by Nehanda.[5]

As in her fiction, so Vera, when interviewed, proclaims the endurance of Nehanda's legend, yet she also says that as the older, spiritualized belief system in which Nehanda's power was rooted has been weakened, the contemporary 'narrative' of liberation has become more masculinist, with a consequent displacement of

---

[2] Eva Hunter, "'Shaping the Truth of the Struggle': An Interview with Yvonne Vera," *Current Writing* 10.1 (April 1998): 78.

[3] Hunter, "'Shaping the Truth of the Struggle'," 79.

[4] Yvonne Vera, *Nehanda* (Harare: Baobab, 1993): 62. Further page references are in the main text.

[5] Hunter, "'Shaping the Truth of the Struggle'," 78.

Nehanda's status as a real political leader, rather than a symbolic entity. The validity of this assertion is attested to, somewhat ironically, by the comments of an appreciative male critic, Eldred D. Jones. Jones praises Vera's literary achievement in *Nehanda*, but he does not, despite Vera's narrating skills, appear able to grasp the "actuality" of Nehanda as a political and cultural hero. For instance, after saying that the novel "is dominated by the life of one woman, Nehanda," he continues, "the novel is really concerned with the spirit of the people" that is linked with "the spirit of the land." He then says little more about the character whose life dominates the novel, but for several paragraphs discusses two male leaders, Ibwe and Mashoko–Moses, who attract his attention.[6] Jones appears not to respond to Nehanda's force as an activist or to Vera's characterization of her as a person of extraordinary gifts.

Vera also said when interviewed that the contemporary downplaying of Nehanda's role as a historical leader and the lesser extent to which women are, in post-independence Zimbabwe, permitted to participate in politics and political leadership, showed that there was "something in the African world, in Zimbabwe, which we had now lost." She added, "I think in Nehanda's time anybody who had been chosen by the ancestors could emerge as a leader."[7] Vera is proposing that custom presented not only problems but also opportunities for women and that women of outstanding character might seize such opportunities to carve distinctive and powerful roles for themselves, a proposition that has been raised in the fiction of other African women. Flora Nwapa's *Efuru* and Buchi Emecheta's *The Rape of Shavi*, for instance, both record such phenomena among the Nigerian Igbo. Importantly, knowledge of the existence of such flexibility in customary practice constitutes an argument for turning to the *African* past, rather than to recent Western wisdom, for a lineage of practices that recognize the worth of women. The value of such an argument lies not only in the fact that indigenous ways may be accounted worthy in relation to 'advanced' modern beliefs about human dignity, in contra-distinction to Africa's supposed inferiority in the sphere of human rights, but also in its usefulness in deflecting the objection (raised usually by male thinkers, who do not voice similar objections to appealing to Western thought when it comes to race and class freedoms) that feminism is yet another imported set of beliefs that asserts the superiority of Western ways.

Vera suggests, in *Nehanda*, how customary practice sanctioned the exercise of unusual influence by a woman: she was viewed as a generic "mother." Once Nehanda's special gifts are recognized, she is freed from the expectation that in order to

---

[6] Eldred Durosimi Jones, "Land, War and Literature in Zimbabwe: A Sampling." *African Literature Today: New Trends and Generations in African Literature: A Review* (Trenton NJ: Africa World Press & London: James Currey, 1996): 50–61.

[7] Hunter, " ' Shaping the Truth of the Struggle'," 78.

attain adult womanhood she should marry and bear children, yet she speaks with the "voice" of "the mothers whom they trust" (47–51; 62). Nwapa and Emecheta, too, suggest a link between the wide scope for women and the flexible nature of the term "mother": a woman need not have given birth to adopt the term and its powers. And in South Africa, too, the writers Ellen Kuzwayo and Miriam Tlali have recorded such flexibility, implying also that it may be crucial, in order for a woman to have her claim to public authority accepted, for her to act and speak precisely through the role of "mother."[8] Among the maShona peoples in the past, even the category 'woman' was not precisely defined, politically, or even along gender lines: For instance, the 'wife' of a king might be a highly respected man, while women close to the king might be given the right to rule over territories, be exempt from bride-price, and exercise a freedom to choose many sexual partners – a privilege normally reserved for powerful and wealthy men. However, as Ane Kirkegaard says, women in influential positions gained their authority due to their relations to important men, and, while women could become spirit-mediums without connections to men, as Vera portrays Nehanda to have done, the most important spirit-mediums were men.[9] Further, Tanya Lyons found, when interviewing women veterans and studying the contrasts between their stories and published (male-authored) representations of their contributions to the Zimbabwean National War of Liberation, although the term 'mother' gained added political and 'military' weight during the war, both during and after the war the term was used to contain women within 'the domestic' and within acceptable (unthreatening) roles, rather than as 'heroic fighters.' As already stated, in the post-independence period these veterans' requests for recognition of the part they played have continued, along with demands for genuine equality with men, have been ignored and suppressed.[10] Zimbabwean women have not, despite

---

[8] On the flexible usage of the term "mother" and the political and social power that women may wield by resorting to this term, see also Dorothy Driver, "M'a-Ngoana O Tsoare Thipa ka Boha-leng – The Child's Mother Grabs the Sharp End of the Knife: 'Women as Writers'," in *Rendering Things Visible: Essays on South African Culture*, ed. Martin Trump (Johannesburg: Ravan, 1990): 225–55, and Eva Hunter, " ' A Mother is Nothing but a Backbone': Women, Tradition and Change in Miriam Tlali's *Footprints in the Quag: Stories and Dialogues from Soweto*," *Current Writing* 5.1 (1993): 60–75, as well as Eva Hunter, " ' What Exactly is Civilisation?': 'Africa,' 'The West' and Gender in Budi Emecheta's *The Rape of Shavi*," *English Studies in Africa* 37.1 (1994): 50. On the contrary aspects of the status of women in Emecheta's *The Rape of Shavi*, see Hunter, " ' What Exactly is Civilisation?'," 53–55.

[9] Ane Kirkegaard; "Gendered History, Gendered Present: Inquiring into the Roots of Some Contemporary Perceptions of Women's Sexuality and Fertility in Zimbabwe," paper presented at conference on Gender and Colonialism, University of the Western Cape (13–15 January 1997).

[10] Tanya Lyons, "Written in the Revolution(s): Zimbabwean Women in the National War of Liberation," paper presented at conference on "Gender and Colonialism in Southern Africa," University of the Western Cape (13–15 January 1997): 5, 15.

decades of long struggles, succeeded in "making their own demands a fundamental part of nationalist and post-independence political agendas."[11]

For her part, Vera, in her next novel, *Without a Name* (1996), opposed the romanticized maternal entity with a figure whose maternity instead involves intense suffering and who even commits infanticide; and she sets this character, Mazvita, on a path to freedom that is independent of ties to fertility, whether her own or that of the land. In doing so, Vera of course manifests through Mazvita a profound mistrust of the belief system she has recreated with profound respect in *Nehanda*. But, Vera's respect for the past is tinged with fear of its pull. She says that writing *Nehanda* was a matter of "re-inventing the history for my current purpose and place," or writing "a contemporary novel which follows our own tradition of legend-making"; but she goes on to say that the cyclic, supernaturally-controlled world view of the past is nowadays a cause of "enormous and fearsome problems" for the maShona.[12]

Discovering Something New: Without a Name *(1994)*

In her next two novels, *Without a Name* and *Under the Tongue* (1996), Vera focuses on the question that, she says, no one has yet asked, "What is happening to the women while we are creating these heroes?"[13] What has been happening to women, according to her novels, is the hardship endured by real as opposed to idealized mothers, women's physical abuse and abandonment by their menfolk, an intensification of their conflicted relationship to the land, their alienation from their bodies and their own fertility, their enforced silencing, and their disillusionment with the family as 'natural' site of the nation's core. What has also been happening is women's discovery of new ways of relating to the land and their fertility, and new ways of liberating themselves. Vera herself, in writing about what she does in the way she does, opens new doors for women: She defies certain strict social codes, most importantly the ban on speaking up about the violence inflicted upon women and children by their own menfolk. Even more provocatively, Vera creates female characters who themselves use violence. And their victims are not white settlers but

---

[11] T. Scarneccia, "Poor Women and Nationalist Politics: Alliances and Fissures in the Formation of a Nationalist Political Movement in Salisbury, Rhodesia, 1950–56," *Journal of African History* 37.2 (1996): 283.

[12] Hunter, " ' Shaping the Truth of the Struggle'," 79, 81. In fact, the narrator of *Nehanda* at times signals less than total fidelity to the "mythical consciousness" the author depicts; Hunter, " ' Shaping the Truth of the Struggle'," 79. In a sentence like "Nehanda's trembling voice reaches them *as though* coming from some distant past, some sacred territory *in their imaginings*. She speaks *as though* they have already triumphed, *as though* they only looked back at their present sorrow" (62, my emphasis), the narrative voice is, as it mediates between legendary world and the reader, at times subtly infused with a critical stance.

[13] Hunter, " ' Shaping the Truth of the Struggle'," 80.

those who deserve their utmost loyalty and protection – in *Without a Name* Mazvita kills her newborn baby; in *Under the Tongue* Runyararo kills her husband – but both women kill as a consequence of male abuse. I will argue that Vera is not glorifying women's use of violence as a means, failing all others, of freeing themselves, although she is allying these women's acts of murder with protests against the physical and emotional abuse of women, and against their continued denial to human rights in the post-independence period.

Without a Name begins with Mazvita waiting for a bus that will take her to her home village and away from the capital, Harare. Mazvita was, we learn, some while back traumatized by an attack on her village by freedom fighters, during which her family were killed and she was raped, but she is, above all, as she waits for her bus, overwhelmed by guilt and remorse: She has strangled her baby. Mazvita's journey home, to the place where her kinsfolk were murdered and she was raped, is a journey to recover memory, for she has rejected her identity, even her name, in order to obliterate her past; it is also a journey of atonement for her own dreadful crime. She now carries on her back her baby's corpse, as a mark of her contrition.

The assault upon Mazvita left her with a sense of dislocation in relation to her body, as is evident in her murdering her baby, but as is also manifest in her relation with the land, and the novel devotes much attention to various and shifting attitudes to the land. The land is a central value in nationalist conceptions of identity, while the Second Chimurenga, the period in which the novel is set, was a struggle for the land. Mazvita's rape by a freedom fighter has left her hating what her attacker was fighting for:

> Mazvita [...] had not seen the man's face [...]. Hate required a face against which it could be flung but searching for the face was futile. Instead, she transferred the hate to the moment itself, to the morning, to the land, to the dew-covered grass that she had felt graze tenderly against her naked elbow in that horrible moment of his approach [...] it was as if she had lost the world [...] mostly, she hated the land that pressed beneath her back as the man moved impatiently above her.[14]

Mazvita believes that not only she herself but all Zimbabweans have been 'betrayed' by the land and the ancestors. In a Zimbabwe ravaged by prolonged colonial occupation, she cannot sustain the kind of faith in spiritual ties with the land that is held by Nyenyedzi, the kind man who is her lover for a time. It is he who is the father of her baby, and he tries to persuade her to marry him and work with him on the tobacco farm where he is employed. Mazvita rejects him, saying,

---

[14] Vera, *Without a Name* (1994; Harare: Baobab, 1996): 30. Further page references are in the main text.

> We live in fear because even those who fight in our name threaten our lives. The land has forgotten us. The strangers plant tobacco where once we buried the dead. The dead remain silent. The land has not rejected [the strangers]. (32)

"The dead remain silent." The ancestors no longer communicate with their descendants. However, while the land may no longer hold for Mazvita the sacredness it does for Nyenyedzi, she had developed an exhilarating conception of her own, one that is crushed by the dislocatedness from the land brought on by her rape:

> [Mazvita] had loved the land, saw it through passionate and intense moments of freedom, but to her the land had no fixed loyalties. She gathered from it her freedom which it delivered to her wholly and specially. Mazvita was ambitious. She wanted to discover something new in her world. (34)

Unlike the traditional belief of her people in continuity as all-important, Mazvita's faith is in discontinuities; she has "no fear of departures" (34). Mazvita resists the fixedness of women's destiny on the land; she is, in fact, a quester, in search of adventure and fulfilment. When she fled from her razed village to Harare, it was to find "freedom." Instead, alone, and confused by the bustle of the capital, she took refuge with a man, Joel, with whom she lived in an arrangement close to prostitution, until he kicked her out when she gave birth to a child he knew was not his. Yet, during her time in Harare, Mazvita tried to find a "Harari" [sic] of her own, rather than Joel's cynical version of the city. She also tried to find work that paid but did not humiliate. And, she has courage and determination enough to take responsibility for her guilt when she ties her baby to her back. Mazvita is a contemporary, flawed hero, grounded firmly in *material* conditions such as abuse, poverty, lack of paid work, unequal privileges between men and women. The obstacles that deflect her from her quest – an unwanted pregnancy, the temptation to accept a 'good' man in marriage, and another man's desertion – are obstacles encountered by women the world over. The fact that pregnancy and marriage are presented *as* obstacles, instead of fitting goals for a proper woman, and the fact that Vera has Mazvita reject a man who both venerates the land and is fertile, signal Vera's challenge to orthodox notions that attribute to heterosexual maternity and marriage "special status and power." Vera refuses to "reduplicate the unchallenged role of the family as the central component of legitimate national identity,"[15] and to locate the most advantageous for the family on the land. The end of the narrative has Mazvita re-connect with the landscape of her past, but not as a final goal in itself. She completes her journey of atonement, and will, perhaps, begin again, alone, lonely, but on her own terms.

---

[15] Rachel Holmes, "All Too Familiar: Gender, Violence, and National Politics in the Fall of Winnie Mandela," in *No Angels: Women who Commit Violence*, ed. Alice Myers & Savak Wright (London: Pandora, 1996): 99.

Vera might be warning that women who wish to break the mould may endure intense suffering, that they may even in desperation commit acts they abhor, but she is also warning against seeking one's destiny on the land and within the heterosexual family. In any culture, however, a writer risks losing her readers' sympathy for a fictional mother who commits infanticide. The idealization of mothers and mother-hood has been widespread – as in the western peace movements and, more recently, in the theories of "difference" feminism – in nationalist and popular discourses on the African continent.[16] In the African discourses the continent may become Mother Africa or Mama Afrika, and women who are prominent in politics or culture may be known as the Mother of the Nation, as was Winnie Mandela, or Mama Afrika, as was Miriam Makeba. Rachel Holmes says, when writing of Winnie Madikizela–Mandela's political disgrace, that a factor complementary to women being sym-bolically linked, as "icons of national liberation," with "nurturing roles such as motherhood and the life-giving properties" of the land itself, is that whilst "the use of forms of violence is naturalized within the dynamics of masculine political activism, the language and symbolism of sexual difference make women's relation-ship to violence more visible and culturally problematic."[17]

Vera's story of Mazvita potentially destabilizes the idealization of mothers and the automatic condemnation of their violent acts. Vera invites sympathy for Mazvita by focalizing the entire novel through her (the narrator in *Nehanda* is, by contrast, more remote from the protagonist and her legendary world), by repeating phrases that underscore the fact that Mazvita suffers appallingly, and, by rooting Mazvita's infanticide largely in the trauma caused by her abuse by men. Mazvita's alienation from her body, herself, and from others following her rape, is reinforced by the dislocatedness she experiences in Harare, with its harsh, unfamiliar mores. Her sole human contact in Harare is Joel, and it is when he deserts her that she murders her baby. Mazvita has been driven beyond the limits of endurance in a chaotic, brutal socio-economic environment that is especially pitiless in its treatment of women. One may compare Toni Morrison's solicitations on behalf of Sethe, in *Beloved*.

The Silences of the Present: Under the Tongue *(1996)*

In her third novel, *Under the Tongue*, Vera continues to show what has been happen-ing to the women while the heroes and their tales of heroism have been created; she continues to speak up and create new war stories that radically attack the claims of the dominant accounts, whether historical or literary, of the struggle for Zimbabwean

---

[16] Katha Pollitt, "Marooned on Gilligan's Island: Are Women Morally Superior to Men?" in *Reasonable Creatures: Essays on Women and Feminism*, ed. Pollitt (New York: Vintage, 1995): 43–44.

[17] Holmes, "All Too Familiar," 97–98.

independence; and she again has a female character commit murder, again in reaction to male abuse. If in *Without a Name* a freedom fighter rapes one of his own womenfolk, in *Under the Tongue* a would-be struggle hero rapes his own young daughter Zhizha. Muroyiwa's incest is a perversion of his frustrated desire to be as much of a war hero as his brother. The truth about some of the heroes of the war is their brutalization and their cowardly abuse of their superior physical strength.

Most of the narrative in *Under the Tongue* is recounted in Zhizha's voice and traces her consciousness. It is a consciousness intended to reflect the pathology that follows both the abuse of women and children and their enforced silencing, and Zhizha's language is suffused with imagery suggesting pain, confusion, stasis, frustration, unnaturalness. Zhizha's mother, Runyararo, also defines her husband's act as unnatural – "He has stolen the light of the moon and its promises of birth."[18] As in her previous novels, Vera amasses behind her protests on behalf of women the phenomena of the geographical universe. Zhizha, reflecting upon her silencing through shame and fear, says: "I know a stone is buried in my mouth [now], carried under my tongue," and "before I learnt to forget there was a river in my mouth" (1). When her grandmother's loving care begins to take effect, she imagines herself once more part of a universe whose features, no matter how vast or remote, are beneficent:

> I am swallowed by the shadow which grows from Grandmother and bends deep into the earth, lifting me from the ground, raising me high. It is warm inside the shadow. It is warm like sleep. I meet the sky in that warm place and the sky is inside Grandmother and it is filled with voiceless stars. (41)

The prevalence of these metaphors from nature may be seen as establishing a context in which Runyararo's killing of her husband follows a course of natural justice, and the narrative suggests, too, that this form of justice is the more desirable since the three women, grandmother, mother, and daughter, know they cannot appeal to human justice. Zhizha's grandmother repeatedly links her granddaughter's and daughter's suffering to that of other women, telling Zhizha "of the many wounds women endure" (2) and that "a woman must swallow [many words] before she can learn to speak her sorrow and be heard" (32). Runyararo, pouring out her grief and rage to her mother, says, "'Did he not teach me silence, this husband, that a woman is not a man?'" (31). Meanwhile, her father refuses to hear of his son-in-law's crime, insisting instead on his daughter's guilt. Allying himself with his son-in-law, he underpins the patriarchal forces of silencing and enforced forgetting that, within families, collude at the abuse of women and girls.

---

[18] Vera, *Under the Tongue* (Harare: Baobab, 1996). Further page references are in the main text.

All three of Vera's novels are distinguished by clusters of metaphors that, on the one hand, connote movement, vitality, and speaking, and on the other, hardness, stasis, and voicelessness. To speak is to live, to follow the lines of a natural life-force. Nehanda's power to move the people lies, precisely, in the exercise of her voice. But if the ancestors are disobeyed (*Nehanda*), or if a crime, such as rape or infanticide (*Without a Name*) or incest (*Under the Tongue*), is committed, what ensues for those affected is a spiritual and emotional death that is represented by images of stone or rock, and of silence.[19] A story-teller herself, Vera focusses in her novels on the dynamism of the voice, the word, and of storytelling, and on the stultification that follows enforced silencing, in particular as these contrary forces affect women. Women must be allowed to speak, of the violence done to them, and by them.

Conclusion

The social scientist Ane Kirkegaard argues in support of the perceptions of Vera and other sub-Saharan women writers that women have, since the colonial period, had their influence and flexibility for negotiating power diminished. While women were previously viewed as "political [and] economic actors," they have, during colonial times, and under pressure of what Kirkegaard terms "colonial re-constructions facilitated by a collusion of [the] interests of the colonial authorities and settlers and maShona male elders," been increasingly perceived as, properly, "domesticated, sexualised and passive," and, most important, such perceptions are today identified as "African" and "cultural."[20] Under colonial rule, the migrant labour system tied women to the land or to domestic work, and so to an economic position more poverty-stricken than their menfolk. Policies aimed at maximizing profit for European farming and mining promoted tighter male control of women, economically and socially (15). Meanwhile, European religious and political systems did not re-cognize authority in the ways used by women among the pre-colonial maShona peoples; as a result, women's political, economic, and religious influence was under-mined, and the liberation struggle of the 1970s did not, despite women's partici-pation in support and combatant roles, improve either the perceived nor actual status

---

[19] But rock and solidity are in *Nehanda* also linked to the written word of the conquering British, as opposed to the oral storytelling of the maShona, which synchronizes with the life force that flows through natural phenomena. Vera herself, though, uses the written medium. She draws upon the legacy of the maShona oral tradition, as in her frequent use of imagery, much of which refers to the natural worlds, and in her use of repetitive, incantatory phrases, rather than linear, progressive sentences and plot. But, since she is attempting to develop effective forms for the con-ditions and needs of the present, she uses the printed form and writes in English, not the vernacular.

[20] Kirkegaard, "Gendered History, Gendered Present," 1. Further page references are in the main text.

of women as much as might have been expected. Women have remained symbolically linked with the nurturing properties of the land and of their own bodies,
guardians of 'culture' rather than agents of change.

This is the context for Vera's assault upon narratives of exclusively male heroism, an assault she allies to a nineteenth-century liberation hero's power to lead
and the 'actuality' of her life as a woman, and to contemporary women's right to
speak about what is done to and by them. Mazvita and Runyararo are neither
leaders in a struggle nor combatants: Their stories reveal a more masculinist
society, and women's ways of reacting to current brutalities. Both express their
despair and rage through murder, and Vera uses these murders not only as a form
of protest against the (silenced) fact of male abuse of women and children, she also
uses them as a warning that women are not merely passive dwarfs, bounded by the
ties of fertility. They have agency; they even, at times, exact revenge, in the face of
patriarchal injustice.

What Vera's Mazvita and Runyararo tell us is that the way in which women act
as mothers is not delimited by universal features but by their material conditions, by
their economic and social circumstances, by the actual power differences between
women and men. Women may, and they do, kill their own children and kill in order
to protect their children. Adopting a humanist perspective, we might claim that Vera
wishes readers to see that maShona women may, when driven beyond what is
tolerable, like their menfolk, and like women elsewhere in the world, commit
murder – and what would then be at issue is women's humanity, their 'realness' in
the 'real' world of experience by contrast with their symbolic veneration as mothers
in nationalist and popular discourses. Being human, women are entitled to full
accommodation of their economic and political rights within society.

WORKS CITED

Driver, Dorothy. "M'a-Ngoana O Tsoare Thipa ka Bohaleng – The Child's Mother Grabs the
    Sharp End of the Knife: Women as Mothers, Women as Writers," in *Rendering Things Visible:
    Essays on South African Culture*, ed. Martin Trump (Johannesburg: Ravan, 1990): 225–55.

Holmes, Rachel. "All too Familiar: Gender, Violence, and National Politics in the Fall of Winnie
    Mandela." in *No Angels: Women who Commit Violence*, ed. Alice Myers & Sarah Wight (Lon-
    don: Pandora, 1996).

Hunter, Eva. "'A Mother is Nothing but a Backbone': Women, Tradition, and Change in Miriam
    Tlali's *Footprints in the Quag: Stories and Dialogues from Soweto*," *Current Writing* 5.1
    (1993): 60–75.

——. "'Shaping the Truth of the Struggle': An Interview with Yvonne Vera," *Current Writing*
    10.1 (April 1998): 75–86.

———. "' What exactly is civilisation?': 'Africa,' 'The West' and Gender in Buchi Emecheta's *The Rape of Shavi*," *English Studies in Africa* 37.1 (1994): 47–61.

Jones, Eldred Durosimi. "Land, War & Literature in Zimbabwe: A Sampling," *African Literature Today: New Trends and Generations in African Literature: A Review* (Trenton NJ: Africa World Press; London: James Currey, 1996) : 50–61.

Kirkegaard, Ane. "Gendered History, Gendered Present: Inquiring into the Roots of Some Contemporary Perceptions of Women's Sexuality and Fertility in Zimbabwe," paper presented at conference on "Gender and Colonialism in Southern Africa," University of the Western Cape (13–15 January 1997).

Lyons, Tanya. "Written in the Revolution(s): Zimbabwean Women in the National War of Liberation," Paper presented at conference on "Gender and Colonialism in Southern Africa," University of the Western Cape (13–15 January 1997).

Pollitt, Katha. "Marooned on Gilligan's Island: Are Women Morally Superior to Men?" in *Reasonable Creatures: Essays on Women and Feminism*, ed. Katha Pollitt (New York: Random House / Vintage, 1995): 42–61.

Scarnecchia, T. "Poor Women and Nationalist Politics: Alliances and Fissures in the Formation of a Nationalist Political Movement in Salisbury, Rhodesia, 1950–56," *Journal of African History* 37.2 (1996): 283–310.

Vera, Yvonne. *Nehanda* (Harare: Baobab, 1993).

———. *Under the Tongue* (Harare: Baobab, 1996).

———. *Without a Name* (1994; Harare: Baobab, 1996).

❧

Tsitsi Dangarembga's Ambiguous Adventure
Nervous Conditions and
the Blandishments of Mission Education

JOHN C. HAWLEY

T HE TITLE OF THIS ESSAY alludes to Cheikh Hamidou Kane's important portrayal of the deracination attendant upon those who find themselves hybridized by the educational process in their country and, eventually, in the country of the colonizer. In Kane's novel, the protagonist, Samba, first endures the rigorous corporal punishment of qur'anic schooling in Senegal, and is then sent by his reluctant father and the enthusiastic "Royal Lady" to France. The idea is to use him as a mole, as someone who will acquaint himself with the methods and secrets of the enemy, and then return unscathed to his homeland and turn powerfully against the oppressor the very knowledge that has been used to enslave Senegal. Things don't work out quite as planned, and Samba returns home a very confused young man – neither French nor the Islamic hero that his village had hoped he would become. In fact, he is recognized by "The Fool," who had also at one time visited France and totally rejected the colonizer's culture in favour of a fundamental embrace of Islam, as the worst sort of enemy, and therefore deserving of the murder that is meted out at novel's end. Kane's novel stands as the model for the diverse portrayals of these hapless encounters, ranging from Richard Rodriguez's *Hunger of Memory* through Camara Laye's *The Dark Child* to Tayeb Salih's *Season of Migration to the North* – with varying degrees of violence in response to the "adventure," but also with varying degrees of discomfort in acknowledging the appeal of the culture that had savaged one's own land and self.

The ambiguity of the response is well expressed by Emmanuel Chukwudi Eze. In summarizing his recent essays on postcolonial African philosophy, he describes the typical condition of what others have called the "transnational intellectual,"[1] and also of those who may not yet have had a direct encounter with the colonizer's home base: "In depression and always on the verge of the tragic," he writes, "our engagement with the West becomes susceptible, and in fact readily transposes itself, to the realm of the radically mythical: The West is against us, yet the West is our savior. In this role the West becomes not just the (objective) West, but the Absolute West – which repels and fascinates us at once [...] The way we live our (post)colonial contradictions is to transpose, project, and elevate our schematizations of the West to the level of the mythical and the fantasmagoric."[2] Eze suggests a level of distortion inevitable in the conceptualization of the West by Africans – that is, a kind of occidentalism.

Dangarembga's *Nervous Conditions* is one of the first and certainly most eloquent embodiments (quite literally, as we shall see) of this predicament written from a woman's point of view. This, of course, complicates the critique of the West by incorporating a strong (and possibly prior) critique of patriarchy. Dangarembga's novel, set in Rhodesia of the 1960s and 1970s, tells the story of the relationship between the narrator, Tambudzai, and her cousin Nyasha. When her brother, Nhamo, dies, Tambu(dzai) is allowed to attend the school run by Nyasha's father, Babamukuru. This schoolmaster's wife, Maiguru, has been well-educated, and she comes to embody the frustration inherent in the situation for women, regardless of their schooling. Nyasha rejects her mother's apparent acceptance of her plight, and chooses a self-destructive rebellion that devastates her body. But in the caveat that Tambu reads in Nyasha's bodily (spiritual, cultural and egoistic) evacuation, Dangarembga shows the growth in consciousness that amounts to an entrance into ambiguity. Thus, as Deepika Bahri writes of Nyasha: "Attracted and repelled in almost equal measure by colonial educational and cultural systems, Nyasha reacts in a forseeably conflicted manner to the variety of concerns weighing on her mind: She becomes obsessed with passing the exams which will test her on the colonizer's version of knowledge even while she is aware that this education is a 'gift' of her father's status, and the 'knowledge' itself is questionable."[3] The approach/avoidance conflict that Nyasha typifies carries with it the danger of pathology, as Dangarembga makes painfully clear in her anorexia (*nervosa*), an emaciation of the indivi-

---

[1] Biman Basu, "Trapped and Troping: Allegories of the Transnational Intellectual in Tsitsi Dangarembga's *Nervous Conditions*," *ARIEL: A Review of International English Literature* 28.3 (1997): 7–24.

[2] Emmanuel Chukwudi Eze, "Toward a Critical Theory of Postcolonial African Identities," in *Postcolonial African Philosophy*, ed. Eze (Oxford: Blackwell, 1997): 343.

[3] Deepika Bahri, "Disembodying the Corpus: Postcolonial Pathology in Tsitsi Dangarembga's Nervous Conditions," *Postmodern Culture: An Electronic Journal of Interdisciplinary Criticism* 5.1 (1994): 22.

dual that serves to transform the book's title into a pun on the novel's epigraph from Fanon's *The Wretched of the Earth*: "The condition of native is a nervous condition."[4] The condition of "female" native, Dangarembga seems to imply, has additional burdens. The pain of the "hybridity" that Nyasha warns Tambu against manifests the barren state that often results from such experimentation. In Eze's analysis of the broader pathology, when "the zone of the social imaginary is 'distorted' or 'diseased' and 'inflamed,' our actions and 'knowledge' become *systematically* distorted as well. Are we surprised, therefore, that our will to freedom is riddled with inconsistencies that have rendered us an enigma – even to ourselves?"[5] It is the enigmatic nature of that "freedom" that dominates Dangarembga's imagination, and that of so many writers who are grappling with transculturation.

There remains a good bit of controversy over the avenues of liberatory action available to the characters in this novel. Deepika Bahri gives one of the strongest readings of the book from a feminist point of view, attempting to apply both Frantz Fanon and Naomi Wolf's logic to the self-defeating "protest" that Nyasha carries out with a vengeance against her father's imposed British cultural invasion. From Fanon she notes that the pathological consequences of colonization manifest themselves in colonized peoples by prompting internal violence, and that these forces "take shape in Nyasha in the need to target herself as the site on which to launch a terrorist attack upon the produced self."[6] Since there is no other object that can be controlled so directly as her own body, Nyasha attacks it as metonymic of the colonial product. Fair enough, but one takes a step too far in implying, as Wolf seems to do, that such self-destruction is, ultimately, to be valorized: "Eating diseases are often interpreted as symptomatic of a neurotic need for control. But surely it is a sign of mental health to try to control something that is trying to control you."[7] The error in logic here implies that Nyasha's body is, in literal fact, a cultural product from which some inner self cannot escape except through mutilation. Bahri does a fine job of isolating those sections of the novel that describe the physical change in body and in clothing that Nyasha has taken on before returning from England. But Dangarembga, for all the attention that is directed to Nyasha in the novel, nonetheless makes this Tambu's story – implying that a change in consciousness (as has certainly happened to Nyasha and is beginning to happen to Tambu at book's end) is the preferred route of escape, and that this consciousness need not imply a hopeless embrace of suicidal

---

[4] Frantz Fanon, *The Wretched of the Earth*, tr. Constance Farrington (New York: Grove, 1963).

[5] Eze, "Toward a Critical Theory of Postcolonial African Identities," 343–44.

[6] Tsitsi Dangarembga, *Nervous Conditions* (Seattle: Seal, 1988): 1. Further page references are in the main text.

[7] Naomi Wolf, *The Beauty Myth: How Images of Beauty are Used Against Women* (New York: Doubleday / Anchor, 1991): 198.

activity. When asked whether she identified more strongly with Tambu or Nyasha, Dangarembga remarked that she would identify with both of them, and that during her own education at Cambridge, before returning to Zimbabwe, her own conscientization had been ongoing.[8] Unlike Nyasha, however, she wrote this novel – an angry and complex protest, but one that has moved beyond the confines of her body.

Deepika Bahri does not seem particularly hopeful regarding Tambu's future, though. "We can assume," she writes, "from her aunt Maiguru's trajectory and her own pursuit of it that she will continue to be schooled in the ways of a societal economy that will use her labour to support and enable the colonial and patriarchal order which will deny her, as it has Maiguru, the fruits of that labor."[9] But others foresee a future that is, at least, not self-destructive.[10] Gilian Gorle points out that Tambu has certain advantages which, somewhat ironically, empower her and help build a bridge between cultures that eluded Nyasha. "The self-mocking humour," she writes, "with which her adult narrative voice portrays her childhood world does imply such an empowerment through language."[11] Nyasha, on the other hand, had not been sufficiently grounded in Zimbabwean culture before travelling overseas, and upon her return (and suffering under an exceptionally anglophile father) she was, in effect, entering a foreign country.[12] While Nyasha has certainly gained the critical apparatus that she aims with precision at the colonizer, she has also picked up English social expectations that disrupt her acceptance of patriarchal social norms within Zimbabwe. Her protest, after all, is not simply against colonialism, but against the cramped possibilities she has as a young woman. She does not wish to accommodate to those expectations, as her mother has had to do. Gorle argues that the adult Tambu, serving in some sense as Nyasha's amanuensis, "demonstrates a victory in this struggle over the word, for she has appropriated the language of colonial domination and deftly used it to expose the workings of that domination on many levels"; in this regard, it is not only a 'postcolonial' triumph, but also a specifically feminist one, since "in the patriarchal setting of this novel, men may be disempowered by English schooling, while woman may stand to gain substantially

---

[8] Flora Veit–Wild, "'Women Write About the Things that Move Them': A Conversation with Tsitsi Dangarembga," in *Moving Beyond Boundaries*, vol. 2, ed. Carole Boyce Davies (New York: New York UP, 1994): 27, 29.

[9] Dangarembga, *Nervous Conditions*, para. 11.

[10] See, for example, Miki Flockemann, "'Not-Quite Insiders and Not-Quite Outsiders': The 'Process of Womanhood' in *Beka Lamb, Nervous Conditions*, and *Daughters of the Twilight*," *Journal of Commonwealth Literature* 27.1 (1992): 37–47.

[11] Gilian Gorle, "Fighting the Good Fight: What Tsitsi Dangarembga's *Nervous Conditions* Says About Language and Power," *Yearbook of English Studies*, ed. Andrew Gurr (Leeds: Mancy, 1997): 186.

[12] Sue Thomas, "Killing the Hysteric in the Colonised's House: Tsitsi Dangarembga's Nervous Conditions," *Journal of Commonwealth Literature* 27.1 (1992): 26–36.

more."[13] But this distinction, one may safely suggest, is one of degree. After all, Babamukuru is pretty safely ensconced; Nhamo, as the young male scholar, is freed from chores; and Maiguru's scholastic talents are wasting on the vine. What Tambu will surely gain, and this is something she demonstrates in the very production of her tale, are the tools of analysis, an informed agenda, and a healthily hybridized view of both cultures.

But this conclusion only serves to emphasize the ambiguity of the "condition." As Biman Basu notes, "postcolonial intellectuals inhabit the 'structures of violence' which define their situatedness and serve as the site of production for this discourse. They inhabit a Western intellectual structure, all the while questioning and ejecting the very structure they inhabit."[14] True enough, as far as it goes. But, as books like *Nervous Conditions* demonstrate, this is only half the story. The other side of the ambiguity is the "situatedness" within their original cultures, encumbered by all the baggage of social expectations that may well have become (internal or external) targets for criticism in a language and in tools supplied by the colonizer. Branding such cultural critique as (simply) neocolonialism can be perfectly appropriate, but it can also be a manifestation of the occidentalism that Eze criticizes.

Nonetheless, in the broader view the personal growth in consciousness and in the ability to apply a critique to a hegemonic culture should not obscure the power of that culture to eviscerate such criticism and to accommodate the critic within the system. This brings us back to Nyasha (and, to a lesser extent Tambu), and to the insistence of Deepika Bahri and others that the body is the site of colonization (and, perhaps, of protest). Biman Basu, for example, notes that

> the exercise of disciplinary power must be apprehended not at the level of the subject endowed with consciousness but in the space of the banal. Disciplinary mechanisms are not aimed at the transformation of consciousness, and discipline is not internalised at the level of consciousness. These mechanisms are aimed at bodies, and discipline is, we might say, epidermalised. In the process, bodies are trained, bodily functions regulated, gestures are acquired, postures cultivated, styles are adopted, and attitudes assumed.[15]

All these "epidermal" manipulations are portrayed in *Nervous Conditions*, apparent not only in the two female protagonists, but in such neocolonial representatives as Babamukuru – who shares the bodily stresses, though in lesser degree, that manifest themselves later in his daughter.[16]

---

[13] Gorle, "Fighting the Good Fight," 192.

[14] Basu, "Trapped and Troping," 7.

[15] Basu, "Trapped and Troping," 11.

[16] See Thomas, "Killing the Hysteric in the Colonised's House," 30.

Basu argues strongly that the hope that seems to be offered at the end of the novel is ephemeral and even self-deceptive, a move, it is implied, that may be typical of transnational intellectuals who wish to criticize the colonial system of education while continuing to enjoy the (relative) freedom (principally economic) that it has provided. Thus, while pointing out that the novel "ostensibly is about Western education, Christian education specifically," and that this education is explicitly associated with emancipation and progress, "the language by which it is articulated unmistakably invokes the grand narratives of emancipation and enlightenment."[17] On these terms, Tambu's story, while incorporating Nyasha's criticisms, nonetheless is a record of the narrator's cooptation by a hegemonic neocolonialism. Basu notes the movement from homestead, to mission, to Convent, as the process by which an individual is offered just enough incentive that she will willingly take the next step into deracination – until, "thoroughly enmeshed in the lines of force that traverse the terrain and the body of the intermediate space [ie, the mission], Tambu turns docile [...] As figure of the transnational intellectual in the making, she yields to the seduction of power and seeks desperately to assert a vestigial agency in masochistic complicity,"[18] This is an argument with a certain appeal, but why would such a complicit narrator include Nyasha's strong denunciation of the colonial notion of "progress"; why would she recognize that the Convent was not necessarily where her sun would rise; and why would "she" go on to publish such a book? Just how "masochistic" is one's pragmatic manipulation of the forces that, of course, also manipulate in turn? There is in many such situations an understandable glorification of the trickster, and they are seldom looked down upon as victims.

There can be no denying, in any case, that Basu's "intermediate" space, that of the mission school, is reasonably described as one of "seduction."[19] Certainly, in *Nervous Conditions*, we see such a process at work in Nhamo, in Tambu, and in Chido. Tambu is especially calculating, however, in her 'surrender' to this seduction, openly embracing the new faith required to become a favourite of the nuns. Tambu writes a self-cautionary tale, constantly reading her possible future in the decline of Nyasha. She had seen it first in her brother, who went to the mission school and soon "forgot" how to speak Shona. But in Nyasha she asked herself "if Nyasha who had everything could not make it, where could I expect to go?" (202) – Nyasha, who had gone to England and returned a confused person. "We shouldn't have gone," Nyasha once told her. "The parents ought to have packed us off home. They should have, you know. Lots of people did that. Maybe that would have been best. For them at least, because now they're stuck with hybrids for children [...] And I don't know

---

[17] Basu, "Trapped and Troping," 14.

[18] Basu, "Trapped and Troping," 17.

[19] Basu, "Trapped and Troping," 18.

what to do about it, Tambu, really I don't. I can't help having been there and grown into the me that has been there" (78). It is somewhat hard to square the inclusion in the narrative of such anguished confessions if we are then to see Tambu as simply coopted by the same process at the end – unless, of course, Dangarembga herself (having gone through the same process and, uniquely, having emerged unbesmirched) is attempting to underscore the power and cunning of the process.

Nyasha ultimately decides it is "the Englishness" that is alienating her and making her bulimic. But in the course of the telling Tambu dissects this cultural clash more specifically, and seems to attribute it more directly to the mission education Nyasha, and now she herself, is receiving. Babamukuru, Nyasha's father who is the Academic Director of the Church's Manicaland region, comes across like a good many other such figures in African fiction – like Wole Soyinka's Soditon, for example – but far more rigid, buying in to the Christian mission wholeheartedly and without reservation. Tambu, clearly, is more sceptical, and as opportunistic as her father. She analyses Nyasha's regular and enthusiastic attendance at church in a way that suggests some element of projection: "Nyasha went," she writes, "because she was at a devout stage of development: she liked having causes and the Christian cause, which was conformist but could clandestinely be translated into a progressive ideology, was ideal for her" (98). Thus, it seems that, at least in Tambu's case, the religious element involved in her education plays second fiddle, at best, to the very "Englishness" that she warns herself against in the narrative: "the books, the games, the films, the debates," she writes, "all these things were things that I wanted" (203), and she goes to great lengths to get them. And why should she not? Yet Dangarembga, by presenting this desire in such juvenile terms, suggests the vulnerability that students bring to mission schools, as well as the 'legitimate' quest for knowledge. For the best students, the ones who might otherwise make trouble, Nyasha tells us that the mission educators offered these enticements (some admittedly intellectual, since the students were the best), and little by little the prizes seemed to glitter all the more.

But one must recall the novel's ambiguity that prompts this essay. As E.A. Ayandele points out, "the Christian missions were more than destroyers; they were builders as well and, to some extent, preservers. Upon the Christian missions devolved the task of preserving the vernacular against the wishes of their converts and the indifference of the administrators who preferred the English language."[20] While Ayandele is speaking about Nigeria, his observations can be extended to a great many of the mission schools throughout the British empire. Tambu, for example, is confused and annoyed to see that missionaries insist on having their own children

---

[20] E.A. Ayandele, _The Missionary Impact on Modern Nigeria 1842–1914_ (London: Longmans, 1966): 283.

speak Shona in the classroom, rather than English. But an example from Nigeria may offer an instructive backdrop for an understanding of Tambu's awkward 'progress.' In his history of the origins of Nigerian nationalism, Ade Ajayi recalls a definitive contest between Edward Blyden and Bishop Crowther:

> a small extremist group, finding the tutelage of European missionaries irksome and frustrating, began to question the whole basis of the partnership between the educated Africans and the missionaries [...]. Crowther, who had just been made a bishop and had the challenge of a vast mission field on the Niger before him was most conscious of the support he needed from Europe and he therefore tried to rally the nationalist forces to the side of the missionaries.[21]

But this backfired in 1890 when imported missionaries humiliated him in trying to europeanize the staff. Blyden then visited Lagos and inspired the foundation of the United Native African Church. The question of indigenization of European-sponsored institutions, like the Church, sparked many splits of this sort and prompted a good deal of internal discussion of the correct role of the indigenous population in assuming leadership positions within the Churches. Something similar, in fact, played a significant role, for example, in the democratization of Zimbabwe.[22]

But Ayandele goes on to demonstrate that the old conflation of guns and the Bible in the colonization of peoples followed in Nigeria the pattern set elsewhere:

> The year 1914 marked the end of an era and the beginning of another in the history of education in Nigeria. Up to this year the missions and Government, the two agencies on whom the development of this most important social service depended, seemed to be drifting apart in their conception of education. But both agencies needed each other [...] In 1914 the beginnings of a fruitful co-operation between the two bodies were symbolized in Lord Lugard [who] sought to co-operate with the missions on terms acceptable to the latter by fostering the teaching of non-denominational Christianity in 'pagan' areas, by increasing grants to the missions and by setting up an efficient inspectorate that would recommend grants on the moral behaviour of pupils and sanitation observed in each school.[23]

Though Ayandele does not seem aware of the fact in his description of the enterprise (he was writing in 1966), the criteria for the issuance of grants to pupils sounds very much like Nyasha's understanding that such admission to the fascinating world of the white man was offered specifically to head off at the pass any promising pupils who might otherwise turn to insurrection. But this fact should not weigh so heavily

---

[21] J.F. Ade Ajayi, "Nineteenth Century Origins of Nigerian Nationalism," *Journal of the Historical Society of Nigeria* 2.2 (1961): 204–205.

[22] David J. Maxwell, "The Church and Democratisation in Africa: The Case of Zimbabwe," in *The Christian Churches and the Democratisation of Africa*, ed. Paul Gifford (Leiden: E.J. Brill, 1995): 168–89.

[23] Ayandele, *The Missionary Impact on Modern Nigeria 1842–1914*, 303.

in our discussion that his hopeful estimate of the enterprise gets dismissed out of hand. The change that was wrought by Lugard and others like him was, as in *Nervous Conditions* and the other books of its kind, ambiguous.

Except in interviews we can only surmise the degree to which this ambiguity defined the lives of the various novelists themselves. But where African 'transnational' or 'transcultural' intellectuals speak out about their hybrid identities, it appears to be painfully unresolved. A young Nigerian who is implicated on many levels in this discussion recently wrote of his ongoing experience in school in the USA, and his words demonstrate the highly nuanced situation that a Nyasha might have been capable of enunciating, had she been speaking as an adult. Uwem Celestine Akpan is a young Nigerian Jesuit who has already successfully completed a good number of years in college. He is now in the graduate training in theology necessary for ordination to priesthood in the Roman Catholic church. He is studying in Berkeley, California, and finding the experience confusing, but multi-layered in meaning. "As children," he writes, "our chief task was to learn [...] cross-bred values":

> We were born into them. This was the only world, the only reality we knew [...]. The parents, teachers, priests and catechists forged a strong and broad collaboratory front that legitimised the new paradigm and discouraged deviance and truancy [...]. Through their roles, they tapped into some objective cultural power. These objectifications took hold of our personal identities, and our biographies became individualised versions of these abstractions.[24]

It is worth recalling the source of these observations. Much like the adult Tambu who recalls her coming-of-age and willing entry into the world that "destroyed" Nyasha, Akpan is still very, very much committed to a hybridized world that he can fully understand and criticize. Some might wonder why; some might echo the sort of implied criticism that concludes Basu's article: "the intellectual is particularly prone to the blandishments offered at the level of the banal, while simultaneously eliding this position by an appeal to a unique subjectivity endowed with consciousness. These texts remind us that as intellectuals trapped in powerful institutional structures, we may in practice be desperately troping."[25] The word "trapped" catches one's attention, because it may suggest there is some other way of being in today's world – that, if the trap could somehow be un-sprung, we could launch off into primal territory. But where would that be?

Certainly, it would not be America, as Akpan discovers. As he takes off for studies there he asks himself, "What will I need to become in order to find God fully

---

[24] Uwem Celestine Akpan, "A Nigerian Roman Catholic 'Something'," *America* (2 November 1996): 23.

[25] Basu, "Trapped and Troping," 22.

in this new environment? What will I outgrow to enter fully into God in this new world? How will I come into God to get fully out of myself? And at what cost?"[26] Whether or not all these questions are directly faced by the various protagonists in novels dealing with expatriation, surely the last one is. Tambu's whole narrative implies the query. Akpan is as eloquent as anyone I have encountered in shaping the personal crisis that the adventure poses:

> I once saw a dragonfly fight to free itself from a spider's web. It fought and flapped so hard its wings cracked, then snagged in defeat. The spider quickly wound its silver thread around the unlucky insect. In the next seconds, the poor thing was twisting its limbs in submission to the thickening silver cocoon. The quarry thus disarmed and handcuffed, the spider closed in and brained it. The dragonfly staged a last feeble struggle, stretched and hung still in its new plastered capsule. Carefully the predator reached out and tapped the corpse and, when nothing moved, it ran a quick frisk over it. I saw it maneuver its powerful mandibles, and I couldn't tell whether this was a triumphant smile or its regular warm-up. I wasn't around to witness the slow dismembering of the carcass as the spider settled into a happy dinner. – Will I snag a wing? Will I lose my head to these questions? Worse still, my giant spider, fear, was closing in. Very soon, I knew, it would fret and frisk my body, finding me guilty. As my people say, 'A fly is never innocent in the spider's web.'[27]

Yes, Akpan identifies the spider as his fears, and this is understandable enough. But what do those fears represent? An entrapment by the demands of a new culture, a dismembering of himself, and then what? As a religious person, he would see the process as God's will, as a purification, as a vivifying stripping away of ego. But as we read his account against those of Tambu and others, do we not hear echoes of the justifiable terror in the face of an obliteration of the self one has come to know and with whom one identifies? If Tambu had hesitations over her entrance in the Convent school, they were naive compared to Akpan's (and therefore so much tamer). Whatever ambiguities there may always be in such cross-cultural encounters, the pain is inescapable and inevitable. The spider closes in. "'It's bad enough,' [Nyasha] said severely, 'when a country gets colonised, but when the people do as well! That's the end, really, that's the end" (147). But as the history of one nation after another would suggest, that is not, in fact, the end. Tambu begins her narrative by telling the reader that "I feel many things these days, much more than I was able to feel in the days when I was young and my brother died, and there are reasons for this more than the mere consequences of age" (1). In those abundant feelings is the urge to tell the story, to piece together, to create anew.

---

[26] Akpan, "A Nigerian Roman Catholic 'Something'," 24.

[27] Akpan, "A Nigerian Roman Catholic 'Something'," 24.

WORKS CITED

Ajayi, J.F. Ade. "Nineteenth Century Origins of Nigerian Nationalism," *Journal of the Historical Society of Nigeria* [Ibadan] 2.2 (1961): 196–210.

Akpan, Uwem Celestine. "A Nigerian Roman Catholic 'Something'," *America* (2 November 1996): 22–26.

Ayandele, E.A. *The Missionary Impact on Modern Nigeria 1842–1914* (London: Longmans, 1966).

Bahri, Deepika. "Disembodying the Corpus: Postcolonial Pathology in Tsitsi Dangarembga's *Nervous Conditions*," *Postmodern Culture: An Electronic Journal of Interdisciplinary Criticism* 5.1 (1994). Muse.jhu.edu/journals/postmodern culture.

Basu, Biman. "Trapped and Troping: Allegories of the Transnational Intellectual in Tsitsi Dangarembga's *Nervous Conditions*," *ARIEL: A Review of International English Literature* 28.3 (1997): 7–24.

Dangarembga, Tsitsi. *Nervous Conditions* (Seattle WA: Seal, 1988).

Eze, Emmanuel Chukwudi. "Toward a Critical Theory of Postcolonial African Identities," in *Postcolonial African Philosophy*, ed. Eze (Oxford: Blackwell, 1997): 339–44.

Fanon, Frantz. *The Wretched of the Earth*, tr. Constance Farrington (New York: Grove, 1963).

Flockemann, Miki. " ' Not-Quite Insiders and Not-Quite Outsiders': The 'Process of Womanhood' in *Beka Lamb*, *Nervous Conditions*, and *Daughters of the Twilight*," *Journal of Commonwealth Literature* 27.1 (1992): 37–47.

Gorle, Gilian. "Fighting the Good Fight: What Tsitsi Dangarembga's *Nervous Conditions* Says About Language and Power," *Yearbook of English Studies*, ed. Andrew Gurr (Leeds: Maney, 1997): 179–92.

Maxwell, David J. "The Church and Democratisation in Africa: The Case of Zimbabwe," in *The Christian Churches and the Democratisation of Africa*, ed. Paul Gifford (Leiden: E.J. Brill, 1995): 168–99.

Thomas, Sue. "Killing the Hysteric in the Colonised's House: Tsitsi Dangarembga's Nervous Conditions," *Journal of Commonwealth Literature* 27.1 (1992): 26–36.

Veit–Wild, Flora. " ' Women Write About the Things that Move Them.' A Conversation with Tsitsi Dangarembga," in *Moving Beyond Boundaries*, ed. Carole Boyce Davies (New York: New York UP, 1994), vol.2: 27–31.

Wolf, Naomi. *The Beauty Myth: How Images of Beauty are Used Against Women* (New York: Doubleday / Anchor, 1991).

❧

  India

Resistance through Sub/mission in the Novels of R.K. Narayan

Hyacinth Cynthia Wyatt

MONG INDIAN AUTHORS WRITING IN ENGLISH, R.K. Narayan was among the first to resist Western cultural dominance. He did so by developing a personal style and using the English language in a unique way (a style which was deceptively simple), in order to deal with themes of national objectives. At that time the Indian intellectuals in general, and the Indian writers in particular, had been emulating the romantic style and literature of the British *hommes de lettres*. By choosing to write about national topics such as the diversity and idiosyncrasies of the people of India, the complexity and the sophistication of its religious philosophy and the wealth of its deep-rooted historical traditions, Narayan deliberately renounced an imported fiction, a utopian one, one which was inappropriate for the Indian reality but which, nevertheless, had prevailed for almost two centuries within the literary circles in India. Narayan's first novel, *Swami and Friends*, was published in 1935 in Great Britain, where it gained unreserved public acclaim by the British critics.[1] In that novel, and in the following ones, Narayan developed an original aesthetic representation of the vicissitudes in the life of the ordinary Indian man, portraying thus the popular ethos in all its authenticity. As a rule, Narayan concerned himself exclusively with Indian characters; all his novels are set in India, within the confined cultural triangle of Mysore, where he studied and lived with his family; Coimbatore, where his wife was born and where he visited his in-laws regularly; and Madras, where he was born and where he spent his childhood under the care of his grandmother and his uncle. Narayan remained in that triangle until the age of fifty, when, his only daughter having just got married, he

---

[1] R.K. Narayan, *Swami and Friends* (London: Hamish Hamilton, 1935); references in this paper follow the Mandarin paperback edition (London: 1993).

thought it "the right time to accept the travel grant the Rockefeller Foundation had offered him," and decided to go to the USA.[2]

That land-rooted stability, and the quietness of Narayan's life – he was widowed at the age of thirty-two and never remarried, his only occupation has been writing and observing people, in order to draw material for his writing – contrast somehow with the violence of the events India went through between 1935, the date of publication of his first novel, and 1956, the date of his first trip abroad. A similar quietness or, in other terms, a kind of tranquil force, can be said to characterize Narayan's resistance to Western cultural dominance. Indeed, Narayan uses gentle humour and literary metaphors, never overtly attacking that culture; rather, his novels show the threatening reality of the growing influence of the West with the psychological effects it has had, and continues to have, on the Indian psyche.

In *The Painter of Signs*,[3] for example, Narayan writes satirically about Raman who, determined to establish the Age of Reason, "wants a logical explanation for everything." However, as the novel develops, Raman is made to realize that (to para-phrase the French philosopher Pascal) cultural logic has a logic that rational logic cannot understand, that is to say, that everything cannot be measured against the same yardstick. This results in his becoming aware that he has to communicate "on two planes, audibly and inaudibly": the subjective one which relates him to Eternal India and the rational one which makes him look for the logic behind all action. One of the episodes in the novel that highlights this is the following: A young lawyer who has just passed his law examinations orders his nameboard to be made and delivered on a certain auspicious day. Raman works feverishly until late in the night for several days in order to have it finished on time. When it is ready, Raman rushes to the lawyer's house to have it put up. There, to his surprise, a grand inaugural ceremony is about to take place for the occasion, and Raman is made to wait for the exact moment which was indicated by an astrologer before he can put up the board. Raman, inclined to spurn the stars' dictum, wants to shout, "Be scientific, please, scientific," but has to remain silent because of the din made by the excited crowd reaching out for the board. Guessing his reluctance to wait, and to prevent him from putting up the board before the auspicious time, the lawyer and his friends propel him gently, but firmly, into the kitchen to be served tea and *idli*.

Raman is upset and dismayed by these "irrational" customs, and by the multitude gazing at the signboard as if it possessed some magical charm. In the kitchen, his every movement being observed, and a host of ears being pricked up to catch his every word, Raman again is compelled to voice his comments inwardly: "good *idli*, up to the mark," thinks Raman; "the coffee is too dilute [...] at a scalding tempera-

[2] R.K. Narayan, *My Days: A Memoir* (1975; Harmondsworth: Penguin, 1989): 163.

[3] R.K. Narayan, *The Painter of Signs* (Harmondsworth: Penguin, 1976).

ture, which benumbs the tongue and one can't notice what one is consuming" (11). Observed as he is by a zealous crowd, Raman only hopes that no one can read his thoughts. Significantly, thus, Raman is unable to communicate with his own people, and he finds himself alienated from his own culture. In other words, Raman has become, under the influence of the West, a "disoriented character, trapped between two cultures, which results in inner confusion."[4]

Another example, found in *The Man Eater of Malgudi*, concerns the character Vasu, who is described as "the perfect enemy." The reader wonders: "the perfect enemy? Enemy of what?" Then the reader remembers: Vasu was born in Junagadh. Significantly, Junagadh is a tiny princely state that refused to sign the Union Act for joining the new Republic for India's accession of Independence. The reader is left with that: an almost unnoticeable political detail. Thus, Narayan's resistance is of a subtle nature and only a close re-reading of his novels can reveal the quality of such resistance, resistance that is nonetheless present and traceable in every one of his novels.

Another example, manifest in *The Vendor of Sweets*, is Jagan's attitude towards his son. Jagan, the protagonist, is the father of Mali, a college drop-out, who after rifling his father's savings from the loft of the house, goes off to America. He returns after three years. His father is, one can easily imagine, overjoyed about his return and goes to meet him at the station. But in the station, Jagan is overwhelmed by the spectacle of Mali wearing a dark suit, with an overcoat, and "carrying an airbag, a camera, an umbrella and what not on his person." Jagan thought that "he was following a stranger."[5] The fact that Mali is dressed like a "European" disconcerts Jagan totally, creates a gap between the father and the son and prevents communication. Here we are reminded of Gandhi, who refused to wear a European suit when he went to England to attend the Round Table Conference. He disembarked in England dressed in his impeccably white *dhoti*, as a sign of affirmation of his Indianness.

However, Narayan's urge to resist Western cultural dominance was not political, rather than that, it seems to have its origin in an early conflict he had to contend with, being, as it were, the only Indian Brahmin in the Albert Mission school, a prestigious school, which he started attending at the age of eight. The other pupils, the offspring of a westernized elite created under the Evangelical Movement and the Utilitarians, were converted Christians. The Lutheran Mission school Narayan attended was the result of Macaulay's "Minute on Education" (1835) implemented by Lord Bentinck, which had made English compulsory in the Indian universities. The Evangelical Movement thus became a 'civilizing mission,' and primary and

---

[4] Michel Pousse has explained this at length in *R.K. Narayan: Romancier et témoin* (Paris: L'Harmattan / Université de la Réunion, 1992): 56.

[5] R.K. Narayan, *The Vendor of Sweets* (1967; Harmondsworth: Penguin, 1983): 43.

secondary schools had been set up in an effort to 'civilize,' supposedly, the Indian people, in order for them to have the beneficial effects of European culture. To that effect, the Bible was a key subject highly praised by the young protagonist's scripture teacher in the novel *Swami and Friends*. The teacher, Ebenezar, a Christian convert, had great admiration for "Jesus who cured the poor" and little respect for "Sri Krishna who only went gadding about with dancing girls" (2).

The Evangelical Mission taught culture and civilization to a portion of the Indian population which actually felt itself as a local élite. Swami is well aware of this every day of his life. In the Mission School, he suffers on the part of those (in this case his teacher and his schoolmates) who have embraced a different faith from their native one. Just as the intellectuals had "borrowed" a literary style which did not, and could not, reproduce an authentic reality, the new converts had also "borrowed" a faith, whose true spirit of charity and generosity of heart they failed to understand. Thus, in the name of "Jesus who cured the poor" the scripture teacher showed little concern about offending and wounding the "weak," or the minority like Swaminathan, who were non-converts. Ebenezar's attacks on Hinduism seem a reflection of ideological fanaticism. We are told that: "he displayed a lot of hatred" and that the Scriptures classes were mostly devoted to attacking and lampooning the Hindu gods; that violent abuses were heaped on idol worshippers as a prelude to glorifying Jesus (note the possessives): "Why do you worship dirty, lifeless, wooden idols and stone images? [...] Did *our* Jesus go about stealing butter like that arch-scoundrel Krishna? Did *our* Jesus go gadding about with dancing girls like *your* Krishna? [...] Did *our* Jesus practice dark tricks on those around him?" (4).

All this seems so intolerable to Swaminathan that he cannot help asking: "If he did not, why was he crucified?" (4). As an answer the teacher suggests that he might come to him at the end of the hour and learn the answer in private. However, this response does not satisfy Swaminathan's curiosity. This curiosity is justified, it seems, not only by his age but also by his understandable lack of knowledge about the facts of the life of Jesus. So Swami boldly puts a second question to the teacher: "If he was a *good* god, why did he eat flesh and drink wine?" As a Brahmin boy, it was inconceivable to him that a god should be a non-vegetarian, a logical question for a young boy of eight years of age more curious about the real facts and more eager to have light thrown on some incomprehensible matter than to dissent. The only answer Swaminathan gets is his teacher "leaving his seat, advancing slowly towards him and trying to wrench his left ear off" (4). That is the most incomprehensible of all answers and the least enlightening into the mysterious alchemy of the transmuting of blood into wine and body into bread. In this dramatic episode, what Narayan calls attention to is the basis for religious intolerance, in this case, an inability to understand or to accept a different notion of the divine. Ebenezar's attitude reveals the "clearly defined limits of any theological discussions."[6]

Thus, as Narayan sees that the concept of the "divine" or the "notion of God" may be strongly influenced by the prevailing culture, on a more superficial level, he shows in *The Vendor of Sweets*, how Jagan's mind has become confused by Mali's adoption of Western clothes. Similarly, in *Swami and Friends*, Rajam's perfect English causes consternation among his schoolmates, including Swami: Rajam is a newcomer to the class, he is very different from the others: well off, well dressed, well educated. Swami, who admires him for all those reasons, is longing to gain his friendship. Furthermore, we are told that Rajam "spoke very good English, exactly like a European, which meant that few in the school could make out what he said" (12). Neither were his schoolmates confident enough to speak back to Rajam. Ironically then, it is precisely the mastering of the English language that separates Rajam from the others, and, consequently, Rajam's arrival starts a rift between Swami and his former friends.

In resisting Western cultural dominance, what Narayan is addressing is "mimetism," the blind, and sometimes servile, imitation of Western customs by Indians who adopt superficial external aspects, without knowing or understanding the true philosophy which underlies those customs. Those who imitate and act according to the models they are exposed to deprive that philosophy or that faith of its essential meaning. They try to "feel" what is impossible for them to feel. They think that by "imitating" a feeling, they will be able to "feel." But that is not possible, as Erich Fromm explains at length, even providing a definition to the process: he refers to it as "pseudo feelings: thoughts about feelings rather than genuine emotional experiences"; in other words, a "faith which is not rooted in one's own experience, in the confidence in one's power of thought, observation, and judgment."[7]

Similarly, the French author René Girard, in his book *Deceit, Desire, and the Novel*,[8] discusses this phenomenon. The example he gives is Cervantes's Don Quixote, who, according to Girard, "borrows" his "feeling" (which Girard calls "desire," meaning his aspiration to be the champion of perfect chivalry) from Amadis the perfect knight. Girard shows how, the moment Don Quixote decides to choose Amadis as a model, he loses one of his fundamental characteristics: his spontaneity, because henceforth all the objects of the "desires" he now pursues are determined for him. It follows that his words and his actions are transformed into mere "performances," just like those of Ebenezar glorifying Jesus. As performances they lack a

---

[6] Pousse, *R. K. Narayan: Romancier et témoin*, 196 (my tr.).

[7] Erich Fromm, *Man for Himself* (1949; London: Routledge, 1990): 183, 205.

[8] René Girard, *Deceit, Desire, and the Novel*, tr. Ivonne Freccero (Baltimore MD: Johns Hopkins UP, 1965).

sense of reality; inherent to performances is the fact that aesthetic judgement as well as common judgement have perforce to be silenced. Thus, in spite of the fact that during the act the performer can actually "feel," the kind of feeling he has does not, and cannot, last. This accounts for our amazement at the performer's "inexplicable indifference" in real life, such as witnessed by the reader at Ebenezar's scanty concern for the non-converted Swami. Evidently, if the feeling is not there from the start, planted inside, rooted, as it were, it cannot express itself spontaneously, nor grow nor expand.

In the same strain of thought, Jules Gaultier has defined "Bovarysm" in this way: "The same ignorance, the same inconsistency, the same absence of individual reaction seem to make them fated to obey the suggestion of an external milieu, for lack of an auto-suggestion from within."[9] And for Girard, in a similar fashion as Don Quixote who desires or "feels" through Amadis, Emma Bovary "desires through the romantic heroines she has read about in the second hand books she has devoured and which have destroyed all her spontaneity."[10]

Narayan seems to hold similar views when it comes to imitating a foreign culture and, consequently, he renounced the romantic topics of the British writers and chose to write about what he knew and felt genuinely: India. Although he expresses himself in English, Narayan refrains from copying the *King's English* used by the British authors. Instead, Narayan devised a spontaneous way of expressing his feelings. His English, an Indian English, is a genuine manifestation of his deep-rooted culture, a culture in which he has a rational faith. And here it may be worth remembering that the term "faith" is used in the Old Testament. "Emunah" means 'firmness' and thereby denotes "a certain character of human experience, a character trait, rather than the content of a belief in something."[11] Narayan can be seen as illustrating this, as someone drawing from his own experience of thought and feeling rather than from a conviction in somebody or something involved in submission, which is another way of expressing conversion.

Narayan submitted to and used British culture, but only superficially. On a deeper level, he refuses to give up the culture that he feels more meaningful and that gave him strength and orientation in his living and writing. For that reason, Narayan could choose to express himself through the novel, which is a European genre; but he used it as a strategic form to 'disclose' his resistance. Indeed, Albert Camus describes this genre thus: "The novel is born simultaneously with the spirit of rebellion

---

[9] Quoted in Girard, *Deceit, Desire, and the Novel*, 5.

[10] Girard, *Deceit, Desire, and the Novel*, 5.

[11] Fromm, *Man for Himself*, 199.

and expresses, on the aesthetic plane, the same ambition."[12] Seen in this light, Narayan's form of 'resistance' is given a larger philosophical dimension.

WORKS CITED

Camus, Albert. *The Rebel*, tr. Anthony Bower (London: Hamish Hamilton, 1953).

Fromm, Erich. *Man for Himself* (1949; London: Routledge, 1990).

Girard, René. *Deceit, Desire, and the Novel*, tr. Ivonne Freccero (Baltimore MD: Johns Hopkins UP, 1965).

Narayan, R.K. *The Man-Eater of Malgudi* (1961; Harmondsworth: Penguin, 1983).

——. *My Days: A Memoir* (Harmondsworth: Penguin, 1989).

——. *The Painter of Signs* (Harmondsworth: Penguin, 1976).

——. *Swami and Friends* (1935; London: Art Mandarin, 1993).

——. *The Vendor of Sweets* (1967; Harmondsworth: Penguin, 1983).

Pousse, Michel. *R.K. Narayan: Romancier et témoin* (Paris: L'Harmattan / Université de la Réunion, 1992).

❧

---

[12] Albert Camus, *The Rebel*, tr. Anthony Bower (London: Hamish Hamilton, 1953).

Manichaeism and Mimicry
in Ruth Prawer Jhabvala's *Heat and Dust*

ISABEL ALONSO BRETO

T HROUGH AN ANALYSIS of Ruth Prawer Jhabvala's novel *Heat and Dust* (1975),[1] I intend to show that the concepts of Manichaeism and mimicry are not opposed or mutually exclusive. Rather, they are complementary, and both may be helpful in describing articulations of the colonial and postcolonial discourses.[2]

This contention acknowledges to the objections that Abdul JanMohamed raises against Homi Bhabha's application of the concept of mimicry. JanMohamed argues that Homi Bhabha "completely ignores Fanon's definition of the conqueror / native relationship as a 'Manichean' struggle."[3] Yet Bhabha does not ignore Fanon's theories. Indeed, he is deeply influenced by them when, in his work *The Location of Culture*, he recalls that, in 1952, Fanon suggested that "an oppositional, differential reading of Lacan's Other might be more relevant for the colonial condition than the Marxisant [sic] reading of the Master–Slave dialectic."[4] As is well known, the Lacanian reading suggested by Fanon is the very sustaining point of Bhabha's theory of mimicry.

Bhabha observes in the colonial subject "a mimicry that mocks the binary structure travestying it,"[5] thus finding a way to overcome dichotomies. According to

---

[1] Ruth Prawer Jhabvala, *Heat and Dust* (1975; London: Futura, 1976). All page references in text refer to this edition.

[2] About the ambiguity and implications of these terms see Ann McClintock, "The Angel of Progress: The Pitfalls of the Term 'Post-Colonialism'," in *Colonial Discourse and Post-Colonial Theory Reader*, ed. Patrick Williams & Laura Chrisman (London: Harvester, 1993): 291–304.

[3] Abdul JanMohamed, "The Economy of Manichean Allegory: The Function of Racial Difference in Colonialist Literature," *Critical Inquiry* 12 (1985): 60.

[4] Homi Bhabha, *The Location of Culture* (London: Routledge, 1996): 32.

[5] Robert Young, *White Mythologies: Writing History and the West* (London: Routledge, 1996): 209.

Bhabha, mimicry lies in the space between Self and Other, or between identity and difference. It lies in the unstable and destabilizing location of Lacanian Desire: "It is not the colonial Self or the colonized Other, but the disturbing distance in-between that constitutes the figure of colonial otherness."[6] Bhabha's concept of mimicry reflects the complexity of the relationship among the elements in the colonial scene, and the ambivalence of the relationship not only between colonizer and colonized, but also the relationship each of these has with him-/herself:

> What they all share is a discursive process by which the excess or slippage produced by the ambivalence of mimicry (almost the same, *but not quite*) does not merely 'rupture' the discourse, but becomes transformed into an uncertainty which fixes the colonial subject as a 'partial' presence.[7]

Thus, Bhabha's conclusion that the colonial subject is marked by an ambivalent mimicry potentially enriches insight on the colonial and the postcolonial scenes. But JanMohamed does not consider mimicry as a further step in the conceptualization of colonialism, since he accuses Bhabha of falling too short and "repressing the political history of colonialism."[8] He is also deeply disturbed by Bhabha's ambiguity with regard to the question of agency, and he wonders: "What does it mean, in practice, to imply as Bhabha does that the native, whose entire economy and culture are destroyed, is somehow in 'possession' of the colonial power?" Bearing this question in mind, I wonder who JanMohamed is referring to when he speaks about "the unity of the colonial subject."[9] This colonial subject seems not to be the colonized, since JanMohamed sees the native as lacking any agency at all.

The distinction JanMohamed makes between different types of postcolonial literary texts implies that he does not deny the existence of ambivalence in the relationship between colonizer and colonized, yet he seems hardly ready to acknowledge it. Should it exist at all, ambivalence is for him merely "a product of deliberate, if at times unconscious, imperialist duplicity, operating very efficiently through the economy of its central trope, the Manichean allegory":[10] a concept ever-present in the colonial scene, which, according to his explicit statements, bears no relation to mimicry, camouflage or hybridity. The manichaean allegory denounces the virtual dismissal of the reality of the colonial object in favour of an artificial reality created in the interests of the colonial subject,[11] and thus, as I have remarked, it is a theory

---

[6] Bhabha, *The Location of Culture*, 45.

[7] *The Location of Culture*, 86.

[8] JanMohamed, "The Economy of Manichean Allegory," 60.

[9] "The Economy of Manichean Allegory," 59.

[10] "The Economy of Manichean Allegory," 61.

[11] Edward Said echoes this when exploring representations of the East in Western culture: "After Napoleon, then, the very language of Orientalism changed radically. Its descriptive realism

which regards the colonizer as the subject and the colonized as the object. This, in my opinion, is too simple a version of the complexity of postcolonial relationships; hence the convenience of combining a 'manichaeistic' scheme with other theories for approaching postcolonial literature.

JanMohamed proposes a distinction between two categories of colonial literature, and he also uses Lacanian terminology to define them. In the first of these, which he calls the 'imaginary,' emphasis is on the colonizer's narcissistic self-recognition. Here, the native is too degraded to be more than a recipient of the negativity bestowed on him. In this category we thus find works in which the word 'native' is automatically associated with negative values. The writer of these texts "tends to fetishize a non-dialectical, fixed opposition between the self and the native."[12]

The second category is the 'symbolic.' Within this type of works, the native becomes a mediator of European desires. These texts tend to be more open to a modifying dialectic between the Self and the Other:

> These authors are willing to examine the specific individual and cultural differences between Europeans and natives and to reflect on the efficacy of European values, assumptions, and habits in contrast to those of the indigenous cultures.[13]

Within the symbolic category, he goes on, two types of texts are to be found: The first one is that which provides syncretic solutions for the colonial encounter. The second type explores the possibility of reaching syncretic solutions for the conflict, but finds them impossible to attain. Somewhat contradicting himself, JanMohamed argues that the texts within the second type escape the Manichean allegory, because, if they conclude that there is no escape from the constraints of power relationships in the colonial society, they tend to reflect on and closely examine these constraints before reaching that conclusion.

If it seems plausible to presuppose the existence of mimicry within symbolic literature (accepting JanMohamed's nomenclature), it is my contention that mimicry is also present in the imaginary. I shall argue further, with Bhabha, that the interaction between two elements, called either subject and object or Self and Other, engenders unending displacements of both; that the space *in-between* them is a space continuously dislocated and thus continuously redefined, a space of *slippage*. If a degree of manichaeism is always present in the colonial scene and texts (and often in the postcolonial), it is my contention that exploring the processes of mimicry in those texts, as postulated by Bhabha, becomes a necessary complement to the mere

---

was upgraded and became not merely a style of representation but a language, indeed a means of *creation*"; Said, *Orientalism* (Harmondsworth: Penguin, 1995): 87 (my emphasis).

[12] JanMohamed, "The Economy of Manichean Allegory," 65.

[13] JanMohamed, "The Economy of Manichean Allegory," 66.

description of "a world divided into compartments, a motionless, Manicheistic world, a world of statues," to use the words of Fanon.[14]

In *Heat and Dust* we read two interwoven stories, one taking place in 1923 and the other in the early 1970s.[15] The two stories share some parallels: In both there is a white woman who settles in India, and who is or becomes involved with both an Indian and an English man.

The first story takes place during the colonial period, and the woman protagonist is Olivia, the wife of an English officer. She falls in love with an Indian, a Nawab, and at the end of the novel she elopes with him. We learn that before eloping she had been pregnant and had aborted, but we never learn whether the baby's father was her English husband or her Indian lover. In this story, manichaeism on the part of narrator and characters is striking to the point of making the reader wonder whether irony is keenly at work. If this should be the case, it is not overtly shown by the text. Throughout, colour and light emphasize a relevant opposition: White and light stand for Englishness, civilization, cleanliness, honesty, and other values depicted as positive. Black and dark, on the other hand, are related to Indianness, and also to superstition, wickedness and dirt.[16] Therefore, borrowing JanMohamed's classification, I shall call this the 'imaginary' story within *Heat and Dust*.

In the other story, which takes place in the postcolonial period, we meet a young woman who travels to India with the intention of finding out about her aunt Olivia, a taboo figure whose name could not even be uttered in the family. We read that "for years, they could not be induced to talk about Olivia. They shied away from her memory as from something dark and terrible" (1–2). Along with this young woman's reviving of Olivia's memory, the book tells her own story, which in several senses parallels her aunt's. This woman, who narrates her own story in first person in the form of a diary, also gets sentimentally involved with both an English and an Indian man, and she also gets pregnant. Parallels can also be found between secondary characters. Dr Gopal is the renewed version of Dr Saunders, as Maji is of the

---

[14] Frantz Fanon, *The Wretched of the Earth*, tr. Constance Farrington (Harmondsworth: Penguin, 1990): 40.

[15] At one point, one of the characters says about India: "Thirty years ago I might have said there is hope: but today – none"; Jhabvala, *Heat and Dust*, 4. We can take her words as a token for the thought, well rooted in the Imperial mind, of India's incapacity to rule itself. Since India has been independent since 1945, the contemporary story takes place not long before the novel's first publication, in 1975. As to the date of the other story, Olivia's letters are "more than fifty years old" (95).

[16] For an analysis of the modes of characterizing race in terms of light / dark related to visibility / invisibility, see David Theo Goldberg, "In / Visibility and Super / Vision: Fanon on Race, Veils, and Discourses of Resistance," in *Fanon: A Critical Reader*, ed. Lewis R. Gordon, T. Denean Sharpley–Whiting & Renee T. White (Oxford: Blackwell, 1996): 179–200.

Begum (the lovers' mothers), Ritu is of Sandy (the lovers' wives), and so on. Hence the claim that this story is a retelling of the first one.

There is a will to redeem in this retelling: The taboo figure of Olivia, in the first place, but, more importantly, there is on the part of the narrator (and, we assume, on the part of the author herself) the will to redeem the extreme manichaeism that once operated in the colonial world. The narrator's diary tells of her attempt to come to terms with Indian culture. I shall call this the 'symbolic' story, since her wish to merge into the native's world overtakes and directs her narration. Now, again: in both stories manichaeism and mimicry coexist.

From the time of her arrival in India, the 'symbolic' woman shows a will to confront stereotypes with reality: "All those memories I've read, all those prints I've seen. I really must forget about them" (2). Although she is "still on English time" (3) when she looks through the window of the Society of Missionaries Hostel, she sees India bright white. This can be understood as a cleansing of prejudice, a will to overcome manichaeism in terms of black and white. Indeed, the process of mimicry she will experience is different from the one experienced by her counterpart in the imaginary story, Olivia, since it will open up a possibility which Olivia could not even contemplate: At the end of her Indian apprenticeship period, the young woman does not have an abortion. Since her baby, like Olivia's, could have either an Indian or an English father (she doesn't know who the real father is), she is both symbolically and literally opening the door to hybridity.

The symbolic story depicts a productive interrelation between the two poles of the colonial system, embodied in a real immersion by the English in Indian culture. The narrator does not show rejection, nor even seem to attempt cultural appropriation. This is reflected in her relationship with Maji, the mother of her Indian lover (a relationship completely different from the absolute estrangement between their counterparts in the imaginary story).[17] Although at the beginning the narrator and Maji are left together "to make what [they] could of each other" (8), we soon read: "After that night the mother and I have drawn closer together. We have become friends" (53).[18] The word 'friendship' is frequently heard in the imaginary story, told to the English by the Nawab in gloomy and mistrustful tones. Yet this is not the case in the symbolic story, as here the interest seems to be mutual and genuine: "she does

---

[17] These two women only look at each other during the abortion, that is, when both are denying the possibility of an Anglo-Indian baby being born. It is a gaze that ends up in a renewal of pain: "Olivia had to shut [her eyes] as the pain below was repeated" (168), a physical reaction which reinforces the psychological estrangement between them.

[18] What happened that night also relates the two stories. Ritu's psychological problems recall Sandy's, the mentally ill wife of the Nawab (Sandy being an English name, not her real one, a mis-naming which could be symbolically read as the cause for her illness).

most of the talking and I like listening to her, especially when she tells me about herself" (53). The same can be said of the relationship between the young narrator and her Indian lover, Inder Lal, who talk to and learn from each other in their frequent conversations before getting sexually involved. Also, in her attempt, though ineffective, to become friends with Ritu, Inder Lal's wife.

Notwithstanding, there is latent manichaeism in the symbolic story, operating subliminally all the way through. An example of this can be found in the description of the Indian community sleeping outdoors (which starts with a stereotyping generalization: "When Indians sleep, they really do sleep," 52). In an apparently casual way, the narrator introduces animal imagery in the same paragraph: "All one hears is occasionally someone crying out in their sleep, or a dog – maybe a jackal – baying at the moon" (52), and the reader may or may not make her or his own connection.[19]

Going back to the narrator's initial relationship with Maji and Ritu, the mother and the wife respectively of her lover-friend, when she meets them the narrator declares her will to come to terms with their Indianness by saying that she "would have preferred to sit on the floor as they did" (8). Nevertheless, it must be noted that she quickly remarks that "the place was certainly very untidy" (8). Another example of subtle manichaeism can be found when she asserts her newly born friendship with Maji: "She has seen to it that everyone charges me the right price" (53), which is a positive comment on Maji's behaviour, but which, at the same time, reinforces the received stereotype of the cheating Indian.

Subtle hints at negativity regarding her lover, Inder Lal, are also ever-present. An example of this can be found at the beginning of their relationship, when the narrator is plainly amazed to discover curiosity and intelligence in his eyes. Even more effective is the scene where the young woman helps an old widow who is dying amid the filth in a street. Although Inder Lal shows up at this moment, he quickly departs, leaving both his lover and the widow buried in the filth. And we see him leaving the women "*clean* in his much *washed* clothes and with his *freshly* cooked food in his tiffin carrier" (110, my emphases). Here, the contrast between cleanliness and dirt reinforces the reader's impression that Inder Lal is selfish and uncharitable.

Finally, covert manichaeism is present in the treatment of the character of Dr Gopal, an interesting case of mimicry within the postcolonial world. He is presented as "a good-looking man in a white coat and an oiled moustache" (111), whereby the white coat exceeds its denotative professional meaning to connote racial implications, for it is the outer covering that symbolizes his will to camouflage himself in whiteness. The oiled moustache also recalls Englishness, and we are told that he is "very polite, even gallant" (111). It is to be noted that the adjective 'gallant' appears

---

[19] This is a *topos* in colonial literature, as Fanon recalls: "when the settler seeks to describe the native fully in exact terms he constantly refers to the bestiary" (*The Wretched of the Earth*, 33).

only one other time in the novel, and on that occasion it refers to the Englishmen who died in the 1857 mutiny. The adverb 'even' used in this context tempts me to reformulate Bhabha's "white, but not quite" as "gallant, but not quite," which eventually come to mean the same thing here.

Upon being informed of the emergency of the widow's case, all Dr Gopal does, after taking the time to smile and stroke his moustache, is to ask her calmly "the standard question: 'Which country are you from?' " (111). If that is not enough to hint at his lack of professionalism, the narrator adds that "he seemed prepared to talk to [her] longer [...] perhaps in order to practise his English" (111). Dr Gopal's mimicry and the narrator's manichaeism merge together in this unsettling scene, while, behind the scenes, the old widow is looking for, and finally finds a place to die.[20]

After having signalled some aspects of the tension between mimicry and manichaeism present in what I have called the symbolic story within *Heat and Dust*, I shall approach the imaginary story in an inverse way. Bearing in mind my initial argument that the manichaean allegory articulates the whole imaginary story, I shall explore the attitudes and behaviour of some characters where different processes of mimicry are to be observed.

Olivia's mimicry is caused by her situation as a powerless subject in the society she inhabits. English wives in the colonizers' microcosm are subjected to their husbands' will, and their only power resides in their command over Indian servants. A stereotype of the woman of her race and class, Olivia does not get on well with the other English wives because of a single difference: age. Thus, since she is deeply bored in India due to her alienation from the colonial society she belongs to, when she meets the Indian Nawab she feels that "at last in India, [she had] come to the right place" (15). By becoming sexually involved with him, she puts an end to her boredom by challenging the laws of marriage and of colonialism, albeit unconsciously. But, most importantly, she will be able to satisfy her narcissistic needs: "Here at last was one person in India to be interested in her the way she was used to" (17). Even so, due to class restrictions, the Nawab is the only Indian with whom she could become involved.

Unlike those of her counterparts in the symbolic story, Olivia's relationship with the Indian man is purely one of romance. The attraction to this physically stereotyped native (who is "very manly and strong," 34) is wholly sexual.[21] Intense phys-

---

[20] I am purposely opening a whole field of speculation in reminding that the conversation between native and settler and the death of the native are taking place at the same time.

[21] In the nineteenth century the native was considered "a creature of instinct, controlled by sexual passions, incapable of the refinement to which the white races had evolved," as Rana Kabbani puts it in *Imperial Fictions: Europe's Myths of Orient* (London: HarperCollins, 1988): 63.

ical sensations are her only reaction when in his company, and she never crosses the distance that separates them except in sexual terms. Thus, her mimicry is strictly informed by the social limitations she is forced to endure as a woman. Olivia's is a gender-restricted mimicry, revealed by the fact that, when the Nawab accuses her of not caring for him, her answer is merely to give him the news of her pregnancy (145). Significantly, only in this situation do we read that "she called his name which she had never used before" (45).[22] Her naming of the Other (hence her recognition of herself as 'Othered') occurs *only* because she is pregnant.[23]

In the end, Olivia chooses to dress in Indian clothes, abandon her English husband, and elope with the Indian Nawab.[24] Yet the fact that she decides to have an abortion works, as I have suggested earlier, in a manichaeistic direction. Olivia's mimicry can only be excused because of the incompleteness to which her society condemns her. Her 'imaginary romance' does not depict any interaction between native and non-native that goes beyond pure sexual drive, nor does the fact that she elopes in the end mean any transgression of the manichaeistic colonial ideology.

Nor are we told whether Olivia's manichaeism, symbolized by the voluntary abortion, is overpowered by mimicry after her elopement, as a result of her plunging into the native's world. The narrator avows in the last pages of the book that she "cannot imagine what she thought about all those years, or how she became" (180). The only thing we know is that Olivia lived the rest of her life isolated in the mountains. On the one hand, this isolation suggests punishment for her disavowal of Englishness. On the other, her living up in the mountains can be read as a symbol of possibly having overcome the manichaeism that, according to my argument, has governed her life.

As for the Indian Nawab, he is a markedly westernized man, but, at the same time, one who stubbornly sticks to his Indianness. There is a difference, though, between him and the English, since he is Indian, and between him and the Indian, since he is a Nawab. Thus, he is condemned to move in a wide empty space which he can only fill with mimicry, to stand out as the loneliest figure in the text. His feeling of dispossession is stated through the poignant irony in the comments he makes about

---

This stereotype seems to lie behind the Nawab's strongly sexual appearance, despite his actual sophistication.

[22] A name which, let me remark, the text itself never pronounces.

[23] The Nawab may well be the father of the creature, as everything leads the reader to think (for instance, there is no allusion to Olivia's sexual relations with her husband). In any case, whether the father is one or the other is never to be known. It is another of the text's ambivalent tricks.

[24] During her abortion, Olivia is covered with a white sheet, and thinks "as if I'm dead" (167). She is indeed dead for the whites, from the moment she has crossed into the "oriental privacies – mysteries that should not be disturbed" (169), to the point of becoming a taboo even for future generations, as I have already noted.

himself and his country to the English. It is a sad irony, the wail of the defeated. Unable to find his own place in colonial society, he makes a pitiful attempt to shift from powerlessness to empowerment by means of romance. It is easy to believe, as the text repeatedly suggests, that in seducing Olivia he is simply trying to recover from his loss. Possession of the white woman is his only way to keep a role in the colonial scene, where he no longer receives a coherent image of himself.[25] If the narratorial voice seems to treat him more gently in terms of manichaeism, it is because he is no threat to colonial power. He is no longer a menace, as Bhabha would put it. "He is a menace to himself, to us, and to the wretched inhabitants of this wretched little state" (148), says Douglas, Olivia's husband, at one point. As is usually the case whenever he intervenes, Douglas is 'not quite' bright: Although the Nawab's gaze of surveillance is turned on the English (he retains some of his political leadership, if only symbolic), the light in his gaze is fading as quickly as that in the widow's eyes, back in the symbolic story. Indeed, at the end of the novel, the Nawab's strongly masculine attributes will have significantly changed, to the point that there is "something womanly about him" (175). This change empathizes his own dispossession with the powerlessness of white women in the colonial sphere.

Like Olivia, the Nawab is closed off from the power-sharing of colonial India, and both his ludicrous gesticulation and his ineffective mimicry are the result of this. His unsteadiness is shown in the hysteria that maps his relationship with Harry, his only male English 'friend.' Harry is depicted as an opportunist, and their relationship mirrors in many senses the Nawab's fake romance with Olivia. Indeed, a homosexual relationship can be interpreted in their friendship.[26]

In short, manichaeism never fails to denigrate the Nawab as an Indian. If this is a covert denigration, it is because, as has been suggested, the Nawab is no real menace to the English, and also because he has to be presented as charismatic enough to captivate an English lady.

These are pictures of a mimicry occurring on the outskirts of colonial power, itself constructed in manichaeistic terms. Major Minnies, though, is an example of one case occurring at the heart of the colonial machine:

> "I'm not *quite* the right kind of person to be in India ... I do realise that in many ways I step over too far."
>
> "Into what?" asked Olivia.

---

[25] See Frantz Fanon, "The Man of Color and the White Woman," in *Black Skin, White Masks,* tr. Charles Lam Markmann (London: Pluto, 1986): 63–82.

[26] The same Nawab says about Harry that "he is a very improper Englishman" (43), an expression where not only Harry's, but also the Nawab's mimicry is hinted at.

"The *other* dimension ... I think I've allowed myself to get too fascinated." (148–49,
my emphases)

If the trap of a stereotyped exotic version of the Orient is present in the use of the
verb 'fascinate,' it is clear that Major Minnies feels his own Englishness undermined
after years in India, after years of contact with the Other. There is ambivalence in
how he feels about this, as he seems to feel a mixture of guilt (he feels *too* fascinated; he has gone *too* far), and of joyful captivation:

The Major didn't see, he was looking up at the sky and reciting in Urdu; his voice was
full of emotion – a sort of mixture of reverence and nostalgia. And afterwards he
sighed: "It gets you," he said. "It really does." (150)

We see through these examples that, despite Abdul JanMohamed's reservations
about Homi Bhabha's theory, mimicry in both colonial and postcolonial texts co-
exists with manichaeism, in the most varied and subtle ways, and that the native is
never fully dispossessed of a degree of agency, albeit symbolic or ineffectual in political terms.

In conclusion, this analysis aims to sustain my contention that different theoretical concepts, such as manichaeism and mimicry, even when employed simultaneously, are useful methodologies for exploring postcolonial fiction and both the
colonial and the postcolonial scene.

WORKS CITED

Bhabha, Homi. *The Location of Culture* (London: Routledge, 1996).

Fanon, Frantz. *Black Skin, White Masks*, tr. Charles Lam Markmann (London: Pluto, 1986).

——. *The Wretched of the Earth*, tr. Constance Farrington (Harmondsworth: Penguin, 1990).

Goldberg, David Theo. "In / Visibility and Super / Vision: Fanon on Race, Veils, and Discourses of
    Resistance," in *Fanon: A Critical Reader*, ed. Lewis R. Gordon, T. Denean Sharpley–Whiting
    & Renee T. White (Oxford: Blackwell, 1996): 179–200.

JanMohamed, Abdul. "The Economy of Manichean Allegory: The Function of Racial Difference in
    Colonialist Literature," *Critical Inquiry* 12 (1985): 59–87.

Kabbani, Rani. *Imperial Fictions: Europe's Myths of Orient* (London: HarperCollins, 1988).

McClintock, Anne. "The Angel of Progress: The Pitfalls of the Term 'Post-colonialism'," in *Colo-
    nial Discourse and Post-Colonial Theory: A Reader*, ed. Patrick Williams & Laura Chrisman
    (Hemel Hempstead: Harvester Wheatsheaf, 1993): 291–304.

Jhabvala, Ruth Prawer. *Heat and Dust* (1975; London: Futura, 1976).

Said, Edward S. *Orientalism* (Harmondsworth: Penguin, 1995).

Young, Robert. *White Mythologies: Writing History and the West* (London: Routledge, 1996).

❧

A Deeper Communion
The Older Women of the Raj Quartet

RAJIVA WIJESINHA

> Old men ought to be explorers
> Here or there does not matter
> We must be still and still moving
> Into another intensity
> For a further union, a deeper communion

The Concept of a Mission

P AUL SCOTT DIED IN 1978, shortly after winning the Booker Prize. His posthumous fame was magnified by the triumph of the televised version of his Raj Quartet.[1] Critical interest in his work however was shortlived, and generally dwelt on the broad outlines. A consideration of the philosophical background to his analysis of empire is still awaited. When it comes, it will surely establish him as one of the most perceptive as well as creative writers of the century.

Such an analysis goes beyond my present brief. I will simply look at some of the characters he presents in assessing the compulsions as well as the articulated motives that drove that extraordinary breed, the British colonials in India. In doing so, what is most significant, and was so to Scott, is the failure of the whole enterprise in terms of its ideals. Yet for Scott that was no reason not to look on it with sympathy. He describes it as "the comic dilemma of the *raj* – the dilemma of men who hoped to inspire trust but couldn't even trust themselves" but adds that laughing at this "would have been laughing for him. I suppose that to laugh for people [...] is a way of expressing affection for them" (*Division* 375).

---

[1] Page references in this essay are to the Panther editions (London, 1984), abbreviated as follows: *Jewel* (= *The Jewel in the Crown*); *Scorpion* (= *The Day of the Scorpion*); *Towers* (= *The Towers of Silence*); *Division* (= *A Division of the Spoils*).

That the British in India were special seems to me beyond doubt. Of course, one realizes colonialism was primarily about exploitation, and exploitation of a clearly differentiated other. That seems to me not even worth arguing about now, and that it is largely Britishers associated with India who still argue the point[2] I think upholds my view – that it was primarily in India that colonialism was accompanied by moralistic assertions of a mission.

The Failure of the Mission: The Perceptions of Women

My focus here will be the characters Scott presents as aware both of a mission and its failure. At first sight surprisingly, these will be women. Yet it makes sense that they should be more actively perceptive in this regard. British men in India were generally part of the imperial enterprise and had a considerable stake in it. The abnegation of self that commitment to a mission involves was therefore impossible for them. To put it simplistically, the concept of love in a comprehensive sense that Scott celebrates elsewhere is generally easier for women than men to assert without also asserting themselves. Previously, this was not apparent because earlier opportunity for independent initiative was lacking. But between the wars changing social circumstances let women, not only the young but even older ones able to transcend their restricted situations, affirm what they found otherwise lacking in the imperial enterprise.

It is the older women I wish to consider here, not least because they are concerned with the mission, a concept treated with scepticism by the girls in whose cases sexuality is used to make the point. There are four of these older women, none of them central except for Barbie Batchelor in *The Towers of Silence*. Yet, in addition to being placed constantly before us, their importance is underlined by the introduction to the work, the first part of the first book, being entitled "Miss Crane." The story of the missionary who saw at the end of her life the failure of its work, and therefore committed suttee, the ritual self-immolation of the Indian widow upon her husband's pyre, thus sets the keynote for the whole work.

Miss Crane: Understanding of the Other, but on Whose Terms?

At its most obvious Miss Crane's act was because of what she saw as the death of the British relationship with India, the publicly proclaimed one to which she subscribed. When the war began she had no doubts about allocating blame for the cracks in the relationship to the Indians. Though generally liberal, when Congress ministries resigned to protest the Viceroy's declaration of war against Germany because he had not consulted the Indians, she took down Gandhi's portrait from her

---

[2] See *Plain Tales fom the Raj*, ed. Charles Allen (London: André Deutsch / BBC, 1975): passim.

wall. Her view was that "if Mr. Gandhi had not [...] seized the moment of Britain's greatest misfortune to press home his demands for political freedom [...] then at this moment [...] an Indian cabinet would have been in control in Delhi" (*Jewel* 45–46). In effect, despite her liberalism, Miss Crane was conventional in believing that the British knew best. Although after the First World War similar expectations had been betrayed, she accepted unquestioningly the British view that Britain's current danger laid on Indians an obligation to support the ruling power. They had to trust that they would receive their reward, while there was no need of any public acknowledgment of obligation from the British.

It was because Miss Crane realized, after her experiences on the road back from Dibrapur, the essential unfairness of this attitude that she saw that her own life had been based on an ideal incapable of fulfilment. And what she sensed was that this incapacity was due to a drawing-back, a failure of commitment, intrinsic to the British position in India, despite its proud claims:

> "For years [...] we have said at home [...] that the day would come when our rule in India will end, not bloodily, but in peace, in – so we made it seem – a perfect gesture of equality and friendship and love [...] For years we have been promising and for years finding means of putting the fulfilment of the promise off." (*Jewel* 72)

The incapacity to trust becomes clearer when, in reaction to what she has suffered, the British soldiers she entertains to tea ignore her old faithful servant. So she takes down, as earlier with Gandhi, the picture of Queen Victoria receiving tribute from Indians, the allegory of 'The Jewel in the Crown.' That was all she could do to make up to the old man for the wound to his self-respect, a wound received despite his loyalty to her because of the colour of his skin.

Significantly, in *The Towers of Silence*, when someone remarks how clever it was of Edwina to use the picture to teach both "'English *and* loyalty'," Barbie will say, "'It always seemed to me to be a picture about love rather than loyalty. Perhaps they amount to the same thing. What do you think?'" (82–83). She receives no response. Long before, Miss Crane had realized the absence of sufficient love on the British side to ensure mutual commitment. Thus, not only could loyalty not be assumed from the Indians, it could not even be recognized when it did occur. It is to try to make up for this basic failure that Miss Crane immolates herself.

Yet apart from the public failure, Miss Crane also recognized an inadequacy in herself, the fact that she too always held something back. She had begun her missionary career with the right ideas, as is shown by her view that its only justification was awareness of "a duty to promote the cause of human dignity and happiness" (*Jewel* 24). Her career was successful and effective. Yet she was at times uneasy about her position, as in her relations with the Dibrapur teacher Mr Chaud-

huri for, though he worked under her, he had a degree and spoke English well, so
she was less at ease with him than with her assistant Mr Narayan, who sounded in
comparison "like a bazaar comedian" (*Jewel* 51). Scott's point here is that the idea
of treating an Indian equally, so that she could accept he was superior in some
ways though subordinate in others, was difficult to take. There was always a lack
of trust, based on the principle that could not be challenged, that she was in charge.
It was that that made it difficult for her to appreciate Gandhi's thinking over the
'Quit India' resolution because, though she thought she shared the aspirations of
the Indians, this was only on British terms. So, too, she cannot heed Chaudhuri's
advice when he tries to stop her driving back to Mayapore after the riots have
begun. She cannot trust his motives, and her own perception of the situation must
take precedence.

Yet during the journey there is a moment when he speaks freely of its absurdity
and she suddenly realizes that she needs neither to pity nor to fear him. For the first
time she can have confidence in him as an individual, for she recognizes both his independence of judgement and his commitment. Yet despite this, despite feeling "she
was about to get over the hump thirty-five years of effort and willingness had never
really got her over [...] which [...] lay in the path of thoughts you sent flowing out to
a man or woman whose skin was a different colour from your own" (*Jewel* 64), her
commitment does not measure up to his. She disobeys his instructions to drive on
through the mob that holds them up, and so he is taken out of the car and killed.

She could not, of course, appreciate the danger in which she was putting him. In
words echoed at the tragic culmination of the Quartet, by an Indian who had no
illusions about the sacrifices demanded of the subject race, she says: "'After all, it's
me they want [...] Not you'" (*Jewel* 66). But, unlike him, she was wrong. As later,
the British were safe; because of their failure to fulfil their 'promise,' it was Indians
committed to them who suffered. All Miss Crane can do, having registered that
"'There's nothing I can do [...]. Nothing. Nothing.'" is to go back to the body and
take its hand to affirm the commitment at which she has at last arrived. "'It's taken
me a long time,' she said, meaning not only Mr Chaudhuri, 'I'm sorry it was too
late'" (*Jewel* 69).

Miss Crane, as already stated, sets the tone for the whole *Quartet*. So her subsequent suttee, after the callous quelling of the riots at Mayapore, is the most extreme example in the book of the need to make up for the failure of the purported
ideal.[3] And it is this failure that is Scott's primary concern. Certainly the most

---

[3] As Janis Tedesco and Janet Popham put it in their *Introduction to 'The Raj Quartet'* (Lanham
MD: UP of America, 1985): "Mr Chaudhuri was dead and with him died her illusions and her
hopes" (12). Gerwin Strobl is sharper: "By recognizing [...] her countrymen's presumption Edwina
explodes the myth of 'the White Man's Burden', revealing it to be nothing but arrogance, cant and

powerful impression in the book is that made by Merrick, the obvious villain of the piece. His denial of any ideal was a major problem to both Indians and the British who believed in an ideal. Yet in the end Scott was more concerned morally with the failure of the idealists to adopt a similar sort of single-mindedness in their approach.

Mabel Layton and Lady Manners: Conflicting Commitments

It was mainly because of the idealist's failure that in the end tragedy could not be avoided. But it is largely women who realize this, or at least express the realization openly. So Edwina Crane, and others, make what recompense they can. By the intensity of their responses Scott shows the intensity of regret about the failure of the ideal, and suggests, too, that the tragedy was as much that of the idealists as of the land they loved, because they did not love enough.

The least dramatic response among these women, if in duration the longest, was that of Mabel Layton. Our first clear perception of her is when she refuses to contribute to the fund for General Dyer. He had been retired on half-pay after firing "on an unarmed crowd of civilians [...] killing several hundred and wounding upwards of a thousand," (*Scorpion* 67). Scott had earlier drawn attention to this cathartic incident, in the comments of the ostensibly liberal Mayapore Deputy Commissioner, Robin White, over the British decision 1919 not to grant

> a major advance towards self-government as a reward for co-operating [...] What in hell was the good of declaring Dominion status as our aim [...] and [...] later instituting trial without jury for political crimes and powers of detention [...] the result: riots, and then General Dyer at Amritsar and a return to distrust and fear and suspicion (*Jewel* 346).

Scott's point is that no easy distinction can be drawn between humane civil administrators and aggressive soldiers. Dyer and those like him could function only in a context, as occurred in Mayapore in 1942, in which the administration had taken provocative decisions based on the assumption that they knew best about India. Even when those like Robin White disagreed, their own commitment to India going deeper, it was not deep enough for them not to carry out the prescribed policy. So it was not surprising that when Dyer was retired for his actions he was seen as a martyr and the ladies of the area busied themselves collecting money for him.

It was to Mabel's credit that her logic went deeper: "'To me it's not a question of choosing between poor old Dyer and the bloody browns. The choice was made for me when we took the country over and got the idea we did so for its own sake

---

self-delusion"; *The Challenge of Cross-Cultural Interpretation in the Anglo-Indian Novel: the Raj Revisited* (Lewiston NY & Lampeter: Edwin Mellen, 1995): 30.

instead of ours. Dyer can look after himself, but according to the rules the browns can't because looking after them is what we get paid for"' (*Scorpion* 69). So she contributed instead to the fund raised by Indians for the victims' families. She kept this quiet, but over time her contributions to Indian charities increased while a sense of guilt haunted her. The reiteration of what sounds like 'Gillian Waller' in her sleep recalls Jallianwallah where Dyer's massacre had occurred, its impact reinforced by Reid's massacres at Mayapore. Finally, moving in its starkness, is her remark when she sees the silver in the mess of her menfolk's regiment: "' I thought there might be some changes, but there aren't [...] I can't even be angry. But someone ought to be' " (*Towers* 235).

Mabel's protest, if muted, could not be easily ignored. Her detachment from society could be attributed to eccentricity, but there remained the "belief that [...] she was among those people who would not regret the flood" (*Towers* 36–37). And after she dies it is felt that her behaviour had constituted "a criticism of the foundation of the edifice, of the sense of duty which kept alive the senses of pride and loyalty and honour" (*Towers* 306). Scott's point, of course, is that all that had been left behind when the 'rules' were broken, the trust forgotten and the Dyers unleashed. Mabel's withdrawal into herself has its more pointed counterpart in Lady Manners' withdrawal from British society to the almost exclusive companionship of her Indian friends.

Of course the British would not have wanted to receive her, after the momentous step she had taken in publicly acknowledging her niece's half-caste child, born after the infamous rape. That was necessarily seen as a much more hostile criticism of the foundations of the edifice of the British presence in India than Mabel's quiet withdrawal was. But for Lady Manners it was the logical extension of the relationship originally proclaimed, in which a period of trusteeship would lead to equality in the end. As such, like Mabel, she inspires the two women who occupy more central positions in the Quartet in actively illustrating the positive attitudes Scott supports. Barbie Batchelor sees her in Pankot and is reminded of Mabel, while Sarah Layton visits her in Kashmir and looks at the baby. Sarah's later confession of this marks the advent of liberation from the stultifying proprieties in which Anglo-Indian society had bound her.

Yet despite the firmness of their responses, it should be noted that both Mabel and Lady Manners were passive in their approach. With Mabel we can understand both her obligation to family and the complications a public course of action might have caused. But we also see, from her assertion that she hated the country now and could not even be angry, that her retreat was as much from herself as from the people around her. Lady Manners, of course, did more, in cutting herself off so resolutely; yet her efforts, too, were limited.

A point, significant also for Scott's wider analysis, at which her limitations become clear is her reaction to partition. *The Jewel in the Crown* concludes with her claiming that "The creation of Pakistan is our crowning failure [...] Our only justification for [...] power was unification. But we've divided one composite nation into two" (473). This, as the Quartet makes clear, was Scott's view too;[4] but while he shows the contribution of British policy towards partition, Lady Manners sees it as an Indian solution to the problem, "abdication on India's terms instead of ours" (475). The suggestion is that Britain should have even stayed longer to sort things out on her own terms. There is no awareness that it was those very terms that had caused the mess.

Scott himself makes clear to us how even a liberal governor could encourage the move towards partition, perhaps the more effectively for being decent. Chief Minister Kasim responds warmly to George Malcolm's goodwill but later he reflects that Malcolm wanted to involve him in intrigue that would destroy the Congress Party and its stand for a united India:

> A reply [...] which makes it clear that the Governor's request that I write to him occasionally wasn't really the friendly gesture [...] I could be out of Premanagar by Christmas if I wrote to him and said I'd changed my mind and was willing to resign from Congress and accept nomination to his executive council. (*Scorpion* 46–47)

This, I think, indicates further the distinction between a liberal sense of duty and the greater commitment based on appreciation of identities and interests separate from one's own. The trouble with the former in British India was that it was so often used on behalf of its British peers, hence against those viewed as alien. Both Mabel and Lady Manners late in life resist this sort of complaisance and, by withdrawing from their peers, express disapproval of the betrayal of an ideal. However, in both cases, more active commitment was beyond them.

Bronowsky's Commitment

It may be as well to consider here the one male character in the Quartet who shares with these women a positive approach based on commitment. By this I refer to Count Bronowsky, Chief Minister of the Nawab, ruler of Mirat. Bronowsky indeed may not seem an exception to the rule, in that Scott suggests a certain femininity by making him a homosexual attracted only to youths "whose attributes were wholly masculine" (*Scorpion* 168). However, the shrewdness we see, and his capacity to

---

[4] As he wrote to Dorothy Ganapathy in 1965, "What is clear to me is that in the end India must be reunited [...] Pakistan always was an impossible concept"; cited in Robin Moore, *Paul Scott's Raj* (London: Heinemann, 1990): 75.

manipulate and control, indicate that he too would have been as capable of domination as others in his position, had not his own choice dictated otherwise.

There are two reasons for the exceptional manner in which Bronowsky exercises
his authority. The first was that he did so by the Nawab's invitation. Secondly,
though he took pride in his achievement, Scott makes clear there is no selfish element in the relationship: "It was part of his pride that Nawab Sahib alone should be
credited" (*Scorpion* 165). So Bronowsky does not impose his own views on the
question of accession to India. Recognition of and respect for another's interests was
an intrinsic part of his commitment, marking it off from an impersonal sense of duty
which, if probed, revealed a personal (indeed, selfish) basis.

Of course, it was easier for Bronowsky, in that he had only himself to commit,
whereas for Englishmen the weight of society always pressed upon them. Ahmed
suggests the institutional limitations of English liberalism when he says that the
"'friendly English [are] more dangerous than the rude'" (*Scorpion* 97), but explains why Bronowsky's friendliness does not cause similar problems:

> It isn't the whiteness that matters. It's the position of the English as rulers that makes
> their friendship dangerous. They are consciously or subconsciously aware of weaken-
> ing their position by friendliness, so this friendliness always has to be on their own
> guarded terms. (*Scorpion* 97)

The fear of being taken advantage of we have seen already in Miss Crane. The
question of solidarity, however, was more important, and perhaps explains why the
men in authority in the Quartet, however liberal their views, fail so signally to fulfil
their ideal of trusteeship. Bronowsky's approach brings this out while his active
commitment contrasts with the more restrained apologia of Mabel Layton and Lady
Manners. Thus, his behaviour emphasizes the inevitable limitations for the two
ladies in terms of the positions they had once occupied.

Despair and Withdrawal: The Consequences of Failure

As to the inadequacy of Lady Manners' commitment, as significant as her regrets
over Britain not interfering about Pakistan was the contrary impulse with regard to
Hari Kumar. Though aware of his suffering, she let a year lapse before asking for
the case to be re-examined; and though that examination made clear the injustice
done him, she does nothing more. Later, on Hari's release, she does nothing to
unite him with his daughter. Her reason is that "'anything else would [...] smack of
condescension'" (*Division* 650). Significantly Rowan agrees, whereas Perron tries
to visit Hari. It therefore seems unlikely that Scott intended to underwrite Lady
Manners' keeping herself apart. Her decisions do not take into account Hari's
views; and earlier Scott had in fact given us the real reason for the failure to com-

mit herself further: "She felt the first wave [...] of an extraordinary tranquillity the nature of which she had no energy to determine [...] the first tranquillity of death" (*Scorpion* 314–15).

This contrasts with T.S. Eliot's prescription in my epigraph, which Scott used in his paper on "India: A Post-Forsterian View."[5] And it recalls Mrs Moore, who also withdrew into herself culpably when her help might have been of use.[6] Later on, Lady Manners could not do quite the same, and her public commitment to the child indicates the greater demands on even a limited response. However, Scott makes clear that, like Mabel Layton, who concealed the workings of her conscience, Lady Manners too withheld something of herself.

Barbie Batchelor: Striving for Fulfilment

In this respect, Barbie Batchelor represents a distinct advance. Though at first sight her silent madness might seem close to Mrs Moore's catatonic trance, that arose from weariness. Such weariness can be seen in Lady Manners and in Mabel Layton too, whereas Barbie's withdrawal was like Edwina Crane's suttee, surrender of self in fulfilment of a commitment.

It is necessary to recognize this to appreciate the significance of the symbolism in the title *The Towers of Silence*. It is clear that Barbie takes over from Edwina after the first book, just as Sarah Layton does from Daphne Manners. As Edwina made clear the meaning of *The Jewel in the Crown*, which represented the traduced ideal relationship between Britain and India, so Barbie shows the significance of *The Towers of Silence*, the book over which she is, as Swinden puts it, "The presiding genius."[7] Unfortunately he does not explain the imagery, while all Bhaskara Rao says is that "The hovering vultures waiting to pick the dead bodies clean symbolize [...] the British Raj waiting to be picked clean."[8] This suggests that dead bodies symbolize the Raj and does not make clear what the Raj will suffer, nor from what source.

Rather, it is clear from what Scott says that it is herself whom Barbie sees as a tower of silence, from which "The birds had picked the words clean" (*Towers* 463). When the idea of being stripped clean in this fashion had first occurred to her, she had been

---

[5] Paul Scott, "India: A Post-Forsterian View," Address to the Royal Society of Literature, 1968 (London: Proceedings of the Royal Society of Literature, 1968).

[6] See "Of Love and Development," in Rajiva Wijesinha, *Inside Limits: Identity and Repression in (Post)-Colonial Fiction* (Colombo: Sabaragamuwa UP, 1998): 64–90.

[7] Patrick Swinden, *Paul Scott: Images of India* (London: Macmillan, 1980): 69.

[8] K. Bhaskara Rao, *Paul Scott* (Boston MA: Twayne, 1971): 83.

> filled with a tiny horror: the idea of someone coming to claim back even one item of
> what was contained [...] if you allowed the possibility of one claim then you had to
> allow the likelihood of several [...] the logical end to the idea was total evacuation of
> room, body and soul, and of oneself dead but erect, like a monument. (206)

But at the end Barbie yields herself to the claims, to the extent of foregoing her own
identity. Instead she takes on the persona of Edwina Crane who had also gone
beyond reason in reaffirming the commitment she had failed to live up to in her
lifetime.

To appreciate the significance of Barbie's transformation we should consider
carefully her shift of perspective as well as its underlying motivation. Early in the
book, Scott mentions her concern about her luggage, because of her need to add
weight to the meaning of her life:

> At the end of her career the tide of affairs which had involved her was on the ebb,
> leaving her revealed [...] apart from herself there was only her luggage [...] without it
> she did not seem to have a shadow. (15–16)

Yet the important thing about her is that she does not rest on her laurels, but continues to reconsider the meaning of what she had done. From the beginning, she
does this in terms of the people she had been in charge of, as we see from her
anxiety about the girl she punished for colouring Jesus' face blue. It is this sort of
anxiety that prepares us for her profound reaction to the news of Edwina Crane
having held Chaudhuri's hand, together with news of

> Miss Manners in some kind of unacceptable relationship with a man of another race
> whom she was intent on saving [...] there emerged a figure [...] of an unknown Indian
> [...] it occurred to her that the unknown Indian was what her life in India had been
> about. (88)

Because of her recognition through this of what real commitment amounts to, she
begins to doubt whether love had ever been among the gifts her mission had brought
to the children of India. Other motives such as pity, she realizes, were irrelevant in
comparison with love, and without that her work could not have the intended meaning: "After many years of believing I knew what love is I now suspect I do not
which means I do not know what God is either" (237).

It is at the time she registers the importance of Edwina's commitment that she
begins to read and be fascinated by Emerson, to see the relations between her own
experiences and those of the society within which she functioned. The image of the
vultures that later pick clean her words is first seen here, with a positive twist that
foreshadows its later significance: "the philosophical life [...] impinged on her own
like the shadow of a hunched bird of prey patiently observing below it the ritual of
survival. The bird should have been an angel" (88). In effect, Barbie begins to understand the need for objective analysis, to go through the various strands in one's life

and assess them in relation to one's ideals and obligations. So, if other English women in Pankot resemble harpies in their reactions to Edwina Crane and Daphne Manners, Barbie recognizes the claims of others, the unknown Indians she had not considered before. Unlike Edwina, however, who acted promptly on her enhanced perceptions, Barbie continues to live within the society she had begun to judge. Through her, we thus see an increasing derogation from the ideals suggested by the titles to the five parts of the book, as a society justified by a sense of obligation abandons it more and more openly: "The charade was finished. Mabel had guessed the word [...] but had refrained from speaking it. The word was 'dead' [...] the edifice had crumbled and the facade fooled nobody" (268).

That, despite this perception, Barbie continues to act is to her credit. Though we cannot criticize Edwina Crane for self-immolation in recognition of the failure of an ideal, the fact that Barbie continues to strive to fulfil the obligations necessary for the pursuit of love surely makes her the more admirable character. Touchingly, Scott allows her a trace of fulfilment in her relations with the little Indian boy whom she calls her unknown Indian. She tries to give him love instead of patronage and is rewarded by what seems a genuine response.

Barbie and Merrick: Different Responses to Despair

The relationship, however, cannot develop, for in the end Barbie, like Edwina, gives up, and her final acknowledgment of the claims upon her leads, if not to suicide, then to a similar negation of herself. The immediate causes of this are twofold. First the trunk, which she still clings to as containing her history, falls on top of her and lays her low. More importantly, she meets Merrick, personifying the devil, desiring her soul as once before it seemed to her he had desired Edwina's. Her characterization of the devil on that occasion made clear the reason she thought it essential to still keep on striving, whatever one's perceptions:

> Barbie's Devil was not a demon but a fallen angel, and his Hell [...] an image of lost heaven. There was no soul lonelier than he. His passion for souls was as great as God's but all he had to offer was his own despair. He offered it as boundlessly as God offered love. He *was* despair as surely as God was love. (*Towers* 112)

At that time, Barbie thought Edwina had killed herself out of "despair not purified by love" (*Towers* 112). It was because of the despair generated by Merrick's brutal certainties with regard to his role in India that Barbie felt him "so purposeful in his desire for her soul that he had thrown away Edwina's" (475). Yet after the accident she feels that she had "been through Hell and come out again by God's mercy," and the reason is that her despair was purified by love. Characteristically she had tried to share this with him by giving him her picture of 'The Jewel in the Crown':

> One should always share one's hopes [...] That represents one of the unfulfilled ones. Oh, not the gold and scarlet uniforms [...] We've had everything in the picture except what got left out."
> "What was that, Miss Batchelor?"
> She said, not wishing to use that emotive word, "I call it the unknown Indian. He isn't *there*. So the picture isn't finished." (453)

I think we see throughout the book that the absence of love affects Merrick as much as it does Barbie. But where she continued to pursue it, he denied it and tried to draw others into the certainties of the despair with which he was left. In the Indian situation at this time, with the illusion of self-denial no longer available, despair was perhaps all that was realistically left to those of the British who still yearned for their ideals. In Barbie's case, however, the despair engendered by recognition of the failure of ideals was purified by love. For that reason I think we are intended to see the state at which she arrived, however sad, as an affirmation of over-riding commitment. Rubin's conclusion then about both Edwina and Barbie – "Their labours had embodied the highest ideals of the British mission, but neither can fulfil those ideals because, as both came to realize, it is nurtured on the usual colonialist self-delusion and upheld by unrelenting racial prejudice"[9] – may be true. But what it omits is Scott's celebration of the recompense they try, vainly yet so movingly, to offer.

WORKS CITED

Allen, Charles, ed. *Plain Tales from the Raj* (London: André Deutsch/BBC, 1975).

Bhaskara Rao, K. *Paul Scott* (Boston MA: Twayne, 1971).

Moore, Robin. *Paul Scott's Raj* (London: Heinemann, 1990).

Rubin, David. *After the Raj: British Novels of India since 1941* (Hanover NH: UP of New England, 1986).

Scott, Paul. *The Day of the Scorpion* (London: Panther, 1984).

——. *A Division of the Spoils* (London: Panther, 1984).

——. "India: A Post-Forsterian View." Address to the Royal Society of Literature, 1968 (London: Proceedings of the Royal Society of Literature, 1968).

——. *The Jewel in the Crown* (London: Panther, 1984).

——. *The Towers of Silence* (London: Panther, 1984).

Strobl, Gerwin. *The Challenge of Cross-Cultural Interpretation in the Anglo-Indian Novel: the Raj Revisited* (Lewiston NY & Lampeter: Edwin Mellen, 1995).

Swinden, Patrick. *Paul Scott: Images of India* (London: Macmillan, 1980).

---

[9] David Rubin, *After the Raj: British Novels of India since 1941* (Hanover NH: UP of New England, 1986): 140.

Tedesco, Janis, & Janet Popham. *Introduction to 'The Raj Quartet'* (Lanham MD: UP of America, 1985).

Wijesinha, Rajiva. *Inside Limits: Identity and Repression in (Post)-Colonial Fiction* (Colombo: Sabaragamuwa UP, 1998).

❧

- dominance of colonial native

- Eurocentric bias that distorts Plunkett's amateur historicism

- potential for historical objectivity

• Is history a narrative or an empirical science

(aka objectivity is possible)

the real Q

overcome the logic of correlation ?

the triumph of unforeseen

complex allusion

original

One might argue that all histories
are narrative — stories that fall
into literary genres of tragedy, action,
adventure, romance, etc.
What is regained are narratives that
are rendered not exclusively from the
perspective of the rulers.

Colonialism, Hegemony and After in Nayantara Sahgal's *Rich Like Us*

CHITRA SANKARAN

T HE PROBLEM OF CONTESTING AND RE-WRITING imperial historical representation, which throughout the colonial period has systematically relegated individual postcolonial societies to the margins, has been widely recognized as one of the predominant tasks awaiting postcolonial societies. The postcolonial task has been conceived of as primarily to engage the medium of narrativity itself, and, as the cultural historian, Hayden White,[1] describes it, to re-inscribe the 'rhetoric' – the heterogeneity of historical representation. However, the task of penetrating a discursive plane which always has 'Europe' inscribed at its centre has been perceived as posing great problems to emerging postcolonial historiographical reinterpretations.

Thus far, one of the greatest impediments to this enterprising project, as 'revisionist' historians have repeatedly discovered, is the deeply embedded myth of the historical narrative as an objective and unvarnished representation of 'true events as they actually happened somewhere out there.' However, with the recognition that nineteenth-century eurocentric historical discourse, seeking to legitimate the imperial enterprise, systemically suppressed the modality of interpretation which gave it its form, the extant historiographic ideology that foregrounds historical discourse as a neutral narrative form came to be deconstructed. Since then the trend has been to favour some relativism, more openness about what constitutes evidence and a less inflexible attitude to the documentary model of knowledge. However, in the opinion of critics such as Hayden White and Dominick LaCapra, the process of rethinking

---

[1] Hayden White, "The Politics of Historical Interpretation: Discipline and De-Sublimation," *Critical Inquiry* 9 (1982): 113–37.

has barely begun.[2] In fact, on occasion the postcolonial commitment to rewriting the received account from imperial powers has itself led to the reinforcement of the essentializing ideology inherent in eurocentric historical discourse.[3] A standing example cited by Philip Darby is that of the eight-volume UNESCO *General History of Africa* published in 1981, whose introduction uses terms such as 'true history' and describes its processes as providing "the best possible guarantee of the scientific objectivity of the general history of Africa.[4] Thus the pitfall of relying entirely on 'official rewritings of history' has come to be recognized. This has led to the exploration of alternative narrative forms that can contribute productively to this process of re-historicizing.

One of the possible sites of entry to construct an alternative historiography, it has been suggested, could be through the medium of literature. Wilson Harris, for instance, believes that "a philosophy of history may well lie buried in the arts of the imagination."[5] However, one of the greatest barriers to accepting this is the traditional dichotomy that exists between 'fiction' and non-fiction.

This fiction/non-fiction dichotomy, however, has increasingly come to be questioned, and the notion that there is a definitive distinction between fiction and non-fiction has become less and less tenable.[6] It is recognized that because the hold of this dichotomy in our minds is deep-rooted we do not attempt to unravel the extent to which they overlap, making the boundaries fuzzy and unrecognizable. The genre of autobiography illustrates this well. It defies clear categorization as fiction, history or psychology.[7] Studies in narratology have further recognized the unreliability of such absolute categorizations.

The argument has been proposed in the field of narratology that narrative involves the telling of a story. So far as the *form* of the story is concerned, there is not

---

[2] See Hayden White, *The Content of the Form: Narrative Discourse and Historical Representation* (Baltimore MA: Johns Hopkins UP, 1987; Dominic LaCapra, *History and Criticism* (Ithaca NY & London: Cornell UP, 1985).

[3] Philip Darby, *The Fiction of Imperialism* (London & Washington: Cassell, 1998): 20.

[4] *General History of Africa*, vol. 1: *Methodology and African Prehistory*, ed. J. Ki Zerbo (UNESCO International Scientific Committee for the Drafting of a General History of Africa; London: Heinemann; Berkeley: U of California P, 1981). The words are those of Professor B.A. Ogot.

[5] Wilson Harris, "History, Fable and Myth in the Caribbean and the Guianas," in *Selected Essays of Wilson Harris: The Unfinished Genesis of the Imagination*, ed. A.J.M. Bundy (London & New York: Routledge, 1999): 152–66.

[6] For example, Barett J. Mandel, in his essay "Full of life now" in *Autobiography: Essays Theoretical and Critical*, ed. James Olney (Princeton NJ: Princeton UP, 1980): 49–72, argues that some categories of narrative defy the simple fiction/non-fiction dichotomy.

[7] As Philip Darby points out, "we might plump for labelling [autobiography] fiction because it imposes on an unformed past a coherent pattern derived from the present (but in what way is this different from history?), or because at the very least some things will be repressed or obfuscated (but in politics is not public testament as likely to conceal or reveal?)"; *The Fiction of Imperialism*, 22.

much to distinguish fiction from non-fiction. Reality is not 'out there' waiting to be discovered, neither is the past 'back there' waiting to be retrieved by the historian. It has been recognized by theorists that it is precisely the narrative impulse that distances an account from the material evidence upon which it draws. Thus, imagination as an element cannot be divorced from historical or political treatises. It seems to be this self-conscious fashioning activity at the centre of constructing a narrative that more or less reduces the distance between historical and literary accounts.

Given these theoretical observations, several postcolonial scholars have turned to imaginative fiction to unearth certain deep-rooted historical attitudes mainly about imperial historical events and / or periods. The work of late-Victorian authors such as Conrad and Kipling have often served as evidential materials for historical reconstructions of the Imperial era. Such attempts have foregrounded the fact that fiction's apprehensions and constructions, far from being merely incidental to or by-products of the imperial era, were in fact fundamental to and contributed substantially to the enterprise of empire itself. Thus, in postcolonial societies literary discourse has been set up as a mode of contesting the hitherto monolithic narrative of history.

It is with the above background in mind that I set out to analyse Nayantara Sahgal's *Rich Like Us*, first published in 1983, five years after the dissolution of the State of Emergency, the period in which the text is set. Winner of the 1985 Sinclair Prize for Literature, the text has been variously described by critics and reviewers as "a poignant lament for the India which is being ruined by stupidity and corruption" (*The Literary Review*) and as "the first significant work of fiction about that tense and self-questioning period" (*British Book News*).[8] The text is significant to our purposes in that it attempts to describe the impact and consequences of a historical epoch on a postcolonial nation-state. My purpose, then, is to analyse the ways in which it attempts to interpret this particular epoch in independent India and the concerns it raises through its interpretation.

Rich Like Us is an overt exploration into the consequences of the State of Emergency declared by the then prime minister Indira Gandhi on 26 June 1975, nearly thirty years after Indian independence. Two narratives, the first-person narrative of Sonali (a civil servant, ignominiously demoted from her post during the Emergency) and an omniscient authorial narrative, alternate with each other, cross-cut by the manuscript of Sonali's paternal grandfather that inscribes the tale of his grandmother, her *sati* or widow-burning, into the text.

At the outset, the pluralistic fictional narrative attempts to bring in these several heterogeneous narratives which as critics have pointed out "counter, but do not

---

[8] The two quotations are taken from the cover page of the text. These and all other references to the text are from Nayantara Sahgal, *Rich Like Us* (1983; London: Sceptre, 1996).

completely displace, the monolithic, linear Christian, European chronology."[9] Time zones alternate between the past and the present. The span of the narrative dealing with the present is only around four months – between July 1975, a month after Indira Gandhi declared a State of Emergency, and the first Divali of the year, roughly around the end of October. However, flashbacks from two predominant characters – Rose and Ram – take us to the pre-World War II era, while the manuscript of Sonali's father relates a tale of 1820s India. This again challenges the limitations of the single narrative perspective at the centre of most historical analyses. Thus, it becomes useful for our purposes to examine these three broad strands of narrative and analyse how they contribute to an understanding of this tense political period in India.

The text begins with the omniscient authorial narrative, which ironically plays up the Self/Other stereotype now identified as a central trope in any East–West encounter. The postcolonial nation-state is shown to be in no way 'free' from this trope despite gaining political autonomy. If anything, in the international market, things have only worsened. There is a humanity to Mr Goldfinkel, who has done business with Dev's father, Ram, that is shown as entirely lacking in Mr Neuman, who is here to do business with Dev. For Mr Neuman, a representative of First-World economies who often finds himself in Third-World settings,

> The walls outside the cool, controlled climate of his hotel room, wherever it happened to be, in a republic, a sheikhdom, or a monarchy, had erupted with predictable regularity into the violent poster paint and purple prose of announcement and celebration, hailing a coup, the return of an old prophet, or the rise of a new messiah [...] Political convulsions left him cold and political clichés bored him. He had no trouble avoiding controversy in the host country as he had been told to do. (10)

Mr Neuman seems emblematic of an economically exploitative West that is shown as purely profit-driven, spreading its acquisitive tentacles over the teeming Third-World markets. This is the state of affairs in the international domain. Things are equally difficult at home, within the nation-state. With independence, the structures of power may have shifted from the imperial centre to the colonies, but only to be duplicated into manichaean dichotomies within the postcolonial state – have(s) and have-not(s), rulers and ruled. Neuman, the clinically detached outsider, unhurriedly notes the signs of this difference as it is manifested, without emotion, merely to record it as significant data for future economic transactions. The abused workforce attempts to grasp at a semblance of empowerment through unionism, but this, too, is effectively curbed. As Nishi, the wife of the criminal and inefficient yet successful entrepreneur Dev (who goes on to become a union minister at the end of the story),

---

[9] Dennis Walder, *Post-Colonial Literatures in English History, Language, Theory* (Oxford: Blackwell, 1998): 106.

artlessly notes, her initial dismay that their tailors were resorting to unionism dissolves, since "Later the emergency solved that problem" (18) with its ban on all unions and meetings.

The State of Emergency declared within the postcolonial nation-state is presented ironically as a thinly veiled attempt to grasp and retain power in the face of stiff opposition. The public face of dominance is displayed in various ways – in the high-handed way in which Sonali, a high-ranking, conscientious civil servant, is replaced by the politico-touting Kachru, in the brutality with which tenements are torn from under slum-dwellers who are packed off out of sight to distant locations, and the diligence with which vans with iron-barred windows roam the streets picking up citizens for vasectomies. The narrative exposes the hate and fear of those inside the vans, the rebelliousness evident in the young man arrested and hustled towards a waiting van, and the desperation of the silent subalterns whisked away for quick sterilization.

The significance of this exposure proffers an important corrective to detached historical accounts of the Emergency. It demonstrates that our understanding of the abstractions of politics is heightened when integrated with life. The likelihood of the reader identifying partially or fully with one or more of the characters means he would have a more direct comprehension of the political predicament that is being described. In *Rich Like Us*, the discourse becomes enabling because it demonstrates the fundamental truth about power relations: that the meaning of dominance cannot be considered apart from the thoughts and behaviour of those who exercise overlordship and those who suffer it; that the two are mutually interdependent. The abused – at least initially, it seems – are shown to be complicit with the abusers. As Sonali observes, "we were all taking part in a thinly disguised masquerade, preparing the stage for family rule" (29). The abused initially enter into a conspiracy of silence with their abusers.

The second strand of the omniscient narrative deals with the marriage of Ram, the wealthy, erudite, highly westernized, Kashmiri Indian, and Rose, the cockney English girl. If, like most interracial marriages in Indo-British novels, we also have to consider this union as symbolizing an allegorical Indo-British union, then Ram's social slide implied in the union itself seems to be a statement about the limitations of the options at the centre available to the margins. Symbolically, Ram can only yearn from afar for his more equal intellectual and social Western counterpart – the eminently eligible Marcella Carlyle, who, predictably enough, goes on to marry a white middle-class male. Apart from exploring the relations between Britain and India, this strand of the narrative also subtly foregrounds the Indo-Pakistan affinity through the relationship of Ram and his close friend Zafar, who later becomes a

political personality in independent Pakistan. At one stage, Rose, watching the two
of them, wonders "what all the uproar of religion these days" was about:

> They could be blood-brothers, she thought, tall and aquiline, unhurried, unhurriable,
> handsome, conceited, loveable and insufferable in all the same ways. You couldn't put
> a grain of rice between them, they were that alike. If Ram was a muslimized Hindu,
> Zafar was a Hinduized Muslim. So what was all the shouting about? (72)

The whole Indo-Pakistan division is exposed as the political plot it essentially was,
rather than as any division based on religious and/or ideological differences. The
narrative foregrounds in several ways the essential hybridizing that was so much a
part of the culture of the subcontinent. If Ram and Zafar are shown to be the male
outcome of a highly hybridized species, the females, too, do not seem to find their
religious differences insurmountable. As Rose sits hosting her cocktail party, the
religious incantations of Mona (Ram's Hindu wife's) come wafting up in the air
joined by Begum Zafar's muttered invocations to Allah to provide a better life for
Mona (74). By presenting the merriment of the two men, Ram and Zafar, the narrative realistically portrays how insubstantial the whole idea of a divided India was
during the pre-independence era. Zafar, in fact, compares it to Cythera, a mere
dream, a Peter-Pan land. In such ways, the novel realistically reclaims the larger
histories of the nation by addressing more intimate personal histories.

Next we approach the first-person narrative of Sonali. Once again, weighing the
narrative from the perspective of history, one is led to ask: how pertinent is Sonali's
private story in the context of history? Our first realization in considering this issue
is the acknowledgement that Sonali's predicament is not unique, but recorded as
fairly representative of the Emergency era. Thus, her private sphere is no longer just
that, but has actually evolved into a site of resistance – in other words, it is a politi-
cized sphere. However, to explore how Sonali's predicament is significant to an
historical reading of the period, one first needs to locate Sonali.

Sonali is from the ruling middle-class elite, aligned on the side of the rulers. She
is part of the civil service, who see themselves as direct inheritors of the British Raj.
The fact that Sonali herself is displaced under the Emergency underscores the prevalence of rampant corruption. A sense of the desperate state of affairs is brought
home to us: no one, it seems, not even the empowered bourgeoisie who have
replaced the imperial rulers, is free of its exploitative and corrupt clutches. Sonali's
narrative traverses the middle ground between internal consciousness and external
public events. Thus, the overt political engagement of the novel is qualified by the
agonized internal searchings of Sonali, providing an important counterweight to a
mere chronicling of events. This section of the narrative thus approximates to the
searching analysis of an historian who attempts to connect events in order to find an
overarching purpose.

Furthermore, it is from Sonali's narrative that we realize that dominance approached from the perspective of geopolitical power exudes an aura of capability and confidence. Thus, several historical accounts – Stanley Wolpert's, for instance[10] – paint the positive side of the Emergency quite expansively, barely touching on the negative:

> The combination of stick and carrot proved quite effective. Within days bureaucrats who had never reached their offices before half-past ten in the morning were hard at work by nine. Black market hoarding and price gouging stopped overnight. Smugglers and tax evaders quickly realised that "Madam" was determined to enforce her program, even if to do so required arresting her former supporters and friends. Within a month the prices of rice and barley fell 5 percent, and they kept falling. Almost miraculously, it seemed to many Indians, [...] the "trains were running on time." (97)

However, Sonali's account balances this by showing that dominance seen from within is marked by elements of pretence, incomprehension and deep insecurity for the peoples of the nation. Once again, the fictional account redresses the balance. As Philip Darby notes in another context, "literature's concentration on the personal can be a corrective to international relations' preoccupation with aggregates."[11]

Sonali's account also raises the question of gender and disempowerment in the postcolonial context. The strategy of the beggar, who escapes the clutches of the sterilizing squad by the simple expedient of slipping in and out of their grasp at lightning speed, illustrates this. The beggar refuses to meet the dominant group, here the sterilizing squad, head-on, because he is canny enough to realize that he would never survive the confrontation intact. Here, the mutilated beggar's positioning vis-à-vis the sterilizing squad is illustrative of the feminine in opposition to the 'dominant masculine.' As theorists point out, dominance essentially works on the principle of the hyper-masculine and the homo-erotic. In other words, as in Nazi ideology, there is no room for defects or defections, for this ideal of the perfect hyper-masculine thrives on self-admiration.

The mutilated beggar does not conform to the hyper-masculine ideal. Therefore, like the unsightly slum-dwellers' tenements blotting the urban landscape, he becomes expendable. In the rigorously dichotomous world of the 'dominant masculine,' the beggar does not conform to the masculine ideal and is therefore by default relegated to the realms of the feminine. Thus he is feminized.

Studies in imperialist ideology have repeatedly exposed the fact that in an autocracy anything that is feminine is derided. The feminine, opposed to and excluded

---

[10] Stanley Wolpert, "A New History of India," in *Offprint Collection for Post-Colonial Literatures in English*, ed. Cicely Palser Havely et al. (Milton Keynes: Open UP, 1989): 95–100.

[11] Darby, *The Fiction of Imperialism*, 42.

from the realm of the 'dominant masculine,' refuses to engage with the rules of the dominant, because it subverts and speaks with a different voice, refusing any overt confrontation, leaving the oppressor nonplussed and helpless.[12]

The sphere of the feminine, once again taken up by the third type of narration in the text – the manuscript of Sonali's paternal grandfather – adds a further dimension to the historical enquiry. It is reproduced in full in Chapter 11, midway through the narrative. Found among her father's papers, it is *his* father's diary written in 1915, which reproduces the event of his grandmother's *sati*, thus taking us back to the nineteenth century. The journal is highly significant, since it interjects into the text a first-hand account of Indian–British interaction, revealing how important international events registered themselves on an educated Indian consciousness. This journal, as a text, serves both to underwrite the contemporary order of its day and to query it. In other words, it sits on the exact site that we earlier allocated to autobiography. This is a site where historiography, fiction and psychoanalysis intersect. The manuscript thus exemplifies the uses of the personalized narrative as testimony of an era and as historiography to future generations.

In her essay "On the Remaking of History," Janet Abu–Lughod talks about the difference between sociological and historical narratives. She observes:

> What sociologists take as a truism – namely, that accounts of social events are "constructions" rather than descriptions isomorphic with some "objective reality" – has yet to be fully assimilated into historical methodology. Just as is the case when studying ongoing social life, in historical reconstruction there is no archimedean point *outside* the system from which to view historic "reality." The only antidote to this dilemma is the same one used in sociological research, namely, triangulation. We assume that *somewhere* between the accounts given, duly discounted for "distortions" due to partial perspectives and vested interests, one can "find" an approximation of social reality that *might have been constructed* by an unbiased and virtually omniscient narrator, had such an observer been possible.[13]

What strikes me about the three-pointed narrative of *Rich Like Us*, where the impersonal omniscient narrator's viewpoint is interwoven with the first-person narrative of Sonali, an insider, and with the third perspective of Sonali's paternal grandfather, who remains complicit within history yet distanced by time, is that it offers just this methodology of triangulation. Therefore, individual or partisan positions

---

[12] For a detailed discussion of gender and politics, see *Gender and International Relations*, ed. Rebecca Grant & Kathleen Newlands (London: Oxford UP, 1991); *Gendered States: Feminist (Re)Visions of International Relations Theory*, ed. V. Spike Peterson (Boulder CO: Lynne Rienner, 1992).

[13] Janet Abu–Lughod, "On the Remaking of History: How to Reinvent the Past," in *Remaking History*, ed. Barbara Kruger & Phil Mariani (Dia Art Foundation Discussions in Contemporary Culture 4; Seattle: Bay Press, 1989): 112.

seem to be countered to an extent by the intersecting trajectories of all three narratives neutralizing the partiality of any one account.

There is one final factor that holds up the efficacy of this fictional site for constructing an alternative historiography. The heterogeneity of the narratives constantly offer 'counterfactuals' that help to avoid one of the perennial pitfalls of historical narratives: namely, the construction of self-fulfilling hypotheses of narratives, built after events have run their course, which appears to make them inevitable.

However, in offering this alternative site, there are problems as well that need to be addressed. Firstly, no voice is given to the *sati* or the subaltern. The handless beggar intrudes upon the First-World businessman as a subhuman creature. He at least, albeit at the tail end of the narrative, gets to tell the bare outline of his *storia*. This, however, is denied to his raped and murdered wife and to the victim of *sati*, who are inscribed in the text only as voiceless subalterns.

This raises questions about the location of the author herself. Sahgal, as an established political journalist and a close relative of Indira Gandhi, occupies a privileged position available to few in India. Gayatri Spivak's point in "Who Claims Alterity?" – about how the old colonial elite, turned into the national bourgeoisie after independence, generate legitimizing narratives that feed an almost seamless national identity, producing a comfortable 'Other' for transnational postmodernity – becomes pertinent to our argument.

Finally, there seems to be one vital blind spot in the narrative. Though all the problems of the Emergency are presented, the problems implicit in the alternative of democratic governance are never voiced. The ideal of democracy held up as a holy cow to be exalted and worshipped is almost entirely Western in its conception. Sonali's father, the experienced civil servant, is the sole exception in hoping to forge a truly Indian system of governance. Both Sonali and Kachru, as representative modern civil servants, display blind acceptance of Western ideological praxis, in one form or another. The idea that the 'Emergency' itself may be an exploration into formulating an alternative form of democracy is never examined. The fact that Western democracy, which gradually evolved over centuries *for*, *of* and *by* the people, may be less suited to a nation where this form of governance was imposed from above by the elite on the masses, who are as yet uninitiated into the responsibilities that accompany it, is never entertained. This seems to detract from the overall balance of the detailed narrative as an historical account.

On balance, then, literary discourses, traditionally considered as inhabiting the realms of fiction and / or 'non-fact,' actually bear up to consideration as historical material. As such, they seem to exhibit neither more limitations nor fewer than those associated with traditional historical narratives.

WORKS CITED

Abu–Lughod, Janet. "On the Remaking of History: How to Reinvent the Past," in *Remaking History*, ed. Barbara Kruger & Phil Mariani (Dia Art Foundation Discussions in Contemporary Culture 4; Seattle: Bay Press, 1989): 111–29.

Darby, Philip. *The Fiction of Imperialism* (London & Washington: Cassell, 1998).

Grant, Rebecca, & Kathleen Newlands, ed. *Gender and International Relations* (London: Oxford UP, 1991).

Harris, Wilson. "History, Fable and Myth in the Caribbean and the Guianas," in *Selected Essays of Wilson Harris: The Unfinished Genesis of the Imagination*, ed. A.J.M. Bundy (London & New York: Routledge, 1999): 152–66.

Ki–Zerbo, J., ed. *General History of Africa*, vol. 1: *Methodology and African Prehistory* (UNESCO International Scientific Committee for the Drafting of a General History of Africa; London: Heinemann; Berkeley: U of California P, 1981).

La Capra, Dominic. *History and Criticism* (Ithaca NY & London: Cornell UP, 1985).

Mandel, Barett J. "Full of Life Now," in *Autobiography: Essays Theoretical and Critical*, ed. James Olney (Princeton NJ: Princeton UP, 1980): 49–72.

Peterson, V. Spike, ed. *Gendered States: Feminist (Re)Visions of International Relations Theory* (Boulder CO: Lynne Rienner, 1992).

Sahgal, Nayantara. *Rich Like Us* (1983; London: Sceptre, 1996).

Walder, Dennis. *Post-Colonial Literatures in English: History, Language, Theory* (Oxford: Blackwell, 1998).

White, Hayden. *The Content of the Form: Narrative Discourse and Historical Representation* (Baltimore MD: Johns Hopkins UP, 1987).

——. "The Politics of Historical Interpretation: Discipline and De-Sublimation," *Critical Inquiry* 9 (1982): 113–37.

Wolpert, Stanley. "A New History of India," in *Offprint Collection for Post-Colonial Literatures in English*, ed. Cicely Palser Havely et al. (Milton Keynes: Open UP, 1989): 95–100.

❧

To Dwell in Travel
Historical Ironies in Amitav Ghosh's *In an Antique Land*

Rocío G. Davis

I N THE MANNER OF HIS PROTAGONISTS, whose lives are a complicated
mesh of departures and arrivals as they hover between territorial boundaries
and belonging, Amitav Ghosh's *In an Antique Land* crosses the frontiers of
traditional ethnographic travel narratives into the more complex field of transcultural
writing. His text – a blend of autobiography and biography, investigative reporting
and palaeography, cultural studies and travel guide – widens the discursive space
within which he delves into historical ironies within the conglomerate that is the
Middle East. There are two main plot-lines: the story of an Indian slave and his
Jewish master in India and the Middle East during the twelfth century; and a second
story, constructed around the author's experiences as an ethnographer in an Egyptian
village in the 1980s. These two stories intersect continuously as Ghosh's research
slowly unravels the chronicle of the medieval travellers, forging a "triangular relationship between historical reconstruction, ethnography, and literary text"[1] that "re-
casts the conventional village study as a multiply-centred account of transnational
relations."[2] Interestingly, Ghosh presents the area around the Egyptian villages as
important "contact zones," in Mary Louise Pratt's definition of the expression as "an
attempt to invoke the spatial and temporal co-presence of subjects previously
separated by geographic and historical disjunctures, and whose trajectories now
intersect," emphasizing how subjects are constituted in and by their relations to each
other, treating the relations among travellers and "travellees" not in terms of sepa-

---

[1] Javed Majeed, "Amitav Ghosh's *In an Antique Land*: The Ethnographer-Historian and the
Limits of Irony," *Journal of Commonwealth Literature* 30.2 (1995): 45.

[2] James Clifford, "Looking for Bomma," *London Review of Books* (24 March 1994): 26.

rateness or apartheid but of "co-presence, interaction, interlocking understandings and practices, often within radically asymmetrical relations of power."[3]

The stories Ghosh presents – his own, those of the villagers he interviews, and the accounts he constructs from the painstakingly deciphered manuscripts stored for centuries in the Geniza and now kept in special collections at Universities in the West – privilege the experience, impulse, obsession, or need for travel. His subtitle "History in the Guise of a Traveller's Tale" becomes almost an understatement. Practically everyone in the narrative travels, making transnational interaction a common experience and one of the central characteristics of the cultures the protagonists belong to, in the twelfth or the twentieth century. Ghosh's poignant, tragic, sometimes comic account connects the time of the Crusaders and Ibn Battuta with current labour migrations and the Gulf War. In the face of brutal geopolitical divisions, it offers a vision of human crossings in the borderlands, engaging a prehistory of postcolonialism.[4] Ghosh first learned about the slave of MS H.6 in 1978. He had left India for Oxford a few months earlier and was working towards a doctorate in social anthropology:

> I had never heard of the Cairo Geniza before that day, but within a few months I was in Tunisia, learning Arabic. About the same time the next year, 1980, I was in Egypt, installed in a village called Lataîfa, a couple of hours journey to the south-east of Alexandria. I knew nothing then about the Slave of MS H.6 except that he had given me the right to be there, a sense of entitlement.[5]

As Ghosh combs the documents for traces of his South Asian alter ego, he discovers a network of extraordinary Arab and Jewish travellers, of "syncretic cultural forms, of commerce in the fullest sense."[6] The transcultural character of the protagonists' experiences foregrounds paradigmatic forms of an entire social formation, highlighting the circulation and exchange of ideas, energies, and visions between different ethnocultural groups.

The characters in Ghosh's writing do not occupy discrete cultures, but "dwell in travel" in cultural spaces that flow across borders – the "shadow lines" drawn around modern nation-states.[7] As Ghosh explains,

> The area around Nashawy had never been a rooted kind of place; at times it seemed to be possessed of all the busy restlessness of an airport's transit lounge. Indeed, a long

---

[3] Mary Louise Pratt, *Imperial Eyes: Travel Writing and Transculturation* (London: Routledge, 1992): 7.

[4] James Clifford, "Looking for Bomma," *London Review of Books* (24 March 1994): 26.

[5] Amitav Ghosh, *In an Antique Land* (New York: Alfred A. Knopf, 1993): 19. Further page references are in the main text.

[6] Clifford, "Looking for Bomma," 26.

[7] Robert Dixon, "'Travelling in the West': The Writing of Amitav Ghosh," *Journal of Comonwealth Literature*, 31.1 (1996): 3–24.

history of travel was recorded in the very names of the area's 'families': they spoke of links with distant parts of the Arab world – cities in the Levant, the Sudan and the Maghreb. That legacy of transience had not ended with their ancestors either: in Zagh-loul's own generation dozens of men had been 'outside,' working in the shaikdoms of the Gulf, or Libya, while many others had been to Saudi Arabia on the Hajj, or to the Yemen, as soldiers – some men had passports so thick they opened out like ink-blackened concertinas. (173–74)

The expression "dwelling in travel" comes from James Clifford's analysis of Ghosh's work. Clifford highlights the irony in the image of the ethnographer who goes to a village in the Middle East expecting to find a place belonging to a settled, 'authentic' culture and encountering instead a centuries-old palimpsest of move-ment, travel, and intercultural crossings. He argues that there could be no better image of postmodernity than this conflation of an Egyptian village with an airport transit lounge. In Ghosh's writing, Clifford explains, fieldwork relations have be-come less a matter of localized dwelling and more like specific travel encounters, as the writer draws attention to the complex "roots" and "routes" that make up the rela-tions between cultures: "Everyone is on the move, as they have been for centuries: dwelling-in-travel."[8]

Ghosh appropriates the central narrative strategy of travel writing – the itine-rary as the basic organizing principle – in his own narrative: The first three chap-ters are names of cities, and tell of Ghosh's stay there: "Lataîfa," "Nashâwy," and "Mangalore." The fourth is called "Going Back." The episodic structure, more than being just a technical device, therefore becomes essential to the genre. More importantly, travel writing has traditionally gone beyond 'mere' ethnography by being insistently autobiographical. The "amalgamations of the lyrical and the prag-matic in travel writing serve both to sustain and to counter impulses toward per-sonal intimacy, on the one hand, and sociological abstraction on the other. 'Travel has less to do with distance,' [Paul] Theroux asserts, 'than with insight'."[9] So twentieth-century Ghosh travels to the Middle East and to the past as he traces the life of a medieval Indian slave who also travels from India to Egypt and, through the manuscripts and the writer's account, to the future. Ghosh himself is no stranger to travel and displacement:

When I was a child we lived in a place that was destined to fall out of the world's atlas like a page ripped in the press: it was East Pakistan, which, after its creation in 1947,

---

[8] James Clifford, "The Transit Lounge of Culture," *TLS* 4596 (3 May 1991): 7.

[9] Michael Kowalewski, "Introduction: The Modern Literature of Travel," *Temperamental Jour-eys: Essays on the Modern Literature of Travel*, ed. Kowalewski (Atlanta & London: U of Georgia P, 1992): 8.

survived only a bare twenty-five years before becoming a new nation, Bangladesh. (204–205)

Moreover,

> there was an element of irony in our living in Dhaka as 'foreigners,' for Dhaka was in fact our ancestral city: both my parents were from families which belonged to the middle-class Hindu community that had once flourished there [...] we were Indians now, and Dhaka was foreign territory to us although we still spoke its dialect and still had several relatives living in the old Hindu neighbourhoods in the heart of the city. (205)

The continual dislocations Ghosh experiences are always set within a larger background of history and exchange – both cultural and material. He often finds himself more in the position of being studied than studying, as all he encounters question him about India and Hinduism, in an effort to understand what to the fervent Muslims is incomprehensible. " 'I know – it's cows you worship isn't that so?' " (47), says a well-meaning Ustaz Mustafa. " 'I have read all about India [...] There is a lot of chilli in the food and when a man dies his wife is dragged away and burnt alive' " (46). But the villagers offer their logical solutions to what they deem his terrible situation: " 'Now that you are here among us you can understand and learn about Islam, and then you can make up your mind whether you want to stay within that religion of yours' " (48). The agnostic Ghosh will also understand the profound religious fervour that unites these people and provides them with an unwavering sense of community:

> A phenomenon on that scale [all Muslims fasting and praying all over the world] was beyond my imagining, but the exercise helped me to understand why so many people in the hamlet had told me not to fast: to belong to that immense community was a privilege which they had to re-earn every year, and the effort made them doubly conscious of the value of its boundaries. (76)

The archetypal characters he meets in the village and describes in his account heighten the presentation of the village as an emblematic tableau with a complex history of transcultural travel. He taps into the folklore mentality of the Egyptian villagers, using the insights he gains to better comprehend the map and figures of the medieval world that are simultaneously opening up to him as he deciphers the manuscripts that had been stored in the Geniza. At the same time, he is made aware of a more contemporary travel impulse. In this ancient cross-roads of cultures, the inclination is now towards the West. As David Spurr points out, the new forms of cultural appropriation have become

> the very nature of reality in the Third World, now seen in its potential as an image of the West. This form of appropriation gives rise to a curious phenomenon: The West

seeks its own identity in Third World attempts to imitate it; it finds its own image, idealised, in the imperfect copies fabricated by other cultures.[10]

At one point, exhausted and irritated by constant questions about cow-worship and cremation, Ghosh begins to argue violently with an imam healer, each stubbornly defending the superiority of their culture, unknowingly "vying with each other to establish prior claim to the technology of modern violence" (236). On later reflection, Ghosh realizes that

> despite the gap that lay between us, we understood each other perfectly. We were both travelling, he and I: we were travelling in the West. The only difference was that I had actually been there, in person: I could have told him a great deal about it, seen at first hand, its libraries, its museums, its theatres, but it wouldn't have mattered. We would have known, both of us, that all that was mere fluff: in the end, for millions and millions of people on the landmasses around us, the West meant only this – science and tanks and guns and bombs. (236)

The contemporary culture of travel Ghosh reconstructs through his study of the village and parallel palaeographic work is set upon a complex layered history of the commerce in the Indian Ocean. In a world not yet structured by centuries of Western economic and cultural expansion, success implied travelling East, as Ghosh discovers in his research on the Jewish merchant Abraham Ben Yiju:

> To the young Ben Yiju, journeying eastwards would have appeared as the simplest and most natural means of availing himself of the most rewarding possibilities his world has to offer [...] When it came to a choice of career the opportunities offered by the eastern trade must have seemed irresistible to [him], reared as he was in a community that made a speciality of it. (153–54)

The merchant travels from Ifriqiya (now a town in Tunisia) to Fustat, to Aden, then to Mangalore, "the port that sat astride the most important sea-routes connecting the Middle East and the Indian Ocean" (154), where he married a local woman, a freed slave who bore his children (her manumission record survives in St Petersburg). He lived on the Malabar Coast for twenty years, in the busy transcultural world of Arabs, Indians, and Jews, finally returning to Egypt in an attempt to reconnect with his dispersed siblings and reunite the family.

This account, which arises from Ghosh's research on Ben Yiju's slave, holds centre-stage in the narrative. The descriptions Ghosh gathers from the letters sent back and forth from Ben Yiju to his friend and business partner in Egypt, Khalaf ibn Ishaq, support Spurr's description of culture as

---

[10] David Spurr, *The Rhetoric of Empire: Colonial Discourse in Journalism, Travel Writing and Imperial Administration* (Durham NC: Duke UP, 1993): 36.

an ongoing phenomenon in human relations arising out of the dialectical play between forces of homogeneity and heterogeneity. The encounter between one culture and another cannot finally be distinguished from any given culture's continued confrontation with its own ruptures and discontinuities.[11]

As Ghosh explains,

> For the synagogue of Ben Ezra [in Egypt] the influx of migrants from Ifriqiya was to prove providential: the newcomers proved to be the most industrious members of the community and they soon assumed its leadership, setting the pattern for the others in matters of language and culture, as well as trade and commerce. The North Africans appear to have had a particular affinity for the flourishing trade between the Mediterranean and the Indian Ocean and over a period of several centuries the Jewish traders of Fustat counted as an integral part of the richly diverse body of merchants who were involved in the conduct of business in Asian waters. Carried along by the movements of that cycle of trade many of them travelled regularly between three continents – men whose surnames often read like the chapter headings of an epic, linked them to sleepy oases and dusty Saharan market towns, places like El Faiyun and Tlemcen. (55)

Ghosh, weaving together stories of the past and of the present, unveils a long history of cultural interpenetration and coexistence where Jews and Arabs shared languages, trading relations, poetry, clothing, and food. This is a world where slavery "was often used as a means of creating fictive ties of kinship between people" and "as an instrument of religious imagination" (260). Though Ben Yiju and his friends were all orthodox, observant Jews, "the everyday language of their religious life was one they shared with the Muslims of the region: when they invoked the name of God in their writing it was usually as Allah, and more often than not their invocations were in Arabic forms, such as inshâ'allâh" (261). The Geniza documents themselves, written in Arabic with Hebrew characters, are an index of currently impossible contacts, a reminder of the long intercultural history of Levantine societies.[12]

But the writer's interest goes beyond mere ethnographic record, as he tries to think beyond the written experience to the personal lives and relations of his subjects:

> Yet, since Ben Yiju chose, despite the obvious alternative, to marry a woman born outside his faith, it can only have been because of another overriding and more important consideration. If I hesitate to call it love it is only because the documents offer no certain proof. (230)

His interest in the slave also arises from a personal need to encounter the personal beyond the historical, the living behind the shards of culture stored in the Geniza. The first preserved reference to the slave comes as no more than a name and a

---

[11] Spurr, *The Rhetoric of Empire*, 140.

[12] Clifford, "Looking for Bomma," 26.

greeting at the end of a letter from Khalaf ibn Ishaq to Ben Yiju. Yet, as Ghosh observes,

> the reference comes to us from a moment in time when the only people for whom we can even begin to imagine properly human, individual, existences are the literate and the consequential, the wazirs and the sultans, the chroniclers and the priests – the people who had the power to inscribe themselves physically upon time. But the slave of Khalaf's letter was not of that company: in his instance it was a mere accident that those barely discernible traces that ordinary people leave upon the world happen to have been preserved. It is nothing less than a miracle that anything is known about him at all. (16–17)

The world of Ben Yiju and his slave is doomed to end with the arrival of the Europeans who effectively destroyed the Indian Ocean trade and the cultures that supported it. As Ghosh explains,

> Transcontinental trade was no longer a shared enterprise; the merchant shipping of the high seas was now entirely controlled by the naval powers of Europe. It no longer fell to Masr to send her traders across the Indian Ocean; instead, the geographical position that had once brought her such great riches had now made her the object of the Great Powers' attentions, as a potential bridge to their territories in the Indian Ocean. (80–81).

This historical eventuality led to yet another, equally important, diaspora:

> the dispersion of manuscript and archival material from an original point of collection [...] Migration in the text is mainly about the uprooting of bodies of archival material, which becomes one measure of the disruptive effects of European colonial expansion.[13]

Ghosh's interest in the diasporic experience of the Cairo Geniza arises from access to the texts made possible by their transportation to European archives and subsequent transcription and study. The narrative abounds with allusions to the materiality of the text, and to the painstaking process of deciphering it. The section where Ghosh describes the steps involved in arriving at a reasonable hypothesis about the slave's name, Bomma, becomes a metaphor for the entire process of historical and imaginative reappropriation – "the act of imaginative relocating is necessary to heal the rupture caused by the physical removal of that material."[14]

Ghosh's travel account thus becomes a valediction for a time, a place, and a way of life doomed to perish. Vasco da Gama landed in India on 17 May 1498, some three hundred and fifty years after Ben Yiju left Mangalore.

---

[13] Majeed, "Amitav Ghosh's *In an Antique Land*," 46.

[14] Majeed, "Amitav Ghosh's *In an Antique Land*," 47.

> Within a few years of that day the knell had been struck for the world that had brought
> Bomma, Ben Yiju and Ashu together, and another age had begun in which the crossing
> of their paths would seem so unlikely that its very possibility would all but disappear
> from human memory. (286)

The history of imperialism would modify the transcultural nature of that twelfth-
century world, paradoxically rendering impossible the complex interaction that
characterized it, and hiding the consequences which still exist today, most painfully
revealed at the Jordanian border for a brief moment late in 1990. But perhaps the
final irony is that "Bomma's story ends in Philadelphia" (348), the "last testament to
the life of Bomma, the toddy-loving fisherman from Tulunad" housed at the Annen-
berg Research Institute, a centre for social and historical research that "owes its
creation to the vast fortune generated by the first and most popular of America's
television magazines, 'TV Guide'" (348). Ghosh ends the account of the discovery
and unearthing of an incredible transcultural history with a wry comment: "Bomma,
I cannot help feeling, would have been hugely amused" (349).

WORKS CITED

Clifford, James. "Looking for Bomma," *London Review of Books* (24 March 1994): 26–27.
——. "The Transit Lounge of Culture," *Times Literary Supplement* (3 May 1991): 7–8.
Dixon, Robert. "'Travelling in the West': The Writing of Amitav Ghosh," *Journal of Common-
    wealth Literature* 31.1 (1996): 3–24.
Ghosh, Amitav. *In an Antique Land* (New York: Alfred A. Knopf, 1993).
Kowalewski, Michael. "Introduction: The Modern Literature of Travel," in *Temperamental Jour-
    neys: Essays on the Modern Literature of Travel*, ed. Kowalewski (London: U of Georgia P,
    1992): 1–16.
Majeed, Javed. "Amitav Ghosh's *In an Antique Land*: The Ethnographer-Historian and the Limits
    of Irony," *Journal of Commonwealth Literature* 30.2 (1995): 45–55.
Pratt, Mary Louise. *Imperial Eyes: Travel Writing and Transculturation* (London: Routledge,
    1992).
Spurr, David. *The Rhetoric of Empire: Colonial Discourse in Journalism, Travel Writing and Im-
    perial Administration* (Durham NC: Duke UP, 1993).

"Dissolving boundaries"
The Woman as Immigrant
in the Fiction of Chitra Banerjee Divakaruni

ROBERT ROSS

> I want to be in America, America where everyone's like me,
> because everyone comes
> from somewhere else.
> (Salman Rushdie, *The Ground Beneath Her Feet*)

The Immigrant Story

NOW THAT THE ONCE-COLONIZED are colonizing the former colonizers and the rest of the world, the literature of the diaspora promises to be one of the most rewarding areas in the future of postcolonial studies. Of course, this move from colony to England has already begun to be recorded. In 1971 Anita Desai published *Bye-Bye Blackbird* and in 1974 Kamala Markandaya's *The Nowhere Man* appeared – both novels that portray the precarious condition of Indians in England. Through the years, V.S. Naipaul and Salman Rushdie have also recounted the vicissitudes of immigration to England in various works and ways. As well, Buchi Emecheta's *In the Ditch* (1972) depicts the African experience in London, and Timothy Mo follows a family from Hong Kong to London in *Sour Sweet* (1982). Expanding the story, the British-born Hanif Kureishi – half-English, half-Pakistani – reveals in novels like *The Buddha of Suburbia* (1990) and *The Black Album* (1995) the trials of an immigrant son. While the story set in England has become a familiar enough one, the full telling of that same experience in the USA has just started. So far the voices are mainly Asian – more specifically East Indian, even though America's new immigrants come from every part of Asia – Viet Nam, Cambodia, China, South Korea, Taiwan, and so on, from the Middle East, Central and South America and the Caribbean, from all corners of Africa.

Indeed, there are endless tales there, and so few are being told. Bharati Mukherjee found a place as the biographer of recent immigrants to America in the collections *Darkness* (1985) and *The Middleman and Other Stories* (1988), neither of
which are limited to the Asian experience. In her novel *Jasmine* (1989), Mukherjee
enlarges the immigrant story into an expansive adventure that delineates the changing shape of American culture. In her more recent work, though, she has moved
away from what she called "the exuberance of immigration"[1] to other themes. A
Pakistani writer, Bapsi Sidhwa, has also taken up the story in *An American Brat*
(1993), which recounts the adventures of a Parsi girl from Lahore, at first wandering
across the American landscape, then finding a place. A publisher in San Francisco,
the Coffee House Press, has published anthologies of immigrant fiction and poetry,
especially Asian. Interestingly, both Bapsi Sidhwa and the Coffee House Press have
received grants from the Lila Wallace–Reader's Digest Fund – that most American
of institutions. Another writer who has emerged recently, and on whom I would like
to focus, is Chitra Banerjee Divakaruni. Born in Calcutta in 1956, she came to the
USA when she was nineteen to further her education. After earning a master's
degree from Wright State University, she completed a doctorate at the University of
California at Berkeley. She now teaches creative writing at the University of Texas
at Houston. Divakaruni first published three volumes of poetry; then in 1995 she
published a collection of short stories, *Arranged Marriage*. Two years later her first
novel appeared, *The Mistress of Spices*. In 1999 another novel was published, *Sister
of My Heart*. She has also edited an anthology, *We, Too, Sing America* (1998), a
book she describes as being "about growing up in America today, about being part
of a rich and complex mix of people of different backgrounds, cultures, interests,
and abilities."[2] It contains fiction, essays, and poetry by writers from varied ethnic
and national backgrounds.

Arranged Marriage

In Divakaruni's volume of short stories, no narrative called "Arranged Marriage"
appears. Instead, the title permeates these accounts of female experience even as it
does not pertain directly to it. The setting for the first story is India; the other nine
shift to the USA. Why "The Bats" should introduce the book becomes obvious as
the others unfold. It relates an account of wife-beating told through the eyes of a
child who witnesses her father's rage, and this action sets the metaphoric stage for
what follows. The narratives explore in varied ways the psychological effect and/or
the physical brutality stemming from a patriarchal order that considers women as

---

[1] Mukherjee, "Introduction" to Mukherjee, *Darkness* (New York: Penguin, 1985): 3.

[2] Divakaruni, ed. *We, Too, Sing America* (Boston MA: McGraw–Hill, 1998): 1.

chattel. And, Divakaruni reveals, immigration fails to reverse the established pattern but often exacerbates the situation.

Although each story develops this theme flawlessly, I will examine just two of them: one that dwells on psychological consequences, the other on physical cruelty. The story simply titled "Clothes" depicts a successful relationship between a couple brought together through an arranged marriage. Sumita and Somesh, once settled in California, look forward to their future in a land full of potential and reject their Indian past through Western clothes – including jeans and a T-shirt of "sunrise orange," which Somesh buys for his wife and which she wears in the privacy of their bedroom. The fantasy and hopes collapse when the husband is murdered during a robbery in the convenience store where he works. Expected to return to India and assume the role of a widow, Sumita rebels: "I know I cannot go back. I don't know yet how I'll manage, here in this new dangerous land. I only know I must. Because all over India, at this very moment widows in white saris are bowing their veiled heads, serving tea to in-laws. Doves with cut-off wings." At the end, she stands before a mirror, wearing a widow's white sari but sees herself reflected in "a blouse and skirt the color of almonds." She readies herself "for the arguments of the coming weeks, the remonstrations."[3] Yet the ending remains open. Does Sumita succumb to the burden of tradition? Or does she survive "in this new dangerous land"? As with all the narratives, America's promise – not to be fulfilled without trials – lingers over the central female character to provide her with an elusive refuge.

In another story, "Silver Pavements, Golden Roofs," an Indian girl arriving in Chicago discovers a bleak edge to the glorious America she had imagined when she moves into a shabby apartment with her aunt and uncle. The uncle, who keeps his wife a prisoner and has turned her into the surrogate victim of his failure, warns the naïve girl: "Things here aren't as perfect as people at home like to think. We all thought we'd become millionaires. But it's not so easy. The Americans hate us. They're always putting us down because we're dark-skinned foreigners, *kala admi.* Blaming us for the damn economy, for taking away their jobs. You'll see it for yourself soon enough."[4] The girl, anxious to explore the city, persuades her aunt to go out, even though it is forbidden; they get lost and wander into a dingy neighbourhood where four blond boys yell "'nigger, nigger'." When they return home, the angry husband strikes his wife as the niece watches, then begs forgiveness. At the story's close, the girl vows that her future in the new world will be fulfilled. Once more the character remains suspended between the reality of immigration – which

---

[3] Divakaruni, *Arranged Marriage* (New York: Doubleday, 1995): 33.

[4] *Arranged Marriage*, 43.

her uncle described so graphically, and its possibilities – which she has constructed in her fantasies.

Each narrative explores the condition of Indian women adrift in a society where the past social rigidity no longer applies but has left a void in the present. The accounts take up relationships between wife and husband, lovers, friends, mother and son, mother and daughter – all affected by the demarcation between past and present, all intensified by the gulf between tradition and the unknown. Although uncertainty prevails as the narratives close, the pivotal female character has experienced a moment of awareness, an epiphany, that will certainly mitigate the pain that the future holds.

While *Arranged Marriage* received favourable reviews as a literary work, its content offended some in the Indian community, who accused Divakaruni of tarnishing their image and reinforcing stereotypes about oppressed Indian women and domineering Indian men. Countering the criticism of her work, Divakaruni insists that her aim is not to create stereotypes but to shatter them by tackling and revealing sensitive topics. She also points out that she sees her fiction as a way of "dissolving boundaries."[5] Through her work with MAITRI, a helpline that assists South Asian women facing abusive situations, she met numerous South Asian women suffering from domestic violence, depression, and cultural alienation. While *Arranged Marriage* does not present case studies of actual women, it does speak for, to, and about all those who face the pain of immigration, as they set aside one society for another, one identity for another, in an adopted country.

The Mistress of Spices

In *The Mistress of Spices*, Divakaruni once more presents the immigrant experience in starkly realistic terms, but at the same time mixes in generous helpings of mythology and fantasy. The dual approaches could well collapse on one another; instead they complement each other and transform this novel into a strikingly original work. The central character – the mistress of spices called Tilo – grew up in an Indian village, where she displayed supernatural powers of healing; then at a young age she was abducted by pirates. After a series of adventures in which she serves as queen of the pirates, she arrives on a mysterious island to attend a spice school. Graduation ceremonies include a walk through fire, which transports Tilo to her assigned post: the proprietor of a spice shop, catering mainly to Asians, in a shabby section of Oakland, California. This industrial city, just across the bay from glittering San Francisco, is not one of America's model urban areas. In fact, its first and probably only literary recognition came from Jack London's radical writing about the struggle of

---

[5] Chitra Divakaruni, "Dissolving Boundaries," *BoldType Online Magazine* 2.12 (1997).

the working class in the early part of the century. Today, along with its large African-American and Chicano population, Oakland is home to extended immigrant communities – Asian, African, South American, and so on. Divakaruni captures the essence of this beleaguered city through her poetic prose:

> But today the light is pink-tinted like just-bloomed *karabi* flowers, and the Indian radio channel spills out a song about a slim-waisted girl who wears silver anklets, and I am hungry for the sight. There is a smell like seabirds in the air. It makes me long to open windows. I pace the front aisle looking out, though there is nothing except a bag lady shuffling behind a grocery cart and a group of boys lounging lazy against the graffitied walls of Myisha's Hair Salon Braiding Done. An impatient voice calls me back to the register. A long low aquamarine Cadillac with shark fins cruises by.[6]

In another passage, Divakaruni balances natural beauty with the city's gritty appearance as the day ends:

> When the sky turns arsenic-red from sunset and smog, and the palm that stands scrawny by the bus stop throws its long ragged shadow in my doorway, I know it is time to close up. I unpleat the wooden shutters and slide them across the pock-marked curve of a pale moon.[7]

One can imagine Tilo then settling down behind the counter and scratching out her exaggerated memoir on a tablet. She could just possibly be an unreliable narrator. Once stripped of the fantastic origins she has designed for herself, she might be a well-meaning busybody whose own immigrant experience helps her to understand her customers' problems. Like the mistress of spices, they have chosen the "new dangerous land," a place that has neither chosen nor accepted them.

Tilo encounters the familiar dilemmas of the immigrant, at first treating them with spices, then intruding into their lives – a practice strictly forbidden in the code governing the conduct of a mistress of spices. An Indian boy, ridiculed by his classmates for being different, gains the protection of members of a street gang and in turn serves as a runner for them. The conflict between generations threatens the happiness of a professional Indian woman who has fallen in love with a Chicano and faces her family's opposition to a marriage outside the Indian community. Indian men working in common jobs like taxi drivers fall victim to the violence and crime that plagues a metropolis, and some leave their wives stranded. One Indian wife faces a brutal husband who assaults her sexually.

Tilo continues to rebel against the strictures of the spice mistress, even explores the alien America into which she has been dropped, including a comic foray into a

---

[6] Divakaruni, *The Mistress of Spices* (New York: Doubleday, 1997): 84.

[7] Divakaruni, *The Mistress of Spices*, 61.

Sears store. And, worst of all, she falls in love with a handsome American who visits her shop. He is, ironically, a Native American Indian, who has shunned his heritage – an odd breed of immigrant in his own land. The novel literally ends in pyrotechnics, and concludes with Tilo and her lover understanding at last what immigrants must do as they confront the fragility of their condition and the demands of their altered lives.

Sister of My Heart

That a writer who could create such perceptive short stories and so inventive a novel would publish the sentimental, cliché-ridden, melodramatic *Sister of My Heart*[8] is surprising. This Bengali soap opera, set in Calcutta for the most part, follows the misfortunes of two girls born on the same day to their recently widowed mothers. Although unrelated except in spirit, they grow up as sisters in a distinguished but impoverished family of bitter, disagreeable women who inhabit a crumbling mansion. At an early age the girls enter arranged marriages, which turn out to be disastrous. One moves to California with her aloof, computer-scientist husband and develops into a shrew with an eating disorder. The other rebels against the classic domineering mother-in-law, who wants her to abort the girl child she is carrying, and leaves her weak-willed husband, who agrees with his mother. She then joins the "sister of her heart" in California to start a new life. All appears blissful when the novel finally ends and they meet at San Francisco airport – except that the shrew's husband is eyeing with unwholesome and questionable interest the new arrival, who possesses an exquisite beauty that far outshines his wife's plainness. A terrible secret hangs over the narrative, but revelation comes during the plane trip from India. Of course, the reader has already solved the mystery back on page 50 or so. The writing itself borders on the cloying. Even though the voices of the "sisters" alternate chapter by chapter, it becomes difficult to distinguish the two narrators because they sound exactly alike. The novel also appears to be an expansion of "The Ultrasound," one of the stories in *Arranged Marriage*, but the narrative was far more successful in its abbreviated form.

Should the immigrant writer, then, not be permitted to draw on her past? Divakaruni has spent her adult life in the USA, where she has been quite successful, so should she be required to write about her adopted home? Not at all. Yet, if she decides to re-create a lost past, she should not depend on exotica, on myths, on a generous sprinkling of foreign words, recipe-like descriptions of food, and all the other literary paraphernalia required to reproduce the mystical and fantastic India. She should instead depend on the truth, and *Sister of My Heart* has little of that.

---

[8] Divakaruni, *Sister of My Heart* (New York: Doubleday, 1999).

Besides, Bharati Mukherjee handled the plight of the spoiled Bengali girl caught up in America much more effectively in *Wife* way back in 1975. Rohinton Mistry, another immigrant writer who has lived in Canada since the 1970s, continues to write about Bombay and the broader India in a *A Fine Balance* (1996). The vision of India that Mistry still holds remains authentic, just as Vikram Seth's depiction of Indian domestic life in *A Suitable Boy* (1993) has a genuine ring. Interestingly, though, Seth's new novel, *An Equal Music* (1999), takes an altogether unexpected direction as it explores the realm of musicians.

Granted, Divakaruni does in *Sister of my Heart* give the immigration theme, that dissolving of boundaries of which she has spoken so nobly, a fresh twist. For immigration somehow becomes entwined with a distorted feminism. By coming to America and joining her "sister," the neophyte arrival and her embittered, disillusioned counterpart will be able to throw off the shackles of Indian tradition and at last free themselves from dependence on males – that is, once they become entrepreneurs in the boutique they dream of opening. Will the US Immigration Service soon include oppressed women running from destructive mothers-in-law and self-centred men on its list of those seeking refugee status? The outlandish premiss that undergirds *Sister of My Heart* contradicts both of Divakaruni's earlier works of fiction.

Perhaps I am being too harsh on the novel, but it is so very disappointing after Divakaruni's impressive debut. Is she falling into the trap of which Indian critics often accuse Indian writers in English, especially those who live abroad: that is, pandering to Western tastes? Although checking reader response to a novel through the website of the Amazon booksellers on the Internet may not be exactly scholarly, it is revealing. Of the forty or so readers who responded, those with non-Asian names praised the novel lavishly, while those with Indian names discredited it, finding the narrative overwrought, false, exaggerated, even amusing. Has Divakaruni been so anxious to succeed that she has succumbed to the lure of attempting to please her Western readers rather than agitate them with a text that truly reveals the immigrant world about which they know so little?

Missions and Colonizations

In the twenty-first century the missions and colonizations of the British will indeed evolve into a postcolonial future of cosmopolitan interdependence – an undertaking in which immigrant writers will play a pivotal role. Those like Bharati Mukherjee, Bapsi Sidhwa and Chitra Banerjee Divakaruni have chosen the USA as their home and have taken citizenship. Mukherjee declared that she is not an immigrant writer or an Indian writer in English, but an American writer, in the tradition of Jewish writers who recorded their plunge into the new world, or in the tradition of a novelist like James T. Farrell who recounted Irish immigrant life. Mukherjee talks about the need for a modern breed of Walt Whitmans, who will hear America singing fresh songs. The USA has a way of appropriating its immigrants, taking their talents, their work, their culture, and absorbing them. So, as Divakaruni sets out on her task of "dissolving boundaries," she may well at the same time be dissolving her Indianness – and that of others – into a cosmopolitan interdependence. She will accomplish this goal if she puts aside the exotic and the melodramatic, and remains true to her mission. American literature has always welcomed the emerging Walt Whitmans, but has little patience with those who look back.

WORKS CITED

Divakaruni, Chitra Banerjee. *Arranged Marriage* (New York: Doubleday, 1995).
——. "Dissolving Boundaries," *BoldType: An Online Literary Magazine* 2.12 (1997).
——. *The Mistress of Spices* (New York: Doubleday, 1997).
——. *Sister of My Heart* (New York: Doubleday, 1999).
——, ed. *We, Too, Sing America* (Boston MA: McGraw–Hill, 1998).
Mukherjee, Bharati. "Introduction" to *Darkness* (New York: Penguin, 1985): 1–4.

❧

Magical Realism, Indian-Style
or, the Case of Multiple Submission
The God of Small Things by Arundhati Roy

ALEXANDRA PODGÓRNIAK

> If you are an extra-territorial writer you select a pedigree for yourself, a
> literary family [...] Swift, Conrad, Marx are as much our literary forebears
> as Tagore or Ram Mohan Roy [...] We are inescapably international writers
> at times when the novel has never been a more international form [...]
> cross-pollination is everywhere.
>
> (Salman Rushdie, *Imaginary Homelands: Essays and Criticism 1981–
> 1991* (London: Granta, 1991): 19)

C OSMOPOLITAN INTERDEPENDENCE REPEATEDLY PROVES to be an indelible phenomenon that shapes literary representation of the postcolonial
reality. Global hybridization of postcolonial cultures results in multi-
layered dependencies, while Salman Rushdie claims that the novel is an international form and "cross-pollination is everywhere."[1] It is in this context that I will
attempt to analyse the submission-related strata in Arundhati Roy's *The God of
Small Things*, a controversial Booker Prize-winning novel published in 1997.[2]

The case of *The God of Small Things* is a spectacular instance of cross-cultural-
ity resulting from multi-faceted cultural submergence. Roy's version points back to
Rushdie, yet Rushdie's work is already an example of double submission, as, on the
one hand, it is heavily indebted to the European literary fantastic as represented by
Laurence Sterne (*Tristram Shandy*) and Günter Grass (*Die Blechtrommel*); on the

---

[1] Salman Rushdie, *Imaginary Homelands: Essays and Criticism 1981–1991* (London: Granta,
1991): 19.

[2] Cf. Tom Deveson, "Much ado about small things," *Sunday Times Review of Books* (15 June
1997): 12.

other, it points back to South American literary tradition – Gabriel García Márquez (*Cien años de soledad*).

Realizing that Latin America and India share, to a certain extent, the postcolonial experience may help to understand the essence of magical realism in its numerous postcolonial interpretations. In countries previously ruled autocratically as colonies, the fact that information can easily be manipulated or even commanded by power groups makes truth a relative entity – relativism which magical realism both mimics and exploits through its own merging of realism and fantasy. By and large, magical realism, South American-style, emerged as an effect of Spanish colonization, its Indian counterpart as an effect of British imperialism.

This essay will first discuss several plot invariants and the version of history as presented by Roy, then analyse narrative technique and the question of language, all of which contribute greatly to the multiple submission of *The God of Small Things*.

"If ever two were one, then surely we"
On the Concept of Magical Twins

Roy's submission to the Rushdie-esque motifs starts with her usage of the concept of twins. *The God of Small Things* centres on telepathically linked twins, who "thought of themselves together as Me, and separately, individually, as We or Us. As if they were a rare breed of Siamese twins, physically separate, but with joint identities." As children, they were able to share memories of experiences, which happened only to one of them and they dreamt each other's dreams, which evokes associations with Rushdie's *Midnight's Children* where Reverend Mother dreamt her daughters' dreams and Saleem entered the thoughts of other people. Along with the flow of time, the twins' "me," "we" or "us" changes into "Them, because separately, the two of them are no longer what *They* were or even thought *They'd* be."[3] This might suggest that the magical abilities (telepathy) are characteristic of children, very much the view that Rushdie shares in *Midnight's Children* and Grass in *Die Blechtromme* (1959). Isabel Allende's *La casa de los espíritus* (1982) proves further that the idea of children having access to other extrasensory forms of reality can be traced back not only to European but also to Latin American magical-realist fiction.

Refusal

Magical realism seems to be especially concerned with the theme of refusal in its many versions: refusal to grow (*The Tin Drum*), refusal to speak (*Midnight's Children, The House of the Spirits*), refusal to eat (*The Tin Drum, Midnight's Children*)

---

[3] Arundhati Roy, *The God of Small Things* (London: Flamingo, 1997): 3. Further page references are in the main text.

refusal to take up a name (*Midnight's Children*). In *The Tin Drum*, Oskar refuses to grow, protesting against his mother's adultery. The latter refuses to eat as a protest against her husband forcing her to eat fish. In *The House of the Spirits*, Clara refuses to speak on two occasions: as a child – because of a traumatic event, and as an adult – because of her husband's violence. In *Midnight's Children*, silence descends on Reverend Mother; Saleem's son is said to be a silent infant as he refuses to cry or whimper. Saleem, in turn, is also a peculiar baby, as he does not close his eyes, and later, in the jungle, already an adult, he refuses to take up a name. Arundhati Roy is attracted by at least three kinds of refusals. Estha ceases to talk after a trauma – "quietness arrived, stayed and spread" (11) in him. This muteness had at least two effects on the protagonist: It returned him to the epoch of "ancient, foetal heartbeat" (11), and "it stripped his thoughts of the words then described them and left them pared and naked. Unspeakable. Numb" (12). The refusal to speak, to use language, can be treated in a metaphoric way, along Lacanian lines, as the refusal to accept the Other.[4] Refusing the Other, Estha recovers the ability to perceive things as they are, the possibility of not confining his perception in the limits of language. Yet, this also means returning to "the amorphous years," to times when "memory had only just begun" (2). Therefore, it additionally signifies his refusal to grow up. Soundlessness appears in Roy's novel once more when Pappachi stops speaking to Mammachi, reminiscent of both *Midnight's Children* and *The House of the Spirits*. Ammu not only refuses to obey the laws that "lay down who should be loved, and how. And how much" (33), but she also refuses to take up a name: She wants neither her father's nor her husband's surname.

"Welcome Home, Our Sophie Mol"
Or, Who Drowns in India and Why

Although the genesis of the tragedy in *The God of Small Things* lies in the days when Love Laws were made, the direct cause of the events is the drowning of Sophie Mol, the twins' cousin. Had it not been for the fact that Sophie was the twins' *English* cousin, there would have been nothing surprising in it. However, oddly enough, Sophie Mol is not the only drowned female in recent Indian fiction: Yet again, her case immediately brings to mind *Midnight's Children*, where Ilse, Adam Aziz's European friend, finds drowning in India the most suitable way of committing suicide. Rushdie even makes it a rule: "There is a tribe of feringee [European] women who come to this water to drown" (17).

---

[4] Jaques Lacan, "The Function and Field of Speech and Language in Psychoanalysis," in *Writing Theory: An Anthology*, ed. Julia Rivkin (Oxford: Blackwell, 1998): 184–90.

Since *The God of Small Things* contains numerous references to the British as colonizers, the fact that Sophie Mol is English, bears particular significance. The twins' grandfather is referred to as "a British CCP" (51), which in Hindi stands for "a shit-wiper" (51) or an anglophile, which in turn means that "his mind had been *brought into a state* which made him like the English" (52). Sophie's Indian father, Chacko, exemplifies a peculiar split, which seems to be characteristic of Indian postcolonial reality. Educated in Oxford, having an English wife, trying to plant all he learnt in Britain on Indian soil, he at the same time loathes the English:

> Chacko told the twins that though he hated to admit it, they were all Anglophiles. Pointed in the wrong direction, trapped outside their own history, and unable to retrace their steps because their footprints had been swept away. (52)

Love Laws

Another concept used by Roy that seems to be common to many magical-realist texts is that of incest. In one of the last scenes of *The God of Small Things*, Rahel makes love to her twin brother Estha, marking thus the union and the closeness the two of them are able to regain, yet at the same time breaking "the laws that lay down who should be loved. And how. And how much" (328). Actual love-making never takes place between Saleem and Jamila in *Midnight's Children*, yet Saleem fantasizes about sex with his sister when he kisses his wife Parvati-the-witch:

> [...] her face changing, becoming the face of forbidden love; the ghostly features of Jamila the Singer replaced those of the witch girl [...] so now the rancid flowers of incest blossomed on my sister's phantasmal features, and I couldn't do it, couldn't kiss, touch, look upon that intolerable spectral face.[5]

Oscar (*The Tin Drum*) is actually a fruit of forbidden love between his mother and her Polish cousin Jan Bronsky. In *The House of the Spirits*, Alba is a victim of rape committed by her cousin Esteban García. The town of Macondo is destroyed as a result of four generations of inbreeding (*One Hundred Years of Solitude*).

Etcetera, or Other Plot Invariants

Let me point to only a few other examples of plot invariants that make Roy's submission to Rushdie even more evident: ie, exile (Estha – is 'Returned,' to his father and later 'Re-Returned' to his mother's family; Saleem is exiled several times); the idea of a tomboy with a propensity to arson (Rahel and Jamila); the similarities in constructing the biographies of Baby Kochamma and Mary Pereira.

---

[5] Rushdie, *Midnight's Children* (1981; London: Random House / Vintage, 1995): 396.

Arundhati Roy's convergence with the Rushdie-esque occurs again in the fact that both *The God of Small Things* and *Midnight's Children* are narrated from the point of view of a thirty-one-year-old. Surprisingly enough, both narrators regard the age of thirty-one as "a viable die-able age."[6]

Chutneys, Pickles & Preserves
Or, Spicing Up History

Since Roy switches back and forth between the time present and various times past, *The God of Small Things* propounds a particular concept of history. This intermingling of the present and the past provides different perspectives of perceiving history: from the inside (the child's perspective) and from the outside (the adult perspective). Thus, the narrator is both an insider and an outsider to the history. Roy's concept of history could be compared to the process of making pickles, especially in view of the fact that the world in *The God of Small Things* is centred on the pickles and preserves factory. History appears to be like pickles: a collection of many different things which need some time to become meaningful or tasteful. If one tries to understand or taste them before their due time, they can only seem meaningless and tasteless, "there would only be incoherence. As though meaning had slunk out of things and left them fragmented" (225). It is the outsider's perspective that provides insight into history. Like the twins, one has to read backwards, one has to find out how separate vegetables became pickles and how separate events constituted history.

Yet this fragmented or 'pickled' version of history makes Roy's submission to the Rushdie-esque even more spectacular, especially with regard to *Midnight's Children*. Rushdie, and later Roy, supplies two insights into the past: from the outside and from the inside, or from the adult's or child's point of view. Not only does Rushdie employ here the idea of getting to know the world via a perforated sheet: ie, seeing only fragments, but he also uses chutney as a metaphor for history. There seems, however, to be a marked difference between Rushdie's treatment and Roy's. Saleem Sinai, Rushdie's *Midnight's Children*, screws the lids on his chutney jars: ie, he tells his story to save "memory, as well as fruit, from the corruption of the clocks,"[7] whereas what Roy proposes is to unscrew the pickle jars, looking back into the past. Therefore, history for Roy is what it was for Herodotus – an act of inquiry. For Roy, telling the story is the act of opening in order to achieve catharsis, whereas for Rushdie every written chapter is like a closed jar put on a shelf:

---

[6] Roy, *The God of Small Things*, 3; Rushdie, *Midnight's Children*, 9.
[7] Rushdie, *Midnight's Children*, 38.

> Twenty-six pickle jars stand gravely on a shelf; twenty-six special blends, each with its
> identifying label, neatly inscribed with familiar phrases: 'Movements Performed by
> Pepperpots', for instance, or 'Alpha and Omega', or 'Commander Sabarmati's Baton.'[8]

Closing the jars (ie, closing the succeeding chapters) justifies, in Rushdie's view, the
process of amnesia:

> Every pickle-jar contains, therefore, the most exalted of possibilities: the feasibility of
> chutnification of history; the grand hope of pickling of time! I, however, have pickled
> chapters. I have immortalized my memories. [...] Thirty jars stand upon a shelf, waiting
> to be unleashed upon the amnesiac nation.[9]

One more aspect, perhaps, needs critical attention: namely, the role of spices in colonial and postcolonial history, postcolonial referring here to both the colonizers and
the colonized. At the beginning of *The Moor's Last Sigh* Rushdie claims that it was
spices, the very lure or the supposed 'essence' of India, which introduced this
country into the European consciousness:

> And to begin with, pass the pepper. [...] I repeat: the pepper if you please; for if it had not
> been for peppercorns, then what is ending now in East and West might never have begun.[10]

Rushdie exploits this idea even further by situating the action of the novel in Cochin,
a place where centuries ago Vasco da Gama came in search of spices, starting, thus,
what is considered by many to be the beginning of common history of the Orient
and the Occident. This historical location is also employed in *The God of Small
Things.* Roy chooses Cochin as a meeting-point for the twins and Sophie Mol, which
could symbolically be read as a meeting of India – the land that is commonly associated with spices and England – the land that is commonly associated with tea. In
this respect, spices represent India and, by extension, the Orient; tea represents England and, by extension, European civilization. However, there may exist a somewhat
paradoxical analogy in the perception of Sophie Mol and the popular perception of
tea, based on semi-conscious mystification, as both are regarded as English though
neither of them actually is. Sophie Mol is only half-British, as her father is the twins'
Indian uncle Chacko. The same half-British origin applies to tea, as it was 'discovered' by the British, but in fact it was the Orient's 'invention.'

"El arte narrativo y la magia" (Narrative Technique and Magic)

The narrative technique in *The God of Small Things* is, in itself, yet another example
of multi-layered submission and submergence not only to European but also to
South American literary representation. Roy uses the tactics described by Borges in

---

[8] Rushdie, *Midnight's Children*, 384.
[9] *Midnight's Children*, 459–60.
[10] Salman Rushdie, *The Moor's Last Sigh* (London: Vintage, 1996): 4.

his essay "El arte narrativo y la magia" (1932), where he claims that it is not the natural but the magical sequence of events that provides a novel with truthfulness. In that kind of writing the details have the power of foretelling the future events which, for the construction of narration, signifies that every episode projects what happens later.[11] At the same time the narration in _The God of Small Things_ is reminiscent of the Indian oral narrative tradition, which – among other narrative techniques – is successfully used in _Midnight's Children_:

> [The oral narrative] is not linear. An oral narrative does not go from the beginning to the middle to the end of the story. It goes in great swoops, it goes in spirals or in loops, it every so often reiterates something that happened earlier to remind you, and then takes you off again, sometimes summarises itself, it frequently digresses off into something that the story teller appears just to have thought of, then it comes back to the main thrust of the narrative. (Rushdie 1985: 8)

In a manner typical also of magical realist fiction, Roy uses the technique of building a tale within a tale, persistently delaying climaxes, intermingling the past and the present. Thus, the chronological time has to be located in alternative ways. To provide just one emblematic example – the process of gradual urbanization is marked by several problematical changes: the transformation of the river into something "that smelled of shit and pesticides brought with World Bank loans" (13), Baby Kochamma's satellite TV, and the tourist hotels where Khathakali dancers perform.

"Prer nun sea ayshun"
On the Question of Language, or Hot Spices are Entering English

Jacques Lacan, who I have already alluded to, claims that acquiring the language means accepting the Other which, in the case of Arundhati Roy, and, by extension, other Indian-English writers, means double contact with the Other, for they are not only submitted to their native languages, but they choose to be submitted to English. This causes a certain paradox. inasmuch as the writers of the sixth-biggest country in the world, the second most populous, with a literary tradition that goes back thousands of years, and definitely many centuries before Christ, with eighteen official languages and at least the same number of non-official ones, have chosen to express themselves in the language of colonizers. The double submission makes one necessarily sceptical about Indian literary representation of reality. If, like Fredric Jameson, we assume that the only access to history we have is via text, then the version of history in _The God of Small Things_, and, by extension, in Indian-English fiction, is falsified twice (via languages) and this is a twofold falsification (because contem-

---

[11] Henryk Markiewicz, _Teorie powiesci za granica_ (Warsaw: PWN, 1995): 329–30.

porary Indian-English writers want to break free of their burdensome colonial label
and stress that they do not belong to British culture any more; yet at the same time
they write in English, get British prizes and thus preserve the British cultural
heritage). Thus, the question of whether Roy's writing is a part of national Indian
literature is bound to be posed. Following Rushdie,[12] one could assume that there is
no such thing as an Indian nation, or, rather, that India is a collection of many different nations, resembling, as it were, a collection of many different spices. Each of
these spices gives a foretaste of what India is, but only the mixture of them all can
supply – let us revert to the previous formulation – the very *essence* of the country.
This reminds us once again of what Rushdie postulates in *The Moor's Last Sigh* –
that India is "not so much sub-continent as sub-condiment."[13]

Magical realism, as a large part of twentieth-century literature, is essentially
eclectic, and so is Roy's fiction. She does not enclose herself – let me remain in the
realm of taste – in one of the spices. She chooses one particular point in time and
space and locates her novel in it, but her spice is permeated with other spices. All
Indian spices spice up the international dish, which is Indian magical-realist fiction.
One could treat *The God of Small Things* either as a case of multiple submission or
as exquisite intertextual play. Whichever it is, in the era of the global hybridization
of cultures, it appears to be an inevitable choice. Let me conclude with a quotation
from Ernest Renan which, although written in the nineteenth century and referring to
language, could be transferred to contemporary literature as a warning against cultural claustrophobia:

> Language invites people to unite, but it does not force them to do so. [...] There is
> something in man which is superior to language, namely the will. [...] This exclusive
> concern with language [...] has its dangers and its drawbacks. Such exaggerations en-
> close one within a specific culture, considered as national; one limits oneself, one hems
> oneself in. One leaves the heady air that one breathes in the vast field of humanity in
> order to enclose oneself in a conventicle with one's compatriots. Nothing could be
> worse for the mind; nothing could be more disturbing for civilisation.[14]

WORKS CITED

Bhabha, Homi. *Location of Culture* (London: Routledge, 1995).
——, ed. *Nation and Narration* (London & New York: Routledge, 1994).
Borges, Jorge Luis, "El arte narrativo y la magia," in Markiewicz, ed. *Teorie powiesci za granica*,
329–30.

---

[12] Rushdie, *Midnight's Children*, 112.

[13] Rushdie, *The Moor's Last Sigh*, 5.

[14] Ernest Renan, "What is a Nation," in *Nation and Narration*, ed. Homi Bhabha (London:
Routledge, 1990): 16–17.

Brennan, Timothy. *Salman Rushdie and the Third World* (London: Macmillan, 1989).

Deveson, Tom. "Much ado about small things," *Sunday Times Review of Books* (15 June 1997): 12.

Lacan, Jacques. "The Function and Field of Speech and Language in Psychoanalysis," in Rivkin, ed. *Writing Theory*, 184–90.

Markiewicz, Henryk. *Teorie powiesci za granica* (Warsaw: PWN, 1995).

Renan, Ernest, "What is a Nation," in *Nation and Narration*, ed. Homi Bhabha (London: Routledge, 1990): 8–23.

Rivkin, Julie, ed. *Writing Theory: An Anthology* (Oxford: Blackwell, 1998).

Roy, Arundhati. *The God of Small Things* (London: Flamingo, 1997).

Rushdie, Salman. *Imaginary Homelands: Essays and Criticism 1981–1991* (London: Granta, 1991).

——. "Interview with Salman Rushdie," *Kunapipi* 7.1 (1985): 8–12.

——. *Midnight's Children* (1981; London: Random House / Vintage, 1995).

——. *The Moor's Last Sigh* (London: Random House / Vintage, 1996).

Walder, Dennis, ed. *Literature in the Modern World: Critical Essays and Documents* (Oxford: Oxford UP, 1993).

♋

ço Australia

Fair Australasia
A Poet's Farewell to Emigrants

OLGA SUDLENKOVA

ROM THE SEVENTEENTH CENTURY ONWARDS, emigration was an integral part of Britain's colonial policy. Besides being a powerful means of conquering and appropriating new territories, emigration helped to solve many internal problems of economic, social and even religious character. With the loss of the American colonies in the 1770s, Britain turned its attention to Australia and New Zealand as objects of its colonial expansion. Colonization of these territories was looked upon as a means of relieving the pressure upon Britain's prisons, of providing Britain with a bastion in the eastern sea, of creating a springboard for economic exploitation of the area. The first convict settlement was founded in New South Wales in 1788. The first governor of Australia, Captain Arthur Philip (1788–92), urged the British government to send free settlers, as "fifty farmers with their families can do more within one year for creating self-providing colonies than a thousand convicts."[1] Yet because of the fear of distance and hard conditions, few people volunteered to go to Australia in the first years of colonization. In 1788–93 only five free families settled there, while the shipment of prisoners continued. The total number of convicts sent to Australia in the course of some eighty years (from 1788 to 1868, when the continent stopped being looked upon as a place of exile) amounted to 155,000.

The aggravation of the economic situation in the second decade of the nineteenth century and the social problems it entailed – pauperism, unemployment, population surplus – gave a new impetus to Britain's emigration policy. Wilmot Horton advocated emigration as a way of dealing with the over-population and urged the govern-

---

[1] Quoted in Helen G. Palmer & John Macleod, *The First Hundred Years* (Melbourne & London: Longmans, Green, 1954): 19. The information that follows is taken from Kim Vladimirovich Malakhovski, *История Австралии* [History of Australia] (Москва: Наука [Moscow: Nauka], 1980): 39.

ment to fund emigration of the poor to the colonies. He calculated that it was chea-per for the government to give a free passage overseas to a pauper family of four and launch it in a new country as a self-supporting unit than to keep it at home. His plan was criticized as his opponents doubted if paupers would be able to turn into self-supporting labourers in the new and difficult conditions. One of Horton's critics, Gibbon Wakefield, argued that "shovelling out" unwanted people made the British think of emigration "with dislike and horror." He considered that emigration should be voluntary, yet state-supervised. To prevent inexperienced labourers from becom-ing landowners he suggested that land in colonies should not be granted free but sold at a sufficient price, and the money raised in this way might be used to fund further emigration. He also demanded that emigrants should be thoroughly selected, there should be a reasonable proportion of both sexes, and young married couples should be given preference.

Wakefield's plan of "systematized emigration" was thought to be more efficient, for it not only relieved the population pressure but also created a labour market in the colonies, provided fields for capital investments and extended the Empire's markets. The project was thoroughly propagated throughout the country and pro-moted departure for the colonies. In the 1820s, the British government began to encourage the emigration of able and well-to-do people to Australia by providing them with substantial grants. Official land sales in Australia in 1824 gave an impetus to "land fever." In 1828, the sale of land increased sixfold in comparison with 1813. From 1824 to 1832, about thirty thousand colonists arrived from Britain.

Very inspiring and influential were Wakefield's *Letters from Sydney, Principal Town of Australia* (1829), which, though this author had not yet been to the country, contained much information about the continent and promoted emigration to Aus-tralasia. In 1838, the number of Britons emigrating to Australia and New Zealand (fourteen thousand) equalled that sailing for the USA.

Yet emigration was a controversial issue, and British society was divided on the question of whether it was beneficial or detrimental to the country.[2] Opponents to emigration held that it deprived Britain of working hands as well as of considerable capital. Others argued that, on the contrary, emigration promoted Britain's economic development, providing new commodity markets and helping to deal with unem-ployment and other social problems. There was no unanimity on emigration even among democrats. Thus, in *Past and Present* (1843), Thomas Carlyle presented "a

---

[2] For surveys of the controversy, see Nikolai Aleksandrovich Erofeyev, *Народная эмиграция и классовая борьба в Англии в 1825–1850 гг.* [People's Emigration and Class Struggle in England in 1825–1850] (Москва [Moscow]: Издательство Академии наук СССР, 1962), and Erofeyev, *Английский колониализм в середине XIX века* [English Colonies in the Mid-Nineteenth Century] (Москва: Наука [Moscow: Nauka], 1977).

proposal for an emigration service to ship off superfluous and potentially trouble-some workers to less populated countries."[3] William Cobbett, a very influential democratic publicist and political figure, was at first a confirmed opponent to emi-gration but later, in the 1820s, changed his point of view and even published his *Emigrant's Guide* (1830), where he treated emigration as a means of protest against the British political system.

Similarly controversial was the attitude towards emigrants. Some reproached them for being unpatriotic, while radical democrats saw in emigration an escape from oppression, poverty, heavy taxes and other ills of the country. The radical magazine *Gorgon* stressed that only the rich could object to emigration as it led to the reduction of their incomes. Emigration, asserted the magazine, did not mean lack of patriotism, as Britain was not worthy of its citizens' love. People could only despise and curse a country whose political and social system was the source of misery and injustice.[4]

Emigration was not only the theme of heated parliamentary debates and publicist essays and pamphlets; it also found its way into the fine arts and literature. The drawing "Emigration a Remedy" by John Leesh (*Punch*, 1848) and Ford Madox Brown's famous picture "The Last of England" (1855) are but two examples of visual representation of the issue. The latter "shows a group of emigrants looking back from their ship as they sail away towards a new life. They seem to wonder anxiously just what their new life might bring and also perhaps to survey in imagina-tion the England that they are leaving behind."[5]

Democratic literature was especially keen on the emigration problem. In his book on English popular poetry, Aleksandr Nikolyukin stated that the second decade of the nineteenth century witnessed the popularity of the genre of poetic farewell messages, which was due to a new wave of emigration following the defeat of the democratic movement in 1817–19.[6] Most of these poems – "The Patriot's Farewell to England" (1818), "Emigrant's Farewell" (1820), "Farmer's Farewell" (1821) – were published in the radical democratic magazine *The Black Dwarf*. The chartist movement heightened the emigration issue, a fact that was immediately reflected in

---

[3] *Great Victorian Poets and Their Paths to Fame. An Arts Council Exhibition of 1978* (Leeds City Art Gallery): 12.

[4] *Gorgon* (31 October 1818): 191.

[5] John Mepham, "What is England?" *Literature Matters* 20 (March 1996): 11. The immediate impulse for the genesis of the picture was the emigration of one of the painter's friends to Australia in 1852 when emigration was at its highest point: 369,000 Britons left for abroad.

[6] Aleksandr Nikolaevich Nikolyukin, *Массовая поэзия в Англии конца XVIII начала XIX веков* [Popular Poetry in England in the Late Eighteenth – Early Nineteenth Centuries] (Москва [Moscow]: Издательство Академии наук СССР, 1961): 136.

numerous, mostly anonymous poems. "The Scottish Emigrant's Farewell,"[7] "Land of Kings and Queens,"[8] "Song of the Chartist Emigrant,"[9] "Emigrant's Argument,"[10] as well as the poems "Emigrants" and "Emigration"[11] by the outstanding Chartist poet William James Linton, exposed the emigrants' motives for quitting their native land:

> It is not because I despise
> The land, or the place of my birth [...]
> My country, my nation I love.
> The birthplace of all that is dear.
> And yet I am tempted to rove
> Across the wide ocean to steer.[12]

Low wages, unemployment, poverty, starvation, exploitation, tyranny, the power of Mammon – these were, according to the poets, the reasons that forced people to leave Britain. "A band of oppressors thus drives me away," reads a line from "The Patriot's Farewell to England." And though the chartists' attitude to emigration was mostly negative (Linton called it "drawing the life-blood of the land") they justified emigrants. In the comments to his poem "Emigration," Linton wrote: "I do not reproach the emigrants. How many, tracked by the bloodhounds of the law for their share in endeavouring to raise their country, are compelled to leave it! How many, too, have no resource but emigration to keep them from dying of famine here!"[13]

But it was not only the hopelessness that Linton summed up as "Plague Despair" which drove the British across the ocean. They all cherished a hope for a better future, for a land free of oppression; they lived by the dream of political, spiritual and religious freedoms. It was also the hope of acquiring land and setting up an independent homestead that made people set out on dangerous, months-long sea voyages.

One of the earliest literary responses to the emigration issue was the poem "Lines on the Departure of Emigrants to New South Wales" (1828) by Thomas Campbell,[14] an English poet of Scottish origin and a contemporary of Wordsworth and Byron. The poem stands apart from those mentioned above: first, it was written

---

[7] *Chartist Circular* (16 May 1840).

[8] *Chartist Circular* (4 July 1840).

[9] *Chartist Circular* (25 June 1842).

[10] *Struggle* (1842).

[11] Both published in *The English Republic* (1851): 252, 253.

[12] "Emigrant's Argument," *Struggle* 48 (1842), in Nikolai Aleksandrovich Erofeyev, People's Emigration and Class Struggle in England in 1825–1850, 195.

[13] *The English Republic* (London, 1851): 253.

[14] *The Complete Poetical Works of Thomas Campbell*, ed. Epes Sargent (Boston MA: Phillips, Sampson, 1854): 327–331.

by a well-established professional poet; secondly, it contained concrete information about the place of destination; thirdly, not only did it deal with the emigrants' motives and feelings, but also depicted the prospects of life in the new country. Unlike other poems on the theme, it was written neither by an emigrant nor in the name of one, but by one who, on witnessing a scene of emigrant departure, was induced to ponder over the future of those people. It should be mentioned that the poet had first touched on emigration to Australia thirty years before in his most famous long didactic poem, "The Pleasures of Hope" (1799), the last episode of which is a dramatic scene of the parting of a convict father, exiled to the southern continent, from his woebegone daughter.

The "Lines on the Departure of Emigrants to New South Wales," 122 verses in heroic couplets, opens with a scene that the poet witnessed in a seaport.

> On England's shore I saw a pensive band,
> With sails unfurled for earth's remotest strand,

The poet's empathy with "poor wanderers" who are "like children parting from a mother" is felt in the mood of the first part of the poem, where words like "grief," "weep," "miss," "regret," "lament," "sorrow" dominate. Yet the next lines contain the poet's appeal to the emigrants to search for consolation in feelings other than love for their native land. He is sure that these able labourers (an "industrious train," he calls them) will soon realize the advantages of life in the new place.[15] He expresses the hope that in this country, with "long sunshine" and fertile land that yields "twice its harvest home," these people's "bosoms shall be changed / And strangers once shall cease to feel estranged." The poet enumerates the benefits the new homeland would grant them: they would be free farmers who would "rear an independent shed," and give their families "an unborrowed bread"; they would have no fear of losing their children through want and famine, and would be able to provide for their posterity's future:

> And call the blooming landscape all our own,
> Our children's heritage, in prospect long.

And nostalgia for England will be assuaged at hearing "the cherub-chorus of the children's mirth," at surveying" with pride beyond a monarch's spoil / His honest arm's own subjugated soil," at "marking o'er his farm's expanding ring / New fleeces whiten and new fruits upspring." It should be noted that the poet's mention

---

[15] G.M. Trevelyan wrote that "the English village was still able to provide an excellent type of colonist to new lands beyond the ocean. The men were accustomed to privation and to long hours of out-of-door work and were ready to turn their hands to tree-felling, agriculture and rough handicraft"; Trevelyan, *Illustrated English Social History* (Harmondsworth: Penguin, 1964), vol. 4: 32.

of sheep-breeding among other farming achievements was not by chance. Sheep-breeding, which started at the turn of the nineteenth century, soon became Australia's leading industry. In 1828, the very year in which the poem was written, the British Parliament acknowledged that Australian wool was the finest and cheapest in the world.

Campbell predicts not only economic well-being for "fair Australasia"; he also prophesies the flourishing of its arts – poetry, music, architecture: "For minstrels thou shalt have of native fire / And maids to sing the songs themselves inspire." In his mind's eye he sees

> Proud temple-domes, with galleries winding high,
> So vast in space, so just in symmetry,
> They widen to the contemplating eye,
> With colonnaded aisles in long array,
> And windows that enrich the flood of day
> O'er tessellated pavements, pictures fair.

The poet looks further into the future, beyond the life-span of these emigrants, and foretells that their descendants, born and brought up in Australia, will not experience any of their fathers' nostalgic feelings, and their love for the new homeland will be no weaker than their ancestors' devotion to England. In Campbell's time, Australia was still to a great extent *terra incognita*, and the poet stresses that there still is a lot of room for human daring and exploration. The poem abounds in adjectives with the prefix "un": in Australia there still were "undiscovered fountains," "tracts untrodden yet by man," "unbeaconed crags," "untracked in deserts" lay "the marble mine," "undug" yet was "the ore" and "unborn" yet were "the hands – but born they are to be," – that would turn "fair Australasia" into a

> Delightful land, in wildness even benign,
> The glorious past is ours, the future thine!
> [...]
> Land of the free! Thy kingdom is to come
> Of states, with laws from Gothic bondage burst,
> And creeds by chartered priesthoods unaccursed.

The poem closes with an appeal to God to bless the emigrants:

> May He, who in the hollow of his hand
> The ocean holds, and rules the whirlwind's sweep,
> Assuage its wrath, and guide you on the deep.

In depicting Australia in colourful scenes, Campbell evidently drew on several sources. They might have been the books *An Account of the English Colony in New South Wales* (1798) by David Collins and the *Description of New South Wales*

(1817) of William Wentworth,[16] which "were literate, informative and impressive," as well as the poems "First Fruits of Australian Poetry" (1819) by Barron Field and Wentworth's "Australasia" (1823) which were well known in England; both poems rendered their authors' "visionary hopes for the peaceful and civilized development of the country."[17] So did Campbell's "Lines on the Departure of Emigrants for New South Wales."

Campbell evidently modelled his idea of Australia's future on the USA, which at that time was still a "promised land" for British emigrants. The phrase "land of the free" was a line from the well-known American poem "The Star-Spangled Banner" by Francis Scott Key (1814), destined later to become the USA's national anthem. The idea of a future Australia as a kingdom of states with civilized laws and religious freedoms, as a country inhabited in future by different nations – all this suggests that in his predictions the poet proceeded from the popular idealized notion of the USA as a bastion of freedom and democracy. As G.M. Trevelyan put it,

> The tide of emigration also ran strongly to the USA, and might have run there almost to the exclusion of British territories but for the organized effort of emigration societies, and the occasional assistance of Government, inspired by the propaganda of Gibbon Wakefield.[18]

The fact that there is almost no mention of any hardships or privations which, as was commonly known, awaited the emigrants on the way to Australia and on their arrival there, as well as the reassuring and mostly optimistic tone of the poem, so different from that of the majority of poems on emigration, suggest that "Lines on the Departure of Emigrants to New South Wales" was also a kind of propaganda, either involuntary or deliberate, aimed at encouraging emigration and emigrants.[19] In literary terms, the poem was a kind of utopian presentation of Australian reality, which probably contributed to the creation of a stereotyped image of "fair Australasia."

Yet, though one of the many poems dedicated to the topical and controversial issue of emigration, Campbell's "Lines" exceeds the limits of a mere public farewell message. The poet casts a prophetic glance into the future of the continent, which at

---

[16] William Charles Wentworth (1790–1872) was the leading political figure during the first half of the nineteenth century. His lifelong work for self-government culminated in the New South Wales Constitution of 1855. His works publicized opportunities for colonization.

[17] *The New Encyclopedia Britannica* (Chicago: Encyclopedia Britannica, 1994), vol. 14: 494.

[18] Trevelyan, *Illustrated English Social History* vol. 4, 163.

[19] It is also noteworthy that Campbell, who all his life was very sensitive to the problem of national oppression (he condemned colonization of India, championed Poland's struggle for independence, etc. in his other works) completely overlooked the problem of relations between the white settlers and the aborigines of Australia in "Lines on the Departure."

his time was a land of both fear and hope, and makes predictions, most of which have eventually come true.

WORKS CITED

Campbell, Thomas. *Complete Poetical Works*, ed. Epes Sargent (Boston MA: Phillips, Sampson, 1854).

Erofeyev, Nikolai Aleksandrovich. *Английский колониализм в середине XIX века* [English Colonies in the Mid-Nineteenth Century] (Москва: Наука [Moscow: Nauka], 1977).

——. *Народная эмиграция и классовая борьба в Англии в 1825–1850 гг.* [Mass Emigration and Class Struggle in England in 1825–1850] (Москва [Moscow]: Издательство Академии наук СССР, 1962).

Great Victorian Poets and Their Paths to Fame: An Arts Council Exhibition of 1978 (Leeds: City Art Gallery, 1978).

Merpham, J. "What is England," *Literature Matters* 20 (March 1996): 10–11.

Malakhovski, Kim Vladimirovich. *История Австралии* [History of Australia] (Москва: Наука [Moscow: Nauka], 1980).

The New Encyclopedia Britannica (Chicago: Encyclopedia Britannica, 1994).

Nikolyukin, Aleksandr Nikolaevich. *Массовая поэзия в Англии конца XVIII начала XIX веков* [Popular Poetry in England in the Late Eighteenth – Early Nineteenth Centuries] (Москва [Moscow]: Издательство Академии наук СССР, 1961).

Palmer, Helen G., & John Macleod, *The First Hundred Years* (Melbourne & London: Longmans, Green, 1954).

Trevelyan, G.M. *Illustrated English Social History*, vol. 4 (Harmondsworth: Penguin, 1964).

◈

Ambivalent Oppositionality
David Malouf's *Fly Away Peter:* A European View

MARC DELREZ

S TEPHEN SLEMON, IN HIS SEMINAL ARTICLE entitled "Unsettling the Empire: Resistance Theory for the Second World," identifies the Second World as a paradigm of a particular kind of ambivalence which may possibly have a generalized relevance for postcolonial literary resistance. Roughly, the argument runs as follows: While most postcolonial theory still seeks to anchor its models of oppositionality in Third-World patterns of frontal resistance to the hegemony of the First World, which tend to lock the writer/critic into the polarity of Self/Other or here/there, a new aesthetic of resistance can be derived from the peculiar cultural schizophrenia inherent in settler culture. As Slemon puts it, what is particular about the white literatures of Australia, New Zealand, or Canada, is that they promote a form of anti-colonialist resistance which "has *never* been directed at an object or a discursive structure which can be seen as purely external to the self." They therefore testify to an "*internalisation* of the object of resistance"[1] which has two important consequences. The first is that the literatures of the Second World must be considered as part and parcel of the oppositional project of postcolonialism itself, a claim that has now become something of a critical truism – which possibly attests to the efficacity of Slemon's interventions and of others of its kind. The second is that these literatures offer a model for a theory of textual resistance which acknowledges at last the compromised nature of all 'writing back,' as always "*necessarily* complicit in the apparatus it seeks to transgress,"[2] and ought therefore to be adopted within any theorizing on literary resistance, in the Third World as well.

The argument is persuasive but complex, relying as it does on a paradox that is left unresolved, but which we are asked to accept as such. The paradox can be

---

[1] Stephen Slemon, "Unsettling the Empire: Resistance Theory for the Second World," *World Literature Written in English* 30.2 (1990): 39.

[2] Slemon, "Unsettling the Empire," 37.

articulated like this: on the one hand, white settler literatures can be seen to further native dispossession, insofar as the authors aim to secure for themselves and for their readership a sense of cultural rootedness which effectively displaces prior claims. To this extent, the 'postcolonial' settler writer aids and abets the project of European appropriation, territorial and otherwise. On the other hand, the white settler's defining predicament becomes one of cultural tension, or dividedness, which can be seen to figure forth a new, dynamic relation between such traditional opposites as colonizer and colonized, invader and indigene, centre and periphery. For Slemon, it is precisely this sort of ambivalence that must be turned into a system of resistance against hegemonic discourses.

Although this argument may seem empowering, it is still not clear to what extent it conveys the implicit suggestion that the reticence displayed by white settler culture on the subject of invasion is sufficient to atone for the continuing realities of oppression and dispossession. Accordingly, it is the aim of this essay to examine ways in which orthodox postcolonial nomenclatures, which only recognize, between the Second and the Third Worlds, a difference of degree and not of kind, in fact promote a looseness of historical fit, a misrepresentation of existing cultural hierarchies, which tend to be concealed behind a rhetorical smoke screen that I like to call the "binge."

I do not wish to claim any particular originality in inventing a concept which is, in fact, as old as the cultural cringe. When A.A. Phillips first proposed his description of the "cringe" in the 1950s, he allowed for the simultaneous existence of an "inverted cringe,"[3] which finds its source in the same inferiority complex as the cringe itself, but takes the unexpected form of a compensatory over-emphasis in the assertion of one's cultural identity. The cultural binge, then, may not be all that different from the inverted cringe, but the coinage offers the advantage of connoting self-indulgence – a certain lack of restraint in the exercise of intellectual expenditure. Moreover, the binge positively differs from the cringe, in that, while Phillips identified only a kind of psychological phenomenon (at the collective level), the binge denotes a much more deliberate gesture, which is both rhetorical and ideologically motivated. The function of the binge has something to do with keeping alive the ghosts of past enemies in order to reaffirm one's "oppositional credentials."[4] This may be why Alan Lawson pointed out that "commentators in Australia and Canada have, perhaps, shown an even greater obsession with the problem of

---

[3] A.A. Phillips, *The Australian Tradition: Studies in a Colonial Culture* (Melbourne: Cheshire, 1959): 89.

[4] David Carter, "Australia / Post: Australian Studies, Literature and Post-Colonialism," in *From a Distance: Australian Writers and Cultural Displacement*, ed. Wenche Ommundsen & Hazel Rowley (Geelong: Deakin UP, 1996): 113.

national identity than those of other emergent colonial or postcolonial nations.[5] Although Lawson puzzles over this, the binge might offer an explanation. While it is of course true that the versatile nature of the culture of Australia, which is largely a nation of immigrants, makes it worth exploring again and again, it can also be argued that the postcolonial desire to oppose, and indeed to reiterate one's opposition to, the traditional bugbear of European imperialism, in fact springs from a perception of embarrassing proximity to that very same Europe.

For example, the proverbial "tyranny of distance," which is usually seen to result in a preoccupation with exile on the part of many writers, possibly indicates, in its more recent literary manifestations, a need for ever-finer distinctions and discriminations, felt to be urgently necessary in order to screen out the emerging awareness of Australia as "a lapsed colonial power locked in an unresolved and undeclared struggle with the original possessors for legitimacy and land."[6] In other words, the theme of exile might fulfil the function of inscribing distance, as an attempt to preserve a postcolonial stance in the context of a new crisis of legitimacy, brought about by the Mabo case but also, partly, by the publication of *Dark Side of the Dream* by Bob Hodge and Vijay Mishra. This book is unlike many others on Australia, in that it presents the construction of national identity in this country as massively determined by the sense of its own complicity with an imperialist enterprise. This is an aspect that most postcolonial criticism overlooks, with the result that, as David Carter suggests, "the boom in career-making 'subversive' readings of canonical authors such as Malouf, Stow and White"[7] only testifies to a dubious form of interpretative agility on the part of critics who all too willingly tone down these writers' metaphysics of transcendence, in order to foist upon them a ready-made postcolonial aesthetic.

The case of David Malouf is particularly interesting, inasmuch as he openly presents himself in interviews as a writer with a mission, which is specifically to create "real spiritual links between us and the landscapes, us and the cities, us and the lives we live here."[8] Naturally, this formulation begs the question of belonging, as one wonders who might be included in Malouf's personal "imagined commu-

---

[5] Alan Lawson, "Patterns, Preferences and Preoccupations: The Discovery of Nationality in Australian and Canadian Literatures," in *Theory and Practice in Comparative Studies: Canada, Australia and New Zealand* (Sydney: ANZACS, 1983): 67.

[6] Bob Hodge & Vijay Mishra, *Dark Side of the Dream: Australian Literature and the Post-Colonial Mind* (Sydney: Allen & Unwin, 1991): xiv.

[7] David Carter, "Australia / Post: Australian Studies, Literature and Post-Colonialism," in *From a Distance: Australian Writers and Cultural Displacement*, ed. Wenche Ommundsen & Hazel Rowley (Geelong: Deakin UP, 1996): 110.

[8] Julie Copeland, interview with David Malouf, *First Edition*, ABC Radio (15 August 1985).

nity." He himself may supply the answer when he concedes, in a nonchalant aside n
his autobiographical *12 Edmonstone Street*, that "we discount the abos."[9] Already,
this alerts one to the possibility that Malouf is deliberately writing to, and on behalf
of, a specific segment of the Australian population, when he engages in the imaginative exploration of a national mythology. It is in keeping with the self-conscious
nature of his project that Malouf should explicitly acknowledge the existence of a
"fated affinity"[10] between the settler and the colonizer, and further, between the
writer and the conqueror. This aspect of Malouf's "mission" has been aptly pin-
pointed by Amanda Nettelbeck, who writes that his poetic "interpretation of Australia's changes as a community" has been regarded as betokening "a gradual national
shift away from England's legacy" that is, in essence, postcolonial; but that commentators have said very little about "the ways in which the processes of mapping,"
which form the core of Malouf's writing, are in fact "still encoded by the politics" of
the *imperium*.[11]

The latter is notably apparent in his privileging of exploration as a metaphor of
cultural attunement to what is perceived as a foreign space. Nettelbeck further suggests, very interestingly, that the notion of "exploration without end," developed by
Paul Carter in his *Living in a New Country*, adequately describes Malouf's aesthetic
project, which consists in rehearsing the evolutionary possibilities contained in the
open narrative of the past. Each of Malouf's novels can be seen as one in a succession of attempts to release from the colonial past a promise of change, of cultural
metamorphosis, which is embraced as the hallmark of Australian identity. This kind
of exploration, indeed, never ends, since what characterizes the subjects under
scrutiny is precisely their inexhaustible capacity to transform themselves. In spatial
terms, this can be represented as a kind of deferred arrival or, perhaps, as an exploration without conquest, in which the activity of investigation becomes an end in
itself. It may be argued that this suspension of conquest is in fact what makes
Malouf's project different from a fully-fledged colonialist one. In my view, this
aspect also feeds the binge, because the "always incomplete or provisional nature"[12]
of his project creates an unstaunchable flow of discourse, literary and otherwise,
which is at once self-justificatory and self-generating.

Nettelbeck, then, warns that the "impulse to explore and map new conceptions
of the world" may, of course, signal an ambition to break from received cultural

---

[9] David Malouf, *12 Edmonstone Street* (Harmondsworth: Penguin, 1986): 44.

[10] David Malouf, "Putting Ourselves on the Map," *Saturday Age Extra* (28 January 1988): 2.

[11] Amanda Nettelbeck, "Cultural Identity and the Narration of Space: A Reading of David
Malouf," in *From a Distance: Australian Writers and Cultural Displacement*, ed. Wenche Or-
mundsen & Hazel Rowley (Geelong: Deakin UP, 1996): 73–82.

[12] Nettelbeck, "Cultural Identity and the Narration of Space," 76.

traditions, such as the "colonial patriarchy's tradition of claiming space,"[13] but it also paradoxically reinscribes them in the very act of possession, albeit an imaginative form of possession. Again, Malouf has the merit of being candid about the extent to which his narrative strategies, which creatively invest the universe of settler culture, also bring about a repression of perspectives that cannot be viewed from his assumed vantage-point. For example, in *The Conversations at Curlow Creek*, there is a sense in which the narrative itself represses its own awareness of Jonas, an Aborigine who emerges as yet another manifestation of the figure of the native guide, that staple of Australian fiction. The novel's impersonal narrator only acknowledges the existence of Jonas as a member of the party when the story is well underway – with a sense of belated (and astonished) discovery:

> He was [...] an opening there into a deeper darkness, into a mystery – of the place, of something else too that was not-place, which might also be worth exploring – but all traffic through it, in either direction, was blocked.[14]

Curiously, Malouf seems to distinguish here between two degrees of inscrutability, perhaps because he *needs* to utilize Jonas as a guide to the mystery of the place, thus recognizing the indigene's exclusive competence in this respect, while not wishing to take on board the constraints that would derive from a consideration of further ethical principles particular to Aboriginal culture(s). This would be in keeping with Malouf's avowed intention of creating links with the place, a project for which he may have to take his cue from the natives, although his ulterior aim is to supersede native culture through the establishment of alternative, white mythologies about Australian history and its landscapes.

On the other hand, the observation that the cultural border is blocked in both directions possibly points to Malouf's acute consciousness of the methodological difficulties encoded in any cross-cultural blueprint. In *The Conversations at Curlow Creek*, the stigma of near-invisibility which sticks to Jonas – "he had been there all this while, but as if he were not there at all"[15] – derives from a deliberate suspension of vision on the part of the author, who knows only too well that, in Australia, "the literary representation of Aborigines by white writers has become a contentious issue."[16] Thus, Malouf's E.M. Forster-like decision to freeze all traffic – not here, not now – with a no-go zone of culture which might, in another context, be "worth exploring" amounts to a well-pondered refusal to lapse into a form of 'Aboriginalism' comparable to the kind of 'Orientalism' denounced by Edward Said. The same

---

[13] Nettelbeck, "Cultural Identity and the Narration of Space," 75, 76.

[14] David Malouf, *The Conversations at Curlow Creek* (London: Chatto & Windus, 1996): 112.

[15] Malouf, *The Conversations at Curlow Creek*, 24.

[16] Justin D'Ath, "White on Black," *Australian Book Review* 154 (1993): 35.

refusal informs *Remembering Babylon* (1993), Malouf's previous novel, which can be regarded as his most committed attempt to acknowledge Aboriginal experience as part of a mixed Australian tradition, but without presuming to pick the lock of a culture which is perceived as out of bounds for the white writer.[17]

This novel's initial image shows the protagonist, Gemmy, hovering in precarious balance on the top rail of a fence which separates the paddock from the bush; white from black; settler from native. On the face of it, then, Malouf here appears to gesture towards a twin representation of Australianness as hybrid or "geminate." However, on closer examination, Gemmy on his fence, "[his] arms outflung as if preparing for flight,"[18] also emerges as an embodiment of the writer's ascensional urge, by virtue of which he ultimately eludes historicity in favour of a metaphorized idealization of cultural metamorphosis. By the same token, I would claim that Malouf's postcolonialism forms a very limited branch of his utopianism; and, while the two can be found to be compatible, it is certainly not the case that they can be equated. In other words, perhaps because of his awareness of political and epistemological boundaries, Malouf is swift to desert the postcolonial battlefield for a superior dimension of sublimated ontologies which can be seen as universal.

My point, then, is that postcolonialism is only a facet, in Malouf, of a much larger scheme; and this is confirmed by the fact that the image of Gemmy on his fence, which signals a striving for a form of cultural equilibrium encompassing white and black, in fact echoes an earlier moment in Malouf's work which, though very similar, ultimately carries different implications. I am thinking of the ending of *Fly Away Peter* (1982), a book which closes on another vision of precarious balance, with the vignette of a young surfer poised on the crest of a wave. This, as the final image of the novel, carries particular resonance. The surfer's figure is "sharply outlined against the sky [...] his arms extended,"[19] as if he, too, had mastered the gift of flying, so that he can be seen as an extension of the bird metaphor which is central in the novel and which, by virtue of the birds' capacity to migrate between hemispheres, signifies a reconciliation of opposites. The surfer brings together the "seemingly opposing elements of change and continuity, motion and immobility,"[20] and, because he reminds the viewer of the late Jim Saddler, who died in the war, he also emerges as an emblem of the future, seen as a creative variation on the past. More-

---

[17] Marc Delrez & Paulette Michel–Michot, "The Politics of Metamorphosis: Cultural Transformation in David Malouf's *Remembering Babylon*," in *The Contact and Culmination: Essays in Honour of Hena Maes–Jelinek*, ed. Marc Delrez & Bénédicte Ledent (Liège: Liège UP, 1997): 155–70.

[18] David Malouf, *Remembering Babylon* (London: Chatto & Windus, 1993): 3.

[19] David Malouf, *Fly Away Peter* (Ringwood, Victoria: Penguin, 1983): 133.

[20] Amanda Nettelbeck, "Languages of War, Class and National History: David Malouf's *Fly Away Peter*," *Kunapipi* 18.2–3 (1996): 258.

over, the surfer keeps falling in the trough of the wave, only to rise up again, so that the novel's final scene ties up another metaphorical loose end – the image of the fall, which is invoked to represent Jim's expulsion from his colonial paradise, while the war is presented as a collective rite of passage from innocence to the harrowing experience of twentieth-century international history. In short, the image of the surfer encapsulates and entwines a variety of discursive threads, which went into the making of Australian identity as constituted through the mythologizing of the First World War. On the one hand, the surfer can be seen as a moving monument to the memory of Jim Saddler, which betokens Malouf's "humbling respect for the experience itself and those who endured it"[21] – an experience that the writer wishes to acknowledge and assimilate. But, on the other hand, the surfer emerges as yet another emblem of novelty, an opening onto the unknown (like Jonas), which implies the need to move beyond the institutionalized myth of ANZAC and its ideological cargo of "Anglo-Celtic xenophobia, militarism and red-necked philistinism."[22]

Amanda Nettelbeck has beautifully unravelled the rich array of discourses which Malouf spins around *his* version of the First World War in *Fly Away Peter*. In particular, she suggests that the myth of pre-war innocence in Australia is a deceptive one "that was always shadowed by its opposite."[23] This becomes clear in the light of Jim's inventory of birds in "The Book," whereby he recognizes "their place in the landscape, or his stretch of it,"[24] in a way that is fraught with imperialist presumptions. Jim's "Book" thus emerges as a metaphor for the activity of colonial exploration or mapping out, in a way which ironically reflects on Malouf's own writing, at the same time as it alerts one to the fact that pastoral innocence in the "Sanctuary" is "complicitous with the invisible exercise of cultural power."[25] In other words, the dream of arcadian innocence in the South Seas simply depends on a silencing of the history of bloodshed that made it possible in the first place. As Nettelbeck puts it, "the absence of Aboriginal presence [...] in either the urban or the 'sanctified' landscape [...] indicates the naturalizing of the settler culture's own violences."[26]

Although I agree that *Fly Away Peter* problematizes the myth of prewar innocence by suggesting that Jim's universe is vulnerable to the Fall – to the point when the Sanctuary begins to tilt "in the direction of Europe"[27] – I am not at all sure that

---

[21] David Malouf, "Statement," *Kunapipi* 18.2–3 (1996): 332.

[22] Malouf, *Fly Away Peter* (Ringwood, Victoria: Penguin, 1983): 331.

[23] Nettelbeck, "Languages of War, Class and National History," 257.

[24] Malouf, *Fly Away Peter*, 44.

[25] Nettelbeck, "Languages of War," 255.

[26] "Languages of War," 256.

[27] *Fly Away Peter*, 36.

Malouf's reader is invited to read the book as an indictment of colonial presence in
Australia. Significantly, when Jim finally punctures the myth of the place as a pre-
lapsarian Eden, it is by coming to terms with a vision of violence which is either
accidental or casual. Looking back on his youth after his initiation into violence in
the war, Jim remembers the violent death of his brother in a harvesting accident, as
well as the cruel torture to which a kestrel is subjected by some "innocent" children.
These memories force Jim to revise his earlier perception of a sunny place: "That
was how it was, even in sunlight. Even there."[28] Thus, even as violence is reinte-
grated into Jim's moral universe, it continues to be depoliticized as a form of inescapable evil. This is a far cry from recognizing the foundations of violence on which
the dream of utopian Australia is in fact constructed.

    This elision of historical responsibility becomes all the more problematic since
the idyllic presentation of Jim's relationship to the land borrows from identifiable
stereotypes of Aboriginal spirituality. In this sense, the narrative undertakes to
dislodge the natives prior to plundering the imaginative privileges which seem to be
theirs by right. Indeed, Jim's claims to the land are justified in terms of his unique
understanding of a place experienced as "unmade." His vision, which goes beyond
"mere convention or the law," is simply presented as inalienable. At the same time,
the authenticity of this vision is attested by Jim's gift for nomenclature, by his
having "names for things, and in that way possessing them," by virtue of a familiar-
ity with the land which is "ancient and deep." Malouf appears to be playing a
curious game here, which consists in deliberately confusing the time-scales, in order
to erase the unfortunate evidence provided by chronology. Similarly, when he introduces the character of Ashley, the British landowner, he insists on the continuity of
ownership, hinting at funeral monuments which are "so chipped and stained that
they might have been real monuments going back centuries rather than a mere score
of years to the first death."[29] Again, the suggestion is that the settlers enjoy a sense of
belonging to the land which, viewed from their own perspective, reveals a tradition
seen as immemorial.

    Because no rival claim is acknowledged in *Fly Away Peter*, this presumption of
belonging is never at any stage seriously contested. One may even argue that the
novel as a whole inscribes itself within a context of self-affirmation which is
strongly coded ideologically, quite in keeping with the rhetorics of roots that I have
called the binge. In as much as Malouf's work in general seeks to rehearse crucial
historical landmarks in settler experience in order to release a sense of imaginative
possession in these same settlers, it also paradoxically responds to a logic of cultural
*dis*possession of the land's original inhabitants. Therefore, any postcolonial cor-

---

[28] Malouf, *Fly Away Peter*, 104.
[29] Malouf, *Fly Away Peter*, 11, 7, 12 (quotations in this paragraph).

struction of the work is bound to appear somewhat shaky, since Malouf's revision-
ary impulse rests on a colonialist substratum, which is possibly inherent in settler
culture itself. Without wishing to deny the settlers' claims a validity of their own (of
course), I would like to point out that this kind of tension raises a number of questions concerning the status of settler literature within the institution of postcolonial
studies. To my mind, by accepting Australia without further ado 'into' the postcolonial mansion we run the risk of overlooking the peculiar slippage that occurred
at the pivotal moment when the beneficiaries of conquest began to "identify with the
conquered land."[30]

On the other hand, David Malouf may not be paradigmatic, in this respect, of all
that is going on in Australian literature, despite his visibility as a living figurehead
on the international scene. This is why I would like to add, as a very brief coda to
this essay, a note on the work of Nicholas Jose – who, perhaps significantly, belongs
to a younger generation of Australian novelists. Jose's latest novel, *The Custodians*
(1997), provides an interesting comparison with and counterpoise to Malouf, on
account of its peculiar structure. Each of the main sections of the novel is followed
by a brief chapter recounting the story of Daniel, an Aborigine whose life was
stolen, quite literally, as a result of child-removal policy. Daniel is a gifted painter
who, unable to endure incarceration, finally commits suicide by ramming the slender
handle of a paint-brush into his right eye. Although he remains, by all accounts, a
minor character in the book, it becomes clear that the denial of Daniel's vision,
which is the other side of Australian history, emerges as the condition on which the
lives of all the other protagonists, white and black, depends. Jose thus acknowledges
the suffering on which Australian society is based, in a way that precludes the possibility of arcadian nostalgia. It is in keeping with this that all the characters, again
white and black, should somehow belong to the land in *The Custodians*, while at the
same time the land itself belongs to no one. Indeed, Nicholas Jose is at pains to replace the notion of exclusive possession by the alternative one of custodianship,
which implies shared responsibility for the land, which in turn extends into a form of
commitment to mankind as a whole. In Australia, then, a renunciation of ownership
would seem to be a prerequisite for any convincing claim to the label 'postcolonial';
a situation which is emblematic of the country's curious predicament.

❧

---

[30] Diana Brydon & Helen Tiffin, *Decolonising Fictions* (Sydney & Mundelstrup: Dangaroo,
1993): 41.

WORKS CITED

Brydon, Diana, & Helen Tiffin. *Decolonising Fictions* (Mundelstrup & Sydney: Dangaroo, 1993).

Carter, David. "Australia / Post: Australian Studies, Literature and Post-Colonialism," in *From a Distance: Australian Writers and Cultural Displacement*, ed. Wenche Ommundsen & Hazel Rowley (Geelong: Deakin UP, 1996): 103–16.

Copeland, Julie. Interview with David Malouf. *First Edition*, ABC Radio (15 August 1985).

D'Ath, Justin. "White on Black," *Australian Book Review* 154 (1993): 35–39.

Delrez, Marc, & Paulette Michel–Michot. "The Politics of Metamorphosis: Cultural Transformation in David Malouf's *Remembering Babylon*," in *The Contact and the Culmination: Essays in Honour of Hena Maes–Jelinek*, ed. Marc Delrez & Bénédicte Ledent (Liège: Liège UP, 1997): 155–70.

Hodge, Bob, & Vijay Mishra. *Dark Side of the Dream: Australian Literature and the Post-Colonial Mind* (Sydney: Allen & Unwin, 1991).

Jose, Nicholas. *The Custodians* (London: Pan / Picador, 1997).

Lawson, Alan. "Patterns, Preferences and Preoccupations: The Discovery of Nationality in Australian and Canadian Literatures." *Theory and Practice in Comparative Studies: Canada, Australia and New Zealand* (Sydney: ANZACS, 1983).

Malouf, David. *The Conversations at Curlow Creek* (London: Chatto & Windus, 1996).

——. *Fly Away Peter* (Ringwood, Victoria: Penguin, 1983).

——. "Putting Ourselves on the Map," *Saturday Age Extra* (28 January 1988): 2.

——. *Remembering Babylon* (London: Chatto & Windus, 1993).

——. "Statement," *Kunapipi* 18.2–3 (1996): 331–32.

——. *12 Edmonstone Street* (Harmondsworth: Penguin, 1986).

Nettelbeck, Amanda. "Cultural Identity and the Narration of Space: A Reading of David Malouf," in *From a Distance: Australian Writers and Cultural Displacement*, ed. Wenche Ommundsen & Hazel Rowley (Geelong: Deakin UP, 1996): 73–82.

——. "Languages of War, Class and National History: David Malouf's *Fly Away Peter*," *Kunapipi* 18.2–3 (1996): 249–60.

Phillips, A.A. *The Australian Tradition: Studies in a Colonial Culture* (Melbourne: Cheshire, 1959)

Slemon, Stephen. "Unsettling the Empire: Resistance Theory for the Second World," *World Literature Written in English* 30.2 (1990): 35–45.

❧

Reinventing the Future(s)
Peter Carey and the Dystopian Tradition in Australian Fiction

RALPH PORDZIK

The Dystopian Strand in Australian Writing

COMPARING THE UTOPIAN TRADITIONS of New Zealand, Canada and Australia, one finds that utopian novels written in Australia lack a clear sense of faith in the creation of an improved society in which peace and stability are universally and permanently obtained.[1] The beginnings of the land as a hell on earth for transported convicts have fuelled an imagery of imprisonment rather than one of a virgin paradise "lowered down from heaven,"[2] effecting a view of the environment as hostile and violent, and creating a dispirited cultural self-image that has figured large in utopian and speculative fiction ever since. This lack of confidence is already reflected in the earliest writings on record; many novels, tracts and poems concerned with the notion of utopia exhibit a bizarre millenarianism (Hannah Boyd, *A Voice From Australia*, 1851; Edward F. Hughes, *The Millenium: An Epic Poem*, 1873), indulge in a thinly disguised racial exclusiveness (James A.K. Mackay, *The Yellow Wave: A Romance of the Asiatic Invasion of Australia*, 1895), or present fictive accounts of mythical kingdoms in the interior of the conti-

---

[1] See Lyman T. Sargent's bibliographies of New Zealand, Australian and Canadian utopian literature for a great variety of fictional and non-fictional writings since the early nineteenth century. For detailed discussions of utopian literature in Britain see Richard Gerber, *Utopian Fantasy Since the End of the 19th Century* (London: Routledge, 1955); Lewis Mumford, "Utopia, the City and the Machine," in *Utopias and Utopian Thought*, ed. Frank E. Manuel (Boston MA: Houghton Mifflin, 1966): 3–24; Hans Ulrich Seeber, *Wandlungen der Form in der literarischen Utopie: Studien zur Entfaltung des utopischen Romans in England* (Göppingen: Kümmerle, 1970); and Ruth Levitas, *The Concept of Utopia* (Syracuse NY: Syracuse UP, 1990). A bibliography of British and American utopian fiction has been compiled by Lyman Tower Sargent, *British and American Utopian Literature: An Annotated Bibliography* (Boston MA: G.K. Hall, 1979).

[2] Mumford, "Utopia, the City and the Machine," 14.

nent peopled either by hostile savages or by technologically advanced, sinister races (Ernest Favenc, *Marooned On Australia*, 1897; Phil Collas, *The Inner Domain*, 1935).[3] Socialist 'eutopias,' such as William Lane's *The Workingman's Paradise* (1892) or Ralph Gibson's *Socialist Melbourne* (1937), are rather the exception and even Barnard Eldershaw's much-acclaimed technocratic far-future utopia *Tomorrow and Tomorrow* (1947) is tinged with a sceptical awareness of the price that social equality might demand.[4] Indeed, most of these novels appear to confirm Nan B. Albinski's argument that

> Australian writing has always had a thread of dystopianism. Its minor aspect is criticism of the plight of the urban working classes in utopian novels [...] It is expressed even more strongly in the avowedly dystopian novels that are thematically dominated either by the sinister, inland 'lost' civilisation, or by the xenophobic fears of an Australian future under an Asian iron heel.[5]

The anti-utopian stance exhibited in many novels continued well into the 1960s and 1970s, when positive utopias were in danger of "fading from the map"[6] of English literature and the field was taken over by science fiction dystopias prophesying with an alarming easiness a most frightening future for mankind.[7] The inevitability of the arrival of hell on earth was no longer called into question in these works; what

---

[3] Many of these writings were inspired by the then widely held notion of Australia being the 'lost' pre-Atlantan continent of Lemuria (J.J. Haley, "The Lemurian Nineties," *Australian Literary Studies* 8 [1978]: 307–16). However, the communities depicted in these novels can hardly be conceived of as having been assigned a truly separate cultural identity or form of life of their own. At best, they are manifestations of the invaders' persistent need to create a colonial exotic or westernized 'other,' a superb race endowed with a modern technology and a set of 'white' notions of utopian perfection. Especially in Australia with its remarkably long tradition of novels written in the 'lost race' vein, this attitude towards the other is tinged with a sense of the writers' own exile and alienation from the continent, the unsettling eeriness and infinitude of its interior and the natives' strange and unfamiliar ways of life.

[4] It is curious to note, however, that among the few published progressive utopias women eutopias play a significant role: As early as 1888 Catherine Helen Spence advocated a system of trial marriage in her future novel *Handfasted*, and Henrietta Dugdale included a detailed feminist eutopia in her narrative *A Few Hours in a Far-Off Age* (1883). The most striking of these works, however, is Mary Moore–Bentley's *A Woman of Mars, or, Australia's Enfranchised Women* (1901) which features a woman from Mars bringing to earth the benefits of an alternative social pattern shaped according to the moral instincts of the female rather than the aggressive physical energies of the male.

[5] Nan Bowman Albinski, "A Survey of Australian Utopian and Dystopian Fiction," *Australian Literary Studies* 13 (1987): 16.

[6] Chad Walsh, *From Utopia to Nightmare* (New York & Evanston: Harper & Row, 1962): 170.

[7] See Albinski, "A Survey of Australian Utopian and Dystopian Fiction," 20: "The watershed between [the utopias of the nineteenth and twentieth centuries] is that loss of faith in the achievability and desirability of utopia that led to the powerful dystopias of the twentieth century: Zamyatin's *We* (1924) and Huxley's *Brave New World* (1934)."

varied instead was the ferocity and assertiveness with which these nightmares were conceived. Not surprisingly, the number of dystopias written and published in Australia since the mid-1960s has increased markedly as well, echoing some of the apocalyptic forecasts of Western writing as well as examining the future prospects of a formerly colonized nation struggling to disabuse itself from its imperial legacy.[8] Novels of the late 1960s and early 1970s such as Bertram Chandler's *False Fatherland* (1968), Geoff Taylor's *Day of the Republic* (1968) and Colin Free's *The Soft Kill* (1973) all reflect the critical attitude of writers towards authoritarianism derived, in more general terms, from their sense of alienation in a morally corrupt world and, in more particular terms, from Australia's involvement in the Vietnam War and the wide-spread intellectual resentment against the prohibition of literature and political commentary published overseas.[9] David Ireland's much-acclaimed *The Unknown Industrial Prisoner* (1971) is by far the most sophisticated dystopian novel of this period to make points about the dangers of global capitalism and the almost unlimited power of multinational corporations. It depicts the life of a large group of workers in an oil refinery located at Botany Bay (where James Cook first landed in 1770) and captures the sickening reality and depressing absurdity of life in this horrid enclave in a series of disconnected passages and units that evoke the atmosphere of a penal colony peopled with the outcasts and rejects of a bleak, profit-oriented society. With particular regard to its uncompromising treatment of violence, Ireland's futuristic novel anticipates some of Peter Carey's early fiction, such as *The Fat Man in History* (1974, reissued 1990) or *War Crimes* (1979). In both cases the reader is confronted with a view of contemporary society as hell, void of any regenerative potential and dominated by the sinister, multiplying technologies of the twentieth century. Both writers employ satire and black comedy in order to show how late industrial capitalism permeates and conditions modern life; both exhibit a desire to register the bizarre and the uncanny as a part of the individual's quotidian social experience. It is in this respect that their work continues earlier strands of modern Australian fiction concerned with nightmares of violence and disintegration.[10]

What distinguishes Carey from Ireland, however, is the fact that he has developed a taste for new modes of expression that seek to break the spell of the tragic ritualized in much dystopian fiction and to put an end to the apocalyptic state of siege that prevents humans from getting anywhere in the future. Some of his earliest stories, such as "The Chance," "Do You Love Me?" or "The Puzzling Nature of

---

[8] Albinski, "A Survey of Australian Utopian and Dystopian Fiction," 26.

[9] Ken Goodwin, *A History of Australian Literature* (London: Macmillan, 1988): 253.

[10] Goodwin, *A History of Australian Literature*, 4; Anthony J. Hassall, *Dancing on Hot Macadam: Peter Carey's Fictions* (St Lucia: U of Queensland P, 1994): 72.

Blue," set out to challenge the claustrophobic posture exhibited in utopian and
science fiction literature and to employ the speculative and the fantastic as a means
of reclaiming a world of difference embedded variously in region, imagination or a
separate cultural history and identity. This attitude is continued in *Bliss* (1981) and
further explored in the more recent *Unusual Life of Tristan Smith* (1994), a complex
story about metamorphosis and about entering a liminal (textual) territory where
established categories constantly get blurred or distorted and current notions about
cross- or interculturality are rendered in most powerful terms. In the following I
would like to pay a visit to some of the future territories in Carey's writings and to
examine the ways in which the characters trapped in these landscapes manage to
escape the grinding, nightmarish routine that surrounds them. Obviously, Carey
seeks to subvert the long established tradition of Australian utopian fiction, which in
the past has restricted itself mainly to fashioning either apocalyptic or purely scientific versions of the future. Inserting a fruitful dialogue between the hardened conventions of genre science fiction and the cross-cultural capacity of more recent postcolonial writing, he transcends what Wilson Harris has termed the "repetitive logic
that sustains our grimmest expectations or fears of unfreedom."[11] The future prospects his fictions offer may at times seem bleak, but they always provide some
extra space for the celebration of human creativity and inventiveness or for the
possibility of escape through a form of 'cathartic' story-telling that offsets the fears
and whims so unproductively embraced by an earlier strand of utopian writing.

Disaffected With Dystopia

In "The Chance," one of the most powerful and haunting of Carey's early stories,
Australia has been invaded by the extraterrestrial Fastalogians. They have replaced
the Americans as the leading colonial superpower and established a Genetic Lottery
that provides people with the opportunity to obtain a new body if they are dissatis-
fied with the one they already have. For the price of "two thousand inter-galactic
dollars"[12] it is possible to try one's luck up and down the genetic scale and to become another person with a different age and a different voice. The world depicted
in this story mockingly reflects the stereotypes of the conventional disaster novel:
"Wild-haired holymen in loincloths, palm-readers, seers, revolutionaries without
followings, [...] Gurus in helicopters [and] bandits roam[ing] the countryside in
search of travellers who [...] moved in nervous groups, well armed and thankful to
be alive when they returned" (57) inhabit this future Australia, motivated by nothing

---

[11] Wilson Harris, *The Womb of Space: The Cross-Cultural Imagination* (Westport CT & London: Greenwood, 1983): xvii.
[12] Carey, *The Fat Man in History* (1974; London: Faber & Faber, 1990): 57. Further page-refer-
ences are in the main text.

but their self-preservation and their blind confidence in the success of the next genetic "Chance."

Paul, the first-person narrator, has already taken four Chances when the story opens. Not entirely unhappy with his body of an "ageing street-fighter" (58) that suits his resolute power, he is, however, taken aback by his girlfriend's bold announcement to move down the genetic scale: She wants to abandon her attractive "upper class" body and acquire instead one from the "misshapen Lumpen Proletariat" as a gesture of solidarity with the forthcoming revolutionary struggle against the "Fastas and their puppets" (62). Paul tries to imprison Carla at home in order to prevent her from taking the Chance but fails and, after Carla's return from the Lottery, rejects her new, unattractive body. Mourning over her loss of a lover, Carla leaves him and embarks on a new career as a leader of the revolution. Her subsequent success as one of the "fiercest fighters" who "attacked and killed without mercy" (88) is outside Paul's experience and so is only sketched in a brief historical summary at the end of the story. The narrator himself, by now a "crazy old man, alone with his books and his beer and his dog" (88), bitterly regrets his decision and his inability to stand the simple test of true love and loyalty to his former girlfriend.

"The Chance" is basically a story about missed opportunities, about alternatives whose potential for change and improvement is not fully realized. Although the abrupt ending leaves it open whether the revolution was for better or for worse or whether the Lottery remained after the take-over, the reader is offered the view of a new quality in individuals aiming to overcome their adherence to fixed notions of identity, solidity and permanence. Compared to other short-story dystopias in Carey's first two collections *War Crimes* (1979) and *The Fat Man in History* (1990), "The Chance" thus confronts the static completion of the vicious nightmares depicted, for instance, in "The Fat Man in History," where the totalitarian regime represents a self-reproducing and self-signifying system, or in "Crabs," where the narrator is trapped in a repetitive pattern of violence and repression which he fuels by constantly fighting against it. In its unexpected forecast of a 'post-dystopian' condition, a new sense of the future which is to replace the eternal twilight of the gods is conveyed, a future that calls for the responsibility of the individual not to miss the chance once it is there and not to give up the continual quest for a new and improved identity – symbolized in Paul's subsequent career as clerk and seller of cars, "pock-marked and ugly, [...] bankrupt and handsome" (88), a haunting image of a de-centred, multiple (postcolonial) personality erasing temporal and cultural boundaries as well as stable inscriptions of the future.

A similar case can be made for some other stories published in *The Fat Man in History*. "The Puzzling Nature of Blue" (89–109), for instance, is about a small

Pacific island abused by a multinational corporation to warehouse a shipment of a banned drug that colours the extremities of those who consume it. The islanders steal the drugs, have their arms and legs turned blue, and, during their subsequent struggle for independence, make blue the trademark of their revolution. Later the colour turns into a symbol of their separate cultural and national identity. The main point at issue, however, is the fact that the protagonist, an ex-member of the company and responsible for the shipment, regrets his deed and adopts the culture of the islanders along with their most prominent feature, the blue hands. By a strange irony of fate, the former colonizer is thus transformed into a living emblem of the decolonization / interculturalization process, providing a model for others to dissociate themselves from their past and their imperial allegiance.

Carey's determination to recycle the familiar concerns of traditional dystopian fiction is even more ambitiously dramatized in *Bliss* (1981) and *The Unusual Life of Tristan Smith*. In one of the last chapters of *Bliss* it is reported that a cancer epidemic is going to change the face of the immediate future:

> But his [Harry's] behaviour was not so different [...] than the panic that was to run through the Western world (and parts of the industrialized East) ten years later when the cancer epidemic really arrived, and then it came at a time of deep recession, material shortages, unemployment and threatening nuclear war, and it proved the last straw for the West which had, until then, still managed to tie its broken pieces together with cotton threads of material optimism which served instead of the older social fabric of religion and established custom. Then the angry cancer victims [...] took to the streets in what began as demonstrations and ended in half-organized bands, looting for heroin first, and then everything else.[13]

Like many other future scenarios in Carey's fictions, this prophetic passage is temporally indeterminate: there is no certain indication of the event's occurrence in the real world. However, whereas Harry Joy's descent into the privacy of his own hell may pass as a symbol of his growing neurosis, the cancer epidemic and the ensuing crisis must be taken as a "cognitive estrangement" in Darko Suvin's definition of the term: ie, as a change or innovation in the structure of the represented world that is based on an "alternative historical hypothesis" and determines the entire logic of the narrative or at least a substantial part of it.[14] Accordingly, the dystopian baseline is

---

[13] Carey, *Bliss* (Brisbane: U of Queensland P, 1981): 262. Further page references are in the main text.

[14] Darko Suvin, *Metamorphoses of Science Fiction: On the Poetics and History of a Literary Genre* (New Haven CT: Yale UP, 1979): 63. A similar approach has been taken by Robert Scholes who conceives of Suvin's novum in terms of the "presence of at least one clear representational discontinuity with life as we know it"; Robert Scholes, *Structural Fabulation: An Essay on the Fiction of the Future* (London: Notre Dame UP, 1975): 61. Utopian works can thus be grasped in terms of a projection of a whole network of changes or innovations on the ontological plane of

continually reflected in the gloomy forecasts reiterated throughout the novel, in the thrilling steps of a late capitalist society towards disintegration as well as in the gripping portrayal of a middle-class family on the verge of self-destruction. Harry's daughter Lucy and her boyfriend Ken are doomsday addicts who believe that they will "go down" with the world, that there is no "escape" (227). Awaiting the arrival of the beast of the apocalypse, they have prepared themselves for survival in the wilderness after the "event," when it's "over." Their overriding obsession with the end of the world finds a climax in Ken's grave recital of C.P. Cafavy's poem "Waiting for the Barbarians" (227) that voices the anxieties and forebodings of the former English 'settler communities' and anticipates their defeat in the forthcoming struggle against the downtrodden and the colonized rising to overthrow the ruling powers.

On the other hand, there is Honey Barbara, the attractive visitor from a hinterland commune who moves into the Joy's family home after having fallen in love with Harry. Personifying the spirit of 'California 1968,' she seeks to cure the world's malignancy with love, meditation and massage. She believes in witchcraft and in the healing powers of herbal teas, and now and then she uses spells to drive away evil spirits. Her home community at Bog Onion is the enchanted New Age 'eutopia' Harry finally manages to escape to after the death of his wife. Critics have been irritated by this optimistic ending, which seems to be out of harmony with the monochromatic and darkly comic fictions of *The Fat Man in History* and *War Crimes*.[15] Indeed, the marital peace Harry and Barbara enjoy at Bog Onion after an interim period of hostility and separation as well as their celebration of a rural life strangely at odds with the pastimes of modern capitalism invites an interpretation that applauds Harry's retreat from society and sympathizes with the utopian views and attitudes embraced by this 'imagined community' of drop-outs and rejects. Although the reader is given to understand that the notion of the 'Good Life' as envisaged by the villagers represents another timeless Western myth profitably recycled by a cynical consumer industry – evident, for instance, in the numerous tongue-in-cheek descriptions of Barbara's esoteric attitudes, her belief in a person's "bad Karma" (130) and in the value of "good food" (214) – he is also made to approve of this nest of alternative life-styles that confronts the cancerous nightmare logic slowly encroaching upon the slick world of profit Harry has left behind. This view is reinforced by the fact that the dwellers at Bog Onion do not appear to have wholly lost their sense of faith in the meaning of a genuine past. Their village is therefore

---

fictional representation that are effective insofar as they enable the reader to relocate familiar structures of the material world he inhabits in an alternative environment "validated by cognitive logic" (63).

[15] See Graham Huggan, *Peter Carey* (Melbourne: Oxford UP, 1996): 60.

not simply a chimerical refuge on the back of the all-devouring capitalist monster. Rather, it creates its own substantial, living past or "enabling myth"[16] through the symbolic meaning it attributes to the art of storytelling. Harry's acknowledged talent for refashioning the tales inherited from his father and for adapting them to the specific needs of the community paves the way for the creation of an entirely different communal spirit that transcends the assimilative designs of the culture it has abolished:

> They were the refugees of a broken culture who had only the flotsam of belief and ceremony to cling to or, sometimes, the looted relics from other people's temples. Harry cut new wood grown on their soil and built something they all felt comfortable with. They were hungry for ceremony and story. (291)

The founding gesture implied in this passage may run the danger of reinforcing the 'bush ethos' of Australian literature,[17] but it also highlights the relevance of stories and legends in the process of forging a collective inheritance that, once called into being, inscribes into history its own views and perceptions. Perceived from this angle, Harry is not one of the conjurers portrayed in *Illywhacker* who "summon up whole pasts and futures in a puff of smoke,"[18] but rather the founding figure of a truly postcolonial culture emancipating itself from the imported tales and legends of the imperial (capitalist) past. Accordingly, Bog Onion is not a timeless utopia of static perfection, but rather a site of exchange between the different versions of its own past circulating among the dwellers, a place that gradually grows into existence with each new story invented and memorized, each tale retold and transferred to the next generation in search of the cultural pattern that suits its perceptions and its hopes for a future in dignity and self-respect.

Travels in Heterotopia

Bliss meticulously deconstructs the binary opposition between the arcadian hinterland and the nightmare of the metropolitan centre reflected in much Australian literature. The most radical challenge to this paradigm, however, is posed by *The Unusual Life of Tristan Smith*, a tale of two cities conjoined and divided in ways which Tristan Smith, who dwells successively in both, painfully traces. Chemin Rouge and Saarlim are respectively the capitals of Efica and Voorstand, the former an ex-colonial southern archipelago still having an uneasy client-state dependence on Voorstand, the latter a former Dutch colony occupying a vast northern continent spreading from arctic circle to hot desert. French, Dutch and English cultures coexist

---

[16] Hassall, *Dancing on Hot Macadam*, 81.

[17] Albinski, "A Survey of Australian Utopian and Dystopian Fiction," 16.

[18] Huggan, *Peter Carey*, 60.

with that of Voorstand, which may be seen as a conglomerate of South African, North American and Southern Pacific colonial history.[19] Voorstand's national mythology revolves around the stories of Bruders Dog, Duck and Mouse, archetypal creaturely emblems of an historical animal-revering cult whose basic religious manifestation is the Franciscan Free Church. The partly sacral, partly mythological nature of these "agents of an enslaving imperial culture"[20] – animated to life in vast "Sirkus Domes" in Voorstand and then beamed via satellite as giant-size projections to the smaller Efican "Simulation Domes" – is confronted by the picaresque quest of Tristan Smith, the hideously stunted actor–narrator born in a theatre in a rather grubby quarter of Chemin Rouge. When his mother, involved in a political campaign against Voorstand domination, is murdered by political agents, Tristan leaves for Saarlim in search of his father, Bill Millefleur. Circumstances enable him to hide his deformed body in a derelict Bruder Mouse cyborg and to enter Voorstand's capital in the guise of one of its most cherished symbolical beasts. Absorbed into Saarlim's corrupt high society, Tristan quickly turns into a celebrity and indulges in a sexual affair with the fabulous Sirkus entrepreneur Peggy Kram, until his career finds a rather abrupt and comical ending in the final unmasking debacle. However, Tristan manages to escape the consequences of his pretence with the help of his father Bill and his nurse Jacqui. Together the party embarks on a symbolic journey to the arctic circle and eventually leaves Voorstand for Bergen in Norway, facing the new life and the challenges that lie ahead of them.

Not only are the "strains of dystopian satire"[21] deployed in the novel subverted by this final, optimistic summation, but the whole idea of a fixed utopian locus is challenged by the design of the book as a heterotopian "zone," in Brian McHale's sense of the term: ie, a site of conflicting perceptions and ontological propositions occupying the imaginative space of the narrative.[22] Thus English, Dutch and North American cultural components are fused with the fictional mythologies of Voorstand and Efica (Peggy Kram's luxurious penthouse, for instance, is hung with Dutch and Flemish masters); the historical facts of Western colonial expansion are interpolated

---

[19] Huggan, *Peter Carey*, 60.

[20] Huggan, *Peter Carey*, 60.

[21] K.V. Bailey, review, "Peter Carey's *The Unusual Life of Tristan Smith*," *Foundation* 63 (1995): 108.

[22] Brian McHale, *Postmodernist Fiction* (London & New York: Routledge, 1991), 44–49, names four distinct strategies employed by writers to (de)construct a fictional zone: *juxtaposition* (relating of geographical and semantic areas shown as non-contiguous in real-world encyclo-paedias or atlases), *interpolation* (introducing an alien space within a familiar space), *superimposi-tion* (two familiar spaces are placed one on top of the other) and *misattribution* (the wilful displacing and rupturing of automatic associations).

with the chronicles of the imagined settler colonies; and the unilateralism of Western imperialist doctrines is juxtaposed with the constantly changing relations between colonizer and colonized as depicted in *Tristan Smith*. In a fictional place like this, Michel Foucault argues, "things are 'laid,' 'placed,' and 'arranged' in sites so very different from one another that it is impossible to find a place of residence for them, to define a *common locus* beneath them all."[23] To put it another way: mutually exclusive worlds are brought together in a fictional zone marked by its peculiar quality of what Utz Riese calls the "differential negativity"[24] of the text, its subtle fabric of spatial relations between different discourses and narratives sustained by an incessant process of re-adjustment and re-negotiation.

In *Tristan Smith* this strategy is put into the service of effectively enacting a postcolonial utopia where the real and the fictional sites of a culture can be located in such a way as to undercut fixed notions of coherence and permanence and to recuperate alternative identities lost or muted in the imperial process. Historical as well as linguistic boundaries are obliterated; displaced individuals are shown to be on the move between heterogeneous cultural spheres; adventurers and outcasts dodge back and forth across a part-dystopian, part-hallucinatory landscape. As yet unimagined postcolonial utopian possibilities are explored and placed in confrontation with the facts and events as rendered by 'real-world' colonial historiographers – visible, for instance, in Voorstand's military triumph over the French and British intruders. The specific character of the book as a mixed locus of events and discursive practices is underlined by Carey's ironic appropriation of the standard glossary used in much postcolonial fiction to draw attention to the writers' culturally formative background: In *Tristan Smith* it is most fruitfully employed as a vehicle for conveying a new and inventive vocabulary in which all those distinct linguistic, cultural and imaginary items are included which the text seeks to valorize. Terms reminiscent of Dutch or Afrikaans, such as *bullschtool* (bullshit) or *Voorwacker* (admirer of Voorstand culture), are mixed with French and English words (*teuf-teuf,* or formulae referring to Baudrillard's notions about the self-signifying nature of the modern media, such as *Simulacrum* or *Simulation*. The reference to "Jacqui's Ph.D. thesis on 'Orientalist Discourses and the Construction of the Arab Nation State'" (268) even suggests the work of Edward Said and the far-reaching topics of postcolonial discourse theory in general. All in all, these references create the impression of a deliberate attempt to render in fictional terms the theoretical and rhetorical premisses of the postcolonial debate, translating the often fatiguing discussions about

---

[23] Michel Foucault, "Of Other Spaces," *Diacritics* 16 (1986): 24.

[24] Utz Riese, "Heterotopien der Komplizenschaft: Räume differentieller Negativität in der amerikanischen Literatur," in *Postmoderne: globale Differenz*, ed. Robert Weimann & Hans Ulrich Gumbrecht (Frankfurt am Main: Suhrkamp, 1991): 281.

'rewriting' and 'writing back' into a discursive mode more suitable to the particulars of a given social and geographical area: namely, the former British colony (and also former Aboriginal homeland and more recent North American 'client-state') of Australia.[25] When finally it becomes evident that in the course of its history Voorstand itself has gradually developed into a colonizing nation that sublimates its expansive aggression by diverting it into entertainment and pleasure, the ambiguous explorations of *Tristan Smith* even begin to transcend the boundaries of the postcolonial debate itself: The futuristic tale metamorphoses into a political allegory about the globalization process that constantly deconstructs and re-adjusts existing power relations and in doing so radically confronts some of postcolonialism's most cherished doctrines about who are the victims and who are the dominating powers in the colonization process.

Conclusion: Towards a Cross-Cultural Utopia

It is self-evident that my reading of *Tristan Smith* fails to account for the different cultural perceptions and fantastic chronotopoi this almost prototypical postcolonial heterotopia abounds with.[26] My primary ambition here was to document Carey's continuing interest in the dystopian genre and to examine the ways in which his fiction challenges the case often made against this mode of writing – that it is "fated to repeat by inversion the categories of the society from which [it] spring[s]."[27] The fundamental limitation of the dystopian mode itself, its antithetical nature that constantly reproduces the social order that it seeks to invert, is confronted by Carey's strategic positioning of a whole series of writing patterns – ranging from the prediction of a 'post-dystopian' condition in some early works and Harry's cathartic story-

---

[25] Cf also Huggan, *Peter Carey*, 61–62: "Carey is clearly aware of current academic debates on postcolonialism [...] [He] seems to tip a wink here at his own academic critics, some of whom have labelled him as a postcolonial writer, speaking out against the evils of transnational (corporate) capitalism and lamenting American inroads into Australian national culture. [...] The view tacitly expressed in later works such as *Tristan Smith* is that Australia's metamorphosis into a postcolonial nation requires a certain sleight of hand and an inventive approach to cultural history." Another dystopian novel engaging the 'client-state' status of Australia is Rodney Hall's thrilling *Kisses of the Enemy* (1987).

[26] The term chronotope is taken from Mikhail Bakhtin's influential study *Voprosy literatury i èstetiki* (1975). Translated into English, it means "the essential connection of temporal and spatial relationships, as shaped in literary art." In the chronotope, "the characteristics of time are unfolded in space, while space is given meaning and measured by time"; quoted in Suvin, *Metamorphoses of Science Fiction*, 78–79.

[27] Simon Dentith, "Imagination and Inversion in Nineteenth-Century Utopian Writing," in *Anticipations: Essays on Early Science Fiction and its Precursors*, ed. David Seed (Liverpool: Liverpool UP, 1995): 143.

telling in *Bliss* to the imaginary voyages of *Tristan Smith* – which denies too close an identification with any unitary sociopolitical background. More than some of his earlier writings, *Tristan Smith* captures Carey's outspoken desire not to transform the genre into some other thing, but rather to turn it *into a richer version of its own possibilities*. It is through Tristan's mask of a Bruder Mouse automaton that we can catch glimpses of a condition of postcoloniality rendered more fertile by its recognition of cross-cultural identities in a global context as well as of a utopian discourse redeemed from the destiny of having to reproduce for all eternity the nightmare of the Orwellian "boot stamping on a human face forever" (*1984*) notable in much Australian utopian literature. In this respect, *Tristan Smith* undertakes to deliberately sum up as well as to rework earlier issues pre-eminent in Australian dystopian writing: In its portrayal of a zone or world fragmented but also enriched by the imperial process, the novel moves beyond conventional transcriptions of reality forever under an obligation to create their own integral and fully developed antithesis; in its attribution of a positive value to ambiguity and elusiveness it lends weight to the concept of a postcolonial or cross-cultural future precluding permanent solutions and therefore ruling out a condition of being that claims an autonomous (national and / or cultural) identity for itself as if it were a timeless and coherent truth recovered from the forgetful waters of history.

WORKS CITED

Bibliography of Anti-Utopian and Dystopian Fiction from Australia

Adams, Glenda. *Games of the Strong* (1982; New York: Cane Hill, 1989).

Bottari, Bridie. *The Last Real Cirkus: A Futuristic Fairytale* (Sydney: Angus & Robertson, 1995).

Boyd, Hannah. *A Voice from Australia* (London: Partridge, 1851).

Buckley, Doug. *State of Play* (Sutherland: Albatross, 1990).

Carey, Peter. *Bliss* (Brisbane: U of Queensland P, 1981).

——. *The Fat Man in History* (1974; London: Faber & Faber, 1990).

——. *The Unusual Life of Tristan Smith* (London: Faber & Faber, 1994).

——. *War Crimes* (Brisbane: U of Queensland P, 1979).

Chandler, Bertram A. *False Fatherland* (Sydney: Horwitz, 1968).

Collas, Phil. *The Inner Domain* (1935; Sydney: Graham Stone, 1989).

Dugdale, Henrietta Augusta. *A Few Hours in a Far-off Age* (Melbourne: McCarron, Bird, 1883).

Eldershaw, M. Barnard. *Tomorrow and Tomorrow* (Melbourne: Georgian House, 1947).

Favenc, Ernest. *Marooned on Australia: Being the Narrative of Diedrich Buys of His Discoveries and Exploits "In Terra Australis Incognita" About the Year 1630* (London: Blackie, 1897).

Free, Colin. *The Soft Kill* (New York: Berkley, 1973).

Hails, Ian McAuley. *Back Door Man* (North Adelaide: Aphelion, 1992).

Hall, Rodney. *Kisses of the Enemy* (New York: Farrar, Straus & Giroux, 1987).

Hughes, Edward F. *The Millenium: An Epic Poem* (Melbourne: Author, 1873).

Ireland, David. *City of Women* (Ringwood, Victoria: Allen Lane, 1981).

——. *The Unknown Industrial Prisoner* (North Ryde, NSW: Angus & Robertson, 1971).

Kocan, Peter. *Flies of a Summer* (North Ryde, NSW: Angus & Robertson, 1988).

Lohrey, Amanda. *The Reading Group* (Sydney: Penguin, 1988).

Lord, Gabrielle. *Salt* (Ringwood, Victoria: McPhee Gribble / Penguin, 1990).

Mackay, James A.K. *The Yellow Wave: A Romance of the Asiatic Invasion of Australia* (London: Richard Bentley, 1895).

Moore–Bentley, Mary. *A Woman of Mars, or, Australia's Enfranchised Women* (Sydney: Edwards, Dunlop, 1901).

Murnane, Gerald. *The Plains* (1982; Ringwood, Victoria: Penguin, 1984).

Page, Geoff. *Winter Vision* (St Lucia: U of Queensland P, 1989).

Spence, Catherine Helen. *Handfasted* (1888; Ringwood, Victoria: Penguin, 1984).

Taylor, Geoff. *Day of the Republic* (London: Peter Davies, 1968).

Turner, George. *Beloved Sun* (London: Faber & Faber, 1978).

——. *The Destiny Makers* (New York: William Morrow, 1993).

——. *Vaneglory* (London: Faber & Faber, 1981).

Wilding, Michael. "Outlines for Urban Fantasies," *Urban Fantasies*, ed. David King & Russell Blackford (Melbourne: Ebony, 1985): 63–69.

Willmot, Eric. *Below the Line* (Milsons Point, NSW: Hutchinson, 1991).

Wongar, Banumbir. *Walg: A Novel of Australia* (New York: George Braziller, 1983).

Secondary Sources

Albinski, Nan Bowman. "A Survey of Australian Utopian and Dystopian Fiction," *Australian Literary Studies* 13 (1987): 15–28.

Bailey, K.V. (Rev.) "Peter Carey's *The Unusual Life of Tristan Smith*," *Foundation* 63 (1995): 107–11.

Dentith, Simon. "Imagination and Inversion in Nineteenth-Century Utopian Writing," in *Anticipations: Essays on Early Science Fiction and its Precursors*, ed. David Seed (Liverpool: Liverpool UP, 1995): 137–53.

Foucault, Michel. "Of Other Spaces," *Diacritics* 16 (1986): 22–27.

Gerber, Richard. *Utopian Fantasy Since the End of the 19th Century* (London: Routledge, 1955).

Goodwin, Ken. *A History of Australian Literature* (London: Macmillan, 1988).

Haley, J.J. "The Lemurian Nineties," *Australian Literary Studies* 8 (1978): 307–16.

Harris, Wilson. *The Womb of Space: The Cross-Cultural Imagination* (Westport CT & London: Greenwood, 1983).

Hassall, Anthony J. *Dancing On Hot Macadam: Peter Carey's Fictions* (St Lucia: U of Queensland P, 1994).

Huggan, Graham. *Peter Carey* (Melbourne: Oxford UP, 1996).

Levitas, Ruth. *The Concept of Utopia* (Syracuse NY: Syracuse UP, 1990).

Manuel, Frank E., & Fritzie P. Manuel, ed. *Utopian Thought in the Western World* (Cambridge: Cambridge UP, 1979).

McHale, Brian. *Postmodernist Fiction* (London & New York: Routledge, 1991).

Mumford, Lewis. "Utopia, the City and the Machine," in *Utopias and Utopian Thought*, ed. Frank E. Manuel (Boston MA: Houghton Mifflin, 1966): 3–24.

Riese, Utz. "Heterotopien der Komplizenschaft: Räume differentieller Negativität in der amerikanischen Literatur," in *Postmoderne: globale Differenz*, ed. Robert Weimann & Hans Ulrich Gumbrecht (Frankfurt am Main: Suhrkamp, 1991): 278–90.

Sargent, Lyman Tower. "Australian Utopian Literature: An Annotated, Chronological Bibliography 1852–1999," *Utopian Studies* 10.2 (1999): 138–73.

——. *British and American Utopian Literature 1516–1979: An Annotated Bibliography* (Boston MA: G.K. Hall, 1979).

——. "New Zealand Utopian Literature: An Annotated Bibliography," *Occasional Paper* 97.1 (Wellington: Stout Research Centre, Victoria U of Wellington, 1996).

——. "Utopian Literature in English Canada: An Annotated, Chronological Bibliography 1667–1999," *Utopian Studies* 10.2 (1999): 174–206.

Scholes, Robert. *Structural Fabulation: An Essay on Fiction of the Future* (London: Notre Dame UP, 1975).

Seeber, Hans Ulrich. *Wandlungen der Form in der literarischen Utopie: Studien zur Entfaltung des utopischen Romans in England* (Göppingen: Kümmerle, 1970).

Suvin, Darko. *Metamorphoses of Science Fiction: On the Poetics and History of a Literary Genre* (New Haven CT: Yale UP, 1979).

Walsh, Chad. *From Utopia to Nightmare* (New York & Evanston IL: Harper & Row, 1962).

Literary Lessons from the Past
Stereotypes and Intertextuality in Peter Carey's *Jack Maggs*

SIGRUN MEINIG

T HE WRY AUTHOR'S NOTE preceding Peter Carey's novel *Jack Maggs* (1997) provides a suitable starting-point for this essay by highlighting two important issues. "The author willingly admits to having once or twice stretched history to suit his own fictional ends." Here, we find an allusion to the difficult relationship between history and fiction alongside the notion of fictional ends, hinting at the functionality of literature. As this paper intends to show, *Jack Maggs'* 'ends' make use of history, fiction and the tensions between both to empha-size that a reassessment of Australian history and cultural heritage is necessary to transform perceptions of identity in Australia.

The history represented in the historical novel *Jack Maggs*, set in London in 1837, is not the 'great' history of historiography to be recounted by the enumeration of great dates, great events and great men. Before the background of a powerfully drawn, "hellish"[1] London of poverty, criminality, overpopulation and dirt, the novel traces the individualized and, as it is called in the novel, the "hidden history" (91) of the protagonist Jack Maggs, a convict from Australia. Maggs has returned to London illegally to find Henry Phipps, whom he regards as his son. His involvement with other characters during his search allows for a variety of other individualized perspectives on the historical time span involved and the relationship between Great Britain and Australia. The history represented in Carey's novel is thus mainly the history of fictional individuals and the cultural history of the setting in Victorian London. There, children like Jack Maggs are trained to recognize and steal valuable silver, while the really poor like the Mudlarks have "never lived inside a house" (75) and do not know what a midwife is, and destitute women like Mercy Larkin can

---

[1] Peter Carey, *Jack Maggs* (London: Faber & Faber, 1997): 291. Further page references are in the main text.

only resort to marriage or prostitution in order to survive. Even more significantly, cultural history in *Jack Maggs* is epitomized by literary history, since the story of the returned convict searching for a boy whom he has provided with great expectations certainly rings a bell. It is reminiscent of the story of the convict Abel Magwitch in Charles Dickens' novel from 1861, *Great Expectations*. Although the relationship between Jack Maggs and the snobbish London gentleman Henry Phipps is an obvious intertextual reference,[2] the novel refrains from any direct comments or epistemological considerations[3] and, consequently, from explicit metafiction. Thus, the pre-text *Great Expectations* serves as a foil to be transformed in *Jack Maggs*, which in Gérard Genette's terminology represents a relationship of hypertextuality rather than one of metatextuality.[4] Nevertheless, the Australian novel's reworking of the foil certainly functions as an interpretation which comments on the pre-text. In order to discuss this not explicitly stated, intertextual commentary in *Jack Maggs* and in order to determine the values and attitudes operative in both novels, this essay offers an analysis of the portrayal of convicts within the narrative framework of each novel. Carey's revision of the convict's characterization is the first of three notable alterations he introduces into his novel which I will explore with regard to their impact on the image of Australia and the representation of its history. Following the discussion of the convict figure and protagonist Jack Maggs, my focus will thus shift to two of the newly introduced characters, first to the great writer Tobias Oates, then to the servant Mercy Larkin.

For Charles Dickens, in a comment on *Great Expectations*, the convict figure is "the pivot of the novel."[5] Indeed, for the protagonist and first-person narrator Pip, the criminal Abel Magwitch, transported to Australia for fraud, embodies "the

---

[2] The understanding of intertextuality in this paper is best described by John Frow: "Intertextual analysis is distinguished by source criticism both by this stress on interpretation rather than on the establishment of particular facts, and by its rejection of unilinear causality (the concept of 'influence') in favour of an account of the work performed upon intertextual material and its functional integration in the later text"; Frow, "Intertextuality and Ontology," in *Intertextuality – Theories and Practices*, ed. Michael Warton & Judith Still (Manchester: Manchester UP, 1990): 46.

[3] The title of Carey's manuscript while writing *Jack Maggs* represents the one explicit hint at the intertext. Thus, in Anthony Hassall's *Dancing on Hot Macadam – Peter Carey's Fiction* (St Lucia: U of Queensland P, 1994) the chronology records for 1992–93: "Work in progress on two novels, [...], and the other, 'Magwitch', dealing, among other things, with Magwitch (from *Great Expectations*) in Australia" (xviii).

[4] Genette, *Palimpsests: Literature in the Second Degree*, tr. Channa Newman & Claude Doubinsky (*Palimpsestes: la littérature au second degré*, 1982; Lincoln: U of Nebraska P, 1997): esp. ch. 1.

[5] Herbert Foltinek, *Charles Dickens und der Zwang des Systems* (Vienna: Verlag der österreichischen Akademie der Wissenschaften, 1987): 5.

turning point of [his] life."[6] The novel traces the development of the good-hearted child Pip who helps the convict despite his great fear. As a young snob in London, however, eager to impress beautiful but cold Estella, Pip has reached the morally deplorable stage of a "gentleman of manners" (204), who incurs debts and cannot recognize the worth of people independently of their fortune and adherence to etiquette. By overcoming this stage, Pip acquires the perfection of the "true gentleman at heart" (204), who can see beneath the social veneer. In *Great Expectations*, Dickens uses the convict's Australian money to provide Pip with the 'great expectations' of the title and to show him the moral insignificance of material wealth. The convict figure and his treatment by the legal system serve to make Pip aware of the social injustices of the English class structure.

While, in terms of plot, Magwitch thus fulfils the function of catalyst for the development of the protagonist, the narrative depiction of the convict figure is circumscribed by the dominance of the first-person narrator Pip. Pip's tone and attributions shape the portrayal to the extent that the description of his emotional reactions to the convict serves as a model for the reader. Readers share the fear of the little boy in the graveyard:

> "Hold your noise!" cried a terrible voice, as a man started up from among the graves at the side of the church porch. "'Keep still, you little devil, or I'll cut your throat!" A fearful man, all in coarse grey, with a great iron on his leg. (36)

Seven-year-old Pip in the graveyard is unable to recognize the iron on the man's leg as an indicator of a convict, and as a consequence the horrible man, who literally turns Pip upside down, appears to be an ogre straight out of a fairy-tale, whose physical hardships allow only for a modicum of pity. Even after the identification of the man as a criminal escaped from the hulks, this first impression remains indelible in the minds of the readers and of Pip, who will be haunted by this childhood experience until he meets the convict again in London at the age of twenty-three. There Pip, in his own words, feels only "unsurmountable aversion" (346). This turns into pity for the misguided criminal only after Magwitch has been allotted a complete chapter for the first-person narration of his criminal history. Although he displays rhetorical brilliance in this chapter, he remains an uneducated man using poor grammar, in stark contrast to the protagonist, whose only asset while being misguided by the lure of money is his incessant reading. The final chapters dealing with the convict figure describe him as a man mellowed by Pip's compassion and love, accepting his own faults as well as the social system, and in his last words: "'I don't

---

[6] Dickens, *Great Expectations* (Harmondsworth: Penguin, 1985): 318. Further page references are in the main text.

complain of none, dear boy' " (469). Thus, Magwitch undergoes a development, too, but it is a development from one stereotype to another.[7] From the violent fairy-tale ogre of the childhood scenes he turns into what is termed by Coral Lansbury the figure of a "romantic convict," "an honest man driven by hunger to crime."[8]

The stereotyping of Magwitch's development results from the limited and limiting frame of reference employed for this portrayal. The convict is associated with animality – for example, in the recurrence of the dog metaphor – and he is linked with amorphous environments like the marshes, the Thames estuary and, of course, the Australian desert. From the outset, he is linked to death, and Pip states rationally: "it was unquestionably best that he should die" (457). Magwitch is connected to material wealth, the superficiality of which he is unable to recognize to his death – unlike the novel's hero Pip. In the framework of binary oppositions governing the colonial relationship,[9] the representative of Australia is thus linked with the category of nature, while Pip occupies the position of culture. While Dickens's novel criticizes the materialism of the English class system and the absence of moral values in the progress of its protagonist, it is blind to the way its ideals of education and morality discriminate against a figure linked with the opposite side of the binary. The logic of the novel demands that he die. The convict has to accept this fate resulting from his linkage with nature, since English ideology and 'objective' history have taught him that he cannot try "to bend the past out of its eternal shape" (465).

Literary criticism has largely mirrored this attitude of acceptance of the novel's ideology sanctioned by history, as Edward Said points out:

> Most, if not all, readings of this remarkable work situate it squarely within the metropolitan history of British fiction, whereas I believe that it belongs in a history both more inclusive and more dynamic than such interpretations allow.[10]

---

[7] 'Stereotype' is taken to refer to limited perceptions produced by a cognitive process of overgeneralization and mental short-cutting; see Emer O'Sullivan, *Das ästhetische Potential nationaler Stereotypen* (Tübingen: Stauffenburg, 1989): 22–25. While such a 'channelling' of perception is to some extent necessary for our everyday living and does not automatically have to be considered harmful, stereotyped perception in a postcolonial context is implicated in power structures which produce discrimination by ascribing inferiority.

[8] Anne Sadrin, *Great Expectations* (London: Guerin Hyman, 1988): 81.

[9] For a pointed outline of the pairs of opposites and the ensuing mechanisms involved in this dichotomy, see Abdul R. JanMohamed, "The Economy of Manichean Allegory: The Function of Racial Difference in Colonialist Literature," in *"Race", Writing, Difference*, ed. Henry Louis Gates, Jr. (Chicago: U of Chicago P, 1986): esp. 82. Following Fanon, JanMohamed diagnoses a binary manichaean allegory as operative in the colonial race relations. In the settler colony Australia, this axis also applies to white Australians like Magwitch, although it of course acquires its greatest power with regard to members of a different ethnicity.

[10] Edward Said, *Culture and Imperialism* (London: Vintage, 1993): xv.

Peter Carey's *Jack Maggs* re-reads the attitudes that have informed *Great Expectations*. The novel transposes its foil by introducing three decisively different features. Firstly, the portrayal of the convict in *Jack Maggs* differs greatly from the dog-like, toothless Magwitch. Jack Maggs is literate, quoting *King Lear* and correcting dropped aitches, and he is powerful. Not only was he renowned for his organizational talents in the colony; he was considered a gentleman deserving the epithet "Esquire" (281) and commanding respect from English people, partly by his sheer presence. Physicality is an important feature in the portrayal of the convict, who possesses a strong body and an affinity with violence. Maggs' cultural skills, as well as the fact that we learn that the greater part of his story from his letters to Henry Phipps, deny a simplistic association with nature. Instead, Maggs is, like the other characters in Carey's novel, a complex, contradictory and not always likeable figure. The novel's foregrounding of his power nevertheless presents Maggs as a figure actively shaping his life's history. Unlike Magwitch, he does not evoke pity as a victim of society, but is, indeed, sexually attractive. Not only the footman Constable falls for him, but also Mercy Larkin, who is one of the novel's most appealing characters. Carey's novel not only endows the convict with a love interest, but emphasizes from the outset that he is capable of development: He is "an oyster working on a pearl" (15). Jack Maggs, during the course of the novel, learns to overcome his blindness, which initially makes him admire England and denigrate Australia: "I am a fucking *Englishman*, and I have English things to settle. I am not to live my life with all that vermin. I am here in London where I belong" (128). In a subtle change of the configuration[11] taken from *Great Expectations*, it is now the London gentleman Henry Phipps, modelled on Pip, who remains static. Furthermore, he is presented as a weak, decadent and snobbish character, whose homosexuality can be read as a metaphoric hint at the impossibility of the continuance of the system he represents. The story of Maggs and Phipps also differs from the structure of *Great Expectations* in its complete lack of childhood scenes, since the novel only starts with the convict's return to London. Here, Maggs' formative encounter is not the one with Henry Phipps, whom he only meets at the very ending of the novel when Phipps tries to shoot him. Instead, the relationship between the famous author Tobias Oates and Maggs is more important in Carey's novel than the one between Maggs and Phipps.

The character Tobias Oates and the configuration connected with him – his wife, his sister-in-law and his son – represent the second divergence in *Jack Maggs*. Since Oates, with his slightly vulgar waistcoats, his vanity, his fastidiousness, his obsession with money and his promising career as an author, is clearly modelled on the

---

[11] The term is Heinrich Plett's. It denotes the "grouping of the characters" – *Intertextuality* (Berlin: de Gruyter, 1991): 114.

young Charles Dickens, the configuration associated with him can be read as a second, non-fictional instance of intertextuality. The biography of Dickens thus serves to balance the fictional intertext *Great Expectations* as represented by the relationship between Maggs and Phipps. With its portrayal of the making of Oates's great literary masterpiece to be written thirty years later, *The Death of Maggs*, which is the fictional equivalent of *Great Expectations*, Carey's novel invites the reader to reconsider the moral value and 'truth' to be found in works of art. After all, in a truly Victorian attitude, Tobias Oates strives to stylize his character sketches and novels as scientific cataloguings of the human species. His office is organized like a laboratory where he can pigeon-hole "Evidence" (43). His method of mesmerism, however, is only seemingly scientific. After hypnotizing Maggs, Oates influences the convict's visions, which leads the reader to suspect that he has planted in Maggs's mind the phantom that haunts him. Oates' exercise of mesmerism most pointedly reveals the main motif of the vain Tobias Oates. He craves power and control: "'Don't you see what I now possess? A memory I can enter and leave. Leave, and then return to. My goodness, my gracious. What a treasure house'" (87). Oates, furthermore, is obsessed with treasures of a most worldly nature: "Money was a subject always on his mind. One can see the evidence on all his manuscripts – their margins marked with calculations headed *£-s-d*" (129). Oates's portrayal consequently reverses the hierarchy existing between materiality and culture, since he calculates with his literary pieces to earn plenty of money. This represents an ironic comment on the great cultural and moral value usually placed on masterpieces of literature – and their authors. Oates is not a morally superior genius: in his affair with his sister-in-law Lizzie he behaves in a cowardly and naive manner. He does not write objective and truthful works of art; instead, his hatred for Jack Maggs affects his portrayal of the convict in *The Death of Maggs*. That the turbulent encounter between Maggs and Oates forms the basis of the convict's portrayal in the Victorian novel serves to emphasize the very specific, subjective and idiosyncratic circumstances informing the creation of a work of art. Furthermore, the reader's trust in the neutrality of the convict's portrayal in *The Death of Maggs* is undermined by the emphasis on the arbitrariness of the creative process of writing, since Oates drafts three beginnings until he settles for the final one.

With this structure, Peter Carey's *Jack Maggs* questions the seemingly transcendental values of its pre-text *Great Expectations* and of the Victorian age as represented by the biography of Charles Dickens by situating them within a specific historical context. In *Jack Maggs*, intertextuality, both of fictional and non-fictional origin, thus becomes a metaphor for discursive dependence. Carey shows that the image of Australia has been determined by the English cultural discourse and by discursive values that are embodied and transmitted in works of art and in exemplary biographies.[12] With the juxtaposition of the two intertextual realms, this mechanism is exposed and the hierarchies involved are eroded, significantly so by placing the convict and his author on the same level in a narrative dominated by an omniscient narrator.

The third and final novelty in Peter Carey's *Jack Maggs* is to be found in the female character Mercy Larkin. The introduction of a second figure to represent Australia alongside the convict allows for additional facets in the image of Australia and for a move beyond discursive dependence. Ironically fulfilling the classical role of the ideal woman in the *Bildungsroman*, the fallen woman, madwoman's daughter and servant, Mercy can help Jack Maggs to recognize his blindness with regard to Australia. She is not only, like Jack Maggs, inferior because of her class; rather, she is doubly powerless because she is also female. As a woman in Victorian society, she can only hope for social status and power from association with a man – for example, by being "My Good Companion" (112) to the grocer-become-gentleman Buckle and hoping to marry him one day like Richardson's Pamela. Courageous like Jack Maggs, Mercy does not wait for fortune to fall into her lap, but actively works towards it by subversively employing and spreading the secret and powerful knowledge of the men in the novel with the help of gossip. Feeling increasingly drawn to Maggs, she finally uses her curiosity and her control of information to help him – for example, in his search for Henry Phipps. Unafraid of the boundaries of a society in which she has no place, she confronts Jack Maggs with the denial of his children in Australia and helps him to recognize the value of his fruitful life there – both in financial and in family terms. Thus, Mercy shifts her position from a relative to a defining creature. In Australia, she "civilizes" the children so that "she who had always been so impatient of 'rules' now became a disciplinarian"; with the happy ending of the novel, the convict figure is superseded by this powerful female character. As the novel states: "it is Mercy who is now remembered best" (327).

Mercy's interference with the circulation of information connects her to the cultural realm, while her insistence on family values provides the link to the field of nature. *Jack Maggs* thus replaces the reductive and discriminatory effects of Australia's association with nature, condemning its representative to death in *Great Expectations*, by intertwining and thus dissolving the oppositional categories of nature and

---

[12] 'Discourse' here refers to "the delimitation of a field of objects, the definition of a legitimate perspective for the agent of knowledge, and the fixing of norms for the elaboration of concepts and theories"; Foucault, quoted in Peter Childs & Patrick Williams, *An Introduction to Post-Colonial Theory* (London: Prentice Hall, 1997): 227. For the Australian context, the colonial discourse is particularly important. Its aim is characterized by Homi Bhabha: "to justify conquest and to establish systems of administration and instruction" (Childs & Williams: 227).

culture in the two representations of Australia. The convict figure survives and is the origin of a new genealogy for Australian identity, while Mercy Larkin, a powerful female figure, participates in the active shaping of their Australian lives. The metaphoric impact of intertextuality, so far interpreted as an indication of discursive dependence, has thus been taken one step further. While intertextuality can certainly function as a 'prison house' when it results in a fixing of meanings and values, it can also present the 'escape key' to discursive fixations.[13] *Jack Maggs* offers such an escape key by introducing, in the words of Anthony Hassall, "a transparently fictional original of Magwitch"[14] which represents a revision of both fiction and history. This fictional revision can be regarded as the main function Peter Carey's novel seeks to fulfil. With this insight we are brought back to the beginning of this essay, the author's note and the two questions raised there, with the question of the difficult relationship between fiction and history remaining. By examining values and attitudes which have proved discriminatory to the history of Australian identity and self-consciousness in a work of fiction, *Jack Maggs* demonstrates that fiction – when regarded as an assembly of great masterpieces of cultural and moral value – is in danger of contributing to the limiting and fixing views involving power and dominance often ascribed to 'objective' history. Thus, the distinction between fiction and history, often used to attribute superiority to the former, collapses.[15] By employing intertextuality, however, *Jack Maggs* underlines the potential for polyvalency, complexity and ambiguity embedded in literary texts, with the power to break up limiting ideological preconceptions. The intertextual novel *Jack Maggs* has to be regarded as a particularly scintillating example of the faculty of intertextual texts sketched out by Jacques Derrida:

> Thus the text overruns all the limits assigned to it so far (not submerging or drowning them in an undifferentiated homogeneity, but rather making them more complex, dividing and multiplying strokes and lines) – all the limits, everything that was to be set up in opposition to writing (speech, life, the world, the real, history, and what not, every field of reference – to body or mind, conscious or unconscious, politics, economics and so forth).[16]

---

[13] For a close discussion of this phenomenon, see Manfred Pfister, "Konzepte der Intertextualität," in *Intertextualität: Formen, Funktionen, anglistische Fallstudien*, ed. Ulrich Broich & Manfred Pfister (Tübingen: Max Niemeyer, 1985): 22.

[14] Anthony Hassall, "A Tale of Two Countries: *Jack Maggs* and Peter Carey's Fiction," *Australian Literary Studies* 18.2 (1997): 128–35.

[15] Drawing attention to a seminal example of this distinction, Peter Widdowson describes how Aristotle's ascription of a "high moral dimension" to poetry and thus literature connects to the philosopher's belief that "its synthetic and generalising tendency [...] is truer to reality than are the particularities of history"; Widdowson, *Literature* (London: Routledge, 1999): 29.

[16] Quoted from Jacques Derrida's essay "Living on / *Border Lines*," in John Frow, "Intertextuality and Ontology," 49.

WORKS CITED

Carey, Peter. *Jack Maggs* (London: Faber & Faber, 1997).

Childs, Peter, & Patrick Williams. *An Introduction to Post-Colonial Theory* (Englewood Cliffs NJ & London: Prentice–Hall, 1997).

Dickens, Charles. *Great Expectations* (Harmondsworth: Penguin, 1985).

Foltinek, Herbert. *Charles Dickens und der Zwang des Systems* (Vienna: Verlag der österreichischen Akademie der Wissenschaften, 1987).

Frow, John. "Intertextuality and Ontology," in *Intertextuality: Theories and Practices*, ed. Michael Worton & Judith Still (Manchester: Manchester UP, 1990).

Genette, Gérard. *Palimpsests: Literature in the Second Degree*, tr, Channa Newman & Claude Doubinsky (*Palimpsestes: la littérature au second degré*, 1982; Lincoln: U of Nebraska P, 1997).

Hassall, Anthony. *Dancing on Hot Macadam: Peter Carey's Fiction* (St Lucia: U of Queensland P, 1994).

——. "A Tale of Two Countries: *Jack Maggs* and Peter Carey's Fiction," *Australian Literary Studies* 18.2 (1997): 128–35.

JanMohamed, Abdul R. "The Economy of Manichean Allegory: The Function of Racial Difference in Colonialist Literature," in *"Race", Writing, Difference*, ed. Henry Louis Gates, Jr. (Chicago: U of Chicago P, 1986).

O'Sullivan, Emer. *Das ästhetische Potential nationaler Stereotypen* (Tübingen: Stauffenburg, 1989).

Pfister, Manfred. "Konzepte der Intertextualität," in *Intertextualität: Formen, Funktionen, anglistische Fallstudien*, ed. Ulrich Broich & Manfred Pfister (Tübingen: Max Niemeyer, 1985): 1–30.

Plett, Heinrich F. *Intertextuality* (Berlin: de Gruyter, 1991).

Sadrin, Anny. *Great Expectations* (London: Unwin Hyman, 1988).

Said, Edward. *Culture and Imperialism* (London: Random House / Vintage, 1993).

Widdowson, Peter. *Literature* (London: Routledge, 1999).

❧

The (Ad)Missions of the Colonizer
Australian Paradigms in Selected Works of Prichard, Malouf and White

CYNTHIA VANDEN DRIESEN

R
UDYARD KIPLING'S IMPASSIONED PLEA addressed to his compatriots in 1899 provides the best backdrop to this essay:

> Take up the White Man's burden –
> send forth the best ye breed –
> Go bind your sons to exile
> To serve your captives' need;
> To wait in heavy harness
> On fluttered folk and wild –
> Your new-caught, sullen peoples,
> Half devil and half child.[1]

One of the motives that instigated and sustained the colonialist project was a belief in 'the White man's burden,' the God-given mission to bring to the savage non-European the enlightened beliefs of the master-race. Meanwhile, several critics of colonialism hold that this creed was only promulgated in order to salve the European conscience for the massive dispossession of colonized peoples. Said's *Orientalism* (1978) shows how the discourse of 'otherness' became entrenched in the cultural texts of Europe, and its implications have been further articulated succinctly by such theorists as Abdul JanMohammed in "The Economy of Manichean Allegory." This essay will explore how that vaunted superiority of the European, in comparison with the endemic inferiority of the non-European, is interrogated by three Australian writers, Katharine Susannah Prichard, David Malouf and Patrick White, through four selected works.

---

[1] Rudyard Kipling, *Complete Verse* (London: Kyle Cathie, 1990): 19.

Because of the constraint of space and my attempt to pursue a complex enquiry examining four texts, a fairly schematic procedure will be adhered; I yet hope to provide some insights into the commonalities, variations and ambivalences underlying the works of these writers as they explore the black/white encounter, which, in the view of J.J. Healy, lies at the heart of much Australian literary self-exploration.[2] With varying success, each work interrogates entrenched Orientalist perceptions of the blacks as savage and uncultured and in need of the whites' civilizing mission. Conversely, the 'heathen' world suggests redemptive potential – that the European's mission could be turned back upon itself. European ad/mission into the culture of the indigene could be productive of tremendous insights.

In his "Introduction" to *Orientalism*, Edward Said outlines the basic strategies for evaluating the Orientalist ideology of a text – such as the positioning of the narrator or the experiencing consciousness in relation to the cultural space being focused on, the motifs and epithets circulating in the text, and the language.[3] My analysis of these strategies in Joseph Conrad's *Heart of Darkness* (1902) shows how this text emerges as a paradigmatic colonialist narrative. Conrad's novella will be compared with each of the Australian works selected in order to show how the same strategies can also be seen to function in an inverted fashion. In Conrad, the Saidian reminder concerning the positioning of the narrator is surprisingly productive. Marlow, observing the landscape from the deck of the steamboat, sees it as an alien observer would; he cannot decipher the landscape or decode its sounds:

> every living bush of the undergrowth might have been changed into stone [...] Not the faintest sound of any kind could be heard. You looked on amazed and began to suspect yourself – of being dead.[4]

The landscape takes on the aspect of total otherness. Equally, Marlow's distanced view of the blacks never allows him to perceive them even as human – he has glimpses of flailing limbs and rolling eye-balls, hears shrieks and groans. Such African figures as emerge from the general chaos are constructed as less than human – a cannibal, a witch-doctor and a female more tigress than woman. Language functions as a pointer in two ways – none of these benighted beings is afforded language; besides, the epithets and images circulating in the text such as "cannibal," "savage" and "devil" demonize the African, justifying Chinua Achebe's rejection of this text as "racist."[5]

What is the outcome of the encounter between black and white? For Kurtz, the experience of Africa is summed up in his dying words, "The horror! The horror!" In

---

[2] J.J. Healy. *Literature and the Aborigine in Australia* (Brisbane, U of Queensland P, 1989).

[3] Edward Said, *Orientalism* (1978; Ringwood, Victoria: Penguin, 1991): 2.

[4] Joseph Conrad, *Heart of Darkness and The Secret Sharer* (New York: Bantam, 1981): 65.

[5] Chinua Achebe, "An Image of Africa," *Massachusetts Review* 18.4 (1977): 783.

essence, it also encapsulates Marlow's own discovery, released by the same experience, of the evil and depravity in the hearts of all men. Finally, the Conrad text never admits the possibility of a reversal of the hegemonic relationship in which the white man consistently stands in relation to the black. Even at death's door, Kurtz asserts the white man's power over the enslaved blacks; the "white man's burden" can never be relinquished.

Prichard's novel *Coonardoo* appeared as an iconoclastic breakthrough in the 1930s. For the first time, a black woman is placed at the centre of a literary work in an attempt to explore the sensitive area of sexual relationships between black and white. Passing over, for the moment, the actual positioning of the narrating consciousness, one notes that in the projection of the landscape the aboriginal figures appear inextricably linked with it. In the opening scene, the child Coonardoo is singing in a spring landscape. Wytaliba station is beginning to prosper. At the end, when her disease-ridden limbs collapse into the soil "like [...] blackened and broken sticks"[6] the station is ruined. As her name signifies, she is 'the well in the shadows' explicitly associated with the land's fertility. Her despoliation by the white man is a trope for the destruction of the land by the white colonizers.

Yet black and white can come together in harmony – for instance, when the boy Hughie plays together with his aboriginal playmates, or when blacks and whites work together, as in the scene of the cattle mustering. In one particularly evocative sequence, when the sick Hughie is being carried by his faithful blacks to the coast for help, Warieda sings the story of the land they are passing through, interpreting it, as it were, for the white man who cannot know it as the blacks do.

How is the black world projected? One of the central motifs of the novel is the contrast between the repressed sexuality of the European and the health-conferring natural sexuality of the black. With the latter, sexuality is aligned to the natural order. The fertility rites enacted are not some kind of savage orgy but part of a religious ritual designed to preserve the fertility of the land and its people. Prichard's text thus subverts the manichaean allegory which would align the black's sexuality to licence and bestiality; transforming it into a natural, healthy, even redemptive force. It is part of a cultural ethos in which human and natural fertility are harmoniously integrated.

Other values of the black world are explicitly articulated as admirable, particularly in contrast to the European. In a formally structured dialogue between Hughie and Saul (with Mollie positioned to offer the stereotypical colonialist perspective), the Aborigines' innate goodness is eulogized: " ' The blacks are like that [...] They

---

[6] Katharine Susannah Prichard, *Coonardoo* (1925; Ringwood, Victoria: Penguin, 1991): 232. Further page references are in the main text..

never kill for sport – only for food or vengeance [...] No black ever did to a white man what white men have done to the blacks'" (117). It is white misdeeds that are recounted: "'White men came, jumped their hunting grounds, went kangaroo shooting for fun [...] The police [...] used to bring the niggers in, in chains, leather straps round the neck, fastened to their stirrup irons'" (118).

The ambivalences in this text begin to emerge when some of the other Saidian criteria are applied, such as the position from within which the aboriginal world is surveyed. Here it becomes apparent that the observer is clearly positioned outside of black culture. As Sue Thomas points out, we are rarely allowed to observe Coonardoo and the other aboriginal figures within the *uloo*.[7] They are observed only as they move about their duties of service to their white masters. The norm that underlies their portraiture is irremediably eurocentric: "Coonardoo's hair, soft, and wavy when it had just been washed, grew dull golden, like wind grass out on the plains" (10). Or, on another occasion, "as she helped him to wash [...] Hugh said, 'What pretty hands you've got, Coonardoo!' So elegant and delicate the slim brown fingers were. [...] He glanced down at the small brown feet which were as straight and well-shaped as her hands" (76).

The same eurocentric values are at work in the projection of black virtues. What Prichard foregrounds for her white audiences is the extreme docility of the blacks.

> Coonardoo, even while nursing her baby, is more anxious to hurry back to serve her white employer: Coonardoo could see Hugh striding about the verandas [...] Coonardoo laughed and pulled a milk-sweet nipple out of her baby's mouth [...] she must hurry to make morning tea for Hugh's woman. (92)

It may be argued that this depiction of the blacks is finally no less demeaning of them than Conrad's was. The stereotype here is of the 'savage' as the "half child" of Kipling's verse – the type portrayed in Joyce Cary's *Mr Johnson* (another stereotype as forcefully rejected by Achebe as the Conradian construction of the black as demonic savage).

Sue Thomas makes the vital point that the aboriginal characters in Prichard's novel are actually denied both voice and agency. Coonardoo herself hardly utters more than a few unintelligible monosyllables. In terms of actual narrative space, the story is much more Hughie's than Coonardoo's; it is essentially the white man's story. In the language of the narration, the recurrence of epithets like "gin" (the derogatory term for aboriginal female) is standard; other terms implying value-judgements about 'primitive' culture are frequent. At best, Prichard perpetuates the stereotype of the intuitive, natural, 'noble' savage. Notably, there is never a reversal

---

[7] Sue Thomas, "Interracial Encounters in Katharine Susannah Prichard's *Coonardoo*," *World Literature Written in English* 27.2 (1987): 234–44.

– however temporary – of the power relationship between black and white. Even at the climactic point of Hughie's assault on Coonardoo, the watching blacks (who include her son) meekly accept the white man's decree.

What of Prichard's most sensational advocacy of the possibility of intimacy between black and white? Note the actual construction of the encounter: sexual intimacy between the two takes place only once in a relationship that lasts over a lifetime, and then at a time when Hughie is caught up in the trauma of his mother's death, in a state of mental breakdown. The language does not suggest the coming together of two sexual beings. Hughie is enfolded by some overpowering force of nature, one that is associated with childhood friendship and innocence. In this way, the 'guilt' of the black / white sexual embrace is exorcized:

> She was Coonardoo, the old playmate; he felt about her as he had when they were children together [...] Deep inexplicable currents of his being flowed towards her [...] her eyes the fathomless shining of a well in the shadows. [Hugh] gave himself to the spirit which drew him. (71)

Despite its iconoclastic resonances, this work projects a vision of the non-European world that still suggests the special onus on the white man to retain the role of responsible adult towards the child-like black. Failing in this role, he fails in his mission to the blacks and therefore in the fulfilment of his own destiny.

In *Remembering Babylon*, David Malouf juxtapositions the black and white worlds in the psyche of the protagonist. The black / white man Gemmy, born English, is inducted into the aboriginal world, returning briefly to his European heritage in the white Australian settlement but electing to rejoin his adoptive Aboriginal community. Gemmy is the occupant of a hybrid space through which insights into both worlds are mediated.

There is an explicit comment on the difference between the blacks' and whites' responses to the landscape in the entries in Mr Frazer's notebook: "We have been wrong to see this continent as hostile and infelicitous [...] The children of this land were made for it, as it was for them [...] We must humble ourselves and learn from them."[8] Through Gemmy, Mr Frazer himself learns the names for the local flora and fauna gaining that oneness with the landscape which characterizes the indigene. Frazer sees Gemmy as "a forerunner [...] no longer a white man, or a European, [...] but a true child of the place" (132). A whole range of perceptions are transmitted. At one end of the spectrum, Gemmy, when with his aboriginal 'kinsfolk,' is transported into the Aboriginal view of their world, "the tribe's home territory, with its pools and

---

[8] David Malouf, *Remembering Babylon* (London: Vintage, 1994): 129–30. Further page references are in the main text.

creeks and underground sources of water, its rock ridges and scrub; its edible fruits and berries and flocks of birds and other creatures, all alive in their names and the stories that contained their spirit" (117).

Jock McIvor moves from a homesickness for England, through a series of encounters which can only be described as epiphanic, to a responsive empathy with the Australian landscape. At first, "He was often homesick [...] The land here never slept. If only he could wake one day and find it, just for a day under a blanket of snow!" (76). As he begins to be more at home in the landscape, he observes "hundreds of wee bright insects [...] the new light they brought to the scene was a lightness in him [...] a form of knowledge [...] Another time [...] he [...] saw a bird [...] he was filled with the most intense and easy pleasure" (107). For Ellen, his wife, the soil of the new land is now precious, since it contains the bodies of her dead children. With her husband, she too begins to respond to the land: "He had turned his gaze from her and was looking, very intently, at a little flower [...] It was the way he held it, the grace of the bit of a thing in his rough hand [...] that touched her and made its whiteness come alive" (109–10).

At the other end of the spectrum are the responses of the occupants of Government House, who revel in their success at superimposing a foreign landscape upon the indigenous one: " ' you should see Herston [...] You would think yourself in England. The peaches! So plump and with such a blush on the skin [...] Our asparagus [...] is quite special' " (173).

The hybridity of Malouf's protagonist enables a curiously complex perception of the Aboriginal world. Where the Conrad text suggests that the acts of cruelty perpetrated by Kurtz are triggered by his submergence in the African world, for Gemmy it is the Aboriginal world that is a healing force after the horrors of his English childhood. Later, the cruelty and rejection he experiences in the Australian white settlement drive him back to his Aboriginal community. The whites' perception of the black man underlines their sense of his 'otherness.' To the children who befriend him, he changes from "the creature, unrecognised and unnamed" to "someone we loved" (194). But to most of the white community, Gemmy appears inalienably 'Other': "For the fact was, when you looked at him sometimes, he was not white [...] Study him, sitting there in the sun with that vacant, in-turned look; heavy-browed, morose [...] he had kept the smell he came with" (40–41).

Language – as always in Malouf's work – is a key marker of affinity. The bizarre detail of Gemmy's inability to speak his own English language fluently reinforces the sense of his alienation from the English world, whereas his induction into the Aboriginal world is facilitated by his easy acquisition of the language. Much of the white community's revulsion against him derives from his inability to speak the language: "when, as sometimes happened, he fell back on the native word, the only one that could express it, their eyes went hard, as if the mere existence of a language they did not know was a provocation, a way of making them helpless" (65).

If this is a text that 'writes back' to Conrad's *Heart of Darkness*, there is an ironic effect in the blacks' perception of the white boy as strange, yet as akin to them (contrasted with Marlow's perception of the blacks as wholly 'Other') and progress towards complete acceptance is swift. He sees his first coming amongst them from their perspective: "half-child, half sea-calf, his hair swarming with spirits in the shape of tiny phosphorescent crabs" (27). Later, when he returns to the white community, "They (his black kinsfolk) were concerned that in coming here, among the ghostly white creatures, he might have slipped back into the thinner world of wraiths and demons that he had escaped" (115).

Unlike Conrad's and Prichard's narratives, *Remembering Babylon* reverses, however briefly, the hegemonic control of white over black. Gemmy's arrival in the Aboriginal world has all the resonances of a birthing process. The Aborigines revive him from his semi-drowned state and induct him into their world:

> One old woman with no sign of personal interest, as if he were a little white hairless thing that could not fend for itself, gave him a mouthful of seeds [...] So he began his life among them [...] They were astonished at the swiftness with which he learned their speech. (25–26)

Malouf manages to project how the whites impinge on native consciousness. It is the white world that is in need of salvation. For Gemmy, the black / white man, it is experience of the white world that is destructive. Having survived the attempt of his white redeemers to murder him, Gemmy makes the decision to retreat again into the world of the indigene, though he has himself been born originally a white man.

What of the impact of this black / white encounter on the whites? For some, the experience has (as with Kurtz in Conrad's work) brought their most destructive tendencies to the surface, but the savagery surfaces within the white community. Juxtaposed with this, the world of the black has its own innocence and humanity. The world that requires redemption from moral depravity would be that of the white community. Yet, for some at least, the encounter with Gemmy has been in some way redemptive and healing: "He [George Abbott] regarded Gemmy very differently now [...] Gemmy had repelled him then [...] He felt humbled now" (179).

In Patrick White's *A Fringe of Leaves* and *Voss*, the protagonists share a quality with Malouf's protagonist Gemmy which perhaps is best described as "incipient indigeneity."[9] Voss and Ellen are also Europeans who gain induction into the black

---

[9] Cynthia Vanden Driesen, " 'Devils, Savages, Nobler Forms': Post-Colonial Re-invention of the Indigene in the Works of Patrick White," in *Australia's Changing Landscapes*, ed. Susan

world, Voss dying in it, while Ellen returns later to the colonial world of Sydney. Their affinity with the black world is first manifested through their response to the landscape. For them, as for Gemmy, positioned as they are in hybrid space, the Australian landscape has all the aspects of home. Voss reprimands Laura and the colonialist society for its rejection of the native landscape: " ' A pity that you huddle [...] Your landscape is of great subtlety' " ; for himself he declares, " ' I am at home [...] It is like the poor parts of Germany. Sandy. It could be the Mark Brandenburg'."[10] Ellen, on her first visit to Sydney, is struck by the resemblances to her home in Gwynor: "The scent of the cow's breath, the thudding of her hooves and the plop of falling dung, filled Ellen with immeasurable home-sickness."[11]

For both, on occasion, encounter with the landscape becomes an erotic encounter: "Fronds of giant ferns caressed her, and she in turn caressed the brown fur which clothed their formal crooks. She was so entranced."[12] In his last moments, Voss's view of "the old man or woman" metamorphoses into a vision of Laura: "Leaves were in her lips, that he bit off, and from her breasts the full, silky, milky buds."[13] For both, landscape also becomes a medium of spiritual insight, a source of mystical illumination. Voss is overwhelmed by the sheer beauty of the land:

> But it was the valley itself which drew Voss. Its mineral splendours were increased in that light. As bronze retreated, veins of silver loomed in the gullies, knobs of amethyst and sapphire glowed on the hills.[14]

In the midst of her misery, Ellen is sustained by the beauty of the natural scene:

> Round her the blacks were proceeding with their various duties, beneath a splendid sky, beside a lake the colour of raw cobalt shot with bronze [...] Mrs Roxburgh could not remain unmoved by the natural beauty surrounding her.[15]

How are the Aboriginal figures and the black culture perceived? Where the Conrad text constructs the blacks as 'demonic,' even sub-human, Voss is shown, from his first meeting with the blacks, to react with respect: "Their bare feet made upon the earth only a slight, but very particular sound, which, to the German's ear, at once established their ownership."[16] While, for Marlow, the mere thought that these beings could be human is repugnant, Ellen, quite early in her experience, experi-

---

Ballyn, Doireann MacDermott & Kathleen Firth (Barcelona: Promociones y Publicaciones Universitarios, 1995): 80–95.

[10] Patrick White, *Voss* (1957; Ringwood, Victoria: Penguin, 1974): 11.
[11] Patrick White, *A Fringe of Leaves* (Ringwood, Victoria: Penguin, 1976): 74.
[12] White, *A Fringe of Leaves*, 82.
[13] White, *Voss*, 383.
[14] White, *Voss*, 128.
[15] White, *A Fringe of Leaves*, 220–21.
[16] White, *Voss*, 169.

ences a sense of bonding with them. Initially revolted by the child she is obliged to nurse, she joins with the women mourning its death: "For the first time since the meeting on the beach, the captive and her masters, especially the women, were united in a common humanity."[17] She recalls the black children with happiness even after her return to civilization: "when the young Lovells broke in, climbed upon the bed [...] Innocence prevailed [...] black was interchangeable with white."[18]

In *Voss* particularly, the blacks' link with the land is constantly emphasized through visual detail. Dugald, the old Aborigine, "could have been a thinking stick, on which the ash had cooled after purification by fire, so wooden was his old, scarified, cauterized body, with its cap of grey, brittle ash."[19] The Aborigines manifest as emanations from trees and the natural world: "Other figures were beginning to appear, their shadows first, followed by a suggestion of skin wedded to the trunk of a tree"[20] or again, "as shreds of dry bark glimpsed between the trunks of the trees, but always drifting, until, finally, they halted in human form."[21] Anthropologists have recorded that, "In the aboriginal cosmos human, plant and spiritual beings co-exist as one."[22] The white colonizer's potential for transformation into the indigene is underlined by the visual physical transformation they both undergo as they are exposed to the elements and compelled to survive as the indigenes do. In Ellen's case, there is a particular irony in that the white woman – the icon of white civilization – is wrenched from her aristocratic English home and tossed into this wildest of surroundings. On her first meeting with the Aboriginal women, she is stripped of her Western clothing, her skin is blackened and her hair shorn: "she had become a stubbled fright such as those around her, or even worse."[23] As Voss journeys into the desert he is similarly transformed: "Blackened and yellowed by the sun, dried in the wind, he now resembled some root, of dark and esoteric purpose."[24]

In each work the white protagonist's final identification with the aboriginal world seems underlined by an act seemingly 'savage,' yet which, as represented in the text, acquires the significance of sacrament, an act of redemptive grace – Ellen's

---

[17] White, *A Fringe of Leaves*, 234.

[18] White, *A Fringe of Leaves*, 342.

[19] White, *Voss*, 170.

[20] White, *Voss*, 191.

[21] White, *Voss*, 204.

[22] R. Tonkinson, *The Mardijara Aborigines: Living the Dream in Australia's Desert* (New York: Holt, Rinehart & Winston, 1978): 115. Myths illustrative of this beliefs are recorded by Ronald M. & Catherine H. Berndt in *The World of the First Australians* (Sydney: Ure Smith, 1964): 185–216.

[23] White, *A Fringe of Leaves*, 224.

[24] White, *Voss*, 168.

partaking of the human remains in the forest and Voss's reception of the witchetty grub on his deathbed.

Both texts record the reversal of the hegemonic relationship of black over white in those sections where the narrative moves into the black world and the very survival of the whites is dependent on the blacks. Dugald's decision to abandon the expedition leads Voss to experience his first real premonition of failure, subsequently Jackie comes and goes at will and Voss is powerless to control him. Finally the remnant of the party is taken captive by the blacks, and Jackie becomes Voss's executor. As soon as Ellen is taken captive she is obliged to serve the blacks as a slave: first compelled to suckle the ailing offspring of one woman, then to carry the group's utensils and equipment or to dive for lily roots and climb trees for possums as she becomes inducted into the life of the tribe. Here, clearly, the colonialist stereotype of the roles of the black / white relationship is completely reversed.

Is this collision of cultures productive of insight – does the subject admit of progress and illumination or the reverse? In the Conrad text, the inescapable result of the encounter with the savage is degradation and 'horror.' As Terry Goldie has pointed out, White (like the Canadian writer Rudy Wiebe) uses the world of the indigene to project spiritual experience and the possibilities of moral and psychic regeneration.[25] In White's novels, as in those by Malouf and Prichard, no simplistic superiority of a black culture is posited, but the Orientalist concept of a non-white world as a savage world in need of the European mission of enlightenment is radically undermined. Along with this, the rich potential for the colonizer's metamorphosis into native Australian, his ad / mission through submergence in the Aboriginal inheritance and the reversal of his original 'mission' is advanced as a fascinating possibility for European salvation and the healing of the psychic "wound" inflicted by the colonial project.[26]

WORKS CITED

Achebe, Chinua. "An Image of Africa," *Massachusetts Review* 18.4 (1997): 783.

Berndt, Ronald M., & Catherine H. "Religious Mythology," in *The World of the First Australians* (Sydney: Ure Smith, 1964): 185–216.

Conrad, Joseph. *Heart of Darkness and The Secret Sharer* (New York: Bantam, 1981).

Fanon, Frantz. *The Wretched of the Earth*, tr. Constance Farrington, intro. Jean–Paul Sartre (*Les damnés de la terre*, 1961; tr. 1965; Harmondsworth: Penguin, 1990).

Goldie, Terry. *Fear and Temptation: The Image of the Indigene in Canadian, Australian and New Zealand Literatures* (Montreal & London: McGill–Queen's UP, 1989).

---

[25] Terry Goldie, *Fear and Temptation* (London: McGill–Queen's UP, 1989): 192.

[26] Frantz Fanon, *The Wretched of the Earth* (1961; Harmondsworth: Penguin, 1990): 200.

Healy, J.J. *Literature and the Aborigine in Australia* (Brisbane: U of Queensland P, 1989).

JanMohammed, Abdul R. "The Economy of Manichean Allegory: The Function of Racial Difference in Colonialist Literature." *Critical Inquiry* 12 (August 1985): 59–87.

Kipling, Rudyard. *Complete Verse* (London: Kyle Cathie, 1990).

Malouf, David. *Remembering Babylon* (London: Random House / Vintage, 1994).

Prichard, Katharine Susannah. *Coonardoo* (1925; Sydney: Angus & Robertson, 1994).

Said, Edward W. *Orientalism* (1978; Ringwood, Victoria: Penguin, 1991).

Vanden Driesen, Cynthia. *Centering the Margins: Perspectives on Literatures from India, Africa, Australia* (New Delhi: Prestige, 1995): 96–107.

——. " 'Devils, Savages, Nobler Forms': Post-Colonial Re-Invention of the Indigene in the Works of Patrick White," in *Australia's Changing Landscapes*, ed. Susan Ballyn, Doireann MacDermott & Kathleen Firth (Barcelona: Promociones y Publicaciones Universitarios, 1995): 80–95.

White, Patrick. *A Fringe of Leaves* (Ringwood, Victoria: Penguin, 1976).

——. *Voss* (1957; Ringwood, Victoria: Penguin, 1974).

Thomas, Sue. "Interracial Encounters in Katharine Susannah Prichard's *Coonardoo*," *World Literature Written in English* 27.2 (1987): 234–44.

Tonkinson, R., *The Mardijara Aborigines: Living the Dream in Australia's Desert* (New York: Holt, Rinehart & Winston, 1978).

∾

Mission Completed?
On Mudrooroo's Contribution to the Politics of Aboriginal Literature in Australia

EVA RASK KNUDSEN

> We are on a mission of God, on a holy mission of salvation [...] These poor
> heathens must be saved and I will save them. I have been ordained to do so
> by God Almighty Himself [...] I am the Truth and the Light; I am the Way
> and the Goal; I am here because I have been summoned to be here. I am
> here because I am here because I am here[1]

LTHOUGH THIS ESSAY WILL BE CONCERNED WITH THE MISSIONS
of cultural survival and human integrity rather than with the mission of
conquest sanctioned by a Christian God, the quotation above serves as a
discursive reference point for the three different but interrelated notions of mission
addressed in the following.[2] With reference to Mudrooroo's two novels *Doctor
Wooreddy's Prescription for Enduring the Ending of the World* (1983) and *Master of
the Ghost Dreaming* (1991), I will will focus on the 'missionary' activities at work
within as well as beyond the texts: First, I will look at how missions, as institutionalized places of segregation, are emblematic of the colonial endeavour to confine
and control Aboriginal people and their means of cultural expression; second, I will

---

[1] George Augustus Robinson in Mudrooroo's *Doctor Wooreddy's Prescription for Enduring the
Ending of the World* (Melbourne: Hyland House, 1983): 72.

[2] This essay deals explicitly with the literary politics of genre and form in relation to two of
Mudrooroo's novels and therefore offers no detailed discussion of the narrative contents. For a
discussion of Mudrooroo's nomadic approach in *Master of the Ghost Dreaming*, see my article
"Clocktime and Dreamtime: A Reading of Mudrooroo's Master of the Ghost Dreaming" in
Aratjara: Aboriginal Culture and Literature in Australia, ed. Dieter Riemenschneider & Geoffrey
V. Davis (Cross/Cultures 28; Amsterdam & Atlanta GA: Rodopi, 1997): 111–21. The literary
developments in Aboriginal writing (including Mudrooroo's work) are also discussed in *The Circle
and the Spiral: A Study of Australian Aboriginal and New Zealand Maori Literature*, forthcoming
in Rodopi's Cross/Cultures series.

examine how Mudrooroo has responded to this in a subversive counter-mission of healing designed to deconstruct the fatal impact of cultural enclosure and let a liberated sense of Aboriginality integrate with the world at large on equal terms. Third, I hope to show how, in the recent critical reception of Mudrooroo's work, many postcolonial critics seem to have regressed to the zealous missionary's stance of protection, denunciation and self-righteousness by confusing his major contribution towards counteracting the callous racism of Australia with a discussion of black genes and genealogy. The opposition to and liberation from colonialist and even postcolonialist hegemonic regimes are inseparable from the politics of fringe writing in Australia. By indicating how the fight for representational freedom extends from the pages of a hybrid narrative to the stages of an essentialist public debate, I hope to also make the point that, in matters of race, Australia appears not to have come to terms with the challenges of cross-culturalism implied by its postcolonial condition.

Missions, or reserves, have a long history in Australia of being physical places that demarcated the limitations in Aboriginal freedom of movement and mental places that regulated accepted cultural behaviour. They enclosed – as well as excluded – a people. In cultural terms they functioned as the colonizer's controlling device of admission and / or dismissal in relation to Aboriginality. According to both historical records and Aboriginal life stories, missions or reserves were closed worlds, 'total' or 'managed' institutions that aimed at reforming and conforming Aborigines to prepare for their subsequent entry into mainstream society. In a monotonous atmosphere of regimentation, disciplinary punishment and civilizing 'drills' the missionaries or reserve managers controlled not only the training of the 'ideal type,' but also the bureaucratic norms that determined the degree of a person's Aboriginality. Entry and exit permits were granted only at the discretion of authoritarian managers; Aboriginal reserve councils, when they came into existence, were at all times "kept subservient to the official will."[3] Aboriginal people became the victims of a seemingly benevolent but utterly disastrous father-knows-best philosophy under which their individual and cultural selves were systematically destroyed because it encouraged them to give up their language, religion, nomadic lifestyle and cultural traditions. Such were the demands, even on a mission station in the 1970s, not for purity but for assimilation, that a mother would scrub her children with solvol to lighten their skin.[4]

---

[3] Kevin Gilbert, *Living Black: Blacks Talk to Kevin Gilbert* (Ringwood: Penguin, 1977): 282.

[4] Ruth Fink, "The Caste-Barrier: An Obstacle to the Assimilation of Part-Aborigines in North-West N.S.W," *Oceania* (1971): 105.

However, one of the major paradoxes of colonialism is, as Ania Loomba has observed, that "it both needs to 'civilize' its 'others' and to fix them in perpetual 'otherness'."[5] Since the early days of Empire in Australia, missions have reflected this ambivalence; with the promise of self-determination and autonomy Aboriginal people were required to adopt European definitions of civilization and cultural acceptability, yet in the very process of internalizing these adverse definitions they would in fact forever cast themselves as estranged and so 'other' to themselves and the surrounding world. They would condemn themselves to being perpetually 'not quite / not right.' This is not entirely the predicament of the protagonist Doctor Wooreddy in Mudrooroo's historical revision of the nineteenth-century Tasmanian holocaust – he dons the mask of accepting European superiority only as a matter of survival and because this will allow him to do his field work among the white barbarians – but his life story seems to be just as imprisoned within the European genre of the historical novel as the life stories of non-fictional Aboriginals have been inside missions and reserves for almost two centuries. There is an obvious parallel between the Christian mission and the historical realist novel, both may be seen as functional extensions of Empire and therefore directly opposed to Aboriginal autonomy and freedom of expression. A sense of entrapment permeates the narrative level of *Doctor Wooreddy's Prescription for Enduring the Ending of the World*, one which certainly originates in the grim historical evidence of genocide on which the story is based but also one which is reinforced by the capturing impulse of 'history' writing and the genre of realism itself.

The Aboriginal world of the novel closes in on itself, not only in line with the development of the tragic plot but also because, despite its reversed perspective and the agency it gives back to Aboriginal historical characters, the novel itself is kept subservient to a conventional idea of recorded history as fact and the verisimilitude of the genre of historical realism. History with its chronological conception of time – ie, time is believed to unfold like a scroll and events are arranged in neat and orderly sequence – imposes itself on the texture of this Aboriginal mission narrative and becomes an infringement on Aboriginality that mirrors the submission – at plot level – of Aboriginals to more mundane yet still universalized standards of 'the right way' such as pious recitals of Christian prayers, tidy line-ups for physical exercise or hand-outs, delicate needlework, dedicated vegetable gardening or other "domestic duties [like] keeping their little family parlours clean and laundering their clothing."[6]

---

[5] Ania Loomba, *Colonialism / Postcolonialism* (New York: Routledge, 1988): 173.

[6] Mudrooroo [Colin Johnson]. *Doctor Wooreddy's Prescription for Enduring the Ending of the World* (Melbourne: Hyland House, 1983): 148). Where clear from the context, further page references are in the main text.

In relation to the shaping of Aboriginal images, the conventions of the genre come into force, not unlike the standards of good missionary work, as repositories of "the Truth and the Light, the Way and the Goal" (72). The telling of past events from an Aboriginal perspective is kept in check by a genre that moves inescapably, as it abides by a linear time frame, towards narrative closure by foreshadowing from the very beginning the sense of an ending (as indeed suggested by the title of the novel). In such a narrative scheme the Aboriginal characters are predestined to be merely the sad victims of a failed and misguided enlightenment project; the narrative form in itself will find Aboriginal people at the receiving end of history. "It must be the times," says Wooreddy, and in this ambivalent and often repeated phrase lies the explanation also for the textual apocalypse of Aboriginal traditions – the genre of historical realism is not conducive to an exploration of the cyclic or mythic Aboriginal perceptions of life and existence, it appears to be "incongruous when tied to Aboriginal subjectivity" as Kateryna Arthur has remarked.[7] The phrase is used by Wooreddy as a stoic, almost withdrawn, comment on genocide (9), the break-down of Aboriginal customs (24) and the loss of self-determination (85), and it echoes through the novel as Mudrooroo's own awareness of how his black words are, despite their celebration of Aboriginality, caught up in a white form. The Aboriginal stories of the novel are contained by the notion of European history.

The only form of opposition, it seems, that is available to Wooreddy – and Mudrooroo – in this novel, is the parodic power of mimicry, and both protagonist and writer to some extent succeed in menacing the power of the missionary, of history and writing, by their shrewd appropriation of colonialist author/ity and its media of submission. Wooreddy keeps the missionary impositions at bay by replicating a colonialist discourse by which the invading European 'other' is cogently constructed as primitive, less than human, and quite often cunning and corrupt while Mudrooroo keeps novelistic dispositions at bay by exposing how history became 'fact' through narrative positioning and how genre is both politically and ideologically implicated.[8] However, like Wooreddy, who realizes that his strategy of survival numbs and disables him to the extent that he passively observes the disintegration of his culture with "all the detachment of a scientist" (20), Mudrooroo realizes that writing realistically is the equivalent of living at a mission: the white form sets the right norm and pacifies the aspirations of this Aboriginal hi/story. Traditional Aboriginal culture in the novel, including the ceremonial song poetry from Arnhem Land, appears to be arrested by genre and a determinist plot, and

---

[7] Kateryna Arthur, "Fiction and the Rewriting of History: A Reading of Colin Johnson," *Westerly* 30.1 (1985): 58.

[8] See Arthur, "Fiction and the Rewriting of History," 40.

deprived of its evocative potential. It cannot do anything to the narrative, it cannot perform. In a drab atmosphere of resignation, it is as framed, fixed and objectified as the Aboriginal inmates of Mister Robinson's mission. In effect, both Mudrooroo and most of his historical Aboriginal characters are serving the proverbial 'sentence of history'; Mudrooroo in the sense that he is "composing in the shadow of death"[9] while having to serve time, or submit to 'the times,' in textual imprisonment, his characters in the capital sense of dying as a consequence of the fatal representational power of the colonizers and their faithful missionary. The description of Wooreddy sitting quietly against a whitewashed wall in the mission church glancing at a piece of writing describing the conditions of Aboriginal life at the settlement is both an emblematic and sadly ironic comment on the missionary enterprise of salvation:

> [He] was getting over an attack of the coughing demon, and stared at the letters form-ing words and sentences that stood at attention in line like red-coated soldiers [...] He stared down at the black marks and his eyes went right through them to the twenty-nine people that had recently died [...] Death was the central fact of their lives – the steady placing of bodies into the cold ground in the Christian way. (145)

Black body up against a white wall, black letters on a white page, black corpses in white graves form a strong image of Aboriginal surrender to Robinson's mission of God and the red colour of the soldiers' uniform only increases the sense of fatality. Like the many inmates of Aboriginal missions throughout history, both Wooreddy and Mudrooroo were aware of the double bind that governed their respective inter-actions with the non-Aboriginal world surrounding them: Their survival or accep-tance in that world depended on their willingness to become mimic men, yet if they gave in to this demand they would at the same time give up on being themselves. They would, to recall Loomba's phrase, have agreed to reside in 'perpetual other-ness.' Mudrooroo's first Tasmanian story may be seen as a case in point, as Woor-eddy, who is destined to survive until the ending of the world, can be granted author-ity only through European or westernized definitions of the term – as a 'Doctor' of tribal lore and philosophy – and Mudrooroo himself can do little to release him from this historical and generic predicament.

In *Master of the Ghost Dreaming*, a persuasive rewriting of the Doctor Woor-eddy story, Mudrooroo clearly intended to counteract this doublebind by exploring a new role for his Aboriginal protagonist – and himself – as shaman. This still involves some degree of controlled mimicry of European learnings, but for Janga-muttuk this is an empowering means to an end: "He was not after a realist copy,

---

[9] Bob Hodge & Vijay Mishra, *Dark Side of the Dream: Australian Literature and the Post-colonial Mind* (North Sydney: Allen & Unwin, 1990): 341.

after all he had no intention of aping the European, but sought for an adaptation of these alien cultural forms appropriate to his own cultural matrix"; however, "things were not the simple black and white he had imagined them to be,"[10] as Wooreddy discovered in a flash of enlightenment just before he died, and this realization spills over into *Master of the Ghost Dreaming* as a hybridizing mantra for the shamanic healer Jangamuttuk. 'The times' cannot be evaded, history cannot be un-done, the power of writing cannot be abolished, but the ideologically constructed dichotomies of 'white superior' and 'black inferior' can be dismantled, and in a counter-mission designed to infiltrate the colonizer's mentality (the Ghost Dream-ing), Mudrooroo sends the shaman Jangamuttuk off on a mental journey of re-covery. Mudrooroo thus shifts from "the heroic to the totemic, transforming [his literature] by design, into functional dreaming."[11] He, like Jangamuttuk, adopts a strategy of resistance which is effective precisely because it lies outside the formal categories of insurgence recognized by Europe and the missionary Fada – the generic reinvention of colonial missionaries like Robinson. Myth swallows history, 'clocktime' is subsumed into Dreamtime, and European letter and alphabet relin-quish their epistemological grip on Aboriginal word and image: "I see in vision [...] that sickness comes from that ghost [...] he writes us down in that big book of his and we are trapped forever. But I watch out, I know what he is doing and I can free" (29–30), says Jangamuttuk, the re-invention of the Wooreddy character, who is no longer the stoic victim of historical circumstance but the creative agent of cultural resurrection. The shaman's insight, however, is by no means converted into a swift and unproblematical change of action as his strategy requires, before he can set his own people free, both a liberation of voice through the demolition of the European semantics found for instance in European convict ballads and the careful healing of the displaced Europeans on the mission.

Jangamuttuk's sub/mission is of a different nature because it makes use of the transformative power of the mind – an expertise by birthright, one might add, for Jangamuttuk and traditional Aboriginals – and so the boulder that eventually demolishes Fada's mission compound leaving of "Fada's monument to history" only "the square outline of what had once been a church" (146) is only a metaphor of the successful completion of a mental dream-journey that has reinitiated Jangamuttuk and his tribe into a sense of cultural belonging which has unhinged itself in the process from European definitions of "the Truth and the Light, the Way and the

---

[10] Mudrooroo, *Master of the Ghost Dreaming* (Sydney: Collins/Angus & Robertson, 1991): 196. Further page references are in the text.

[11] J.J. Healy, "Colin Johnson/Mudrooroo Narogin," in *International Literature in English: Essays on the Major Writers*, ed. Robert L. Ross (New York: Garland, 1991): 34.

Goal." Jangamuttuk, however, has transgressed the confines of the Christian mission long before the premises fall apart, and this is due to the fact that Mudrooroo bursts the confines of the European realist genre from the very first page of *Master of the Ghost Dreaming* by inserting the story into the narrative framework of myth and a performative context of decolonizing ceremonies. The literary mode of historical realism has been replaced by Mudrooroo's mimicry in writing of an oral Aboriginal storytelling practice that is intrinsically opposed to fixity and the stagnant perceptions of the world engendered by institutionalized mission life. Oral stories of cultural belonging know no boundaries as they are as long as the land they stretch across in polyphonic reverberations of mythic events that unite the fluid notions of past and present in a mental view to the future. An Aboriginal story may be best understood as "words going somewhere" in nomadic movements of stopping and starting and "its authority comes from the territory covered, not the person temporarily in charge of the pen. It cannot be imperial [...] because it has to abandon the traces it leaves behind"[12] until the traveller – the writer or the reader – returns for another 'track up.'

In the context of *Master of the Ghost Dreaming* and the stories of dispossession and despair that need to be healed, this original strategy of retelling the Aboriginal experience, past and present, enables the characters not only to transcend missionary confinement but also to go back in time and space and 'track up' colonization and redefine the prejudiced thinking that led to this confinement. And this is the Way and the Goal of the shaman's cure to the painful infliction of European Truth and Light. From within the empire of the novel, Mudrooroo works deconstructively towards narrative disclosure and renegotiations of Aboriginality in the same vein. From within the premises of the mission, Jangamuttuk works subversively towards representational disclosure and cultural survival. The synchronic movements of the traditional nomad and the postcolonial bricoleur pave the way for an opening, a way out, and the power and authority held by European mission and Western genre in their capacity of being 'total' or 'managed institutions' is contested if not undermined. This way out leads towards more spacious territories and to the very different notion of Aboriginal textuality that rests in the speaking land.

Although this land has been rendered palimpsestic by colonial expansionism and the multiple stories of diaspora related to it by Aboriginals, missionaries and convicts – even ex-slaves and descendants of the Middle Passage – Jangamuttuk is still able to seek out "a few ancient nodes [...] that he can accept as the footprints of his Dreaming ancestors who had passed through [it]" (21), and this in turn allows Mud-

---

[2] Kim Benterrak, Stephen Muecke & Paddy Roe, *Reading the Country: Introduction to Nomadology* (Fremantle: Fremantle Arts Centre P, 1984): 22.

rooroo to decolonize it by letting the interwoven stories of diaspora be spoken through and by land in the traditional Aboriginal way. Through the replication of the Aboriginal formula of 'land as text' the geography of Australia becomes in fact the metaphysical master-narrative of liberation – and postcolonial initiation – not just for Aboriginals but for every displaced character in this novel of convergence, including the Afro-American character Wadawaka who, in keeping with a common traditional Aboriginal kinship practice, becomes Aboriginal by affiliation: "you come with us [...] you belong us mob now" (83), as Jangamuttuk tells him. Whereas mission life ruthlessly accustomed its people to a caste system based on the shades of blackness and the false dichotomy of self and 'other,' the land has taught its first-born people to be inclusive rather than exclusive, because, characteristically, in every aspect of the Aboriginal world view nothing is nothing; everything is, and must be, something, and everybody is, and must be, somebody.

Accordingly, the nomadic Dreaming perception of life and being is in itself emancipating, it shuns fixity and framing, and whereas in the realistic mission setting of *Doctor Wooreddy's Prescription for Enduring the Ending of the World* this came to be seen as a cultural impulse that halted Aboriginal integration into the colonial world, it turns into Aboriginal advantage in the decolonizing enterprise of *Master of the Ghost Dreaming*. In both novels, the Aboriginal characters have been silenced, rendered 'Other' to themselves, and inauthentic on the margins of chaos and disorder, yet in the narratives of the dream-journeys and the concurrent ceremony of healing choreographed by Jangamuttuk, this is rationalized, not as the unfortunate side effect of a civilizing mission of God, but as the first phase of a rite of passage. By going through – indeed, by travelling through – ordeals of chaos and disorder that are both ritualistic and historical, Mudrooroo's characters are reborn and re-emerge triumphantly from the colonial encounter before they set off into a new story in another novel. In the context of the pantheistic nomadic mind, there is no background and foreground in the representation of the world, no split between self and Other. The mental dream-journeys carried out within the physical location of a European mission transcend this sheltered and secluded environment and bring the characters into 'Other' being, an 'otherness' of a very different kind from that offered by colonialism. Here intensity and association, having overruled European notions of, and colonizations of, time and place, bring about an ultimate act of identification with land in which the characters may reunite with the parts of themselves that were lost in 'history.' This is a double act of re-membering, and when the characters merge with the experienced geography of Australia they slide into "a warm sense of well-being in which there is no separation between inner and outer [...] pulsing slowly, pulsing rhythmically" (111). With this mending of the sacred bond between culture and nature, man and land – and in recalling the contrast of imagery found in *Doctor Wooreddy's Prescription for Enduring the Ending of the World* with its "steady placing [dead] bodies in the cold ground in the Christian way" (145) – it seems that Mudrooroo has successfully explored means of decolonizing both a culture and a text while pinpointing in the process a subtle but basic tenet of black and white encounters, past and present: A culture will remain forever submitted to the colonizers' control as long as both colonizers and colonized remain fixed in a politics of identity that focuses on essential notions of being at the expense of cross-cultural processes of becoming.

Whereas the cultural traditions of Aboriginal people seemed to be merely on anthropological display, captured by the genre in premodernity in *Doctor Wooreddy's Prescription for Enduring the Ending of the World*, they release themselves and their potential in *Master of the Ghost Dreaming*; they are not merely in the story, they *are* the story, in fact the story being told. With its focus on process, passage and renewal, the strategy of writing nomadically can be, it appears, the equivalent of living, not outside of white institutions, but certainly within them and without the encroachments of 'missionary' conventions. Like few other black writers in Australia, Mudrooroo has contributed to the politics of cross-cultures. Not only does his own personal history of having 'done the round' as an inmate of Australia's variety of managed institutions bestow the hi/stories he has written with authenticity, but indeed his entire writing career reflects the development of Aboriginal writing – through the early stages of writing that were documentary and searching to the later stages of writing that are archaeological and reconstructive.[13] It would be absurd to evaluate the creative force and the visionary perspectives of black Australian (indeed, Aboriginal) writing without paying tribute to his enormous contribution to the exploration of black being in a white world. Mudrooroo has been at the strategic forefront of the struggle to combat the bigotry of racism, and his writings have been an important means of making the historical plight and the neglected rights of Australia's indigenous people heard throughout the world. His outstanding literary career is testimony to the fact that although cultural identity is a highly ambiguous subject it may in fact be both discovered and recovered through a conscious engagement with 'otherness.'

However, the mood and oppressive atmosphere of 'missionary' regimes may still be with us, and, in a highly ironic sense, things are indeed not the simple black-and-white or in-between some of us perhaps imagined them to be. New missions of the right faith have emerged and although they come in more covert forms than those of

---

[13] See Healy, "Colin Johnson / Mudrooroo Narogin."

the past – they range from university departments to academic conferences and post-colonial forums and chat rooms in cyberspace – they, like the missions of the past, can be serious violations of authenticity and quite often as hermetically closed off from genuine interactions between cultures, or races, as Mister Robinson's mission in *Doctor Wooreddy's Prescription for Enduring the Ending of the World*. In colonial times, the missionaries seized the power of denaming and renaming in the successful endeavour to define and so control a person's – indeed, a people's – identity. The question needs to be addressed whether in these postcolonial times the members of the critical establishment are not in fact reiterating a strategy of submission by assuming that, like the missionaries, they are called upon to replicate the old power game that once determined who should be admitted onto and who should be ejected from the premises of Aboriginality.

I am not addressing here the issue of Mudrooroo's contested Aboriginality, but the critical preoccupation with his identity and the urge – in the name of political correctness, a new faith no less self-righteous and self-indulgent than missionary Christianity – to rename his status and so defame his position as a writer of Aboriginality because his blackness is no longer of the right kind. This calls, I argue, for self-introspection and a revaluation of our professional rights (if not of something as good old-fashioned decency). When some critics – outside as well as inside Aboriginal Australia – have converted to the belief that the literary persona of Mudrooroo is a hoax which can be dealt with in the same way as the Australian public has dealt with a Malley or a Burrup, a Wongar or a Demidenko – or when the issues of native title to land and human title to integrity are confused – it looks like a cultural backlash of major colonialist proportions. A person who has spent a lifetime inside Aboriginal culture believing himself to be Aboriginal and accepted as such speaks with an authority engendered by often harsh personal experiences, and that is something literary hoaxes tend to lack. This practice of exclusion, this apparent need to purify, translates into a politics of cultural essentialism. What is identity in a postcolonial society, if not hybrid or multiple, and something that out of sheer political, social and cultural necessity has to be embraced as such? The curiously inverted application of the 'biology is destiny' doctrine to Mudrooroo's persona makes sense only if it is seen as an example of how, as Loomba has indicated in relation to cultural identity, "colonial empires both fear and engender biological as well as intellectual hybridities"; it may, in fact, be indicative of an unwillingness to come to terms with the fact that "identities – on both sides of the divide – are unstable, agonised, and in constant flux" and how this "undercuts [...] claims to a unified self and warns us against interpreting cultural difference in absolute or reductive terms."[14]

This essay has engaged in the complex web of meanings related to the notion of 'mission,' and it would appear that the various types of mission discussed are connected through the central issues of representational control and the power of naming: How does 'otherness' come into being, how may the 'Other' come to terms with his 'otherness,' who has the right to write as 'other,' and who has the power to determine the 'otherness' of the 'Other.' It appears that such a debate engenders more ambivalent questions than unequivocal answers. However, while the critics engaging in such a discussion should be observant of the many theoretical ambiguities of 'otherness,' they should never, however, lose sight of the practical, indeed ethical, implications of their academic exercises. Before they engage in beguiling language games of un/author/ization and de/ab/originalization they should recall that there is nothing more degrading and more reminiscent of the old missionary days than assuming that one has the right to dissect another person's, another people's, being as if that can be eradicated with the stroke of a pen or the insertion of a slash. Mudrooroo once remarked about the cultural environment in Australia that it took "a referendum to bring the Aboriginal people into the human race."[15] Let us hope it does not take yet another referendum to grant people the right to their own sense of being. And let us more than hope that it will be nothing more than an unbecoming inter-mission when we as critics, speaking from our privileged positions within academic institutions, feel called upon to profess the "Truth and the Light, the Way and the Goal." If not, we, as contemporary reincarnations of Mister Robinson, will have summoned ourselves to be part of a new mission of oppression while, in terms of the appropriateness of our work, we can lay claim only to the dubious and immoderate fame of being here because we are here because we are here.

WORKS CITED

Arthur, Kateryna. "Fiction and the Rewriting of History: A Reading of Colin Johnson." *Westerly* 30.1 (1985): 55–60.

——. "Neither Here Nor There: Towards Nomadic Reading." *New Literatures Review* 17 (1989): 31–42.

Benterrak, Kim, Stephen Muecke & Paddy Roe. *Reading the Country: Introduction to Nomadology* (Fremantle: Fremantle Arts Centre P, 1984).

---

[14] Loomba, *Colonialism / Postcolonialism*, 173, 178.

[15] Mudrooroo, "Guerilla Poetry: Lionel Fogarty's Response to Language Genocide." *Westerly* 3 (1986): 50.

Fink, Ruth. "The Caste-Barrier – An Obstacle to the Assimilation of Part-Aborigines in North-West N.S.W.," *Oceania* (1971): 28–29.

Gilbert, Kevin. *Living Black: Blacks Talk to Kevin Gilbert* (Ringwood, Victoria: Penguin, 1977).

Healy, J. J. "Colin Johnson / Mudrooroo Narogin," in *International Literature in English: Essays on the Major Writers*, ed. Robert L. Ross (New York: Garland, 1991).

Hodge, Bob, & Vijay Mishra: *Dark Side of the Dream: Australian Literature and the Postcolonial Mind* (North Sydney: Allen & Unwin, 1990).

Loomba, Ania. *Colonialism / Postcolonialism* (New York: Routledge, 1998).

Mudrooroo [Colin Johnson]. *Doctor Wooreddy's Prescription for Enduring the Ending of the World* (Melbourne: Hyland House, 1983).

——. "Guerilla Poetry: Lionel Fogarty's Response to Language Genocide," *Westerly* 3 (1986).

Mudrooroo. *Master of the Ghost Dreaming* (Sydney: Collins / Angus & Robertson, 1991).

✍

Mission Impossible
Mudrooroo's Gothic Inter/Mission Statement

GERRY TURCOTTE

Re-Mastering the Ghosts
Generically Dis/Figuring Majority Cultural Codes

I N THIS ESSAY I AM ATTEMPTING to (un)cover a fair bit of ground. I would like to discuss briefly the question of the Gothic as it has been used to construct a eurocentric notion of Aboriginality, but more importantly, I would like to look at the way the mode has been turned on its head, as it were, by indigenous artists, to produce an oppositional, revisionist discourse that undermines European historiography. The chief example in this reading will be a series of novels by the writer Mudrooroo, who is interesting in the context of this collection because he locates his ghost and vampire tales at the site of the invasion of Australia by Europeans, and around a battle that was frequently effected through missionary activities.

Particularly fascinating is his rewriting of the "conciliating" efforts of George Augustus Robinson, in what was then called Van Diemen's Land (until 1855 – now Tasmania), and his disastrous attempts to establish what he called a "Friendly Mission" that would effectively rid the small island of its Aboriginal inhabitants and so leave it free for white settlement. This mission would see the death of most of its inhabitants, including that of "Truganini [...] regarded at the time as 'the last of her race'."[1]

Tasmania is a particularly apt place to begin a discussion of the Gothic, since it has so often been figured, in the Australian mainland imaginary, as a space of terror, of backwardness, of depravity. Australia itself, however, long before it was ever 'discovered' by European explorers and cartographers, was constructed as a

---

[1] Henry Reynolds, *Fate of a Free People: A Radical Re-Examination of the Tasmanian Wars* (Melbourne: Penguin, 1995): 5.

space of monstrosity.[2] Tasmania, owing to its notorious convict prisons, was seen
to be even darker.

Indeed, Ken Gelder begins his study *Reading the Vampire* by mentioning a coincidental yet no less fascinating moment in the European naming of that island. The
first map of Van Diemen's Land, by Thomas Scott in 1830, was produced when
"over half" of the island was colonized. "But although the remainder," as Gelder
puts it, "was left blank, it was nevertheless given a name: *Transylvania*." And
though this naming "precedes the popularised association of Transylvania and vam-
pires" effected by Bram Stoker's *Dracula*, "it also, perhaps, anticipates that later
association." If it is true, as Gelder maintains, that "One of the peculiarities of vampire fiction is that it has – with great success – turned a real place into a fantasy,"[3] it
is certainly true that European epistemologies have persistently enacted a similar
refiguration of the 'Other': constructing and inventing a fantastic identity for 'undiscovered' or recently 'discovered' lands and peoples.

Many contemporary Indigenous writers respond to such constructions by explicitly hijacking familiar European stories, tropes and figurations – and 'disfiguring'
them through satire, parody, and other forms of ritual dismemberment. The Dracula
myth is particularly appropriate in this context. If we accept that *Dracula* enacts
what one critic has called the "anxiety of reverse colonization" by "bringing the
terror of the Gothic home," in contradistinction to the usual flow of the Gothic into
'displaced' lands, times and spaces,[4] then it is possible to read Mudrooroo's ongoing account of the invasion of Australia as a particularly powerful elaboration and
satire of that fear – relocated into the orientalized space itself.

In *Master of the Ghost Dreaming* (1991) and in the three more recent books, *The
Undying* (1998), *The Underground* (1999), and *The Promised Land* (2000), Mudrooroo re-animates the figure of the vampire as a European presence which descends
upon the Australian landscape to suck it dry, and to contaminate its spaces. The Indigenous figures who meet this invading force are alternatively perplexed and
continuously adaptable, transforming themselves, their songlines, their very world,
in order to resist acculturation into what is presented as a devilish, impoverished and
ultimately soul-destroying enterprise. At the same time, Mudrooroo cleverly signals

---

[2] See my development of this idea in relation to the Gothic in *Handbook to Gothic Literature*,
ed. Marie Mulvey Roberts (London: Macmillan, 1998): 10–19. The idea of the Antipodes was
controversial, but the belief that "a separate human race" might live there "was distinctly heretical." See C. Raymond Beazley, *The Dawn of Modern Geography* (New York: Peter Smith, 1949),
vol. 1: 372.

[3] Ken Gelder, *Reading the Vampire* (London: Routledge, 1994): 1 (all quotations here).

[4] Stephen D. Arata, "The Occidental Tourist: *Dracula* and the Anxiety of Reverse Colonization," *Victorian Studies* 33 (Summer 1990): 621–45.

the way the 'Other' is fetishized in that process of projection so typical of European Gothic narratives.

The Gothic began by locating its darkest narratives 'elsewhere'; but its most terrifying accounts were those which returned to the home, or the self, as the source of the monstrous. *Dracula* is one of many Gothic narratives which chill by alerting its readers to the enemy without, whose greatest power is its ability to colonize from within. How fitting, then, that Mudrooroo should seize on this narrative trope and turn it against the invading culture. For Mudrooroo, Australia is filled with spiritual forces, but the ghostly – the *otherworldly* – is logically identified as a white invading presence, literally from another world. Much has been made of his artful figuration of the white man as *num* – a term suggesting both a ghostliness and a lack of feeling.[5]

In *Doctor Wooreddy's Prescription for Enduring the Ending of the World* (1983) and in *Master of the Ghost Dreaming*, Mudrooroo mobilizes the metaphor of ghostliness to speak of competing dreamings, white and black, and to meditate on the ability of Aboriginal cultures to respond to invasive forces through adaptability. Wooreddy and Jangamuttuk learn the dreamings of whites in order to resist their power. They become Masters of the Ghost Dreaming to counter the bad "magic" of invasion.

In *Doctor Wooreddy* and *Master of the Ghost Dreaming* (hereafter referred to as *Ghost*), which retell the missionary tale of George Augustus Robinson and his attempts to replace ancient Aboriginal beliefs with his own Christian God, Mudrooroo charts the devastating consequences of these *supposedly* well-meaning European policies. Robinson is an especially relevant target both because of his actual impact on the Tasmanian Aborigines as well as because of the way he scripted himself into history. Robinson invented himself, as it were, and this heroicized and fictive persona determined for a long time how his accomplishments were read. Mudrooroo's interrogation of this figure, therefore, becomes a specifically textual deconstruction of what, for the Tasmanian Aborigines, was one of the most disabling 'texts' of empire.

The vision of Robinson as a godly hero is without foundation. Robinson was a voluminous writer who used lengthy reports, based on his own jealously guarded and more detailed journals, as a way of securing his own advancement. This advancement was attempted through a construction of himself as a consummate mediator, philanthropist and negotiator, effected through "often exaggerated and inaccu-

---

[5] See, for example, Adam Shoemaker's reading of *Wooreddy*, where "The European invaders are not human at all – they are 'ghosts' or 'num' "; *Mudrooroo: A Critical Study* (Sydney: Angus & Robertson, 1993): 48.

rate accounts of his activities [...]." As Vivienne Rae–Ellis makes clear, "Robinson's journals are a confusing mixture of false and factual information."[6]

Mudrooroo's rewriting of this character is blistering in its ridicule. In *Dr Wooreddy* and *Ghost* Robinson is refigured as a bumbling, hopelessly inefficient, hypocritical failure of a human being. Robinson lusts after his charges whom he admonishes with religious diatribes about modesty; he pontificates endlessly; he loses himself in the bush or contracts severe skin ailments. All the while he is tended to and saved from himself by mocking, and infinitely wiser counterparts, Wooreddy and Jangamuttuk, who are shown to be spiritual advisers to their people. They humour the incompetent missionary, while simultaneously labouring to find a way to survive the Government's genocidal activities. And so another important element enters into this discussion. As well as a 'real' white figure of history, there are also 'real-life' Aboriginal leaders who are profoundly implicated in this story, and who are reintroduced by Mudrooroo in his re / vision of Black History.

Specifically, Mudrooroo retells the story of the role of Wooreddy and, to a lesser extent, of Trucannini,[7] in the campaign to assist "The Great Conciliator" to carry out his plans. He effectively and aggressively rewrites the white historical account of Aborigines as failed or inefficient warriors. Building on admittedly white documentary evidence,[8] Mudrooroo re-writes the roles of Aboriginal warriors, showing that they were cunning and effective adversaries despite the insurmountable odds.

Ghost is important for a number of reasons. As Shoemaker has noted, it is fascinating first because it marks Mudrooroo's return, after some eight years, to the theme of the Aboriginal Tasmanians,[9] a return visit that allows him to re-write, perhaps more militantly and more optimistically, his earlier account of Aboriginal resistance. Where, in the first text, the vision was one of inevitable collapse, a prescription to endure the ending of the world, in *Ghost* "the novel resonates with the

---

[6] Vivienne Rae–Ellis, *Black Robinson: Protector of Aborigines* (Melbourne: Melbourne UP, 1996): xiv. The variation in the spelling of Rae–Ellis's name reflects the author's own practice. Her name is spelled without a hyphen in the 1981 book, and with a hyphen in the 1996 volume. I have used the latter spelling except in reference to the earlier edition.

[7] Trucannini is a European appropriation of the woman's name and is spelled in a variety of ways, as this article will show. I have adopted one of the more common spellings. For a fuller discussion of this issue of naming practice, see Ian Anderson, "Reclaiming Tru-ger-nan-ner: De-Colonising The Symbol," in *Speaking Positions: Aboriginality, Gender and Ethnicity in Australian Cultural Studies*, ed. Penny van Toorn & David English (Melbourne: Victoria U of Technology, 1995): 31–42.

[8] Mudrooroo's principal source for his rewritings is N.J.B. Plomley, *Friendly Mission: The Tasmanian Journals and Papers of George Augustus Robinson, 1829–1834* (NSW: Halstead Press, 1966). (Source: interview with the author.)

[9] See Shoemaker, *Mudrooroo: A Critical Study*, ch. 4, "Turning the Circle."

rhythms of a different Australia and a different mental universe." If in the earlier novel "Robinson's version of Christianity [...] seems to succeed," the latter book "decentres the whole concept of proselytising." As Shoemaker goes on to say, "If anything, it is Jangamuttuk and his wife Ludjee (Mudrooroo's reinvention of Wooreddy and Truganinni) who convert Fada and Mada (the ironic echo of 'The Great Conciliator' and his spouse)."[10]

Jangamuttuk's chief weapon is parodic mimicry, usually of key ritualistic moments. The novel opens, in fact, with a ceremonial exorcism of sorts, where the tribes people have painted European costumes – lapels, insignia, even pockets – onto their bodies. Jangamuttuk's purpose is not to reproduce "a realist copy"; he has "no intention of aping the European" (*Ghost* 3). Jangamuttuk is seeking to adapt the "alien cultural forms" in order to "possess" the European. He is preparing the groundwork so that his people can enter "into the realm of the ghosts" to possess "the essence of health and well-being" of the invaders. Mudrooroo here is literally describing a ghostly type of possession, a reverse colonization of the European invader.

Master of the Ghost Dreaming destabilizes the historical accounts the earlier novel was based on, by more radically distorting the names by which the familiar figures were known, but also by deviating more distinctly from the documented history. One such gesture is the inclusion of an African character, Wadawaka, which, for Shoemaker, is a sign of Mudrooroo's attempts to create "a parable about the colonial experience anywhere [...] This seems to imply a post-colonial solidarity between the formerly oppressed."[11]

Where *Wooreddy* had signalled a quiescent defeat before the European onslaught, *Ghost* enacts a specific, hallucinogenic and unqualified conquering of the mission, where a large boulder, propelled by a pulsing crystal, rolls down a steep slope until "It reached the mission compound, flattened the cemetery and rolled onwards. Fada's monument to history, the chapel, stood directly in its path. The huge boulder pressed it into the earth. All that was left was the square outline of what had once been a church" (146). As well as a type of wish-fulfilment narrative, what the ending of *Ghost* puts in place is a jarring, non-realist fusion of narrative types. As soon as the dust clears, the novel ends by announcing that "The dismal period was over" (147). The novel concludes with a note about the Aboriginal heroes of the tale: "As for our band of intrepid voyagers, their further adventures on the way to and in their promised land await to be chronicled, and will be the subject of further volumes" (148).

---

[10] Shoemaker, *Mudrooroo: A Critical Study*, 67–68.

[11] Shoemaker, *Mudrooroo: A Critical Study*, 71.

The abrupt ending and peculiar postscript signal Mudrooroo's refusal to play by the rules. They underscore his insistence on blurring generic categories so that the very literary guidelines which, elsewhere, he has identified as prisoning – the laws of genre for example – are contested and, if not overturned then at least destabilized. They are, in point of fact, made unfamiliar, precisely at the point where they begin to become identifiable. Generic categories, in other words, are made uncanny: familiar and yet unfamiliar, simultaneously.[12]

This is why Mudrooroo, particularly in *Ghost*, focuses so frequently on rituals and ritual re-enactments. What is often enacted at the level of ritualistic or celebratory protest, however, is frequently attended by or articulated through the manipulation of genre and generic stability. Genre, of course, is ritual as well. It allows for the rehearsal of social and literary conventions according to seemingly binding rules. Genre is a guideline for how things should be and operate. It has also been read, not least by Mudrooroo himself, as a way of policing Aboriginal writing. As Mudrooroo observed in *Writing from the Fringe* (1990), for example,

> Genres have developed as a European way of categorising works of literature. In themselves, they are ways of manipulating the text so that the reader is led from an intuitive to a logical response to the work. Not only this, but the Aboriginal writer is led to believe that there are fixed categories of literature to which he or she must conform. If we as writers accept this we, in effect, dilute the Aboriginality of our work. (170)

Mudrooroo's generic rewriting is most interesting when he turns his hand to the Gothic mode. Gothic tales are usually about oppression and violence, narratives that blur and contest the very certainties which contextualize and make possible such narratives. Just as interesting for the purposes of this essay is the fact that the Gothic has frequently been used by imperial agencies to identify Aboriginality as primitive, pagan and unenlightened, precisely by returning to the origins of the word, so that in one easy gesture the "Dark Ages" and Aboriginal Australia are equated. Both are dark – unenlightened.[13]

---

[12] I am alluding here to Freud's well-known essay "Das Unheimliche" ("The Uncanny"), *Collected Papers: Papers on Metapsychology, Papers on Applied Psycho-Analysis*, tr. Joan Rivière (London: Hogarth Press, 1956) vol. 4: 368–407. For a development of Freud's theory of the uncanny through readings of Australian and Aboriginal literature see "How Dark is My Valley? Canadian and Australian Gothic," *Scarp* 22 (May 1993): 26–32 and "Footnotes to an Australian Gothic Script: The Gothic in Australia," *Antipodes* 7.2 (December 1993): 127–34). See a more recent reading of the Aboriginal sacred and the uncanny in Ken Gelder & Jane M. Jacobs, *Uncanny Australia: Sacredness and Identity in a Postcolonial Nation* (Melbourne: Melbourne UP, 1998).

[13] For more extended readings of this particular issue, see Penny van Toorn, "The Terrors of *Terra Nullius*: Gothicising and De-Gothicising Aboriginality," *World Literature Written in English*, 33.2–33.1 (1992–93): 87–97; and also Gerry Turcotte, "Australian Gothic," in *Handbook to Gothic Literature*, ed. Marie Mulvey Roberts (London: Macmillan, 1998): 10–19.

Given Mudrooroo's interest in re-writing disabling European forms, and dis-
lodging their authoritative hold over the Aboriginal imaginary, it is not surprising
that he should turn increasingly towards this mode of writing. And in his sequels to
Ghost, he embraces the Gothic's most recognizable form – the vampire story – as a
way of acknowledging and overturning this association.

The Undying: *The Vampire Bites Back?*

The images of the ghostly and predatory, of the vampiric and demonic, are everywhere in Mudrooroo's writing, but it isn't until *The Undying* (1998) that he creates
an actual vampire, Amelia, in a way which is particularly fascinating. At the end of
Ghost, Jangamuttuk, Ludgee, their children and Wadawaka, together with a small
group of Aboriginal survivors, take over a ship and sail away from the Tasmanian
mission that has entrapped them. In *The Undying* they arrive at mainland Australia,
hoping, presumably, for a fresh start. Instead, they find that the country is being
preyed upon by a female European vampire who enjoys the taste of eucalyptus in the
Australian blood (137) and who has a predilection for consuming male genitals.
More confusing still is that her accomplice is an Aboriginal man named Renfiel, in a
spelling so close to Stoker's that we are not meant to miss the connection. Finally, to
make the figure even more complex, Amelia is said to be Eliza Fraser's sister.

Fraser, as Mudrooroo well knows, is one of the most controversial and overloaded figures in Australian settlement history, a woman shipwrecked in 1836, and
putatively kidnapped and victimized by her Aboriginal captors. Fraser would become a signifier for the evilness of Aboriginal Australians, a justification for punitive expeditions to rescue her. Later, in a dramatic change of fortune, she would go
from mother of empire to symbol of female moral degradation, being blamed (perhaps as Trucannini had been) for her own violation at the hands of her captors and
rescuers. Perhaps most like Trucannini, she would be resented for taking charge of
her life, for speaking for herself, and for refusing to be silenced by patriarchy and
by history.[14]

---

[14] For an account of the Fraser legend and for a critical analysis of the way she has been 'read,'
see Kay Schaffer, *In the Wake of the First Contact: The Eliza Fraser Stories* (Melbourne: Cam-
bridge UP, 1995) and *Constructions of Colonialism: Perspectives on Eliza Fraser's Shipwreck*, ed.
Ian McNiven, Lynette Russell & Kay Schaffer (London: Leicester UP, 1998). See also Gerry
Turcotte, "Mrs Fraser's Ravenous Appetite: The Taste for Cannibalism in Captivity Narratives," in
*Crossing Lines: Formations of Australian Culture: Proceedings of the Association for the Study
of Australian Literature Conference, Adelaide, 1995*, ed. Caroline Guerin, Philip Butters &
Amanda Nettelbeck (Adelaide: ASAL, 1996): 165–74; "Coming Out of the Closet: Sexual Politic
in Michael Ondaatje's *the man with seven toes*," in *La création biographique / Biographical Creation*, ed. Marta Dvorak (Rennes: Presses Universitaires de France, 1997): 101–10, and "'Fears of

That Mudrooroo would invoke her in this elliptical way is a sign of his brilliant understanding of the fetishism of the sign of Eliza. In *The Undying*, Amelia's power becomes entangled in some oddly misogynistic, and not unfamiliar figurations of women, particularly in Gothic texts. Amelia is an embodiment of a type of *vagina dentata*, of the female as monstrous. This leads to one particularly troubling scene in which the African character, Wadawaka, subdues her through his virile, black sexuality. The scene moves oddly between romance and outright porn, where Amelia explains that her attempts to subdue Wadawaka fail because he tears

> past whatever defences still remain and pierc[es] me to my very vitals. I give a shriek. I have never known a man in this way and am afraid. Then I feel my body responding and try to rake his face with my nails, try to get at him with my fangs, but I am mortified when he laughs as he continues to violate me. (188)

Mudrooroo manages to represent Amelia as simultaneously promiscuous and virginal, ironically echoing the construction of Eliza in many of the 'rewritings' of the latter's story. If Mudrooroo is known for his refusal to conform, and for his determination to defy expectations, this penultimate chapter of *The Undying* seems to push him to new extremes. To understand what he is doing, it is necessary to return to the beginning of the novel, and to listen to the story told by Jangamuttuk's son George.

The Undying begins as a yarn – a song cycle. A stranger, George, named after a mad King, approaches a fire by night and offers to "exchange my yarn for your company" (1). We discover in this "prologue" within Chapter One that George is "the undying," all that is left "at the end of [the] western voyage" (1). George is a vampire who has to "avoid the full light of day" (1) ever since "an old granny ghost touched me with her teeth and followed after us" (2). The effect of this is to replace his Aboriginal visions with hers: "She gave me dreams that were not my dreams, and that is part of my story" (2).

This line is important because the book is about the power and battle over dreamings. And it is particularly significant when read in the context of *Master of the Ghost Dreaming*, which ends with the escape from Fada's – George Augustus Robinson's – prison island. What saves them all in *Ghost*, of course, is Jangamuttuk's Ghost Dreaming. But in *The Undying* we are told that he failed: "never did we escape the influence of the ghosts" (19). For every possession, there is a disposses-

---

Primitive Otherness': 'Race' in Michael Ondaatje's *the man with seven toes*," in *Constructions of Colonialism*, ed. McNiven et al., 138–50, for, respectively, a reading of the 'cannibalizing' of Eliza Fraser by critics and a contextualizing of this story according to both 'race' and 'gender' in Michael Ondaatje's *the man with seven toes*. My articles discuss the sort of readings of Aboriginal sexual and cultural depravity and objectification that Mudrooroo is writing against.

sion. For a ghost to take over a soul, a soul must be lost. For land to be taken, some-one must be dispossessed. For Aboriginal people, this moment of invasion is particularly uncanny. They are simultaneously possessed and dispossessed; they are taken over and disowned.

The Undying is a darker, more confusing narrative than *Ghost*, because it begins by refusing the optimism of the latter's ending. It begins by *announcing* the end, and in this way returns us to the tone of *Doctor Wooreddy.* In *Ghost* the small group of people who escaped Flinder's Island on a stolen ship have died or disappeared. Augustus, George's brother, has fallen from the mast and drowned. The others, one by one, have perished. The ship has become specifically Gothic: The breeze rattles "like dead men's bones," the rigging sounds like "giant bat wings" (3). The narrator becomes a type of Ancient Mariner, announcing the end of the "songline": "I don't want tea. I want your ears so that I can tell you of those days which we thought belonged to us, for we were powerful in song" (4). George, the undying, is the last of his mob, strangely echoing – and hence cleverly refuting – a range of colonial narratives, from *The Last of the Mohicans* to the obscene fiction that Trucannini was the last of the Aboriginal Tasmanians.

This, then, is where the prologue ends, and where the tale begins. The story that George tells is 'ruptured' when they meet Amelia Fraser who takes over as narrator after she has bitten George. At the moment of infection, the narrative slips out of George's sole control. The voice of the narrative, in other words, is possessed, just as his body has been, by the European vampire.

Where, in Bram Stoker's *Dracula* (1897), the Count's designs on England, metaphorically represented by his importing of his dark earth, suggests the possible colonization of the centre by the feared Other, in *The Undying* Mudrooroo reverses this model to embody England's devastating visitation as the feared vampiric force. Amelia's journey to Australia is an odd refiguration of the Dracula legend, conjoined with a number of other European narratives.

There are two other major players who need to be briefly introduced into this tale before a full stocktaking can be made. One of these is a violent military commander, Captain Torrens, who is at his most cruel when the moon is full – which is when he becomes a werebear. Torrens' job is to defend the new colony from the attacks of the Aborigines, though, unbeknownst to him, his retaliation is in response to acts of violence committed by Amelia.

At one stage, as he surveys the "mutilated bodies" of the Aboriginal men he has slaughtered and disembowelled, "hanging all in a row" as a warning to the blacks, he searches for a missing soldier and thinks: "A flogging will add to the romance of this desolate shore. The stinking savages hanging dead and the thud of the lash upon a deserter's flesh – what else could we do to realise this Gothic scene?" (124).

It is as though Mudrooroo has asked himself this same question. He provides one last ingredient, perhaps by way of an answer – a figure of ridicule who is an outcast among his people. Gunatinga (Dungeater), is a hopeless figure who is rejected by his tribe, is crippled by a spear wound to his leg, and has made himself central to his people through duplicity and luck. It is he who first stumbles on the wreck of the *Kore* which brought Amelia to Australia, and significantly, as he approaches it, he is said to have "entered the uncanny" (81).

Dungeater is a "man of many names," redefining himself as he progresses through the story, gaining an increasing sense of self-importance that 'real' shamans, such as Jangamuttuk and Waai can easily see through. Dungeater makes two important discoveries when he first approaches the ship. The first is its severed figurehead, "a woman coloured like *moma*, a spirit all white with red painted lips and nipples. Long flowing yellow hair had been carved about the features" (80). This iconographic representation of Amelia herself is also an intertextual gesture towards the figurehead that was central to the white woman of Gippsland story, another putative tale of a kidnapped white woman which justified a series of punitive expeditions until it was discovered that the woman never existed; that she was merely a ship's figurehead which a local Aboriginal tribe had used as a centrepiece for its corroborees.[15] The second major discovery is Amelia herself. Or, to be more precise, Amelia, sensing Dungeater's malleability, discovers him, and calls him to her cave. Amelia realizes that she will need an assistant and, instead of killing him, she speaks to him telepathically – "in pictures." She names him Renfield and asks, "Can you pronounce that in your rude language?" (93). The answer, clearly, is no, and so he becomes "Renfiel." When she makes him drink her blood she re-enacts the famous scene in *Dracula* where the Count forces Mina to drink. Amelia holds him "tightly so that he must fill his mouth with my blood then swallow it" (93). Unlike Mina, where the enforced fellatio cannot be spoken, here the para-sexual element is fixated upon. Indeed, it could easily be said that the entire narrative has an oral fixation.

Dungeater, then, is a peculiar figure between worlds. He is a Spirit Master to his people, and a "trusty servant" to Amelia. He is, in fact, an overloaded figure, invoking the limping grotesque assistant of so many monster narratives, a type of "dark" Quasimodo. He is also, of course, a gesture towards the original Renfield from *Dracula*, the betrayer of his own people who allows Dracula into the asylum to

---

[15] For more information on this tale, see Kate Darian–Smith, Roslyn Poignant & Kay Schaffer, *Captured Lives: Australian Captivity Narratives* (London: Sir Robert Menzies Centre for Australian Studies, 1993).

feast on Mina. More intriguingly, he invokes another Bram Stoker character, the figure of Oolanga, from *The Lair of the White Worm* (1914), a black servant who similarly served a white female demon, Arabella (and the parallel in names may not be accidental).

All these characters move towards a final resolution. The werebear is defeated (though not killed) by Amelia, who in turn is subdued by Wadawaka. The distant and local Aboriginal groups combine their power to wipe out the ghost settlement, yet somehow Amelia escapes. The books ends with an allusion to a new songline, "The Song of the Nomad," a story which begins, "He came from the sea, from the cool, cool sea, he rose to hurry us west" (201). These are the unmistakable tones of the Western, perhaps a dark parody – a reclaiming of *Pale Rider* – as Wadawaka assumes his spirit shape and goes in search of Amelia – to annihilate the one who is worse than all of them. George, who has not showed an inability to tolerate the sun after he has been contaminated, has presumably progressively worsened. The last page returns us to the first, with the conclusion of the yarn he promised to tell – and the hint of the next to come.

So what are we to make of this extraordinary tale? A superficial reading of this complex text might lead us to conclude that it was generically and intertextually 'promiscuous' to its peril; that the metaphoric and postmodern play collapses upon itself into a nihilistic scenario, speaking the defeat of the Aboriginal people at the hands of white culture. Instead, I would like to suggest that in *The Undying*, Mudrooroo specifically invokes a range of master-narratives in order to expose their hidden agendas. He invokes the codes of representation that so frequently frame female sexuality as predatory, available and compromised. Similarly, the fetishized black male body is brought to life in this tale, with every imaginable stereotype and cliché.[16]

Many of the nineteenth- and early twentieth-century texts that are gestured towards, or which are cleverly plagiarized in *The Undying*, are tremendously undercoded at the level of performance. Like *Dracula* they allude to an uncontrollable desire, but they vie away from expressing it. The texts, therefore, are redolent with contradiction – they are contra / dictions: against utterance. Similarly, the project of Empire has been both explicit and indirect – admitting to its totalitarian vision of colonization, and yet simultaneously couching this desire / design within a rhetoric

---

[16] For an examination of this figuration see bell hook's argument, building on Michael Dyson, that in the tales of Empire, Black men are constructed as " ' peripatetic phalluses with unrequited desire for their denied object – white women.' As the story goes, this desire is not based on longing for sexual pleasure. It is a story of revenge, rape as the weapon by which black men, the dominated, reverse their circumstance, regain power over white men." bell hooks, *Yearnings: Race, Gender, and Cultural Politics* (Boston MA: South End Press, 1990): 58.

of, dare one say, missionary purpose – of colonizing for the good of the colonized. This double vision is expressed through many of the narratives which Mudrooroo invokes in his novel. In *The Undying* Mudrooroo reveals the hidden – he enacts the unperformed – he declares the unspoken.

If Stephen Arata is correct when he argues that *Dracula*, published in 1897, articulated a *fin de siècle* fear of "reverse colonization," how fitting that Mudrooroo's *The Undying*, published almost exactly a century later, should speak to a similar centennial terror, though articulated in a specifically Australian context.

Ken Gelder's and Jane Jacob's *Uncanny Australia* (1998) identifies the way the Aboriginal sacred, reinforced by the Australian High Court's Native Title Act (or Mabo) decision has led to many white Australians feeling dispossessed in their own country. There is a misinformed yet pervading fear that Aboriginal people will reclaim their land – that they will rise from nothingness – from *terra nullius* – and avenge themselves. Mudrooroo plays with these fears of 'reverse colonization' and allows them to haunt the Australian imaginary.

Finally, like an Anne Rice novel perhaps, Mudrooroo writes *The Undying* in the style of an autobiography of sorts, a self-scripting which refuses the construction of the Aborigine as other. This story is told by the vampire himself – to a specifically white audience. And the story George tells us is distressing yet hopeful. Far from registering the optimistic voyage promised at the conclusion of *Master of the Ghost Dreaming*, we are alerted in *The Undying* to the dire fact of contamination. It is fitting that the story should shift from the perspective of Jangamuttuk, a full-blood Aboriginal character, to George, a man who is Aboriginal but who also carries "a bit of old England in Me" (1), as he points out at the start of the next book in the series, *The Underground* (1999).[17]

The Undying is a novel that acknowledges the virulent contamination of Aboriginal culture by the European settlers, a contagion which is enacted both biologically and narratively. Aboriginal culture is irredeemably changed because of the predations of the otherworldly ghosts, just as the songlines are forever different because of the texts of Empire. It is for this reason that *The Undying* is haunted by European references – not to signal how it has been dispossessed by an unavoidable intertextuality, but, rather, that it has survived this spectral legacy. And perhaps, in a mischievously reassuring note to all those anxious Australians in terror of their own imminent dispossession at the hands of Aboriginal land-rights activists, Mudrooroo also makes the point that the Aboriginal *spirit* is not identical to the European *num*. As George puts it in the closing words of *The Undying*, in exchange for the Abori-

---

[17] Indeed, as is revealed in *The Underground*, George's real father is Augustus Robinson himself!

ginal stories which will entertain and enrich the listeners, he "will exact something in return, but do not be afraid – I am not that greedy!" (202).

WORKS CITED

Anderson, Ian. "Reclaiming Tru-ger-nan-ner: De-Colonising The Symbol," in *Speaking Positions: Aboriginality, Gender and Ethnicity in Australian Cultural Studies*, ed. Penny van Toorn & David English (Melbourne: Victoria U of Technology, 1995): 31–42.

Arata, Stephen D. "The Occidental Tourist: *Dracula* and the Anxiety of Reverse Colonization," *Victorian Studies* 33 (Summer 1990): 621–45.

Beazley, C. Raymond. *The Dawn of Modern Geography*, vol. 1 (New York: Peter Smith, 1949).

Darian–Smith, Kate, Roslyn Poignant & Kay Schaffer. *Captured Lives: Australian Captivity Narratives* (Working Papers in Australian Studies 85–87; London: Sir Robert Menzies Centre for Australian Studies, 1993).

Freud, Sigmund. "The Uncanny," *Collected Papers: Papers on Metapsychology, Papers on Applied Psycho-Analysis*, tr. Joan Rivière (London: Hogarth, 1956), vol. 4: 368–407.

Gelder, Ken. *Reading the Vampire* (London: Routledge, 1994).

——, & Jane M. Jacobs. *Uncanny Australia: Sacredness and Identity in a Postcolonial Nation* (Melbourne: Melbourne UP, 1998).

hooks, bell. *Yearnings: Race, Gender, and Cultural Politics* (Boston MA: South End, 1990).

McNiven, Ian, Lynette Russell, & Kay Schaffer. *Constructions of Colonialism: Perspectives on Eliza Fraser's Shipwreck* (London: Leicester UP, 1998).

Melville, Henry. *The History of Van Diemen's Land: From the Year 1824 to 1835, inclusive, During the Administration of Lieutenant-Governor George Arthur*, Part II, ed. & intro. George Mackaness (Sydney: D.S. Ford, 1959).

Mudrooroo. *Doctor Wooreddy's Prescription for Enduring the Ending of the World* (Melbourne: Hyland House, 1983).

——. *Master of the Ghost Dreaming* (Sydney: Angus & Robertson, 1991).

——. *The Promised Land* (Sydney: Angus & Robertson, 2000).

——. *The Underground* (Sydney: Angus & Robertson, 1999).

——. *The Undying* (Sydney: Angus & Robertson, 1998).

——. *Writing from the Fringe* (Melbourne: Hyland House, 1990).

Plomley, N.J.B. *Friendly Mission: The Tasmanian Journals and Papers of George Augustus Robinson, 1829–1834* (NSW: Halstead Press, 1966).

Rae Ellis, Vivienne. *Black Robinson: Protector of Aborigines* (Melbourne: Melbourne UP, 1996).

——. *Trucanini: Queen or Traitor?* (Canberra: Australian Institute of Aboriginal Studies, 1981).

Reynolds, Henry. *Fate of a Free People: A Radical Re-Examination of the Tasmanian Wars* (Melbourne: Penguin, 1995).

——. *This Whispering in Our Hearts* (Sydney: Allen & Unwin, 1998).

Ryan, Lyndall. *The Aboriginal Tasmanians* (Sydney: Allen & Unwin, 2nd ed. 1996).

Schaffer, Kay. *In the Wake of First Contact: The Eliza Fraser Stories* (Melbourne: Cambridge UP, 1995).

Shoemaker, Adam. *Mudrooroo: A Critical Study* (Sydney: Angus & Robertson, 1993).

Stoker, Bram. *Dracula* (Harmondsworth: Penguin, 1993).

Turcotte, Gerry. "Australian Gothic," in *Handbook to Gothic Literature*, ed. Marie Mulvey Roberts (London: Macmillan, 1998): 10–19.

——. "Coming Out of the Closet: Sexual Politic in Michael Ondaatje's *the man with seven toes*," in *La création biographique: Biographical Creation*, ed. Marta Dvorak (Rennes: Presses Universitaires, 1997): 101–10.

——. "'Fears of Primitive Otherness': 'Race' in Michael Ondaatje's *the man with seven toes*," in McNiven et al., ed. *Constructions of Colonialism*, 138–50.

——. "Footnotes to an Australian Gothic Script: The Gothic in Australia," *Antipodes* 7.2 (December 1993): 127–34.

——. "How Dark is My Valley? Canadian and Australian Gothic," *Scarp* 22 (May 1993): 26–32.

——. "Mrs Fraser's Ravenous Appetite: The Taste for Cannibalism in Captivity Narratives," in *Crossing Lines: Formations of Australian Culture: Proceedings of the Association for the Study of Australian Literature Conference, Adelaide, 1995*, ed. Caroline Guerin, Philip Butters & Amanda Nettelbeck (Adelaide: ASAL, 1996): 165–74.

Van Toorn, Penny. "The Terrors of *Terra Nullius*: Gothicising and De-Gothicising Aboriginality," *World Literature Written in English* 32.2–33.1 (1992–1993): 87–97.

❧

New Zealand and the Pacific

Missionaries of the British Muse
Concepts of Literary Nation-Building in Early New Zealand Poetry in English

BÄRBEL CZENNIA

Introduction

L EAVING PARTICULAR HISTORICAL CIRCUMSTANCES aside, national
identity can be defined as the construction of a collective identity in a field
of polarities halfway between politics and culture.[1] To a certain extent
national identity always depends on, or relates to, *cultural* identity, the word *culture*
in this context including all sorts of material, social as well as mental expressions of
human life, with language, religion, education, art, and the collective memory of a
shared past as its most prominent aspects.

The history of English literature(s) shows how thoroughly interrelated the fields
of politics and art have always been: From the outset, literature, as one among
numerous interconnected fields of public discourse (along with political and theological debate, philosophy, early historiography, aesthetics or literary criticism) not
only reflected contemporary perceptions of a collective cultural 'self' as opposed to
a cultural 'other'; in many important ways it influenced or even accelerated the process of nation-building, because it helped to invent, confirm, perpetuate, modify or
question the – constantly changing – identities of countries.[2] English, Scottish, and

---

[1] Bernhard Giesen, ed. *Nationale und kulturelle Identität: Studien zur Entwicklung des kollektiven Bewußtseins in der Neuzeit* (Frankfurt am Main: Suhrkamp, 1991).

[2] Aleida Assmann, "This blessed plot, this earth, this realm, this England: Zur Entstehung des
Englischen Nationalbewußtseins in der Tudor-Zeit," in *Nation und Literatur im Europa der frühen
Neuzeit: Akten des I. Internationalen Osnabrücker Kongresses zur Kulturgeschichte der Frühen
Neuzeit*, ed. Klaus Garber (Tübingen: Max Niemeyer, 1989): 429–52; Bärbel Czennia, "Nation-
building Down Under: Repräsentationen von Geschichte in der englischsprachigen Lyrik Neu-
seelands, 1890–1990," in *Fiktion und Geschichte in der anglo-amerikanischen Literatur: Fest-
schrift für Heinz–Joachim Müllenbrock zum 60. Geburtstag*, ed. Rüdiger Ahrens & Fritz–Wilhelm
Neumann (Heidelberg: Carl Winter, 1998): 479–514.

Irish writers like Dryden in the seventeenth century, Defoe, Pope, Thomson, and Burns in the eighteenth, Tennyson and Kipling in the nineteenth, Yeats and Hugh MacDiarmid in the early twentieth century, inscribed their views on collective identity into their poetry, and thus bore witness to an eminently political function of literature. Many eighteenth-century writers concentrated on the invention of coherent histories[3] for their 'imagined communities,'[4] either defined as English, British, or Scottish; conjectures concerning the possibilities of a future exportation of the increasingly self-confident British model were still comparatively modest. Yet, with the foundation of English-speaking white settler-communities overseas – starting in North America and later expanding to Australia and New Zealand – some writers not only helped to advocate a fully-fledged British imperialism, but eventually took an active part in the colonial enterprise.

In New Zealand it started in 1840, the year of the Treaty of Waitangi. Writers from all over the British Isles thus became missionaries of British culture in a double sense of the word:

on the one hand, by using literature as a *medium*, a means to an end for the propagation of the (supposedly superior) political, social and cultural values of Britain which they shared with the rest of the emigrants;

on the other hand, by exporting 'British Literature' (including the concept of literacy as opposed to orality, and a distinctive tradition of literary modes of expression) as a cultural and aesthetic value in its own right – a *mental* tool, equivalent to the pioneer farmers' more material pickaxes and spades, both echoed in Thomas Bracken's gardening metaphor of the "bold planters of that noble British tree."[5]

Literary History and Literary Criticism: The Traditional View

A little over a century-and-a-half later, the modern, internationally acknowledged, politically independent island state, with a (multi-)cultural identity of its own, displays a remarkable sense of embarrassment when looking back on its literary beginnings, initiated by the British-born pioneer generation of writers. This impression is reinforced by at least two popular and representative histories of New Zealand literature in English, written by New Zealanders since the beginning of the 1990s:

---

[3] Eric J. Hobsbawm & Terence Ranger, *The Invention of Tradition* (Cambridge: Cambridge UP, 1983).

[4] Benedict Anderson, *Imagined Communities: Reflections on the Origin and Spread of Nationalism* (London & New York: Verso, rev. ed. 1993).

[5] Thomas Bracken, "The Golden Jubilee [Sydney Exhibition, 1879]," in *Lays of the Land of the Maori and Moa* (London: Sampson Low, 1884): 53.

For Victorian colonials [...] literature was a gift received rather than a mechanism to
tinker with: the right way of doing things had long been perfected by the great figures
of the age, Tennyson, Browning, and to a lesser extent Arnold [...] With Tennyson's
death in 1892, the last of the great Victorian poets was gone: the new poets all seemed
minor [...] So imitative had English poetry become [...] that it barely mattered where it
was written: in London or in Auckland, it was simply "emotional slither," "rhetorical
din and luxurious riot," as Ezra Pound wonderfully said of it in 1912.[6]

Most nineteenth century New Zealand poets had not only brought with them moribund
Victorian poetic modes and disabling conceptions of the poet's role as comforter,
moralist, or dreamer, but also lacked talent.[7]

Both critics seem to regard New Zealand's pioneer poets as inferior copies of British
originals, hardly worth remembering at all. Evaluations applied to particular authors
reveal even more scathing judgments. This can be illustrated by focusing on three
'missionaries of the British muse' still frequently anthologized. A brief examination
of their treatment in modern literary histories will be followed by a first annotated
reading of their poems, in order to find out how far the criticism may be justified.

John Barr of Craigilee (1809–89) was of Scottish origin and emigrated to New
Zealand in 1852; according to the *The Penguin History of New Zealand Literarture*
"Dialect poetry," as first practised by Barr, is "especially tiresome to read now" (45).
MacDonald P. Jackson, in *The Oxford History of New Zealand Literature English*,
gives another turn to the screw, disqualifying Barr's poems as "hamely Scottish
jingle," "firmly based within his provincial community" (353).

Jessie Mackay (1864–1938), also of Scottish descent but belonging to the second
generation already born in the colony, was famous for her poetry in Scots as well as
in standard English. In contrast to John Barr, who "registers his environment as
social setting and workplace, not as landscape,"[8] so that in many of his poems New
Zealand is not an explicit issue, Mackay was one of the first writers to make New
Zealand's scenery, inhabitants (including its Maori population), and their stories
themes of her poetry. Patrick Evans criticizes Mackay's "fervently idealistic and
quite unfocussed nationalism" (27) and sums up her poetry as "of no time, of no
place" (50–51). The seasoning of his literary criticism with highly subjective comments on Mackay's biography, however, does not make Evans's statement all too
convincing. Judgments such as "Jessie Mackay [...] declined marriage for good
works and bad poetry" (33) tell us more about the male attitudes of the critic than

---

[6] Patrick Evans, *The Penguin History of New Zealand Literature* (Auckland: Penguin, 1990): 42.

[7] MacDonald P. Jackson, "Poetry: Beginnings to 1945," in *The Oxford History of New Zealand
Literature in English*, ed. Terry Sturm (Auckland: Oxford UP, 1991): 343.

[8] Jackson, "Poetry: Beginnings to 1945," 353–54.

the literary characteristics of the female writer in question. Jackson also offers his readers a personal judgment on Mackay's way of life rather than a descriptive approach to her writing:

> throughout Mackay's career 'dreaming' and 'doing' were in conflict [...] An ardent prohibitionist, defender of the underprivileged, and 'advocate of Irish and Scottish Home Rule, of Liberalism, feminism, and internationalism,' she at times felt an impulse to make her poetry serve a social function. (358)

Thomas Bracken (1843–98), born in Ireland, author of the country's national anthem ("God defend New Zealand") and one of the most popular poets in the second half of the nineteenth century, is the most harshly criticized of the pioneer generation of writers. The more successful a New Zealand poet was before 1890, the more he seems in danger of being condemned in late twentieth-century literary histories: In the *Oxford History*, Bracken gets an even worse lashing than Mackay; more, it seems, for his 'politically incorrect' behaviour than for lack of talent:

> The complete opportunist, he had Irish blarney enough to twice win the Caledonian society of Otago Prize Poem competition with "The Exile's Lament," in which he revealed more nostalgia for heather and glen than he had ever shown for a shamrock. (353–54)

The *Penguin History* 'characterizes' Bracken as "an ambitious Irishman who had pursued the muse to Australia before cornering it in New Zealand." To Bracken, Evans goes on,

> poetry was like a lot of things the Victorians had brought with them to the new colony, portable and, because so little engaged with anything real in the first place, easily adapted to the new situation. (42)

Less pardonable than imitating English poetry of the Romantic or Victorian period, according to the *Oxford History*, is the sin of regression into even deeper folds of Britain's literary past:

> [Bracken's] chief poetic strategies are Augustan, rather than Romantic [...] For sheer mawkishness he is hard to match, and *Musings in Maoriland* (1890), with its fey illustrations, is the essence of kitsch. (355)

A First Annotated Poetry-Reading

Confronting the judgments pronounced on early New Zealand poets with a first reading of their poems indicates that the literary criticism quoted so far cannot simply be dismissed as mere back-biting: John Barr was indeed clearly influenced by his Scottish compatriot Burns in his experiments with a literary version of Scots as his main stylistic device. Like Burns, he used a stylized form of dialect, combining grammatical and syntactical structures which are mostly, though not entirely, English, with a variable blend of Scots and English on the lexical level. For both of them, this seems to be part of a consciously planned strategy: On the one hand, it keeps the potential readership as large as possible, while, on the other, enabling the writer to own up to his personal loyalties, both in a cultural and a political sense. And yet, literary critics may have wondered, is it really possible to transfer this stylistic technique from one time and place to another without turning it into a weak copy of a splendid original? Various remarks in the modern literary histories quoted so far add up to the overall impression of a fairly epigonous figure. The poem "Grub Away, Tug Away" (1861)[9] is well suited to confirming that impression: It consists of an antithetical juxtapositon of an idealized Scotland, vaguely stereotyped as "land of the heather-bell, mountain, and foggy dell," connected with the persona's youth, and an even less distinct New Zealand, only to be guessed at by the annoying "ferns" that impede the pioneer's attempt to transform the native wilderness into a civilized agriculture.

In the same way, Jessie Mackay's poem "The Charge at Parihaka" (1889)[10] seems to confirm some of the worst assumptions of critics, as it clearly is an imitation of the English laureate Tennyson's famous "The Charge of the Light Brigade" (1854), the patriotic account of a military disaster during the Crimean War in 1854, ending with the death of close to 600 British soldiers. There can be no denying Mackay's minute copying of rhyme, rhythm, and metre, even half-sentences, from the successful English model: Is this not excellent proof of the deficiency of "New Zealand verse before 1890," its lack of "development," and the assertion that "there are few literary occupations more depressing and less rewarding then the study of it," as the *Oxford History* has it (344)?

Browsing through Thomas Bracken's "Jubilee Day,"[11] which in 150 lines celebrates the fiftieth anniversary of the British colony in 1890, it would be difficult not to register the strong influence of Alexander Pope and James Thomson. While Pope's "Windsor Forest" (1713) may safely be called its immediate pre-text, echoes of Thomson's "Liberty" (1736) are less obvious, although they can be traced in emotional key-passages. It would also be difficult to overlook Bracken's extensive use of many stylistic devices dear to Augustan poets, which readers of the twentieth century – owing to a change of literary taste – have come to despise as unnatural, as the frequent occurrence of personified abstractions, as a weakness for periphrasis,

---

[9] *An Anthology of New Zealand Poetry in English*, ed. Jenny Bornholt, Gregory O'Brien & Mark Williams (Auckland: Oxford UP, 1997): 510.

[10] *100 New Zealand Poems*, ed. Bill Manhire (Auckland: Godwit, 1994): no. 11.

[11] *Musings in Maoriland* (Dunedin, Wellington & Sydney: Arthur T. Keirle, 1890): 25–30.

and as a tiring amount of ornamental epithets, to mention just a few. Borrowing, however, is not limited to the rhetorical and stylistic micro-level; more important are structural and conceptual adoptions that in one respect justify characterizing Bracken's poem as an *imitation* of Pope's panegyric on good old England in the golden days of Queen Anne (1702–14). Even the political loyalties seem to be preserved, as Bracken does not yet opt for political independence but still situates the colony within the ideological and geographical bounds of the British Empire. Additionally, where Pope compares the Forests of Windsor and their surroundings to a second Garden of Eden (7–28, 37–40), Bracken has no problem transplanting this rural idyll into the southern hemisphere, including the aesthetic concept of 'order in variety' borrowed from eighteenth-century English landscape gardens. Pope's patriotic pride, contrasting British "Liberty" with foreign "Slav'ry," and British "Peace" with foreign "Conquest" (l. 407–408), his belief in the universal applicability of aesthetic norms belonging to Augustan England, all of this cultural baggage and much more reappears in Bracken's "Jubilee Day."

Three Arguments in Favour of a Reconsideration

There are several reasons, however, why what at first sight looks like an unequivocal case of colonial lack of originality may yet be worth a closer examination, and why many early New Zealand poets (despite indisputable flaws) may be worth reconsidering:

1.   One reason is the uncompromising harshness as well as the apparent homogeneity of opinion in various literary history-books published lately. Is this kind of 'poet-bashing' just another expression of a former colony's cultural cringe, long believed dead? Is it possible that today's New Zealand critics even out-do their European colleagues of yesteryear in killing artists' reputations from an unreflectingly eurocentric point of view?

2.   Just as literature has its traditions, so has literary criticism, the latter functioning not only as a 'store of knowledge' of a culture's literary past but also as a store of value-judgements, even prejudices, often perpetuated over long periods of time. A key figure in the formation of a literary tradition as well as of literary criticism in New Zealand was Allen Curnow, the country's most famous, internationally acclaimed poet of the twentieth century. It was Curnow who, in the 1940s, started the first serious discussion of concepts such as cultural and national identity in New Zealand literature. Combining the activities of an author, literary critic and academic teacher, he became an authority whose opinions were highly respected, frequently referred to, and sometimes also misunderstood or misquoted by other members of New Zealand's literary scene. Curnow's activities as the editor of anthologies of

New Zealand poetry may have been of even greater importance for later generations of poets and critics than his own poetry. His introductions to *A Book of New Zealand Verse* (1945), and to *The Penguin Book of New Zealand Verse* (1960) were among the first surveys of New Zealand poetry with an historical perspective and also among the first to take the colonial authors severely to task from a modernist point of view. Echoes of what might be called 'the curse of Curnow' can clearly be heard in modern literary histories, although the man himself is least to blame.[12] In his double role of literary creator and mediator, however, Curnow was not an unbiased critic, but – at least as a poet – found himself in a serious state of competition with Bracken. Just as the Irish immigrant had written poetry to commemorate political events of public concern, like the colony's 1890 jubilee, and had reaped enthusiastic support from colonial politicians, so Curnow commemorated the tercentenary of Abel Tasman's arrival in New Zealand with his famous ode, "Landfall in Unknown Seas" (1942), commissioned by the New Zealand Department of Internal Affairs. Although very different in tone and attitude, it resembles Bracken's "Jubilee-Day" in its fusion of poetry and politics and its attempt to forge a collective identity for a young nation-state trying to come to terms with its growing political independence.[13] At least partly due to Curnow's long-lived influence, even the most recent histories of New Zealand literature, written from a postcolonial point of view, still seem to be pervaded by a concept of 'historical progress'; the idea of 'progress' in its turn implying that of 'improvement,' of a succession of stages leading from 'bad' to 'good.' One possible explanation for the survival of a concept otherwise long since dismissed because of its ideological implications is the close interdependence in New Zealand of literary production and literary criticism.

3. Yet there may be yet another reason for the condescending attitude of modern literary criticism towards New Zealand's pioneer poets: As long as an approach to the early literature of New Zealand focuses on 'influence-studies,' perceiving 'influence' as a one-directional move from the culture of a 'mother-country'

---

[12] It is due to the selectivity of many quotations in modern literary histories that the (wrong) impression of an unrestricted condemnation of colonial poetry is brought about, whereas Curnow himself has given much more balanced statements than his critical successors, see, for instance, the "Introduction" to *The Penguin Book of New Zealand Verse* (Harmondsworth: Penguin, 1960): "At least, if many of those writers now appear colonial geese, whom that older New Zealand esteemed swans, we are not released from our debt to the colonial and prenational generations. Their assumption that if there was to be a nation there had also to be literature – not at all the same thing as arguing that literatures have to be national – was an entirely reasonable one, and did credit to the temper of their minds. We may catch them in absurd postures, trying to concoct the 'national' by colonial pressure-cookery, with much sentimental steam and scraps from Victorian kitchens. But if they had not dared to be silly then, we should be sillier today" (22).

[13] See Bärbel Czennia, "Nation-building" (1998).

to that of a dependent territory, it will not be able to register anything but similarities, hence will constantly confirm the derivative qualitiy of the colony's culture.
An approach, however, that focuses on colonial writers first and foremost as *readers*
of British literature, who in various ways inscribe in their texts a whole range of
attitudes towards their predecessors, may be able to detect more than similarities,
because it pays just as much attention to the manifold *additions* to, and *reinterpretations* of, adopted material, as to *omissions*.[14] It may thus come to a more comprehensive understanding of its 'Anglo-colonial' heritage as a complex literary response
to British literature whereby New Zealand authors "transformed" the British pre-
texts "from models into [...] points of departure."[15] A second reading of the poems
mentioned above will therefore try to point out various strategies of "inscribing
deviating responses to British 'correlative works' [and other manifestations of
British culture,] into their own"[16] that so far have nearly gone unnoticed.

An Annotated Re-Reading of the Poetry

A second look at John Barr will be preceded by a closer scrutiny of his chosen
model. According to Robert Crawford,[17] Robert Burns's use of Scottish dialect for
literary purposes can be interpreted as a statement in favour of a concept of *Britishness*, affirming the new *political* entity of Great Britain after 1707 (Union of Parlia-
ments) without giving up one's own *cultural*, regionally defined *Scottish* identity.
Following Crawford, Burns's mixing of the English and the Scottish idiom led to the
creation of a third idiom, expressing true "linguistic Britishness," and was a highly
conscious act of defiance in order to "upset established categories," like 'high' vs.
'low' culture, 'big' vs. 'small' and 'centre' vs. 'periphery.' What have Barr's Otago
poems to do with Burns's provincial resistance to England's pressure for cultural
assimilation?

Although the poem "Rise Oot Your Bed" (1861)[18] is so unspecific in its setting
that it could theoretically be located in Scotland as well as in any other country of an
emigrated Scot, from Canada to Australia, there is some – rather circumstantial –

---

[14] For this and several related differentiations I am indebted to Armin Paul Frank and his long-
standing work on the trans-Atlantic reading culture in English, shared by Britain and (former
British) US-America, and to his concept of *"Writer Response Criticism."* See Frank, "Writing
Literary Independence: The Case of Cooper – the 'American Scott' and the un-Scottish American,"
Comparative Literature Studies 34.1 (1997): 41–70.

[15] Frank, "Writing Literary Independence," 47.

[16] Frank, "Writing Literary Independence," 47.

[17] Robert Crawford, *Devolving English Literature* (Oxford: Clarendon, 1992): 88–110.

[18] *The Anthology of New Zealand Poetry in English*, 508–09.

evidence that Barr is still in New Zealand and that this poem is a more cheerful rendering of the story already told in "Grub Away, Tug Away": the nagging wife in the second stanza of "Grub Away" pops up again; the exhausting everyday work of pioneer farmers – the main concern of "Grub Away" – is a subordinate topic in the fourth and fifth stanza of "Rise Oot"; inversely, a subordinate topic of "Grub Away" – the 'wee dram' as the pioneer's only occasional amusement (l. 8) – becomes the dominant theme of "Rise Oot Your Bed." Written as a dialogue with alternating stanzas given to a male and a female persona, the poem is a near-dramatic encounter between a Scottish housewife calling her (still intoxicated) husband to account after a night of heavy drinking. Although there is insufficient evidence to call Burns's famous mock-epic poem "Tam O'Shanter" (1791)[19] the immediate pre-text of Barr's poem, there are numerous references to it on the plot level, as well as lexical echoes. Thus, one may read Barr's text as a *continuation* of "Tam O'Shanter," much like the principle of the serial novel, and taking up at exactly the moment when Burns's narrative of the heroic Scottish farmer left off. While Burns concentrated on the nightly adventures of fearless Tam, riding back home from town after market-day, completely drunk yet outwitting the Scottish brownies and witches who take up his pursuit, Barr's poem can be summarized as 'the day after': Tam Maut, as he is now called, suffers a rude awakening from a grumpy wife who is endlessly blaming him for his bad habits and ignoring his allusions to the fearful night he has barely survived. While, in Burns's poem, Tam's narrow escape from the forces of hell was brought about by his faithful horse Maggie, in Barr's text, in a surprising and witty *tour de force*, the author himself enters the poem to rescue Tam from the fists of his increasingly menacing wife.

"There's Nae Place Like Otago Yet" (1861),[20] more serious in tone than "Rise Oot" and explicitly situated in New Zealand, shows that the settling-in of Barr's fictitious Scottish colonist in the Antipodes has made considerable progress since "Grub Away," where Scotland was still his unequivocal emotional 'home.' Pulling out the "toot roots" of New Zealand's bush and momentarily overwhelmed by the hardships of his pioneer existence, he had felt culturally uprooted and homesick; an emotional state linguistically illustrated by his clinging to the Scottish dialect as the only 'living root' remaining to link him to the far-away country of his ancestors. In "There's Nae Place," however, Otago takes on positive connotations precisely because everything is different from the old country. Associating Otago with social justice and the egalitarian values of the French Revolution as opposed to Scottish

---

[19] *The Poetry of Robert Burns*, ed. William Ernest Henley & Thomas F. Henderson (Edinburgh: T.C. & E.C. Jack, 1896): 278–87.

[20] *An Anthology of New Zealand Poetry in English*, 509–10.

poverty, oppression and feudalism, John Barr voices expectations Scottish emigrants shared with fellow-emigrants from other places in Britain, and which later New Zealand writers were to develop into the new myth of 'The Just City.'

In contrast to "Grub Away," the Scottish dialect is now primarily linked to the *negative* sphere of Old-World Scotland and dominates the first half of the poem, which deals with a past everybody is happy to have left behind – the idiom of the second half of the poem, dealing with "Otago" and representing the New World and the future, is *English*, as the more appropriate means for linguistic integration in a colonial melting-pot; yet this is clearly not the English with a capital E associated with the poetic diction of Pope or the elaborate style of Tennyson. Barr, rather, advocates a more demotic, sub-standard version of English (including curses, colloquial elisions and some faint relics of Old-World dialects) which is demonstratively shown to be acceptable as the language of a new poetry, thereby symbolizing the deviating social and cultural values of the new home.

Setting aside an undeniable tendency towards sentimentalism, one can view Barr's attitude towards his Scottish model as in some respects creative: The type of reference found in "Rise Oot" – an implicit "reference to a canonized text" – could be called a *perpetuation* of Burns's "Tam O'Shanter." "There's Nae Place," while it cannot be traced back to any immediate pre-text of Burns, belongs to another group of references relating to "various kinds of commentary originating in the source-culture,"[21] in other words: public, and often institutionalized *discourses* (including poetic-aesthetic, political and cultural-political discourses, such as those of nation-building and imperialism). Once again, Barr does not simply copy Burns's challenge of England's linguistic, poetic and cultural norms. This would have been impossible anyway, as the eighteenth-century Scottish struggle for cultural survival was too specific to be transplanted to the southern hemisphere. Although the main enemy is still the same, the allies confronting him have changed and start to dilute Burns's basic opposition: In the colony, it is not primarily a culture somewhere between *Scottish* and *English* but, rather, between a self-complacent British Establishment in the northern hemisphere and the disaffected, impoverished lower classes (including Scottish members alongside English and Irish) who emigrate to build a "fairer England [...] / 'Neath speckless skies of sunny blue."[22]

---

[21] Barbara Buchenau, *Zwischen Windschattenfahrt und Eigenständigkeit: Vergleichende Studien zum historischen Roman in den USA des frühen 19. Jahrhunderts* (doctoral dissertation, University of Göttingen: 1999): 3 (my tr.).

[22] Thomas Bracken, "The Canterbury Pilgrims," in *Lays of the Land of the Maoris and Moa* (London: Sampson Low et al., 1884): 117.

As the struggle between *European* centre and *colonial* periphery takes on an additional political dimension (shifting more and more towards 'Old World despotism and tyranny' vs. 'New World egalitarianism and liberty'), Barr starts to *modify* Burns' technique by *reversing* the connotations of the Scottish and the English idiom in the colonial context. At least in the Otago poem, his handling of Burns's stylistic devices can be called a productive adaptation, a technical advancement, paving the way for New Zealand's later collective identity as a more democratic, multicultural nation. Using different techniques in different poems, Barr himself is an example of a pioneer poet gradually settling in and, starting out as a mere missionary of the British muse, imperceptibly developing into a forerunner of a distinctive vernacular literary mode belonging to New Zealand.

Jessie Mackay's poem "The Charge at Parihaka" (1889) not only features explicit references to a canonized text but also the third (and so far undiscussed) type of literary reference relating her text to a particular well-established form in the sense of a specific literary sub-genre: parody. The judgment on Mackay as either derivative or creative will depend partly on how important the achievement of a colonial author is thought to be when strict adherence to an English pre-text is limited to formal characteristics, while the 'content' has been radically changed with a clearly *parodistic* intention. The poem

> mocks the excessive caution shown when in November 1881 large numbers of European troops marched on Parihaka to arrest Te Whiti and Tohu. They met no resistance. As Jessie Mackay observes in a note, "the campaign terminated without a scratch. The affair caused some real apprehension in the North Island and a good deal of burlesque sentiment in the South.[23]

One way to explain the substitution of the mock-heroic for the heroic mode of the pre-text seems to be the banality of this particular 'culture-clash' as well as the general over-reaction of North Island Pakeha during the landwars against the Maori of Southern Taranaki. Whereas England's soldiers unflinchingly sacrificed their lives for their country in a serious international conflict, New Zealand's Imperial regulars and settler militia had nothing to fear right from the start (l. 12). Using the rhetorical strategy of comic exaggeration, Mackay doubles the number of opponents engaged in the conflict from six hundred cavalry against an unspecified superior force (Tennyson) to twelve hundred foot-soldiers "marching" against a village of unarmed Maori – mostly women and children – and capturing three who offer no resistance. Whereas Tennyson's heroes stoically keep up the fight to the bitter end, Mackay's troops display very unheroic attitudes as they approach the end of their mission,

---

[23] Bill Manhire's un-paginated editor's note in *100 New Zealand Poems*, 1994.

when "honour to hunger yields" (l. 32) and the colonial "Volunteers" turn into a bunch of potato- and cattle- (or, rather, pig-) thieves. It is a poetic anecdote rendered from the clearly biased perspective of a South Islander, which can be interpreted as a remarkably early indication of new *regional identities within* the country, as well as a first attempt to put New Zealand on an international map of literature(s) in English.

On a second, more general level, Mackay's ironic treatment of traditional English values like 'military glory' and 'male bravery' can also be read as an attempt to establish a sense of colonial difference. Her concentration on an internal conflict can be likewise interpreted as a first sign of a withdrawal of political loyalties from the imperial 'centre.' Mackay's deliberate choice of a sacred text, written by the most highly respected Victorian poet, for satirical purposes may also indicate a critical attitude either towards Tennyson in particular or, more generally, towards the mixture of political and literary obligations he represented as Britain's poet laureate. More obviously than any other case so far discussed, Mackay's poem is an example of colonial *counter-writing*, illustrating how New Zealand poets gradually develop strategies to 'alienate' British literature, and – by inscribing deviant responses in their poems – create "bridgeheads"[24] for what will later develop into New Zealand's poetic tradition.

Even in Bracken's Jubilee-poem, which seems at first sight perfectly loyal towards the British Empire and the values it represented, a careful reading will detect several strategies of inscribing difference. Though much more subtle than Mackay's open counter-discourse, Bracken's poems reveal an unexpected sense of cultural independence. Paradoxically, he was a precursor of later literary nation-builders in New Zealand, *because* he was trying to remain as close as possible to his English pre-text, Pope's "Windsor Forest": choosing, consciously or not, a canonical text of the Augustan rather than the Romantic or Victorian period, he opted for a text written at a time when English nation-building was reaching its peak and pervaded every conceivable form of cultural commentary, including pamphlets, political and moral essays, newspapers, early forms of literary criticism, and contemporary poetry.[25]

Although both authors based their texts on the concept (rather: construct) of a national history and, accordingly, equipped them with a temporal structure, distinguishing a past with negative connotations from a positive present (including a brief glimpse of the future), there is a fundamental difference. Pope needed a negative

---

[24] Frank, "Writing Literary Independence," 47.

[25] Bärbel Czennia, "Nationale und kulturelle Identitätsbildung in Großbritannien, 1660–1750. Eine historische Verlaufsbeschreibung," in *Muster und Funktionen der Selbst- und Fremdwahrnehmung bei der Herausbildung 'nationaler' Sprachen und Literaturen (Emanzipationstopoi)*, ed. Fritz Paul & Christine Sander (Göttingen: Wallstein, 2000): 355–90.

past – presented, under the heading of "Peace and Plenty," as a constant succession of external and internal conflicts caused by ruthless political leaders – to justify the 'divine' rule of the Stuart Queen Anne and her controversial Peace of Utrecht (1713). Bracken adopted this differentiation, yet *adapted* it to New Zealand's needs by distinguishing a 'black' New Zealand past, presented as a time of violent conflict between savage tribes, from a 'white' present – subsumed under the heading of "Peace and Progress" – to justify British rule and the subsequent displacement of the indigenous population by British settlers.

Bracken, in his "Golden Jubilee," invents a white history for New Zealand, negating that of the Maori, whose prehistoric Polynesian ancestors had discovered uninhabited islands and settled them in the true sense of a *colonization* (Latin *colonus* 'farmer,' 'settler'), in contrast to the British latecomers' *colonialism*, aiming at the expropriation of New Zealand's first nation in favour of Britain. Insinuating that the first settlers of Aotearoa were "Dark navigators, fired with conquest's flame" (l. 89), an expression that more appropriately describes what white settlers practised from 1840 onwards (the word 'conquest' implying the establishment of permanent political rule and the subjugation of earlier inhabitants), Bracken makes the Maori look more British in their *attitudes* towards the country in order to weaken their morally superior claim to the land. At the same time, by focusing on New Zealand-born white settlers as "children of the soil" and using the same adjectives (such as "noble," "bold") for both ethnic groups, he makes the British look more Maori in *character*. In order to strengthen their foothold on the land, he literally 'indigenizes' them.

Often Bracken inscribes difference into his poem by *reinterpretation* and *modification* of seemingly subordinate elements on the microtextual level: An example of this is his treatment of the virgin nymphs populating Pope's Forests of Windsor. As in ancient mythology, Pope's nymphs – as soon as they put their virginity at risk by crossing the boundaries of the forest – share their Mediterranean sisters' tragic fate: Instead of being transformed into Greek or Roman rivers, they end up as English ones. Bracken, however – due to the concept of progress and the selfishness of the British immigrants – has not much forest left to settle nymphs. Instead, he passes the virgin-imagery on to a female personification of New Zealand as a whole whose behaviour towards male pursuers differs greatly from that of their European counterparts ancient or modern. While the English nymphs fled in desperation from the god Pan's sexual harassment (ll. 165–205) to save their innocence, the half-naked virgin called New Zealand, stirred from her slumbers by members of the British New Zealand Company, willingly (even cheerfully) offers up her virginity to them. This is clearly indicated by the sexual innuendo in the description of the first approach of "gallant Wakefield and his comrades" to the bay of (later) Wellington, anticipated by their "delighted and amazed" gazing from afar at New Zealand's appealing "breast" (ll. 30–31): "The virgin started as thy captain steer'd / His noble vessel through the restless Strait / That leads to wide Poneke's open gate" (ll. 40–42).

The justification for what at first sight looks like shockingly loose morals on the part of the New World Maid, who, instead of committing suicide, feels "New life and vigor" in her "joyous heart" (l. 45) after her defloration, is postponed to the end of Bracken's text. New Zealand knew well what was good for her, as the painful act was a natural precondition for her future maturity, symbolizing political independence: "The virgin now [ie, in 1890] to womanhood has grown; / Her strength developed she can stand alone" (l. 32).

Bracken also adopts central images which Pope had used to express the superiority of Great Britain in its fierce competition with European neighbours, but consciously *reverses* them to advertise a new centre of cultural and economic interest situated in another hemisphere, addressed as "Queen of Southern lands" (l. 10) and "ocean queen" (l. 100). While Pope boasts "Augusta's [ie, London's] glitt'ring Spires" and its "two fair Cities" (ie, Westminster and the City of London; ll. 377–79), Bracken surpasses him by claiming twice that number of urban centres for New Zealand: starting with the North Island, he first names the "Central City" (l. 55) of Wellington as an equivalent to London before praising "fair Auckland" (l. 75) for being "proud" of its own tradition (l. 95–96) and its unique scenery (ll. 97–99); he continues with the South Island, introducing Dunedin as "Edina [Edinburgh] of the South" (l. 109) and Christchurch as the equivalent of England's Oxford (l. 106).

Bracken's New Zealand, however, is not only a new centre of material values and that kind of "commerce" James Thomson had eagerly welcomed in his poem "Liberty" (1736).[26] Had Pope believed the Ancient Muses of the Fine Arts he had transplanted from Greek "Olympus" to English "Cooper's Hill" (near Windsor) would remain there for ever, he was seriously mistaken; "winging southward" (ll. 101–102) – ie, to the southern hemisphere as well as to New Zealand's South Island – they are already on their way to the "bright land [...] of sunny isles" (ll. 77–79).

It is high time they did, because it is their domain in particular which is still most in need of development: "Oh, for some master's brush, some poet's pen, / To sketch the bridge connecting Now and Then!" (ll. 51–52). And it goes without saying that, speaking from the imaginary perspective of later generations, destined to crown present-day *cultural* efforts with New Zealand's *political* independence, Bracken

---

[26] James Thomson, "Liberty: A Poem in Five Parts" (1736), in *The Complete Poetical Works of James Thomson*, ed. J. Logie Robertson (London: Oxford UP, 1961): 309–421; Pt. IV, l. 432–38, l. 910–21.

wanted to be numbered among its literary "builders" (ll. 141–42) who "firmly laid the keystone of a State" (l. 147). The concept of English or British nation-building – imported with a literary pre-text – has finally collapsed, and turned against itself, gradually releasing a different self-perception, more closely connected with the new environment.

Bracken's divergent response to Pope is also reflected in selective *omissions* of pre-textual elements which can be interpreted as deliberate *rejections*, presenting New Zealand as a country that has no room for ancient Gods (like Pope's Ceres, Flora, Pan and Pomona) nor for aristocratic rulers (addressed by Pope as "earthly gods," l. 230) or aristocratic poets with country-retreats (Pope's "God-like poets," l. 270). It is a place whose "happy homesteads" and "fruitful fields" (ll. 69–70) are run exclusively by earthly creatures, busily constructing a collective identity of their own.

WORKS CITED

Anderson, Benedict. *Imagined Communities: Reflections on the Origin and Spread of Nationalism* (London & New York: Verso, rev. & ext. ed. 1993).

Assmann, Aleida."This blessed plot, this earth, this realm, this England: Zur Entstehung des eng-lischen Nationalbewußtseins in der Tudor-Zeit," in *Nation und Literatur im Europa der Frühen Neuzeit; Akten des I. Internationalen Osnabrücker Kongresses zur Kulturgeschichte der Frühen Neuzeit*, ed. Klaus Garber (Tübingen: Max Niemeyer, 1989): 429–452.

Buchenau, Barbara. *Zwischen Windschattenfahrt und Eigenständigkeit: Vergleichende Studien zum historischen Roman in den USA des frühen 19. Jahrhunderts* (dissertation, University of Göt-tingen, 1999).

Barr, John of Craigilee (1861)."Grub Away, Tug Away"; "Rise Oot Your Bed"; "There's Nae Place Like Otago Yet," in *An Anthology of New Zealand Poetry in English*, ed. Jenny Bornholdt, Gregory O'Brien & Mark Williams (Auckland: Oxford UP, 1997): 508–10.

Bracken, Thomas (1884). "The Golden Jubilee [Sydney Exhibition, 1879]"; "The Canterbury Pilgrims," in *Lays of the Land of the Maori and Moa* (London: Sampson Low, Marston, Searle, & Rivington, 1884): 53–63; 117–18.

——. "Jubilee Day," in *Musings in Maoriland* (Dunedin, Wellington, Sydney: Arthur T. Keirle, 1890): 25–30.

Burns, Robert (1791). "Tam O' Shanter," in *The Poetry of Robert Burns*, ed. William Ernest Henley & Thomas F. Henderson (Edinburgh: T.C. & E.C. Jack, 1896): 278–87.

Crawford, Robert. *Devolving English Literature* (Oxford: Clarendon, 1992).

Curnow, Allen, ed. "Introduction" to *The Penguin Book of New Zealand Verse* (Harmondsworth: Penguin, 1960): 17–67.

Czennia, Bärbel. "Nation-building Down Under: Repräsentationen von Geschichte in der englisch-sprachigen Lyrik Neuseelands, 1890–1990," in *Fiktion und Geschichte in der anglo-amerika-*

nischen Literatur. Festschrift für Heinz-Joachim Müllenbrock zum 60. Geburtstag, ed. Rüdiger Ahrens & Fritz–Wilhelm Neumann (Heidelberg: Carl Winter, 1998): 479–514.

——. "Nationale und kulturelle Identitätsbildung in Großbritannien, 1660–1750: Eine historische Verlaufsbeschreibung," in *Muster und Funktionen der Selbst- und Fremdwahrnehmung bei der Herausbildung 'nationaler' Sprachen und Literaturen (Emanzipationstopoi)*, ed. Fritz Paul & Christine Sander (Göttingen: Wallstein, 2000): 355–90.

Evans, Patrick. *The Penguin History of New Zealand Literature* (Auckland: Penguin, 1990).

Frank, Armin Paul. "Writing Literary Independence: The Case of Cooper – the 'American Scott' and the un-Scottish American," *Comparative Literature Studies* 34.1 (1997): 41–70.

Giesen, Bernhard, ed. *Nationale und kulturelle Identität: Studien zur Entwicklung des kollektiven Bewußtseins in der Neuzeit* (Frankfurt am Main: Suhrkamp, 1991).

Jackson, MacDonald P. "Poetry: Beginnings to 1945," in *The Oxford History of New Zealand Literature in English*, ed. Terry Sturm (Auckland: Oxford UP): 335–84.

Hobsbawm, Eric J., & Terence Ranger, ed. *The Invention of Tradition* (Cambridge: Cambridge UP, 1983).

Mackay, Jessie. "The Charge at Parihaka," (1889), in *100 New Zealand Poems*, sel. Bill Manhire (1993; Auckland: Godwit, 1994): np (no. 11).

Pope, Alexander. "Windsor Forest" (1713), in *The Poems of Alexander Pope: A One-Volume Edition of the Twickenham Pope*, ed. John Butt (1963; London: Routledge, 1996): 195–210.

Thomson, James. "Liberty: A Poem in Five Parts" (1736), in *The Complete Poetical Works*, ed. J. Logie Robertson (1963; London: Oxford UP): 309–421.

❧

From Erewhon to Nowhere
A Leitmotif of New Zealand Poetry?

PETER H. MARSDEN

I N THE RECENTLY PUBLISHED *Oxford Companion to New Zealand Litera-ture*, the entry for Samuel Butler's novel *Erewhon* (1872) comments that while this satire is "generally regarded as ranking with Moore's *Utopia* and Swift's *Gulliver's Travels* as an ironic fiction of lasting importance [...], its significance as a major text of New Zealand literature has received little attention, apart from documentary interest in the opening section on sheep farming and exploration."[1] The classic of world literature may have a hitherto underrated importance within the more local context of national literature.

One of the principal aims of this essay is to explore that significance, particularly in terms of the traces left on both subsequent texts and intellectual history by the central conceit of the novel. I share the *Oxford Companion's* implicit assumption that status as a major text of New Zealand literature does not necessarily require the author to be a New Zealander, whether by birth or by acquired citizenship.

In respect of geographical location, Butler's narrator almost leans over backwards to avoid using the name New Zealand while enumerating countless recognizable features of the country, pertaining to distances, land use and economy.[2] This establishment of geographical coordinates via rather unsubtle hints does not over-tax the reader's imagination; indeed, it would be hard not to identify the terrain quite specifically as the Canterbury Plains at the foot of the Southern Alps. And the same might be said for the subsequent evocation of the way that region was colonized by sheep- and cattle-farmers (10).

---

[1] *The Oxford Companion to New Zealand Literature*, ed. Roger Robinson & Nelson Wattie (Auckland: Oxford UP New Zealand, 1998): 166. Entry by Roger Robinson.

[2] Samuel Butler, *Erewhon / Erewhon Revisited*, intro. Desmond McCarthy (1872 / 1901; Everyman's Library; London: Dent / New York: Dutton, 1932): 9–10. Further page references are in the main text.

Attitudinally, the phrasing (eg, "in a few years there was not an acre between the sea and the front ranges which was not taken up," 10) hovers somewhere between an unquestioning taking for granted of the process of conquest and possession and a light ironic tone. It is precisely in such uncertainties and indirections that the significance of the novel emerges. As Roger Robinson comments: "The downbeat humour has also become a national characteristic: 'Exploring is delightful to look forward to and back upon, but it is not comfortable at the time'."[3] He also evaluates the significance of the novel in the following more general terms:

> The narrative in these five chapters is of more than biographical interest, as the taut laconic lyricism of its descriptive passages, its counterpointing of local vernacular with European cultural allusion and its subverting of the rhapsodic by the pragmatic all established an imaginative literary relationship to the New Zealand landscape that has remained current.[4]

In its upgrading of Butler's novel, the *Oxford Companion* may well, in fact, be recurring to, and re-affirming, a much earlier judgement enunciated by Allen Curnow in his programmatic, seminal introduction to the *Penguin Book of New Zealand Verse*. There, Curnow classed Butler as

> a great Victorian who was neither a poet nor a New Zealander, [who] has left us a written record, with more than ordinary insight, of a kind of experience that is the primitive stuff of New Zealand mind.
> Samuel Butler arrived in Canterbury in January 1860. He stayed four years, a young sheep farmer in the fierce-fronted, scarce-trodden foothill ranges of the Southern Alps. [...] it was across the main divide of the Southern Alps that [he] located the country of his satiric fantasy, *Erewhon*.[5]

In the context, the somewhat eccentric zero-article usage: "New Zealand mind" seems to connote a peculiarly appropriate collectivity of consciousness.

The early sections of *Erewhon* certainly offer plenty of local colour in terms of flora and fauna, though the local colour often bears an uncanny resemblance to more distant locations and climes (39). On the linguistic level, local colour is transmitted or evoked for instance via the vocabulary of New Zealand sheep farming: *squatters* (in the antipodean sense of 'landowners') (10); *mob* (for StE 'flock') (11); *paddock* (in the general antipodean sense of 'any piece of land marked off by a fence or natural boundary') (11); *swag* (meaning 'blanket-wrapped roll or bundle of posses-

---

[3] Robinson & Wattie, ed. *Oxford Companion to New Zealand Literature*, 166. The passage quoted from *Erewhon* appears at the end of Chapter IV (27).

[4] Robinson & Wattie, ed. *Oxford Companion*, 166.

[5] *The Penguin Book of New Zealand Verse*, sel. & intro. Allen Curnow (Harmondsworth: Penguin, 1960): 23.

sions carried by an itinerant worker or traveller on foot') (28); *sheep-run* ('tract of land [often extensive] used for grazing sheep') (39).[6] These are all familiar "English" words, but words not used in England (or only used in particular dialects) in that sense. At once like and unlike, as G.D.H. Cole puts it in his characterization of *Erewhon* as "Butler's account of a strange people living in isolation 'over the range,' who were at once so like and so unlike the author's Victorian contemporaries."[7] This may be Butler's way of evoking the New Zealand conception of 'Home' as a place very much like the "mother country" but at the same time very far removed from it, a "home from home," as it were: 'This Other England.'[8] And that, I think, is what Curnow means when he says: "The first few chapters of that book are vivid and substantial New Zealand; and by spelling 'nowhere' backwards, Butler may have expressed more of the experience than he meant."[9]

At any rate, Curnow exemplifies the colonial cultural situation by referring to the narrator's dream about the organ (in Chapter IV, 26–27) somewhat incongruously placed in his master's wool-shed and apparently being played by none other than Handel – that archetypal English composer–musician:

> In Butler's dream vision in the Alps we get a sense of that violent and disabling oppugnancy between a Victorian sensibility and an antipodean situation, which so stultified the endeavours of colonial versifiers to set imagination at work in their new surroundings.[10]

Practising what he preaches, Curnow writes back to Butler, as it were, in his poem "On the Road to Erewhon."[11] Curnow starts off with an epigraph taken from Butler's own preface and goes on to incorporate a whole raft of quotations from the body of the novel, which he explicitly identifies both by italicizing them in the poem and by adding annotations. In an interesting profession of deliberate intertextuality, he remarks that he has "lifted" lines from Butler. The epigraph[12] runs:

---

[6] Definitions taken from *The New Zealand Pocket Oxford Dictionary*, ed. Tony Deverson (1994: Auckland, Oxford: Oxford UP New Zealand, 2nd ed. 1997) and from *The New Zealand Dictionary: Educational Edition*, ed. Elizabeth & Harry Orsman (Auckland: New House, 1994).

[7] *The Essential Samuel Butler*, sel. & intro. G.D.H. Cole (London: Jonathan Cape, 1950): 11 ("Introduction").

[8] See, *inter alia*, an article with this title by Terry Coleman, *The Guardian* (24 April 1977): 19.

[9] Curnow, *New Zealand Verse*, 23.

[10] Curnow, *New Zealand Verse*, 23. Cf Bill Manhire's gentle inveighing against "the Tennysonian warblings which once weighed upon the spirit of the land" in the "Introduction" to his *100 New Zealand Poems* (Auckland: Godwit, 1993): 2.

[11] Allen Curnow, *Selected Poems 1940–1989* (London & New York: Viking Penguin, 1990): 162–63. Originally in Curnow, *The Loop in Lone Kauri Road: Poems 1983–85* (Auckland: Auckland UP, 1986).

[12] Curnow, *Selected Poems*, 162.

The Author wishes it to be understood that Erewhon is pronounced *as a word of three syllables, all short – thus, Ĕ-rĕ-whŏn.*

Curnow, in other words, very consciously recuperates both the theme and the actual text of Butler's novel. The theme is also explored in his poems "You Will Know When You Get There," "Landfall in Unknown Seas,"[13] "House and Land," "The Un-historic Story" and "To Introduce the Landscape," but in "On the Road to Erewhon" the relation is at its most evident. It is probably significant that Curnow's title refers less to the place Erewhon – the destination – than to the way there, the process of travel and discovery. And this "road to Erewhon" has a dual meaning, alluding as it does to geographical location and symbolic significance:

> Once past the icefalls and the teeth of
> noon, already descending the pass,
> out of a cloud blackened by lightning,
> if mirrors can spell and maps don't lie,
> that's the Erewhon road, the ambush
>
> can't be far. [...]

> [...] Goat-tracks, lost writings.
> [...] ... If it were just one of those dreams
> where running gets you nowhere! This is
> the mirrored map, the Erewhon road,
> where you came from is where you're going [...][14]

In his own Note to the poem, Curnow remarks:

> The young Butler's four New Zealand years (1859–1863) were spent sheep-farming on his own high-country station between the headwaters of the Rakaia and Rangitata rivers, flowing east from the Southern Alps to the Pacific Ocean; he called his land Mesopotamia, after the 'between rivers' of antiquity, and the name has stuck, at least for the trifle of another century and a quarter.[15]

As, indeed, has the name "Erewhon." There are real-life sheep stations named after these two Butlerian designations, whose location is printed on common-or-garden maps[16] – not *literary*, but *literal* road and motoring maps of the country.

---

[13] David Eggleton's "Landfall in Unknown Seas Revisited," *Empty Orchestra* (Auckland: Auckland UP, 1995): 30–31, 'writes back' to Curnow's poem.

[14] Curnow, *Selected Poems*, 162–63.

[15] Curnow, *Selected Poems*, 202–203 (the Note is dated 1986, 1989). Cf. Robinson's *Oxford Companion* entry on Samuel Butler, whose "distinction in exploration history is commemorated in names in that area such as Mount Butler, the Butler Range and Butler's Saddle (from which he first looked across the Rakaia to see the Pass, as described in *Erewhon*, 1872)"; Robinson & Wattie, 82.

[16] Such as the *AA New Zealand Illustrated Atlas* (Auckland: Hodder Moa Beckett, 1995).

So Samuel Butler in a very real sense put Erewhon 'on the map' and as a result of that literary cartography, Erewhon (= Nowhere) is now, paradoxically enough, somewhere. It 'exists' because somebody has named it and is now at once part of a 'mental map'[17] and a point on the physical map: "if [...] maps don't lie..." There is a place on the map called (a version of) "nowhere" and it is *somewhere*. And it is a place to which a New Zealander like Curnow can very much relate:

> Anyone born and bred, as I was, in sight of the same sea and mountains [Timaru; 1911], enjoys privileged access to the region of Butler's opening chapters, drawn (as he tells us) from 'the Upper Rangitata district of the Canterbury Province (as it then was) of New Zealand'. [...] The terrifying statues guard the summit of the pass which Butler's narrator crosses, from the landscapes of reality, westward into the 'nowhere' of *Erewhon*.[18]

So much for the descriptive dimension of Butler's novel, his representation of the New Zealand landscape. I would now like to turn to more formal aspects. According to the *Oxford Companion*,

> the main New Zealand element is the basic metaphor of inversion, the Erewhonian equivalent of Swift's manipulations of scale. This provides not only a disturbingly unpredictable ironic device, but an imaginative version of antipodean colonial experience, at various times absurdist, black comic and near-tragic. The uneasy alliance between reversed English names and romanticised Maori ones, as with Higgs's eventual wife, Arowhena Nosnibor, is only the most obvious of several signs of disjunction.[19]

Examples of such reversed names are Yram, Nosnibor, Thims, Senoj, Ydgrun. The simple anagrammatic trick is emblematic of the way in which a simple kaleidoscopic reshuffling of constituents can make the familiar unfamiliar, analogously perhaps to mirror-writing ("if mirrors can spell").

Echoing Curnow, the *Oxford Companion* remarks that the title of Butler's novel "inverts 'Nowhere' and thus echoes the true meaning of 'Utopia,' following More and Swift in using a journey to an imaginary [and – one might add – distant] country to highlight and ridicule contemporary customs and deeper human shortcomings"[20] – in Butler's case to situate a critique of Victorian 'respectability' and hypocrisy. But the principle of inversion also operates on the level of beliefs, patterns of behaviour,

---

[17] The concept was coined by Peter Gould & Rodney White, *Mental Maps* (Harmondsworth: Penguin, 1974).

[18] Curnow, *Selected Poems*, 203.

[19] Robinson & Wattie, *Oxford Companion*, 167. Higgs is the narrator, who actually remains unnamed in *Erewhon* itself but whose name is revealed in Butler's sequel *Erewhon Revisited* (1901). Some meta-irony might be seen in the fact that the critic cited here is himself called Robinson.

[20] Robinson & Wattie, *Oxford Companion*, 166.

social structure and the like. In general, with regard to both the Utopian and the geographical frame, it is not just the name of the country that is back to front but – 'down under' – *everything* is back-to-front, upside-down, topsy-turvy. Take, for instance, the relative status of, and relative attitudes to, (ill) health and (im)morality in Erewhonian society. Such matters are treated as if they were no more than arbitrary conventions: "Illness of any sort was considered in Erewhon to be highly criminal and immoral; and [...] I was liable, even for catching cold, to be had up before the magistrates and imprisoned for a considerable period" (51). The corollary of this view of ill health is illustrated by the following passage:

> one of the leading merchants had sent me an invitation to repair to his house and to consider myself his guest for as long a time as I chose. 'He is a delightful man,' continued the interpreter, 'but has suffered terribly from' (here there came a long word which I could not quite catch, only it was much longer than kleptomania), 'and has but lately recovered from embezzling a large sum of money under singularly distressing circumstances.' (52)

Ever since Thomas More, 'Utopia' has meant both desirable paradise and unattainable ideal. Utopian literature:

> has a rich tradition in New Zealand, both in writing by New Zealanders and by others using a New Zealand setting. [...] New Zealand utopian literature is a living tradition that has now been established for over 150 years. It includes almost 150 adult titles and many more for young adult readers; and is being added to regularly.[21]

At the beginning of that tradition stands Butler's *Erewhon*. This national myth-making, this long-term process of projecting New Zealand as a distant and remote place, with little identity of its own apart from the borrowed glory of being 'This Other England,'[22] nevertheless providing the site for a distant and remote vision of the future – whether positive or negative, eu-topian or dys-topian – conceptualizes the country, as it conceptualizes its constituent landscapes. Mental maps arise out of mental landscapes, which, if we are to believe Simon Schama, are always constructs. In this process, the image or leitmotif of Erewhon / Nowhere is a central element.

A recent instance is a sort of concrete poem distributed in postcard form by the expatriate New Zealander Jason Lofts, resident in "the unlikely place of the Principality of Liechtenstein," who "has designed an alternative souvenir of his home country. [...] Lofts [...] literally took New Zealand apart and produced a 'poem' consisting of seven anagrams of the words New Zealand and has made it into a postcard." The result looks like this:

---

[21] Lyman Tower Sargent, in Robinson & Wattie, *Oxford Companion*, 555–56; entry on 'Utopian literature.'

[22] Cf. above, fn 8.

NEW ZEALAND
EZ A NEW LAND
NEW AND ZEAL
WEL AND ZANE
NZ NEED A LAW
Z, ELAN WANED
EZE AND LAWN
NZ: A WEE LAND[23]

In thus defamiliarizing the familiar, alienating the everyday reality of New Zealand by reshuffling its component parts – re-constructing, as it were, national identity – Lofts is availing himself of a device that was first instituted by Butler.[24]

Patrick Evans, quoting from *Erewhon* (18) a purplish passage in which the river is not the only thing that is rushing (nay, gushing), comments that:

> Many Victorian New Zealanders wrote in this way, in a language that fictionalised what was seen even before it was described. [Butler's] example [shows] so well how easily 'facts' could tumble into fiction and how vague the distinction between the two of them could be. The paradisean vision of the country was deep in the culture; and literature, that legal way of lying, was the logical end-point of the process set off by the pioneers' rosy pictures – literature totally detached from reality, like Julius Vogel's mad utopian fantasy *Anno Domini 2000* (1889), in which the Duchess of New Zealand ends up marrying the Emperor of the World.[25]

This is quite the opposite of the *Oxford Companion*'s reading of Butler's landscapes as down to earth in tone, "subverting [...] the rhapsodic by the pragmatic" and proving a seminal influence on the subsequent "imaginative literary relationship to the landscape." As far as the sheep-farming economy is concerned, Evans also writes of the many and various tributes paid in New Zealand literature to a "lost way of life" represented by growing up in the bush and the (often concomitant) attempts to "come to terms with a less innocent urban experience, symbolized by the advent of the frozen-meat trade in 1882," amounting to a myth that grew ever more popular from the end of the nineteenth century onwards – "the idea that institutionalized animal slaughter is New Zealand's own Fall from Eden[...]."[26] Simon Garrett has identified

---

[23] "Poetry in the Post," *New Zealand News UK* (4 December 1996): 1.

[24] Lofts in turn might well (consciously or not) be quoting Janet Frame, who has Godfrey, the protagonist of her novel *The Rainbirds*, muse in a sub-Joycean interior monologue: "No doubt my name is Dogrey Brainrid of Feelt Rived, Resonsand Bay, Dunndie, Ogoat, Shuto Sanlid, *Wen Lazeland*, Rotushen he-mis-phere, the Drowl"; Frame, *The Rainbirds* (1968), also published as *Yellow Flowers in the Antipodean Room* (New York: George Braziller, 1969): 161 (my emphasis).

[25] Evans, *Penguin History of New Zealand Literature*, 21.

[26] Evans, *Penguin History*, 61.

two major areas of thematic concern in New Zealand literature [as being] the 'man alone' theme, the individual versus society and all that is entailed in the idea that New Zealanders are shipwrecked outcasts; and the concern with the sort of society in which we live – Paradise or slaughterhouse, as Patrick Evans has succinctly stated the alternatives.[27]

The point about the 'man alone' theme (first explicitly formulated as the title of John Mulgan's classic 1939 novel) is also made by Robinson in his *Oxford Companion* entry on *Erewhon* (166), with the significant difference that he expressly attributes the establishment of the theme to *Butler*'s novel, *avant la lettre*.

The dichotomous theme of 'Paradise or slaughterhouse,' of the tension between eu- and dystopia, has been provocatively explored by David Eggleton in many poems, in particular "Life and Death in Pig State, 1978"; or the sarcastically entitled "Utopia," with its Curnow-echoing refrain "Utopia's further on up the road."[28] The whole notion of 'Erewhon' – the new word for a place that means a version of 'nowhere' as a new variant on the idea of Utopia – fits in very well with such dichotomies. It was picked up by Peter Bland, an English writer who spent the last forty years or so of his life commuting between Britain and New Zealand and who developed a correspondingly keen sense of dislocation and bifocal vision. Bland has a poem entitled "Erewhon Revisited" – *Erewhon Revisited* revisited, as it were – which starts:

> There's a new blue vacancy to the day. Once again
> the main street runs out of itself
> with dazzling clarity, its turn-of-the-century
> shop fronts peeled to the bone. [...]

and concludes:

> The light though – should you care to stroll in it
> and not rush blinking from door to door –
> imposes a brilliance no one lives up to, one
> even the town drunk (wearing a halo
> as he blunders into the sun) can't disturb.[29]

---

[27] Simon Garrett, "A Maori Place in New Zealand Writing: Recovery and Discovery in the Novels of Witi Ihimaera," in *A Sense of Place in the New Literatures in English*, ed. Peggy Nightingale (St Lucia: U of Queensland P, 1986): 121. The article by Evans referred to is "Paradise or Slaughterhouse: Some Aspects of New Zealand Proletarian Fiction," *Islands* 28 (1980): 71–85. Garrett goes on to say: "In discovering this tradition, Ihimaera, and indeed all Maori writers who start from the basis of a Maori cultural tradition and make the journey into a European literature, radically change the assumptions upon which these themes are built" (121–22):

[28] Both from David Eggleton, *South Pacific Sunrise* (Auckland: Penguin, 1986): 21–24 and 28–30, respectively.

[29] Peter Bland, *Paper Boats* (Dunedin: John McIndoe, 1991): 20.

In this latter-day Erewhon, the lost Utopia is still felt, but as "a brilliance no one lives up to." Elsewhere, like Curnow, Bland also uses a quotation from *Erewhon* as epigraph. In his case, he prefaces a section entitled "EMBARKATIONS 1991– 1996" with the following sentence from Butler's novel:

> *'I was in an inhabited country,*
> *but one which was as yet unknown.*'[30]

Ian Wedde tackles the subject of 'nowhereness' in the title poem – programmatically subtitled "The Art of Poetry" – of his collection *Driving Into the Storm*:

> All language is a place, all
> landscapes
>
> mean something.
> [...] we too
> have places we arrive at
> and sometimes we can't
> drive through.
> [...]
> If you've been everywhere
> this was worth waiting for. If you've been nowhere, this
> feels like everywhere, your free brochure
> 'How To Get Lost & Found In New Zealand'
> where you stop for lunch at a
> 'tavern' that plunks you into Europe
> till you get the bill. $8. *For two*! Where you
> travel through farmland, 'cattle
> ranches' and
> 'meadows' full of sheep.
> If you believe this
> you're really
> nowhere, the language sees to that
> whereas somewhere
> you're still driving
> into storms the mountains are about
> to hurl down upon the nowhere brochure
> imported trees and washbrick haciendas.[31]

---

[30] Peter Bland, *Selected Poems* (Manchester: Carcanet, 1998): 103 (his italics). See also Peter H. Marsden, "When Does an Immigrant Cease to Be an Immigrant?: Or: How do you define a New Zealand poet? The Case of Peter Bland," in *Being/s in Transit: Travelling ∗ Migration ∗ Dislocation*, ed. Liselotte Glage (Cross / Cultures 41 / ASNEL Papers 5; Amsterdam & Atlanta GA: Rodopi: 1999): 173–91.

Wedde also has an essay entitled *How to be Nowhere* – itself the title of a whole
book of poetics in prose form. This essay was originally commissioned to appear in
the catalogue for an exhibition with the Italian title *In Nessun Luogo* (*Erewnon*)
mounted at the Municipal Gallery of Ljubljana, Republic of Slovenia (June–July
1992). It is a sophisticated piece about art, as process rather than product, conveyed
via the metaphoric notion that it is better to travel than to arrive:

> nowhere is not a place you arrive at, it is a place you travel to. That is why representa-
> tion is the vehicle, because representation drives always toward lack, toward absence,
> toward desire. The traveller who knows all about nowhere knows this, and says so:
> 'You know it's nowhere because you're not there – because it's what you want!
> There's no mistaking it.' [...]
>
> In English, the name of the station where representation defers an arrival, is Ere-
> whon; in Italian, *In Nessun Luogo*.
>
> 'There you are!' cries the [fourth] traveller, panicking: 'I told you we were on the
> wrong track! *In Nessun Luogo* does not translate *Erewhon*! It would have to be *Ogoul
> Nussen!*'
>
> [...]
>
> 'Relax,' says the first traveller, the one with the answers, whose name we have
> already guessed is Samuel Butler. 'Enjoy the view. You might like to try looking across
> the surface of it, as if it were Holbein's 'Ambassadors'. *Then* you'd see something
> different! Look: the skeleton of a Tuatara!'
>
> 'What's different about that?' asks the semiotician, who doubts that representation
> can differ with its instruction.
>
> Whereupon Samuel Butler, speaking sometimes in Italian and sometimes in Eng-
> lish, explains that the Porirua Plaza, and a certain Piazza Grande, pass the vehicle of
> representation as though drawn by a shared history. Frame by frame, as the passengers
> look out the window and scan across the surface of this view, they see that the piazza
> and the plaza will not be still with themselves, will not be closed off, will not be
> arrived at; but instead, continuously substitute each other's signs, utter the other's loca-
> tion in terms of their own [...].
>
> [...] another layer of signage and of time has emerged – a Maori hei tiki, which
> seems to locate the plaza in New Zealand, where Samuel Butler discovered how to be
> nowhere.[32]

After 'nowhereness' experienced possibly as a neurosis akin to the legendary New
Zealand fear of falling off the edge of the world, we here have a very self-conscious

---

[31] Ian Wedde, *Driving Into the Storm: Selected Poems* (Auckland: Oxford UP, 1987): 99–101;
here 100. Note Wedde's self-conscious enclosing of cliché concepts such as "'meadow'" in
'scare quotes' – presumably to highlight their inauthenticity in the context.

[32] Ian Wedde, *How To Be Nowhere: Essays and Texts 1971–1994* (Wellington: Victoria UP,
1995): 293.

but at the same time very self-confident New Zealand poet taking the dilemma by the horns, as it were, and resolving to see nowhereness as not necessarily something to be taken at face value. It is revealing to discover the editors of a recent anthology of New Zealand poetry addressing the issue in a similarly upbeat manner:

> Paul Sharrad has suggested that we abandon the notion of the Pacific Basin as an emptiness surrounded by a fullness from which important things come. It is the scene of journeys, encounter, traffic and exchange. Extraordinarily, in 1995 the French, justifying continued nuclear testing, reiterated the colonial belief that the Pacific was a void, 'a desert.'[33]

Sharrad's actual words were: "The [Pacific] Basin is full, and it is defined not only by its rim but by its contents" [34]– ie, what we are looking at is not so much a supposed *terra nullius* as a putative *mare nullius*. Particularly for their inhabitants, the Antipodes are increasingly definable not as nowhere but as an *anagram* of 'nowhere'; as Erewhon. And *that* might just be an identity.

WORKS CITED

AA New Zealand Illustrated Atlas (Auckland: Hodder Moa Beckett, 1995).

Anon. "Poetry in the Post," *New Zealand News UK* (4 December 1996): 1.

Bland, Peter. *Paper Boats* (Dunedin: John McIndoe, 1991).

——. *Selected Poems* (Manchester: Carcanet, 1998).

Bornholdt, Jenny, Gregory O'Brien & Mark Williams, ed. *An Anthology of New Zealand Poetry in English* (Auckland: Oxford UP New Zealand, 1997).

Butler, Samuel. *Erewhon / Erewhon Revisited*, intro. Desmond McCarthy (1872 / 1901; Everyman's Library; London: Dent, New York: Dutton, 1932).

——. *The Essential Samuel Butler*, sel. &. ed. G.D.H. Cole (London: Jonathan Cape, 1950). [Includes Butler, *The Note-Books* and *The Way of All Flesh*.]

Coleman, Terry. "This Other England," *Guardian* (24 April 1997): 19.

Curnow, Allen. *The Loop in Lone Kauri Road: Poems 1983–85* (Auckland: Auckland UP, 1986).

——. *Selected Poems 1940–1989* (London & New York: Viking Penguin, 1990).

——, sel. & intro. *The Penguin Book of New Zealand Verse* (Harmondsworth: Penguin, 1960).

Czennia, Bärbel. "Nation-Building Down Under: Repräsentationen von Geschichte in der englischsprachigen Lyrik Neuseelands, 1890–1990," in *Fiktion und Geschichte in der anglo-amerikanischen Literatur: Festschrift für Heinz-Joachim Müllenbrock zum 60. Geburtstag*, ed. Rüdiger Ahrens & Fritz–Wilhelm Neumann (Heidelberg: Carl Winter, 1998): 481–515.

---

[33] *An Anthology of New Zealand Poetry in English*, ed. Jenny Bornholdt, Gregory O'Brien & Mark Williams (Auckland: Oxford UP, 19–): xxxiii ("Introduction").

[34] Paul Sharrad, "Imagining the Pacific," *Meanjin* 49.4 (Summer 1990): 605; quoted by Bornholdt et al., ed. *Anthology of New Zealand Poetry in English*, xxxiii (16).

Deverson, Tony, ed. *The New Zealand Pocket Oxford Dictionary: Second Edition* (1994; Auckland: Oxford UP New Zealand, 1997).

Eggleton, David. *Empty Orchestra* (Auckland: Auckland UP, 1995).

——. *South Pacific Sunrise* (Auckland: Penguin, 1986).

Evans, Patrick. "Paradise or Slaughterhouse: Some Aspects of New Zealand Proletarian Fiction," *Islands* 28 (1980): 71–85.

——. *The Penguin History of New Zealand Literature* (Auckland: Penguin, 1990).

Frame, Janet. *Yellow Flowers in the Antipodean Room* (1968; New York: George Braziller, 1969).

Garrett, Simon. "A Maori Place in New Zealand Writing: Recovery and Discovery in the Novels of Witi Ihimaera," in *A Sense of Place in the New Literatures in English*, ed. Peggy Nightingale (St Lucia: U of Queensland P, 1986): 112–22.

Gould, Peter, & Rodney White. *Mental Maps* (Harmondsworth: Penguin, 1974).

Manhire, Bill, sel. *100 New Zealand Poems* (Auckland: Godwit, 1993).

Marsden, Peter H. "When Does an Immigrant Cease to Be an Immigrant?: Or: How do you define a New Zealand poet? The case of Peter Bland," in *Being/s in Transit: Travelling * Migration * Dislocation*, ed. Liselotte Glage (Cross / Cultures 41 / ASNEL Papers 5; Amsterdam & Atlanta GA: Rodopi, 1999): 173–91.

Mulgan, John. *Man Alone* (1939; Auckland: Penguin, 1990).

Orsman, Elizabeth, & Harry, ed. *The New Zealand Dictionary: Educational Edition* (Auckland: New House, 1994).

Robinson, Roger, & Nelson Wattie, ed. *The Oxford Companion to New Zealand Literature* (Auckland: Oxford UP New Zealand, 1998).

Sharrad, Paul. "Imagining the Pacific," *Meanjin* 49.4 (1990): 605.

Wedde, Ian. *Driving Into the Storm: Selected Poems* (Auckland: Oxford UP, 1987).

——. *How To Be Nowhere: Essays and Texts 1971–1994* (Wellington: Victoria UP, 1995).

❧

A Sovereign Mission
Maori Maids, Maidens, and Mothers

REINA WHAITIRI

K
O TAKITIMU TE WAKA, KO WAIAU TE AWA, ko Aoraki te maunga, ko Ruapuke te motu, ko Kaitahu me Waitaha nga iwi, ko Ngatimamoe te hapu, ko Whaitiri te whanau. This is my genealogy, my whakapapa. My people lay claim to Te Waipounamu, the South Island of New Zealand, and Rakiura, known as Stewart Island. My position on the subjects discussed in the following paper is that of a Maori woman born in 1943 to a Maori father and a Pakeha mother.

The content of my essay covers that period of intense colonization from the mid-nineteenth century to the early 1970s. The period will be framed and commented on by the prose and poetry of Maori women who were coerced into playing a particular role in the colonization process. The missionaries played their part by setting up boarding schools especially for Maori, where pupils were taught the skills and attitudes necessary to service the homes of the European settlers. Maori women also became the mothers of several generations of illegitimate children with Pakeha fathers. Many Maori women did not become wives and were often rejected by their own men as well in favour of Pakeha women who brought status and economic advancement.

First Contact

In 1642, the Dutchman Abel Tasman was the first recorded Pakeha to visit our shores. This visit decided the Pakeha/Dutch name for our country, Niuew Zeeland. There may also have been sail-bys by Spanish, French and English explorers, but their visits were not recorded. The indigenous people of New Zealand, the Maori, call this place Aotearoa – the land of the long white cloud.

The missionaries first arrived in Aotearoa in the early nineteenth century. Samuel Marsden, a founding missionary, was active in Maori communities as early as 1807. Due mainly to the efforts of these missionaries, Maori readily and eagerly adopted the Christian god, and quickly learnt to read and write. They could see the practical benefits of the new tools, and high numbers learnt English; there were more literate Maori in those early days than Pakeha. A letter written in 1833 by a Maori called Titore to King William and published in *Maori is my Name* demonstrates his grasp of the language and his business acumen. Titore understood the usefulness of gifting items to those you wish to do business with and his generosity illustrates the usual custom amongst Maori of the time:

> Here am I, the friend of Captain Saddler. The ship is full, and is now about to sail. I have heard that you aforetime were the captain of a ship. Do you therefore examine the spars whether they are good or whether they are bad. Should you and the French quarrel here are some trees for your battle-ships. I have put on board the *Buffalo* a greenstone battleaxe and two garments. These are all the things the New Zealanders possess. If I had anything better I would give it to Captain Saddler for you. This is all mine to you. Mine.[1]

The Treaty of Waitangi

On 6 February 1840 the Treaty of Waitangi was signed by two parties: the Crown and Maori. The Treaty entitled representatives of the Crown to have governorship over their own Pakeha people, and ensured sovereignty for Maori, over themselves, their land, and their resources. Since that time, the struggle has been to have this document recognized. Until 1975 Pakeha endeavoured to forget the Treaty which was conveniently buried in some dusty government archive. But over the last 20 years, mainly due to the efforts of so-called radical Maori, the Treaty has come to be acknowledged by the Government as the founding document of Aotearoa. This recognition and acceptance has greatly strengthened the political and moral position of Maori. It is also true to say, however, that there are still many Pakeha who refuse to accept the Treaty as a valid and legally binding document. They see no advantages in acknowledging the rightful owners of Aotearoa.

In Patricia Grace's novel *Baby No Eyes*, we are reminded why the Treaty was signed by Maori, why it was deemed necessary:

> Because of this Treaty there would be a government. There would be laws. Maori would stop their warring and their grievances against each other. Pakeha would stop stealing land. Maori and Pakeha would not fight each other any more. All trouble would end and there would be peace forever. These were the promises made by Pakeha but alas that's not the way things turned out. However, after the Treaty was signed there was more stealing of land, much worse than before. Pakeha were now arriving in shiploads from across the sea and they had been promised land by the settler govern-

---

[1] John Caselberg, *Maori is My Name* (Dunedin: John McIndoe, 1975): 29.

ment. And although some Maori had sold land, or given land, they wanted all the land.
So, now this new government became the biggest stealer of land. Making more and
more laws to steal by. Once they had the land they sold it to the new settlers and made
themselves wealthy.[2]

Without land, Maori have no place on which to stand, to call our own, without land
there is nowhere for our *pito* (afterbirth) to be buried when we are born, nowhere for
our *mate* (dead) to be buried when we die. Without land we have no rights, no
resting place, no speaking rights, no place to declare our connections, with other
tribes, with our past, our future. We are like dust in the wind.

Assimilation

By 1870 the colonization of New Zealand by the British was well under way. With
ever-growing numbers of immigrants and with superior weapons, the colonizers had
all but vanquished the Maori whose numbers were beginning to decrease rapidly.
The drastic population decline amongst Maori was due to the introduction of guns,
loss of land, displacement, imprisonment, poor health, being cut off from traditional
food sources and subsequent starvation. The population decline convinced Pakeha
that Maori would not survive as a race. Indeed, so drastically had the Maori population declined, that by the turn of the century Pakeha commentators believed that all
that could be done was to "smooth the pillow of a dying race."[3] Deliberate racist
policies based on social Darwinism[4] were implemented to assimilate Maori into the
general Pakeha population. I think Maori were meant to be grateful for these efforts.
History, however, has proved that the assimilation policy was doomed to failure.

Since 1970, Maori women, many hundreds of whom are solo mothers, have
risen to the challenge, and today the birth rate of Maori and Pacific Islanders far
exceeds that of Pakeha. With the majority of the Polynesian population under 21
years of age, the associated societal problems related to this phenomenon has triggered major reforms within Maoridom and the wider society, not all of which are
successful or beneficial to those most affected. In the 1980s, the economic restruc-
turing of New Zealand allowed market forces to determine the shape and well-being

---

[2] Patricia Grace, *Baby No Eyes* (Auckland: Penguin, 1998): 113.

[3] Dr Isaac Featherston was Superintendent of the Province in Wellington in 1856. In a public
speech he is quoted saying: "A barbarous and coloured race must inevitably die out by mere
contact with the civilised white; our business, therefore, and all we can do is to smooth the pillow
of the dying Maori race"; Ed. Harry Orsman & Jan Moore, *Heinemann Dictionary of New Zealand
Quotations* (Auckland: Heinemann, 1988): entry F00042.

[4] Social Darwinism states that when two cultures come together the more technically advanced
absorbs the less advanced.

of our society. This has led to the breakdown of the established social structure and to increased poverty, and has put enormous pressure on families. Those most affected by these policies are Maori and Pacific Islanders in the areas of unemployment, health, education, and housing, all made worse since the 1980s. The prisons in Aotearoa are full of Maori men and growing numbers of male Pacific Islanders. This is yet another situation that leaves women raising children alone.

As part of the assimilation policy, missionaries, mainly Church of England, Catholic, Wesleyan, and more recently, the Mormon Church, set about building boarding schools for Maori. A total of eight were built, which is a high number for such a small population base. Rural and small-town Maori communities were encouraged to send their children away to be educated. The achievements of the first generation of Maori leaders who emerged from these boarding schools near the turn of the century enriched the mainstream of New Zealand life and letters. Four of those early leaders were awarded knighthoods: James Carroll, Apirana Ngata, Maui Pomare and Peter Buck. The awarding of knighthoods suited the Pakeha at the time, as they needed Maori leaders and scholars to demonstrate the results and benefits of assimilation. It should be noted that it was only men who received the kind of education which enabled them to achieve academically.

Later the focus of these same Maori boarding schools changed. Maori girls were trained to be domestics, good wives and mothers, whereas Maori boys were trained as woodworkers, metalworkers, and menial labourers. There was strong religious indoctrination, inculcating English and Christian morals, values and attitudes. Later still, Maori girls were trained in typing, with the highest achievers becoming nurses and teachers. In *Baby No Eyes*, Patricia Grace describes a scene in a high school where it is decided who will take which subjects:

> Chop went the principal's arm at our first assembly when we'd entered High School in the third form. I don't know if it would've made any difference if I'd been on the left-hand side of the outstretched arm instead of the right.
>
> 'This half move to the right,' he'd said, looking along his long arm, 'and this half to the left.' Wave wave, went his arm this way, Wave wave, went his arm that way, until we had all moved further enough one way or the other to form a good aisle down the middle of the hall, ready for his next announcement.
>
> 'Those to the right will do cooking, sewing, metalwork and arts, and will go to the Manual Block to be given classes, stationery lists and timetables,' he said. 'Those to the left will do shorthand, typing, woodwork and tech drawing and will remain here.' Teachers prowled up and down the aisle to make sure there were no defections. (88)

Boarding schools did prepare Maori for life in the Pakeha world though, as Makareta says in Patricia Grace's *Cousins*: "Boarding school had prepared me for some of it."[5]

What boarding school had not prepared her for was the racism she would encounter. If a Maori topped an academic course she must automatically be a princess; ordinary Maori did not achieve high academic results:

> Boarding school hadn't prepared me for that. I seemed to be always set apart, people stood off from me. It was rumoured that I was a princess. 'And because you're Maori and you're top of the class. It's hard for them to understand that, a Maori being top of the class, that's why they have to make you a princess.' (204)

Why was there a change of focus from when the schools were first set up? Was it believed that Maori were better with their hands than their minds? Those Maori men who were awarded knighthoods disprove this hypothesis. Whatever the rationale, the racist attitudes set our academic growth and development back twenty or thirty years.

Intermarriage

Other, more obvious forms of racism operated in New Zealand. Following is an extract from Noel Hilliard's novel *Maori Woman* (1974). Hilliard, although Pakeha, was married to a Maori woman and wrote against racism as it operated in Aotearoa. In the novel, Paul shows his mother a photo of Netta, the woman he is going to marry:

> 'Is she a full Maori?'
> A full Maori. Hah! he thought, thank God I'd made up my mind to enjoy this. Isn't there just one teeny weeny drop of white blood – white blood, what next? – to make this girl just that much more acceptable? Can I offer her that small concession, to fasten on and magnify? She was thinking now of how this could be explained to friends of the family, and relatives in distant parts where the proper order of things was understood and respected rather more than here: she has the blood of the early church fathers in her veins, at least! Or some other bewhiskered befeathered nincompoop. She was pleading: Give me some loophole, give me some chance to conceal my failure, leave a few shreds of my self-respect intact – you are cruel but at least you might do that for your mother!
> He hardened. 'Yes, full Maori,' he said, and heard with satisfaction there was no hesitancy in his voice now. Full or not, he didn't know; had never asked. [...]
> 'Some of the half-castes look just like the full ones, you know.' [...] 'There's nothing half or quarter or any other caste about her,' he said. How could she get around

---

[5] Patricia Grace, *Cousins* (Auckland: Penguin, 1992): 204.

that? Bring in the whalers of long ago, perhaps – how one of them might have sneaked into Netta's family and planted his seed and sneaked out again, a lot of that used to go on.[6]

There was, and still is to some extent, a horror of intermarriage between Maori and Pakeha. In Patricia Grace's first novel, *Mutuwhenua* (1978), the grandmother refuses to go to her granddaughter's wedding because marrying a Pakeha will dilute the *whanau* blood. And in Mihipeka's *The Early Years* her *kuia* warns against allowing Pakeha men to get too close.[7]

There were other reasons for warning young Maori maidens to keep away from Pakeha men. Many Maori women lost their land because of their relationships with Pakeha whom they had married under Maori custom. Thinking the marriage was binding, the women never dreamed they had to protect their land, that it would be stolen from under them. Mihipeka recalls what her *kuia* said:

> She used to tell me stories about Pakeha men coming to our country in the early days. They would ask for a Maori girl for a wife. They would dangle a gift, or the family would see an advantage of the girl having a Pakeha husband. The family would hand over the daughter. The couple would be united according to laws of the Maori, which was law to us, believing this was for always. The daughter would live as a real wife. Poor naive Maori girl, she would believe in her husband and then he would take off. Leave her and the children. She was just a Maori. He didn't have to have any responsibility. (96)

Even well-bred, aristocratic men took advantage of their station and the generosity of Maori, stealing land without compunction and with no consideration for the long-term effects of their greed:

> My father came from a very aristocratic line on his Pakeha side. His grandfather was Sir William Fitzherbert. He was in the Upper House in London. That does not mean my grandfather, my Kuia's husband, was a gentleman. No. He was a first-class thief, pretending to love my Kuia and at the same time he used his knowledge and position to steal her land. After he had taken all the best land, Kuia only had thirty acres of swampland left. (96)

In many cases, this method of colonization enabled Pakeha to steal hundreds, in some cases thousands, of acres of Maori land. Often, the men abandoned the women and children of the union, leaving the women without male protection and without their birthright, the land. This practice also cut Maori women off from their traditional *whanau* (extended families) and *iwi* (tribes). Maori hospitality was ruthlessly exploited by greedy and immoral colonizers who believed they could make more of

---

[6] Noel Hilliard, *Maori Woman* (London: Robert Hale, 1974): 216–17.

[7] Mihi Edwards, *Mihipeka: Early Years* (Auckland: Penguin, 1990): 96.

the land than the rightful Maori owners. Pakeha farmers were often driven to distraction by Maori who sometimes had neighbouring land but didn't work it, content to simply leave the land as it was, unable or unwilling to see the point of clearing it, running sheep or cattle on it, exploiting it. Retaining the land, caring for it, ensuring that it remains intact for future generations, is all important.

Postcolonialism

If the prefix post-, as in postcolonial, defines something that is past or over, its use does not apply to Maori. The effects of colonization are always devastating and continue into, and long past, the so-called postcolonial period. An Aboriginal woman was heard to say at a recent conference where the term 'postcolonial' was being bandied about: "*Post* colonial! – Did I miss something?"

For the colonized people of the world, including those of us who live in the South Pacific, colonization remains a fact of life. While the more brutal and destructive elements of colonialism may be obscured or glossed over by successive governments, for the people whose sovereignty has been usurped, colonialism is very much alive. Postcolonialism is not a reality and never can be. There is absolutely nothing 'post-' about our situation. Unless all indigenous people are eliminated or successfully colonized – that is, to the point where they no longer remember or accept as true their history and experiences under colonialism – there can never be a 'postcolonial' state.

While there are some Pacific nations such as Samoa, Tonga, Fiji, Vanuatu and Papua New Guinea that have managed to retain or regain their political independence, most have not. America, Indonesia, France, Australia, Chile, and New Zealand still control many Pacific Island nations. The indigenous people of Australia and New Zealand have no sovereign power. When the previous New Zealand Prime Minister Jim Bolger was asked why Maori were not represented at a Pacific Forum, he replied: "Maori are not a sovereign nation."

The term 'postcolonialism' suggests that the business of colonizing is over, complete, a *fait accompli*. By looking at the literature of some of New Zealand's most successful writers, who also happen to be Maori, it is clear that most Maori do not consider themselves in a state of postcolonialism. Rather, we see our future stretching out before us, beyond our lifetime, and beyond our children's lifetime, as a continual struggle to regain the legal sovereignty we never surrendered. Our sovereignty was taken from us by stealth, by trickery, and by force, and to this very day Pakeha still want to deny us the right to exercise it. We are not so naive as to believe that we will ever be able to return to a true sovereign state, but we firmly believe that an enormous debt is owed to us, and an apology. To be treated like second-class citizens in the country we call ours will no longer be tolerated. While Maori are in a minority, we have never surrendered our sovereign power – even though the shiploads and, more lately, planeloads of immigrants, once from Europe and now from Asia, continue to pour into the country and outnumber us many times over.

Most Pakeha New Zealanders would never consider themselves colonizers; indeed, most like to think that they and Maori together are New Zealanders. I believe Maori make a clear distinction between New Zealanders and Maori. We claim a unique position in our country. As Maori we are the *tangata whenua*, we are the original, indigenous people of Aotearoa and, perhaps most importantly, we are one of the two parties that signed the Treaty of Waitangi. All those who came to our shores after the late eighteenth century are Pakeha and are considered by us as colonizers and as part of the colonizing government.

Wahine Toa/Warrior Women

While the missionaries had some success in christianizing and domesticating Maori women between the late nineteenth and early twentieth centuries, since the 1970s there have been some dramatic and radical transformations. Maori women have clambered out of the kitchen, debunked the promiscuous dusky-maiden stereotype, denied the earth-mother label, and pushed themselves to the forefront of some of the most important and radical changes Aotearoa has ever seen. Maori women have, over the last twenty-five years especially, made serious and sometimes controversial changes to education, law, politics, art, social sciences, conservation, religion, science and sport. In the last national elections, for example, Maori women gained four of the twelve seats won by Maori. All of these areas have been influenced to a larger or lesser degree by Maori women in a way never foreseen by those early Pakeha missionaries and colonizers who had less ambitious plans for 'our Maori maidens.'[8]

The Kohanga Reo (total-immersion Maori-language nests) movement was started by Maori women who recognized the precarious state of *te reo* (Maori language) and began setting up pre-school groups where those grandmothers who still spoke Maori as their first language cared for the children and where only Maori was spoken. These *kohanga reo* sprang up all over the country, and it was not long before schools at the next level were needed for the graduates of the *kohanga*. Hence the Kura Kaupapa Maori schools were started. Now, there is a growing need for

---

[8] Pakeha liked to make statements about the healthy state of race relations in Aotearoa, often referring to Maori by using the possessive 'our.'

secondary schools to be set up to accommodate graduates from the *kura*. The hope is that this system will save the language and contribute to its development. Already, there is a whole generation of young Maori who are bilingual, Maori in their thinking and fiercely proud to be Maori. While most Maori today can claim Pakeha blood, more and more are unashamedly Maori first, Pakeha second. This is a far cry from the situation described in *Baby No Eyes*, where the five-year-old Riripeti is literally killed by school.

Each day Riripeti goes to school, she is humiliated and punished for speaking Maori, for not understanding English. The teacher's intolerance is sufficient to silence the child forever:

> 'Do I have to shake that language out of you, do I do I?' the teacher would say, shaking and shaking her. Then Riripeti would be smacked and sent to stand in the bad place. She did mimi there sometimes. Sometimes she sicked there, then cleaned it all up with a cloth and bucket. (34)

Riripeti's cousins learn to play the game, they learn to second-guess the teacher and come up with the correct things to say; but Riripeti cannot. She simply becomes more and more miserable and withdrawn. The old people never learn what kills Riripeti, because the other children keep it a secret. They understand how important school is to their old people and they try their best to learn and to succeed, for they can see that is what their old people want for them. They are too ashamed to tell what is happening to Riripeti; and so she dies.

Language

One of the first things a colonizing power must do is teach those being colonized their language; a people cannot be controlled unless they understand you. And then there are the issues of domination, not only in a military, political, spiritual, educational and social sense, but linguistically also. Of course, the colonizer could always learn the language of the colonized, but somehow one's authority does not have the same effect, the same authority, in the language of those you are trying to control. In the early days of contact, it was necessary for Pakeha to learn Maori. The early missionaries needed to reach the hearts and minds of their newly found flock; traders needed to communicate with Maori for timber, fresh food, fish, and water, and they needed information about tides, sand bars, channels, and weather patterns. The language used in these cases was, of necessity, Maori. But once Pakeha had 'dug in' and accepted they had come to stay, English was quickly established as the dominant language.

Much has been written about our loss of language, and the shock-waves resulting from that loss travel down through time to touch even the youngest members of
the present generation. But it is in Patricia Grace's novel *Baby No Eyes* that we hear
and see just how truly devastating that policy was. The revelation is one of the most
moving descriptions I have read and supports what Mihipeka has written in her non-
fiction. When the colonizers decided to set up schools for Maori children the main
object of the exercise was to expunge *te reo*; they wanted everyone speaking English. There may have been altruistic reasons for forcing Maori to speak English on
one level, but on the ground and in the classroom, it was one of the cruellest and
most damaging policies of the colonizing government.[9]

But in Grace's earlier novel *Potiki*,[10] one solution at least is offered. Roimata, the
archetypal mother, chooses to keep her son Manu home from school because he
seems to be falling between the cracks. He cannot understand the Pakeha stories, he
finds the hissing language, English, unpleasant and difficult to comprehend. At
home he will be educated by his whole *whanau*. This reveals just how far Maori
have come in terms of taking over the education of their children. It seems to be one
solution for Maori families who, for too long, allowed their children go to Pakeha
schools, and indeed insisted that they do so, with the view that they would succeed
in the future. That the children are damaged, even to death, as in *Baby No Eyes*, still
does not get through to some Maori families who send their children off to schools
in the belief that they are being prepared for a successful adult life. Too often this is
not the case. Of course, in New Zealand, we have a policy which demands that every
child attend school until they are fifteen, but now parents can teach their children at
home or send them to a range of alternative schools. The Kura Kaupapa Maori
schools are one such alternative, and they are flourishing all over the country. This
has been a long time coming, for Maori especially. We are now aware that all
schools are not appropriate for all children, especially Maori children.

But there are more subtle ways in which the Maori language was subverted
linguistically and 'christianized.' Take the word *maa*, for example. This is the word
everyone today translates as 'white'; it actually means 'clean.' The true word for
'white' in Maori is *tea* as in Ao*tea*roa. It is not difficult to see why missionaries, who
first wrote Maori down, considered 'white' and 'clean' as being next to godliness,
and brown and dirty as unholy. The worry is that this missionized, sanitized whiten-
ing of the language has been adopted by native speakers of *te reo*. My mokopuna
now use *maa* for white.

---

[9] Grace, *Baby No Eyes*, 31.
[10] Patricia Grace, *Potiki* (Auckland: Penguin, 1986).

New Zealand English is at an interesting stage of development at the moment, as there are more and more Maori words being incorporated into the language. The lexicographer Harry Orsman has recently completed a massive dictionary of New Zealand English and predicts that Maori words and usage will only continue to increase, changing English forever as it is spoken and used in Aotearoa. There is also a Maori Language Commission which is charged with developing *te reo*. Where once transliterations were acceptable for words such as *motoka* for 'car,' *huka* for 'sugar' and *hoiho* for 'horse,' the Commission creates new Maori words, drawing on the wealth and richness of *te reo* of our *tipuna* and shunning all transliterations.

Maori Women and the Colonizing Process

With the advent of colonialism, women were forced, or taught, to play a subservient role to men. The first Pakeha to arrive on our shores came with their Victorian attitudes, values and beliefs. Whatever the previous system may have been in Aotearoa concerning the social status of men and women, Maori soon adopted the Pakeha way. Victorian attitudes dictated that men were dominant in the family. Men worked, women stayed at home and cared for the children and the husband, women did not have the vote, women were not encouraged to be academics, women were educated and trained to be domestics, cleaners, mothers, wives; certainly not to be leaders. And whatever the attitude towards Pakeha women, Maori women were treated even more unfairly because of the racist attitudes prevalent in Aotearoa at the time. In his novels *Maori Girl* (1960) and *Maori Woman* (1974), Noel Hilliard demonstrates very clearly the racist and insulting attitudes Pakeha men had, and still have to some extent, toward Maori women.

In *Maori Girl*, Netta is asked by her drunken boyfriend, Nick, to put on the dress and shoes she wore on their first date. No matter that the dress is a summer dress and white shoes don't suit the winter weather. She puts these things on to please him. But then we find out what Nick is really thinking:

> That's the trouble with these Maori sheilas, of course – no idea of taste. Can't blame them. I suppose you got to be brought up to that kind of thing. But Christ! what a fool it makes a man feel. They haven't a clue how to dress. It's less than a hundred years since they were running around in grass skirts, eating each other. And I'm stuck with her for the night. Every bastard in town'll stare at her and think she's mad, and me, too, for being so hard up as to get around with anyone in a get-up like it. 'Well, it's my own fault. I ought to know better.' (150)

The position of Maori women today is not much better than that demonstrated above; in fact, the situation has deteriorated. For many years now, Maori women have had to struggle against the attitudes not only of Pakeha men but of Maori men

as well who preferred to marry Pakeha women. Of course, Maori men had relationships with Maori women and fathered children with them, but they married Pakeha
women. Perhaps they believed that by marrying a Pakeha they would be accepted
into Pakeha society, gaining credit and credibility. Maori men turned their backs on
their own, and Maori women have had to endure the humiliation and degradation of
this rejection. This is not to say that Maori women did not deliberately choose
Pakeha husbands for similar reasons, as Mihi Edwards recounts:

> My husband had an eighth Maori blood running through his veins, but he is a Pakeha.
> He looks and behaves like one. There is no room in his heart for anything Maori.
>   I was quite happy, suited my plans for the future. I didn't want my children to be
> Maori in any way, to be treated like I was as a child, made to feel ashamed of being
> born with a brown skin. I had three children – my daughter and two sons. They were
> not born white like my husband, but no matter, they had me to protect them. They were
> my babies. They were beautiful and I loved them dearly.[11]

Nonetheless, the practice left many hundreds of women raising children alone, without the support of the fathers of their children or their traditional *whanau*. This is
having, and will continue to have, a dramatic and terrible effect on Maori and,
indeed, New Zealand society as a whole. This phenomenon is a direct result of the
colonization and displacement that has taken place over two hundred years.

Once, Maori women were the acknowledged bearers of future generations and
held high status. Women of child-bearing age were protected from harm by a system
which ensured their safety above all others. They were never exposed to warrior
parties which came onto the *marae*; they were hidden from view when *manuhiri*
came visiting. It was the older women who had, and still have, the responsibility of
welcoming *manuhiri* on to a *marae*, it is the older women who stand to *waiata* the
speakers at public occasions. This system ensured that young women were out of
harm's way, thus protecting the future of the tribe.

Sovereignty

We have been struggling to stand upright again after being put down, deprived,
exploited, ripped off, and weakened by illness, poverty, and loss of land and sovereignty. However, we have been quietly and steadily strengthening our position,
educating ourselves, gathering our forces, preparing our young, our documentation,
and we have been winning land and resource claims in court.

---

[11]   Mihi Edwards, *Mihipeka: Early Years*, 164.

This is a poem by a young Maori woman. The poet Jacq Carter is a rising talent, and although she looks Pakeha – she has blue, blue eyes, blond hair and very European features – her heart and soul are Maori, as are her pain and her anger:

Aroha

I gave to you a rock
from which you built a wall
then you stood there at the top
making me feel small

I gave to you a seed
from which you grew a tree
then you told me all its fruit
did not belong to me

kss kss aue ha

I took you to a mountain
you did not want to climb
instead you tunnelled deep inside
for treasures that were mine

I led you to the ocean
and taught you about the tides
now I go down to the shore
and all the fish have died

kss kss aue ha

I told you all my stories
you wrote down every word
now I find my stories
are no longer to be heard

I carved a piece of greenstone
and hung it round your neck
then you made a thousand more
only yours were made of plastic

kss kss aue ha

I gave birth to a daughter
a child for you and me
but you did all the parenting
so she wouldn't turn out like me

So I signed your piece of paper
some kind of guarantee
that while you would watch over them
these things belonged to me

kss kss aue ha

I gave to you kawanatanga
the right to govern me
but I didn't give you mana
because there's mana in being me

I embrace my own uniqueness
my rangatirangtanga too
I will have the rights that you have
without having to be like you

kss kss aue ha

And one day I will walk again
the lands you stole from me
only this time I'll be standing tall
and Papatuanuku will be free

WORKS CITED

Carter, Jacq. "Aroha" (unpublished).

Caselberg, John. *Maori is My Name* (Dunedin: John McIndoe, 1975).

Edwards, Mihi. *Mihipeka: Early Years* (Auckland: Penguin, 1990).

Grace, Patricia. *Baby No Eyes* (Auckland: Penguin, 1998).

——. *Cousins* (Auckland: Penguin, 1992).

——. *Mutuwhenua* (Auckland: Longman Paul, 1978).

——. *Potiki* (Auckland: Penguin, 1986).

Hilliard, Noel. *Maori Girl* (London: Heinemann, 1960).

——. *Maori Woman* (London: Robert Hale, 1974).

Orsman, Harry W., ed. *The Dictionary of New Zealand English* (Auckland: Oxford UP, 1997).

——, & Jan Moore, ed. *Heinemann Dictionary of New Zealand Quotations* (Auckland: Heinemann, 1988).

❧

The Sky-Piercers, Lions and Aitu
Missions and 'Traditions'
in Albert Wendt's Vision of a New Pacific

JEAN–PIERRE DURIX

T HE REV. JOHN WILLIAMS of the London Missionary Society brought the first missionaries to Samoa from the Cook and Society Islands in 1830. The missionaries' authority was accepted almost immediately because their arrival was considered by some Samoans as the fulfilment of a prophecy foretelling that chief Malietoa would gain power from heaven.[1] The missionaries soon became welcome accessories in the different chiefs' struggle for control of Samoa. According to Malama Meleisea, a major Samoan historian,

> The distribution of Polynesian missionary teachers among the various chiefs who asked for them was eventually organised by the English missionaries who established themselves in Samoa in 1836. But some chiefs, having failed to obtain one of the missionaries between 1830 and 1832, sent requests to their family connections in Tonga for Wesleyan teachers [...]. Thus, sectarian rivalry was introduced by way of competition between the chiefs for access to the new religion which they now saw as enduring, a new mana leading to rapid acceptance of Christianity as a result.[2]

The struggle between chiefs continued throughout the 1840s and 1850s when foreigners started to settle around Apia, an area which provided reasonable anchorage and was not very densely populated.

---

[1] In *Lagalaga: A Short History of Western Samoa* (Suva, Fiji: U of the South Pacific, 1987), Malama Meleisea retells a Samoan legend about the goddess Nafanua who was given a major part in sharing out the government of Samoa between different chiefs: "When Malietoa Fitisemanu arrived at Falealupo to ask for his share of the government, Nafanua apologized that the 'head' of the government had been given to Leulumoega and only a 'tail' was left. Nafanua urged Malietoa to accept it and to wait for a 'head' to come from the heavens [...] Malietoa Vainu'upo [his successor] [...] accepted the arrival of John Williams as the fulfilment of nafanua's prophecy (57–58). See also Malama Meleisea, *Change and Adaptations in Western Samoa* (n.p. 1992): 20.

[2] Meleisea, *Change and Adaptations in Western Samoa*, 20–21.

As happened elsewhere, the settlers' occupation of land was not initially under-stood by the Samoans, which resulted in land alienation, since customary laws governing land tenure did not include the possibility of the land being permanently given away to somebody outside the *aiga* or extended family to which it belonged. German planters set up coconut plantations in the late 1860s and early 1870s.[3] The British, who wished to include Samoa as part of the British Empire, had appointed a consul. The Americans had growing interests in the harbour of Pago Pago. The different foreign powers present in Samoa wished to have a single Samoan author-ity to negotiate with. The Samoans also had a similar desire to keep the various settlers from overseas under control. Thus the system of having the archipelago ruled by various rival chiefs gradually gave way to a centralized system more in conformity with European practices.

With the signing of the Berlin Act of 1889 the USA took Eastern Samoa (Tutu-ila and the Manu'a group) and the Germans gained authority over the western islands, while Britain withdrew in exchange for German concessions in the Solo-mon Islands and Tonga. In 1914, New Zealand troops occupied Western Samoa, which was given to them as a mandate by the League of Nations after the defeat of Germany. They became the new colonial rulers until independence was granted to Western Samoa in 1962.

The Samoan writer Albert Wendt[4] is the best-known literary figure in the South Pacific, where he has had a major influence on the development of the arts through the organization of literary and artistic events as well as the encouragement and publication of works by Pacific writers.

Although some anthropologists such as Jean Guiart[5] claim that Wendt's novels can serve as a perfect introduction to Samoan society, Wendt does not pretend that his creative work can replace that of a scientist trained in ethnology or sociology. Reacting against the idyllic visions of his region vehicled by many European travel-lers, he refuses to reduce the diversity of the South Pacific to a few clichés such as

---

[3] "It was during this period [1869–72] that Theodor Weber, the local Godeffroy agent and manager, acquired the valuable estates at Vaitele in Faleata district close to Apia. Weber trans-formed the commercial economy of Samoa by concentrating on coconut planting, and he pioneered the practice of exporting dried copra rather than locally extracted coconut oil"; M. Meleisea, *The Making of Modern Samoa* (Suva, Fiji, Institute of Pacific Studies of the U of the South Pacific, 1987): 35.

[4] See Jean–Pierre Durix, "Albert Wendt: The Attempt 'to Snare the Void and Give it Word'," *International Literature in English: Essays on the Major Writers*, ed. Robert Ross (New York: Garland 1991): 63–73.

[5] A specialist in South Pacific cultures who was director of the laboratory of ethnology at the Musée de l'Homme in Paris until he retired.

that of the South Seas Eden or the fashionable notion of the 'Pacific Way' used by some local entrepreneurs to exploit a romantic, tourist-oriented image. What knowledge he does claim concerning the region is of a basically poetic nature. In his 1976 essay "Towards a New Oceania," he prefers to use the term "Oceania" for this homeland of the heart, this new "Hawaiki":[6]

> So vast, so fabulously varied a scatter of islands, nations, cultures, mythologies and myths, so dazzling a creature, Oceania deserves more than an attempt at mundane fact; only the imagination in free flight can hope [...] to grasp some of her shape, plumage, and pain.[7]

Wendt has brushed aside any attempt to recover the 'traditional' culture of his land, which, to him, is largely a colonial fabrication. Similarly, he repudiates the validity of the town vs. village opposition in terms of culture. He fully acknowledges the perverse use made of such binary distinctions by demagogues who take the pretext of searching for cultural purity in order to serve their own private interests.

Albert Wendt's essay "Towards a New Oceania" witnesses to his maturity as a postcolonial writer and thinker who is fully conscious of the rhetorical and ideological oversimplifications associated with some of the exponents of negritude or the search for unadulterated roots in a pure precolonial past. Though he rejects the term 'hybridity' – perhaps because it implicitly echoes racial categories such as '*afakasi*' (half-caste) which are so familiar in his native Samoa – Wendt has no respect for 'purity' or 'authenticity.' He does not believe in a simple return to unproblematical past origins, though he stresses the importance of imaginary rootedness.

Though the Christian religions loom large in Albert Wendt's works, no doubt because they are, strictly speaking, central to Samoan culture, missionaries – in the sense of foreign missionaries evangelizing a non-Christian territory – play a relatively minor part in his novels or stories. This may be due to the fact that, in Samoa, Christianity has long been nativized and is no longer perceived as foreign. The various denominations present (Congregational,[8] Roman Catholic, Methodist, Mormon, and others) have become an integral part of community life. Unsurprisingly, references to missionary influence are more abundant in Wendt's early works, in

---

[6] The name of the mythic land where Polynesian peoples claim they originate.

[7] Albert Wendt, "Towards a New Oceania" (originally published in *Mana* 1.1 [1976]), in *Readings in Pacific Literature*, ed. Paul Sharrad (Wollongong: New Literatures Research Centre 1993) A: 9.

[8] "The congregational Church was different from some other non-conformist churches because it preferred decision concerning church government to be made by the congregation rather than by bishops or ministers"; Meleisea, *Lagalaga: A Short History of Western Samoa*, 55.

which the re-creation of 'traditional' Samoan society is an essential task.[9] However, Wendt's attitude towards missionaries cannot be simply considered as oppositional; unlike some earlier African postcolonial writers who blamed the missionaries for most of the ills that affected colonial societies, Wendt has a more measured judgement. He is fully conversant with the theories of Césaire and Fanon and has a thorough knowledge of Lamming, Achebe, Ngugi et al. Yet he avoids pointing out the missionaries or the colonists as scapegoats for all the ills of contemporary Samoan society. He keeps clear of any oversimplified polarized interpretation of the history of colonization.

Instead of adopting a division between the universe of native people and that of outsiders, he stresses his multiple ancestry in his poem "Inside us the Dead."[10] His approach stresses his belief in the importance of genealogy, in the notion of the individual as a link in an historical chain whose vagaries he acknowledges. Perhaps following the example of Césaire and Senghor, Wendt retraces his diverse roots, starting with his Polynesian ancestors, going on to the missionaries and his German beachcomber ancestor, then moving on to the "maternal myth."

The missionaries, who are called the "sky piercers," rank immediately second after the Polynesian navigators. This denomination is a free translation of the term *papalagi* (literally 'sky bursters') which Samoans apply to anybody of European origin. For the old Samoans, the visible world was believed to be self-enclosed and surrounded by nine heavens. Unable to understand where the missionaries might have come from, the Samoans deduced that they were supernatural beings who had managed to break through the sky.[11]

In "Inside us the Dead," these missionaries, linked with fire and iron, wield the cross as they would a fateful weapon. They appear as predators who break the shells of resistance of the local people and search about for their souls as do collectors of coconuts in breaking the fruit open for the milk inside. The new religion emasculates the local men, who are taught that one of the worst sins is the sin of the flesh. Abuse of alcohol comes second in this hierarchy of insults to the new Christian God.

In the poem, Wendt evokes the missionaries' well-known practice of distributing beads, nails, axes and lengths of material in exchange for the people's conversion to the new religion. Where Wendt's evocation may be idiosyncratic is in his insistence

---

[9] See, in particular, his novel *Leaves of the Banyan Tree* (Auckland: Longman Paul, 1979) and his collection of poetry entitled *Inside us the Dead* (Auckland: Longman Paul, 1976).

[10] Initially published in *Landfall* 95 (September 1965); repr. in *Inside us the Dead*, 7–14.

[11] Meleisea, *Change and Adaptations in Western Samoa*, 20.

on images of self-contained spherical enclosures:[12] the missionaries break "from the sun's yoke through / the turtle-shell of sky."[13] The reader is reminded of other circular shapes which are at variance with common custom. An example can be found in *Sons for the Return Home*, Wendt's first published novel: the protagonist, a young Samoan man raised in New Zealand, goes back to Samoa with his parents and, one day, accidentally discovers his grandfather's grave in the centre of a circular palm grove which contrasts with the normal alignment of such trees favoured by the local people. Intrigued by his relatives' guarded references to his grandfather's "love of the darkness," the protagonist is reduced to imagining his grandfather as "an eccentric loner who treasured solitude," a figure with whom he can easily identify. The unusual arrangement of palms leads the hero to remark that "the grave gave the circle of palms a feeling of completion."[14]

Wendt's imaginary world frequently contains these types of circular shapes, which might be related to the Samoan belief that the individual's physical appearance is surrounded by his invisible *mana* (supernatural power). Here, one may relate these to the position of the individual in a social structure where the individual has traditionally little existence as such and counts essentially as part of a structure of family and lineage relationships. Images of circles frequently penetrated by intruders may well refer to this paradox of a situation in which the individual treasures individual integrity and solitude, but where his desire for this is regularly challenged by the demands of community or the violation of imposed foreign structures.

In "Inside us the Dead," the arrival of the outsiders is thus experienced as a sort of violation which leads to the unmanning of the local populations, who have to resort to secret practices in order to preserve their old customs:

> My father's
>
> gods who had found voice
>
> in wood, lizard, and bird,
>
>
>
> slid
>
> into the dark like sleek eels
>
> into sanctuary of bleeding coral. (9)

---

[12] See, on this theme, Carole Durix, "Networks and Itineraries in Albert Wendt's Poetry," in *Echos du Commonwealth* 8 (1982) [a special issue on Albert Wendt]: 27–37. This essay is also available online at the following address: http://www.u-bourgogne.fr/ITL/echo_w1.htlm

[13] *Inside us the Dead*, 8.

[14] *Sons for the Return Home* (Auckland: Longman Paul, 1973): 186, 185.

Here, Wendt evokes the way in which Samoan families each had their own particular gods, who might assume the form of an animal (an owl[15] or flying fox, for example). These gods did not disappear but simply remained in a part of their memories kept secret from the missionaries.

In the works of Albert Wendt, the eel recurs as a subversive image from the past. It plays a major part in an episode of *Leaves of the Banyan Tree* (1979) when Pepesa, the rebellious son of a successful traditional chief become a businessman and capitalist, hears Toasa, the village *tuua* (senior orator), an old man revered for his knowledge of ancient customs and stories and the last "sacred sanction,"[16] tell about the original gods: Tane, the father of humankind, was in love with a very beautiful girl called Sina, without knowing that she was his granddaughter. In order to win her, Tane turns into an eel whom Sina feeds as a pet in a pool where she bathes every day. When Tane reverts to the form of a good-looking man, she takes him as a husband. Such cases of incest are frequent in mythological tales. What matters here is that Wendt should use the eel as a subversive motif related to the old religion. Such deceptions abound in his works, generally in the form of rebellion against the hypocrisies of established power.

In *Leaves of the Banyan Tree*, the old gods are presented as a refuge from the pressure and corruption of the new elites, who, with the utmost cynicism, use their traditional authority as chiefs to further their financial prosperity. Tauilopepe, the father of the rebellious hero Pepesa, does not hesitate to preach in church the new gospel of "god, money and success," while committing adultery with his rival's wife Moa. He takes advantage of the situation to obtain credit from Malo, Moa's husband, then destroys Malo by having him and his *aiga* banished from the village.

Pepesa sees through his father's hypocrisy and turns into a rebel who attacks the symbols of power on the island: he robs his father's store, an image of ruthless materialism, and sets fire to the Protestant hall which represents the collusion of church and capital. At his trial, Pepesa behaves as a perfect, popular hero who breaks all the conventions of decency, braves authority and speaks aloud the truths that most people dare not express because of the repressive power of society. In his defence, he weaves a wonderful story full of humour and despair, the sort of act that

---

[15] The owl is the particular god in the author's family. This appears in *Sons for the Return Home*, in which the protagonist, who falls in love with a Pakeha student in New Zealand, remembers "his father telling him that their family god in the 'days of darkness' (as he called the time before the missionaries came to Samoa) was the owl" (94).

[16] Wendt, *Leaves of the Banyan Tree*, 114. Further page references are in the main text.

appeals to the audience, eager for excitement and bravery.[17] Following a pattern frequent in Wendt's fiction, Pepesa, the iconoclast, endangers his safety and his life for the sake of denouncing false values. Possibly modelled on the tricksters of traditional Samoan tales, Pepesa also owes a lot to French existentialism.[18]

Pepesa's rebellion leads him to transgress against the most sacred principles of morality in the smug 'Bible-ridden' Samoa which appears in Wendt's works. In a society that treasures the virginity of its daughters until they reach the age when they can marry, the favourite activity of such tricksters is to 'corrupt' as many young females as possible. Besides being a man's proof of virility in a rather macho society, physical love-making also plays the part of "soothing a man's ache," the only way for male characters to admit that their physical and emotional balance depends on their female partners.

In different novels, Albert Wendt's protagonists retell (or invent) ancient Samoan or Maori myths (or sometimes a mixture of the two).[19] Yet, far from being the result of mere anthropological curiosity, the mythic episodes mentioned generally have to do with rebellious heroes who break taboos.

Addressing his judge, Pepesa "[puts] on a good show like in the movies" and declares that his name is that of "the Sapepe hero who challenged all the gods and won" (199), no doubt revenge for the fate that befell the unlucky Sisyphus. Pepesa condemns the collusion of judicial and religious power represented by "the Black Dress," his humorous way of referring to the judge. "The Black Dress" seems as scandalized by Pepesa's profession of atheism as by his crime. When the judge reminds Pepesa that there is only one God and asks him whether he knows who the missionaries were, Pepesa answers: " ' They break through the skies of our world and bring guns and the new religion and the new God and drive my gods into the bush and mountains where they live today' " (200). This is meant to scandalize those Samoans whom the protagonist of *Sons for the Return Home* describes as having a blind literal belief in everything they read in the Bible.[20]

Although, on the surface, Wendt's fictional Samoa is wholly immersed in Christianity, at a deeper level the landscape is composed of separate zones which correspond to a hidden spiritual geography. In Wendt's fiction, Samoa is divided up into

---

[17] This episode may also be read as an ironical way of thematizing one type of relationship between writer and reader, that of the trickster-narrator who uses all the recipes in his cookbook to titillate and amuse his audience.

[18] In his university days, the author was an avid reader of Albert Camus's *The Plague* and *The Myth of Sisyphus.*

[19] The author readily admits that he made up many of the myths told by the characters, much to the confusion of the reader eager to take the fictional text as a scientific document.

[20] See *Sons for the Return Home,* 184.

coastal areas, which were occupied and developed by the missionaries and colonists, and forests and mountains of the interior, where the ancient gods still survive. Yet such a simple dichotomy does not mean that rebels against the Christian gods can simply seek refuge in the interior and recover their lost heritage. The link with the old beliefs has been almost severed and one can only hanker after the relics of this lost civilization. The ancient faith is like some kind of archaeological remnant which no one can teach any longer but which may be the source of a dreaming reconstruction by people eager for an escape from the stifling conformity of today's society. The deep forest of the interior, which is supposed to be the refuge of the old gods forced into retreat by the missionaries, serves as a refuge for some characters in times of crisis. In "Daughter of the Mango Season," the female protagonist has her own favourite tree (the Tahitian chestnut) which "heal[s] her hurt":

> she had heard Filivai, the Satoa taulasea [bush doctor], say that certain trees, in pre-Christian times, had been the home of aitu [ghost, spirit] and atua [god] [...] Her ifi tree had an aitu, she came to believe after hours of relaxing in its green healing.[21]

Yet, when she tries to bring these *aitu* back to life, she can only think of forms inspired by English romantic poets, Walt Disney creations, or the gods of the Greek or Celtic traditions. The modern Samoan imagination is also fashioned by all the influences of world literature and the cinema. Yet this is not perceived as a failure, for, "in her search for her tree's aitu, she had explored and groped her way towards the wisdom of her imagination, to a faith that lay beyond logic and belief."[22]

There is a difference between those like Tauilopepe in *Leaves of the Banyan Tree*, for whom "the past had no real meaning" (63), and Toasa, who remembers the time when he and Tauilopepe's father, challenging the recommendations of "missionaries and traders [who] nailed us to the seashore" (66), set off for the mountains in the interior. When they reached the top of the range, they found two old brown conch shells on a rock platform. When Toasa proceeded to pick up one conch and put his lips to it to blow it, Tauilopepe's father tore it out of his grasp and put it gently back on the platform. "In many villages [conch shells] were symbols of the gods, the voices of a certain god" (68). Toasa and Tauilopepe agree to keep this adventure secret and refer to what they had met up there in sacred code, saying there were "lions and aitu." A similar scene, though in a different context, appears in the poem "Conch Shell,"[23] where the speaker's daughter picks up one such shell from the bookshelf and asks her father to blow it:

---

[21] In *The Birth and Death of the Miracle Man* (Harmondsworth: Viking, 1986): 146.

[22] Wendt, *The Birth and Death of the Miracle Man*, 147.

[23] First published in *Landfall* 96 (December 1970): 338.

> I curl myself where fear
>
> falls club-footed on shattered memory:
>
> to give this curled shell its voice
>
> is to reconstruct in my frail house
>
> a pantheon of gods it won't
>
> be able to contain. I tell her
>
> I don't know how to blow it.

The same sacred fear seizes the narrator, who shudders when his wife eventually blows it, sending him back

> to the palm grove deserted, the sinnet
>
> thread dangling headless in the Void,
>
> and I drown in the dreaming
>
> of a priest without hands.[24]

The modern Samoan can no longer unproblematically resurrect the past culture, however much he would like to. He feels awed, unworthy and powerless when it comes to reviving the old *atua*.

In regard to tradition, Wendt's characters fall into two categories: those who live only in the present, without any concern for their community's history, and who use the power that the Christian church can give them, resorting to bastardized forms of tradition whenever these will serve their material interests; and those for whom the past counts, however much this may raise questions concerning the way people live in the present. Tauilopepe in *Leaves of the Banyan Tree* will have nothing to do with the taboo that applies to certain places or the respect of the sacredness of the bush. All he cares for is increasing his wealth, even if this means using his *aiga* as a little-paid workforce. Unlike him, Toasa treasures history and ancient traditions.

Most positive heroes in Wendt's works are on Toasa's side. They value life as a continuum in which human beings are only one component in a system of interdependent forces. In this sense, materialistic capitalism is viewed as a doctrine that separates human beings from their past and their community. The simple effort made by some heroes to become acquainted with ancient customs appears to be a redeeming force, even though they remain relatively powerless to bring them back to life.

---

[24] Wendt, *Inside us the Dead*, 32, 33.

Pepe's bold recitation of the phrase Toasa has taught him continues to ring as a brave challenge despite its relative irrelevance to most people at present:

> My name is Pepe Tauilopepe, descendant of the House of Sapepe, Heir to the Estate of the Dead, future protector of the Living, Guardian of the Unborn [...] Our duty is to uphold what the Dead bequeathed to us to guard and bequeath to the Unborn when we join the Dead. (72–73)

In the world of the novel, though, such beliefs are threatened and may not survive the disappearance of old Toasa.

Wendt's modern protagonists no longer believe in the God revered by the Christian pastors and Samoan society in general. Yet they cannot seek refuge in an alternative system of belief which the disappearance of the old customs has rendered inaccessible. The closest they can get to making sense of their world is through an exploration of this absurd situation with the help of existentialist philosophies which they sometimes see prefigured in ancient Polynesian stories. Toasa's retelling of the myth of origins bears a resemblance to the importance of the absurd in existentialist philosophy. According to Toasa,

> In the beginning there was only the Void [...] Different colours formed in the Void. These colours turned into solid matter, combined and formed the world. The gods then covered the world's nakedness with creepers. After centuries of light and darkness the creepers rotted and turned into maggots. Out of these maggots emerged Man, who, on his death and the falling of the dark, turned into maggots again. (73)

This forces men to face a world in which man was not created in God's image and cannot hope for eternal bliss in heaven. Here the rearrangement of ancient beliefs and Camus' myth of Sisyphus coalesce. Yet the absolute despair that might emerge from such hopelessness does not seem to destroy the characters, who express fascination for barren landscapes such as lava fields[25] and deserts. The darkness has a strange attraction for those who contemplate the soothing effect of a bare reality devoid of the vain trappings of 'civilization.'

One might be tempted to interpret Wendt's works in terms of a simple manichaean opposition between an imported religion used cynically by power-seekers and the desperate oppositional quest of young rebels. Yet some degree of compassion and respect frequently emerges from situations in which the sons seem to be most eager to overthrow the new complacent order. They rant and rave about the apparently irresistible attraction of the *Book* which most people interpret literally. The protagonist in *Sons for the Return Home* deplores this religious fundamentalism, yet admits that

---

[25] See, in particular, the poem "Lava Field and Road, Savaii," in *Inside us the Dead*, 23.

> The Book was also poetry, and [the Samoan people's] main source of reading [...] At
> night and on Sunday he spent pleasant hours listening to the old people reading aloud
> from Psalms and Ecclesiastes, his favourite books in the Bible. They made the words,
> the music, and the images come alive like beautiful birds hovering in a clear windless
> sky, or multicoloured fish darting in and out of the fabulous corals of the reefs.[26]

What originally came as a foreign form of belief is now a structuring element in
contemporary Samoan culture. The eponymous heroine of Wendt's novel *Ola* (1991)
takes the initiative of accompanying her ageing father on a pilgrimage to the Holy
Land whose ancient geography he seems to know better than that of his own island.
Though she herself has grown to doubt the value of Christianity, she respects her
father's generation enough to ignore her doubts for a few weeks and fulfil the desire
of an ageing father.

Finally, what is important in Wendt's works may be not so much the denunciation of colonial imposition as the fascinating interplay of two apparently antagonistic
forces: ancient cultural relics reappropriated by some modern Samoans eager to find
a continuum with the past appear inextricably interwoven with originally foreign
cultural and religious features. For particular pragmatic reasons, they may dissociate
the two at times. However, what to narrow-minded outsiders may seem like incom-
patible systems actually do cohabit within Wendt's characters and are in no way a
source of inner division or schizoid tendencies. The author manages to create an
imaginary world in which the past and its pre-Christian traditions are not radically
excluded from syncretic modernity.

WORKS CITED

Durix, Carole. "Networks and Itineraries in Albert Wendt's Poetry," *Echos du Commonwealth* 8
(1982): 27–37.

Durix, Jean–Pierre. "Albert Wendt: The Attempt to Snare the Void and Give it Word," in *International Literature in English: Essays on Major Writers*, ed. Robert Ross (New York: Garland,
1991): 63–73.

Meleisea, Malama. *Change and Adaptations in Western Samoa* (n.p., 1992).

——. *Lagalaga: A Short History of Western Samoa* (Suva, Fiji: U of the South Pacific, 1987).

——. *The Making of Modern Samoa* (Suva, Fiji: Institute of Pacific Studies of the U of the South
Pacific, 1987).

Wendt, Albert. *The Birth and Death of the Miracle Man* (Harmondsworth: Viking, 1986).

——. *Inside us the Dead* (Auckland: Longman Paul, 1976).

——. *Leaves of the Banyan Tree* (Auckland: Longman Paul, 1979).

---

[26] Wendt, *Sons for the Return Home*, 184.

——. *Ola* (Auckland: Penguin, 1991).

——. *Sons for the Return Home* (Auckland: Longman Paul, 1973).

——. "Towards a New Oceania," *Mana* 1.1 (1976), repr. in *Readings in Pacific Literature*, ed. Paul Sharrad (Wollongong: New Literatures Research Centre, 1993) A: 9.

❧❧

Contributors

ISABEL ALONSO BRETO holds a degree in English from the University of Barcelona. She has studied at the University of Paris X (Nanterre) and at the Centre for Critical and Cultural Theory of the University of Wales (Cardiff). With academic interests and publications centred on the postcolonial area, she is also a translator and a fiction and travel writer. At present she is completing a doctorate on the writing of the Afro-Caribbean–Canadian author Marlene Nourbese Philip. She currently teaches at the University of Barcelona.

JACQUELINE BARDOLPH was emeritus professor of English at the Université de Nice, where she pioneered postcolonial literature. She spent many years in West Africa, an experience that helped her become one of the most renowned specialists in African literature. Her *Ngugi wa Thiong'o* (Présence Africaine, 1991) is still one of the best studies on the subject. A dedicated teacher, she organized, at Nice, one of the most successful EACLALS conferences ever. In her generation, she was one of the most distinguished scholars to entertain a global view of the different postcolonial literatures of the world. She played a major role in breathing new life into SEPC, the French association for Commonwealth studies. After a long and courageous fight against cancer (she was terminally ill in Tübingen when she delivered what was to be her last public paper), she died in Nice on 7 July 1999.

ANNE COLLETT teaches literatures written and spoken in English. She has a particular interest in the nineteenth and twentieth centuries, inclusive of romanticism, imperialism, modernism, postcolonialism, and has co-edited a book with Lars Jensen and Anna Rutherford on *Teaching Post-Colonialism and Post-Colonial Literatures*. Her research interests lie primarily in the exploration of relationship between politics and poetics, and the intersection of race and gender. Her recent publications and conference papers have concentrated on the Caribbean writers Jamaica Kincaid, Olive Senior and Kamau Brathwaite, the First Nations poets Pauline Tekahionwake Johnson and Joan Crate, the Canadian writers Margaret Atwood and Hiromi Goto, the Australian poets Judith Wright and Oodgeroo, and the Irish poet Seamus Heaney. She is currently co-editor of *Kunapipi*.

PILAR CUDER DOMÍNGUEZ is Senior Lecturer at the University of Huelva, Spain, where she teaches courses on English literature, women's writing in English, and English-Canadian literature. She has edited two collections of articles, *La mujer del texto al contexto* (1996) and *Exilios femeninos* (2000), and has published articles in *Essays on Canadian*

Writing, the *International Journal of Canadian Studies*, *Annales de l'Université de Savoie*, *Facsimile*, and other international journals. She was visiting scholar at McGill University (Montreal, Quebec) in 1997 and at Dalhousie University (Halifax, Nova Scotia) in 1999.

BÄRBEL CZENNIA did her doctoral research on the translation of novels from English into German. She has been a member of the English Department at Göttingen University since 1994 and is currently working on a postdoctoral thesis on concepts of collective identity in English, Scottish, and New Zealand poetry. Her fields of teaching are English literature (sixteenth to twentieth century), Scottish and New Zealand literature in English; her research interests include literature in comparative contexts and intercultural studies.

ROCÍO G. DAVIS has degrees from the Ateneo de Manila University (Philippines) and the University of Navarre (Spain), where she is Professor of American and Postcolonial Literature. She has recently published *Transcultural Reinventions: Asian American and Asian Canadian Short Story Cycles* (2001), and is the co-editor of *Small Worlds: Transcultural Visions of Childhood* (2000), *Tricks with a Glass: Writing Ethnicity in Canada* (Cross / Cultures, 2000), and *Asian American Literature in the International Context: Readings on Fiction, Poetry, and Performance* (2002). Her research interests include the writing of the Asian diaspora, children's literature, and autobiography.

MARC DELREZ (M.A. Adelaide; Ph.D. Liège) is a professor of literature in English (new and established) at the University of Liège, Belgium. In the postcolonial field, he has published articles on Salman Rushdie, Randolph Stow, David Malouf, Nicholas Jose and Janet Frame. His monograph on Janet Frame, *Manifold Utopia*, has recently appeared in Rodopi's Cross / Cultures series.

HEILNA DU PLOOY is professor in the School of Languages at the Potchefstroom University for Christian Higher Education (South Africa). She teaches Afrikaans and Dutch literature and literary theory. She has written a book on twentieth-century narrative theories and has published extensively on aspects of narrative literature. She has been a guest lecturer in Limburg and Leiden in the Netherlands. She writes poetry and short stories.

JEAN–PIERRE DURIX is professor of English at the Université de Bourgogne in Dijon, France. After writing his doctorate on the British novelist James Hanley, he specialized in postcolonial literature. Over the past twenty-five years he has published widely, especially on writers from the Caribbean (Wilson Harris, Derek Walcott), the South Pacific (Frank Sargeson, Albert Wendt, Witi Ihimaera, Patricia Grace), Australia (Patrick White), Africa (Ngugi wa Thiong'o, Wole Soyinka, J.M. Coetzee) and India (Salman Rushdie). His most recent books include *The Writer Written: Images of the Artist in the New Literatures in English* (1987), *The New Literatures in English* (1993, in collaboration with Carole Durix) and *Mimesis, Genres and Post-Colonial Discourse* (1998). He has been editor of the journal *Commonwealth: Essays and Studies* since 1984. He also translated into French Wilson

Harris's *Palace of the Peacock, The Secret Ladder* and *Angel at the Gate*, Witi Ihimaera's *Tangi*, and a collection of poems by Albert Wendt.

ULRIKE ERICHSEN studied English, German and pedagogy in Hamburg and at Hertford College, Oxford. She was a lecturer with the German Academic Exchange Service at Sidney Sussex College, Cambridge. Since 1995 she has been a member of the English Department of the Technical University, Darmstadt. Her doctoral dissertation on re-writings of colonial history and colonial experience in selected contemporary Caribbean novels was published in 2001. She is currently working on a postdoctoral study of the 'Condition of England' novel.

ULLA HASELSTEIN is a professor of American literature at the University of Munich. Her research interests include nineteenth- and twentieth-century literature, the avantgarde, postcolonial literature, and literary theory. She has published *Entziffernde Hermeneutik. Studien zum Begriff der Lektüre in der psychoanalytischen Theorie des Unbewussten* (1991) and *Die Gabe der Zivilisation: Interkultureller Austausch und literarische Textpraxis in Amerika, 1661–1862* (2000), as well as articles on Poe, Hawthorne, Gertrude Stein and Thomas Pynchon, and on slave narratives, Native American literature, psychoanalysis, and the media.

JOHN C. HAWLEY is Associate Professor of English at Santa Clara University. He is the editor of ten books, most recently the *Encyclopedia of Postcolonial Studies* (2001) and *Postcolonial, Queer: Theoretical Intersection* (2001).

EVA HUNTER is an Associate Professor in the English Department of the University of Western Cape, an institution that established itself as "an intellectual home of the left" during the apartheid era. She has published widely in overseas and local journals on problems of feminist literary theory in South Africa, and on South African and African women writers. More recently, her teaching and research have taken her into the fields of culture studies.

MIRKO JURAK, Professor of English and American literature at the Faculty of Arts, University of Ljubljana, was a postgraduate student at the University of Sussex (1963–64), obtained his doctorate in English poetic drama in 1967 at the University of Ljubljana, and held the offices of Dean of the Faculty and Vice-Rector at this University. He has published four books of articles and essays, four textbooks and over eighty scholarly articles in various journals (including *Modern Drama, Educational Theatre Journal, Melus, BELLS, Acta Neophilologica, Acta Universitatis Upsaliensis, Slovene Studies*). He has also edited books of conference procedings (*Australian Papers*, 1983; *Cross-Cultural Studies: American, Canadian and European Literatures, 1945–1985*, 1988, and *Literature, Culture and Ethnicity*, 1992).

BRUCE KING has been a professor of English in Canada, New Zealand, Nigeria, Scotland, and the USA. His many publications include, more recently, *Modern Indian Poetry in English* (1987), *Coriolanus* (1989), *Three Indian Poets: Ezekiel, Ramanujan and Moraes* (1991), *Derek Walcott and West Indian Drama – 'Not Only a Playwright But a Company': The Trinidad Theatre Workhop, 1959–1993* (1993), and *Derek Walcott: A Caribbean Life* (2000).

EVA RASK KNUDSEN teaches postcolonial literature and theory in the University of Copenhagen. Her main research interests are indigenous literatures, cultural creolization, and the issue of orality and / in writing. She has published widely within the field of indigenous literature, in particular Aboriginal literature. Her doctoral dissertation *The Spiral and the Circle* (on Aboriginal and Maori writing in English) is forthcoming in the Cross / Cultures series. She was one of the organizers of the Aratjara Aboriginal arts exhibition at Louisiana in Copenhagen in 1994 and has taken part in Danish radio and television programmes on Aboriginal culture.

SARAH LAWSON WELSH is a Senior Lecturer at University College Northampton, England. She is the co-editor of the *Routledge Reader in Caribbean Literature* (1996) and the author of numerous chapters and articles on Caribbean and Black British literature. She compiles the annual "West Indies" bibliography for the *Journal of Commonwealth Literature* and is co-editor of the newly re-aunched journal, *World Literature Written in English*. She is presently working on a critical study of the writings of Grace Nichols.

BÉNÉDICTE LEDENT teaches English for Special Purposes and Caribbean Literature at the Univerity of Liège (Belgium), where she completed a doctoral dissertation on the fiction of Caryl Phillips, forthcoming in Manchester University Press's World Writers Series. She has published articles on Caryl Phillips, Fred D'Aguiar, Jamaica Kincaid, Joan Riley and Michelle Cliff. Her current research interests include contemporary Caribbean fiction and cross-Caribbean criticism.

PETER H. MARSDEN is a member of the Department of English Studies at Aachen University of Technology. His teaching and research interests embrace both linguistics (such as varieties of Engish and translation studies) and literature, with a particular focus on Australian and New Zealand poetry. He has published on individual authors such as Les Murray and Peter Goldsworthy, and on the oral tradition in Aboriginal and Maori culture.

SIGRUN MEINIG is completing a doctorate on the representation of history in Australian historical novels by Henry Handel Richardson, Patrick White, Peter Carey and Rodney Hall. She teaches in the area of postcolonial literatures at the University of Mannheim, Germany. She holds an interisciplinary degree in English philology and business from the University of Mannheim and an M.A. in Modern Literature from the University of Kent, England.

THENGANI H. NGWENYA is a Senior Lecturer in the School of Languages and Literature at the University of Durban–Westville, South Africa. His doctoral dissertation focused on South African autobiography. Ngwenya has published journal articles and reviews in the field of South African autobiographical writing. He is currently working on a biography of the famous Zulu critic and writer, B.W. Vilakazi.

MARI PEEPRE, a professor at York University, is co-director of a project on cross-cultural contacts and postcolonial writing in English. Her research interests are Canadian literature, postcolonial literature, diaspora studies, and cultural studies. Her publications include *Transcultural Travels: Essays in Canadian Literature and Society* (1994), and, with Nely Keinänen, *Reading Our World: A Guide to Practical and Theoretical Criticism* (revised edition, 2000).

MAYA PETRUKHINA is Professor of English Language and American Literature at the Diplomatic Academy, Department of English, in Moscow. Her research interests are comparative literary studies in Russian and American cultures, multiculturalism and identity in American and Canadian fiction, and translations of fiction and poetry (including that of Timothy Findley). She has pubished widely and translated several books.

ALEXANDRA PODGÓRNIAK obtained her M.A. in 1997 and B.A. in Spanish in 2000. Currently she is an assistant lecturer at the Institute of British and American Literature and Culture and a member of the Colonial and Postcolonial Studies Centre at the University of Silesia, Poland. She is currently working on a doctorate on magical-realist fiction in postcolonial literatures.

RALPH PORDZIK received his doctorate from the Free University Berlin, and his postdoctoral study *Ästhetische Funktion und kulturelles Handeln: Transformationsprozesse in der modernen englischsprachigen Lyrik Südafrikas 1950 bis 1980* has been submitted at the Ludwig Maximilians University, Munich. He has recently launched a new research project on "Future Projection and Utopian Imagination in Postcolonial English Fiction" funded by the German Research Foundation.

ROBERT ROSS, currently resident in Aachen, Germany, is an associate of the Edward A. Clark Centre for Australian Studies at the Universtiy of Texas at Austin. He is the founding editor (now retired) of *Antipodes*, a North America journal of Australian literature, and recently published *Colonial and Postcolonial Fiction: An Anthology*. Apart from his special interest in Australian literature, Ross has also published articles on Canadian, New Zealand, African, and Indian literature. He is currently working on a book on the Australian novelist Thea Astley.

CHITRA SANKARAN is currently on joint appointment as Assistant Professor in the Department of English Language and Literature and the University Scholars Programme, National University of Singapore. Her research areas include feminist theory and writing, postcolonial theory and criticism, Indian fiction in English, Singaporean fiction and East–West comparative literatures. Her publications include a book, *The Myth Connection: A Comparative Study of R.K. Narayan and Raja Rao*, and articles published in the *Journal of Commonwealth Literature*, *Journal of South Asian Literature*, *World Englishes*, *World Literature Written in English*, and others. She has book chapters forthcoming with Peter Lang (New York), SUNY Press (New York), and Oxford University Press (Singapore).

MARK SHACKLETON is currently Professor of American Literature in the Department of English, University of Helsinki. He has published widely on Native North American literature, including articles on Tomson Highway, Gerald Vizenor, Thomas King, Monique Mojica and Simon Ortiz. He is also the author of *Moving Outward: The Development of Charles Olson's Use of Myth* (1994), and has edited three collections of short stories and a collection of one-act plays.

OLGA SUDLENKOVA was born in Brest (Belarus). She graduated from Minsk State Linguistics University in 1965 and has since taught English and American literature at the MSLU and the European Humanities University (Minsk). In 1985, she was awarded her doctorate by St Petersburg State University for a dissertation on the poetry of Thomas Campbell. Major publications include *Thomas Campbell's Poetry in Russia* (1990), *English Literature*, a textbook for senior schoolchildren (1996), and *100 British Writers*, a reference book (1997).

JOHN THIEME is Professor Emeritus at South Bank University, London. His books include *The Web of Tradition* (1987), *The Arnold Anthology of Post-Colonial Literatures in English* (1996), *Derek Walcott* (1999) and *Postcolonial Con-texts: Writing back to the Canon*. He is currently working on a study of R.K. Narayan. He is co-editor of the *Journal of Commonwealth Literature*, General Editor of the Manchester University Press Contemporary World Writers Series, and an editor for the on-line *Literary Encyclopedia* and the *Annotated Bibliography of English Studies*.

GERRY TURCOTTE is Associate Professor and Head of the English Studies Program at the University of Wollongong, Australia. He is the author and editor of numerous articles and monographs, including *Jack Davis: The Maker of History*, *Neighbourhood of Memory* and *Writers in Action*. His new novel, *Flying in Silence*, was published in Canada by Cormorant Books and in Australia by Brandl & Schlesinger in 2001 and was shortlisted for the *Age* Book of the Year. He is the winner of the OCTAL Vice-Chancellor's Award for Excellence in Teaching (2000) and the ACE/State Government Award for Teaching Excellence (2001). He is past President of the Association for Canadian Studies in Australia and New Zealand (ACSANZ), and past Secretary of the International Council for Canadian Studies (ICCS).

CYNTHIA VANDEN DRIESEN , born in Sri Lanka, later lived and taught in Nigeria and now lives in Australia. She completed her postgraduate studies at the University of Western

Australia and teaches English, Australian and other new literatures in English at Edith Cowan University, Perth, Western Australia. Her publications include *The Novels of R.K Narayan* (1986), *An Anthology of Australian Literature for Korean Readers*, tr. Jin Young Choi (1995), *Centering The Margins: Perspectives on Literatures in English from India, Africa, Australia* (1995), *Celebrations: Fifty Years of Australia/Sri Lanka Interactions, 1948–1998* (co-edited with Ian Vanden Driesen, 1998), and *New Directions in Australian Studies* (co-edited with Adrian Mitchell, 1999). She is the Australian Co-President of the Asian–Australian Association for the Study of Australia and is currently co-editing the papers of the AASA Conference held in Mysore, India, September 2000.

REINA WHAITIRI, Ngaitahu, was born in 1943 to a Pakeha mother and Maori father. She was educated at High Church of England boarding schools: St Mary's Collegiate School in Stratford Taranaki, and St Hilda's Diocesan School in Dunedin. She started her academic career late in life, completing her M.A. in English at the University of Auckland in 1986. She gained her Diploma of Teaching in 1989. Since 1990 she has worked in the English Department at the University of Auckland, teaching English and Pacific literature and coordinating a programme which encourages students to return to tertiary education. For the Manoa series she has, with Robert Sullivan, co-edited the volume *Homeland: New Writing from America, the Pacific, and Asia*, which focuses on contemporary Maori writing. She is currently editing an anthology of Polynesian poetry with Robert Sullivan and Albert Wendt, the first collection of Polynesian poetry written and edited by Polynesians. Her areas of interest are Maori women's poetry and writing from the Pacific.

RAJIVA WIJESINHA is currently Professor of Languages at Sabaragamuwa University in Sri Lanka. He is also Coordinating Manager of the English and Foreign Languages Unit of the Sri Lankan Ministry of Education. He read Classics and then obtained a doctorate in English at Oxford University, and has worked for the British Council in between teaching at various universities. Publications include several novels and books of political history in addition to literary criticism and anthologies of Sri Lankan writing in English.

HYACINTH CYNTHIA WYATT was born in Trinidad and went to France at the age of eleven. She studied in Paris and received her B.A., M.A. and D.E.A. at the Sorbonne. She now lives in Spain, where she did her doctorate on R.K. Narayan at the University of Barcelona. She has published on Commonwealth culture and literature, and edited, with C.D. Narasimhaiah, *The Vitality of West Indian Literature* (2000). She is currently teaching in the Department of Anglo-Germanic Philology at the University of Rovira i Virgili, Tarragona, and working on a book about myth and symbol in the work of R.K. Narayan, as well as dedicating time to writing and publishing poetry.

☙❧

Index

This index is a key to the texts and footnotes. It does not include references to the editor's introduction or the critical works cited by the contributors. In the first part, terms and concepts are listed which seemed relevant in the context of the "missions of interdependence" addressed in this book. This includes historical events, nationalities, languages, ethnical groups and religious denominations as well as conceptual signposts for the discussion of cultural conflict and religious or secular missions. The list of names includes major figures from public and cultural life as well as authors. References to their books are added as sub-entries. For a full list of authors and critics mentioned in the book, the bibliographies and footnotes to the individual contributions should be consulted.

Terms and Concepts

Names and Titles